Criminal Justice in Action
THE CORE

Seventh Edition

LARRY K. GAINES
California State University
San Bernardino

ROGER LeROY MILLER
Institute for University Studies
Arlington, Texas

WADSWORTH
CENGAGE Learning

Australia • Brazil • Japan • Korea • Mexico • Singapore • Spain • United Kingdom • United States

Criminal Justice in Action
The Core, 7th Edition
Larry K. Gaines and **Roger LeRoy Miller**

Editor-in-Chief: Michelle Julet

Senior Publisher: Linda Schreiber Ganster

Senior Acquisitions Editor:
Carolyn Henderson-Meier

Senior Developmental Editor: Bob Jucha

Assistant Editor: Rachel McDonald

Editorial Assistant: Casey Lozier

Senior Marketing Manager:
Michelle Williams

Marketing Assistant: Jack Ward

Production Manager: Brenda Ginty

Senior Content Project Manager:
Ann Borman

Photo Researcher: Anne Sheroff

Copyeditor: Mary Berry

Indexer: Terry Casey

Media Editor: Andy Yap

Manufacturing Planner: Judy Inouye

Art Director: Maria Epes

Interior Designer: Riezebos Holzbaur

Cover Designer: Riezebos Holzbaur/
Tim Heraldo

Cover Image: Scott Olson/
2011 Getty Images

Compositor: Parkwood Composition
Service

For product information and technology assistance, contact us at
Cengage Learning Customer & Sales Support 1-800-354-9706

For permission to use material from this text or product, submit all requests online at **www.cengage.com/permissions** Further permissions questions can be emailed to **permissionrequest@cengage.com**

Library of Congress Control Number: 2012952536

Student Edition ISBN-13: 978-1-285-06915-9
Student Edition ISBN-10: 1-285-06915-3

Looseleaf Edition ISBN-13: 978-1-285-06917-3
Looseleaf Edition ISBN-10: 1-285-06917-X

Wadsworth Cengage Learning
20 Davis Drive
Belmont, CA 94002-3098
USA

Cengage Learning is a leading provider of customized learning solutions with office locations around the globe, including Singapore, the United Kingdom, Australia, Mexico, Brazil, and Japan. Locate your local office at **www.cengage.com/global**.

Cengage Learning products are represented in Canada by Nelson Education, Ltd.

To learn more about Wadsworth, visit **www.cengage.com/Wadsworth** Purchase any of our products at your local college store or at our preferred online store **www.CengageBrain.com**

Printed in the United States of America

1 2 3 4 5 6 7 16 15 14 13 12

CONTENTS IN BRIEF

PREFACE xiii

Part One: The Criminal Justice System

CHAPTER 1: Criminal Justice Today 2
CHAPTER 2   Measuring and Explaining Crime 30
CHAPTER 3: Inside Criminal Law 64

Part Two: The Police and Law Enforcement

CHAPTER 4: Law Enforcement Today 96
CHAPTER 5: Problems and Solutions in Modern Policing 126
CHAPTER 6: Police and the Constitution—
The Rules of Law Enforcement 158

Part Three: Criminal Courts

CHAPTER 7: Courts and the Quest for Justice 186
CHAPTER 8: Pretrial Procedures and the Criminal Trial 214
CHAPTER 9: Punishment and Sentencing 250

Part Four: Corrections

CHAPTER 10: Probation and Intermediate Sanctions 284
CHAPTER 11: Prisons and Jails 308
CHAPTER 12: Behind Bars—The Life of an Inmate 334

Part Five: Special Issues

Chapter 13: The Juvenile Justice System 364
Chapter 14: Today's Challenges in Criminal Justice 394

THE CONSTITUTION A-1

YOU BE THE _____: ACTUAL OUTCOMES AND COURT DECISIONS B-1

TABLE OF CASES C-1

GLOSSARY G-1

NAME INDEX I-1

SUBJECT INDEX I-5

CONTENTS

Features of Special Interest xi

Preface xiii

Part One: The Criminal Justice System

CHAPTER 1:
Criminal Justice Today 2

WHAT IS CRIME? 5

Determining Criminal Behavior 5
An Integrated Definition of Crime 7

THE PURPOSE OF THE CRIMINAL JUSTICE SYSTEM 7

Maintaining Justice 8
Protecting Society 8

THE STRUCTURE OF THE CRIMINAL JUSTICE SYSTEM 9

The Importance of Federalism 9
The Criminal Justice Process 13

DISCRETION AND ETHICS 15

Informal Decision Making 15
The Pitfalls of Discretion 15
Ethics and Justice 16

CRIMINAL JUSTICE TODAY 17

Crime and Law Enforcement: The Bottom Line 17
Homeland Security and Individual Rights 20
Inmate Populations: A New Trend 21
The Social Media Revolution 24

Chapter Summary • Questions for Critical Analysis • Key Terms • Self-Assessment Answer Key • CourseMate • Notes

Chapter One Appendix
How to Read Case Citations and Find Court Decisions 29

Lucy Nicholson/Reuters /Landov

CHAPTER 2:
Measuring and Explaining Crime 30

TYPES OF CRIME 33

Violent Crime 33
Property Crime 33
Public Order Crime 33
White-Collar Crime 34
Organized Crime 34
High-Tech Crime 34

CRIME MEASUREMENT IN THE UNITED STATES 35

The Uniform Crime Report 36
Victim Surveys 37
Self-Reported Surveys 39

CRIME TRENDS 40

Looking Good: Crime in the 1990s and 2000s 41
Crime, Race, and Poverty 42
Women and Crime 44

WHAT CAUSES CRIME? 45

Correlation and Cause 45
The Role of Theory 46
The Brain and the Body 46
Bad Neighborhoods and Other Economic
    Disadvantages 49
Life Lessons and Criminal Behavior 50
Victims of Crime 53
From Theory to Practice 55

THE LINK BETWEEN DRUGS AND CRIME 55

The Criminology of Drug Use 56
Drug Addiction and Dependency 56
The Drug–Crime Relationship 57

Chapter Summary • Questions for Critical Analysis • Key Terms •
Self-Assessment Answer Key • CourseMate • Notes

CHAPTER 3:

Inside Criminal Law 64

WRITTEN SOURCES OF AMERICAN CRIMINAL LAW 67

Constitutional Law 67
Statutory Law 67
Administrative Law 69
Case Law 69

THE PURPOSES OF CRIMINAL LAW 70

Protect and Punish: The Legal Function of the Law 70
Maintain and Teach: The Social Function of the Law 70

CLASSIFICATION OF CRIMES 71

Civil Law and Criminal Law 71
Felonies and Misdemeanors 74
Mala in Se and *Mala Prohibita* 75

THE ELEMENTS OF A CRIME 77

Criminal Act: *Actus Reus* 77
Mental State: *Mens Rea* 77
Concurrence 80
Causation 80
Attendant Circumstances 81
Harm 82

DEFENSES UNDER CRIMINAL LAW 82

Criminal Responsibility and the Law 83
Justification Criminal Defenses and the Law 86

PROTECTING CIVIL LIBERTIES 88

The Bill of Rights 89
Due Process 89

Chapter Summary • Questions for Critical Analysis • Key
Terms • Self-Assessment Answer Key • CourseMate • Notes

Part Two: The Police and Law Enforcement

CHAPTER 4:

Law Enforcement Today 96

THE RESPONSIBILITIES OF THE POLICE 99

Enforcing Laws 99
Providing Services 100

Preventing Crime 101
Preserving the Peace 101

A SHORT HISTORY OF THE AMERICAN POLICE 102

The Evolution of American Law Enforcement 102
Policing Today: Intelligence, Terrorism, and
    Technology 105

RECRUITMENT AND TRAINING: BECOMING A POLICE OFFICER 107

Basic Requirements 108
Training 109

WOMEN AND MINORITIES IN POLICING TODAY 110

Antidiscrimination Law and Affirmative Action 110
Working Women: Gender and Law Enforcement 111
Minority Report: Race and Ethnicity in Law
    Enforcement 111

PUBLIC AND PRIVATE LAW ENFORCEMENT 114

Municipal Law Enforcement Agencies 114

Scott Olson/Getty Images

Sheriffs and County Law Enforcement 114
State Police and Highway Patrols 115
Federal Law Enforcement Agencies 116
Private Security 120

Chapter Summary • Questions for Critical Analysis • Key Terms •
Self-Assessment Answer Key • CourseMate • Notes

CHAPTER 5:

Problems and Solutions in Modern Policing 126

POLICE ORGANIZATION AND FIELD OPERATIONS 129

The Structure of the Police Department 129
Police on Patrol: The Backbone of the Department 131
Police Investigations 133
Aggressive Investigation Strategies 133
Clearance Rates and Cold Cases 134
Forensic Investigations and DNA 134

POLICE STRATEGIES: WHAT WORKS 137

Response Time to 911 Calls 138
Patrol Strategies 139
Predictive Policing and Crime Mapping 139
Arrest Strategies 140
Community Policing and Problem Solving 141

"US VERSUS THEM": ISSUES IN MODERN POLICING 143

Police Subculture 144
The Physical Dangers of Police Work 144
Stress and the Mental Dangers of Police Work 145
Authority and the Use of Force 146

POLICE MISCONDUCT AND ETHICS 149

Police Corruption 149
Police Accountability 150
Ethics in Law Enforcement 151

Chapter Summary • Questions for Critical Analysis • Key Terms •
Self-Assessment Answer Key • CourseMate • Notes

CHAPTER 6:

Police and the Constitution—The Rules of Law Enforcement 158

THE FOURTH AMENDMENT 161

Reasonableness 161
Probable Cause 161
The Exclusionary Rule 163

STOPS AND FRISKS 165

The Elusive Definition of Reasonable Suspicion 165
A Stop 167
A Frisk 167

ARRESTS 168

Elements of an Arrest 168
Arrests with a Warrant 169
Arrests without a Warrant 170

LAWFUL SEARCHES AND SEIZURES 170

The Role of Privacy in Searches 171
Search and Seizure Warrants 171
Searches and Seizures without a Warrant 172
Searches of Automobiles 174
The Plain View Doctrine 175
Electronic Surveillance 176
Social Media Searches 178

THE INTERROGATION PROCESS AND MIRANDA 178

The Legal Basis for *Miranda* 179
When a *Miranda* Warning Is Required 179
When a *Miranda* Warning Is Not Required 180
The Future of *Miranda* 181

Chapter Summary • Questions for Critical Analysis • Key Terms •
Self-Assessment Answer Key • CourseMate • Notes

Part Three: Criminal Courts

CHAPTER 7:

Courts and the Quest for Justice 186

FUNCTIONS OF THE COURTS 189

Due Process and Crime Control in the Courts 189
The Rehabilitation Function 190
The Bureaucratic Function 190

THE BASIC PRINCIPLES OF THE AMERICAN JUDICIAL SYSTEM 190

Jurisdiction 191
Trial and Appellate Courts 192
The Dual Court System 193

STATE COURT SYSTEMS 194

Courts of Limited Jurisdiction 194
Trial Courts of General Jurisdiction 195
State Courts of Appeals 195

THE FEDERAL COURT SYSTEM 196

U.S. District Courts 196
U.S. Courts of Appeals 196
The United States Supreme Court 196

JUDGES IN THE COURT SYSTEM 199

The Roles and Responsibilities of Trial Judges 199
Selection of Judges 201
Diversity on the Bench 202

THE COURTROOM WORK GROUP 203

Members of the Courtroom Work Group 204
The Judge in the Courtroom Work Group 205
The Prosecution 205
The Defense Attorney 207

Chapter Summary • Questions for Critical Analysis • Key Terms •
Self-Assessment Answer Key • CourseMate • Notes

CHAPTER 8:
Pretrial Procedures and the Criminal Trial 214

PRETRIAL DETENTION 217

The Purpose of Bail 217
Gaining Pretrial Release 219

ESTABLISHING PROBABLE CAUSE 220

The Preliminary Hearing 220
The Grand Jury 220

THE PROSECUTORIAL SCREENING PROCESS 221

Case Attrition 221
Screening Factors 222

PLEADING GUILTY 223

Plea Bargaining in the Criminal Justice System 224
Motivations for Plea Bargaining 225

SPECIAL FEATURES OF CRIMINAL TRIALS 227

A "Speedy" Trial 227
The Role of the Jury 228
The Privilege against Self-Incrimination 229
The Presumption of a Defendant's Innocence 229
A Strict Standard of Proof 230

JURY SELECTION 231

Voir Dire 231
Race and Gender Issues in Jury Selection 232

THE TRIAL 235

Opening Statements 235
The Role of Evidence 235
The Prosecution's Case 238
Cross-Examination 239
The Defendant's Case 239
Rebuttal and Surrebuttal 241
Closing Arguments 241

THE FINAL STEPS OF THE TRIAL AND POSTCONVICTION PROCEDURES 242

Jury Deliberation 242
The Verdict 243
Appeals 244
Wrongful Convictions 245

Chapter Summary • Questions for Critical Analysis • Key Terms •
Self-Assessment Answer Key • CourseMate • Notes

CHAPTER 9:
Punishment and Sentencing 250

THE PURPOSE OF SENTENCING 253

Retribution 253
Deterrence 254
Incapacitation 254
Rehabilitation 255
Restorative Justice 256

THE STRUCTURE OF SENTENCING 256

Legislative Sentencing Authority 256
Judicial Sentencing Authority 258
The Sentencing Process 259
Factors of Sentencing 260

INCONSISTENCIES IN SENTENCING 262

Sentencing Disparity 262
Sentencing Discrimination 263

SENTENCING REFORM 265

Sentencing Guidelines 265
Mandatory Sentencing Guidelines 267
Victim Impact Evidence 268

CAPITAL PUNISHMENT— THE ULTIMATE SENTENCE 269

Methods of Execution 269
The Death Penalty and the Supreme Court 270
Still Cruel and Unusual? 273
Debating the Sentence of Death 274
The Immediate Future of the Death Penalty 277

Chapter Summary • Questions for Critical Analysis • Key Terms •
Self-Assessment Answer Key • CourseMate • Notes

Part Four: Corrections

CHAPTER 10:
Probation and Intermediate Sanctions 284

THE JUSTIFICATION FOR COMMUNITY CORRECTIONS 287

Reintegration 287
Diversion 287
The "Low-Cost Alternative" 288

PROBATION: DOING TIME IN THE COMMUNITY 288

Sentencing Choices and Probation 289
Conditions of Probation 290
The Supervisory Role of the Probation Officer 292
Revocation of Probation 293
New Models of Probation 295

INTERMEDIATE SANCTIONS 295

Judicially Administered Sanctions 296
Day Reporting Centers 299
Intensive Supervision Probation 299
Shock Incarceration 299
Home Confinement and Electronic Monitoring 300
Widening the Net 302

THE PARADOX OF COMMUNITY CORRECTIONS 303

Chapter Summary • Questions for Critical Analysis • Key Terms • Self-Assessment Answer Key • CourseMate • Notes

CHAPTER 11:
Prisons and Jails 308

A SHORT HISTORY OF AMERICAN PRISONS 311

Walnut Street Prison: The First Penitentiary 311
The Great Penitentiary Rivalry:
    Pennsylvania versus New York 311
The Reformers and the Progressives 312
The Reassertion of Punishment 313

INMATE POPULATION TRENDS 314

Factors in Prison Population Growth 314
The Costs of Incarceration 315
Decarceration 316

PRISON ORGANIZATION AND MANAGEMENT 316

Prison Administration 317
Types of Prisons 319

THE EMERGENCE OF PRIVATE PRISONS 322

Why Privatize? 322
The Argument against Private Prisons 324
The Future of Privatization
    in the Corrections Industry 325

JAILS 325

The Jail Population 326
Jail Administration 328
New-Generation Jails 328

THE CONSEQUENCES OF OUR HIGH RATES OF INCARCERATION 330

Chapter Summary • Questions for Critical Analysis • Key Terms • Self-Assessment Answer Key • CourseMate • Notes

CHAPTER 12:
Behind Bars— The Life of an Inmate 334

PRISON CULTURE 337

Adapting to Prison Society 337
Who Is in Prison? 338
Rehabilitation and Prison Programs 339
Violence in Prison Culture 339
Issues of Race and Ethnicity 341

CORRECTIONAL OFFICERS AND DISCIPLINE 342

Rank and Duties of Correctional Officers 342
Discipline 344
Female Correctional Officers 345
Protecting Prisoners' Rights 346

Photo Courtesy Bergen County Sheriff's Office, Bergen, NJ

INSIDE A WOMEN'S PRISON 347

Characteristics of Female Inmates 348
The Motherhood Problem 349
The Culture of Women's Prisons 349

PAROLE AND RELEASE FROM PRISON 350

Discretionary Release 351
Parole Guidelines 353
Parole Supervision 354

Other Types of Prison Release 355

REENTRY INTO SOCIETY 356

Barriers to Reentry 356
Promoting Desistance 357
The Special Case of Sex Offenders 358

Chapter Summary • Questions for Critical Analysis • Key Terms •
Self-Assessment Answer Key • CourseMate • Notes

Part Five: Special Issues

CHAPTER 13:

The Juvenile Justice System 364

**THE EVOLUTION OF AMERICAN JUVENILE
JUSTICE 367**

The Child-Saving Movement 367
The Illinois Juvenile Court 367
Juvenile Delinquency 368
Constitutional Protections and the Juvenile Court 369

DETERMINING DELINQUENCY TODAY 371

The Age Question 371
The Culpability Question 372

TRENDS IN JUVENILE DELINQUENCY 373

Delinquency by the Numbers 373
The Rise and Fall of Juvenile Crime 373
Girls in the Juvenile Justice System 374
School Violence and Bullying 375

FACTORS IN JUVENILE DELINQUENCY 377

The Age-Crime Relationship 377
Substance Abuse 378
Child Abuse and Neglect 379
Gangs 379

**FIRST CONTACT: THE POLICE AND PRETRIAL
PROCEDURES 381**

Police Discretion and Juvenile Crime 381
Intake 382
Pretrial Diversion 383
Transfer to Adult Court 383
Detention 384

TRYING AND PUNISHING JUVENILES 384

Adjudication 385
Disposition 386
Juvenile Corrections 386

Chapter Summary • Questions for Critical Analysis • Key Terms •
Self-Assessment Answer Key • CourseMate • Notes

CHAPTER 14:

Today's Challenges in Criminal Justice 394

HOMELAND SECURITY 397

The Global Context of Terrorism 397
The Antiterrorism and Effective Death Penalty Act 399
The Patriot Act 400
The Department of Homeland Security 401
Federal Agencies outside the DHS 401
Counterterrorism Challenges and Strategies 402
Security versus Civil Liberties 405

CYBER CRIME 408

Computer Crime and the Internet 408
Cyber Crimes against Persons and Property 409
Cyber Crimes in the Business World 411
Cyber Crimes against the Community 413

**THE CRIMINALIZATION OF IMMIGRATION
LAW 414**

Immigration Law Basics 414
Enforcing Immigration Law 417

WHITE-COLLAR CRIME 418

What Is White-Collar Crime? 418
Regulating and Policing White-Collar Crime 420
White-Collar Crime in the 2000s 421

Chapter Summary • Questions for Critical Analysis • Key Terms •
Self-Assessment Answer Key • CourseMate • Notes

THE CONSTITUTION A-1

YOU BE THE _____: ACTUAL OUTCOMES
AND COURT DECISIONS B-1

TABLE OF CASES C-1

GLOSSARY G-1

NAME INDEX I-1

SUBJECT INDEX I-5

Features of Special Interest

CHAPTER OPENING STORIES

Ch 1: NEIGHBORHOOD BOTCH 4
Trayvon Martin shooting in Florida

Ch 2: TIME FOR A CHANGE 32
Justice Dept changes the definition of rape

Ch 3: DEADLY HEAT 66
Arizona sweat lodge deaths

Ch 4: LIFE ON THE TWEET 98
Police officer's indiscretion on Twitter

Ch 5: TEXAS TRAGEDY 128
Officer uses deadly force on a minor

Ch 6: WHAT'S THAT SMELL? 160
When is warrentless entry justified?

Ch 7: A PRANK OR A CRIME? 188
Invasion of privacy at Rutgers

Ch 8: NO EXCUSES 216
Murder v. manslaughter at Univ of VA

Ch 9: A LIFETIME FOR LOOKING 252
Sentencing for child pornography

Ch 10: A TRIAL OF FAITH 286
A child's death and probation

Ch 11: THE WAKE-UP CALL 310
Overcrowding in California's prisons

Ch 12: TRIPLE FRAY 336
Violent outbreaks at Folsom Prison

Ch 13: THE END OF INNOCENCE 366
Life without parole for juvenile offenders

Ch 14: THE HACKTIVIST 396
Prosecuting computer hackers

LANDMARK CASES

Brown v. Entertainment Merchants Association (EMA) Ch 2, p 52
Miranda v. Arizona Ch 6, p 180
Baze v. Rees Ch 9, p 275
In Re Gault Ch 13, p 370

COMPARATIVE CRIMINAL JUSTICE

CH 1: **TRASH TALK 6**
CH 2: **A REAL WAR ON DRUGS 58**
CH 6: **EXTENDING A FIRM HAND 164**
CH 7: **BACK TO SCHOOL 202**
CH 8: **JAPAN'S ALL-POWERFUL PROSECUTORS 224**
CH 9: **THE NORWEGIAN WAY 255**
CH 10: **SWEDISH DAY-FINES 298**
CH 14: **THE NOT-SO-FRIENDLY SKIES 405**

YOU BE THE _____

SENATOR
Banning Texting While Driving Ch 1, p 10

JUDGE
A Voluntary Act? Ch 3, p 78

POLICE COMMISSIONER
Occupational Hazard Ch 4, p 100

SHERIFF'S DEPUTY
Threat Level Ch 5, p 148

JUDGE
A Valid Pretext? Ch 6, p 176

DEFENSE ATTORNEY
A Gang Murder Ch 8, p 240

PROBATION OFFICER
A Judgment Call Ch 10, p 294

PAROLE BOARD MEMBER
Threat Level Ch 12, p 353

Badge: Rasmus Rasmusson/iStockphoto;
Handcuffs: Photodisc; Gavel: Shutterstock; Scale: James Stadl/iStockphoto

ANTI-TERRORISM IN ACTION

Trapping a Lone Wolf Ch 1, p 22
Due Justice? Ch 3, p 90
Under Suspicion Ch 4, p 106
Trying Times Ch 8, p 230
Prislam Ch 12, p 348

CAREERS IN CJ

Crime Scene Photographer Ch 1, p 12

Criminologist Ch 2, p 35

Gang Investigator Ch 3, p 72

Federal Bureau of Investigation (FBI) Agent Ch 4, p 119

Forensic Scientist Ch 5, p 136

Police Detective Ch 6, p 162

Bailiff Ch 7, p 204

Public Defender Ch 8, p 234

National Victim Advocate Ch 9, p 270

Lead Probation Officer Ch 10, p 296

Prison Warden Ch 11, p 323

Halfway House Program Manager Ch 12, p 358

Resident Youth Worker Ch 13, p 388

Customs and Border Protection Agent Ch 14, p 416

A QUESTION OF ETHICS

Kidney Compensation Ch 3, p 68

The "Dirty Harry" Problem Ch 5, p 152

The Right Decision? Ch 7, p 209

Canvas Incarceration Ch 11, p 328

The Million-Dollar Man Ch 12, p 340

MYTH VS. REALITY

Race Stereotyping and Drug Crime Ch 2, p 43

Are Too Many Criminals Found Not Guilty
   by Reason of Insanity? Ch 3, p 85

Women Make Bad Cops Ch 4, p 112

Does Putting Criminals in Prison
   Reduce Crime? Ch 11, p 317

Soft Time for White-Collar Crime Ch 14, p 422

MASTERINGCONCEPTS

How Discretion Works, Ch 1, p 16

Civil Law versus Criminal Law, Ch 3, p 73

The Difference between a Stop and
   an Arrest, Ch 6, p 168

The Bifurcated Death Penalty Process,
   Ch 9, p 272

The Main Differences between
   Prisons and Jails, Ch 11, p 326

Probation versus Parole, Ch 12, p 351

The Juvenile Justice System versus
   the Criminal Justice System, Ch 13, p 385

CJ & TECHNOLOGY

Mobile Offender Recognition and Identification
   System (MORIS) Ch 1, p 18

Transdermal Alcohol Testing Ch 2, p 40

Electronic Eavesdropping Ch 3, p 76

High-Tech Cop Cars Ch 4, p 104

Self-Surveillance Ch 5, p 151

Automatic License Plate Recognition Ch 6, p 177

New Fingerprinting Techniques Ch 7, p 200

Wireless Devices in the Courtroom Ch 8, p 243

Global Positioning System (GPS) Ch 10, p 301

Tracking Inmates Ch 12, p 344

Cyberbullying Ch 13, p 376

Hacking Cars Ch 14, p 412

of *measuring* crime, including the FBI's Uniform Crime Reports and the U.S. Department of Justice's National Crime Victimization Survey, and (2) *criminology,* providing students with insight into why crime occurs before, in the chapters that follow, shifting their attention toward how society goes about fighting it.

- To give students an idea of how crime statistics shape our perception of crime in the United States, the chapter includes a section entitled **"Crime Trends Today,"** which has been **expanded** to show the historical and contemporary links between violent crime rates and factors such as guns, gangs, illegal drugs, the economy, and the national birth rate.

- A **new** discussion of **life course theories of crime,** which posit that antisocial behavioral patterns established in early childhood are useful predictors of juvenile delinquency and adult criminality.

Chapter 3 Inside Criminal Law lays the foundation

of *criminal law.* It addresses constitutional law, statutory law, and other sources of American criminal law before shifting its focus to the legal framework that allows the criminal justice system to determine and punish criminal guilt.

- An **updated** discussion of self-defense concepts and so-called Stand Your Ground laws in the wake of George Zimmerman's controversial February 2012 fatal shooting of African American teenager Trayvon Martin in Sanford, Florida.

- A **new** Anti-Terrorism in Action feature ("Due Justice") examines the due process questions raised by American drone strikes against terrorism suspects in foreign countries, particularly the strike that killed U.S. citizen Anwar al-Awlaki in Yemen.

PART 2: THE POLICE AND LAW ENFORCEMENT

Chapter 4 Law Enforcement Today acts as an

introduction to law enforcement in the United States today. This chapter offers a detailed description of the country's numerous local, state, and federal law enforcement agencies and examines the responsibilities and duties that come with a career in law enforcement.

- As part of a new discussion on the landscape of **policing today,** students will learn about the strategies that make up **intelligence-led policing,** the challenges of **anti-terrorism,** and **"Law Enforcement 2.0,"** in which law enforcement agents gather information about criminal activity by accessing social networks on the Internet.

- A **new** section, entitled **"Women and Minorities in Policing Today,"** provides an extended discussion of diversity issues in policing, including antidiscrimination law, affirmative action, consent decrees, recruiting challenges, tokenism, and double marginality.

Chapter 5 Problems And Solutions In Modern Policing puts students on the streets and gives them a

gritty look at the many *challenges of being a law enforcement officer.* It starts with a discussion of police organization and field services and then moves on to law enforcement strategies and issues in modern policing, such as crime mapping, the mental dangers of police work, and use of force.

- A **new** You Be the Sheriff 's Deputy feature ("Threat Level") addresses the subject of police use of deadly force by placing the student in a dangerous situation where such force may—or may not—be called for.

- A **new** CJ and Technology feature ("Self-Surveillance") describes how some law enforcement agencies are considering a drastic measure to curb employee misconduct: placing small cameras on the heads of police officers to record their every move.

Chapter 6 Police and the Constitution examines

the sometimes uneasy *relationship between law enforcement and the U.S. Constitution* by explaining the rules of being a police officer. Particular emphasis is placed on the Fourth, Fifth, and Sixth Amendments, giving students an understanding of crucial concepts such as probable cause, reasonableness, and custodial interrogation.

- An **updated** section entitled "Video and Digital Surveillance" illuminates the constitutional issues surrounding law enforcement use of closed-circuit television (CCTV) cameras as crime-fighting tools. The discussion includes a **new** CJ and Technology feature ("Automatic License Plate Recognition") that introduces students to one of the latest, and most-effective, new force multipliers available to American police.

- In the context of the Supreme Court's recent ruling on Arizona's immigration law S.B. 1070, an **updated** discussion of **racial profiling** and the burden on law enforcement officers to determine if a person is in the United States unlawfully.

PART 3: CRIMINAL COURTS

Chapter 7 Courts and the Quest for Justice takes

a big-picture approach in describing the *American court system,* giving students an overview of the basic principles of our judicial system, the state and federal court systems, and the role of judges, prosecutors, and defense attorneys in the criminal justice system.

- The court system's ability to live up to societal expectations of truth and justice, a running theme of the third part of this textbook, is explored with a close look at the trial of Dharun Ravi. The chapter's **new** introductory vignette examines why, in 2012, a New Jersey jury found Ravi guilty of invasion of privacy and bias intimidation for using a webcam to view his Rutgers University roommate, Tyler Clementi, embracing another man.

- A **new** discussion designed to give students an understanding of **how the U.S. Supreme Court "makes" criminal justice policy** through judicial review. The discussion focuses on a recent case in which the Court invalidated a federal law banning the Internet sale of "crush" videos, which show the brutal slaughter of small animals, on First Amendment grounds.

Chapter 8 Pretrial Procedures and the Criminal Trial provides students with a rundown of *pretrial procedures* and highlights the role that these procedures play in America's *adversary system*. Chapter materials also place the student in the courtroom and give her or him a comprehensive understanding of the steps in the *criminal trial*.

- Three **new** Figures use excerpts from actual court records to give students a first-hand understanding of three crucial aspects of the criminal trial: jury selection, the opening statement, and the closing statement.

- A **new** You Be the Defense Attorney feature ("A Gang Murder") challenges the student to create reasonable doubt in the minds of jurors who will decide the fate of a client who is on trial for assisting in the murder of a fellow gang member.

Chapter 9 Punishment and Sentencing links the many different *punishment options* for those who have been convicted of a crime with the theoretical justifications for those punishments. The chapter also examines punishment in the policy context, weighing the costs and benefits to society of such controversial practices as mandatory minimum sentences and the death penalty.

- A **new** Comparative Criminal Justice feature ("The Norwegian Way") explains the philosophy behind a seemingly light potential punishment for Anders Bering Breivik, who massacred nearly eighty people in Norway in the summer of 2011.

- An **updated** discussion on the short-term future of capital punishment in the United States takes into account such factors as a nationwide reduction in death sentences, the burdensome costs of execution, an evident juror preference for life-without-parole, and recent steps taken by several states to abolish the practice.

PART 4: CORRECTIONS

Chapter 10 Probation and Intermediate Sanctions makes an important point, and one that is often overlooked in the larger discussion of the American corrections system: not all of those who are punished need to be placed behind bars. This chapter explores the *community corrections* options, from probation to intermediate sanctions such as intensive supervision and home confinement.

- A **new** discussion of innovative probations strategies focuses on Hawaii's attempt to encourage compliance through "swift and certain" punishment and a California ballot initiative that requires certain low-level drug offenders in that state to receive treatment in the community rather than be incarcerated.

- A **new** You Be the Probation Officer feature ("A Judgment Call") asks students whether they would revoke the probation of an offender who tests positive for marijuana use and violates his probation agreement in other minor ways.

Chapter 11 Prisons and Jails focuses on *prisons and jails*. After four decades of growth, high incarceration rates have pushed these institutions to the forefront of the criminal justice system, and this chapter explores the various issues—such as severe overcrowding and the emergence of private prisons—that have resulted from the prison population boom.

- A **new** section entitled **"Inmate Population Trends"** describes a surprising recent decrease in the American prison population as well as efforts by certain states to reduce their inmate numbers in order to lower the unfeasible costs of expensive corrections systems.

- A **new** Mastering Concepts feature gives students a clear idea of the different roles that prisons and jails play in the American corrections system.

Chapter 12 Behind Bars is another example of our efforts to get students "into the action" of the criminal justice system, this time putting them in the uncomfortable position of being behind bars. It also answers the

increasingly important question, "What happens when the inmate is released back into society?"

- **New** sections on **female correctional guards** and **women's prisons** provide insight into the challenges faced by women on both sides of prison bars.

- **New** discussions of various aspects of life behind bars, such as prison programs designed to prepare inmates for life "on the outside" and the increased use of solitary confinement for "problem" inmates.

PART 5: SPECIAL ISSUES

Chapter 13 The Juvenile Justice System examines the *juvenile justice system*, giving students a comprehensive description of the path taken by delinquents from first contact with police to trial and punishment. The chapter contains a strong criminological component as well, scrutinizing the various theories of why certain juveniles turn to delinquency.

- A **new** chapter-opening vignette that uses the example of Omer Ninham, who was fourteen-years-old when he killed a playmate in Green Bay, Wisconsin, to explore the subject of life-without-parole prison sentences for juvenile violent offenders.

- A **new** section, **"Bullied to Death,"** that addresses the growing national awareness of the negative consequences of bullying, as well as a a **new** CJ and Technology feature ("Cyberbullying") that describes how increased use of social media by juveniles has exacerbated the problem.

Chapter 14 Today's Challenges in Criminal Justice concludes the text by taking an expanded look at four crucial criminal justice topics: (1) homeland security, (2) cyber crime, (3) immigration law, and (4) white-collar crime.

- A **new** section on the **criminalization of immigration law** provides students with the basics of immigration law and an understanding of how the actions of federal immigration agents are impacting local law enforcement and crime prevention.

- Another **new** section on **white-collar crime** describes the myriad of wrongdoing covered by this umbrella term and provides an overview of recent law enforcement efforts to combat economic crimes. The section also includes a **new** Myth v. Reality feature ("Soft on White-Collar Crime") that challenges the popular notion that the criminal justice system is "soft" when it comes to punishing white-collar criminals.

SPECIAL FEATURES

Supplementing the main text of *Criminal Justice in Action, The Core,* Seventh Edition, are approximately seventy eye-catching, instructive, and penetrating special features. These features, described below with examples, have been designed to enhance the student's understanding of a particular criminal justice issue.

CAREERS IN CJ As stated before, many students reading this book are planning a career in criminal justice. We have provided them with an insight into some of these careers by offering first-person accounts of what it is like to work as a criminal justice professional.

- In Chapter 6, William Howe describes the thrill that he experiences when he solves a crime "puzzle" as a detective.

- In Chapter 10, Peggy McCarthy, a probation officer, provides an inside look at the many duties involved with her profession, from assisting in the arrest of hardened criminals to helping defendants make "a positive change in their lives."

ANTI-TERRORISM IN ACTION This new feature focuses on various law enforcement strategies to promote homeland security.

- "Trapping a Lone Wolf" (Chapter 1) details the strategies favored by American law enforcement when confronted with the homegrown, would-be terrorists that have evolved into a constant threat to homeland security.

- "Trying Times" (Chapter 8) explains how the prosecution's "failure" regarding the criminal trial of Ahmed Khalfan Ghailani ensures that high-level terrorist suspects will be tried before military tribunals for the foreseeable future.

MASTERINGCONCEPTS Some criminal justice topics require additional explanation before they become crystal clear in the minds of students. This feature helps students to master many of the essential concepts in the textbook.

- In Chapter 6, the feature helps students understand the legal differences between a police stop and a police frisk.
- In Chapter 13, the feature compares and contrasts the juvenile justice system with the criminal justice system.

YOU BE THE _____ This new feature, as noted earlier in the Preface, puts students into the position of a criminal justice professional in a hypothetical case or situation that is based on a real-life event. The facts of the case or situation are presented with alternative possible outcomes, and the student is asked to "be the _____" and make a decision. Students can then consult Appendix B at the end of the text to learn what actually happened in the offered scenario.

- You Be the Police Commissioner, "Occupational Hazard" (Chapter 4) asks students what tactics they would use to disperse a peaceful but law-breaking group of protestors.
- You Be the Parole Board Member, "Cause of Compassion?" (Chapter 12) challenges students to decide the fate of a model prisoner who has been behind bars for nearly four decades because of her participation in a grisly murder spree.

CJ & TECHNOLOGY Advances in technology are constantly transforming the face of criminal justice. In these features, which appear in nearly every chapter, students learn of one such emergent technology and are asked to critically evaluate its effects.

- This feature in Chapter 1 describes how a biometrics smartphone application allows law enforcement agents to quickly identify a suspect simply by taking a photo of her or his face.
- This feature in Chapter 8 explores the problems caused when jurors make use of small wireless devices to text, tweet, blog, take photos, and conduct Internet research during a criminal trial.

COMPARATIVE CRIMINAL JUSTICE The world offers a dizzying array of different criminal customs and codes, many of which are in stark contrast to those accepted in the United States. This feature provides dramatic and sometimes perplexing examples of foreign criminal justice practices in order to give students a better understanding of our domestic ways.

- "Back to School" (Chapter 7) contrasts the American method of electing judges with the French method of training judges and asks students to determine if one approach is superior to the other.
- "The Not-So Friendly-Skies" (Chapter 14) describes security measures used to screen airplane passengers in Israel, including a level of racial profiling that would be unacceptable to many in the United States.

A QUESTION OF ETHICS Ethical dilemmas occur in every profession, but the challenges facing criminal justice professionals often have repercussions beyond their own lives and careers. In this feature, students are asked to place themselves in the shoes of police officers, prosecutors, defense attorneys, and other criminal justice professionals facing ethical dilemmas: Will they do the right thing?

- In "Kidney Compensation" (Chapter 3), students consider the ethical considerations behind a U.S. ban on selling kidneys and are asked to decide whether this criminal law does more harm than good.
- In "The 'Dirty Harry' Problem" (Chapter 5), a police detective is trying to save the life of a young girl who has been buried alive with only enough oxygen to survive for a few hours. Is he justified in torturing the one person—the kidnapper—who knows where the girl is buried?

LANDMARK CASES Rulings by the United States Supreme Court have shaped every area of the criminal justice system. In this feature, students learn about and analyze the most influential of these cases.

- In Chapter 2's *Brown v. Entertainment Merchants Association*, the Supreme Court rejected the argument that violent video games cause violent behavior and invalidated a California law banning the sale of such games to minors.
- In Chapter 13's *In re Gault* (1967), the Supreme Court held that juveniles are entitled to many of the same due process rights granted to adult offenders—a decision that caused a seismic shift in America's juvenile justice system.

MYTH vs. REALITY Nothing endures like a good myth. In this feature, we try to dispel some of the more enduring myths in the criminal justice system while at the same time asking students to think critically about their consequences.

- "Race Stereotyping and Crime" (Chapter 2) challenges the perceived wisdom that members of certain minority groups, particularly African Americans, are prone to violence and therefore more likely to be criminals than other racial or ethnic groups.

- "Are Too Many Criminals Found Not Guilty by Reason of Insanity?" (Chapter 3) dispels the notion that the criminal justice is "soft" because it lets scores of "crazy" defendants go free due to insanity.

EXTENSIVE STUDY AIDS

Criminal Justice in Action, The Core, Seventh Edition, includes a number of pedagogical devices designed to complete the student's active learning experience. These devices include:

- Concise **chapter outlines** at the beginning of each chapter. The outlines give students an idea of what to expect in the pages ahead, as well as a quick source of review when needed.

- Dozens of **key terms** and a **running glossary** focus students' attention on major concepts and help them master the vocabulary of criminal justice. The chosen terms are boldfaced in the text, allowing students to notice their importance without breaking the flow of reading. On the same page that a key term is highlighted, a margin note provides a succinct definition of the term. For further reference, a glossary at the end of the text provides a full list of all the key terms and their definitions. This edition includes over forty new key terms.

- Each chapter has at least three **figures,** which include graphs, charts, and other forms of colorful art that reinforce a point made in the text. This edition includes sixteen new figures.

- Hundreds of **photographs** add to the overall readability and design of the text. Each photo has a caption, and most of these captions include a **critical-thinking question** dealing with the topic at hand. This edition includes nearly ninety new photos.

- At the end of each chapter, students will find five **Questions for Critical Analysis.** These questions will help the student assess his or her understanding of the just-completed chapter, as well as develop critical-thinking skills.

ANCILLARY MATERIALS

Wadsworth provides a number of supplements to help instructors use *Criminal Justice in Action, The Core,* Seventh Edition, in their courses and to aid students in preparing for exams. Supplements are available to qualified adopters. Please consult your local Wadsworth/Cengage sales representative for details.

FOR THE INSTRUCTOR

- **Annotated Instructor's Edition.** This essential resource features teaching tips, discussion tips, and technology tips to help professors engage students with the course material. Prepared by Carly Hilinski of Governers State University.

- **Instructor's Resource Manual with Test Bank.** The manual includes learning objectives, key terms, a detailed chapter outline, a chapter summary, discussion topics, student activities, media tools and a newly expanded test bank. The learning objectives are correlated with the discussion topics, student activities and media tools. Each chapter's test bank contains questions in multiple-choice, true false, completion, and essay formats, with a full answer key. The test bank is coded to the learning objectives that appear in the main text, and includes the page numbers in the main text where the answers can be found. Finally, each question in the test bank has been carefully reviewed by experienced criminal justice instructors for quality, accuracy, and content coverage. Our Instructor Approved seal, which appears on the front cover, is our assurance that you are working with an assessment and grading resource of the highest caliber.

The manual is available for download on the password-protected website and can also be obtained by e-mailing your local Cengage Learning representative. Prepared by Samantha Carlo of Miami-Dade College and Rosemary Arway of Hodges University.

- **Online Lesson Plans.** The Lesson Plans bring accessible, masterful suggestions to every lesson. This supplement includes a sample syllabus, learning objectives, lecture notes, discussion topics & in-class activities, a detailed lecture outline, assignments, media tools, and "What if . . ." scenarios. The learning objectives are integrated throughout the Lesson Plans and current events and real-life examples in the form of articles, websites and video links are incorporated into the class discussion topics, activities and assignments. The lecture outlines are correlated with PowerPoint slides for ease of classroom use. Lesson Plans are available on the PowerLecture resource and the instructor Web site. Prepared by Bernard Zadrowski of College Of Southern Nevada- Cheyenne.

- **Online PowerPoints.** Helping you make your lectures more engaging while effectively reaching your visually oriented students, these handy Microsoft PowerPoint® slides outline the chapters of the main text in a classroom-ready presentation. The PowerPoint® slides are updated to reflect the content and organization of the new edition of the text and feature some additional examples and real world cases for application and discussion. Available for download on the password-protected instructor book companion website, the presentations and can also be obtained by e-mailing your local Cengage Learning representative. Prepared by Jaclyn Smith of University of Maryland— College Park.

- **PowerLecture DVD with ExamView.** The fastest, easiest way to build customized, media-rich lectures, PowerLecture™ provides a collection of book-specific Microsoft® PowerPoint® lecture and class tools to enhance the educational experience. PowerLecture™ includes lesson plans, lecture outlines linked to the learning objectives for each chapter, art from the text, new videos, animations, and more. The DVD-ROM also contains electronic copies of the Instructor's Resource Manual, Test Bank, and Lesson Plans; and ExamView® testing software, which allows you to create customized tests in minutes using items from the test bank in computerized format.

REAL WORLD RESOURCES: TOOLS TO ENHANCE RELEVANCY

The media tools from across all the supplements are gathered into one location and organized by chapter and Learning Objective. Each item has a description of the resource and a directed learning activity. Available on the companion website, WebTutor and CourseMate, these can be used as resources for additional learning or as assignments.

- **WebTutor™ on Blackboard® and WebCT®.** Jump-start your course with customizable, rich, text-specific content within your Course Management System. Whether you want to web-enable your class or put an entire course online, WebTutor delivers. WebTutor offers a wide array of resources, including media assets, test banks, practice quizzes linked to chapter learning objectives, and additional study aids. Visit www.cengage.com/webtutor to learn more.

- **The Wadsworth Criminal Justice Video Library.** So many exciting new videos—so many great ways to enrich your lectures and spark discussion of the material in this text. Your Cengage Learning representative will be happy to provide details on our video policy by adoption size. The library includes these selections and many others.

- **ABC® Videos.** ABC videos feature short, high-interest clips from current news events as well as historic raw footage going back 40 years. Perfect for discussion starters or to enrich your lectures and spark interest in the material in the text, these brief videos provide students with a new lens through which to view the past and present, one that will greatly enhance their knowledge and understanding of significant events and open up to them new dimensions in learning. Clips are drawn from such programs as World News Tonight, Good Morning America, This Week, PrimeTime Live, 20/20, and Nightline, as well as numerous ABC News specials and material from the Associated Press Television News and British Movietone News collections.

- **Cengage Learning's "Introduction to Criminal Justice Video Series"** features videos supplied by the BBC Motion Gallery. These short, high-interest clips from CBS and BBC news programs—everything from nightly news broadcasts and specials to CBS News Special Reports, CBS Sunday Morning, 60 Minutes, and more—are perfect classroom discussion starters. Designed to enrich your lectures and spark interest in the material in the text, these brief videos provide students with a new lens through which to view the past and present, one that will greatly enhance their knowledge and understanding of significant events and open up to them new dimensions in learning. Clips are drawn from BBC Motion Gallery.

- **Classroom Activities for Criminal Justice.** This valuable booklet contains both tried-and-true favorites and exciting new projects; activities are drawn from across the spectrum of criminal justice subjects and can be customized to fit any course.

- **Internet Activities for Criminal Justice.** This useful booklet helps familiarize students with Internet resources and allows instructors to integrate resources into their course materials.

CRIMINAL JUSTICE MEDIA LIBRARY

Cengage Learning's Criminal Justice Media Library includes nearly 300 media assets on the topics you cover in your courses. Available to stream from any Web-enabled computer, the Criminal Justice Media Library's assets include such valuable resources as; Career Profile Videos featuring interviews with criminal justice professionals from a range of roles and locations, simulations that allow students to step into various roles and practice their decision-making skills, video clips on current topics from ABC® and other sources, animations that illustrate key concepts, interactive learning modules that help students check their knowledge of important topics and Reality Check exercises that compare expectations and preconceived notions against the real-life thoughts and experiences of criminal justice professionals. The Criminal Justice Media Library can be uploaded and used within many popular Learning Management Systems. You can also customize it with your own course material. Please contact your Cengage Learning representative for ordering and pricing information.

FOR THE STUDENT

- **Cengage Learning's Criminal Justice CourseMate** brings course concepts to life with interactive learning, study, and exam preparation tools that support the printed textbook. CourseMate includes an integrated eBook, quizzes mapped to chapter Learning Objectives, flashcards, videos, and more, and EngagementTracker, a first-of-its-kind tool that monitors student engagement in the course. The accompanying instructor website offers access to password-protected resources such as an electronic version of the instructor's manual and PowerPoint® slides.

- **Study Guide.** An extensive student guide has been developed for this edition. Because students learn in different ways, the guide includes a variety of pedagogical aids to help them. Each chapter is outlined and summarized, major terms and figures are defined, plus media tools for directed learning and self-tests are provided. Prepared by William Head of Indiana University.

- **Careers in Criminal Justice Web Site: www.cengage.com/criminaljustice/careers.** This unique Web site gives students information on a wide variety of career paths, including requirements, salaries, training, contact information for key agencies, and employment outlooks.

  Several important tools help students investigate the criminal justice career choices that are right for them.

  —Career Profiles: Video testimonials from a variety of practicing professionals in the field as well as information on many criminal justice careers, including job descriptions, requirements, training, salary and benefits, and the application process.

  —Interest Assessment: Self-assessment tool to help students decide which careers suit their personalities and interests.

  —Career Planner: Résumé-writing tips and work sheets, interviewing techniques, and successful job search strategies.

  —Links for Reference: Direct links to federal, state, and local agencies where students can get contact information and learn more about current job opportunities.

- **Handbook of Selected Supreme Court Cases, Third Edition.** This supplementary handbook covers almost forty landmark cases, with a full case citation, an introduction, a summary from WestLaw, and excerpts and the decision for each case.

- **Current Perspectives: Readings from InfoTrac®.** These readers, designed to give you a deeper taste of special topics in criminal justice, include free access to InfoTrac® College Edition. The timely articles are selected by experts in each topic from within InfoTrac College Edition.

—*Cybercrime*

—*Introduction to Criminal Justice*

—*Forensics and Criminal Investigations*

—*Community Corrections*

—*Policy in Criminal Justice*

—*Technology and Criminal Justice*

—*Law and Courts*

—*Ethics in Criminal Justice*

—*Corrections*

—*Victimology*

—*Policy in Criminal Justice*

—*Terrorism and Homeland Security*

—*New Technologies and Criminal Justice*

—*Racial Profiling*

—*White Collar Crime*

—*Crisis Management and National Emergency Response*

—*Juvenile Justice*

- **CLeBook.** CLeBook allows students to access Cengage Learning textbooks in an easy-to-use online format. Highlight, take notes, bookmark, search your text, and (in some titles) link directly into multimedia: CLeBook combines the best aspects of paper books and ebooks in one package.

- **Course360—Online Learning to the Next Degree.** Course360 from Cengage Learning is a complete turn key solution that teaches course outcomes through student interaction in a highly customizable online learning environment. Course360 blends relevant content with rich media and builds upon your course design, needs, and objectives. With a wide variety of media elements including audio, video, interactives, simulations, and more, Course360 is the way today's students learn.

ACKNOWLEDGMENTS

Throughout the creation of the seven editions of this text, we have been aided by hundreds of experts in various criminal justice fields and by professors throughout the country, as well as by numerous students who have used the text. We list below the reviewers for this Seventh Edition, followed by the class-test participants and reviewers for the first six editions. We sincerely thank all who participated on the revision of *Criminal Justice in Action, The Core*. We believe that the Seventh Edition is even more responsive to the needs of today's criminal justice instructors and students alike because we have taken into account the constructive comments and criticisms of our reviewers and the helpful suggestions of our survey respondents.

REVIEWERS FOR THE SEVENTH EDITION

We are grateful for the participation of the reviewers who read and reviewed portions of our manuscript throughout its development, and for those who gave us valuable insights through their responses to our survey.

Sheri Chapel
Ridley Lowell Technical College

Thomas Chuda
Bunker Hill Community College

Tomasina Cook
Eerie Community College

Gary Ebels
Grand Rapids Community College

Carl Franklin
Southern Utah University

Kelly Gould
Sacramento City College

Gerald Hildebrand
Austin Community College

Arthur Jipson
University of Dayton

Jon Mandrell
Sauk Valley Community College

Joe Morris
Northwestern State
University of Louisiana

Debra Ross
Grand Valley State University

Jason Waller
Tyler Junior College

Michelle Watkins
El Paso Community College

Jesse Weins
Dakota Wesleyan University

CLASS-TEST PARTICIPANTS

We also want to acknowledge the participation of the professors and their students who agreed to class-test portions of the text. Our thanks go to:

Tom Arnold
College of Lake County

Paula M. Broussard
University of Southwestern Louisiana

Mike Higginson
Suffolk Community College

Andrew Karmen
John Jay College of Criminal Justice

Fred Kramer
John Jay College of Criminal Justice

Anthony P. LaRose
Western Oregon University

Anne Lawrence
Kean University

Jerry E. Loar
Walters State Community College

Phil Reichel
University of Northern Colorado

Albert Sproule
Allentown College

Gregory B. Talley
Broome Community College

Karen Terry
John Jay College of Criminal Justice

Angelo Tritini
Passaic County Community College

Gary Uhrin
Westmoreland County
Community College

Robert Vodde
Fairleigh Dickinson University

REVIEWERS OF THE FIRST, SECOND, THIRD, FOURTH, FIFTH AND SIXTH EDITIONS

We appreciate the assistance of the following reviewers whose guidance helped create the foundation for this best seller. We are grateful to all.

Angela Ambers-Henderson
Montgomery County
Community College

Lorna Alvarez-Rivera
Ohio University

Gaylene Armstrong
Southern Illnois University

Judge James Bachman
Bowling Green State University

Tom Barclay
University of South Alabama

Julia Beeman
University of North
Carolina at Charlotte

Lee Roy Black
California University of Pennsylvania

Anita Blowers
University of North
Carolina at Charlotte

Stefan Bosworth
Hostos Community College

Michael E. Boyko
Cuyahoga Community College

John Bower
Bethel College

Scott Brantley
Chancellor University

Steven Brandl
University of Wisconsin–Milwaukee

Charles Brawner III
Heartland Community College

Timothy M. Bray
University of Texas–Dallas

Susan Brinkley
University of Tampa

Paula Broussard
University of Southwestern Louisiana

Michael Brown
Ball State College

Theodore Byrne
California State University,
Dominguez Hills

Patrick Buckley
San Bernardino Valley College

Joseph Bunce
Montgomery College–Rockville

James T. Burnett
SUNY, Rockland Community College

Ronald Burns
Texas Christian University

Paul Campbell
Wayne State College

Dae Chang
Wichita State University

Sheri Chapel
Ridley-Lowell Business and Technical
Institute and Keystone College

Steven Chermak
Indiana University

Charlie Chukwudolue
Northern Kentucky University

Monte Clampett
Asheville-Buncombe
Community College

John Cochran
University of South Florida

Ellen G. Cohn
Florida International University

Mark Correia
University of Nevada–Reno

Corey Colyer
West Virginia University

Theodore Darden
College of Du Page

John del Nero
Lane Community College

Richard H. De Lung
Wayland Baptist University

John Dempsey
Suffolk County Community College

Tom Dempsey
Christopher Newport University

Joyce Dozier
Wilmington College

Frank J. Drummond
Modesto Junior College

M. G. Eichenberg
Wayne State College

Frank L. Fischer
Kankakee Community College

Linda L. Fleischer
The Community College
of Baltimore County

Aric Steven Frazier
Vincennes University

Frederick Galt
Dutchess Community College

Phyllis Gerstenfeld
California State University Stanislaus

James Gilbert
University of Nebraska–Kearney

Dean Golding
West Chester University
of Pennsylvania

Debbie Goodman
Miami-Dade Community College

Cecil Greek
Florida State University

Donald Grubb
Northern Virginia Community College

Sharon Halford
Community College of Aurora

Michael Hallett
Middle Tennessee State University

Mark Hansel
Moorhead State University

Pati Hendrickson
Tarleton State University

Michelle Heward
Weber State University

Gerald Hildebrand
Austin Community College

Dennis Hoffman
University of Nebraska–Omaha

Richard Holden
Central Missouri State University

Ronald Holmes
University of Louisville

Marilyn Horace-Moore
Eastern Michigan University

Matrice Hurrah
Shelby State Community College

Robert Jerin
Endicott College

Jason R. Jolicoeur
Cincinnati State Technical
and Community College

Nicholas Irons
County College of Morris

Michael Israel
Kean University

J. D. Jamieson
Southwest Texas State University

James Jengeleski
Shippensburg University

Paul Johnson
Weber State University

Casey Jordan
Western Connecticut State University

Matthew Kanjirathinkal
Texas A & M University–Commerce

Bill Kelly
University of Texas–Austin

Paul Klenowski
Clarion University

David Kotajarvi
Lakeshore Technical College

John H. Kramer
Pennsylvania State University

Janine Kremling
California State University
at San Bernardino

Kristen Kuehnle
Salem State University

Karl Kunkel
Southwest Missouri State

James G. Larson
National University

Barry Latzer
John Jay College of Criminal Justice

Deborah Laufersweiler-Dwyer
University of Arkansas at Little Rock

Paul Lawson
Montana State University

Nella Lee
Portland State University

Walter Lewis
St. Louis Community
College–Meramec

Larry Linville
Northern Virginia Community College

Faith Lutze
Washington State University

Richard Martin
Elgin Community College

Richard H. Martin
University of Findlay

William J. Mathias
University of South Carolina

Janet McClellan
Southwestern Oregon
Community College

Pat Murphy
State University of New York–Geneseo

Rebecca Nathanson
Housatonic Community
Technical College

Ellyn Ness
Mesa Community College

Kenneth O'Keefe
Prairie State College

Michael Palmiotto
Wichita State University

Rebecca D. Petersen
University of Texas, San Antonio

Gary Prawel
Monroe Community College

Mark Robarge
Mansfield University

Matt Robinson
Appalachian State University

Debra Ross
Buffalo State College

William Ruefle
University of South Carolina

Gregory Russell
Washington State University

John Scheb II
University of Tennessee–Knoxville

Melinda Schlager
University of Texas at Arlington

Ed Selby
Southwestern College

Larry Snyder
Herkimer County Community College

Ronald Sopenoff
Brookdale Community College

Domenick Stampone
Raritan Valley Community College

Katherine Steinbeck
Lakeland Community College

Hallie Stephens
Southeastern Oklahoma
State University

Kathleen M. Sweet
St. Cloud State University

Gregory Talley
Broome Community College

Karen Terry
John Jay College of Criminal Justice

Amy B. Thistlethwaite
Northern Kentucky University

Rebecca Titus
New Mexico Junior College

Lawrence F. Travis III
University of Cincinnati

Kimberly Vogt
University of Wisconsin–La Crosse

Robert Wadman
Weber State University

Ron Walker
Trinity Valley Community College

John Wyant
Illinois Central College

Others were instrumental in bringing this Seventh Edition to fruition. We continue to appreciate the extensive research efforts of Shawn G. Miller and the additional legal assistance of William Eric Hollowell. Robert Jucha, our developmental editor, provided equal parts elbow grease and creative energy; it was a pleasure to work with him. Editor Carolyn Hendersen Meier supplied crucial guidance to the project through her suggestions and recommendations. At the production end, we once again feel fortunate to have enjoyed the services of our tireless production manager, Ann Borman, who oversaw virtually all aspects of this book. How she was able to make all of the schedules on time never ceased to amaze us. Additionally, we wish to thank the designer of this new edition, RHDG of San Francisco, who has created what we believe to be the most dazzling and student-friendly design of any text in the field. Photo researcher Anne Sheroff went to great lengths to satisfy our requests, and we sincerely appreciate her efforts. We are also thankful for the services of all those at Parkwood Composition who worked on the Seventh Edition, particularly Debbie Mealey. The eagle eyes of Mary Berry, Loretta Palagi, and Sue Bradley who shared the duties of proofreading and copy editing, were invaluable.

A special word of thanks must also go to the team responsible for the extensive multimedia package included in this project, including media editor for Criminal Justice, Andy Yap, and writer Robert C. De Lucia of John Jay College of Criminal Justice. In addition, we appreciate the work of Carly Hilinkski of Governers State University, who created annotations for the *Annotated Instructor's Edition*, Samantha Carlo of Miami-Dade College, and Rosemary Arway of Hodges University, who revised the *Instructor's Resource Manual*, Bernard Zadrowski of College of Southern Nevada—Cheyenne, who created the *Lesson Plans*, and Jacyln Smith of University of Maryland—College Park, who created the *PowerPoints*. We also appreciate the work of William Head of Indiana University for revising the Study Guide and for revising the web quizzing. We are also grateful for the aid of assistant editor Rachel McDonald and editorial assistant Virginette Acacio who ensured the timely publication of supplements. A final thanks to all of the great people in marketing and advertising who helped to get the word out about the book, including marketing manager Michelle Williams, who has been tireless in her attention to this project, and marketing communications manager Heather Baxley for keeping everything on track.

Any criminal justice text has to be considered a work in progress. We know that there are improvements that we can make. Therefore, write us with any suggestions that you may have.

L. K. G.
R. L. M.

DEDICATION

This book is dedicated to my good friend and colleague, Lawrence Walsh, of the Lexington, Kentucky Police Department. When I was a rookie, he taught me about policing. When I became a researcher, he taught me about the practical applications of knowledge. He is truly an inspiring professional in our field.

L.K.G.

To Eric,

Thanks for all of your hard work for so many years.

R.L.M.

Criminal Justice Today

AP Photo/John Minchillo

LEARNING OBJECTIVES

After reading this chapter, you should be able to...

1 Describe the two most common models of how society determines which acts are criminal.

2 Define *crime*.

3 Outline the three levels of law enforcement.

4 List the essential elements of the corrections system.

5 Explain the difference between the formal and informal criminal justice processes.

6 Define *ethics* and describe the role that they play in discretionary decision making.

7 Contrast the crime control and due process models.

8 List the major issues in criminal justice today.

Throughout the chapter you will see each learning objective repeated in the margin next to the content it relates to. The chapter summary on pages 25 and 26 includes all of the learning objectives for review.

CHAPTER OUTLINE

- What Is Crime?
- The Purpose of the Criminal Justice System
- The Structure of the Criminal Justice System
- Discretion and Ethics
- Criminal Justice Today

NEIGHBORHOOD BOTCH

The Retreat at Twin Lakes, a small community of about 260 town houses in Sanford, Florida, was experiencing a crime wave. Dozens of attempted break-ins and the common sight of would-be burglars casing potential targets had created an atmosphere of fear that permeated the neighborhood. After an incident on August 3, 2011, in which two men tried to steal resident Olivia Bertalan's television while she hid upstairs with her infant son, the local homeowners' association decided to set up a neighborhood watch. The members asked George Zimmerman, a twenty-eight-year-old insurance-fraud investigator with a good reputation, to head the new venture. Zimmerman, who legally owned a 9mm handgun, agreed.

On February 26, 2012, Zimmerman, who was patrolling Twin Lakes in his SUV, saw a young African American male walking down the street. He called 911 and reported a "suspicious guy." The dispatcher told Zimmerman to stop following the young man, a seventeen-year-old named Trayvon Martin, and let law enforcement handle the situation. Several weeks earlier, however, the police had failed to apprehend another "suspicious" suspect identified by Zimmerman, and that suspect was eventually arrested with a stolen laptop computer. "These a**holes," Zimmerman muttered over the phone. "They always get away."

What happened next is a matter of dispute. A lawyer for Martin's family says that Martin, on his way to the home of his father's girlfriend, was speaking to his own girlfriend on a cell phone when he noticed Zimmerman nearby on foot. Martin told his girlfriend that he was being followed, and she told him to run. Martin said that he would "walk fast." Zimmerman claims that he lost track of Martin and was headed back to his car when Martin attacked him from behind. In any case, witnesses saw the two men scuffle, and heard one crying for help. Within seconds, Martin lay dead with a bullet from Zimmerman's handgun in his chest.

George Zimmerman, charged with second degree murder for the shooting death of Trayvon Martin, appears in a Sanford, Florida, courthouse.

Pool/Reuters/Landov

When authorities initially refused to arrest George Zimmerman in connection with Trayvon Martin's death, a national outcry ensued. Anger focused on two aspects of incident that seemed to indicate racial bias. First, did Zimmerman assume that Martin was a criminal because of the teenager's skin color? Second, was Zimmerman avoiding arrest because he had killed a black man? Sanford police responded that they *could not* arrest Zimmerman, who claimed that he had been acting in self-defense. Under Florida law, persons in public places who reasonably believe that they are in imminent danger of death or severe injury can use deadly force to defend themselves without fear of being charged with a crime.[1]

Supporters of this so-called Stand Your Ground statute say that it allows people to confront attackers in dangerous situations. Critics say that such laws, which exist in nearly half the states, "create a nation where disputes are settled by guns instead of gavels, and where suspects are shot by civilians instead of arrested by police."[2] Some observers insisted that, by his actions, Zimmerman lost his right to a self-defense claim. "Stand your ground means stand your ground," said former Florida governor Jeb Bush. "It doesn't mean chase after somebody who's turned their back."[3]

Six weeks after the shooting incident, a special prosecutor charged Zimmerman with second degree murder for Martin's death. In Chapter 3, we will take a closer look at Stand Your Ground laws and the role they play in self-defense claims such as Zimmerman's.

We will examine several other issues highlighted by this controversial case in upcoming chapters. How do prosecutors reach the decision to charge a suspect like Zimmerman with a crime (Chapter 8)? Given all the publicity surrounding Martin's death, can a high-profile defendant such as Zimmerman possibly get a fair trial (Chapter 8)? As you proceed through this textbook, you will come to understand that few aspects of American criminal justice are simple, even if you have clear opinions about them. In this opening chapter, we introduce you to the criminal justice system by discussing its structure, the values it is designed to promote, and the important issues that define it today.

WHAT IS CRIME?

Of course, it is generally illegal for one person to kill another person. Exceptions to this rule are known as *justifiable homicides,* which are killings that occur under circumstances that remove criminal guilt. One example of a justifiable homicide is when a law enforcement officer kills a suspect in the line of duty. Another is when a person is acting in self-defense, as claimed by George Zimmerman. Indeed, justifiable homicides in Florida increased from an average of twelve a year before the state passed its Stand Your Ground law in 2005 to an average of thirty-three a year afterward.[4]

Do such laws really provide "a license to kill," as their critics contend? Consider the Miami case of Greyston Garcia, who chased down and stabbed to death a person suspected of stealing his car radio. In 2012, a Florida judge dismissed murder charges against Garcia, stating that the bag of radios brandished by the burglary suspect amounted to a lethal weapon.[5] In a state that does not have a Stand Your Ground law, it is unlikely that Garcia's act would be deemed a justifiable homicide.[6] Thus, a **crime** is not merely an act that seems illegal. It is a wrong against society that is proclaimed by law and that, if committed under specific circumstances, is punishable by the criminal justice system.

DETERMINING CRIMINAL BEHAVIOR

One problem with the definition of *crime* just provided is that it obscures the complex nature of societies. A society is not static—it evolves and changes, and its concept of criminality changes as well. For example, due to political and cultural shifts in the United States, a person is much more likely to face criminal charges for lying in a business or immigration context today than was the case even a decade ago.

Furthermore, different societies can have vastly different ideas of what constitutes criminal behavior. In 2011, France passed a criminal law that essentially prevents Muslim women from wearing garments in public that cover their faces. Because the First Amendment to the U.S. Constitution forbids any government action "prohibiting the free exercise of religion," such a ban in this country is highly unlikely. (See the feature *Comparative Criminal Justice—Trash Talk* on the following page for details about another foreign criminal law that runs counter to American legal tradition.) To more fully understand the concept of crime, it will help to examine the two most common models of how society "decides" which acts are criminal: the consensus model and the conflict model.

THE CONSENSUS MODEL The term *consensus* refers to general agreement among the majority of any particular group. Thus, the **consensus model** rests on the assumption that as people gather together to form a society, its members will naturally come to a basic agreement with regard to shared norms and values. Those individuals whose actions deviate from the established norms and values are considered to pose a threat to the well-being

Crime An act that violates criminal law and is punishable by criminal sanctions.

Consensus Model A criminal justice model in which the majority of citizens in a society share the same values and beliefs. Criminal acts are acts that conflict with these values and beliefs and that are deemed harmful to society.

Learning Objective **1** Describe the two most common models of how society determines which acts are criminal.

COMPARATIVE CRIMINAL JUSTICE

TRASH TALK

The two incidents, occurring on two different continents several months apart, were strikingly similar. On October 23, 2011, in London, England, Chelsea soccer player John Terry appeared to yell two obscenities and the word "black" at Anton Ferdinand of the opposing Queens Park Rangers. Then, on December 31, in Miami, Krys Barch of the Florida Panthers was ejected from a professional hockey game after aiming a racial slur at P. K. Subban of the Montreal Canadiens.

The consequences of the actions, however, were quite different. The National Hockey League suspended Barch—who admitted that his comments might have been "inappropriate"—for one game. Terry, meanwhile, found himself charged with committing a "racially aggravated public order offense" for violating a section of England's Crime and Disorder Act. The law, passed in 1998, prohibits "threatening, abusive, or insulting words" within the "hearing or sight" of someone "likely to be caused harassment, alarm, or distress which was racially aggravated." Terry, who was found innocent of any wrongdoing in July 2012, faced a maximum fine of about $4,000 if he had been found guilty.

Criminal charges were never considered against Barch, the hockey player. As interpreted by American courts, the First Amendment to the U.S. Constitution does not allow laws punishing speech unless that speech is likely to produce imminent violence. English criminal codes, in contrast, allow a maximum penalty of seven years for certain forms of verbal racial or religious harassment. The goal of these laws, according to one British legal expert, is to "promote justice by attempting to mould the collective conscience."

FOR CRITICAL ANALYSIS Do you think that the United States should criminalize "threatening, abusive, or insulting words" aimed at members of a minority group? What would be the consequences—both intended and unintended—of such a law?

---

of society as a whole and must be sanctioned (punished). The society passes laws to control and prevent unacceptable behavior, thereby setting the boundaries for acceptable behavior within the group.[7]

Morals Principles of right and wrong behavior, as practiced by individuals or by society.

Conflict Model A criminal justice model in which the content of criminal law is determined by the groups that hold economic, political, and social power in a community.

The consensus model, to a certain extent, assumes that a diverse group of people can have similar **morals.** In other words, they share an ideal of what is "right" and "wrong." Consequently, as public attitudes toward morality change, so do laws. In sixteenth-century America, a person found guilty of *adultery* (having sexual relations with someone other than one's spouse) could expect to be publicly whipped, branded, or even executed. Furthermore, a century ago, one could walk into a pharmacy and purchase heroin. Today, social attitudes have shifted to consider adultery a personal issue, beyond the reach of the state, and to consider the sale of heroin a criminal act.

THE CONFLICT MODEL Some people reject the consensus model on the ground that moral attitudes are not constant or even consistent. In large, democratic societies such as the United States, different groups of citizens have widely varying opinions on controversial issues of morality and criminality such as abortion, the war on drugs, immigration, and assisted suicide. These groups and their elected representatives are constantly coming into conflict with one another. According to the **conflict model,** then, the most politically powerful segments of society—based on class, income, age, and race—have the most influence on criminal laws and are therefore able to impose their values on the rest of the community.

Consequently, what is deemed criminal activity is determined by whichever group happens to be holding power at any given time. Because certain groups do not have access to political power, their interests are not served by the criminal justice system. To give one example, with the exception of Oregon and Washington State, physician-assisted suicide is illegal in the United States. Although opinion polls show that the general public is evenly divided on the issue,[8] several highly motivated interest groups have been able to convince lawmakers that the practice goes against America's shared moral and religious values.

AN INTEGRATED DEFINITION OF CRIME

Learning Objective 2 — Define *crime*.

Considering both the consensus and conflict models, we can construct a definition of *crime* that will be useful throughout this textbook. For our purposes, crime is an action or activity that is:

1. Punishable under criminal law, as determined by the majority or, in some instances, by a powerful minority.
2. Considered an *offense against society as a whole* and prosecuted by public officials, not by victims and their relatives or friends.
3. Punishable by sanctions based on laws that bring about the loss of personal freedom or life.

At this point, it is important to understand the difference between crime and **deviance,** or behavior that does not conform to the norms of a given community or society. Deviance is a subjective concept. For example, some segments of society may think that smoking marijuana or killing animals for clothing and food is deviant behavior. Deviant acts become crimes only when society as a whole, through its legislatures, determines that those acts should be punished—as is the situation today in the United States with using illegal drugs but not with eating meat.

Furthermore, not all crimes are considered particularly deviant—little social disapprobation is attached to those who fail to follow the letter of parking laws. In essence, criminal law reflects those acts that we, as a society, agree are so unacceptable that steps must be taken to prevent them from occurring.

Deviance Behavior that is considered to go against the norms established by society.

Criminal Justice System The interlocking network of law enforcement agencies, courts, and corrections institutions designed to enforce criminal laws and protect society from criminal behavior.

SELFASSESSMENT

Fill in the blanks and check your answers on page 26.

The consensus model of crime assumes that diverse members of society share similar _____, or ideals of right and wrong. The _____ model, in contrast, focuses on dissimilarities of such attitudes within society. A criminal act is a wrong against _____ and therefore is "avenged," or prosecuted, by _____ _____, not by the individual victims of a crime. A crime is not the same as an act of _____, the term for behavior that is nonconformist but not necessarily criminal.

Several years ago, the federal government and several state governments banned the sale of Four Loko, here being enjoyed by college students in Fort Collins, Colorado. The drink, known as "blackout in a can," combines the alcohol content of nearly six beers with a strong dose of caffeine. Why might society demand that the sale of this product be made a criminal offense?

Matthew Staver/Landov

THE PURPOSE OF THE CRIMINAL JUSTICE SYSTEM

Defining which actions are to be labeled "crimes" is only the first step in safeguarding society from criminal behavior. Institutions must be created to apprehend alleged wrongdoers, to determine whether these persons have indeed committed crimes, and to punish those who are found guilty according to society's wishes. These institutions combine to form the **criminal justice system.** As

we begin our examination of the American criminal justice system in this introductory chapter, it is important to have an idea of its purpose.

MAINTAINING JUSTICE

The explicit goal of the criminal justice system is to provide *justice* to all members of society. Because **justice** is a difficult concept to define, this goal can be challenging, if not impossible, to meet. Broadly stated, justice means that all individuals are equal before the law and that they are free from arbitrary arrest or seizure as defined by the law. In other words, the idea of justice is linked with the idea of fairness. Above all, we want our laws and the means by which they are carried out to be fair.

Justice and fairness are subjective terms, which is to say that people may have different concepts of what is just and fair. If a woman who has been beaten by her husband retaliates by killing him, what is her just punishment? Reasonable persons could disagree, with some thinking that the homicide was justified and that she should be treated leniently. Others might insist that she should not have taken the law into her own hands. Police officers, judges, prosecutors, prison administrators, and other employees of the criminal justice system must decide what is "fair." Sometimes, their course of action is obvious, but often, as we shall see, it is not.

PROTECTING SOCIETY

Within the broad mandate of "maintaining justice," Megan Kurlychek of the University at Albany, New York, has identified four specific goals of our criminal justice system:

1. To protect society from potential future crimes of the most dangerous or "risky" offenders.
2. To determine when an offense has been committed and provide the appropriate punishment for that offense.
3. To rehabilitate those offenders who have been punished so that it is safe to return them to the community.
4. To support crime victims and, to the extent possible, return them to their pre-crime status.[9]

Review the four goals of the criminal justice system at right. Which of the goals would be met by rehabilitating James Holmes, shown here with his attorney in a Colorado court, and returning him to society? Which would be met by putting him in prison for life?
RJ Sangosti-Pool/Getty Images

Again, though these goals may seem straightforward, they are fraught with difficulty. Take the example of James Holmes, who was charged with twenty-four counts of murder and 116 counts of attempted murder by law enforcement officials on July 30, 2012. Ten days earlier, Holmes—armed with an assault rifle and three other guns—had apparently opened fire on the audience at a late-night screening of a Batman movie in Aurora, Colorado. Following the incident, authorities at the University of Colorado, where Holmes had been a graduate student, came under heavy criticism for not reacting more forcefully to staff concerns about his behavior. In the next chapter, we will study the challenges of predicting criminality.

In August 2012, Holmes's defense attorneys told a district judge that their client was mentally ill, causing many in Aurora and elsewhere to worry that he would *never* receive an appropriate punishment for his actions (see the photo alongside). In Chapter 3, you will learn how insanity can be used as a defense to criminal wrongdoing. Furthermore,

regardless of his mental state, should Holmes ever be set free? In Chapters 9 and 12 we will discuss the concept of rehabilitation and the role that victims play in the eventual return of offenders to the community. Throughout this textbook, you will come to better understand the criminal justice system by exposure to differing opinions on these topics and many others.

SELF ASSESSMENT

Fill in the blanks and check your answers on page 26.

The concept of _____ is closely linked with ideas of fairness and equal treatment for all, and it is a primary goal of American police officers, judges, and prison administrators. Other goals include _____ society from criminal behavior, _____ those who are guilty of criminal wrongdoing, and supporting the _____ of crime.

THE STRUCTURE OF THE CRIMINAL JUSTICE SYSTEM

Society places the burden of maintaining justice and protecting our communities on those who work for the three main institutions of the criminal justice system: law enforcement, the courts, and corrections. In this section, we take an introductory look at these institutions and their role in the criminal justice system as a whole.

THE IMPORTANCE OF FEDERALISM

To understand the structure of the criminal justice system, you must understand the concept of **federalism,** which means that government powers are shared by the national (federal) government and the states. The framers of the U.S. Constitution, fearful of tyranny and a too-powerful central government, chose the system of federalism as a compromise.

The appeal of federalism was that it established a strong national government capable of handling large-scale problems while allowing for state powers and local traditions. For example, earlier in the chapter we noted that physician-assisted suicide, though banned in most of the country, is legal in Oregon and Washington State. In 2006, the federal government challenged the decision made by voters in these two states to allow the practice. The United States Supreme Court sided with the states, ruling that the principle of federalism supported their freedom to differ from the majority viewpoint in this instance.[10]

The Constitution gave the national government certain express powers, such as the power to coin money, raise an army, and regulate interstate commerce. All other powers were left to the states, including the express power to enact whatever laws are necessary to protect the health, morals, safety, and welfare of their citizens. As the American criminal justice system has evolved, the ideals of federalism have ebbed somewhat. In particular, the powers of the national government have expanded significantly. (For a better understanding of how federalism works, see the feature *You Be the Senator—Banning Texting While Driving* on the following page.)

Federalism A form of government in which a written constitution provides for a division of powers between a central government and several regional governments.

LAW ENFORCEMENT The ideals of federalism can be clearly seen at the local, state, and federal levels of law enforcement. Although agencies from the different levels cooperate if the need arises, they have their own organizational structures and tend to operate independently of one another. We briefly introduce each level of law enforcement here and cover them in more detail in Chapters 4, 5, and 6.

Local and County Law Enforcement On the local level, the duties of law enforcement agencies are split between counties and municipalities. The chief law enforcement officer of most counties is the county sheriff. The sheriff is usually elected, with a two- or four-year term. In some areas, where city and county governments have merged, there is a county police force, headed by a chief of police. As Figure 1.1 on the facing page shows, the bulk of all police officers in the United States are employed at the local level. The majority work in departments that consist of fewer than 10 officers, though a large city such as New York may have a police force of about 36,000.

Local police are responsible for the "nuts and bolts" of law enforcement work. They investigate most crimes and attempt to deter crime through patrol activities. They apprehend criminals and participate in trial proceedings, if necessary. Local police are also charged with "keeping the peace," a broad set of duties that includes crowd and traffic control and the resolution of minor conflicts between citizens. In many areas, local police have the added obligation of providing social services such as dealing with domestic violence and child abuse.

State Law Enforcement Hawaii is the only state that does not have a state law enforcement agency. Generally, there are two types of state law enforcement agencies: those designated simply as "state police" and those designated as "highway patrols." State highway patrols concern themselves mainly with infractions on public highways and freeways. Other state law enforcers include fire marshals, who investigate suspicious

YOU BE THE SENATOR

Banning Texting While Driving

THE SITUATION According to a recent poll, one in five American drivers—and half of those between the ages of sixteen and twenty-four—admits to having texted on a smartphone or other electronic device while driving. Texting while behind the wheel makes our roads less safe—one study found that such behavior is twice as risky as driving with a 0.08 blood alcohol level, the general standard for drunk driving. The U.S. Transportation Department estimates that every year nearly 6,000 people are killed and another 530,000 are injured in car crashes connected to "distracted driving," which often involves cell phones or other mobile devices.

THE LAW More than thirty states ban texting while driving. Punishments vary: in California, the offense warrants a $20 fine, while in Utah it can result in three months in jail. The effectiveness of these state laws is somewhat questionable, however. In Missouri, state patrol officers, finding it difficult to determine when a person was texting behind the wheel, cited only eight offenders in the first five months after that state's prohibition went into effect. Furthermore, texting bans did nothing to reduce the number of auto accidents in four states surveyed recently, as most drivers appeared to be ignoring the laws.

YOUR DECISION Suppose that you are a U.S. senator representing your home state, and another senator introduces a bill that would give the federal government the power to force *all* states to ban texting while driving. Would you support this bill? Why or why not? What are the benefits and drawbacks of letting each state decide its own response to this problem?

To see how the U.S. Senate has responded to state texting bans, go to Example 1.1 in Appendix B.

Rasmus Rasmusson/iStockphoto/Photodisc/Shutterstock/James Stadl/iStockphoto

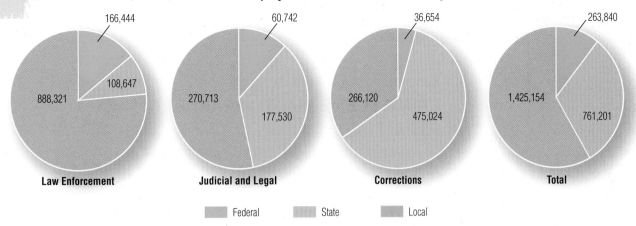

166,444

108,647

888,321

Law Enforcement

60,742

270,713

177,530

Judicial and Legal

36,654

266,120

475,024

Corrections

263,840

1,425,154

761,201

Total

Federal State Local

Source: Bureau of Justice Statistics, *Justice Expenditure and Employment in the United States, 2007* (Washington, D.C.: U.S. Department of Justice, September 2010), Table 2.

fires and educate the public on fire prevention, and fish, game, and watercraft wardens, who police a state's natural resources and often oversee its firearms laws. Some states also have alcoholic beverage control officers, as well as agents who investigate welfare and food stamp fraud.

Federal Law Enforcement The enactment of new national anti-terrorism, gun, drug, and violent crime laws over the past forty years has led to an expansion in the size and scope of the federal government's participation in the criminal justice system. The Department of Homeland Security, which we will examine in detail in Chapters 4 and 14, combines the police powers of twenty-four federal agencies to protect the United States from terrorist attacks. Other federal agencies with police powers include the Federal Bureau of Investigation (FBI), the Drug Enforcement Administration (DEA), the U.S. Secret Service, and the Bureau of Alcohol, Tobacco, Firearms and Explosives (ATF). In fact, almost every federal agency, including the postal and forest services, has some kind of police power.

Unlike their local and state counterparts, federal law enforcement agencies operate throughout the United States. In May 2012, for example, the FBI conducted a nationwide sweep targeting health care fraud, arresting more than one hundred doctors, nurses, and other medical professionals in seven cities ranging from Los Angeles to Chicago to Miami. Federal agencies are also able to provide support for local police departments, as happened in July 2011 when agents from the ATF joined forces with the Tulsa (Oklahoma) Police Department to combat a string of armed robberies that had plagued the city for nearly six months.

THE COURTS The United States has a *dual court system,* which means that we have two independent judicial systems, one at the federal level and one at the state level. In practice, this translates into fifty-two different court systems: one federal court system and fifty different state court systems, plus that of the District of Columbia.

As allowed under the rules of federalism, the U.S. (federal) criminal code lists about 4,500 crimes, while each state has its own criminal statutes that determine illegal acts under state law. In general, those defendants charged with violating federal criminal law will face trial in federal court, while those defendants charged with violating state law will appear in state court. The federal system consists of district courts, circuit courts of

CAREERS IN CJ

DIANA TABOR
CRIME SCENE PHOTOGRAPHER

A crime scene photographer's job is invaluable to those who are not present at the scene, yet need to be able to observe the scene as accurately as possible. I like the variety of my work. No two scenes are exactly alike, and the conditions pose different challenges. I have photographed scenes in cramped mobile homes, spacious homes, and out in the woods where we had to hike because there were no roads leading directly to the scene. I've been really hot and sweaty, fogging up the viewfinder. Then I have been so cold that I had to go sit in the van to let my hands and the camera warm up because they had stopped working.

I do wonder what the people at the gas stations think when we come in there after we're done to clean up and get something to drink. Fingerprint powder gets everywhere—I have found that nothing less than a shower really gets rid of it completely. It is sometimes difficult to accept that there is nothing to prevent the crime that has already happened, but I take pride in representing the victim when he or she cannot speak.

Social Media Career Tip

When you are posting on Facebook, assume that it will be published in your local newspaper and read by a potential employer. So, if you think the post might reflect poorly on you as a potential employee, keep it offline. **f** **Linked in**

FAST FACTS

CRIME SCENE PHOTOGRAPHER, JOB DESCRIPTION:

- Photograph physical evidence and crime scenes related to criminal investigations.
- Also must be able to compose reports, testify in court, and understand basic computer software and terminology.

WHAT KIND OF TRAINING IS REQUIRED?

- One year in law enforcement or commercial photography OR a degree or certificate in photography and darkroom techniques OR some combination of the above training or experience totaling one year.

ANNUAL SALARY RANGE?

- $45,780 – $53,290

---

appeals, and the United States Supreme Court. The state systems include trial courts, intermediate courts of appeals, and state supreme courts.

The *criminal court* and its work group—the judge, prosecutors, and defense attorneys—are charged with the weighty responsibility of determining the innocence or guilt of criminal suspects. We will cover these important participants, their roles in the criminal trial, and the court system as a whole in Chapters 7, 8, and 9.

Learning Objective 4 List the essential elements of the corrections system.

CORRECTIONS Once the court system convicts and sentences an offender, he or she is assigned to the corrections system. (Those convicted in a state court will be under the control of that state's corrections system, and those convicted of a federal crime will find themselves under the control of the federal corrections system.) Depending on the seriousness of the crime and their individual needs, offenders are placed on probation, incarcerated, or transferred to community-based correctional facilities.

- *Probation,* the most common correctional treatment, allows the offender to return to the community and remain under the supervision of an agent of the court known as a probation officer. While on probation, the offender must follow certain rules of conduct. When probationers fail to follow these rules, they may be incarcerated.

- If the offender's sentence includes a period of *incarceration,* he or she will be remanded to a correctional facility for a certain amount of time. *Jails* hold those convicted of minor crimes with relatively short sentences, as well as those awaiting trial or involved in certain court proceedings. *Prisons* house those convicted of more serious crimes with longer sentences. Generally speaking, counties and municipalities administer jails, while prisons are the responsibility of federal and state governments.

- *Community-based corrections* have increased in popularity as jails and prisons have been plagued with problems of funding and overcrowding. Community-based correctional facilities include halfway houses, residential centers, and work-release centers. They operate on the assumption that all convicts do not need, and are not benefited by, incarceration in jail or prison.

At midyear 2011, America's jails held approximately 730,000 inmates, including these residents of the Orange County jail in Santa Ana, California. What are the basic differences between jails and prisons?
Lucy Nicholson/Reuters/Landov

The majority of those inmates released from incarceration are not finished with the corrections system. The most frequent type of release from a jail or prison is *parole,* in which an inmate, after serving part of his or her sentence in a correctional facility, is allowed to serve the rest of the term in the community. Like someone on probation, a parolee must conform to certain conditions of freedom, with the same consequences if these conditions are not followed. Issues of probation, incarceration, community-based corrections, and parole will be covered in Chapters 10, 11, and 12.

THE CRIMINAL JUSTICE PROCESS

In its 1967 report, the President's Commission on Law Enforcement and Administration of Justice asserted that the criminal justice system

> is not a hodgepodge of random actions. It is rather a continuum—an orderly progression of events—some of which, like arrest and trial, are highly visible and some of which, though of great importance, occur out of public view.[11]

The commission's assertion that the criminal justice system is a "continuum" is one that many observers would challenge.[12] Some liken the criminal justice system to a sports team, which is the sum of an indeterminable number of decisions, relationships, conflicts, and adjustments.[13] Such a volatile mix is not what we generally associate with a "system." For most, the word **system** indicates a certain degree of order and discipline. That we refer to our law enforcement agencies, courts, and correctional facilities as part of a "system" may reflect our hopes rather than reality. Still, it will be helpful to familiarize yourself with the basic steps of the *criminal justice process,* or the procedures through which the criminal justice system meets the expectations of society. These basic steps are provided in Figure 1.2 on the following page.

In his classic study of the criminal justice system, Herbert Packer, a professor at Stanford University, compared the ideal criminal justice process to an assembly line,

System A set of interacting parts that, when functioning properly, achieve a desired result.

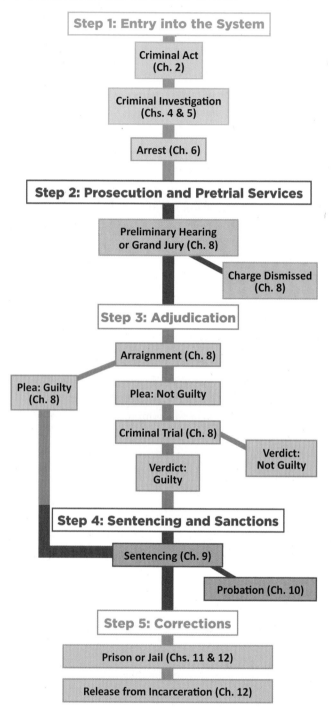

FIGURE 1.2 The Criminal Justice Process
This diagram provides a simplified overview of the basic steps of the criminal justice process, from criminal act to release from incarceration. Next to each step, you will find the chapter of this textbook in which the event is covered.

Step 1: Entry into the System

Criminal Act (Ch. 2)

Criminal Investigation (Chs. 4 & 5)

Arrest (Ch. 6)

Step 2: Prosecution and Pretrial Services

Preliminary Hearing or Grand Jury (Ch. 8)

Charge Dismissed (Ch. 8)

Step 3: Adjudication

Arraignment (Ch. 8)

Plea: Guilty (Ch. 8)

Plea: Not Guilty

Criminal Trial (Ch. 8)

Verdict: Not Guilty

Verdict: Guilty

Step 4: Sentencing and Sanctions

Sentencing (Ch. 9)

Probation (Ch. 10)

Step 5: Corrections

Prison or Jail (Chs. 11 & 12)

Release from Incarceration (Ch. 12)

Formal Criminal Justice Process The model of the criminal justice process in which participants follow formal rules to create a smoothly functioning disposition of cases from arrest to punishment.

"down which moves an endless stream of cases, never stopping."[14] In Packer's image of assembly-line justice, each step of the **formal criminal justice process** involves a series of "routinized operations" with the end goal of getting the criminal defendant from point A (his or her arrest by law enforcement) to point B (the criminal trial) to point C (if guilty, her or his punishment).[15] As Packer himself was wont to point out, the daily operations of criminal justice rarely operate so smoothly. In this textbook, the criminal justice process will be examined as the end product of many different decisions made by many different criminal justice professionals in law enforcement, the courts, and corrections.

SELFASSESSMENT

Fill in the blanks and check your answers on page 27.

To protect against a too-powerful central government, the framers of the U.S. Constitution relied on the principle of _____ to balance power between the national government and the states. Consequently, the United States has a _____ court system—one at the federal level and one at the _____ level. One expert has compared the _____ criminal justice process to an assembly line involving a series of routine operations.

> "It is the spirit and not the form of the law that keeps justice alive."
>
> **—Earl Warren,**
> American judge
> (1891–1974)

DISCRETION AND ETHICS

Learning Objective 5 Explain the difference between the formal and informal criminal justice processes.

Practically, the formal criminal justice process suffers from a serious drawback: it is unrealistic. Law enforcement agencies do not have the staff or funds to investigate *every* crime, so they must decide where to direct their limited resources. Increasing caseloads and a limited amount of time in which to dispose of them constrict many of our nation's courts. Overcrowding in prisons and jails affects both law enforcement agencies and the courts—there is simply not enough room for all convicts.

The criminal justice system relies on *discretion* to alleviate these pressures. By **discretion,** we mean the authority to choose between and among alternative courses of action, based on individual judgment and conscience. Collectively, the discretionary decisions made by criminal justice professionals are said to produce an **informal criminal justice process** that does not operate within the rigid confines of formal rules and laws.

INFORMAL DECISION MAKING

By their nature, many, if not most, criminal statutes require informal decision making. To take just one example, rule 1050(7)(J) of New York City's transit code criminalizes the act of putting one's feet on a subway seat or taking up more than one seat if it interferes with other passengers' comfort.[16] Each year, nearly 1.6 billion riders use New York's subway system,[17] and many of them, at some point, violate rule 1050(7)(J). If each offender were arrested for doing so, the city's police officers would have little time to prevent other crimes, and the city's courts and jails would be overwhelmed.

In 2011, New York police officers handed out only 6,000 tickets and made only about 1,600 arrests for violations of this particular criminal offense.[18] Obviously, in the vast majority of cases, officers used their discretion to merely issue a warning or "look the other way" when confronted with inconsiderate subway riders. In Chapters 4, 5, and 6, we will examine many other circumstances that call for discretionary decision making by law enforcement officers. (See *Mastering Concepts—How Discretion Works* on the following page to get a better idea of discretion's role in the informal criminal justice process.)

Discretion The ability of individuals in the criminal justice system to make operational decisions based on personal judgment instead of formal rules or official information.

Informal Criminal Justice Process A model of the criminal justice system that recognizes the informal authority exercised by individuals at each step of the criminal justice process.

THE PITFALLS OF DISCRETION

Unfortunately, the informal criminal justice system does not always benefit from measured, rational decision making. Individual judgment can be tainted by personal bias, erroneous or irrational thinking, and plain ill will. When this occurs, discretion becomes "the power to *get away* with alternative decisions (emphasis added)."[19] Indeed, many of the rules

Laura is a hypothetical fifteen-year-old living in Northport, Alabama. She recently decided to impress her boyfriend, Tim, also fifteen, by taking sexually suggestive photos of herself and sending them to his smartphone. One day, after Tim uses it in class, the device is confiscated, and a teacher discovers Laura's racy photos.

Alabama state law prohibits the "electronic reproduction of minors engaged in real or simulated sexual activity." Technically, Laura has broken this law. Without discretion, a state prosecutor would be forced to charge her with disseminating child pornography. State prosecutors do have discretion in this area, however, and can choose from several different options, such as sending Laura to counseling or allowing her parents to handle the matter. In making this discretionary decision, an Alabama prosecutor might consider the following factors:

- State law is designed to punish adult child pornographers, not inappropriately romantic juveniles.
- Laura did not mean for anybody but Tim to see the photos.
- The punishment for this crime can be quite harsh, including jail time, a fine, and registration as a sex offender (discussed in Chapter 12).
- This behavior, sometimes known as "sexting," is widespread among Northport teens, and punishing Laura for it might have a strong deterrent effect.

iStockphoto/Sean Locke

According to a recent survey, one in five American teenagers admits to having sexted. In most instances, law enforcement professionals have used their discretion to refrain from arresting and prosecuting teens involved in this type of behavior when no adults are involved. As one legal expert noted, "What are we going to do? Lock up 20 percent of America's teens?"

of the formal criminal justice process are designed to keep its employees from substituting their own judgment for that of the general public, as expressed by the law.

Regarding the New York subway statute discussed above, one judge denounced what he saw as a "disconnect between the code's goals and its enforcement."[20] Problematically, most of the arrests seemed to take place late at night or early in the morning, when the subway cars were least crowded and most riders were members of minority groups on their way to work. Furthermore, associate Supreme Court justice Antonin Scalia has criticized discretion in the courts for its tendency to cause discriminatory and disparate criminal sentences, a subject we will discuss in Chapter 9. According to Scalia, the need for fairness and certainty in the criminal justice system outweighs the practical benefits of widespread and unpredictable discretionary decision making.[21]

ETHICS AND JUSTICE

Learning
Objective **6** Define *ethics* and describe the role that they play in discretionary decision making.

How can we reconcile the need for some sort of discretion in criminal justice with the ever-present potential for abuse? Part of the answer lies in our initial definition of discretion (see page 15), which mentions not only individual judgment but also *conscience*. Ideally, actors in the criminal justice system will make moral choices about what is right and wrong based on the norms that have been established by society. In other words, they will behave *ethically*.

Ethics in criminal justice are closely related to the concept of justice. Because criminal justice professionals are representatives of the state, they have the power to determine whether the state is treating its citizens fairly. If some New York police officers are in fact making the decision to arrest discourteous subway riders based on appearance, then they are not only acting unethically but also unjustly.

ETHICS AND THE LAW The line between ethics and justice is often difficult to discern, as ethical standards are usually not written into criminal statutes. Consequently, individuals must often "fill in" the ethical blanks. To make this point, ethics expert John Kleinig

Ethics The moral principles that govern a person's perception of right and wrong.

uses the real-life example of a police officer who refused to arrest a homeless person for sleeping in a private parking garage. Despite a local ordinance that clearly forbids such behavior, the officer felt it would be unethical to make an arrest in that situation unless the homeless person was disturbing the peace or otherwise acting in a disorderly manner. The officer's supervisors were unsympathetic to his ethical stance, and he was suspended from duty without pay.[22]

ETHICS AND CRITICAL THINKING Did the police officer in the above example behave ethically by inserting his own beliefs into the letter of the criminal law? Would an officer who arrested peaceful homeless trespassers be acting unethically? In some cases, the ethical decision will be *intuitive*, reflecting an automatic response determined by a person's background and experiences. In other cases, however, intuition is not enough. *Critical thinking* is needed for an ethical response.[23] Throughout this textbook, we will use the principle of critical thinking—which involves developing analytical skills and reasoning—to address the many ethical challenges inherent in the criminal justice system.

SELFASSESSMENT

Fill in the blanks and check your answers on page 27.
At every level, the criminal justice system relies on the _____ of its employees to keep it from being bogged down by formal rules. Some critics think that this freedom to make decisions leads to the dominance of an _____ criminal justice system, which can, in some cases, result in unequal treatment and even discrimination. Ideally, to avoid this kind of injustice, criminal justice professionals will incorporate proper _____ in their decision-making process.

CRIMINAL JUSTICE TODAY

Learning Objective 7 Contrast the crime control and due process models.

In describing the general direction of the criminal justice system as a whole, many observers point to two models introduced by Herbert Packer: the *crime control model* and the *due process model*.[24] The underlying value of the **crime control model** is that the most important function of the criminal justice process is to punish and repress criminal conduct. The system must be quick and efficient, placing as few restrictions as possible on the ability of law enforcement officers to make discretionary decisions in apprehending criminals.

Although not in direct conflict with crime control, the underlying values of the **due process model** focus more on protecting the rights of the accused through formal, legal restraints on the police, courts, and corrections. That is, the due process model relies on the courts to make it more difficult to prove guilt. It rests on the belief that it is more desirable for society that ninety-nine guilty suspects go free than that a single innocent person be condemned.[25]

Crime Control Model A criminal justice model that places primary emphasis on the right of society to be protected from crime and violent criminals.

Due Process Model A criminal justice model that places primacy on the right of the individual to be protected from the power of the government.

CRIME AND LAW ENFORCEMENT: THE BOTTOM LINE

It is difficult to say which of Packer's two models has the upper hand today. As we will see later in the section, homeland security concerns have brought much of the criminal justice system in line with crime control values. At the same time, dropping arrest and imprisonment rates suggest that due process values are strong, as well. Indeed, in 2011, the number of violent crimes committed in the United States decreased for the fifth straight year, reaching the lowest level in four decades.[26]

Property crimes also declined slightly in 2011, contradicting the conventional wisdom that when people are out of work and need money, they turn to crime as a last resort. Despite the economic downturn that has gripped the country for several years, the expected higher levels of criminality did not occur. Juvenile crime rates are also declining, a subject we will address in Chapter 13. Alfred Blumstein of Carnegie Mellon University in Pittsburgh has called all this good news "striking," because it comes "at a time when everyone anticipated [crime rates] could be going up because of the recession."[27]

SMARTER POLICING Just as law enforcement inevitably gets a great deal of the blame when crime rates are high, American police forces have received much credit for the apparent decline in criminality. The consensus is that the police have become smarter and more disciplined over the past two decades, putting into practice strategies that allow them to more effectively prevent crime. For example, the widespread use of *proactive policing* promotes more rigorous enforcement of minor offenses—such as drunkenness and public disorder—with an eye toward preventing more serious wrongdoing.[28] In addition, *hot-spot policing* has law enforcement officers focusing on high-crime areas rather than spreading their resources evenly throughout a metropolitan area.[29] These and other policing strategies will be explored more fully in Chapter 5.

IDENTIFYING CRIMINALS Technology has also played a significant role in improving law enforcement efficiency. Police investigators are reaping the benefits of perhaps the most effective new crime-fighting tool since fingerprint identification: DNA profiling.[30] This technology allows law enforcement agents to identify a suspect from body fluid evidence (such as blood, saliva, or semen) or biological evidence (such as hair strands or fingernail clippings). As we will see in Chapter 5, by collecting DNA from convicts and storing the information in databases, investigators have been able to reach across hundreds of miles and back in time to catch wrongdoers.

Law enforcement's ability to identify criminal suspects is set to receive another boost with the increased use of **biometrics.** The term refers to the various technological devices that read a person's unique physical characteristics and report his or her identity to authorities. The most common biometric devices record a suspect's fingerprints, but hand geometry, facial features, and the minute details of the human eye can also provide biometric identification.[31]

Biometrics Methods to identify a person based on his or her unique physical characteristics, such as fingerprints or facial configuration.

CJ&TECHNOLOGY

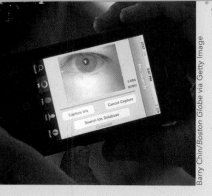

Mobile Offender Recognition and Identification System (MORIS)

It seems as though there is an app for everything these days—even biometrics. Recently, law enforcement agents in about forty counties began using the Mobile Offender Recognition and Identification System (MORIS). With the device, which weighs about twelve ounces and attaches to an iPhone, the police officer takes a photograph of a suspect's face from five feet away, or of the suspect's eyes from a distance of six inches. The app is then engaged to search for a facial or iris match from a national database to determine whether the suspect has a previous record.

Barry Chin/Boston Globe via Getty Image

Without MORIS, a police officer must transport the suspect back to the station house, take her or his fingerprints, and then wait up to a week to hear if the FBI was able to produce a match. With MORIS, the digital search is completed within seconds. "This is a game changer for law enforcement," says Pinal County (Arizona) sheriff Paul Babeu, who was happy to pay the $3,000 cost of each MORIS unit. "It's worth its weight in gold."

THINKING ABOUT MORIS: Why is MORIS a "game changer" for law enforcement? Should this technology be made available to ordinary citizens? Why or why not?

CONTINUING CHALLENGES FOR LAW ENFORCEMENT Not every policing trend is positive. Due to the worsening economic conditions discussed above, according to one recent survey, about half of the nation's local law enforcement agencies have been subject to budget cuts in recent years.[32] The impact of these cuts, which include officer layoffs and resource reductions, could seriously hamper efforts to combat three of the major challenges facing today's police: gangs, guns, and illegal drugs.

The Scourge of Street Gangs For many local law enforcement agencies, particularly those in large metropolitan areas, success is measured by their ability to control **street gangs.** These gangs are often identified as groups of offenders who band together to engage in violent, unlawful, or criminal activity. According to the most recent data, more than 33,000 gangs, with approximately 1.4 million members, are criminally active in the United States. The same study estimates that gangs are responsible for an average of 48 percent of violent crime in most cities, and for up to 90 percent in the worst-hit areas.[33] The FBI's "Safe Streets" initiative—in which the federal agency teams up with local police forces—has resulted in the arrest of more than 23,000 gang members over the past decade, but such efforts are threatened by budget cuts at the municipal and county levels.

Gun Sales and Gun Control In many cities, high levels of gang activity have led to high levels of gun violence.[34] Even though overall weapons violations have decreased along with other criminal activity, Carnegie Mellon's Alfred Blumstein suggests that the most serious threat to America's positive crime outlook is not the economy but an increase in the number of guns in high-crime neighborhoods.[35]

Overall, about 30,000 people are killed by gunfire in the United States each year, and illegally obtained firearms are a constant concern for law enforcement officials. At the same time, legal ownership of guns is widespread, with almost one-third of American households possessing at least one gun.[36] In 2008, the United States Supreme Court further solidified the legal basis for this practice by ruling that the U.S. Constitution protects an individual's right to "bear arms."[37] The Court's decision has done little to lessen the debate over **gun control,** a blanket term used to describe the policies that the government implements to keep firearms out of the hands of the wrong people.

Street Gang A group of people, usually three or more, who share a common identity and engage in illegal activities.

Gun Control Efforts by a government to regulate or control the sale of guns.

Two police officers in Salinas, California, question a male suspect about his gang affiliation. Why might an extra law enforcement presence in gang-ridden neighborhoods lead to a reduction in crime in those areas?

Monica Almeida/*New York Times*/Redux Pictures

The Illegal Drugs Problem One area in which the nation's crime outlook has not been particularly encouraging involves illegal drugs. Between 1980 and 2009, while arrests for most criminal behavior declined, the arrest rate for illegal drug possession and use increased by 122 percent.[38]

The broadest possible definition of a **drug,** which includes alcohol, is any substance that modifies biological, psychological, or social behavior. In popular terminology, however, the word *drug* has a specific connotation. When people speak of the "drug problem," or the "war on drugs," or "drug abuse," they are referring specifically to illegal **psychoactive drugs,** which alter the consciousness or perception of the user. Almost all of the drugs that we will be discussing in this textbook, such as marijuana, cocaine, heroin, and amphetamines, are illegal and psychoactive.

The main source of drug use data is the National Survey on Drug Use and Health, conducted annually by the National Institute on Drug Abuse (see Figure 1.3 on the facing page). According to the survey, only about 9 percent of those questioned had used an illegal drug in the past month. Even so, this means that a significant number of Americans—nearly 23 million—are regularly using illegal drugs, and the figure mushrooms when users of legal substances such as alcohol (131 million users) and tobacco (70 million users) are included.[39] Drug abuse often leads to further criminal behavior in adolescents, as we will see when we look at the juvenile justice system in Chapter 13. In general, the growing market for illegal drugs causes significant damage both in the United States and in countries such as Mexico that supply America with its "fix."

HOMELAND SECURITY AND INDIVIDUAL RIGHTS

"September 11 is the day that never ends," wrote journalist Richard Cohen on the occasion of the tenth anniversary of the events of that day in 2001.[40] Without question, the attacks of September 11, 2001—when terrorists hijacked four commercial airlines and used them to kill nearly three thousand people in New York City, northern Virginia, and rural Pennsylvania—were the most significant events of the first decade of the 2000s as far as crime fighting is concerned. As we will see throughout this textbook, the resulting **homeland security** movement has touched nearly every aspect of criminal justice. This movement has the ultimate goal of protecting America from **terrorism,** which can be broadly defined as the random use of staged violence to achieve political goals.

THE PATRIOT ACT The need to respond to the terrorist threat led American politicians and police officials to turn sharply toward crime control principles, as discussed on page 17. In particular, the USA Patriot Act,[41] passed six weeks after the 9/11 attacks, strengthened the ability of federal law enforcement agents to investigate and incarcerate suspects. The 342-page piece of legislation is difficult to summarize, but some of its key provisions include the following:

- An expansion of the definition of what it means to "engage in terrorist activity" to include providing "material support" through such activities as fund-raising or operating Web sites for suspected terrorist organizations.
- Greater leeway for law enforcement agents to track Internet use, access private financial records, and wiretap those suspected of terrorist activity.
- A reduction in the amount of evidence that law enforcement agents need to gather before taking a terrorist suspect into custody.

In addition to this kind of legislative action, billions of dollars have been funneled into America's homeland security apparatus, with the majority of the funds going to federal agencies under the control of the Department of Homeland Security. Local police departments are also crucial participants in this area of law enforcement. The worry, discussed in Chapter 4, is that the homeland security burden on local police will become too great—especially if budget cuts related to the economic downturn continue to stretch the departments' already limited resources.

A "THREAT" OR A "TOOL"? In a 2011 poll, 34 percent of those questioned about the Patriot Act felt that the law "goes too far and poses a threat too civil liberties." The term **civil liberties** refers to the personal freedom from government interference guaranteed to all Americans by the U.S. Constitution, particularly the first ten amendments, known as the Bill of Rights. Another 42 percent polled considered the legislation "a necessary tool that helps the government find terrorists."[42]

Concerns about balancing personal freedoms and personal safety permeate our criminal justice system. In fact, an entire chapter of this textbook—Chapter 6—is needed to discuss the rules that law enforcement must follow to protect the civil liberties of crime suspects. As we will discuss in more depth in Chapter 14, the topic is particularly important, and widely debated, when it comes to homeland security. Here are just a few examples:

1. The First Amendment to the U.S. Constitution states that the government shall not interfere with citizens' "freedom of speech." Does this mean that individuals should be allowed to support terrorist causes on the Internet?

2. The Fourth Amendment protects against "unreasonable searches and seizures." Does this mean that law enforcement agents should be able to seize the computer of a terrorist subject without any actual proof of wrongdoing?

3. The Sixth Amendment guarantees a trial by jury to a person accused of a crime. Does this mean that the U.S. military can find a suspect guilty of terrorist actions without providing a jury trial?

Critics of counterterrorism measures, such as intercepting suspected terrorists' e-mails and increasing security at airports, believe that the government has overstepped its bounds. Supporters of these and other tactics point out that as of September 2012, such efforts have succeeded in protecting Americans from another large-scale terrorist attack. The feature *Anti-Terrorism in Action—Trapping a Lone Wolf* on the following page provides an introduction to the tactics that law enforcement employs to fight homegrown terrorism, a subject we will return to in Chapters 5 and 14.

INMATE POPULATIONS: A NEW TREND

The proposition seems logical: if more criminals spend more time behind bars, crime rates will decline. Rising incarceration rates cannot be credited for the recent crime decline, however—for the first time in four decades, incarceration rates are not rising.

FIGURE 1.3 Drug Use in the United States

According to the National Survey on Drug Use and Health, nearly 23 million Americans, or about 9 percent of those over twelve years old, can be considered "illicit drug users." As you can see, most of these people used marijuana exclusively. Furthermore, eighteen- to twenty-five-year-olds were more likely to have used illegal drugs than any other segment of the population.

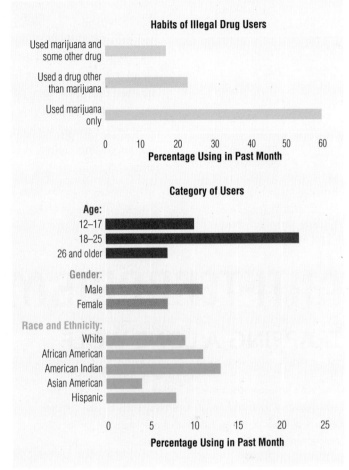

Source: National Survey on Drug Use and Health, 2011.

Civil Liberties The basic rights and freedoms for American citizens guaranteed by the U.S. Constitution, particularly in the Bill of Rights.

After increasing by 500 percent from 1980 to 2008, the inmate population in the United States has leveled off and, as you can see in Figure 1.4 on the facing page, has even decreased slightly over the past several years. Certainly, these decreases have been small, and the American corrections system remains immense, with nearly 2.3 million offenders in prison or jail and another 4.9 million under community supervision.[43] Still, the new trend reflects a series of crucial changes in the American criminal justice system.

THE ECONOMICS OF INCARCERATION For many years, the growing prison population was fed by a number of "get tough on crime" laws passed by politicians in response to the crime wave of the late 1980s and early 1990s. These sentencing laws—discussed in Chapter 9—made it more likely that a person arrested for a crime would wind up behind bars and that once there, he or she would not be back in the community for a long while. The recent reversal of this pattern does not mean that American politicians no longer want to "get tough" with criminals. Rather, as Ram Cnaan, a professor at the University of Pennsylvania, notes, it reflects a painful truth about prison and jail inmates: "They simply cost too much."[44]

ANTI-TERRORISM IN ACTION

TRAPPING A LONE WOLF

Following the terrorist attacks of September 11, 2001, America's anti-terrorism efforts initially focused on stopping radicalized groups of foreign enemies, such as Osama bin Laden's al Qaeda. Now, authorities are increasingly focusing their attention closer to home, on "lone wolf" suspects such as Sami Osmakac.

A twenty-five-year-old U.S. citizen living with his parents in Pinellas Park, Florida, Osmakac first appeared on the homeland security radar in September 2011, when he walked into a Tampa store looking for al Qaeda flags. The store owner alerted the FBI to the request. Two months later, the same store owner told the federal agency that Osmakac had wanted to obtain weapons and attack targets in Tampa. Because of their inexperience, Osmakac and other homegrown "wannabe" terrorists are natural targets for well-placed insiders. According to the Center on Law and Security at New York University, 62 percent of the federal government's most significant terrorism prosecutions have relied on evidence provided by informants such as the store owner.

On December 21, Osmakac met with an undercover FBI agent, from whom he attempted to buy an AK-47-style machine gun, Uzi submachine guns, high-capacity magazines, grenades, and an explosive belt. Osmakac then bragged that he wanted to bomb local nightclubs and the Hillsborough

County sheriff's office, while the explosive belt would help him to "get in somewhere where there's lots of people" and take hostages.

FOILED AGAIN

Because of the potential for widespread loss of life, the goal in counterterrorism operations is not to solve a crime after it has occurred but rather to prevent the crime from happening in the first place. Consequently, federal authorities arrested Osmakac on January 7, 2012, after he purchased explosive devices and firearms from the FBI undercover agent. He was charged with one count of attempted use of a weapon of mass destruction. If convicted, Osmakac could spend the rest of his life in federal prison. According to the Heritage Foundation, a conservative think tank in Washington, D.C., Osmakac's arrest marked the forty-fourth terrorist attack against the United States that has been thwarted since September 11, 2001.

FOR CRITICAL ANALYSIS Federal authorities disabled the explosive devices and firearms before selling them to Osmakac. So, he never posed an imminent danger to the Tampa community. Why are law enforcement officers justified in making an arrest even if a terrorist plot, or any criminal enterprise, is still in the planning stages?

FIGURE 1.4 Prison and Jail Populations in the United States, 1985–2011

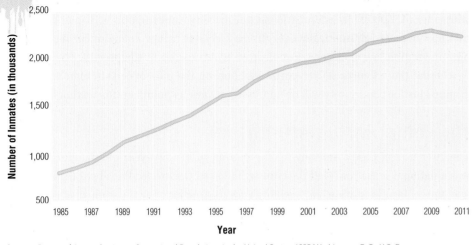

Sources: Bureau of Justice Statistics, *Correctional Populations in the United States, 1995* (Washington, D.C.: U.S. Department of Justice, June 1997), Table 1.1, page 12; and Bureau of Justice Statistics, *Correctional Population in the United States, 2011* (Washington, D.C.: U.S. Department of Justice, 2012), 2.

A recent survey of state corrections officials found "budget cuts" to be the most pressing issue in the field.[45] One way of bringing corrections spending under control is to grant early release to nonviolent offenders. Another is to divert offenders from jail and prison through special courts that promote rehabilitation rather than punishment for certain offenders. Also, corrections officials are implementing a number of programs to reduce the *recidivism rate* of ex-convicts, which stands at about 45 percent.[46] **Recidivism** refers to the act of committing another crime after a person has already been punished for previous criminal behavior. We will examine these policies and their ramifications for the nation's prisons and jails in Chapters 10, 11, and 12.

DNA AND THE DEATH PENALTY On April 30, 2012, after spending sixteen years in prison, Robert Dewey was released by a Colorado judge when DNA evidence showed that he most likely was not responsible for the murder and rape of a woman found strangled with a dog collar. Dewey is part of a small but important subset of former prisoners: those released after postconviction DNA testing. As of August 2012, such testing had freed 297 people who had been arrested by police, found guilty at trial, and placed behind bars.[47] Earlier in this section we noted the benefits of DNA testing as a crime-fighting tool. Here, we see that it can also act as a corrective for law enforcement and prosecutorial mistakes.

Another interesting corrections trend involves death row inmates, who are in prison awaiting execution after having been found guilty of committing a **capital crime.** In April 2012, the death row population in American prisons stood at 3,170, down from 3,652 in 2000. From 2000 to 2011, the number of executions in this country dropped from 85 to 43.[48] Judges and juries, it seems, have become less willing to sentence the "worst of the worst" criminals to death. In 2011, the number of death sentences fell below one hundred for the first time since the early 1970s.[49] We will further explore *capital punishment,* one of the most controversial issues concerning the criminal justice system, in Chapter 9.

INCARCERATION AND RACE One troublesome aspect of capital punishment is that a black defendant is much more likely to be sentenced to death for killing a white victim than a white defendant is for killing a black victim.[50] Indeed, looking at the general statistics, a bleak picture of minority incarceration emerges. Even though African Americans

Recidivism The act of committing a new crime after a person has already been punished for a previous crime by being convicted and sent to jail or prison.

Capital Crime A criminal act that makes the offender eligible to receive the death penalty.

make up only 13 percent of the general population in the United States, the number of black men in state and federal prisons (561,000) is significantly larger than the number of white men (452,000).[51] In federal prisons, one in every three inmates is Hispanic,[52] a ratio that has increased dramatically over the past decade as law enforcement has focused on immigration law violations, a subject we will consider in Chapter 14. The question of whether these figures reflect purposeful bias on the part of certain members of the criminal justice community will be addressed at various points in this textbook.

Learning Objective 8 List the major issues in criminal justice today.

THE SOCIAL MEDIA REVOLUTION

The 2011 trial of Casey Anthony for the murder of her two-year-old daughter, Caylee, was a national sensation. Half the country followed the proceedings on a regular basis, and one cable news station had 5 million viewers tune in to see the somewhat surprising announcement that a Florida jury had found Anthony not guilty. Part of the reason for this interest was undoubtedly the lurid, dramatic tone to the case. But, thanks to *social media,* more Americans were able to follow the trial more closely than would have been possible even in the recent past.

Social media are Internet-based technologies that allow users to interact with each other and with the larger community of users. The most popular are social networking sites, such as Facebook and Google+, through which users can create and share personal profiles, and microblogs such as Twitter, where they can post short comments for public consumption. The most reliable news source for the Anthony trial was not a traditional media outlet but rather a Twitter account set up by the Ninth Judicial Circuit Court of Florida.[53] After the verdict, a Facebook event post asking people to turn on their porch lights in Caylee's memory had 2.5 million respondents within forty-eight hours.[54]

TECHNOLOGICAL STRATEGIES The social media's impact on the criminal justice system goes well beyond stimulating public interest in high-profile court cases. Criminal justice professionals are increasingly adapting the technology to their specific endeavors. Casey Anthony's defense attorneys hired a consultant to read through the tens of thousands of social media comments generated by the trial. Then, the lawyers adjusted their strategy according to public opinion. For example, the social media community was quite critical of Anthony's father, George, mostly due to his alleged extramarital affair. As a result, Anthony's lawyers became much more aggressive in challenging her father's testimony during the trial.[55] Prosecutors have also begun to mine social media, scouring the sites for relevant information on defendants and witnesses.

As we will discuss in Chapter 5, law enforcement agents are benefiting from social media as an investigative tool. Departmental Facebook pages have proved to be a popular thoroughfare for anonymous crime tips, and police officers can develop important leads on suspects without leaving their desks. Law enforcement agencies are also using social media to provide information. The Hillsborough (New Jersey) Police Department, for example, has created a Twitter feed that allows residents to receive instant alerts about dangerous weather conditions, road closures, and "hot spots" of criminal activity.

TECHNOLOGICAL OFFENSES As a rule, technology that helps law enforcement provides new outlets for criminals as well. Social media are no exception. Groups of shoplifters employ

On June 15, 2011, thousands of Canadian hockey fans, including this one, went on a violent rampage in downtown Vancouver, British Columbia. How can law enforcement agencies take advantage of social media to identify offenders in these kinds of acts of mass violence?

Anthony Bolante/Reuters/Landov

Twitter and Facebook to organize "flash-robs," in which a certain establishment is targeted and raided within minutes. Street gangs go to the Internet to recruit new members and organize criminal enterprises. Because of the anonymity they provide, social media are also natural outlets for stalking, bullying, and harassment, topics we address in Chapter 14's section on cyber crime. "The fascinating thing about technology is that once we open the door, it's going to move in ways that we can't always predict and are slow to control," says Scott Decker, a criminal justice professor at Arizona State University.[56]

SELFASSESSMENT

Fill in the blanks and check your answers on page 27.

The _____ _____ model of criminal justice places great importance on high rates of apprehension and conviction of criminal suspects. In contrast, the _____ _____ model emphasizes the rights of the _____ over the powers of the government. Despite predictions to the contrary, crime rates in the United States have steadily _____ over the past several years. At the same time, _____ populations are also decreasing for the first time since the early 1970s. Legislation known as the _____ Act was the initial, and the most comprehensive, reaction to the _____ attacks against the United States on September 11, 2001.

CHAPTER SUMMARY

Learning Objective 1 **Describe the two most common models of how society determines which acts are criminal.** The consensus model argues that the majority of citizens will agree on which activities should be outlawed and punished as crimes. It rests on the assumption that a diverse group of people can have similar morals. In contrast, the conflict model argues that in a diverse society, the dominant groups exercise power by codifying their value systems into criminal laws.

Learning Objective 2 **Define *crime*.** Crime is any action punishable under criminal statutes and is considered an offense against society. Therefore, alleged criminals are prosecuted by the state rather than by victims. Crimes are punishable by sanctions that bring about a loss of personal freedom or, in some cases, fines.

Learning Objective 3 **Outline the three levels of law enforcement.** Because we have a federal system of government, law enforcement occurs at the (a) national, or federal, level and the (b) state level and within the states at (c) local and county levels. Because crime is mostly a local concern, most employees in the criminal justice system work for local governments. Agencies at the federal level include the FBI, the DEA, and the U.S. Secret Service, among others.

Learning Objective 4 **List the essential elements of the corrections system.** Criminal offenders are placed on probation, incarcerated in a jail or prison, transferred to community-based corrections facilities, or released on parole.

Learning Objective 5 **Explain the difference between the formal and informal criminal justice processes.** The formal criminal justice process involves the somewhat mechanical steps that are designed to guide criminal defendants from arrest to possible punishment. For every step in the formal process, though, someone has discretion, and such discretion leads to an informal process. Even when prosecutors believe that a suspect is guilty, they have the discretion not to prosecute, for example.

Learning Objective 6 **Define *ethics* and describe the role that they play in discretionary decision making.** Ethics are the moral principles that guide a person's perception of right and wrong. Most criminal justice professionals have a great deal of discretionary leeway in their day-to-day decision making, and their ethical beliefs can help ensure that they make such decisions in keeping with society's established values.

Contrast the crime control and due process models. The crime control model assumes that the criminal justice system is designed to protect the public from criminals. Thus, its most important function is to punish and repress criminal conduct. The due process model presumes that the accused are innocent and provides them with the most complete safeguards, usually within the court system.

List the major issues in criminal justice today. (a) Falling violent and property crime rates; (b) the impact of an extended recession on crime rates; (c) improved policing strategies; (d) street gangs; (e) gun sales and gun control; (f) use of illegal drugs; (g) homeland security; (h) the Patriot Act and civil liberties; (i) America's shrinking, though still massive, inmate population; (j) cost-cutting measures in the corrections system; (k) possible bias against minorities in the criminal justice system; and (l) social media in the criminal justice system.

QUESTIONS FOR CRITICAL ANALYSIS

1. How is it possible to have a consensus about what should or should not be illegal in a country with several hundred million adults from all races, religions, and walks of life?

2. What would be some of the drawbacks of having the victims of a crime, rather than the state (through its public officials), prosecute criminals?

3. Several years ago, lawmakers in Arkansas and New York considered passing laws against "distracted walkers," or pedestrians who use cell phones, iPods, and other electronic devices while walking on city streets. What would be some of the reasons for instituting these kinds of laws? What is your opinion of any law that prohibits "distracted walking" (or "jogging" or "bicycling")?

4. Refer back to the discussion of the police officer who refused to arrest the nonviolent homeless person on pages 16 and 17. Did the officer act properly in this situation, or should he have carried out the law regardless of his personal ethical beliefs? Explain your answer.

5. As noted in the chapter, over the past several years crime rates have decreased even as the American economy has suffered through the "Great Recession." One theory for this development is that as overall economic activity slows, more people who would otherwise be at work are unemployed and thus are spending more time at home. Consequently, their residences are no longer easy targets for burglaries, and because they themselves are at home, they are no longer victimized by street robberies. What is your opinion of this theory? What other explanation could there be for decreasing crime rates during a recession?

KEY TERMS

biometrics **18**
capital crime **23**
civil liberties **21**
conflict model **6**
consensus model **5**
crime **5**
crime control model **17**
criminal justice system **7**
deviance **7**

discretion **15**
drug **20**
due process model **17**
ethics **16**
federalism **9**
formal criminal justice process **14**
gun control **19**
homeland security **20**
informal criminal justice process **15**

justice **8**
morals **6**
psychoactive drugs **20**
recidivism **23**
street gang **19**
system **13**
terrorism **20**

SELF ASSESSMENT ANSWER KEY

Page 7: i. morals; **ii.** conflict; **iii.** society;
     iv. public officials/the government; **v.** deviance

Page 9: i. justice; **ii.** protecting; **iii.** punishing;
     iv. victims

Page 15: i. federalism; **ii.** dual; **iii.** state; **iv.** formal

Page 17: i. discretion; **ii.** informal; **iii.** ethics

Page 25: i. crime control; **ii.** due process; **iii.** individual; **iv.** decreased; **v.** prison; **vi.** Patriot; **vii.** terrorist

COURSEMATE

For online help and access to resources that accompany *Criminal Justice in Action: The Core,* go to **www.cengage-brain.com/shop/ISBN/978-1-285-06915-9**. Click "Access Now," where you will find flashcards, an online quiz, and other helpful study aids. If you have an access code for CourseMate, log in and go to the chapter of your choice for additional online study aids.

NOTES

1. Florida Statutes Sections 776.012-776.013 and 776.031-776.032.

2. Michael Bloomberg, quoted in "A Lethal Right to Self-Defense," *The Week* (May 4, 2012), 13.

3. Quoted in Lauren Ritchie, "'Stand your Ground' Shouldn't Give Pursuers the Right to Kill," *Orlando Sentinel* (April 8, 2012), A18.

4. Joe Palazzolo and Rob Barry, "More Killings Called Self-Defense," *Wall Street Journal* (March 31-April 1, 2012), A2.

5. *Ibid.*

6. For a list of states that have passed Stand Your Ground laws, see *ibid.*

7. Herman Bianchi, *Justice as Sanctuary: Toward a New System of Crime Control* (Bloomington: Indiana University Press, 1994), 72.

8. "Americans Split on Doctor-Assisted Suicide," *Associated Press* (May 29, 2007).

9. Megan Kurlychek, "What Is My Left Hand Doing? The Need for Unifying Purpose and Policy in the Criminal Justice System," *Criminology & Public Policy* (November 2011), 909.

10. *Gonzales v. Oregon,* 546 U.S. 243 (2006). Many United States Supreme Court cases will be cited in this book, and it is important to understand these citations. *Gonzales v. Oregon* refers to the parties in the case that the Court is reviewing. "U.S." is the abbreviation for *United States Reports,* the official publication of United States Supreme Court decisions. "546" refers to the volume of the *United States Reports* in which the case appears, and "243" is the page number. The citation ends with the year the case was decided, in parentheses. Most, though not all, Supreme Court case citations in this book will follow this formula.

11. President's Commission on Law Enforcement and Administration of Justice, *The Challenge of Crime in a Free Society* (Washington, D.C.: Government Printing Office, 1967), 7.

12. John Heinz and Peter Manikas, "Networks among Elites in a Local Criminal Justice System," *Law and Society Review* 26 (1992), 831–861.

13. James Q. Wilson, "What to Do about Crime: Blaming Crime on Root Causes," *Vital Speeches* (April 1, 1995), 373.

14. Herbert Packer, *The Limits of the Criminal Sanction* (Stanford, CA: Stanford University Press, 1968), 154–173.

15. *Ibid.*

16. Joseph Goldstein and Christine Haughney, "Bad Manners Then, Cause for Arrest Today," *New York Times* (January 7, 2012), A17.

17. "NYC Statistics," *NYC: The Official Guide,* at **www.nycgo.com/articles/nyc-statistics-page**.

18. Goldstein and Haughney.

19. George P. Fletcher, "Some Unwise Reflections about Discretion," *Law & Contemporary Problems* (Autumn 1984), 279.

20. Quoted in Goldstein and Haughney.

21. Antonin Scalia, "The Rule of Law as a Law of Rules," *University of Chicago Law Review* 56 (1989), 1178–1180.

22. John Kleinig, *Ethics and Criminal Justice: An Introduction* (New York: Cambridge University Press, 2008), 33–35.

23. Elizabeth Banks, *Criminal Justice Ethics: Theory and Practice* (Los Angeles: Sage Publications, 2008), 13.

24. Packer, 154–173.

25. *Ibid.*

26. "FBI: U.S. Violent Crime Down in 2011, Fewer Murders, Rapes," *Reuters* (December 19, 2011).

27. Quoted in Richard Oppel, Jr., "Steady Decline in Major Crime Baffles Experts," *New York Times* (May 24, 2011), A1.

28. Charis E. Kubrin et al., "Proactive Policing and Robbery Rates across U.S. Cities," *Criminology* (February 2010), 57–91.

29. James Q. Wilson, "Hard Times, Fewer Crimes," *Wall Street Journal* (May 31, 2011), 9.

30. David B. Wilson, David Weisburd, and David McClure, "Use of DNA Testing in Police Investigative Work for Increasing Offender Identification, Arrest, Conviction, and Case Clearance," *Campbell Systematic Reviews* (2011), 7.

31. Thomas J. Baker, "Biometrics for Intelligence-Led Policing: The Coming Trends," *The Police Chief* (April 2011), 38–45.

32. Police Executive Research Forum, "Is the Economic Downturn Fundamentally Changing How We Police?" *Critical Issues in Policing,* vol. 16 (Washington, D.C.: Police Executive Research Forum, 2010).

33. Federal Bureau of Investigation, "2011 National Gang Threat Assessment Issued," *FBI National Press Office* (October 21, 2011).

34. James C. Howell, Arlen Egley, Jr., George E. Tita, and Elizabeth Griffiths, *U.S. Gang Problems Trends and Seriousness, 1996–2009* (Washington, D.C.: National Gang Center, May 2011), 6–9.

35. Alfred Blumstein, "The Crime Drop in America: An Exploration of Some Recent Crime Trends," *Journal of Scandinavian Studies in Criminology and Crime Prevention* (December 2006), 17–35.

36. James Lindgren, "Fall from Grace: Arming America and the Bellesiles Scandal," *Yale Law Journal* 111 (2002), 2203.

37. *District of Columbia v. Heller,* 554 U.S. 570 (2008).

38. Howard Snyder, *Arrests in the United States, 1980–2009* (Washington, D.C.: Bureau of Justice Statistics, September 2011), 12.

39. Substance Abuse and Mental Health Services Administration, *Results from the 2010 National Survey on Drug Use and Health: Summary of National Findings* (Washington, D.C.: National Institute on Drug Abuse, September 2011), 1, 3, 4.

40. Quoted in "9/11: Ten Years Later, How America Has Changed," *The Week* (September 16, 2011), 18.

41. Uniting and Strengthening America by Providing Appropriate Tools Required to Intercept and Obstruct Terrorism (USA PATRIOT) Act of 2001, Pub. L. No. 107-56, 115 Stat. 272 (2001).

42. Pew Research Center for the People and the Press, "Public Remains Divided over the Patriot Act" (February 15, 2011), at **pewresearch.org/pubs/1893/poll-patriot-act-renewal**.

43. Lauren E. Glaze, *Correctional Populations in the United States, 2010* (Washington, D.C.: Bureau of Justice Statistics, December 2011), Table 1, page 3.

44. Quoted in "U.S. Prison Population Rises Despite a Drop in 20 States," *Associated Press* (December 9, 2009).

45. Association of State Correctional Administrators, "ASCA June 2011 Current Issues in Corrections," at **www.asca.net/ system/assets/attachments/3505/ ASCA%20June%202011%20Current%20 Issues%20in%20Corrections%20Survey. pdf?1316119987**.

46. Pew Center on the States, *State of Recidivism: The Revolving Door of America's Prisons* (Washington, D.C.: The Pew Charitable Trusts, April 2011), 2.

47. See **www.innocenceproject.org**.

48. *The Death Penalty in 2011: Year End Report* (Washington, D.C.: Death Penalty Information Center, December 2011), 1.

49. *Ibid.*

50. Death Penalty Information Center, "National Statistics on Death Penalty and Race," at **www .deathpenaltyinfo.org/race-death-row- inmates-executed-1976**.

51. Bureau of Justice Statistics, *Prisoners in 2010* (Washington, D.C.: U.S. Department of Justice, December 2011), Appendix Table 12, page 26.

52. Federal Bureau of Prisons, "Inmate Breakdown," at **www.bop.gov/news/quick. jsp#2**.

53. John Cloud, "How the Casey Anthony Murder Case Became the Social-Media Trial of the Century," *Time* (June 16, 2011), at **www.time.com/time/nation/article/ 0,8599,2077969,00.html**.

54. Marisol Bello, "For Most, Anthony Verdict Doesn't Sit Well," *USA Today* (July 8, 2011), 3A.

55. "How Casey Anthony Used Social Media, Blogs," *South Florida Sun-Sentinel* (July 14, 2011), 1A.

56. Quoted in Patrik Jonsson, "'Flash Robs': How Twitter Is Being Twisted for Criminal Gain," *Christian Science Monitor* (August 3, 2011), at **www.csmonitor.com/USA/2011/0803/ Flash-robs-How-Twitter-is-being-twisted -for-criminal-gain-VIDEO**.

CHAPTER ONE APPENDIX

HOW TO READ CASE CITATIONS AND FIND COURT DECISIONS

Many important court cases are discussed throughout this book. Every time a court case is mentioned, you will be able to check its citation using the endnotes on the final pages of the chapter. Court decisions are recorded and published on paper and on the Internet. When a court case is mentioned, the notation that is used to refer to, or to *cite*, the case denotes where the published decision can be found.

Decisions of state courts of appeals are usually published in two places, the state reports of that particular state and the more widely used *National Reporter System* published by West Group. Some states no longer publish their own reports. The *National Reporter System* divides the states into the following geographic areas: Atlantic (A. or A.2d), North Eastern (N.E. or N.E.2d), North Western (N.W. or N.W.2d), Pacific (P., P.2d, or P.3d), Southern (So. or So.2d), and South Western (S.W., S.W.2d, or S.W.3d). The 2d and 3d in these abbreviations refer to the *Second Series* and *Third Series,* respectively.

Federal trial court decisions are published unofficially in West's *Federal Supplement* (F.Supp. or F.Supp.2d), and opinions from the circuit courts of appeals are reported unofficially in West's *Federal Reporter* (F., F.2d, or F.3d). Opinions from the United States Supreme Court are reported in the *United States Reports* (U.S.), the *Lawyers' Edition of the Supreme Court Reports* (L.Ed.), West's *Supreme Court Reporter* (S.Ct.), and other publications. The *United States Reports* is the official publication of United States Supreme Court decisions. It is published by the federal government. Many early decisions are missing from these volumes. The citations of the early volumes of the *United States Reports* include the names of the actual reporters, such as Dallas, Cranch, or Wheaton. *McCulloch v. Maryland,* for example, is cited as 17 U.S. (4 Wheat.) 316. Only after 1874 did the present citation system, in which cases are cited based solely on their volume and page numbers in the *United States Reports,* come into being. The *Lawyers' Edition of the Supreme Court Reports* is an unofficial and more complete edition of Supreme Court decisions. West's *Supreme Court Reporter* is an unofficial edition of decisions dating from October 1882. These volumes contain headnotes and numerous brief editorial statements of the law involved in the case.

Citations to decisions of state courts of appeals give the name of the case; the volume, name, and page number of the state's official report (if the state publishes its own reports); and the volume, unit, and page number of the *National Reporter.* Federal court citations also give the name of the case and the volume, name, and page number of the reports. In addition to the citation, this textbook lists the year of the decision, in parentheses. Consider, for example, the case *Miranda v. Arizona,* 384 U.S. 436 (1966). The Supreme Court's decision in this case may be found in volume 384 of the *United States Reports* on page 436. The case was decided in 1966.

CHAPTER

2

Measuring and Explaining Crime

Jason Henry/New York Times/Redux Pictures

LEARNING OBJECTIVES

After reading this chapter, you should be able to...

1 Identify the six main categories of crime.

2 Distinguish between Part I and Part II offenses as defined by the Uniform Crime Report (UCR).

3 Distinguish between the National Crime Victimization Survey (NCVS) and self-reported surveys.

4 Discuss the prevailing explanation for the rising number of women incarcerated in the United States.

5 Discuss the difference between a hypothesis and a theory in the context of criminology.

6 List and briefly explain two important branches of social process theory.

7 Explain the theory of the chronic offender and its importance for the criminal justice system.

8 Discuss the connection between learning theory and the start of an individual's drug use.

Throughout the chapter you will see each learning objective repeated in the margin next to the content it relates to. The chapter summary on page 59 includes all of the learning objectives for review.

CHAPTER OUTLINE

- Types of Crime
- Crime Measurement in the United States
- Crime Trends
- What Causes Crime?
- The Link between Drugs and Crime

TIME FOR A CHANGE

In 1769, English judge William Blackstone described rape as "the carnal knowledge of a woman forcibly against her will." "Forcibly" meant that the male rapist had to use physical force or its threat to penetrate his female victim. "Against her will" meant that the victim had to strenuously resist the attack. To many, this definition may seem outdated, reflecting the values and prejudices of an early age. Nearly two and a half centuries later, however, in determining national rape statistics, the U.S. government was using almost exactly the same terminology as did Blackstone—"carnal knowledge of a female forcibly and against her will."

For years, experts have criticized this definition of rape as "narrow, outmoded, steeped in gender-based stereotypes, and seriously understat[ing] the true incidence of serious sex crimes." The definition limited rape to actions against adult women by men, meaning that incidents in which the victim was a child or male were not counted. It did not take into consideration situations where the victim was rendered defenseless with liquor or date-rape drugs, and it required women to "fight back" for rape to have occurred. Finally, the definition did not include forcible anal or oral penetration or the rape of a woman by another woman.

In 2010, a federal survey using a much broader definition found that about 1 percent of women reported having been the target of actual or attempted rape. This suggests that as many as 1.3 million American women are victims of the crime annually. That same year, official Federal Bureau of Investigation (FBI) statistics counted 84,767 rapes. Partially as a result of this discrepancy, on January 6, 2012, the U.S. Department of Justice announced a new definition of the crime that is more detailed and graphic. Now, for the purposes of government statistics, almost any sexual act committed against a person—female or male—without her or his consent will meet the standard for rape.

For decades, observers have contended that the outdated federal definition of rape reflected a lack of seriousness regarding the crime in the American criminal justice system.

Santos for New York Daily News

The federal government's decision regarding its official definition of rape was met with widespread approval. The new definition "comes much closer to reflecting the reality of the crime," said Scott Berkowitz, head of the Rape, Abuse, and Incest National Network. "It happens to men and women, young and old, but in every case, it's an incredibly violent crime and we owe it to victims to acknowledge and count every one."[1] The change will have a practical impact as well. National measurements of sexual assault, which dropped 2.5 percent in 2011 from the previous year using the old definition, will undoubtedly increase using the new, broader language.

The measurement of crime is not simply about producing a record of what has happened in the past. Lawmakers and other government officials use crime statistics to allocate public funds and other resources for crime prevention and victim assistance. In the first part of this chapter, we first look closely at the different categories of crime and the most common methods of collecting data on criminal offenders in the United States. The second part of the chapter is devoted to exploring one of the most interesting questions in all of criminal justice: What causes criminal behavior?

TYPES OF CRIME

At the same time that federal officials were debating whether to change the official definition of rape, the nation was absorbed by the arrest of Jerry Sandusky. In June 2012, a Pennsylvania jury convicted Sandusky, a former football coach at Penn State University, of forty-five sex abuse counts for sexually assaulting ten young male victims over the course of fifteen years. As more than one commentator noted, because Sandusky's alleged victims were all male, none of the acts would have been counted in national rape statistics under the old definition.[2]

Just because rapes against males have not been counted in federal crime statistics does not mean that such behavior goes unpunished. The majority of actual federal and state crime laws are not restricted by the gender of the victim. Under Pennsylvania criminal code, Sandusky was charged with forty-eight counts of indecent assault of a *person* younger than sixteen years of age.[3] In general, American criminal law focuses on six categories of misconduct: violent crime, property crime, public order crime, white-collar crime, organized crime, and high-tech crime. The following overview of these categories will cover most, if not all, of the criminal activity discussed in this textbook.

Learning Objective 1 Identify the six main categories of crime.

VIOLENT CRIME

Crimes against persons, or *violent crimes*, have come to dominate our perspectives on crime. There are four major categories of violent crime:

- **Murder,** or the unlawful killing of a human being.
- **Sexual assault,** or *rape,* which refers to coerced actions of a sexual nature against an unwilling participant.
- **Assault** and **battery,** two separate acts that cover situations in which one person physically attacks another (battery) or, through threats, intentionally leads another to believe that he or she will be physically harmed (assault).
- **Robbery,** or the taking of funds, personal property, or any other article of value from a person by means of force or fear.

As you will see in Chapter 3, these violent crimes are further classified by *degree,* depending on the circumstances surrounding the criminal act. These circumstances include the intent of the person committing the crime, whether a weapon was used, and (in cases other than murder) the level of pain and suffering experienced by the victim.

PROPERTY CRIME

The most common form of criminal activity is *property crime,* or those crimes in which the goal of the offender is some form of economic gain or the damaging of property. Pocket picking, shoplifting, and the stealing of any property that is not accomplished by force are covered by laws against **larceny,** also known as *theft.* **Burglary** refers to the unlawful entry of a structure with the intention of committing a serious crime such as theft. *Motor vehicle theft* describes the theft or attempted theft of a motor vehicle, including all cases in which automobiles are taken by persons not having lawful access to them. *Arson* is also a property crime. It involves the willful and malicious burning of a home, automobile, commercial building, or any other construction.

PUBLIC ORDER CRIME

The concept of **public order crimes** is linked to the consensus model discussed in Chapter 1. Historically, societies have always outlawed activities that are considered contrary to public values and morals. Today, the most common public order crimes include public drunkenness, prostitution, gambling, and illicit drug use. These crimes

Murder The unlawful killing of one human being by another.

Sexual Assault Forced or coerced sexual intercourse (or other sexual acts).

Assault A threat or an attempt to do violence to another person that causes that person to fear immediate physical harm.

Battery The act of physically contacting another person with the intent to do harm, even if the resulting injury is insubstantial.

Robbery The act of taking property from another person through force, threat of force, or intimidation.

Larceny The act of taking property from another person without the use of force with the intent of keeping that property.

Burglary The act of breaking into or entering a structure (such as a home or office) without permission for the purpose of committing a crime.

Public Order Crime Behavior that has been labeled criminal because it is contrary to shared social values, customs, and norms.

A heroin user injects the drug into his right arm. How might illegal drug use—considered a public order crime—lead directly or indirectly to violent and property crimes?

Stephen Ferry/Liaison/Getty

are sometimes referred to as *victimless crimes* because they often harm only the offender. As you will see throughout this textbook, however, that term is rather misleading. Public order crimes may create an environment that gives rise to property and violent crimes.

WHITE-COLLAR CRIME

Business-related crimes are popularly referred to as **white-collar crimes.** The term *white-collar crime* is broadly used to describe an illegal act or series of acts committed by an individual or business entity using some nonviolent means to obtain a personal or business advantage. As you will see in Chapter 14, when we consider the topic in much greater detail, certain property crimes fall into this category when committed in a business context. Although the extent of this criminal activity is difficult to determine with any certainty, the Association of Certified Fraud Examiners estimates that white-collar crime costs businesses worldwide as much as $2.9 trillion a year.[4]

ORGANIZED CRIME

White-collar crime involves the use of legal business facilities and employees to commit illegal acts. For example, a bank teller can't embezzle (steal funds placed in his or her trust) unless he or she is first hired as a legal employee of the bank. In contrast, **organized crime** describes illegal acts by illegal organizations, usually geared toward satisfying the public's demand for unlawful goods and services. Organized crime broadly implies a conspiratorial and illegal relationship among any number of persons engaged in unlawful acts. More specifically, groups engaged in organized crime employ criminal tactics such as violence, corruption, and intimidation for economic gain.

The hierarchical structure of organized crime operations often mirrors that of legitimate businesses, and, like any corporation, these groups attempt to capture a sufficient percentage of any given market to make a profit. For organized crime, the traditional preferred markets are gambling, prostitution, illegal narcotics, and loan sharking (lending funds at higher-than-legal interest rates), along with more recent ventures into counterfeiting and credit-card scams.

HIGH-TECH CRIME

The newest variation on crime is directly related to the increased presence of computers and social networking in everyday life. The Internet, with approximately 2.3 billion users worldwide, is the site of numerous *cyber crimes,* such as selling pornographic materials, soliciting minors, and defrauding consumers through bogus financial investments. The dependence of businesses on computer operations has left corporations vulnerable to sabotage, fraud, embezzlement, and theft of proprietary data. We will address this particular criminal activity in much greater detail in Chapter 14.

SELFASSESSMENT

Fill in the blanks and check your answers on page 60.

Murder, assault, and robbery are labeled _____ crimes because they are committed against persons. The category of crime that includes larceny, motor vehicle theft, and arson is called _____ crime. When a criminal acts to gain an illegal business advantage, he or she has committed what is commonly known as a _____-_____ crime.

White-Collar Crime Nonviolent crimes committed by business entities or individuals to gain a personal or business advantage.

Organized Crime Illegal acts carried out by illegal organizations engaged in the market for illegal goods or services, such as illicit drugs or firearms.

CAREERS IN CJ

ROBERT AGNEW
CRIMINOLOGIST

When I first became interested in criminology, my research led me to "strain" or anomie theories that said when a person stumbles in achieving financial success or middle-class status due to social factors beyond his or her control, he or she may turn to crime. While strain theory made a lot of sense to me, I felt that the theory was incomplete. When I looked around me, it was easy to spot other sources of frustration and anger, such as harassment by peers, conflict with parents or romantic partners, poor grades in school, or poor working conditions.

I outlined sources of strain as the loss of "positively valued stimuli" such as romantic relationships, or the threat of "negatively valued stimuli" such as an insult or physical assault. I also pointed out that monetary success was just one among many "positively valued goals" that might cause strain when not achieved. Furthermore, I noted that people who experience strain may turn to crime for several reasons—crime might allow them to achieve their monetary and status goals, protect positively valued stimuli, escape negative stimuli, achieve revenge against wrongs, or simply deal with the strain (such as taking drugs to forget problems). I drew on these observations and my own experiences to develop a new "general strain theory."

Social Media Career Tip

Find groups on Facebook and LinkedIn in which people are discussing the criminal justice career or careers that interest you. Participate in the discussions to get information and build contacts. **f** **Linked** in.

FAST FACTS

CRIMINOLOGIST, JOB DESCRIPTION:

- Work for local, state, and federal governments, on policy advisory boards, or for legislative committees. In some cases, he or she may work for privately funded think tanks or for a criminal justice or law enforcement agency. Most often, employment as a criminologist will be through a college or university, where both teaching and research will be conducted.

WHAT KIND OF TRAINING IS REQUIRED?

- An advanced degree is required. Specifically, some combination of degrees in criminology, criminal justice, sociology, or psychology is preferable. Graduate level education is a must for any research position.

ANNUAL SALARY RANGE?

- $40,000–$122,000

CRIME MEASUREMENT IN THE UNITED STATES

Crime experts are constantly producing studies of criminal behavior. Many of these analyses deal with narrow topics such as the prevalence of kidnapping by nonfamily members, the impact of dropping out of school on juvenile delinquency, or the role of alcoholism in domestic violence. The best-known annual survey of criminal behavior, however, tries to answer the broadest of questions: How much crime is there in the United States?

THE UNIFORM CRIME REPORT

Uniform Crime Report (UCR) An annual report compiled by the FBI to give an indication of criminal activity in the United States.

Uniform Crime Report (UCR) An annual report compiled by the FBI to give an indication of criminal activity in the United States.

Part I Offenses Crimes reported annually by the FBI in its Uniform Crime Report. Part I offenses include murder, rape, robbery, aggravated assault, burglary, larceny, motor vehicle theft, and arson.

Each year, the U.S. Department of Justice releases the **Uniform Crime Report (UCR).** Since its inception in 1930, the UCR has attempted to measure the overall rate of crime in the United States by organizing "offenses known to the police."[5] To produce the UCR, the FBI relies on the voluntary participation of local law enforcement agencies. These agencies—approximately 17,500 in total, covering 95 percent of the population—base their information on three measurements:

1. The number of persons arrested.
2. The number of crimes reported by victims, witnesses, or the police themselves.
3. The number of law enforcement officers.

Problems arise in this system when the FBI and local police departments fail to use the same benchmarks in measuring certain crimes. As we saw in the opening of this chapter, until recently the FBI employed a very narrow definition of rape. This situation would force employees at local police departments to sift through yearly reports of sexual assaults and discard those that did not "match" the FBI's definition before sending total figures to the agency. Sometimes, the resulting discrepancies could be dramatic. In 2010, for example, the Chicago Police Department investigated nearly 1,400 sexual assaults, yet did not report a single one to the FBI for inclusion in the UCR because of differences in definitions.[6]

ANNUAL PUBLICATION Once the FBI has collected all the local reports for a given year, the agency presents the crime data in two important ways:

1. As a *rate* per 100,000 people. In 2011, for example, the crime rate was 3,295. In other words, for every 100,000 inhabitants of the United States, 3,295 *Part I offenses* (explained below) were reported to the FBI. This statistic is known as the *crime rate* and is often cited by media sources when discussing the level of crime in the United States.
2. As a *percentage* change from the previous year or other time periods. From 2010 to 2011, there was a 3.8 percent decrease in the violent crime rate and a 0.5 percent decrease in the property crime rate.[7]

The Department of Justice publishes these data annually in *Crime in the United States.* Along with the basic statistics, this publication offers an exhaustive array of crime information, including breakdowns of crimes committed by city, county, and other geographic designations and by the demographics (gender, race, age) of the individuals who have been arrested for crimes.

Learning Objective 2 Distinguish between Part I and Part II offenses as defined by the Uniform Crime Report (UCR).

PART I OFFENSES The UCR divides the criminal offenses it measures into two major categories: Part I and Part II offenses. **Part I offenses** are those crimes that, due to their seriousness and frequency, are recorded by the FBI to give a general idea of the "crime picture" in the United States in any given year. For a description of the seven Part I offenses, see Figure 2.1 on the facing page.

Part I offenses are those most likely to be covered by the media and, consequently, inspire the most fear of crime in the population. These crimes have come to dominate crime coverage to such an extent that, for most Americans, the first image that comes to mind at the mention of "crime" is one person physically attacking another person or a robbery taking place with the use or threat of force.[8] Furthermore, in the stereotypical crime, the offender and the victim usually do not know each other.

FIGURE 2.1 Part I Offenses

Every month local law enforcement agencies voluntarily provide information on serious offenses in their jurisdiction to the FBI. These serious offenses, known as Part I offenses, are defined here. (Arson is not included in the national crime report data, but it is sometimes considered a Part I offense nonetheless, so its definition is included here.) As the graph shows, most Part I offenses reported by local police departments in any given year are property crimes.

Murder. The willful (nonnegligent) killing of one human being by another.

Forcible rape. The carnal knowledge of a female forcibly and against her will.*

Robbery. The taking or attempting to take of anything of value from the care, custody, or control of a person or persons by force or threat of force or violence and/or by putting the victim in fear.

Aggravated assault. An unlawful attack by one person on another for the purpose of inflicting severe or aggravated bodily injury. This type of assault is usually accompanied by the use of a weapon or by means likely to produce death or great bodily harm.

Burglary—breaking or entering. The unlawful entry of a structure to commit a felony or a theft. Attempted forcible entry is included.

Larceny/theft (except motor vehicle theft). The unlawful taking, carrying, leading, or riding away of property from the possession or constructive possession of another.

Motor vehicle theft. The theft or attempted theft of a motor vehicle.

Arson. Any willful or malicious burning or attempt to burn, with or without intent to defraud, a dwelling house, public building, motor vehicle or aircraft, personal property of another, and the like.

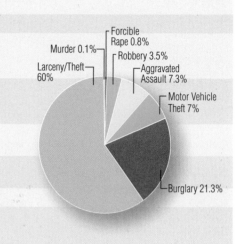

*The new definition of rape, as indicated in the opening to this chapter, had not yet gone into effect for these data.
Sources: Federal Bureau of Investigation, *Crime in the United States, 2011* (Washington, D.C.: U.S. Department of Justice, 2012), at www.fbi.gov/about-us/cjis/ucr/crime-in-the-u.s/2011/crime-in-the-u.s.-2011/offense-definitions and www.fbi.gov/about-us/cjis/ucr/crime-in-the-u.s/2011/crime-in-the-u.s.-2011/tables/table-1.

Given the trauma of violent crimes, this perception is understandable, but it is not accurate. According to UCR statistics, a relative or other acquaintance of the victim commits at least 44 percent of the homicides in the United States.[9] Furthermore, as is evident from Figure 2.1, the majority of Part I offenses committed are property crimes. Notice that 60 percent of all reported Part I offenses are larceny/thefts, and another 21 percent are burglaries.[10]

PART II OFFENSES Not only do violent crimes represent the minority of Part I offenses, but Part I offenses are far outweighed by **Part II offenses,** which include all crimes recorded by the FBI that do not fall into the category of Part I offenses. While information gathered on Part I offenses reflects those offenses "known," or reported to the FBI by local agencies, Part II offenses are measured only by arrest data. In 2011, the FBI recorded about 2.1 million arrests for Part I offenses in the United States. That same year, about 10.2 million arrests for Part II offenses took place.[11] In other words, a Part II offense was approximately five times more common than a Part I offense. (For a description of Part II offenses and their rates, see Figure 2.2 on the following page.) Such statistics have prompted Marcus Felson, a professor at Rutgers University School of Criminal Justice, to comment that "most crime is very ordinary."[12]

Part II Offenses All crimes recorded by the FBI that do not fall into the category of Part I offenses. These crimes include both misdemeanors and felonies.

Victim Surveys A method of gathering crime data that directly surveys participants to determine their experiences as victims of crime.

VICTIM SURVEYS

The UCR relies on official reports of crime. In contrast, **victim surveys** allow the victims of crime to speak directly to crime experts about their experiences. Initially, such surveys were usually conducted as part of face-to-face interviews or over the telephone. Today, researchers take advantage of technologies such as e-mail and social media for access to a deeper pool of potential interviewees on a broader range of possible subjects.

THE DARK FIGURE OF CRIME The first large-scale victim survey took place in 1966, when members of 10,000 households answered questionnaires as part of the President's

FIGURE 2.2 Part II Offenses

Offense	Estimated Annual Arrests	Offense	Estimated Annual Arrests
Drug abuse violations	1,531,251	Offenses against family and children	116,723
Driving under the influence	1,215,077	Stolen property	93,234
Other assaults	1,241,722	Forgery and counterfeiting	70,211
Disorderly conduct	582,158	Sex offenses (except forcible rape and prostitution)	69,225
Liquor law violations	500,648	Prostitution and commercialized vice	57,345
Drunkenness	534,218	Vagrancy	29,203
Fraud	168,217	Embezzlement	16,190
Vandalism	237,638	Gambling	8,596
Weapons	153,519	Suspicion	1,424
Curfew and loitering law violations	76,942	All other offenses	3,532,195

Curfew and loitering law violations (persons under age eighteen)—Offenses relating to violations of local curfew or loitering ordinances.

Disorderly conduct—Behavior that disturbs the public peace.

Driving under the influence—Driving or operating any vehicle or common carrier while mentally or physically impaired under the influence of liquor or narcotics.

Drug abuse violations—State and/or local offenses relating to the unlawful possession, sale, use, growing, and manufacturing of narcotic drugs. The following drug categories are specified: opium or cocaine and their derivatives (morphine, heroin, codeine); marijuana; synthetic narcotics—manufactured narcotics that can cause true addiction (Demerol, methadone); and dangerous nonnarcotic drugs (barbiturates, Benzedrine).

Drunkenness—Offenses relating to drunkenness or intoxication. Excluded is "driving under the influence."

Embezzlement—Misappropriation or misapplication of funds or property entrusted to one's care, custody, or control.

Forgery and counterfeiting—The altering, copying, imitating, selling, or possessing of something, without authority or right, with the intent to deceive or defraud. Attempts are included.

Fraud—The intentional perversion of the truth for the purpose of inducing another person or other entity in reliance upon it to part with something of value or to surrender a legal right.

Gambling—Promoting, permitting, or engaging in illegal gambling.

Liquor law violations—The violation of state or local laws or ordinances prohibiting the manufacture, sale, purchase, transportation, possession, or use of alcoholic beverages.

Offenses against family and children—Nonsupport, neglect, desertion, or abuse of family and children.

Other assaults (simple)—Assaults and attempted assaults where no weapon is used and that do not result in serious or aggravated injury to the victim.

Prostitution and commercialized vice—The unlawful promotion of or participation in sexual activities for profit, including soliciting customers, operating an establishment for such activities, or otherwise promoting prostitution.

Sex offenses (except forcible rape, prostitution, and commercialized vice)—Statutory rape and offenses against chastity, common decency, morals, and the like. Attempts are included.

Stolen property: buying, receiving, possessing—Buying, receiving, and possessing stolen property, including attempts.

Suspicion—No specific offense; suspect released without formal charges being placed.

Vagrancy—Vagabondage, begging, loitering, and the like.

Vandalism—Willful or malicious destruction, injury, disfigurement, or defacement of any public or private property, real or personal, without consent of the owner or persons having custody or control.

Weapons: carrying, possessing, and the like—All violations of regulations or statutes controlling the carrying, using, possessing, furnishing, and manufacturing of firearms, cutting instruments, explosives, or other deadly weapons.

All other offenses—All violations of state or local laws not specifically identified as Part I or Part II offenses, except traffic violations.

Sources: Federal Bureau of Investigation, *Crime in the United States, 2011* (Washington, D.C.: U.S. Department of Justice, 2012), at **www.fbi.gov/about-us/cjis/ucr/crime-in-the-u.s/2011/crime-in-the-u.s.-2011/tables/table-29** and **www.fbi.gov/about-us/cjis/ucr/crime-in-the-u.s/2011/crime-in-the-u.s.-2011/offense-definitions**.

Dark Figure of Crime A term used to describe the actual amount of crime that takes place. The "figure" is "dark," or impossible to detect, because a great number of crimes are never reported to the police.

Commission on Law Enforcement and the Administration of Justice. The results indicated a much higher victimization rate than had been previously expected, and researchers felt the process gave them a better understanding of the **dark figure of crime,** or the actual amount of crime that occurs in the country.

Criminologists were so encouraged by the results of the 1966 experiment that the federal government decided to institute an ongoing victim survey. The result was the National Crime Victimization Survey (NCVS), which started in 1972. Conducted by the U.S. Bureau of the Census in cooperation with the Bureau of Justice Statistics of the Justice Department, the NCVS conducts an annual survey of about 41,000 households with nearly 73,500 occupants over twelve years of age. Participants are interviewed twice a year over the course of three years concerning their experiences with crimes in the prior six months. As you can see in Figure 2.3 on the facing page, the questions cover a wide array of possible victimization.

FIGURE 2.3 Sample Questions from the NCVS (National Crime Victimization Survey)

36a. Was something belonging to YOU stolen, such as:

a. Things that you carry, like luggage, a wallet, purse, briefcase, book—

b. Clothing, jewelry, or cell phone—

c. Bicycle or sports equipment—

d. Things in your home—like a TV, stereo, or tools—

e. Things from outside your home, such as a garden hose or lawn furniture—

f. Things belonging to children in the household—

g. Things from a vehicle, such as a package, groceries, camera, or CDs—

h. Did anyone ATTEMPT to steal anything belonging to you?

41a. Has anyone attacked or threatened you in any of these ways:

a. With any weapon, for instance, a gun or knife—

b. With anything like a baseball bat, frying pan, scissors, or stick—

c. By something thrown, such as a rock or bottle—

d. Include any grabbing, punching, or choking,

e. Any rape, attempted rape, or other type of sexual attack—

f. Any face-to-face threats—OR

g. Any attack or threat or use of force by anyone at all? Please mention it even if you are not certain it was a crime.

42a. People often don't think of incidents committed by someone they know. Other than the incidents already mentioned, did you have something stolen from you OR were you attacked or threatened by:

a. Someone at work or school—

b. A neighbor or friend—

c. A relative or family member—

d. Any other person you've met or known?

43a. Incidents involving forced or unwanted sexual acts are often difficult to talk about. Have you been forced or coerced to engage in unwanted sexual activity by—

a. someone you didn't know before—

b. a casual acquaintance—OR

c. someone you know well?

44a. During the last 6 months (other than any incidents already mentioned), did you call the police to report something that happened to YOU which you thought was a crime?

45a. During the last 6 months (other than any incidents already mentioned), did anything which you thought was a crime happen to YOU, but you did NOT report to the police?

Source: U.S. Department of Justice, *National Crime Victimization Survey* (Washington, D.C.: Bureau of Justice Statistics, 2009).

A VOICE FOR VICTIMS Supporters of the NCVS highlight a number of aspects in which the victim survey is superior to the UCR:

1. It measures both reported and unreported crime.
2. It is unaffected by police bias and distortions in reporting crime to the FBI.
3. It does not rely on victims directly reporting crime to the police.[13]

Most important, some supporters say, is that the NCVS gives victims a voice in the criminal justice process. This "voice" was certainly heard in the debate over rape statistics that we have focused on in the early part of this chapter. In 2010, the NCVS reported more than 188,000 sexual assaults, compared with the approximately 85,000 indicated by the UCR.[14] These figures provided a measure of proof that the FBI was underreporting rape in its annual publication.

SELF-REPORTED SURVEYS

Based on many of the same principles as victim surveys, but focusing instead on offenders, **self-reported surveys** are a third source of data for criminologists. In this form of data collection, participants are asked directly—through personal interviews or questionnaires, or over the telephone—about specific criminal activity to which they may have been a party. Self-reported surveys are most useful in situations in which the group to be studied is already gathered in an institutional setting, such as a juvenile facility or a prison. One of the most widespread self-reported surveys in the United States, the Drug Use Forecasting Program, collects information on narcotics use from arrestees who have been brought into booking facilities.

Because there is no penalty for admitting to criminal activity in a self-reported survey, subjects tend to be forthcoming in discussing their behavior. Researchers interviewing a group of male students at a state university, for example, found that a significant number of them admitted to committing minor crimes for which they had never been

Learning Objective 3 Distinguish between the National Crime Victimization Survey (NCVS) and self-reported surveys.

Self-Reported Survey A method of gathering crime data that relies on participants to reveal and detail their own criminal or delinquent behavior.

arrested.[15] This fact points to the most striking finding of self-reported surveys: the dark figure of crime, referred to earlier as the *actual* amount of crime that takes place, appears to be much larger than the UCR or NCVS would suggest.

CJ&TECHNOLOGY

UPI/Landov

Transdermal Alcohol Testing

Sweat, it seems, is one source of self-reported data that never lies, at least when it comes to alcohol consumption. That's the logic behind the Secure Continuous Remote Alcohol Monitor, otherwise known as the SCRAM bracelet or the "bling with a ping." This eight-ounce bracelet, usually worn around the subject's ankle, relies on a process called *transdermal alcohol testing* to measure the levels of alcohol vapor that show up in perspiration when alcohol has been consumed. The measurements are then transmitted and posted on a Web site via a wireless modem, allowing the subject to prove—or disprove—that he or she remains sober. The SCRAM bracelet gained notoriety several years ago when actress and socialite Lindsay Lohan voluntarily donned one to show her commitment to sobriety. Most wearers, however, are not celebrities but rather offenders who are required by a court to undergo the testing after an arrest for drunk driving, domestic violence, or some other alcohol-related wrongdoing.

THINKING ABOUT TRANSDERMAL ALCOHOL TESTING

Coming soon: passive transdermal detectors in steering wheels. These devices will measure the sweat on the driver's hands to determine whether she or he has been ingesting drugs or alcohol. How could this technology be used to keep someone from driving under the influence?

SELFASSESSMENT

Fill in the blanks and check your answers on page 60.
To produce its annual _____ _____ _____, the FBI relies on the cooperation of local law enforcement agencies. _____ surveys rely on those who have been the subject of criminal activity to discuss the incidents with researchers. _____-_____ surveys ask participants to detail their own criminal behavior. Both methods show that the _____ _____ of crime, or the actual amount of crime that takes place in this country, is much _____ than official crime data would suggest.

CRIME TRENDS

The UCR, NCVS, and other statistical measures we have discussed so far in this chapter, though important, represent only the tip of the iceberg of crime data. Thanks to the efforts of government law enforcement agencies, educational institutions, and private individuals, more information on crime is available today than at any time in the nation's history. When interpreting and predicting general crime trends, experts usually focus on what University of California at Berkeley law professor Franklin Zimring calls the three "usual suspects" of rate variation:

1. *Imprisonment,* based on the principle that (a) an offender in prison or jail is unable to commit a crime on the street, and (b) a potential offender on the street will not commit a crime because he or she does not want to wind up behind bars.
2. *Youth populations,* because offenders commit fewer crimes as they grow older.
3. The *economy,* because when legitimate opportunities to earn income become scarce, some people will turn to illegitimate methods such as crime.[16]

Pure statistics do not always tell the whole story, however, and crime rates often fail to behave in the ways that the experts predict.

LOOKING GOOD: CRIME IN THE 1990s AND 2000s

In 1995, eminent crime expert James Q. Wilson (1931–2012), noting that the number of young males was set to increase dramatically over the next decade, predicted that "30,000 more young muggers, killers, and thieves" would be on the streets by 2000. "Get ready," he warned.[17] Fortunately for the country, Wilson's prediction was wrong. As is evident from Figure 2.4 below, starting in 1994 the United States experienced a steep crime decline that we are still enjoying, though to a somewhat lesser degree, today.

THE GREAT CRIME DECLINE The crime statistics of the 1990s are startling. Even with the upswing at the beginning of the decade, from 1990 to 2000 the homicide rate dropped 39 percent, the robbery rate 44 percent, the burglary rate 41 percent, and the auto theft rate 37 percent. By most measures, this decline was the longest and deepest of the twentieth century.[18] In retrospect, the 1990s seem to have encompassed a "golden era" for the leading indicators of low crime rates. The economy was robust. The prison population was skyrocketing. Plus, despite the misgivings of James Q. Wilson, the percentage of the population in the high-risk age bracket in 1995 was actually lower than it had been in 1980.[19]

A "WELCOME PUZZLE" In the early years of the 2000s, the nation's crime rate flattened for a time before resuming its downward trend. By 2011, property crime rates had dropped for the eighth straight year, and violent crime rates had shrunk to their lowest levels since the early 1970s. As noted in the previous chapter, given that the economy has been mired in a recession, with unemployment running at unusually high levels, the positive

FIGURE 2.4 Violent Crime in the United States, 1990–2011
According to statistics gathered each year by the FBI, American violent crime rates dropped steadily in the second half of the 1990s, leveled off for several years, and now have begun to decrease anew.

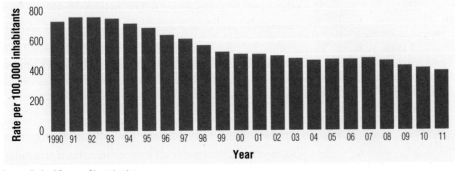

Source: Federal Bureau of Investigation.

crime figures have come as something of a surprise. Richard Rosenfeld, president of the American Society of Criminology, calls the trend "one of those welcome puzzles" and suggests that his colleagues reconsider "under what conditions economic activity influences crime."[20]

CRIME, RACE, AND POVERTY

One group has noticeably failed to benefit from the positive crime trends of the past fifteen years: young African American males. According to data compiled by Alexia Cooper and Erica L. Smith of the Bureau of Justice Statistics, black males between the ages of fourteen and twenty-four, who represent 1 percent of the country's total population, make up a quarter of its homicide offenders and 16 percent of its homicide victims.[21]

Furthermore, James A. Fox of Northeastern University in Boston and Marc L. Swatt of the University of Nebraska at Omaha estimate that from 2002 to 2007, the number of murders committed by black males under the age of eighteen rose 43 percent. Over the same time period, the number of young black males who were victims of murder also increased significantly, by 31 percent. In both categories, levels for young white males remained the same or declined.[22]

RACE AND CRIME Youth homicide rates are not the only area in which there is a "worrisome divergence"[23]—to use Professor Fox's term—in crime trends between the races. Official crime data seem to indicate a strong correlation between minority status and crime: African Americans—who make up 13 percent of the population—constitute 38 percent of those arrested for violent crimes and 30 percent of those arrested for property crimes.[24] A black man is almost twelve times more likely than a white man to be sent to prison for a drug-related conviction, while black women are about five times more likely than white women to be incarcerated for a drug offense.[25] (See the feature *Myth versus Reality—Race Stereotyping and Drug Crime* on the facing page.) Furthermore, a black juvenile in the United States is nearly three times more likely than a white juvenile to wind up in delinquency court.[26]

The racial differences in the crime rate are one of the most controversial areas of the criminal justice system. At first glance, crime statistics seem to support the idea that the subculture of African Americans in the United States is disposed toward criminal behavior. Not all of the data, however, support that assertion. A research project led by sociologist Robert J. Sampson of Harvard University collected extensive data on more than 11,000 residents living in 180 Chicago neighborhoods. Sampson and his colleagues found that 60 percent of the "gap" in levels of violence between whites and African Americans could be attributed to neighborhood and family conditions.[27]

In other words, regardless of race, a person would have a much higher risk of violent behavior if he or she lived in a poverty-stricken neighborhood or in a household run by a single parent.[28] Given that African Americans are two times more likely than whites to live in poverty and hold low-wage-earning jobs, they are, as a group, more susceptible to the factors that contribute to criminal behavior.[29]

CLASS AND CRIME Indeed, a wealth of information suggests that income level is more important than skin color when it comes to crime trends. A 2002 study of

By some measures, black citizens are twice as likely as whites to live in poverty and hold low-wage jobs. What is your opinion of the theory that economic disadvantage, rather than skin color, accounts for the disproportionate number of African Americans in U.S. prisons, such as these inmates at Florida's Dade County Correctional Facility?

Joe Sohm/Visions of America/Newscom

Crack-related violence spread like wildfire through the nation's inner cities in the 1980s. In response, then president Ronald Reagan vowed to escalate the "war on drugs." As a consequence, law enforcement efforts focused on arresting and incarcerating the wrongdoers in those communities, most of whom were African American. Even though this urban violence has largely subsided, the tactics continue: every year between 1980 and 2010, blacks were arrested on drug charges at rates between 2.8 and 5.5 times higher than whites. Today, even though African Americans make up about 13 percent of the U.S. population, they represent more than 50 percent of sentenced drug offenders.

THE MYTH African Americans are sent to prison for drug crimes in greater numbers than whites because more of them buy, sell, and use drugs.

THE REALITY The use of illegal drugs by blacks and whites in the United States is roughly equal. According to data gathered by the federal government, about 10.7 percent of African Americans and about 9.1 percent of whites admit to using drugs within the previous month. A recently released study conducted by Duke University researchers showed that black adolescents are only about half as likely as their white counterparts to become dependent on illegal drugs and alcohol.

These figures are not reflected in criminal justice trends. African Americans who use drugs are arrested at about three times the rate of whites who use drugs. Furthermore, although blacks account for only 28 percent of all drug arrests, they represent 49 percent of those convicted of drug crimes and 44 percent of all Americans incarcerated for drug crimes. Finally, more than four out of every five drug arrests are for possession of the banned substance, not for its sale or manufacture. Thus, the racial disparity in arrests cannot be due to a large class of African American drug dealers.

Although these statistics leave the criminal justice system open to charges of institutionalized racism, the disparities are more likely the result of practical considerations. "There is as much cocaine in the Stock Exchange as there is in the black community," admits one Chicago police chief. "But those guys are harder to catch. Those deals are done in office buildings [and] in someone's home. But the guy standing on the corner, he's almost got a sign on his back. These guys are just arrestable." In addition, residents of low-income neighborhoods are unlikely to hire expensive legal help to contest police action. Quite simply, the inner city is an easy place for police to rack up impressive arrest numbers with little fear for consequences if mistakes are made.

FOR CRITICAL ANALYSIS Heather Mac Donald, a crime expert at the Manhattan Institute in New York, suggests that the racial disparities in the "war on drugs" make sense because the urban street trade often leads to violence and other crimes that harm inner-city communities. Drug use by whites, in contrast, generally takes place in suburban homes, hidden from view, without the same level of negative side effects. What is your opinion of Mac Donald's theory?

---

nearly 900 African American children (400 boys and 467 girls) from neighborhoods with varying income levels showed that family earning power had the only significant connection to violent behavior.[30] More recent research conducted by William A. Pridemore of Indiana University found a "positive and significant association" between poverty and homicide.[31] Lack of education, another handicap most often faced by low-income citizens, also seems to correspond to criminal behavior. Forty-one percent of all inmates in state and federal prisons failed to obtain a high school education, compared with 18 percent of the population at large.[32]

It might seem logical that those without the financial means to acquire the consumer goods and services that dominate our society would turn to illegal methods to "steal" purchasing power. But, logic aside, many experts are skeptical of such an obvious class-crime relationship. After all, poverty does not *cause* crime. The majority of residents in low-income neighborhoods are law-abiding. Furthermore, self-reported surveys indicate that high-income citizens are involved in all sorts of criminal activities[33] and are

A **tribal officer** takes a suspect into custody on the Oneida Indian Reservation in Hobart, Wisconsin. By some measures, Native Americans are the victims of violent crime at twice the national average. Why, then, do many crime studies fail to provide specific statistics concerning this group, instead focusing only on whites, African Americans, and Hispanics?

AP Photo/Mike Roemer

far more likely to commit white-collar crimes, which are not included in national crime statistics. These facts tend to support the theory that high crime rates in low-income communities are at least partly the result of a greater willingness of police to arrest poor citizens and of the court system to convict them.

ETHNICITY AND CRIME Another point to remember when reviewing statistical studies of minority offenders and victims is that these studies tend to focus on race, which distinguishes groups based on physical characteristics such as skin color, rather than *ethnicity*, which denotes national or cultural background. Thus, the bulk of criminological research in this area has focused on the differences between European Americans and African Americans, both because the latter have been the largest minority group in the United States for most of its history and because the racial differences between the two groups are easily identifiable. Americans of Hispanic descent have either been excluded from many crime studies or been linked with whites or blacks based on racial characteristics.[34] Other minority groups, such as Asian Americans, Native Americans, and immigrants from the South Pacific or Eastern Europe, have been similarly underreported in crime studies.

This state of affairs will more than likely change in the near future. At present rates of growth, the Hispanic population will triple by 2050, when it will account for approximately one-third of the total U.S. population. In addition, Hispanics are the fastest-growing minority group in the U.S. prison population.[35] Because of an increased emphasis on immigration law enforcement, more than half of the people sent to federal prisons in this country today are Hispanic.[36]

In fact, crime experts have already begun to focus on issues of Hispanic criminality. For example, Robert Sampson's research project, mentioned earlier on page 42, found lower rates of violence among Mexican Americans than among either whites or blacks living in Chicago. The authors theorize that strong social ties in immigrant populations create an environment that is incompatible with crime.[37]

Learning Objective 4
Discuss the prevailing explanation for the rising number of women incarcerated in the United States.

WOMEN AND CRIME

To put it bluntly, crime is an overwhelmingly male activity. About 68 percent of all murders involve a male victim and a male perpetrator, and in only 2.2 percent of homicides are both the offender and the victim female.[38] Only 12 percent of the national jail population and 7 percent of the national prison population are female, and in 2011 only about a quarter of all arrests involved women.[39]

These statistics fail to convey the startling rate at which the female presence in the criminal justice system has been increasing. Over the past thirty years, the male arrest rate for aggravated assault has not changed, while the female arrest rate for aggravated assault has doubled. In that same time period, the male arrest rate for burglary has dropped 61 percent, while the female arrest rate for that crime has remained constant.[40] In 1970, there were about 6,000 women in federal and state prisons, but today, there are nearly 113,000.[41]

There are two possible explanations for these increases. Either (1) the life circumstances and behavior of women have changed dramatically in the past forty years, or (2) the criminal justice system's attitude toward women has changed over that time period.[42] In the 1970s, when female crime rates started surging upward, many observers accepted the former explanation. "You can't get involved in a bar fight if you're not allowed in the bar," said feminist theorist Freda Adler in 1975.[43] It has become clear, however, that a significant percentage of women arrested are involved in a narrow band of wrongdoing, mostly drug- and alcohol-related offenses or property crimes.[44] Research shows that as recently as the 1980s, many of the women now in prison would not have been arrested or would have received lighter sentences for their crimes.[45] Consequently, more scholars are convinced that rising female criminality is the result of a criminal justice system that is "more willing to incarcerate women."[46]

SELFASSESSMENT

Fill in the blanks and check your answers on page 60.

According to many experts, the three factors that most strongly affect national crime figures are the rate at which offenders are _____, the percentage of the population that is _____ the age of twenty-four, and the economy. Despite continued declining crime rates in the 2000s, young _____ _____ males continue to experience high levels of offending and victimization. Also, because of _____ law offenses, Hispanics are now the fastest-growing minority group in federal prisons.

WHAT CAUSES CRIME?

Jessica Wolpaw Reyes, an economist at Amherst College in Massachusetts, has put forth an intriguing reason for the nation's crime decline. Numerous studies, Reyes points out, show that children with elevated levels of lead in their blood are more likely to act aggressively as adults. In the 1970s, the federal government banned lead in gasoline and many types of paint. A generation of lead-free children has reached adulthood since then, and, Reyes believes, its nonviolent tendencies are responsible for half of the recent drop in violent crime rates.[47]

The scientific study of crime, known as **criminology,** is rich in different explanations as to why people commit crimes, from lead in the bloodstream to violent video games to low self-control. In this section, we discuss the most influential of these explanations put forth by **criminologists,** or researchers who study the causes of crime.

CORRELATION AND CAUSE

At the start, it is important to understand the difference between *correlation* and *causation.* **Correlation** between two variables means that they tend to vary together. **Causation,** in contrast, means that one variable is responsible for the change in the other. In her research described above, Reyes relied on the correlation between lead in the bloodstream and aggressive behavior to reach her conclusions about violent crime rates. No criminologist, however, has proved that high levels of lead *cause* criminal behavior. Rather, it is one variable that may contribute to violent behavior when combined with other variables.

So, correlation does not equal cause. Sales of ice cream and crime rates both rise in the summer, but nobody would say that increased ice cream sales cause higher crime rates. Such is the quandary for criminologists. We can say that there is a correlation between many factors and criminal behavior, but it is quite difficult to prove that the factors directly cause criminal behavior. Consequently, the question that is the underpinning of criminology—What causes crime?—has yet to be definitively answered.

Criminology The scientific study of crime and the causes of criminal behavior.

Criminologist A specialist in the field of crime and the causes of criminal behavior.

Correlation The relationship between two measurements or behaviors that tend to move in the same direction.

Causation The relationship in which a change in one measurement or behavior creates a recognizable change in another measurement or behavior.

FIGURE 2.5
The Scientific Method

The scientific method is a process through which researchers test the accuracy of a hypothesis. This simple example should provide an idea of how the scientific method works.

 Observation: I left my home at 7:00 this morning, and I was on time for class.

 Hypothesis: If I leave home at 7:00 every morning, then I will never be late for class.
(Hypotheses are often presented in this "If . . . , then . . ." format.)

 Test: For three straight weeks, I left home at 7:00 every morning. Not one time was I late for class.

 Verification: Four of my neighbors have the same morning class. They agree that they are never late if they leave by 7:00 A.M.

 Theory: As long as I leave home at 7:00 A.M., I don't have to worry about being late for class.

 Prediction: Tomorrow morning I'll leave at 7:00, and I will be on time for my class.

Note that even a sound theory supported by the scientific method such as this one does not *prove* that the prediction will be correct. Other factors not accounted for in the test and verification stages, such as an unexpected traffic accident, may disprove the theory. Predictions based on complex theories such as the criminological ones we will be discussing in this chapter are often challenged in such a manner.

THE ROLE OF THEORY

Criminologists have uncovered a wealth of information concerning a different, and more practically applicable, inquiry: Given a certain set of circumstances, why do individuals commit criminal acts? This information has allowed criminologists to develop a number of *theories* concerning the causes of crime.

Most of us tend to think of a *theory* as some sort of guess or a statement that is lacking in credibility. In the academic world, and therefore for our purposes, a **theory** is an explanation of a happening or circumstance that is based on observation, experimentation, and reasoning. Scientific and academic researchers observe facts and their consequences to develop *hypotheses* about what will occur when a similar fact pattern is present in the future. A **hypothesis** is a proposition that can be tested by researchers or observers to determine if it is valid. If enough authorities do find the hypothesis valid, it will be accepted as a theory. See Figure 2.5 alongside for an example of this process, known as the *scientific method,* in action.

Criminological theories are primarily concerned with attempting to determine the reason for criminal behavior, but they also provide practical guidance for law enforcement, the courts, and corrections officials. In the remainder of this section, we examine the mostly widely recognized of these theories, starting with one that relies on freedom of choice.

Theory An explanation of a happening or circumstance that is based on observation, experimentation, and reasoning.

Hypothesis A possible explanation for an observed occurrence that can be tested by further investigation.

Rational Choice Theory A school of criminology that holds that wrongdoers act as if they weigh the possible benefits of criminal or delinquent activity against the expected costs of being apprehended.

THE BRAIN AND THE BODY

Perhaps the most basic answer to the question of why a person commits a crime is that he or she makes a willful decision to do so. This is the underpinning of the **rational choice theory** of crime, summed up by criminologist James Q. Wilson as follows:

> At any given moment, a person can choose between committing a crime and not committing it. The consequences of committing a crime consist of rewards (what psychologists call "reinforcers") and punishments; the consequences of not committing the crime also entail gains and losses. The larger the ratio of the net rewards of crime to the net rewards of [not committing a crime], the greater the tendency to commit a crime.[48]

In other words, a person, before committing a crime, acts as if she or he is weighing the benefits (which may be money, in the case of a robbery) against the costs (the possibility of being caught and going to prison or jail). If the perceived benefit is greater than the potential costs, the person is more likely to commit the crime.

"THRILL OFFENDERS" In expanding on rational choice theory, sociologist Jack Katz has stated that the "rewards" of crime may be sensual as well as financial. The inherent danger of criminal activity, according to Katz, increases the "rush" a criminal experiences on successfully committing a crime. Katz labels the rewards of this "rush" the *seduction of crime.*[49] For example, the National Coalition for the Homeless documented nearly 900 unprovoked attacks against the homeless in the decade that ended in 2010, including 244 fatalities.[50] In most of these incidents, the assailants were "thrill offenders" who kicked, punched, or set on fire homeless persons for the sport of it. Katz believes that such seemingly "senseless" crimes can be explained by rational choice theory only if the intrinsic (inner) reward of the crime itself is considered.

RATIONAL CHOICE THEORY AND PUNISHMENT The theory that wrongdoers choose to commit crimes is a cornerstone of the American criminal justice system. Because crime is seen as the end result of a series of rational choices, policymakers have reasoned that severe punishment can deter criminal activity by adding another variable to the decision-making process. Supporters of the death penalty—carried out in thirty-three states and by the federal government—emphasize its deterrent effects, and legislators have used harsh prison sentences to control illegal drug use and trafficking.

TRAIT THEORIES OF CRIME If society is willing to punish crimes that are the result of a rational decision-making process, what should be its response to criminal behavior that is irrational or even unintentional? What if, for example, a schoolteacher who made sexual advances to young girls, including his stepdaughter, could prove that his wrongdoing was actually caused by an egg-sized tumor in his brain? [51]

Somewhat in contrast to rational choice theory, *trait theories* suggest that certain *biological* or *psychological* attributes in individuals could incline them toward criminal behavior given a certain set of circumstances. **Biology** is a very broad term that refers to the scientific study of living organisms, while **psychology** pertains more specifically to the study of the mind and its processes. "All behavior is biological," pointed out geneticist David C. Rowe. "All behavior is represented in the brain, in its biochemistry, electrical activity, structure, and growth and decline." [52]

Hormones and Aggression One trait theory holds that *biochemistry,* or the chemistry of living matter, can influence criminal behavior. For example, chemical messengers known as **hormones** have been the subject of much criminological study. Criminal activity in males has been linked to elevated levels of hormones—specifically, **testosterone,** which controls secondary sex characteristics and has been associated with traits of aggression. Testing of inmate populations shows that those incarcerated for violent crimes exhibit higher testosterone levels than other prisoners. [53] Elevated testosterone levels have also been used to explain the age-crime relationship, as the average testosterone level of men under the age of twenty-eight is double that of men between thirty-one and sixty-six years old. [54]

A very specific form of female violent behavior is believed to stem from hormones. In 2010, defense attorneys for Stephanie Rochester of Superior, Colorado, claimed that their client was not criminally responsible for smothering her six-month-old son to death. Rochester was, they said, suffering from *postpartum psychosis* at the time of her action. This temporary illness, believed to be caused partly by the hormonal changes that women experience after childbirth, triggers abnormal behavior in a small percentage of new mothers. [55]

The Brain and Crime The study of brain activity, or *neurophysiology*, has also found a place in criminology. Cells in the brain known as *neurons* communicate with each other by releasing chemicals called **neurotransmitters.** Criminologists have isolated three neurotransmitters that seem to be particularly related to aggressive behavior:

1. Serotonin, which regulates moods, appetite, and memory.
2. Norepinephrine, which regulates sleep-wake cycles and controls how we respond to anxiety, fear, and stress.
3. Dopamine, which regulates perceptions of pleasure and reward. [56]

Biology The science of living organisms, including their structure, function, growth, and origin.

Psychology The scientific study of mental processes and behavior.

Hormone A chemical substance, produced in tissue and conveyed in the bloodstream, that controls certain cellular and body functions such as growth and reproduction.

Testosterone The hormone primarily responsible for the production of sperm and the development of male secondary sex characteristics such as the growth of facial and pubic hair and the change of voice pitch.

Neurotransmitter A chemical that transmits nerve impulses between nerve cells and from nerve cells to the brain.

In 2011, Christopher Gribble, right, was convicted of murdering a Mount Vernon, New Hampshire, woman with a machete. Gribble's attorneys claimed that he was suffering from mental illness at the time of the crime. If true, should this fact have any bearing on Gribble's guilt or innocence?

AP Photo/Don Himsel, Pool

Researchers have established that, under certain circumstances, low levels of serotonin and high levels of norepinephrine are correlated with aggressive behavior.[57] Dopamine plays a crucial role in drug addiction, a condition that will be described later in the chapter.

Before fatally shooting six people and wounding fourteen others on January 8, 2011, in Tucson, Arizona, Jared Loughner had exhibited signs of mental illness. Specifically, Loughner is believed to suffer from *schizophrenia,* a chronic and severe brain disorder that can lead to erratic, uncontrollable behavior. In fact, persons suffering from this disease are at an unusually high risk for committing suicide or harming others.

Psychiatrist E. Fuller Torrey estimates that schizophrenics commit about a thousand homicides each year.[58] Further research shows that even moderate use of alcohol or drugs increases the chances that a schizophrenic will behave violently.[59] Still, it is important to note that about 2.4 million Americans—1 percent of the adult population—have been diagnosed with schizophrenia, and the vast majority of them will never commit a violent crime. That is, there may be a correlation between schizophrenia and violence, but the brain disorder cannot generally be said to cause violence.

Psychology and Crime Like biological theories of crime, psychological theories of crime operate under the assumption that individuals have traits that make them more or less predisposed to criminal activity. To a certain extent, however, psychology rests more heavily on abstract ideas than does biology. Even Sigmund Freud (1856–1939), perhaps the most influential of all psychologists, considered the operations of the mind to be, like an iceberg, mostly hidden.

One influential branch of psychology—*social psychology*—focuses on human behavior in the context of how human beings relate to and influence one another. Social psychology rests on the assumption that the way we view ourselves is shaped to a large degree by how we think others view us. Generally, we act in the same manner as those we like or admire because we want them to like or admire us. Thus, to a certain extent, social psychology tries to explain the influence of crowds on individual behavior.

About three decades ago, psychologist Philip Zimbardo highlighted the power of group behavior in dramatic fashion. Zimbardo randomly selected some Stanford University undergraduate students to act as "guards" and other students to act as "inmates" in an artificial prison environment. Before long, the students began to act as if these designations were real, with the "guards" physically mistreating the "inmates," who rebelled with equal violence. Within six days, Zimbardo was forced to discontinue the experiment out of fear for its participants' safety.[60] One of the basic assumptions of social psychology is that people are able to justify improper or even criminal behavior by convincing themselves that it is actually acceptable behavior. This delusion, researchers have found, is much easier to accomplish with the support of others behaving in the same manner.[61]

Trait Theory and Public Policy Whereas rational choice theory justifies punishing wrongdoers, biological and psychological views of criminality suggest that antisocial behavior should be identified and treated before it manifests itself in criminal activity.

Though the focus on treatment diminished somewhat in the 1990s, rehabilitation practices in corrections have made somewhat of a comeback over the past few years. The primary motivation for this new outlook, as we will see in Chapters 9 through 12, is the pressing need to divert nonviolent offenders from the nation's overburdened prison and jail system. Trait theories also provide the basis for the insanity defense in criminal trials, which we will discuss in the next chapter.

BAD NEIGHBORHOODS AND OTHER ECONOMIC DISADVANTAGES

While America's current economic problems have not, as yet, resulted in national crime increases, the same cannot be said for local trouble spots. In determining the most dangerous cities in the United States, researchers Douglas McIntyre, Michael Sauter, and Charles Stockdale observe that their list is dominated by cities with "fortresses of crime." These neighborhoods—including Baltimore's Front Street, Detroit's Palmer Avenue, and Memphis's Lamar Avenue—are marked by long-term financial hardship, unemployment, and high levels of violent criminality.[62]

> "The common argument that crime is caused by poverty is a kind of slander on the poor."
>
> —**H.L. Mencken,** American journalist (1956)

Indeed, for decades, criminologists focusing on **sociology** have argued that neighborhood conditions, be they of wealth or poverty, are perhaps the most important variable in predicting criminal behavior.

SOCIAL DISORGANIZATION THEORY In the early twentieth century, juvenile crime researchers Clifford Shaw and Henry McKay popularized sociological explanations for crime with their **social disorganization theory.** Shaw and McKay studied various high-crime neighborhoods in Chicago and discovered certain "zones" that exhibited high rates of crime. These zones were characterized by "disorganization," or a breakdown of the traditional institutions of social control such as family, school systems, and local businesses. In contrast, in the city's "organized" communities, residents had developed certain agreements about fundamental values and norms.[63]

Shaw and McKay found that residents in high-crime neighborhoods had to a large degree abandoned these fundamental values and norms. Also, a lack of social controls had led to increased levels of antisocial, or criminal, behavior.[64] According to social disorganization theory, ecological factors that lead to crime in these neighborhoods are perpetuated by continued elevated levels of high school dropouts, unemployment, deteriorating infrastructures, and single-parent families. (See Figure 2.6 on the following page to better understand social disorganization theory.)

STRAIN THEORY Another self-perpetuating aspect of disorganized neighborhoods is that once residents gain the financial means to leave a high-crime community, they usually do so. This desire to escape the inner city is related to another branch of sociological crime theory: **strain theory.** Most Americans have similar life goals, which include gaining a certain measure of wealth and financial freedom. The means of attaining these goals, however, are not universally available. Many citizens do not have access to the education or training necessary for financial success. This often results in frustration and anger, or *strain.*

Strain theory has its roots in the works of French sociologist Emile Durkheim (1858–1917) and his concept of *anomie* (derived from the Greek word for "without norms"). Durkheim believed that *anomie* resulted when social change threw behavioral

Sociology The study of the development and functioning of groups of people who live together within a society.

Social Disorganization Theory The theory that deviant behavior is more likely in communities where social institutions such as the family, schools, and the criminal justice system fail to exert control over the population.

Strain Theory The assumption that crime is the result of frustration felt by individuals who cannot reach their financial and personal goals through legitimate means.

Anomie A condition in which the individual suffers from the breakdown or absence of social norms.

FIGURE 2.6 The Stages of Social Disorganization Theory

Social disorganization theory holds that crime is related to the environmental pressures that exist in certain communities or neighborhoods. These areas are marked by the desire of many of their inhabitants to "get out" at the first possible opportunity. Consequently, residents tend to ignore the important institutions in the community, such as businesses and education, causing further erosion and an increase in the conditions that lead to crime.

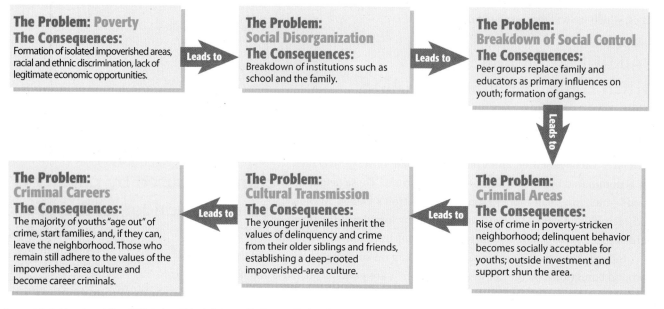

The Problem: Poverty
The Consequences:
Formation of isolated impoverished areas, racial and ethnic discrimination, lack of legitimate economic opportunities.

Leads to

The Problem:
Social Disorganization
The Consequences:
Breakdown of institutions such as school and the family.

Leads to

The Problem:
Breakdown of Social Control
The Consequences:
Peer groups replace family and educators as primary influences on youth; formation of gangs.

Leads to

The Problem:
Criminal Careers
The Consequences:
The majority of youths "age out" of crime, start families, and, if they can, leave the neighborhood. Those who remain still adhere to the values of the impoverished-area culture and become career criminals.

Leads to

The Problem:
Cultural Transmission
The Consequences:
The younger juveniles inherit the values of delinquency and crime from their older siblings and friends, establishing a deep-rooted impoverished-area culture.

Leads to

The Problem:
Criminal Areas
The Consequences:
Rise of crime in poverty-stricken neighborhood; delinquent behavior becomes socially acceptable for youths; outside investment and support shun the area.

Source: Adapted from Larry J. Siegel, *Criminology*, 10th ed. (Belmont, CA: Thomson/Wadsworth, 2009), 180.

norms into a flux, leading to a weakening of social controls and an increase in deviant behavior.[65] Another sociologist, American Robert K. Merton, expanded on Durkheim's ideas in his own theory of strain. Merton believed that *anomie* was caused by a social structure in which all citizens have similar goals without equal means to achieve them.[66] One way to alleviate this strain is to gain wealth by the means that are available to the residents of disorganized communities: drug trafficking, burglary, and other criminal activities.

SOCIAL CONFLICT THEORIES Strain theory and the concept of *anomie* seem to suggest that the unequal structure of our society is, in part, to blame for criminal behavior. This argument forms the bedrock of **social conflict theories** of crime. These theories, which entered mainstream criminology in the 1960s, hold capitalism responsible for high levels of violence and crime because of the disparity of income that it encourages.

According to social conflict theory, the poor commit property crimes for reasons of need and because, as members of a capitalist society, they desire the same financial rewards as everybody else. They commit violent crimes because of the frustration and rage they feel when those rewards seem unattainable. Laws, instead of reflecting the values of society as a whole, reflect only the values of the segment of society that has achieved power and is willing to use the criminal justice system as a tool to keep that power.[67] Thus, the harsh penalties for "lower-class" crimes such as burglary can be seen as a means of protecting the privileges of the haves from the aspirations of the have-nots.

LIFE LESSONS AND CRIMINAL BEHAVIOR

Some criminologists find class theories of crime overly narrow. Surveys that ask people directly about their criminal behavior have shown that the criminal instinct is consistent throughout all income levels, even if the actual crime rate is higher in low-income

Social Conflict Theories
A school of criminology that views criminal behavior as the result of class conflict.

communities. Anybody, these criminologists argue, has the potential to act out criminal behavior, regardless of the socioeconomic class to which they belong.

THE ABANDONED CAR EXPERIMENT Philip Zimbardo conducted a well-known, if rather unscientific, experiment to make this point. Zimbardo placed an abandoned automobile with its hood up on the campus of Stanford University. The car remained in place, untouched, for a week. Then, the psychologist smashed the car's window with a sledgehammer. Within minutes, passersby had joined in the destruction of the automobile, eventually stripping its valuable parts.[68] **Social process theories** function on the same basis as Zimbardo's "interdependence of decisions experiment": the potential for criminal behavior exists in everyone and will be realized depending on an individual's interaction with various institutions and processes of society. Two major branches of social process theory are (1) learning theory and (2) control theory.

LEARNING THEORY Popularized by Edwin Sutherland in the 1940s, **learning theory** contends that criminal activity is a learned behavior. In other words, a criminal is taught both the practical methods of crime (such as how to pick a lock) and the psychological aspects of crime (how to deal with the guilt of wrongdoing). Sutherland's *theory of differential association* held that individuals are exposed to the values of family and peers such as school friends or co-workers. If the dominant values one is exposed to favor criminal behavior, then that person is more likely to mimic such behavior.[69]

More recently, learning theory has been expanded to include the growing influence of the media. In the latest in a long series of studies, psychologists at the University of Michigan's Institute for Social Research released data showing that exposure to high levels of televised violence erodes a natural aversion to violence and increases aggressive behavior among young children.[70] Such findings have spurred a number of legislative attempts to curb violence on television.[71] The controversy surrounding the violent attributes of another medium—video games—reached all the way to the United States Supreme Court, as shown in the feature *Landmark Cases—Brown v. EMA* on the following page.

CONTROL THEORY Criminologist Travis Hirschi focuses on the reasons why individuals do not engage in criminal acts, rather than why they do. According to Hirschi, social bonds promote conformity to social norms. The stronger these social bonds—which include

Social Process Theories A school of criminology that considers criminal behavior to be the predictable result of a person's interaction with his or her environment.

Learning Theory The hypothesis that delinquents and criminals must be taught both the practical and the emotional skills necessary to participate in illegal activity.

Learning Objective **6** List and briefly explain two important branches of social process theory.

attachment to, commitment to, involvement with, and belief in societal values—the less likely that any individual will commit a crime.[72] **Control theory** holds that although we all have the potential to commit crimes, most of us are dissuaded from doing so because we care about the opinions of our family and peers.

James Q. Wilson and George Kelling described control theory in terms of the "broken windows" effect. Neighborhoods in poor condition are filled with cues of lack of social control (for example, broken windows) that invite further vandalism and other deviant behavior.[73] If these cues are removed, according to Wilson and Kelling, so is the implied acceptance of crime within a community.

LIFE COURSE THEORIES OF CRIME If crime is indeed learned behavior, some criminologists are asking, Shouldn't we be focusing on early childhood—the time when humans do

LANDMARK CASES: *Brown v. Entertainment Merchants Association (EMA)*

Reacting to studies linking violent video games to violent behavior in children, in 2006 former California governor Arnold Schwarzenegger signed a bill prohibiting the sale or rental of games that portray "killing, maiming, dismembering or sexually assaulting an image of a human being" to people younger than eighteen years old. The law imposed a $1,000 fine on violators. Immediately, video game sellers sued the state, saying it had violated their constitutional right to freedom of speech. After two lower courts accepted this argument and invalidated California's law, the issue finally arrived before the United States Supreme Court.

Brown v. EMA
United States Supreme Court
559 S.Ct. 1448 (2010)
www.supremecourt.gov/opinions/10pdf/08-1448.pdf

IN THE WORDS OF THE COURT...
JUSTICE SCALIA, MAJORITY OPINION
* * * *

Like the protected books, plays, and movies that preceded them, video games communicate ideas—and even social messages—through many familiar literary devices (such as characters, dialogue, plot, and music) and through features distinctive to the medium (such as the player's interaction with the virtual world). That suffices to confer First Amendment protection. Under our Constitution, "esthetic and moral judgments about art and literature * * * are for the individual to make, not for the Government to decree, even with the mandate or approval of a majority."
* * * *

No doubt a State possesses legitimate power to protect children from harm, but that does not include a free-floating power to restrict the ideas to which children may be exposed. * * * California's argument would fare better if there were a longstanding tradition in this country of specially restricting children's access to depictions of violence, but there is none. Certainly the *books* we give children to read—or read to them when they are younger—contain no shortage of gore. Grimm's Fairy Tales, for example, are grim indeed.

* * * *

California relies primarily on * * * psychologists whose studies purport to show a connection between exposure to violent video games and harmful effects on children. These studies have been rejected by every court to consider them, and with good reason: They do not prove that violent video games *cause* minors to act aggressively (which would at least be a beginning). Instead, "[n]early all of the research is based on correlation, not evidence of causation * * *" They show at best some correlation between exposure to violent entertainment and minuscule real-world effects, such as children's feeling more aggressive or making louder noises in the few minutes after playing a violent game than after playing a nonviolent game.

Decision
In the absence of any provable negative effects on minors, from violent video games, the Court ruled that California's ban was unconstitutional and therefore could not be enforced.

FOR CRITICAL ANALYSIS
If states have the "legitimate power" to "protect children from harm," why did the Court invalidate California's violent video game law? How did Justice Scalia use the concepts of *cause* and *correlation* to support the Court's decision? (You can review those terms on page 45.)

the most learning? Practitioners of **life course criminology** believe that lying, stealing, bullying, and other conduct problems that occur in childhood are the strongest predictors of future criminal behavior and have been seriously undervalued in the examination of why crime occurs.[74]

Self-Control Theory Focusing on childhood behavior raises the question of whether conduct problems established at a young age can be changed over time. Michael Gottfredson and Travis Hirschi, whose 1990 publication *A General Theory of Crime* is one of the foundations of life course criminology, think not.[75] Gottfredson and Hirschi believe that criminal behavior is linked to "low self-control," a personality trait that is formed before a child reaches the age of ten and can usually be attributed to poor parenting.[76]

Someone with low self-control is generally impulsive, thrill seeking, and likely to solve problems with violence rather than his or her intellect. Gottfredson and Hirschi think that once low self-control has been established, it will persist. In other words, childhood behavioral problems are not "solved" by positive developments later in life, such as healthy personal relationships or a good job.[77] Thus, these two criminologists ascribe to what has been called the *continuity theory of crime,* which essentially says that once negative behavior patterns have been established, they cannot be changed.

The Possibility of Change Not all of those who practice life course criminology follow the continuity theory. Robert Sampson and John Laub, for example, have gathered a great deal of data showing, in their opinion, that offenders may experience "turning points" when they are able to veer off the road from a life of crime.[78] A good deal of research in this area has concentrated on the positive impact of getting married, having children, and finding a job, but other turning points are also being explored. John F. Frana of Indiana State University and Ryan D. Schroeder of the University of Louisville argue that military service can act as a "rehabilitative agent."[79] Several researchers have studied the role that religion and spirituality can play as "hooks for change."[80]

VICTIMS OF CRIME

Since its founding days, criminology has focused almost exclusively on one-half of the crime equation: the offender. If you review our discussion of criminology up to this point, you will find little mention of the other half: the victim. Indeed, only in the past several decades has **victimology** become an essential component of criminology. The growing emphasis on the victim has had a profound impact on the police, the courts, and corrections administrators in this country. Accordingly, Andrew Karmen, a professor of sociology at the John Jay College of Criminal Justice in New York City, has defined *victimology* as the study of "relationships between victims and offenders [and] the interactions between victims and the criminal justice system."[81]

THE RISKS OF VICTIMIZATION Anybody can be a victim of crime. This does not mean, however, that everybody is at an equal risk of being victimized. For example, because mental illnesses such as schizophrenia (see page 48) interfere with a person's ability to make smart decisions in risky situations, those who suffer from such disabilities are eleven times more likely to be the victims of violent crimes than nonsufferers.[82]

To better explain the circumstances surrounding victimization, in the late 1970s, criminologists Larry Cohen and Marcus Felson devised the *routine activities theory.* According to Cohen and Felson, most criminal acts require the following:

Life Course Criminology The study of crime based on the belief that behavioral patterns developed in childhood can predict delinquent and criminal behavior later in life.

Victimology A school of criminology that studies why certain people are the victims of crimes and the optimal role for victims in the criminal justice system.

Social Media and CJ The American Society of Criminology operates **Critical Criminology** as a forum for ideas and information relating to the causes of crime. To browse the wide variety of posts on this Facebook page, visit the *Criminal Justice CourseMate* at **cengagebrain.com** and select the *Web Links* for this chapter.

1. A likely offender.
2. A suitable target (a person or an object).
3. The absence of a capable guardian—that is, any person (not necessarily a law enforcement agent) whose presence or proximity prevents a crime from happening.[83]

When these three factors are present, the likelihood of crime rises. Cohen and Felson believe that routine activities often contribute to this "perfect storm" of criminal opportunity. So, for example, when a person leaves for work, her or his home becomes a suitable target for a likely offender because the guardian is absent.

THE VICTIM–OFFENDER CONNECTION Early on the morning of August 14, 2010, a lone gunman shot eight people outside a nightclub in Buffalo, New York. Of the eight victims, four of whom died, seven had previously been arrested or convicted of a crime. This incident underscores an important point: criminals and victims are often the same people. Recently gathered data show, for example, that 92 percent of murder suspects and 72 percent of murder victims in Chicago have previously been convicted of a crime.[84] Of Baltimore's 234 murder victims in 2008, 194 had criminal records.[85]

"The notion that [violent crimes] are random bolts of lightning, which is the commonly held image, is not the reality at all," says David Kennedy, a professor at New York's John Jay College of Criminal Justice.[86] Kennedy's point is further made by Figure 2.7 below, which shows that the most vulnerable demographic groups—particularly young, low-income African American males—are also those with the highest rates of criminality.

FIGURE 2.7
Crime Victims in the United States
According to the U.S. Department of Justice, African Americans, households with annual incomes of less than $15,000, and young people between the ages of eighteen and twenty are most likely to be victims of crime in this country.

Source: Bureau of Justice Statistics, *Criminal Victimization, 2010* (Washington, D.C.: U.S. Department of Justice, September 2011), 11, 12.

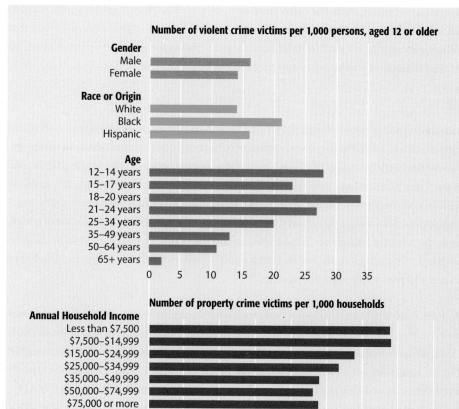

FROM THEORY TO PRACTICE

For the criminological theories we have studied in this chapter to be worthwhile, they must do more than simply offer themselves for academic debate. They must be used, in the field, by criminal justice professionals to prevent crime. On numerous occasions, this has been the case. James Q. Wilson's and George Kelling's "broken windows" theory, mentioned in conjunction with control theory on page 52, reshaped policing strategies in the 1990s, as we will discuss further in Chapter 5. Justice reinvestment, a relatively new strategy, draws on social disorganization theory (page 49) in urging the federal and state governments to redirect tax dollars spent on prisons to the local communities hardest hit by crime and cycles of incarceration.[87]

Perhaps the most far-reaching criminological contribution to crime fighting in the past half century was *Delinquency in a Birth Cohort,* published in 1972 by the pioneering trio of Marvin Wolfgang, Robert Figlio, and Thorsten Sellin. This research established the idea of the **chronic offender,** or career criminal, by showing that a small group of juvenile offenders—6 percent—was responsible for about 70 percent of the violent crime attributed to a group of nearly 10,000 young males.[88]

Further research has supported the idea of a "chronic 6 percent,"[89] requiring law enforcement agencies and district attorney's offices to devise strategies for repeat offenders. Dozens of police departments, for example, operate career criminal units to deal with chronic criminals. Legislators have also reacted to this research: habitual offender laws that provide harsher sentences for repeat offenders are quite popular. We will discuss these statutes, including the controversial "three-strikes-and-you're-out" laws, in Chapter 9.

Chronic Offender A delinquent or criminal who commits multiple offenses and is considered part of a small group of wrongdoers who are responsible for a majority of the antisocial activity in any given community.

Learning Objective 7 Explain the theory of the chronic offender and its importance for the criminal justice system.

SELFASSESSMENT

Fill in the blanks and check your answers on page 60.

_____ _____ theory holds that criminals make a deliberate decision to commit a crime after weighing the possible rewards and punishments of the act. _____ _____ theory focuses on unfavorable neighborhood conditions, while _____ _____ theories of criminal behavior address the influence of friends and family. Supporters of _____ course theories of crime believe that stealing, bullying, and other conduct problems that occur during _____ can, in some instances, predict adult offending. _____ is the study of the relationship between victims and offenders in the criminal justice system.

THE LINK BETWEEN DRUGS AND CRIME

Earlier in this chapter, we discussed the difference between correlations and causes. As you may recall, criminologists are generally reluctant to declare that any one factor causes a certain result. Richard B. Felson of Penn State University and Keri B. Burchfield of Northern Illinois University, however, believe that alcohol consumption has a causal effect on victimization under certain circumstances.[90] Felson and Burchfield found that "frequent and heavy" drinkers are at a great risk of assault when they are drinking, but do not show abnormal rates of victimization when sober. They hypothesize that consuming alcohol leads to aggressive and offensive behavior, particularly in men, which in turn triggers violent reactions from others.

Do you feel that the behavior of celebrities such as socialite Paris Hilton, who was arrested for cocaine possession in Las Vegas, "teaches" adolescents that such behavior is acceptable or even desirable? Explain your answer.

AP Photo/Mark Damon

In Chapter 1, we learned that nearly 23 million Americans regularly use illegal drugs such as marijuana and cocaine, with another 200 million using legal drugs such as alcohol and nicotine. Here, we will discuss two questions concerning these habits. First, why do people use drugs? Second, what are the consequences for the criminal justice system?

THE CRIMINOLOGY OF DRUG USE

At first glance, the reason people use drugs, including legal drugs such as alcohol, is obvious: such drugs give the user pleasure and provide a temporary escape for those who may feel tension or anxiety. Ultimately, though, such explanations are unsatisfactory because they fail to explain why some people use drugs while others do not.

Several of the theories we discussed earlier in the chapter have been used by experts to explain drug use. *Social disorganization theory* (page 49) holds that rapid social change can cause people to become disaffiliated from mainstream society, causing them to turn to drugs. *Learning theory* (page 51) sees drug use as taught behavior. *Control theory* (pages 51–52) suggests that a lack of social control, as provided by entities such as the family or school, can lead to antisocial behavior.

Focusing on the question of why first-time drug users become habitual users, sociologist Howard Becker sees three factors in the "learning process." He believes first-time users:

1. Learn the techniques of drug use.
2. Learn to perceive the pleasurable effects of drug use.
3. Learn to enjoy the social experience of drug use.[91]

Becker's assumptions are evident in the widespread belief that positive images of drug use in popular culture "teach" adolescents that such behavior is not only acceptable but also desirable. The entertainment industry, in particular, has been criticized for glamorizing various forms of drug use.

DRUG ADDICTION AND DEPENDENCY

Another theory rests on the assumption that some people possess overly sensitive drug receptors in their brains and are therefore biologically disposed toward drug use.[92] Though there is little conclusive evidence that biological factors can explain initial drug experimentation, scientific research has provided a great deal of insight into patterns of long-term drug use.

DRUG USE AND DRUG ABUSE In particular, science has aided in understanding the difference between drug *use* and drug *abuse*. **Drug abuse** can be defined as the use of any drug—licit or illicit—that causes either psychological or bodily harm to the abuser or to third parties. Just as most people who drink beer or wine avoid abusing alcohol, most users of illegal substances are not abusers. For most drugs except nicotine, between 7 and 20 percent of all users suffer from compulsive abuse.[93]

Despite their relatively small numbers, drug abusers have a disparate impact on the drug market. The 20 percent of Americans, for example, who drink the most frequently

Learning Objective 8 Discuss the connection between learning theory and the start of an individual's drug use.

Drug Abuse The use of drugs that results in physical or psychological problems for the user, as well as disruption of personal relationships and employment.

consume more than 80 percent of all alcoholic beverages sold in the United States. The data are similar for illicit substance abusers, leading to the conclusion that, to a large extent, abusers and addicts sustain the market for illegal drugs.

ADDICTION BASICS The most extreme abusers are addicted to, or physically dependent on, a drug. To understand the basics of addiction and physical dependence, you must understand the role of *dopamine* in the brain. Dopamine, mentioned earlier in the chapter on page 48, is the neurotransmitter responsible for delivering pleasure signals to brain nerve endings in response to behavior—such as eating good food or engaging in sex—that makes us feel good. The bloodstream delivers drugs to the area of the brain that produces dopamine, thereby triggering the production of a large amount of the substance in the brain. Over time, the continued use of drugs physically changes the nerve endings, called *receptors*. To continue operating in the presence of large amounts of dopamine, the receptors become less sensitive, meaning that greater amounts of any particular drug are required to create the amount of dopamine needed for the same levels of pleasure. When the supply of the drug is cut off, the brain strongly feels the lack of dopamine stimulation, and the abuser will suffer symptoms of withdrawal until the receptors readjust.[94]

THE DRUG—CRIME RELATIONSHIP

Of course, because many drugs are illegal, anybody who sells, uses, or in any way promotes the use of these drugs is, under most circumstances, breaking the law. The drug-crime relationship goes beyond the language of criminal drug statutes, however. About 37 percent of state prisoners and 33 percent of jail inmates incarcerated for a violent crime were under the influence of alcohol at the time of their arrest.[95] Similarly, according to one recent study, between 52 and 83 percent of all arrestees in ten major American cities tested positive for illicit drugs when apprehended.[96] As we will see throughout this textbook, the prosecution of illegal drug users and suppliers has been one of the primary factors in the enormous growth of the American correctional industry. (To learn about a country where the violent crime caused by the drug trade has reached catastrophic levels, see the feature *Comparative Criminal Justice—A Real War on Drugs* on the following page.)

"LEGAL" DRUG ABUSE New forms of drug-related crime are appearing as well. According to federal data, the number of deaths related to painkillers such as OxyContin, Vicodin, and methadone increased from 4,000 in 1999 to almost 15,000 in 2008.[97] The increased demand for these **prescription drugs** has, in the words of one Maine law enforcement official, led to "home invasions, robberies, assaults, homicides, thefts—all kinds of crime."[98] The improper use of controlled prescription drugs has increased to the point where these drugs are second only to marijuana in government rankings of the most-abused drugs in the United States.[99]

Furthermore, legal, over-the-counter substances are the main ingredient in the manufacture of **methamphetamine (meth),** a highly addictive stimulant to the central nervous system. Meth is relatively easy to make in home laboratories using the ingredients of common cold medicines and farm chemicals. Consequently, the drug provides a "cheap high" and has become the scourge of many poor rural areas, particularly in the western half of the United States.

SYNTHETIC DRUGS Numerous drug manufacturers—at least one thousand in the United States alone—have found an innovative way to circumvent drug laws. They produce *synthetic drugs* that simulate the effects of illicit substances but are created using legal

Prescription Drugs
Medical drugs that require a physician's permission for purchase.

Methamphetamine (meth)
An easily produced, relatively inexpensive stimulant that creates a strong feeling of euphoria in the user and is highly addictive.

COMPARATIVE CRIMINAL JUSTICE

A REAL WAR ON DRUGS

For most of the past decade, Mexico and its citizens have suffered through a bloody and seemingly endless "war on drugs." Each year, illegal drugs worth from $25 to $40 billion are smuggled over the border into the United States, and various cartels are willing to fight—and kill—for their cut. From 2007 to 2012, more than 47,500 Mexicans were murdered in drug-related slayings. "I really characterize this as a civil war," says Howard Campbell of the University of Texas at El Paso. "We're seeing all the casualties of a war, people murdered, people wounded, people fleeing their homes, disintegration and chaos."

Mexico's leaders have not stood idly by in the face of this carnage. Mistrustful of corrupt local police, the federal government has sent tens of thousands of federal troops to the areas where the drug trade is most active, primarily along the U.S.–Mexican border. Although numerous drug kingpins have been captured, these efforts have apparently only exacerbated the problem.

FOR CRITICAL ANALYSIS

According to Tony Garza, who spent six years (2002–2008) as the U.S. ambassador to Mexico, the country would not "be experiencing this level of violence were the United States not the largest consumer of illicit drugs and the main supplier of weapons to the cartels." The U.S. government has provided Mexico with $1.4 billion in aid to use in its war on drugs, and numerous American federal, state, and local law enforcement agencies are working with their Mexican counterparts to stem the violence. Is the United States morally obligated to provide this financial and tactical aid? What other steps could our government take to weaken the link between illegal drugs and crime in Mexico?

A soldier stands guard over fifty tons of burning marijuana seized from drug dealers by the Mexican army.

Keith Dannemiller/Corbis

---

chemical compounds. Synthetic cannabinoids, for example, mimic the active ingredient in marijuana, and methadrone crystals, packaged as "bath salts," can be snorted to produce the same "rush" as cocaine or meth.

Even though more than thirty states have passed legislation banning these substances, it is fairly easy for manufacturers to create new variations. Spurred by Internet orders, the use of synthetic drugs has spread rapidly. By one estimate, synthetic cannibinoid sales are now approaching $5 billion annually.[100] In 2010, the nation's poison control centers handled 303 calls linked to "bath salt" use. In the first half of 2011, that number spiked to 3,470.[101]

SELFASSESSMENT

Fill in the blanks and check your answers on page 60.

Drug _____ is defined as the use of any drug that causes harm to the user or a third party. People who are _____, meaning that they desire the drug long after use has stopped, need greater amounts of the drug to stimulate a neurotransmitter in the brain called _____. Harms associated with the abuse of _____ drugs, which require a physician's permission, and _____ drugs, which mimic the effects of substances such as marijuana and cocaine, have increased in recent years.

CHAPTER SUMMARY

Learning
Objective
1 **Identify the six main categories of crime.**
The six main categories of crime are (a) violent crimes—murder, rape, assault, battery, and robbery; (b) property crimes—pocket picking, shoplifting, larceny/theft, burglary, and arson; (c) public order crimes—public drunkenness, prostitution, gambling, and illicit drug use; (d) white-collar crime—fraud and embezzlement; (e) organized crime—crime undertaken by a number of persons who operate their activities much as legal businesses do; and (f) high-tech crimes—sabotage, fraud, embezzlement, and theft of proprietary data from computer systems, as well as cyber crimes, such as selling child pornography over the Internet.

2 **Distinguish between Part I and Part II offenses as defined by the Uniform Crime Report (UCR).** Part I offenses include the most violent crimes and several property crimes. Part II offenses include all other crimes recorded in the UCR. They generally cover less serious crimes and constitute the majority of crimes committed.

3 **Distinguish between the National Crime Victimization Survey (NCVS) and self-reported surveys.** The NCVS involves an annual survey of more than 40,000 households conducted by the Bureau of the Census along with the Bureau of Justice Statistics. The survey queries citizens on crimes that have been committed against them. As such, the NCVS includes crimes not necessarily reported to police. Self-reported surveys, in contrast, ask individuals about criminal activity to which they may have been a party.

4 **Discuss the prevailing explanation for the rising number of women incarcerated in the United States.** Experts believe that many women are arrested and given harsh punishment for activity that would not have put them behind bars several decades ago. For the most part, this activity is nonviolent: the majority of female arrestees are involved in drug- and alcohol-related offenses and property crimes.

5 **Discuss the difference between a hypothesis and a theory in the context of criminology.** A hypothesis is a proposition, usually presented in an "If . . . , then . . ." format, that can be tested by researchers. If enough different authorities are able to test and verify a hypothesis, it will usually be accepted as a theory. Because theories can offer explanations for behavior, criminologists often rely on them when trying to determine the causes of criminal behavior.

6 **List and briefly explain two important branches of social process theory.**
(a) Learning theory, which contends that people learn to be criminals from their family and peers. (b) Control theory, which holds that most of us are dissuaded from a life of crime because we place importance on the opinions of family and peers.

7 **Explain the theory of the chronic offender and its importance for the criminal justice system.** A chronic offender is a juvenile or adult who commits multiple offenses. According to research conducted by Marvin Wolfgang and others in the 1970s, chronic offenders are responsible for a disproportionately large percentage of all crime. In the decades since, law enforcement agencies and public prosecutors have developed strategies to identify and convict chronic offenders with the goal of lessening overall crime rates. In addition, legislators have passed laws that provide longer sentences for chronic offenders in an attempt to keep them off the streets.

8 **Discuss the connection between learning theory and the start of an individual's drug use.** One criminologist believes that first-time illegal drug users go through a "learning process" in taking up the habit. That is, more experienced users teach them the techniques of drug use, the pleasurable aspects of drug use, and the social experience of drug use.

QUESTIONS FOR CRITICAL ANALYSIS

1. Do you agree that public order crimes such as prostitution and illegal gambling are "victimless" crimes? Why or why not?

2. Assume that you are a criminologist who wants to determine the extent to which high school students engage in risky behaviors such as abusing alcohol and illegal

drugs, carrying weapons, and contemplating suicide. How would you go about gathering these data?

3. What are some of the problems with the assumption that there is a link between race and criminal behavior? What are some of the problems with the assumption that there is a link between poverty and criminal behavior?

4. Research shows that when levels of single-family mortgage foreclosures rise in a neighborhood, so do levels of violent crime. Explain the correlation between these two sets of statistics. Why is it incorrect to say that single-family mortgage foreclosures cause violent crimes to occur?

5. Why would someone who subscribes to rational choice theory (see pages 46–47) believe that increasing the harshness of a penalty for a particular crime would necessarily lead to fewer such crimes being committed?

KEY TERMS

anomie **49**
assault **33**
battery **33**
biology **47**
burglary **33**
causation **45**
chronic offender **55**
control theory **52**
correlation **45**
criminologist **45**
criminology **45**
dark figure of crime **38**
drug abuse **56**
hormone **47**

hypothesis **46**
larceny **33**
learning theory **51**
life course criminology **53**
methamphetamine (meth) **57**
murder **33**
neurotransmitter **47**
organized crime **34**
Part I offenses **36**
Part II offenses **37**
prescription drugs **57**
psychology **47**
public order crime **33**
rational choice theory **46**

robbery **33**
self-reported survey **39**
sexual assault **33**
social conflict theories **50**
social disorganization theory **49**
social process theories **51**
sociology **49**
strain theory **49**
testosterone **47**
theory **46**
Uniform Crime Report (UCR) **36**
victimology **53**
victim surveys **37**
white-collar crime **34**

SELF ASSESSMENT ANSWER KEY

Page 34: **i.** violent; **ii.** property; **iii.** white-collar

Page 40: **i.** Uniform Crime Report; **ii.** Victim; **iii.** Self-reported; **iv.** dark figure; **v.** larger

Page 45: **i.** imprisoned/incarcerated; **ii.** under; **iii.** African American; **iv.** immigration

Page 55: **i.** Rational choice; **ii.** Social disorganization; **iii.** social process; **iv.** life; **v.** childhood; **vii.** Victimology

Page 58: **i.** abuse; **ii.** addicted; **iii.** dopamine; **iv.** prescription; **v.** synthetic

COURSEMATE

For online help and access to resources that accompany *Criminal Justice in Action: The Core*, go to **www.cengage-brain.com/shop/ISBN/978-1-285-06915-9**. Click "Access Now," where you will find flashcards, an online quiz, and other helpful study aids. If you have an access code for CourseMate, log in and go to the chapter of your choice for additional online study aids.

NOTES

1. Quoted in "Justice Department Redefines Rape," National Public Radio, January 6, 2012, transcript at **www.npr.org/2012/01/06/144801667/justice-department-redefines-rape**.

2. Charlie Savage, "U.S. to Expand Its Definition of Rape in Statistics," *New York Times* (January 7, 2012), A10.

3. "Jerry Sandusky Case: Summary of the Investigation and the Charges against the Former Penn State University Defensive Coordinator," *York Daily Record/Sunday News* (January 22, 2012), at **www.ydr.com/ci_19280635**.

4. *2010 Report to the Nations: Occupational Fraud and Abuse* (Austin, TX: Association of Certified Fraud Examiners, 2010), 8.

5. Federal Bureau of Investigation, *Crime in the United States, 2011* (Washington, D.C.: U.S. Department of Justice, 2012), at **www.fbi.gov/about-us/cjis/ucr/crime-in-the-u.s/2011/crime-in-the-u.s.-2011**.

6. Savage.

7. *Crime in the United States, 2011*, at **www.fbi.gov/about-us/cjis/ucr/crime-in-the-u.s/2011/crime-in-the-u.s.-2011/tables/table-1**.

8. Jeffery Reiman, *The Rich Get Richer and the Poor Get Prison,* 4th ed. (Boston: Allyn & Bacon, 1995), 59–60.

9. *Crime in the United States, 2011*, at **www.fbi.gov/about-us/cjis/ucr/crime-in-the-u.s/2011/crime-in-the-u.s.-2011/tables/expanded-homicide-data-table-10**.

10. *Ibid.,* at **www.fbi.gov/about-us/cjis/ucr/crime-in-the-u.s/2011/crime-in-the-u.s.-2011/tables/table-1**.

11. *Ibid.,* at **www.fbi.gov/about-us/cjis/ucr/crime-in-the-u.s/2011/crime-in-the-u.s.-2011/tables/table-29**.

12. Marcus Felson, *Crime in Everyday Life* (Thousand Oaks, CA: Pine Forge Press, 1994), 3.

13. Victor E. Kappeler, Mark Blumberg, and Gary W. Potter, *The Mythology of Crime and Criminal Justice,* 2d ed. (Prospect Heights, IL: Waveland Press, 1993), 31.

14. Federal Bureau of Investigation, *Crime in the United States, 2010* (Washington, D.C.: U.S. Department of Justice, 2011), at **www.fbi.gov/about-us/cjis/ucr/crime-in-the-u.s/2010/crime-in-the-u.s.-2010/violent-crime/rapemain**; and Bureau of Justice Statistics, *Criminal Victimization, 2010* (Washington, D.C.: U.S. Department of Justice, September 11, 2011), Table 1, page 2.

15. Peter B. Wood, Walter R. Grove, James A. Wilson, and John K. Cochran, "Nonsocial Reinforcement and Criminal Conduct: An Extension of Learning Theory," *Criminology* 35 (May 1997), 335–366.

16. Franklin E. Zimring, *The Great American Crime Decline* (New York: Oxford University Press, 2007), 45–72.

17. James Q. Wilson, "Concluding Essay in Crime," in James Q. Wilson and Joan Petersilia, eds., *Crime* (San Francisco: Institute for Contemporary Studies Press, 1995), 507.

18. Zimring, 6.

19. *Ibid.,* 197–198.

20. Quoted in Pete Yost, "Violent Crime Falls for Third Straight Year," *San Jose Mercury News* (September 15, 2010), 2B.

21. Alexia Cooper and Erica L. Smith, *Homicide Trends in the United States, 1980–2008* (Washington, D.C.: Bureau of Justice Statistics, November 2011), 16.

22. James Alan Fox and Marc L. Swatt, *The Recent Surge in Homicides Involving Young Black Males and Guns: Time to Reinvest in Prevention and Crime Control* (December 2008), 2, available at **www.jfox.neu.edu/Documents/Fox%20Swatt%20Homicide%20Report%20Dec%2029%202008.pdf**.

23. Quoted in Erik Eckholm, "Murders by Black Teenagers Rise This Decade, Bucking a Trend," *New York Times* (December 29, 2008), A12.

24. *Crime in the United States, 2011*, at **www.fbi.gov/about-us/cjis/ucr/crime-in-the-u.s/2011/crime-in-the-u.s.-2011/tables/table-43**.

25. *Targeting Blacks: Drug Law Enforcement and Race in the United States* (New York: Human Rights Watch, May 2008), 3.

26. Charles Puzzanchera, Benjamin Adams, and Melissa Sickmund, *Juvenile Court Statistics, 2008* (Washington, D.C.: National Center for Juvenile Justice, July 2011), 20.

27. Robert J. Sampson, Jeffrey Morenoff, and Stephen W. Raudenbush, "Social Anatomy of Racial and Ethnic Disparities in Violence," *American Journal of Public Health* 95 (2005), 224–232.

28. John R. Hipp, "Spreading the Wealth: The Effect of the Distribution of Income and Race/Ethnicity across Households and Neighborhoods on City Crime Trajectories," *Criminology* (August 2011), 633–634.

29. Patricia Y. Warren, "Inequality by Design: The Connection between Race, Crime, Victimization, and Social Policy," *Criminology & Public Policy* (November 2010), 715.

30. Eric A. Stewart, Ronald L. Simons, and Rand D. Donger, "Assessing Neighborhood and Social Psychological Influence on Childhood Violence in an African American Sample," *Criminology* (November 2002), 801–829.

31. William Alex Pridemore, "A Methodological Addition to the Cross-National Empirical Literature on Social Structure and Homicide: A First Test of the Poverty-Homicide Thesis," *Criminology* (February 2008), 133.

32. Caroline Wolf Harlow, *Education and Correctional Populations* (Washington, D.C.: Bureau of Justice Statistics, January 2003), 1.

33. Charles Tittle and Robert Meier, "Specifying the SES/Delinquency Relationship," *Criminology* 28 (1990), 270–301.

34. Darrell Steffensmeier, et al., "Reassessing Trends in Black Violent Crime, 1980–2008: Sorting Out the 'Hispanic Effect' in Uniform Crime Reports Arrests, National Crime Victimization Survey Offender Estimates, and U.S. Prisoner Counts," *Criminology* (February 2011), 201.

35. Marguerite Moeller, *America's Tomorrow: A Profile of Latino Youth* (New York: National Council of La Raza), 2010.

36. *Preliminary Fiscal Year 2011 Data* (Washington, D.C.: U.S. Sentencing Commission, September 2011), Table 23, page 44.

37. Sampson, Morenoff, and Raudenbush, 231.

38. Cooper and Smith, Table 4, page 9.

39. Bureau of Justice Statistics, *Jail Inmates at Midyear 2010—Statistical Tables* (Washington, D.C.: U.S. Department of Justice, April 2011), Table 6, page 7; Bureau of Justice Statistics, *Prisoners in 2010* (Washington, D.C.: U.S. Department of Justice, December 2011), Appendix table 12, page 26; and *Crime in the United States, 2011*, at **www.fbi.gov/about-us/cjis/ucr/crime-in-the-u.s/2011/crime-in-the-u.s.-2011/persons-arrested/persons-arrested**.

40. Howard N. Snyder, *Arrests in the United States, 1980–2009* (Washington, D.C.: Bureau of Justice Statistics, September 2011), 1.

41. Bureau of Justice Statistics, *Prisoners in 2010,* Table 1, page 2.

42. Jennifer Schwartz and Bryan D. Rookey, "The Narrowing Gender Gap in Arrests: Assessing Competing Explanations Using Self-Report, Traffic Fatality, and Official Data on Drunk Driving, 1980–2004," *Criminology* (August 2008), 637–638.

43. Quoted in Barry Yeoman, "Violent Tendencies: Crime by Women Has Skyrocketed in Recent Years," *Chicago Tribune* (March 15, 2000), 3.

44. *Crime in the United States, 2011*, at **www.fbi.gov/about-us/cjis/ucr/crime-in-the-u.s/2011/crime-in-the-u.s.-2011/tables/table-42**.

45. Schwarz and Rookey, 637–671.

46. Meda Chesney-Lind, "Patriarchy, Prisons, and Jails: A Critical Look at Trends in Women's Incarceration," *Prison Journal* (Spring/Summer 1991), 57.

47. Jessica Wolpaw Reyes, *Environmental Policy as Social Policy? The Impact of Childhood Lead Exposure on Crime* (Cambridge, MA:

National Bureau of Economic Research, May 2007), at **www.nber.org/papers/w13097.pdf**.

48. James Q. Wilson and Richard J. Hernstein, *Crime and Human Nature: The Definitive Study of the Causes of Crime* (New York: Simon & Schuster, 1985), 44.

49. Jack Katz, *Seductions of Crime: Moral and Sensual Attractions of Doing Evil* (New York: Basic Books, 1988).

50. National Coalition for the Homeless, "Hate Crimes and Violence against People Experiencing Homelessness," at **www.nationalhomeless.org/factsheets/hate-crimes.html**.

51. Jeffrey M. Burns and Russell H. Swerdlow, "Right Orbifrontal Tumor with Pedophilia Symptom and Constructional Apraxia Sign," *Archives of Neurology* (March 2003), 437.

52. David C. Rowe, *Biology and Crime* (Los Angeles: Roxbury, 2002), 2.

53. L. E. Kreuz and R. M. Rose, "Assessment of Aggressive Behavior and Plasma Testosterone in Young Criminal Population," *Psychosomatic Medicine* 34 (1972), 321–332.

54. H. Persky, K. Smith, and G. Basu, "Relation of Psychological Measures of Aggression and Hostility to Testosterone Production in Men," *Psychosomatic Medicine* 33 (1971), 265, 276.

55. Benjamin J. Sadock, Harold I. Kaplan, and Virginia A. Sadock, *Kaplan & Sadock's Synopsis of Psychiatry* (Philadelphia: Lippincott Williams & Wilkins, 2007), 865.

56. Robert J. Meadows and Julie Kuehnel, *Evil Minds: Understanding and Responding to Violent Predators* (Upper Saddle River, NJ: Pearson Prentice Hall, 2005), 156–157.

57. *Ibid.,* 157, 169.

58. Quoted in Eileen Sullivan, "Loners Like Tucson Gunman 'Fly below the Radar,'" *Associated Press* (January 17, 2011).

59. Herman Bianchi, *Justice as Sanctuary: Toward a New System of Crime Control* (Bloomington: Indiana University Press, 1994), 72.

60. Philip Zimbardo, "Pathology of Imprisonment," *Society* (April 1972), 4–8.

61. David Canter and Laurence Alison, "The Social Psychology of Crime: Groups, Teams, and Networks," in *The Social Psychology of Crime: Groups, Teams, and Networks,* ed. David Canter and Laurence Alison (Hanover, NH: Dartmouth, 2000), 3–4.

62. Douglas McIntyre, Michael Sauter, and Charles Stockdale, "The Most Dangerous Cities in America," *24/7 Wall ST* (May 25, 2011), at **finance.yahoo.com/news/pf_article_112804.html**.

63. Clifford R. Shaw, Henry D. McKay, and Leonard S. Cottrell, *Delinquency Areas* (Chicago: University of Chicago Press, 1929).

64. Clifford R. Shaw and Henry D. McKay, *Report on the Causes of Crime,* vol. 2: *Social Factors in Juvenile Delinquency* (Washington, D.C.: National Commission on Law Observance and Enforcement, 1931).

65. Emile Durkheim, *The Rules of Sociological Method,* trans. Sarah A. Solovay and John

H. Mueller (New York: Free Press, 1964).

66. Robert K. Merton, *Social Theory and Social Structure* (New York: Free Press, 1957). See the chapter on "Social Structure and Anomie."

67. Robert Meier, "The New Criminology: Continuity in Criminology Theory," *Journal of Criminal Law and Criminology* 67 (1977), 461–469.

68. Philip G. Zimbardo, "The Human Choice: Individuation, Reason, and Order versus Deindividuation, Impulse, and Chaos," in *Nebraska Symposium on Motivation,* ed. William J. Arnold and David Levie (Lincoln: University of Nebraska Press, 1969), 287–293.

69. Edwin H. Sutherland, *Criminology,* 4th ed. (Philadelphia: Lippincott, 1947).

70. L. Rowell Huesmann, Jessica Moise-Titus, Cheryl-Lynn Podolski, and Leonard D. Eron, "Longitudinal Relations between Children's Exposure to TV Violence and Their Aggressive and Violent Behavior in Young Adulthood: 1977–1992," *Developmental Psychology* (March 2003), 201.

71. Telecommunications Act of 1996, 47 U.S.C. Section 303 (1999).

72. Travis Hirschi, *Causes of Delinquency* (Berkeley: University of California Press, 1969).

73. James Q. Wilson and George L. Kelling, "Broken Windows," *Atlantic Monthly* (March 1982), 29.

74. Francis T. Cullen and Robert Agnew, *Criminological Theory, Past to Present: Essential Readings,* 2d ed. (Los Angeles: Roxbury Publishing Co., 2003), 443.

75. Michael R. Gottfredson and Travis Hirschi, *A General Theory of Crime* (Stanford, CA: Stanford University Press, 1990).

76. *Ibid.,* 90.

77. *Ibid.*

78. Robert J. Sampson and John H. Laub, *Crime in the Making: Pathways and Turning Points through Life* (Cambridge, MA: Harvard University Press, 1993), 11.

79. John F. Frana and Ryan D. Schroeder, "Alternatives to Incarceration," *Justice Policy Journal* (Fall 2008), available at **www.cjcj.org/files/alternatives_to.pdf**.

80. Peggy C. Giordano, Monica A. Longmore, Ryan D. Schroeder, and Patrick M. Seffrin, "A Life-Course Perspective on Spirituality and Desistance from Crime," *Criminology* (February 2008), 99–132.

81. Andrew Karmen, *Crime Victims: An Introduction to Victimology* (Belmont, CA: Wadsworth, 2003).

82. Linda A. Teplin et al., "Crime Victimization in Adults with Severe Mental Illness: Comparison with the National Crime Victimization Survey," *Archives of General Psychiatry* (August 2005), 911–921.

83. Larry Cohen and Marcus Felson, "Social Change and Crime Rate Trends: A Routine Activity Approach," *American Sociological Review* (1979), 588–608.

84. Angela Rozas, "Crime Up for City in 2008,"

Chicago Tribune (January 17, 2009), 12.

85. Peter Hermann, "Statistics Tell a Violent Story That We've Heard Before," *Baltimore Sun* (January 4, 2009), 6A.

86. Quoted in Kevin Johnson, "Criminals Target Each Other, Trend Shows," *USA Today* (August 31, 2007), 1A.

87. Todd R. Clear, "A Private Sector, Incentives-Based Model for Justice Reinvestment," *Criminology & Public Policy* (August 2011), 585–587.

88. Marvin Wolfgang, Robert Figlio, and Thorsten Sellin, *Delinquency in a Birth Cohort* (Chicago: University of Chicago Press, 1972).

89. Lawrence W. Sherman, "Attacking Crime: Police and Crime Control," in *Modern Policing,* ed. Michael Tonry and Norval Morris (Chicago: University of Chicago Press, 1992), 159.

90. Richard B. Felson and Keri B. Burchfield, "Alcohol and the Risk of Physical and Sexual Assault Victimization," *Criminology* (November 1, 2004), 837.

91. Howard S. Becker, *Outsiders: Studies in the Sociology of Deviance* (New York: Free Press, 1963).

92. David G. Myers, *Psychology,* 7th ed. (New York: Worth, 2004), 75–76.

93. Peter B. Kraska, "The Unmentionable Alternative: The Need for and Argument against the Decriminalization of Drug Laws," in *Drugs, Crime, and the Criminal Justice System,* ed. Ralph Weisheit (Cincinnati, OH: Anderson Publishing, 1990).

94. Anthony A. Grace, "The Tonic/Phasal Model of Dopamine System Regulation," *Drugs and Alcohol* 37 (1995), 111.

95. Bureau of Justice Statistics, "Alcohol and Crime: Data from 2002 to 2008," at **bjs.ojp.usdoj.gov/content/acf/29_prisoners_and_alcoholuse.cfm and bjs.ojp.usdoj.gov/content/acf/30_jails_and_alcohol-use.cfm**.

96. *ADAM II: 2010 Annual Report* (Washington, D.C.: Office of National Drug Policy, May 2011), xii.

97. Centers for Disease Control and Prevention, "Prescription Painkiller Overdoses in the US," November 2011, at **www.cdc.gov/vitalsigns/PainkillerOverdoses/index.html#LatestFindings**.

98. Quoted in Abby Goodnough, "A Wave of Addiction and Crime, with the Medicine Cabinet to Blame," *New York Times* (September 24, 2010), A14.

99. National Drug Intelligence Center, *National Drug Threat Assessment, 2011* (Washington, D.C.: U.S. Department of Justice, August 2011), 1.

100. Ben Paynter, "The Money Is Huge: The Unlicensed, Ingenious, and Increasingly Scary World of Synthetic Drugs," *Bloomberg Businessweek* (June 20–26, 2011).

101. Abby Goodnough and Katie Zezima, "An Alarming New Stimulant, Legal in Many States," *New York Times* (July 17, 2011), A1.

CHAPTER

3

Inside Criminal Law

David H. Lewis/iStockphoto

CHAPTER OUTLINE

- Written Sources of American Criminal Law
- The Purposes of Criminal Law
- Classification of Crimes
- The Elements of a Crime
- Defenses under Criminal Law
- Protecting Civil Liberties

LEARNING OBJECTIVES

After reading this chapter, you should be able to...

1 List the four written sources of American criminal law.

2 Explain the two basic functions of criminal law.

3 Discuss the primary goals of civil law and criminal law, and explain how these goals are realized.

4 Explain the differences between crimes *mala in se* and *mala prohibita.*

5 Delineate the elements required to establish *mens rea* (a guilty mental state).

6 List and briefly define the most important excuse defenses for crimes.

7 Describe the four most important justification criminal defenses.

8 Explain the importance of the due process clause in the criminal justice system.

Throughout the chapter you will see each learning objective repeated in the margin next to the content it relates to. The chapter summary on page 92 includes all of the learning objectives for review.

DEADLY HEAT

As a nationally known self-help guru, financial wizard, and motivational speaker, James Arthur Ray prides himself on being right. Ray was tragically wrong, however, on an autumn day in 2009 when he told more than fifty participants in a sweat lodge ceremony he was leading, "You are not going to die. You might think you are, but you're not going to die." About halfway through the two-hour ceremony, the final event of Ray's five-day "Spiritual Warrior" retreat near Sedona, Arizona, people began to vomit and pass out in the extreme heat. When it was over, despite Ray's reassuring words, Kirby Brown, James Shore, and Liz Neuman never regained consciousness and died in a local hospital. Twenty other participants required medical treatment, suffering from burns, dehydration, kidney failure, and respiratory arrest.

"I did everything I could to help," Ray told an interviewer following the incident. "I held people's hands, I stroked their hair, I talked to them, I held the IV for paramedics." According to some witnesses, Ray was not quite so helpful during the ceremony. Beverly Bunn, who was inside the sweat lodge, said that people were gasping for air, collapsing, and crying out for water while Ray, positioned near the entrance, "did nothing. He just stood there."

Megan Frederickson, an employee at the Angel Valley Retreat (the site of the sweat lodge), admitted that before the ceremony, Ray told her not to worry if participants vomited or fainted, because such responses were to be expected.

After a four-month investigation, law enforcement officials decided that the sweat lodge was, in fact, a crime scene. On February 3, 2010, Yavapai County sheriff's deputies arrested Ray and charged him with three counts of manslaughter for the deaths of Brown, Shore, and Neuman. In June 2011, a Campe Verde jury found Ray guilty of three counts of the lesser crime of negligent homicide. Several months later, Judge Warren Darrow sentenced him to two years in prison.

James Arthur Ray—shown here in a Campe Verde, Arizona, courtroom—was convicted of three charges of negligent homicide for his actions during a sweat lodge ceremony over which he presided.

AP Photo/Ross D. Franklin, Pool

Was James Arthur Ray treated fairly? Nobody involved with the situation believes that he wanted any of the Spiritual Warriors to die. The sweat lodge, built in 2008, had been used numerous times previously without incident. "This was a terrible accident," said Luis Ri, Ray's attorney, "but it was an accident, not a criminal act."[1] In this chapter, we will learn that a defendant usually must have a guilty state of mind, or *mens rea*, to have committed a crime. Ray may have acted irresponsibly, but he certainly had no intent to injure or kill.

At the same time, society needs to protect its citizens from harm, even if that harm was not intentionally inflicted. According to the criminal code of Arizona, a person is guilty of a form of illegal homicide if he or she "negligently" causes the death of another person.[2] Later in the chapter, we define *negligence* as ignoring a foreseeable risk. Given the circumstances of the sweat lodge ceremony, Arizona officials felt that Ray *should have known* that he was placing others in grave danger, and therefore he had committed a criminal act. As this example suggests, criminal law must be flexible enough to encompass behavior that is not marked by criminal intent yet still poses a threat to society and therefore may warrant punishment. In this chapter, we will examine how these threats to society are identified and focus on the guidelines that the American criminal justice system uses to determine and punish criminal guilt.

WRITTEN SOURCES OF AMERICAN CRIMINAL LAW

Originally, American criminal law was *uncodified*. That is, it relied primarily on judges following previous judicial decisions, and the body of the law was not written down in any single place. Uncodified law, however, presents a number of drawbacks. For one, if the law is not recorded in a manner or a place in which the citizenry has access to it, then it is difficult, if not impossible, for people to know exactly which acts are legal and which acts are illegal. Furthermore, citizens have no way of determining or understanding the procedures that must be followed to establish innocence or guilt. Consequently, U.S. history has seen the development of several written sources of American criminal law, also known as "substantive" criminal law. These sources include the following:

Learning Objective 1 List the four written sources of American criminal law.

1. The U.S. Constitution and the constitutions of the various states.
2. Statutes, or laws, passed by Congress and by state legislatures, plus local ordinances.
3. Regulations, created by regulatory agencies such as the federal Food and Drug Administration.
4. Case law (court decisions).

We describe each of these important written sources of law in the following pages.

CONSTITUTIONAL LAW

The federal government and the states have separate written constitutions that set forth the general organization and powers of, and the limits on, their respective governments. **Constitutional law** is the law as expressed in these constitutions.

The U.S. Constitution is the supreme law of the land. As such, it is the basis of all law in the United States. Any law that violates the Constitution, as ultimately determined by the United States Supreme Court, will be declared unconstitutional and will not be enforced. The Tenth Amendment, which defines the powers and limitations of the federal government, reserves to the states all powers not granted to the federal government. Under our system of federalism (see Chapter 1), each state also has its own constitution. Unless they conflict with the U.S. Constitution or a federal law, state constitutions are supreme within their respective borders. (You will learn more about how constitutional law applies to our criminal justice system in later chapters.)

Constitutional Law Law based on the U.S. Constitution and the constitutions of the various states.

Statutory Law The body of law enacted by legislative bodies.

STATUTORY LAW

Statutes enacted by legislative bodies at any level of government make up another source of law, which is generally referred to as **statutory law.** *Federal statutes* are laws that are enacted by the U.S. Congress. *State statutes* are laws enacted by state legislatures, and statutory law also includes the ordinances passed by cities and counties. A federal statute, of course, applies to all states. A state statute, in contrast, applies only within that state's borders. City or county ordinances (statutes) apply only to those jurisdictions where they are enacted.

> "Justice?—You get justice in the next world. In this world you have the law."
>
> **—William Gaddis,** American novelist

LEGAL SUPREMACY It is important to keep in mind that there are essentially fifty-two different criminal codes in this country—one for each state, the District of Columbia, and the federal government. Originally, the federal criminal code was quite small. The U.S. Constitution mentions only three federal crimes: treason, piracy, and counterfeiting.

Supremacy Clause A clause in the U.S. Constitution establishing that federal law is the "supreme law of the land" and shall prevail when in conflict with state constitutions or statutes.

Ballot Initiative A procedure in which citizens, by collecting enough signatures, can force a public vote on a proposed change to state or local law.

Today, according to a recent study, federal law includes about 4,500 offenses that carry criminal penalties.[3] Inevitably, these federal criminal statutes are bound to overlap or even contradict state statutes. In such cases, thanks to the **supremacy clause** of the Constitution, federal law will almost always prevail. Simply put, the supremacy clause holds that federal law is the "supreme law of the land."

So, in January 2012, U.S. district judge Donald Molloy ruled that federal law enforcement agents were justified in arresting Montana residents for possessing medical marijuana, even though use of the drug for medicinal purposes is legal under the law of that state. Federal drug law does not allow for medical marijuana use, and as Judge Molloy stated, "we are all bound by federal law, like it or not."[4] Along the same lines, any statutory law—federal or state—that violates the Constitution will be overturned. In the late 1980s, for example, the United States Supreme Court ruled that any state laws banning the burning of the American flag were unconstitutional because they impinged on the individual's right to freedom of expression.[5] (To learn how one federal statute regulates a particular type of medical crime, see the feature *A Question of Ethics—Kidney Compensation* below.)

BALLOT INITIATIVES On a state and local level, voters can write or rewrite criminal statutes through a form of direct democracy known as the **ballot initiative.** In this process, a group of citizens draft a proposed law and then gather a certain number of signatures to get the proposal on that year's ballot. If a majority of the voters approve the measure, it is enacted into law. Currently, twenty-four states and the District of Columbia accept ballot initiatives, and these special elections have played a crucial role in shaping criminal law in those jurisdictions.

A QUESTION OF ETHICS: *Kidney Compensation*

THE SITUATION Located on each side of the spine, just above the waist, kidneys are small, bean-shaped organs that perform crucial functions such as keeping blood healthy and excreting urine. At any given time, more than 80,000 Americans with faulty kidneys need a new kidney to be transplanted into their bodies. Until this happens, they must rely on an expensive, painful process called dialysis to survive. Each year, about 4,500 people in the United States die while waiting for a healthy kidney.

THE ETHICAL DILEMMA Each person has two kidneys but can manage with just one, meaning that, at least theoretically, there is a huge supply of the organs for transplant. In reality, however, the supply of available healthy kidneys is severely limited. Sometimes, an organ donor who has died can provide the necessary transplant, or a living person may choose to donate a kidney to a person in need. Even so, as a lengthy waiting list suggests, the supply of available kidneys does not come close to meeting demand. There is a way to alleviate this shortage: allow people to sell one of their kidneys for transplantation. In the United States, however, as in most of the world, the exchange of any bodily organ for money or other kinds of payment is a crime. Under the 1984 National Organ Transplant Act, anybody who sells a kidney faces a $50,000 fine and five years in prison. This law is based on the idea that it is immoral to sell one's organs. As George Anas, a professor of health, law, bioethics, and human rights at Boston University, puts it, "We do not want to live in a society in which the rich live off the bodies of the poor."

WHAT IS THE SOLUTION? Iran is the only country in the world that has a government-regulated, open market for kidneys. Donors receive between $2,000 and $4,000 for each organ, and Iran has no waiting list for those needing transplants. Do you think that we should adopt this system in the United States? Why or why not? What ethical concerns do you have about the sale of kidneys? (Keep in mind that Americans are allowed to sell their blood, sperm, and, to infertile women, ovarian eggs.)

In the mid-1990s, for example, California voters approved a "three-strikes" measure (discussed in Chapter 9) that increased penalties for third-time felons, transforming the state's criminal justice system in the process. In 2010, Arizona residents voted in favor of a ballot initiative to require that their state join fifteen other states and Washington, D.C., in allowing the use of marijuana for medicinal purposes.[6] As we just noted, however, ballot initiatives do not supercede federal law, and medical marijuana sellers and users in these states are subject to arrest under federal drug laws.

ADMINISTRATIVE LAW

A third source of American criminal law consists of **administrative law**—the rules, orders, and decisions of *regulatory agencies.* A regulatory agency is a federal, state, or local government agency established to perform a specific function. The Occupational Safety and Health Administration, for example, oversees the safety and health of American workers. The Environmental Protection Agency (EPA) is concerned with protecting the natural environment, and the Food and Drug Administration regulates food and drugs produced in the United States.

Disregarding certain laws created by regulatory agencies can be a criminal violation. Federal statutes, such as the Clean Water Act, authorize a specific regulatory agency, such as the EPA, to enforce regulations to which criminal sanctions are attached.[7] So, in February 2012, following a criminal investigation led by the EPA, a North Carolina hog farm was found guilty of discharging waste into the Waccamaw River watershed. As punishment, a federal judge sentenced the company to pay $1.5 million in fines and sent its president to prison for six months.

Al and Leslie Wilcox, shown here in San Francisco's Golden Gate Park, are permitted by the state to smoke marijuana. More than a decade ago, a majority of Californians approved medical marijuana for those with debilitating illnesses. What are the benefits and drawbacks to allowing voters to create or amend their state's criminal laws?
Jim Wilson/*New York Times*/Redux

CASE LAW

Another basic source of American law consists of the rules of law announced in court decisions, or **precedents.** These rules of law include interpretations of constitutional provisions, of statutes enacted by legislatures, and of regulations created by administrative agencies. Today, this body of law is referred to variously as the common law, judge-made law, or **case law.**

Case law relies to a certain extent on how courts interpret a particular statute. If you wanted to learn about the coverage and applicability of a particular statute, for example, you would need to locate the statute and study it. You would also need to see how the courts in your jurisdiction have interpreted the statute—in other words, what precedents have been established in regard to that statute. The use of precedent means that judge-made law varies from jurisdiction to jurisdiction.

Administrative Law The body of law created by regulatory (administrative) agencies (in the form of rules, regulations, orders, and decisions) in order to carry out their duties and responsibilities.

Precedent A court decision that furnishes an example or authority for deciding subsequent cases involving similar facts.

Case Law The rules of law announced in court decisions.

SELFASSESSMENT

Fill in the blanks and check your answers on page 93.
The U.S. _____ is the supreme law of this country. Any law that violates this document will be declared _____ by the United States Supreme Court. Laws enacted by legislative bodies are known as _____, while the body of law created by judicial decisions is known as _____ law.

THE PURPOSES OF CRIMINAL LAW

Learning Objective 2 Explain the two basic functions of criminal law.

Why do societies need laws? Many criminologists believe that criminal law has two basic functions: one relates to the legal requirements of a society, and the other pertains to the society's need to maintain and promote social values.

PROTECT AND PUNISH: THE LEGAL FUNCTION OF THE LAW

The primary legal function of the law is to maintain social order by protecting citizens from *criminal harm*. This term refers to a variety of harms that can be generalized to fit into two categories:

1. Harms to individual citizens' physical safety and property, such as the harm caused by murder, theft, or arson.
2. Harms to society's interests collectively, such as the harm caused by unsafe foods or consumer products, a polluted environment, or poorly constructed buildings.[8]

The first category is self-evident, although even murder has different degrees, or grades, of offense to which different punishments are assigned. The second category, however, has proved more problematic, for it is difficult to measure society's "collective" interests.

MAINTAIN AND TEACH: THE SOCIAL FUNCTION OF THE LAW

If criminal laws against acts that cause harm or injury to others are almost universally accepted, the same cannot be said for laws that criminalize "morally" wrongful activities that may do no obvious, physical harm outside the families of those involved. Why criminalize gambling or prostitution if the participants are consenting?

EXPRESSING PUBLIC MORALITY The answer lies in the social function of criminal law. Many observers believe that the main purpose of criminal law is to reflect the values and norms of society, or at least of those segments of society that hold power. Legal scholar Henry Hart has stated that the only justification for criminal law and punishment is "the judgment of community condemnation."[9]

Take, for example, the misdemeanor of bigamy, which occurs when someone knowingly marries a second person without terminating her or his marriage to an original husband or wife. Apart from moral considerations, there would appear to be no victims in a bigamous relationship, and indeed many foreign societies have allowed and continue to allow bigamy to exist. In the American social tradition, however, as John L. Diamond of the University of California's Hastings College of the Law points out:

> Marriage is an institution encouraged and supported by society. The structural importance of the integrity of the family and a monogamous marriage requires unflinching enforcement of the criminal laws against bigamy. The immorality is not in choosing to do wrong, but in transgressing, even innocently, a fundamental social boundary that lies at the core of social order.[10]

Of course, public morals are not uniform across the entire nation, and a state's criminal code often reflects the values of its residents. Alaska, Arizona, and Vermont, for example, are the only states that do not require citizens to obtain a permit to carry a concealed firearm. Sometimes, local values and federal law will conflict with one another. In South Carolina, operating a cockfighting operation is a misdemeanor, and violators are often let off with a fine. Under federal animal welfare laws, however, the same activity carries a potential five-year prison term.[11] In 2012, five South Carolinians arrested by federal agents for cockfighting argued before a federal judge that their convictions were illegitimate because the federal government has no authority to regulate the "sport" within state borders (see photo alongside).[12]

TEACHING SOCIETAL BOUNDARIES Some scholars believe that criminal laws not only express the expectations of society but "teach" them as well. Professor Lawrence M. Friedman of Stanford University thinks that just as parents teach children behavioral norms through punishment, criminal justice "'teaches a lesson' to the people it punishes, and to society at large." Making burglary a crime, arresting burglars, putting them in jail—each step in the criminal justice process reinforces the idea that burglary is unacceptable and is deserving of punishment.[13]

This teaching function can also be seen in traffic laws. There is nothing "natural" about most traffic laws: Americans drive on the right side of the street, the British on the left side, with no obvious difference in the results. These laws, such as stopping at intersections, using headlights at night, and following speed limits, do lead to a more orderly flow of traffic and fewer accidents—certainly socially desirable goals. The laws can also be updated when needed. Over the past few years, several states have banned the use of handheld cell phones while driving because of the safety hazards associated with that behavior. Various forms of punishment for breaking traffic laws teach drivers the social order of the road.

Why does the supremacy clause make it unlikely that residents of states with lenient cockfighting laws will be able to escape the harsher punishments of federal animal welfare legislation that prohibits the practice?
Al Bello/Getty Images

SELFASSESSMENT
Fill in the blanks and check your answers on page 93.
The _____ function of the law is to protect citizens from _____ harm by ensuring their physical safety. The _____ function of the law is to teach citizens proper behavior and express public _____ by codifying the norms and values of the community.

CLASSIFICATION OF CRIMES

The huge body of the law can be broken down according to various classifications. Three of the most important distinctions are those between (1) civil law and criminal law, (2) felonies and misdemeanors, and (3) crimes *mala in se* and *mala prohibita*.

CIVIL LAW AND CRIMINAL LAW

All law can be divided into two categories: civil law and criminal law. As U.S. criminal law has evolved, it has diverged from U.S. civil law. These two categories of law are distinguished by their primary goals. The criminal justice system is concerned with protecting

CAREERS IN CJ

Photo Courtesy of F. W. Gill

F. W. GILL
GANG INVESTIGATOR

The problem, for most of these kids, is that nobody cares. Their parents don't, or can't, get involved in their children's lives. Teachers are in the business of teaching and don't, or can't, take the time to get to know their most troubled students. So, when I'm dealing with gang members, the first thing I do is listen. I don't lecture them, I don't tell them that they are throwing away their lives. I just listen. You'd be amazed how effective this can be— these kids, who look so tough on the outside, just want an adult to care.

Not that there is any magic formula for convincing a gang member to go straight. It is very difficult to get someone to change his or her lifestyle. If they don't want to change—really want to change—then nothing I can say or do is going to make much of a difference. Unfortunately, there are many lost causes. I've even had a couple of cases in which a juvenile was afraid to leave the gang because his father was a gang member, and he insisted that the boy stay in the gang. I have had some success in convincing gang members to turn their lives around by joining the military. The military provides discipline and a new outlook on life, things that these kids badly need.

Social Media Career Tip

Think about your online presence as your online personal brand. You create your personal brand online through the sum of all the posts you make on different Web sites and social media tools. [f] Linked[in]. [twitter]

FAST FACTS

YOUTH INTERVENTION SPECIALIST/ GANG INVESTIGATOR, JOB DESCRIPTION:

- Conducts assessments and refers at-risk youth to appropriate activities, programs, or agencies.
- Serves as a liaison between the police department, schools, other agencies, and the community.

WHAT KIND OF TRAINING IS REQUIRED?

- A bachelor's degree in counseling, criminal justice, or other social science–related field. Bilingual (English/Spanish) skills are desired.

ANNUAL SALARY RANGE?

- $40,000–$49,000

Civil Law The branch of law dealing with the definition and enforcement of all private or public rights, as opposed to criminal matters.

Plaintiff The person or institution that initiates a lawsuit in civil court proceedings by filing a complaint.

Learning Objective 3 Discuss the primary goals of civil law and criminal law, and explain how these goals are realized.

society from harm by preventing and prosecuting crimes. A crime is an act so reprehensible that it is considered a wrong against society as a whole, as well as against the individual victim. Therefore, the state prosecutes a person who commits a criminal act. If the state is able to prove that a person is guilty of a crime, the government will punish her or him with imprisonment or fines, or both.

Civil law, which includes all types of law other than criminal law, is concerned with disputes between private individuals and between entities. Proceedings in civil lawsuits are normally initiated by an individual or a corporation (in contrast to criminal proceedings, which are initiated by public prosecutors). Such disputes may involve, for example, the terms of a contract, the ownership of property, or an automobile accident. Under civil law, the government provides a forum for the resolution of *torts*—or private wrongs—in which the injured party, called the **plaintiff,** tries to prove that a wrong has been committed by the accused party, or the **defendant.** (Note that the accused party in both criminal and civil cases is known as the *defendant*.)

GUILT AND RESPONSIBILITY A criminal court is convened to determine whether the defendant is *guilty*—that is, whether the defendant has, in fact, committed the offense charged. In contrast, civil law is concerned with *responsibility,* a much more flexible concept. For example, after Kevin Black was killed while cycling in Ballard, Washington, a civil court blamed the driver of the van that struck him for the death. The driver had attempted to make an illegal U-turn by crossing into the bicycle lane where Black was riding, causing the fatal accident. Even though the driver was never charged with any crime, the court decided that he and his employer, Ambient Control Company, should be held **liable,** or legally responsible, for Black's death because of the improper U-turn.

Most civil cases involve a request for monetary damages to compensate for the wrong that has been committed. Thus, in 2011, the civil court ordered Ambient Control Company to pay $1.5 million to Kevin Black's family as compensation for the financial and emotional consequences of his death. (See *Mastering Concepts—Civil Law versus Criminal Law* below for a comparison of civil and criminal law.)

THE BURDEN OF PROOF Although criminal law proceedings are completely separate from civil law proceedings in the modern legal system, the two systems do have some similarities. Both attempt to control behavior by imposing sanctions on those who violate society's definition of acceptable behavior. Furthermore, criminal and civil law often supplement each other. In certain instances, a victim may file a civil suit against an individual who is also the target of a criminal prosecution by the government.

Because the burden of proof is much greater in criminal trials than civil ones, it is almost always easier to win monetary damages than a criminal conviction. In September 2011, for example, store manager Richard Moore was found not guilty of sexually abusing an employee in O'Fallon, Illinois, because investigators could not match his DNA to a semen stain found near the alleged incident. Three months earlier, however, a civil court ruled that Moore had indeed sexually abused the woman and ordered his employer, the furniture chain Aaron's, to pay her $41 million in damages. During the later trial, the criminal court did not find enough evidence to prove **beyond a reasonable doubt** (the burden of proof in criminal cases) that Moore was guilty of any crime. Nevertheless, the civil trial established by a **preponderance of the evidence** (the burden of proof in civil cases) that Moore had thrown the employee to the floor and sexually abused her.

Defendant In a civil court, the person or institution against whom an action is brought. In a criminal court, the person or entity who has been formally accused of violating a criminal law.

Liability In a civil court, legal responsibility for one's own or another's actions.

Beyond a Reasonable Doubt The degree of proof required to find the defendant in a criminal trial guilty of committing the crime. The defendant's guilt must be the only reasonable explanation for the criminal act before the court.

Preponderance of the Evidence The degree of proof required to decide in favor of one side or the other in a civil case. In general, this requirement is met when a plaintiff proves that a fact more likely than not is true.

MASTERING**CONCEPTS**

CIVIL LAW VERSUS CRIMINAL LAW

ISSUE	CIVIL LAW	CRIMINAL LAW
Area of concern	Rights and duties between individuals	Offenses against society as a whole
Wrongful act	Harm to a person or business entity	Violation of a statute that prohibits some type of activity
Party who brings suit	Person who suffered harm (plaintiff)	The state (prosecutor)
Party who responds	Person who supposedly caused harm (defendant)	Person who allegedly committed a crime (defendant)
Standard of proof	Preponderance of the evidence	Beyond a reasonable doubt
Remedy	Damages to compensate for the harm	Punishment (fine or incarceration)

FELONIES AND MISDEMEANORS

Depending on their degree of seriousness, crimes are classified as *felonies* or *misdemeanors*. **Felonies** are serious crimes punishable by death or by imprisonment in a federal or state penitentiary for one year or longer (though some states, such as North Carolina, consider felonies to be punishable by at least two years' incarceration). The Model Penal Code, a general guide for criminal law, provides for four degrees of felony:

1. Capital offenses, for which the maximum penalty is death.
2. First degree felonies, punishable by a maximum penalty of life imprisonment.
3. Second degree felonies, punishable by a maximum of ten years' imprisonment.
4. Third degree felonies, punishable by a maximum of five years' imprisonment.[14]

DEGREES OF CRIME Though specifics vary from state to state, some general rules apply when grading crimes. For example, most jurisdictions punish a burglary that involves a nighttime forced entry into a home more seriously than one that takes place during the day and involves a nonresidential building or structure. Furthermore, the seriousness of any crime is, to a large extent, determined by the mental state of the offender. That is, the law punishes those who plan and intend to do harm more harshly than it does those who act wrongfully because of strong emotions or other extreme circumstances. We will address the importance of mental state in crime more extensively later in this chapter, but here we can see how it affects the degrees of murder.

Murder in the first degree occurs under two circumstances:

1. When the crime is *premeditated,* or considered (contemplated) beforehand by the offender, instead of being a spontaneous act of violence.
2. When the crime is *deliberate,* meaning that it was planned and decided on after a process of decision making. Deliberation does not require a lengthy planning process. A person can be found guilty of first degree murder even if she or he made the decision to murder only seconds before committing the crime.

Second degree murder, generally punishable by fifteen years to life in prison, occurs when no premeditation or deliberation was present, but the offender did have **malice aforethought** toward the victim. In other words, the offender acted with wanton disregard for the consequences of his or her actions. (In general, *malice* means "wrongful intention" or "the desire to do evil.")

The difference between first and second degree murder is clearly illustrated in a case involving a California man who beat a neighbor to death with a partially full brandy bottle. The crime took place after Ricky McDonald, the victim, complained to Kazi Cooksey, the offender, about the noise coming from a late-night barbecue Cooksey and his friends were holding. The jury could not find sufficient evidence that Cooksey's actions were premeditated, but he certainly acted with wanton disregard for his victim's safety. Therefore, the jury convicted Cooksey of second degree murder rather than first degree murder.

TYPES OF MANSLAUGHTER A homicide committed without malice toward the victim is known as *manslaughter* and is usually punishable by up to fifteen years in prison. **Voluntary manslaughter** occurs when the intent to kill may be present, but malice was lacking. Voluntary manslaughter covers crimes of passion, in which the emotion of an argument between two friends may lead to a homicide. Voluntary manslaughter can also occur when the victim provoked the offender to act violently.

Involuntary manslaughter covers incidents in which the offender's acts may have been careless, but he or she had no intent to kill. In 2011, for example, Dr. Conrad

---

Felony A serious crime, usually punishable by death or imprisonment for a year or longer.

Malice Aforethought A depraved state of mind in which the offender's behavior reflected a wanton disregard for the well-being of his or her victim.

Voluntary Manslaughter A homicide in which the intent to kill was present in the mind of the offender, but malice was lacking.

Involuntary Manslaughter A negligent homicide, in which the offender had no intent to kill her or his victim.

Social Media and CJ NBCNews.com provides a constant stream of tweets concerning criminal law topics and other crime news and stories of interest. To access its Twitter Web page, visit the *Criminal Justice CourseMate* at **cengagebrain.com** and select the *Web Links* for this chapter.

Murray (see photo alongside) was convicted of involuntary manslaughter for his role in the death of pop star Michael Jackson. Murray had provided Jackson with a powerful anesthetic to help Jackson sleep, and the dosage proved fatal. Although Murray had certainly not intended for Jackson to die, he was held criminally responsible for the singer's death and sentenced to four years in prison.

DEGREES OF MISDEMEANOR Under federal law and in most states, any crime that is not a felony is considered a **misdemeanor.** Misdemeanors are crimes punishable by a fine or by confinement for up to a year. If imprisoned, the guilty party goes to a local jail instead of a penitentiary. Disorderly conduct and trespassing are common misdemeanors. Like felonies, misdemeanors are graded by level of seriousness. In Illinois, for example, misdemeanors are either Class A (confinement for up to a year), Class B (not more than six months), or Class C (not more than thirty days).

Most states similarly distinguish between *gross misdemeanors,* which are offenses punishable by thirty days to a year in jail, and *petty misdemeanors,* or offenses punishable by fewer than thirty days in jail. Whether a crime is a felony or a misdemeanor can also determine whether the case is tried in a magistrate's court (for example, by a justice of the peace) or in a general trial court (for example, a superior court). Probation and community service are often imposed on those who commit misdemeanors, especially juveniles.

INFRACTIONS The least serious form of wrongdoing is often called an **infraction** and is punishable only by a small fine. Even though infractions such as parking or traffic violations technically represent illegal activity, they generally are not considered "crimes." Therefore, infractions rarely lead to jury trials and are deemed to be so minor that they do not appear on the offender's criminal record. In some jurisdictions, the terms *infraction* and *petty offense* are interchangeable. In others, however, they are different. Under federal guidelines, for example, an infraction can be punished by up to five days of prison time, while a petty offender is only liable for a fine.[15] Finally, those who string together a series of infractions (or fail to pay the fines that come with such offenses) are in danger of being criminally charged. In Illinois, having three or more speeding violations in one year is considered criminal behavior.[16]

MALA IN SE AND MALA PROHIBITA

Criminologists often express the social function of criminal law in terms of *mala in se* or *mala prohibita* crimes. A criminal act is referred to as ***mala in se*** if it would be considered wrong even if there were no law prohibiting it. *Mala in se* crimes are said to go against "natural laws"—that is, against the "natural, moral, and public" principles of a society. Murder, rape, and theft are examples of *mala in se* crimes. These crimes are generally the same from country to country or culture to culture.

In contrast, the term ***mala prohibita*** refers to acts that are considered crimes only because they have been codified as such through statute—"human-made" laws. A *mala prohibita* crime is considered wrong only because it has been prohibited. It is not inherently a wrong, though it may reflect the moral standards of a society at a given time. Thus, the definition of a *mala prohibita* crime can vary from country to country and even from state to state. Bigamy, or the offense of having two legal spouses, could be considered a *mala prohibita* crime.

Why was Dr. Conrad Murray, right, convicted of involuntary manslaughter rather than murder or voluntary manslaughter for his role in the death of pop star Michael Jackson?

Mario Anzuoni/Pool/EPA/Newscom

Misdemeanor A criminal offense that is not a felony; usually punishable by a fine and/or a jail term of less than one year.

Infraction In most jurisdictions, a noncriminal offense for which the penalty is a fine rather than incarceration.

Mala in Se A descriptive term for acts that are inherently wrong, regardless of whether they are prohibited by law.

Mala Prohibita A descriptive term for acts that are made illegal by criminal statute and are not necessarily wrong in and of themselves.

Learning Objective 4 Explain the differences between crimes *mala in se* and *mala prohibita.*

Some observers question the distinction between *mala in se* and *mala prohibita*. In many instances, it is difficult to define a "pure" *mala in se* crime. That is, it is difficult to separate a crime from the culture that has deemed it a crime.[17] Even murder, under certain cultural circumstances, is not considered a criminal act. In a number of poor, traditional areas of the Middle East and Asia, the law excuses "honor killings" in which men kill female family members suspected of sexual indiscretion. As we discussed in Chapter 1, our own legal system excuses homicide in extreme situations, such as self-defense or when a law enforcement agent kills in the line of duty. Therefore, "natural" laws can be seen as culturally specific. Similar difficulties occur in trying to define a "pure" *mala prohibita* crime. More than 150 countries, including most members of the European Union, have legalized prostitution. With the exception of seven rural counties of Nevada, prostitution is illegal in the United States.

CJ&TECHNOLOGY

Andrea Zanchi/iStockphoto

Electronic Eavesdropping

"Our society is going through a technological transformation," notes Adam Schwartz, a civil liberties lawyer. "We are at a time where tens of millions of Americans carry around a telephone or other device in their pocket that has an audio-video capacity. Ten years ago, [we] weren't walking around with all these devices." This widespread ability to record interactions with others has increased the possibility that Americans are breaking the law, often without their knowledge. The criminal codes of twelve states require the consent of all parties involved before any conversation can be recorded.

In some cases, the penalties for breaking these laws can be quite harsh. Under the Illinois Eavesdropping Act, audio-recording a civilian without consent is a Class 4 felony, punishable by up to three years in prison. Audio-recording an Illinois law enforcement official who is performing her or his duties without consent is a Class 1 felony, punishable by up to fifteen years in prison.

THINKING ABOUT ELECTRONIC EAVESDROPPING: Are these
eavesdropping statutes *mala in se* laws or *mala prohibita* laws? While explaining your answer, remember that smartphones and other easily portable devices with one-touch recording capabilities did not exist when most eavesdropping statutes were initially passed.

SELFASSESSMENT
Fill in the blanks and check your answers on page 93.
_____ law is concerned with disputes between private individuals and other entities, whereas criminal law involves the _____'s duty to protect society by preventing and prosecuting crimes. A _____ is a serious crime punishable by more than a year in prison or the death penalty, while a person found guilty of a _____ will usually spend less than a year in jail or pay a fine. _____ _____ _____ occurs when a homicide is premeditated and deliberate. If there is no premeditation or malice on the part of the offender toward the victim, the homicide is classified as _____.

THE ELEMENTS OF A CRIME

In fictional accounts of police work, the admission of guilt is often portrayed as the crucial element of a criminal investigation. Although an admission is certainly useful to police and prosecutors, it alone cannot establish the innocence or guilt of a suspect. Criminal law normally requires that the *corpus delicti,* a Latin phrase for "the body of the crime," be proved before a person can be convicted of wrongdoing. *Corpus delicti* can be defined as "proof that a specific crime has actually been committed by someone."[18] It consists of the basic elements of any crime, which include (1) *actus reus,* or a guilty act, (2) *mens rea,* or a guilty intent, (3) concurrence, or the coming together of the criminal act and the guilty mind, (4) a link between the act and the legal definition of the crime, (5) any attendant circumstances, and (6) the harm done, or the result of the criminal act.

CRIMINAL ACT: *ACTUS REUS*

Suppose Mr. Smith walks into a police department and announces that he just killed his wife. In and of itself, the confession is insufficient for conviction unless the police find Mrs. Smith's corpse, for example, with a bullet in her brain and establish through evidence that Mr. Smith fired the gun. (This does not mean that an actual dead body has to be found in every homicide case. Rather, it is the fact of the death that must be established in such cases.)

Most crimes require an act of *commission,* meaning that a person must *do* something in order to be accused of a crime. The prohibited act is referred to as the *actus reus,* or guilty act. Furthermore, the act of commission must be voluntary. For example, if Mr. Smith had an epileptic seizure while holding a hunting rifle and accidentally shot his wife, he normally would not be held criminally liable for her death. (To better understand this principle, see the feature *You Be the Judge—A Voluntary Act?* on the following page.)

A LEGAL DUTY In some cases, an act of *omission* can be a crime, but only when a person has a legal duty to perform the omitted act. One such legal duty is assumed to exist based on a "special relationship" between two parties, such as a parent and child, adult children and their aged parents, and spouses.[19] Those persons involved in contractual relationships with others, such as physicians and lifeguards, must also perform legal duties to avoid criminal penalty. Hawaii, Minnesota, Rhode Island, Vermont, and Wisconsin have even passed "duty to aid" statutes requiring their citizens to report criminal conduct and help victims of such conduct if possible.[20] Another example of a criminal act of omission is failure to file a federal income tax return when required by law to do so.

A PLAN OR ATTEMPT The guilty act requirement is based on one of the premises of criminal law—that a person is punished for harm done to society. Planning to kill someone or to steal a car may be wrong, but just the thoughts themselves do no harm and are therefore not criminal until they are translated into action. Of course, a person can be punished for *attempting* murder or robbery, but normally only if he or she took substantial steps toward the criminal objective and the government can prove that the desire to commit the crime was present. Furthermore, the punishment for an **attempt** normally is less severe than if the act had succeeded.

MENTAL STATE: *MENS REA*

A wrongful mental state—*mens rea*—is usually as necessary as a wrongful act in determining guilt. The mental state, or requisite *intent,* required to establish guilt of a crime is indicated in the applicable statute or law. For theft, the wrongful act is the taking of

Corpus Delicti The body of circumstances that must exist for a criminal act to have occurred.

Actus Reus (pronounced *ak*-tus *ray*-uhs). A guilty (prohibited) act.

Attempt The act of taking substantial steps toward committing a crime while having the ability and the intent to commit the crime, even if the crime never takes place.

Mens Rea (pronounced *mehns ray*-uh). Mental state, or intent. A wrongful mental state is usually as necessary as a wrongful act to establish criminal liability.

another person's property, and the required mental state involves both the awareness that the property belongs to another and the desire to deprive the owner of it.

Learning Objective 5 Delineate the elements required to establish *mens rea* (a guilty mental state).

THE CATEGORIES OF *MENS REA* A guilty mental state includes elements of purpose, knowledge, negligence, and recklessness. A defendant is said to have *purposefully* committed a criminal act when she or he desires to engage in certain criminal conduct or to cause a certain criminal result. For a defendant to have *knowingly* committed an illegal act, he or she must be aware of the illegality, must believe that the illegality exists, or must correctly suspect that the illegality exists but fail to do anything to dispel (or confirm) his or her belief. Criminal **negligence** involves the mental state in which the defendant grossly deviates from the standard of care that a reasonable person would use under the same circumstances. The defendant is accused of taking an unjustified, substantial, and foreseeable risk that resulted in harm. In Texas, for example, a parent commits a felony if she or he fails to secure a loaded firearm or leaves it in such a manner that it could easily be accessed by a child.[21]

A defendant who commits an act recklessly is more blameworthy than one who is criminally negligent. Criminal **recklessness** can be defined as "consciously disregard[ing] a substantial and unjustifiable risk."[22] During the trial of James Arthur Ray discussed at the beginning of this chapter, prosecutors presented a witness who testified that Ray did nothing to help those who became ill or lost consciousness in the sweat lodge. This testimony, if true, would have helped establish that the defendant was aware of the dangers faced by the ceremony participants and that, therefore, his actions were reckless rather than simply negligent.

Negligence A failure to exercise the standard of care that a reasonable person would exercise in similar circumstances.

Recklessness The state of being aware that a risk does or will exist and nevertheless acting in a way that consciously disregards this risk.

YOU BE THE JUDGE

A Voluntary Act?

THE FACTS On a bright, sunny afternoon, Emil was driving on Delaware Avenue in Buffalo, New York. As he was making a turn, Emil suffered an epileptic seizure and lost control of his automobile. The car careened onto the sidewalk and struck a group of six schoolgirls, killing four of them. Emil knew that he was subject to epileptic attacks that rendered him likely to lose consciousness.

THE LAW An "act" committed while one is unconscious is in reality not an act at all. It is merely a physical event or occurrence over which the defendant has no control—that is, such an act is involuntary. If the defendant voluntarily causes the loss of consciousness by, for example, using drugs or alcohol, however, then he or she will usually be held criminally responsible for any consequences.

YOUR DECISION Emil was charged in the deaths of the four girls. He asked the court to dismiss the charges, as he was unconscious at the time of the accident and therefore had not committed a voluntary act. In your opinion, is there an *actus reus* in this situation, or should the charges against Emil be dismissed?

To see how the appellate court in New York ruled in this case, go to Example 3.1 in Appendix B.

CRIMINAL LIABILITY Intent plays an important part in allowing the law to differentiate among varying degrees of criminal liability for similar, though not identical, guilty acts. The role of intent is clearly seen in the different classifications of homicide, defined generally as the willful killing of one human being by another. It is important to emphasize the word *willful*, as it precludes deaths caused by accident or negligence and those deemed justifiable. A death that results from negligence or accident generally is considered a private wrong and a matter for civil law. Nevertheless, some statutes allow for certain negligent homicides to be criminalized.

As we saw earlier in the chapter, when the act of killing is willful, deliberate, and premeditated (planned beforehand), it is considered first degree murder. When premeditation does not exist but intent does, the act is usually considered second degree murder. When intent is absent, the act is generally considered involuntary manslaughter. As Figure 3.1 below shows, the distinction between involuntary manslaughter and second degree murder is not always clear. Often, prosecutors must rely on discretion in deciding what level of intent exists on the part of the defendant.

STRICT LIABILITY For certain crimes, criminal law holds the defendant to be guilty even if intent to commit the offense is lacking. These acts are known as **strict liability crimes** and generally involve endangering the public welfare in some way. Drug-control statutes, health and safety regulations, and traffic laws are all strict liability laws.

Protecting the Public To a certain extent, the concept of strict liability is inconsistent with the traditional principles of criminal law, which hold that *mens rea* is required for an act to be criminal. The goal of strict liability laws is to protect the public by eliminating the possibility that wrongdoers could claim ignorance or mistake to absolve themselves of criminal responsibility.[23] Thus, a person caught dumping waste in a protected pond or driving 70 miles per hour in a 55 miles-per-hour zone cannot plead a lack of intent in his or her defense.

Given the importance of the *mens rea* requirement in our tradition of criminal law, American courts are often wary of overreaching strict liability statutes. In 2002, for example, the Florida legislature removed the "guilty mind" requirement from its illegal drug laws.[24] Theoretically, then, a U.S. Postal Service employee could be arrested by state

Strict Liability Crimes
Certain crimes, such as traffic violations, in which the defendant is guilty regardless of her or his state of mind at the time of the act.

FIGURE 3.1 Intent and Homicide

Six-week-old Michael Wortmon died after being found unresponsive at his home in Loleta, California. The boy had significant levels of methamphetamine in his system, and his mother, Maggie Jean Wortmon, admitted to having ingested large amounts of the drug before breastfeeding her son. Doctors believe that the toxic breast milk killed Michael.

Humboldt County prosecutors have several options with regard to Maggie Jean Wortmon:

- Accept Michael's death as a tragic accident and file **no criminal charges** against Wortmon.

- Charge Wortmon with **involuntary manslaughter,** defined under state law as an unintended killing that takes place during the commission of a lawful act involving a high risk of death and is committed without due caution. The punishment for involuntary manslaughter in California is two, three, or four years in prison.

- Charge Wortmon with **second degree murder,** defined under state law as a willful killing but one that is not deliberate and premeditated. The punishment for second degree murder in California is fifteen years to life in prison.

Even though Wortmon did not intend to kill Michael, prosecutors charged her with second degree murder. "I think that her conduct [was] so intentionally reckless that it rises to the level of implied malice," explained deputy district attorney Ben McLaughlin.

Source: Jesse McKinley, "Woman Is Accused of Murder after Breast-Fed Son Is Found to Have Meth in His System," *New York Times* (August 5, 2011), A12.

James Menard's mother, right, reaches to hug him at the end of his 2011 trial in Collier County, Florida, for the murder of Jake Couture. Among other charges, Menard was found guilty of felony armed trespass before he shot Couture. Why did this make him subject to a felony-murder charge?

Lexey Swall/Naples Daily News

Statutory Rape A strict liability crime in which an adult engages in a sexual act with a minor.

Felony-Murder An unlawful homicide that occurs during the attempted commission of a felony.

law enforcement agents for unknowingly delivering a package of marijuana or illegal prescription drugs. In 2011, a federal judge declared these laws unconstitutional, calling Florida's attempt to remove intent from the criminal equation "repugnant."[25]

Protecting Minors One of the most controversial strict liability crimes is **statutory rape,** in which an adult engages in a sexual relationship with a minor. In most states, even if the minor consents to the sexual act, the crime still exists because, being underage, she or he is considered incapable of making a rational decision on the matter.[26] Therefore, statutory rape has been committed even if the adult was unaware of the minor's age or was misled to believe that the minor was older.

ACCOMPLICE LIABILITY Under certain circumstances, a person can be charged with and convicted of a crime that he or she did not actually commit. This occurs when the suspect has acted as an *accomplice,* helping another person commit the crime. Generally, to be found guilty as an accomplice, a person must have the "dual intent" (1) to aid the person who committed the crime and (2) that such aid would lead to the commission of the crime.[27] As for the *actus reus,* the accomplice must have helped the primary defendant in either a physical sense (for example, by providing the getaway car) or a psychological sense (for example, by encouraging her or him to commit the crime).[28]

In some states, a person can be convicted as an accomplice even without intent if the crime was a "natural and probable consequence" of his or her actions.[29] This principle has led to a proliferation of **felony-murder** legislation. Felony-murder is a form of first degree murder that applies when a person participates in any of a list of serious felonies that results in the unlawful killing of a human being. Under felony-murder law, a person can be convicted as an accomplice to an intentional killing, even when there is no intent. So, for example, if a person intentionally burns down a building, unintentionally killing an inhabitant, he or she will be charged with first degree murder because, in most jurisdictions, arson is a felony.

CONCURRENCE

According to criminal law, there must be *concurrence* between the guilty act and the guilty intent. In other words, the guilty act and the guilty intent must occur together. Suppose, for example, that a woman intends to murder her husband with poison in order to collect his life insurance. Every evening, this woman drives her husband home from work. On the night she plans to poison him, however, she swerves to avoid a cat crossing the road and runs into a tree. She survives the accident, but her husband is killed. Even though her intent was realized, the incident would be considered an accidental death because she had not planned to kill him by driving the car into a tree.

CAUSATION

Criminal law also requires that the criminal act cause the harm suffered. In 1989, nineteen-year-old Mike Wells shook his two-year-old daughter, Christina, so violently that she suffered brain damage. Soon after the incident, Wells served prison time for aggravated child abuse. Seventeen years later, in 2006, Christina died. When a coroner ruled that the cause of death was the earlier brain injury, Pasco County (Florida) authorities decided that, despite the passage of time, Wells was criminally responsible for his daughter's death. In 2010, Wells pleaded guilty to second degree murder and received a fifteen-year prison sentence.

ATTENDANT CIRCUMSTANCES

In certain crimes, **attendant circumstances**—also known as accompanying circumstances—are relevant to the *corpus delicti*. Most states, for example, differentiate between simple assault and the more serious offense of aggravated assault depending on the attendant circumstance of whether the defendant used a weapon such as a gun or a knife while committing the crime. Criminal law also classifies degrees of property crimes based on the attendant circumstance of the amount stolen. According to federal statutes, the theft of less than $1,000 from a bank is a misdemeanor, while the theft of any amount over $1,000 is a felony.[30] (To get a better understanding of the role of attendant circumstances in criminal statutes, see Figure 3.2 below.)

REQUIREMENTS OF PROOF AND INTENT Attendant circumstances must be proved beyond a reasonable doubt, just like any other element of a crime. Furthermore, the *mens rea* of the defendant regarding each attendant circumstance must be proved as well. Consider the case of Christopher Jones, who was recently convicted of third degree rape in a South Dakota criminal court. Under state law, third degree rape occurs when the victim is incapable of giving consent to the sex act due to severe intoxication.

A South Dakota appeals court overturned Jones's conviction, ruling that prosecutors did not prove beyond a reasonable doubt that the defendant knew of his victim's drunken state and, thus, her inability to give consent. The court added that if the state legislature wanted to remove such knowledge from the definition of the crime, it must say so in the statute, thus making awareness of the victim's intoxication a *strict liability* (see the previous discussion) attendant circumstance.[31]

HATE CRIME LAWS In most cases, a person's motive for committing a crime is irrelevant—a court will not try to read the accused's mind. Over the past few decades, however, nearly every state and the federal government have passed *hate crime laws* that make the suspect's motive an important attendant circumstance to his or her criminal act. In general, **hate crime laws** provide for greater sanctions against those who commit crimes motivated by bias against a person based on race, ethnicity, religion, gender, sexual orientation, disability, or age.

In 2011, for example, Paul Beebe pleaded guilty to federal and state criminal charges stemming from an incident in which he branded a swastika onto the arm of a disabled

Attendant Circumstances The facts surrounding a criminal event that must be proved to convict the defendant of the underlying crime.

Hate Crime Law A statute that provides for greater sanctions against those who commit crimes motivated by bias against an individual or a group based on race, ethnicity, religion, gender, sexual orientation, disability, or age.

FIGURE 3.2 Attendant Circumstances in Criminal Law

Most criminal statutes incorporate three of the elements we have discussed in this section: the act (*actus reus*), the intent (*mens rea*), and attendant circumstances. This diagram of Wisconsin's false imprisonment statute should give you an idea of how these elements combine to create the totality of a crime.

Intent	Act	Attendant Circumstances

Whoever intentionally confines or restrains another without the person's consent is guilty of false imprisonment.

Source: Wisconsin Statutes Section 940.30 (2001).

Native American man in Albuquerque, New Mexico. Because the victim was a member of two protected classes and the act was obviously motivated by bias, Beebe was sentenced to eight and a half years in prison, a tougher punishment than he would have received if he had committed the aggravated battery without the element of hate. According to the National Crime Victimization Survey, nearly 200,000 hate crimes take place in the United States each year.[32]

HARM

For most crimes to occur, some harm must have been done to a person or to property. A certain number of crimes are actually categorized depending on the harm done to the victim, regardless of the intent behind the criminal act. Take two offenses, both of which involve one person hitting another in the back of the head with a tire iron. In the first instance, the victim dies, and the offender is charged with murder. In the second, the victim is only knocked unconscious, and the offender is charged with battery. Because the harm in the second instance was less severe, so was the crime with which the offender was charged, even though the act was exactly the same. Furthermore, most states have different degrees of battery depending on the extent of the injuries suffered by the victim.

Many acts are deemed criminal if they could do harm that the laws try to prevent. Such acts are called **inchoate offenses.** They exist when only an attempt at a criminal act was made. If Jenkins solicits Peterson to murder Jenkins's business partner, this is an inchoate offense on the part of Jenkins, even though Peterson fails to carry out the act. *Conspiracies* also fall into the category of inchoate offenses. In 2003, the United States Supreme Court ruled that a person could be convicted of criminal **conspiracy** even though police intervention made the completion of the illegal plan impossible.[33]

Inchoate Offenses Conduct deemed criminal without actual harm being done, provided that the harm that would have occurred is one the law tries to prevent.

Conspiracy A secret plot by two or more people to carry out an illegal or harmful act.

SELFASSESSMENT

Fill in the blanks and check your answers on page 93.

Proof that a crime has been committed is established through the elements of the crime, which include the _____, or the physical act of the crime; the _____ _____, or the intent to commit the crime; and the _____ of the guilty act and the guilty intent. With _____ _____ crimes, the law determines that a defendant is guilty even if he or she lacked the _____ to perform a criminal act. _____ circumstances are those circumstances that accompany the main criminal act in a criminal code, and they must be proved _____ _____ _____ _____, just like any other elements of a crime.

DEFENSES UNDER CRIMINAL LAW

When Tammy Gibson of Tacoma, Washington, saw a convicted sex offender named William A. Baldwin talking to her ten-year-old daughter, she leaped into action. Grabbing a baseball bat, she went after Baldwin, striking him repeatedly on the arm. A local judge rejected Gibson's excuse that her victim "got what was coming to him" and sentenced the overly protective mother to three months behind bars for committing assault. A number of other defenses for wrongdoing, however, can be raised in the course of a criminal trial. These defenses generally rely on one of two arguments: (1) the defendant is not responsible for the crime, or (2) the defendant was justified in committing the crime.

CRIMINAL RESPONSIBILITY AND THE LAW

The idea of responsibility plays a significant role in criminal law. In certain circumstances, the law recognizes that even though an act is inherently criminal, society will not punish the actor because he or she does not have the requisite mental condition. In other words, the law "excuses" the person for his or her behavior. Insanity, intoxication, and mistake are the most important excuse defenses today, but we start our discussion of the subject with one of the first such defenses recognized by American law: infancy.

INFANCY Under the earliest state criminal codes of the United States, children younger than seven years of age could never be held legally accountable for crimes. Those between seven and fourteen years old were presumed to lack the capacity for criminal behavior, while anyone over the age of fourteen was tried as an adult. Thus, early American criminal law recognized **infancy** as a defense in which the accused's wrongdoing is excused because he or she is too young to fully understand the consequences of his or her actions.

With the creation of the juvenile justice system in the early 1900s, the infancy defense became redundant, as youthful delinquents were automatically treated differently from adult offenders. Today, most states either designate an age (eighteen or below) under which wrongdoers are sent to juvenile court or allow prosecutors to decide whether a minor will be charged as an adult on a case-by-case basis. We will explore the concept of infancy as it applies to the modern American juvenile justice system in much greater detail in Chapter 13.

INSANITY For nearly two years, Stephen Morgan stalked and harassed Johanna Justin-Jinich, a student at Wesleyan University in Middletown, Connecticut. Finally, Morgan fatally shot Justin-Jinich seven times at the bookstore café where she worked. In 2011, a three-judge panel ruled that Morgan's paranoid schizophrenia kept him from knowing that his actions were wrong, and he was sent to a maximum-security psychiatric hospital rather than prison. Thus, **insanity** may be a defense to a criminal charge when the defendant's state of mind is such that she or he cannot claim legal responsibility for her or his actions.

Measuring Sanity The general principle of the insanity defense is that a person is excused for his or her criminal wrongdoing if, as a result of a mental disease or defect, he or she

- Does not perceive the physical nature or consequences of his or her conduct;
- Does not know that his or her conduct is wrong or criminal; or
- Is not sufficiently able to control his or her conduct so as to be held accountable for it.[34]

Although criminal law has traditionally accepted the idea that an insane person cannot be held responsible for criminal acts, society has long debated what standards should be used to measure sanity for the purposes of a criminal trial. This lack of consensus is reflected in the diverse tests employed by different American jurisdictions to determine insanity. The tests include the following:

1. *The* M'Naghten *rule.* Derived from an 1843 British murder case, the **M'Naghten rule** states that a person is legally insane and therefore not criminally responsible if, at the time of the offense, she or he was not able to distinguish

Learning Objective 6 List and briefly define the most important excuse defenses for crimes.

Infancy A condition that, under early American law, excused young wrongdoers of criminal behavior because presumably they could not understand the consequences of their actions.

Insanity A defense for criminal liability that asserts a lack of criminal responsibility due to mental instability.

***M'Naghten* Rule** A common law test of criminal responsibility, derived from *M'Naghten's* Case in 1843, that relies on the defendant's inability to distinguish right from wrong.

In March 2011, a New Jersey judge found Jenny Erazo-Rodriguez not guilty by reason of insanity for fatally strangling her four-year-old daughter. Erazo-Rodriguez claimed that God had ordered the death of her child. Why is someone like Erazo-Rodriguez "not responsible" for behavior that would otherwise be considered criminal?

Robert Sciarrino/*Star-Ledger*

between right and wrong.[35] As Figure 3.3 below shows, half of the states still use a version of the *M'Naghten* rule.

2. *The ALI/MPC test.* In the early 1960s, the American Law Institute (ALI) included an insanity standard in its exhaustive criminal law guidebook, the Model Penal Code (MPC). Also known as the **substantial-capacity test,** the **ALI/MPC test** requires that the defendant lack "substantial capacity" to either "appreciate the wrongfulness" of his or her conduct or to conform that conduct "to the requirements of the law."[36]

3. *The irresistible-impulse test.* Under the **irresistible-impulse test,** a person may be found insane even if he or she was aware that a criminal act was "wrong," provided that some "irresistible impulse" resulting from a mental deficiency drove him or her to commit the crime.[37]

Public backlash against the insanity defense has caused seven state legislatures to pass "guilty but mentally ill" statutes. Under these laws, a jury can determine that a defendant is "mentally ill" rather than insane, and therefore responsible for her or his actions.[38] Defendants who are found guilty but mentally ill generally spend the early part of their sentences in a psychiatric hospital and the rest of the time in prison, or they receive treatment while in prison.

Determining Competency Whatever the standard, the insanity defense is rarely entered and is even less likely to result in an acquittal, as it is difficult to prove. (See the feature *Myth versus Reality—Are Too Many Criminals Found Not Guilty by Reason of Insanity?* on the facing page.) Psychiatry is far more commonly used in the courtroom

Substantial-Capacity Test (ALI/MPC Test) A test for the insanity defense that states that a person is not responsible for criminal behavior when he or she "lacks substantial capacity" to understand that the behavior is wrong or know how to behave properly.

Irresistible-Impulse Test A test for the insanity defense under which a defendant who knew her or his action was wrong may still be found insane if she or he was unable, as a result of a mental deficiency, to control the urge to complete the act.

FIGURE 3.3 Insanity Defenses

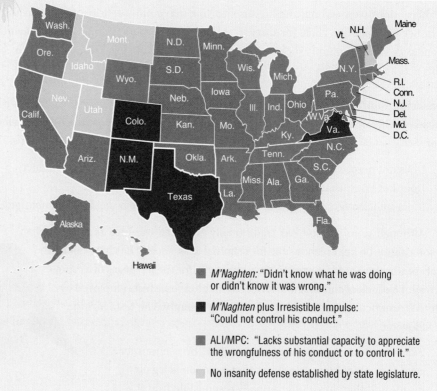

M'Naghten: "Didn't know what he was doing or didn't know it was wrong."

M'Naghten plus Irresistible Impulse: "Could not control his conduct."

ALI/MPC: "Lacks substantial capacity to appreciate the wrongfulness of his conduct or to control it."

No insanity defense established by state legislature.

Source: Bureau of Justice Statistics, *The Defense of Insanity: Standards and Procedures, State Court Organization, 1998* (Washington, D.C.: U.S. Department of Justice, June 2000), Table 38.

MYTH vs. REALITY

Are Too Many Criminals Found Not Guilty by Reason of Insanity?

To many Americans, it seems likely that any person who commits a gruesome murder or any other sort of violent crime has psychological problems. The question, then, is, How do we balance the need to punish such a person with the possibility that he or she may be seriously ill?

THE MYTH The American system of criminal justice answers this question by stating that a person may not be tried for an offense if that person cannot be held legally responsible for her or his actions. Because of the publicity surrounding the insanity defense, many people are under the impression that it is a major loophole in our system, allowing criminals to be "let off" no matter how heinous their crimes.

THE REALITY In fact, the insanity defense is raised in only about 1 percent of felony trials, and it is successful only one out of every four times it is raised. The reason: it is extremely difficult to prove insanity under the law. For example, Andre Thomas cut out the hearts of his

wife, their young son, and his wife's thirteen-month-old daughter. Before his murder trial, Thomas pulled his right eye out of its socket. (Several years later, while on death row, he ripped out the other eye and apparently ate it.) Nonetheless, prosecutors were able to convince a Texas jury that Thomas understood the difference between right and wrong at the time of the murders, and an appeals court upheld the conviction. Thomas is "clearly 'crazy,'" said one of the appellate judges who heard his case, "but he is also 'sane' under Texas law."

Even if Thomas had succeeded with the insanity defense, he would not have been "let off" in the sense that he would have been set free. Many defendants found not guilty by reason of insanity spend more time in mental hospitals than criminals who are convicted of similar acts spend in prison.

FOR CRITICAL ANALYSIS What is your opinion of the insanity defense? Does it protect the interests of society? Why or why not?

---

to determine the "competency" of a defendant to stand trial. If a judge believes that the defendant is unable to understand the nature of the proceedings or to assist in his or her own defense, the trial will not take place.

When **competency hearings** (which may also take place after the initial arrest and before sentencing) reveal that the defendant is in fact incompetent, the court may decide to place the defendant under treatment. For example, nearly eighteen months after his shooting rampage in Tucson, Arizona (discussed in Chapter 2), Jared Loughner was still being forcibly medicated at a federal prison facility in preparation for his criminal trial. Once competency has been restored to the defendant, the proceedings may recommence.[39]

INTOXICATION The law recognizes two types of **intoxication,** whether from drugs or from alcohol: *voluntary* and *involuntary.* Involuntary intoxication occurs when a person is physically forced to ingest or is injected with an intoxicating substance, or is unaware that a substance contains drugs or alcohol. Involuntary intoxication is a viable defense to a crime if the substance leaves the person unable to form the mental state necessary to understand that the act committed while under the influence was wrong.[40]

In Colorado, for example, the murder conviction of a man who shot a neighbor was overturned on the basis that the jury in the initial trial was not informed of the possibility of involuntary intoxication. At the time of the crime, the man had been taking a prescription decongestant that contained phenylpropanolamine, which has been known to cause psychotic episodes.

Voluntary drug or alcohol intoxication is also used to excuse a defendant's actions, though it is not a defense in itself. Rather, it is used when the defense attorney wants to show that the defendant was so intoxicated that *mens rea* was negated. In other words,

Competency Hearing A court proceeding to determine whether the defendant is mentally well enough to understand the charges filed against her or him and cooperate with a lawyer in presenting a defense.

Intoxication A defense for criminal liability in which the defendant claims that the taking of intoxicants rendered him or her unable to form the requisite intent to commit a criminal act.

> **"You know how it is, Dr. Ellsworth. You go to a party, have a few drinks, somebody gets killed."**
>
> —Letter from a death row inmate to **Professor Phoebe Ellsworth,** University of Michigan

the defendant could not possibly have had the state of mind that a crime requires. Many courts are reluctant to allow voluntary intoxication arguments to be presented to juries, however. After all, the defendant, by definition, voluntarily chose to enter an intoxicated state. Twelve states have eliminated voluntary intoxication as a possible defense, a step that has been criticized by many legal scholars but was upheld by the United States Supreme Court in *Montana v. Egelhoff* (1996).[41]

MISTAKE Everyone has heard the saying, "Ignorance of the law is no excuse." Ordinarily, ignorance of the law or a *mistaken idea* about what the law requires is not a valid defense.[42] For example, several years ago retired science teacher Eddie Leroy Anderson and his son dug for arrowheads near their favorite campground site in Idaho, unaware that the land was a federally protected archaeological site. Facing two years in prison for this mistake, they pleaded guilty and were given a year's probation and a $1,500 fine each. "Folks need to pay attention to where they are," said U.S. attorney Wendy Olson.[43]

Mistake of Law As the above example suggests, strict liability crimes specifically preclude the *mistake of law* defense, because the offender's intent is irrelevant. For practical reasons, the mistake of law defense is rarely allowed. If "I didn't know" was a valid defense, the courts would be clogged with defendants claiming ignorance of all aspects of criminal law. In some rare instances, however, people who claim that they honestly did not know that they were breaking a law may have a valid defense if (1) the law was not published or reasonably known to the public or (2) the person relied on an official statement of the law that was erroneous.[44]

Mistake of Fact A *mistake of fact,* as opposed to a mistake of law, operates as a defense if it negates the mental state necessary to commit a crime. If, for example, Oliver mistakenly walks off with Julie's briefcase because he thinks it is his, there is no theft. Theft requires knowledge that the property belongs to another. In some instances, mistake of fact is not an excuse but does allow for a lighter sentence. Several years ago, a Skagit County (Washington) judge sentenced teenage hunter Tyler Kales to thirty days in juvenile detention and 120 hours of community service for shooting and killing a hiker he mistook for a bear. Normally, of course, homicide with a firearm brings a much harsher punishment.

JUSTIFICATION CRIMINAL DEFENSES AND THE LAW

Learning Objective 7 Describe the four most important justification criminal defenses.

In certain instances, a defendant will accept responsibility for committing an illegal act, but contend that—given the circumstances—the act was justified. In other words, even though the guilty act and the guilty intent are present, the particulars of the case relieve the defendant of criminal liability. In 2011, for example, there were 653 "justified" killings of those who were in the process of committing a felony: 393 were killed by law enforcement officers and 260 by private citizens.[45] Four of the most important justification defenses are duress, self-defense, necessity, and entrapment.

Duress Unlawful pressure brought to bear on a person, causing the person to perform an act that he or she would not otherwise perform.

DURESS **Duress** exists when the *wrongful* threat of one person induces another person to perform an act that she or he would otherwise not perform. In such a situation, duress is said to negate the *mens rea* necessary to commit a crime. For duress to qualify as a defense, the following requirements must be met:

1. The threat must be of serious bodily harm or death.
2. The harm threatened must be greater than the harm caused by the crime.
3. The threat must be immediate and inescapable.
4. The defendant must have become involved in the situation through no fault of his or her own.[46]

Note that some scholars consider duress to be an excuse defense, because the threat of bodily harm negates any guilty intent on the part of the defendant.[47]

When ruling on the duress defense, courts often examine whether the defendant had the opportunity to avoid the threat in question. Two narcotics cases illustrate this point. In the first, the defendant claimed that an associate threatened to kill him and his wife unless he participated in a marijuana deal. Although this contention was proved true during the course of the trial, the court rejected the duress defense because the defendant made no apparent effort to escape, nor did he report his dilemma to the police. In sum, the drug deal was avoidable—the defendant could have made an effort to extricate himself, but he did not, thereby surrendering the protection of the duress defense.[48]

In the second case, a taxi driver in Bogotá, Colombia, was ordered by a passenger to swallow cocaine-filled balloons and take them to the United States. The taxi driver was warned that if he refused, his wife and three-year-old daughter would be killed. After a series of similar threats, the taxi driver agreed to transport the drugs. On arriving at customs at the Los Angeles airport, the defendant consented to have his stomach X-rayed, which led to discovery of the contraband and his arrest. During his trial, the defendant told the court that he was afraid to notify the police in Colombia because he believed them to be corrupt. The court accepted his duress defense, on the grounds that it met the four requirements listed above and the defendant had notified American authorities when given the opportunity to do so.[49]

JUSTIFIABLE USE OF FORCE—SELF-DEFENSE A person who believes she or he is in danger of being harmed by another is justified in defending herself or himself with the use of force, and any criminal act committed in such circumstances can be justified as **self-defense.** Other situations that also justify the use of force include the defense of one's dwelling, the defense of other property, and the prevention of a crime. In all these situations, it is important to distinguish between deadly and nondeadly force. Deadly force is likely to result in death or serious bodily harm.

The Amount of Force Generally speaking, people can use the amount of nondeadly force that seems necessary to protect themselves, their dwellings, or other property or to prevent the commission of a crime. Deadly force can be used in self-defense if there is a *reasonable belief* that imminent death or bodily harm will otherwise result, if the attacker is using unlawful force (an example of lawful force is that exerted by a police officer), if the defender has not initiated or provoked the attack, and if there is no other possible response or alternative way out of the life-threatening situation.[50] Deadly force normally can be used to defend a dwelling only if the unlawful entry is violent and the person believes deadly force is necessary to prevent imminent death or great bodily harm. In some jurisdictions, it is also a viable defense if the person believes deadly force is necessary to prevent the commission of a felony (such as arson) in the dwelling.

Self-Defense The legally recognized privilege to protect one's self or property from injury by another.

Confronted by two holdup men at his pharmacy in Oklahoma City, Oklahoma, Jerome Ersland shot one in the head and chased the other away. He then walked out from behind the counter and shot the wounded robber—who was unarmed—five more times, killing him. In May 2011, Ersland, right, was convicted of first degree murder for his actions. What is your opinion of this verdict? How can you argue that Ersland was acting in self-defense?

AP Photo/Sue Ogrocki, File

The Duty to Retreat When a person is outside the home or in a public space, the rules for self-defense change somewhat. Until relatively recently, almost all jurisdictions required someone who is attacked under these circumstances to "retreat to the wall" before fighting back. In other words, under this **duty to retreat,** one who is being assaulted may not resort to deadly force if he or she has a reasonable opportunity to "run away" and thus avoid the conflict. Only when this person has run into a "wall," literally or otherwise, may deadly force be used in self-defense.

Recently, sixteen states have adopted "stand your ground" laws that eliminate this duty to retreat. George Zimmerman's claim of self-defense for his killing of Trayvon Martin, discussed in Chapter 1, relied on one such law, a Florida statute stating that citizens have "the right to stand [their] ground and meet force with force, including deadly force," if they "reasonably" fear for their safety.[51] Zimmerman's attorneys presented evidence, such as photos of their client's bloodied head taken by police after the incident, to show that he had been attacked by Martin and thus "reasonably" used deadly force to defend himself.[52]

NECESSITY The **necessity** defense requires courts to weigh the harm caused by the crime actually committed against the harm that would have been caused by the criminal act avoided. If the avoided harm is greater than the committed harm, then the defense has a chance of succeeding. In 2011, for example, a San Francisco jury acquitted a defendant of carrying a concealed weapon because he was avoiding the "greater evil" of getting shot himself. The defendant had testified that he needed the gun for protection while entering a high-crime neighborhood to buy baby food and diapers for his crying niece.[53] Murder is the one crime for which the necessity defense is not applicable under any circumstances.[54]

ENTRAPMENT **Entrapment** is a justification defense that criminal law allows when a police officer or government agent deceives a defendant into wrongdoing. Although law enforcement agents can legitimately use various forms of subterfuge—such as informants or undercover agents—to gain information or apprehend a suspect in a criminal act, the law places limits on these strategies. Police cannot persuade an innocent person to commit a crime, nor can they coerce a suspect into doing so, even if they are certain he or she is a criminal.

SELFASSESSMENT
Fill in the blanks and check your answers on page 93.

Criminal law recognizes that a defendant may not be _____ for a criminal act if her or his mental state was impaired, by either _____—the psychological inability to separate right from wrong—or _____ due to drugs or alcohol. Defendants may also claim that they were _____ in committing an act either because they were under _____ to perform an act that they would not otherwise have performed or because they were acting in _____-_____ to protect themselves from deadly harm. _____ occurs when a government agent deceives a defendant into committing a crime.

PROTECTING CIVIL LIBERTIES

To this point, we have focused on **substantive criminal law,** which defines the acts that the government will punish. We will now turn our attention to **procedural criminal law.** (The section that follows will provide only a short overview of criminal procedure. In later chapters, many other constitutional issues will be examined in more detail.)

Sidebar definitions:

Duty to Retreat The requirement that a person claiming self-defense prove that she or he first took reasonable steps to avoid the conflict that resulted in the use of deadly force.

Necessity A defense against criminal liability in which the defendant asserts that circumstances required him or her to commit an illegal act.

Entrapment A defense in which the defendant claims that he or she was induced by a public official—usually an undercover agent or police officer—to commit a crime that he or she would otherwise not have committed.

Substantive Criminal Law Law that defines the rights and duties of individuals with respect to one another.

Procedural Criminal Law Rules that define the manner in which the rights and duties of individuals may be enforced.

Criminal law brings the force of the state, with all its resources, to bear against the individual. Criminal procedures, drawn from the ideals stated in the Bill of Rights, are designed to protect the constitutional rights of individuals and to prevent the arbitrary use of power by the government.

THE BILL OF RIGHTS

For various reasons, proposals related to the rights of individuals were rejected during the framing of the U.S. Constitution in 1787. The need for a written declaration of civil liberties of individuals eventually caused the first Congress to draft twelve amendments to the Constitution and submit them for approval by the states. Ten of these amendments, commonly known as the **Bill of Rights,** were adopted in 1791. Since then, seventeen more amendments have been added.

The Bill of Rights, as interpreted by the United States Supreme Court, has served as the basis for procedural safeguards of the accused in this country. These safeguards include the following:

1. The Fourth Amendment protection from unreasonable searches and seizures.
2. The Fourth Amendment requirement that no warrants for a search or an arrest can be issued without probable cause.
3. The Fifth Amendment requirement that no one can be deprived of life, liberty, or property without "due process" of law.
4. The Fifth Amendment prohibition against *double jeopardy* (trying someone twice for the same criminal offense).
5. The Fifth Amendment guarantee that no person can be required to be a witness against (incriminate) himself or herself.
6. The Sixth Amendment guarantees of a speedy trial, a trial by jury, a public trial, the right to confront witnesses, and the right to a lawyer at various stages of criminal proceedings.
7. The Eighth Amendment prohibitions against excessive bails and fines and cruel and unusual punishments. (For the full text of the Bill of Rights, see Appendix A.)

The Bill of Rights initially offered citizens protection only against the federal government. Over the years, however, the procedural safeguards of most of the provisions of the Bill of Rights have been applied to the actions of state governments through the Fourteenth Amendment. Furthermore, the states, under certain circumstances, have the option to grant even more protections than are required by the federal Constitution. As these protections are crucial to criminal justice procedures in the United States, they will be afforded much more attention in Chapter 6, with regard to police action, and in Chapter 8, with regard to the criminal trial.

DUE PROCESS

Both the Fifth and Fourteenth Amendments provide that no person should be deprived of "life, liberty, or property without due process of law." This **due process clause** basically requires that the government not act unfairly or arbitrarily. In other words, the government cannot rely on individual judgment and impulse when making

Bill of Rights The first ten amendments to the U.S. Constitution.

Due Process Clause The provisions of the Fifth and Fourteenth Amendments to the Constitution that guarantee that no person shall be deprived of life, liberty, or property without due process of law.

Why do most citizens accept certain steps taken by the federal government that restrict our individual freedoms—such as limiting the amount of liquids and gels passengers can carry on airplanes to prevent such substances from being used in terrorist attacks?
AP Photo/Gene Blyth

Procedural Due Process
The constitutional requirement that the law must be carried out in a fair and orderly manner.

decisions, but must stay within the boundaries of reason and the law. Of course, disagreements as to the meaning of these provisions have plagued courts, politicians, and citizens since this nation was founded, and will undoubtedly continue to do so.

To understand due process, it is important to consider its two types: procedural due process and substantive due process.

PROCEDURAL DUE PROCESS According to **procedural due process,** the law must be carried out by a *method* that is fair and orderly. It requires that certain procedures be followed in administering and executing a law so that an individual's basic freedoms are not violated.

The American criminal justice system's adherence to due process principles is evident in its treatment of the death penalty. To ensure that the process is fair, as we will see in Chapter 9, a number of procedural safeguards have been built into capital punishment. Much to the dismay of many victims' groups, these procedures make the process expensive and lengthy. In California, for example, the average time between conviction for a capital crime and execution is twenty-five years. Furthermore, each execution costs state taxpayers an average of about $308 million.[55] (The controversy surrounding a government killing that did not follow accepted due process procedures is explored in the feature *Anti-Terrorism in Action—Due Justice?* below.)

SUBSTANTIVE DUE PROCESS Fair procedures would obviously be of little use if they were used to administer unfair laws. For example, suppose a law requires everyone to wear a red shirt on Mondays. You wear a blue shirt on Monday, and you are arrested, convicted, and sentenced to one year in prison. The fact that all proper procedures were followed and your rights were given their proper protections would mean very little, because the law that you broke was unfair and arbitrary.

ANTI-TERRORISM IN ACTION

DUE JUSTICE?

After Islamist cleric Anwar al-Awlaki was killed by an American drone strike in the Middle Eastern country of Yemen on September 30, 2011, President Barack Obama did not hesitate to show his pleasure. The president called Awlaki's death a "milestone in the broader effort to defeat" international terrorism. Through his online sermons in English, Awlaki had been linked to more than a dozen terrorist operations, including a 2010 plot to blow up cargo airplanes bound for the United States.

There was a legal problem with the killing, however. Awlaki was born in New Mexico and was therefore a citizen of the United States. Consequently, critics argued that the drone attack that killed him was illegal, given that the U.S. Constitution forbids the execution of American citizens without due process of law. Legal expert Glenn Greenwald noted that there had been no effort to charge Awlaki with committing any crime, and he had not been

afforded a trial to prove his innocence. "[Awlaki] was simply ordered killed by the president: his judge, jury and executioner," Greenwald said.

FOR CRITICAL ANALYSIS In a secret legal memorandum, the Obama administration justified the killing of Anwar al-Awlaki without a trial on several grounds. Primarily, the memo asserts that Awlaki was no ordinary American citizen. Rather, he was a member of terrorist organizations that were, essentially, at war with the United States. Furthermore, federal attorneys claim that the execution, without trial, of a man who is plotting to kill Americans is a legitimate act of self-defense, particularly given that Yemeni officials were making no effort to apprehend Awlaki. Do you agree that the Obama administration was justified in this action? Or, do you think that the assassination of U.S. citizens without charges is never acceptable? Explain your answer.

Thus, **substantive due process** requires that the laws themselves be reasonable. The idea is that if a law is unfair or arbitrary, even if properly passed by a legislature, it must be declared unconstitutional. In the 1930s, for example, Oklahoma instituted the Habitual Criminal Sterilization Act. Under this statute, a person who had been convicted of three felonies could be "rendered sexually sterile" by the state (that is, the person would no longer be able to produce children). The United States Supreme Court held that the law was unconstitutional, as there are "limits to the extent which a legislatively represented majority may conduct biological experiments at the expense of the dignity and personality and natural powers of a minority."[56]

Substantive Due Process
The constitutional requirement that laws used to accuse and convict persons of crimes must be fair.

THE SUPREME COURT'S ROLE IN DUE PROCESS As the last example suggests, the United States Supreme Court often plays the important role of ultimately deciding when due process has been violated and when it has not. (See Figure 3.4 below for a list of important Supreme Court due process cases.) As we will see throughout this textbook, the Court has recently had to make a number of important decisions regarding the due process rights that should be afforded to terrorist suspects by the American government. In particular, in Chapters 8 and 14, we will look at the due process ramifications of the federal government's efforts to bring terrorist suspects to justice.

SELFASSESSMENT

Fill in the blanks and check your answers on page 93.

The basis for procedural safeguards for the accused is found in the _____ _____ _____ of the U.S. Constitution. According to these safeguards, no person shall be deprived of life or liberty without _____ _____ of law. This means that the _____ by which the law is carried out must be fair and orderly and the laws themselves must be _____. The _____ _____ _____ _____ ultimately decides whether these rights have been violated.

FIGURE 3.4 **Important United States Supreme Court Due Process Decisions**

YEAR	ISSUE	AMENDMENT INVOLVED	COURT CASE
1948	Right to a public trial	VI	*In re Oliver*, 333 U.S. 257
1952	Police searches cannot be so invasive as to "shock the conscience"	IV	*Rochin v. California*, 342 U.S. 165
1961	Exclusionary rule	IV	*Mapp v. Ohio*, 367 U.S. 643
1963	Right to a lawyer in all criminal felony cases	VI	*Gideon v. Wainwright*, 372 U.S. 335
1964	No compulsory self-incrimination	V	*Malloy v. Hogan*, 378 U.S. 1
1964	Right to have counsel when taken into police custody and subjected to questioning	VI	*Escobedo v. Illinois*, 378 U.S. 478
1965	Right to confront and cross-examine witnesses	VI	*Pointer v. Texas*, 380 U.S. 400
1966	Right to an impartial jury	VI	*Parker v. Gladden*, 385 U.S. 363
1966	Confessions of suspects not notified of due process rights ruled invalid	V	*Miranda v. Arizona*, 384 U.S. 436
1967	Right to a speedy trial	VI	*Klopfer v. North Carolina*, 386 U.S. 21
1967	Juveniles have due process rights, too	V	*In re Gault*, 387 U.S. 1
1968	Right to a jury trial ruled a fundamental right	VI	*Duncan v. Louisiana*, 391 U.S. 145
1969	No double jeopardy	V	*Benton v. Maryland*, 395 U.S. 784

CHAPTER SUMMARY

Learning Objective 1 **List the four written sources of American criminal law.** (a) The U.S. Constitution and state constitutions; (b) statutes passed by Congress and state legislatures (plus local ordinances); (c) administrative agency regulations; and (d) case law.

Learning Objective 2 **Explain the two basic functions of criminal law.** The primary function is to protect citizens from harms to their safety and property and from harms to society's interest collectively. The second function is to maintain and teach social values as well as social boundaries—for example, speed limits and laws against bigamy.

Learning Objective 3 **Discuss the primary goals of civil law and criminal law, and explain how these goals are realized.** Civil law is designed to resolve disputes between private individuals and other entities, such as corporations. In these disputes, one party, called the plaintiff, tries to gain monetary damages by proving that the accused party, or the defendant, is to blame for a tort, or wrongful act. In contrast, criminal law exists to protect society from criminal behavior. To that end, the government prosecutes defendants, or persons who have been charged with committing a crime.

Learning Objective 4 **Explain the differences between crimes *mala in se* and *mala prohibita*.** A criminal act is *mala in se* if it is inherently wrong, while a criminal act *mala prohibita* is illegal only because it is prohibited by the laws of a particular society. It is sometimes difficult to distinguish between these two sorts of crimes because it is difficult to define a "pure" *mala in se* crime; that is, it is difficult to separate a crime from the culture that has deemed it a crime.

Learning Objective 5 **Delineate the elements required to establish *mens rea* (a guilty mental state).** (a) Purpose, (b) knowledge, (c) negligence, or (d) recklessness.

Learning Objective 6 **List and briefly define the most important excuse defenses for crimes. Insanity**—different tests of insanity can be used, including (a) the *M'Naghten* rule (right-wrong test); (b) the ALI/MPC test, also known as the substantial-capacity test; and (c) the irresistible-impulse test. **Intoxication**—voluntary and involuntary, the latter being a possible criminal defense. **Mistake**—sometimes valid if the law was not published or reasonably known or if the alleged offender relied on an official statement of the law that was erroneous. Also, a mistake of fact may negate the mental state necessary to commit a crime.

Learning Objective 7 **Describe the four most important justification criminal defenses. Duress**—requires that (a) the threat is of serious bodily harm or death, (b) the harm is greater than that caused by the crime; (c) the threat is immediate and inescapable; and (d) the defendant became involved in the situation through no fault of his or her own. **Justifiable use of force**—the defense of one's person, dwelling, or property, or the prevention of a crime. **Necessity**—justifiable if the harm sought to be avoided is greater than that sought to be prevented by the law defining the offense charged. **Entrapment**—the criminal action was induced by certain governmental persuasion or trickery.

Learning Objective 8 **Explain the importance of the due process clause in the criminal justice system.** The due process clause acts to limit the power of government. In the criminal justice system, the due process clause requires that certain procedures be followed to ensure the fairness of criminal proceedings and that all criminal laws be reasonable and in the interest of the public good.

QUESTIONS FOR CRITICAL ANALYSIS

1. Give an example of a criminal law whose main purpose seems to be teaching societal boundaries rather than protecting citizens from harm. By searching the Internet, can you find examples of other countries where this behavior is not considered criminal? How is the behavior perceived in those countries?

2. Give an example of how one person could be involved in a civil lawsuit and a criminal lawsuit for the same action.

3. Two fathers, John and Phil, get in a heated argument following a dispute between their sons in a Little League baseball game. They come to blows, and John strikes Phil in the temple, killing him. Will John be charged with voluntary manslaughter or involuntary manslaughter? What other details might you need to be sure of your answer?

4. Why does the absence of a *mens rea* provision make it easier for prosecutors to convict defendants charged with strict liability crimes?

5. Critics have derogatorily labeled the "stand your ground laws" passed by Florida and many other states (see page 88) "license to kill" laws. Why would they do so? What is your opinion of these laws?

KEY TERMS

actus reus **77**

administrative law **69**

attempt **77**

attendant circumstances **81**

ballot initiative **68**

beyond a reasonable doubt **73**

Bill of Rights **89**

case law **69**

civil law **72**

competency hearing **85**

conspiracy **82**

constitutional law **67**

corpus delicti **77**

defendant **73**

due process clause **89**

duress **86**

duty to retreat **88**

entrapment **88**

felony **74**

felony-murder **80**

hate crime law **81**

inchoate offenses **82**

infancy **83**

infraction **75**

insanity **83**

intoxication **85**

involuntary manslaughter **74**

irresistible-impulse test **84**

liability **73**

mala in se **75**

mala prohibita **75**

malice aforethought **74**

mens rea **77**

misdemeanor **75**

M'Naghten rule **83**

necessity **88**

negligence **78**

plaintiff **72**

precedent **69**

preponderance of the evidence **73**

procedural criminal law **88**

procedural due process **90**

recklessness **78**

self-defense **87**

statutory law **67**

statutory rape **80**

strict liability crimes **79**

substantial-capacity test (ALI/MPC test) **84**

substantive criminal law **88**

substantive due process **91**

supremacy clause **68**

voluntary manslaughter **74**

SELF ASSESSMENT ANSWER KEY

Page 69: i. Constitution; **ii.** unconstitutional; **iii.** statutes; **iv.** case/judge-made/common

Page 71: i. legal; **ii.** criminal; **iii.** social; **iv.** morality

Page 76: i. Civil; **ii.** state/government; **iii.** felony; **iv.** misdemeanor; **v.** First degree murder; **vi.** manslaughter

Page 82: i. *actus reus;* **ii.** *mens rea;* **iii.** concurrence; **iv.** strict liability; **v.** intent/*mens rea*/mental state; **vi.** Attendant; **vii.** beyond a reasonable doubt

Page 88: i. responsible; **ii.** insanity; **iii.** intoxication; **iv.** justified; **v.** duress; **vi.** self-defense; **vii.** Entrapment

Page 91: i. Bill of Rights; **ii.** due process; **iii.** procedures; **iv.** reasonable/fair; **v.** United States Supreme Court

COURSEMATE

For online help and access to resources that accompany *Criminal Justice in Action: The Core*, go to **www.cengage-brain.com/shop/ISBN/978-1-285-06915-9**. Click "Access Now," where you will find flashcards, an online quiz, and other helpful study aids. If you have an access code for CourseMate, log in and go to the chapter of your choice for additional online study aids.

NOTES

1. Quoted in DeeDee Correll, "Sweat Lodge Guru Is Held in Three Deaths," *Los Angeles Times* (February 4, 2010), 1.

2. Arizona Revised Statutes Section 31–1102(A).

3. John S. Baker, Jr., *Measuring the Explosive Growth of Federal Crime Legislation* (Washington, D.C.: The Federalist Society for Law and Public Policy Studies, 2008), 1.

4. Quoted in "Judge: Federal Law Trumps Montana's Medical Pot Law," *Associated Press* (January 23, 2012).

5. *Texas v. Johnson,* 491 U.S. 397 (1989).

6. "Arizona Voters OK Medical-Marijuana Bill," *Boston Globe* (November 15, 2010), 2.

7. Clean Water Act Section 309, 33 U.S.C.A. Section 1319 (1987).

8. Joel Feinberg, *The Moral Limits of the Criminal Law: Harm to Others* (New York: Oxford University Press, 1984), 221–232.

9. Henry M. Hart, Jr., "The Aims of the Criminal Law," *Law & Contemporary Problems* 23 (1958), 405–406.

10. John L. Diamond, "The Myth of Morality and Fault in Criminal Law Doctrine," *American Criminal Law Review* 34 (Fall 1996), 111.

11. The Humane Society of the United States, "Ranking of State Cockfighting Laws," June 2010, at **www.humanesociety.org/assets/pdfs/animal_fighting/cockfighting_statelaws.pdf**; and Animal Welfare Act Amendments of 2007, Pub. L. 110-246, 122 Statute 223 (2007).

12. John Monk, "Cockfighters Take Fight to Federal Appeals Court," *Columbia (SC) State* (December 4, 2011), A1.

13. Lawrence M. Friedman, *Crime and Punishments in American History* (New York: Basic Books, 1993), 10.

14. Model Penal Code Section 1.04 (2).

15. *Federal Criminal Rules Handbook,* Section 2.1 (St. Paul, MN: West, 2008).

16. 625 Illinois Compiled Statutes Annotated Section 5/16-104 (St. Paul, MN: West, 2002).

17. Johannes Andenaes, "The Moral or Educative Influence of Criminal Law," *Journal of Social Issues* 27 (Spring 1971), 17, 26.

18. *Hawkins v. State,* 219 Ind. 116, 129, 37 N.E.2d 79 (1941).

19. David C. Biggs, "'The Good Samaritan Is Packing': An Overview of the Broadened Duty to Aid Your Fellowman, with the Modern Desire to Possess Concealed Weapons," *University of Dayton Law Review* 22 (Winter 1997), 225.

20. Terry Halbert and Elaine Ingulli, *Law and Ethics in the Business Environment,* 6th ed. (Mason, OH: South-Western Cengage Learning, 2009), 8.

21. Texas Penal Code Section 46.13 (1995).

22. Model Penal Code Section 2.02(c).

23. *United States v. Dotterweich,* 320 U.S. 277 (1943).

24. Florida Statutes Section 893.101 (2002).

25. John Schwartz, "Florida: Drug Laws Ruled Unconstitutional," *New York Times* (July 28, 2011), A20.

26. *State v. Stiffler,* 763 P.2d 308, 311 (Idaho Ct.App. 1988).

27. *State v. Harrison,* 425 A.2d 111 (1979).

28. Richard G. Singer and John Q. LaFond, *Criminal Law: Examples and Explanations* (New York: Aspen Law & Business, 1997), 322.

29. *State v. Linscott,* 520 A.2d 1067 (1987).

30. Federal Bank Robbery Act, 18 U.S.C.A. Section 2113.

31. *State v. Jones,* 2011 S.D. 60 (2011).

32. Bureau of Justice Statistics, *Hate Crime, 2003–2009* (Washington, D.C.: U.S. Department of Justice, June 2011), 1.

33. *United States v. Jiminez Recio,* 537 U.S. 270 (2003).

34. Paul H. Robinson, *Criminal Law Defenses* (St. Paul, MN: West, 2008), Section 173, Ch. 5Bl.

35. *M'Naghten's* Case, 10 Cl.&F. 200, Eng.Rep. 718 (1843). Note that the name is also spelled M'Naughten and McNaughten.

36. Model Penal Code Section 401 (1952).

37. Joshua Dressler, *Cases and Materials on Criminal Law,* 2d ed. (St. Paul, MN: West Group, 1999), 599.

38. South Carolina Code Annotated Section 17-24-20(A) (Law. Co-op. Supp., 1997).

39. Bruce J. Winick, "Presumptions and Burdens of Proof in Determining Competency to Stand Trial: An Analysis of *Medina v. California* and the Supreme Court's New Due Process Methodology in Criminal Cases," *University of Miami Law Review* 47 (1993), 817.

40. Lawrence P. Tiffany and Mary Tiffany, "Nosologic Objections to the Criminal Defense of Pathological Intoxication: What Do the Doubters Doubt?" *International Journal of Law and Psychiatry* 13 (1990), 49.

41. 518 U.S. 37 (1996).

42. Kenneth W. Simons, "Mistake and Impossibility, Law and Fact, and Culpability: A Speculative Essay," *Journal of Criminal Law and Criminology* 81 (1990), 447.

43. Quoted in Gary Fields and John R. Emshwiller, "As Criminal Laws Proliferate, More Are Ensnared," *Wall Street Journal* (July 23, 2011), at **online.wsj.com/article/SB10001424052748703749504576172714184601654.html**.

44. *Lambert v. California,* 335 U.S. 225 (1957).

45. Federal Bureau of Investigation, *Crime in the United States, 2011* (Washington, D.C.: U.S. Department of Justice, 2012), at **www.fbi.gov/about-us/cjis/ucr/crime-in-the-u.s./2011/crime-in-the-u.s.-2011/tables/expanded-homicide-data-table-14**; and **www.fbi.gov/about-us/cjis/ucr/ucr/crime-in-the-u.s/2011/crime-in-the-u.s.-2011/tables/expanded-homicide-data-table-15.**

46. Craig L. Carr, "Duress and Criminal Responsibility," *Law and Philosophy* 10 (1990), 161.

47. Arnold N. Enker, "In Supporting the Distinction between Justification and Excuse," *Texas Tech Law Review* 42 (2009), 277.

48. *United States v. May,* 727 F.2d 764 (1984).

49. *United States v. Contento-Pachon,* 723 F.2d 691 (1984).

50. *People v. Murillo,* 587 N.E.2d 1199, 1204 (Ill. App.Ct. 1992).

51. Florida Statutes Section 776.03 (2005).

52. Kyle Hightower and Mike Schneider, "Evidence Shows Violent Fight Preceded Fla. Shooting Death," *Associated Press* (May 19, 2012).

53. "Man Acquitted of Concealed Weapon Charge on 'Necessity' Defense," *San Francisco Examiner* (July 10, 2011), at **www.sfexaminer.com/local/crime/2011/07/man-acquitted-conceealed-weapon-charge-necessity-defense**.

54. *People v. Petro,* 56 P.2d 984 (Cal.Ct.App. 1936); and *Regina v. Dudley and Stephens,* 14 Q.B.D. 173 (1884).

55. Arthur L. Alarcon and Paula M. Mitchell, "Executing the Will of the Voters? A Roadmap to Mend or End the California Legislature's Multi-Billion Dollar Death Penalty Debacle," *Loyola of Los Angeles Law Review* 44 (2011), S109.

56. *Skinner v. Oklahoma,* 316 U.S. 535, 546–547 (1942).

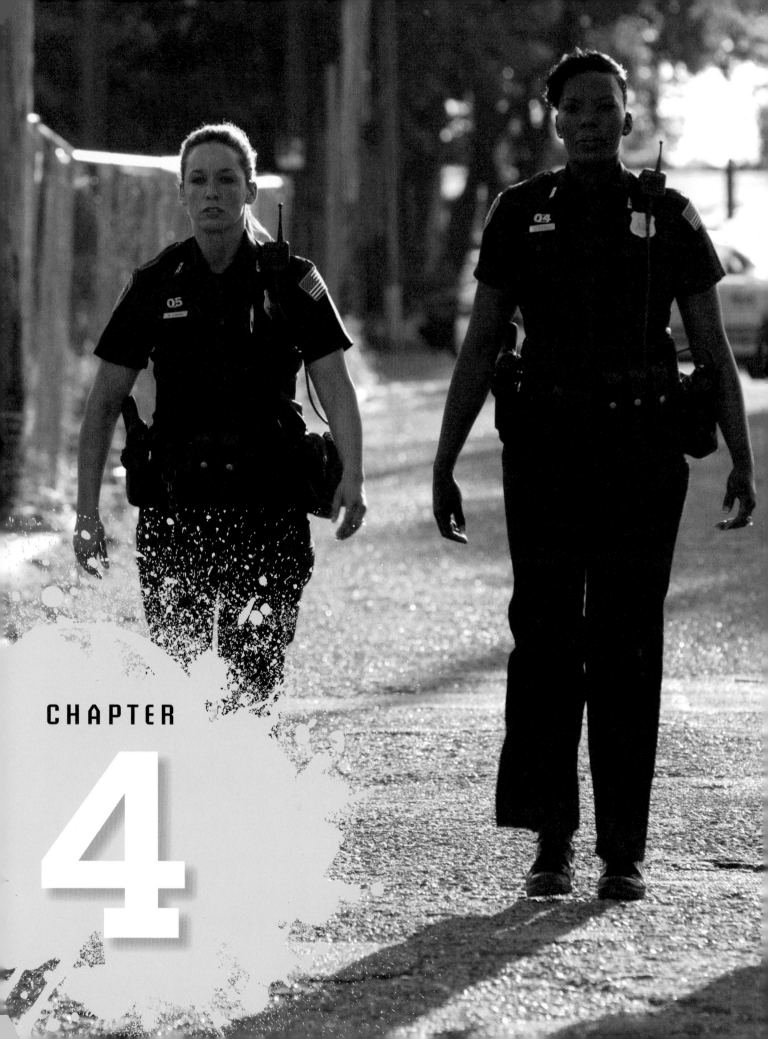

CHAPTER

4

Law Enforcement Today

TLC/Walling McGarity

LEARNING OBJECTIVES

After reading this chapter, you should be able to...

1 List the four basic responsibilities of the police.

2 Tell how the patronage system affected policing.

3 Explain how intelligence-led policing works and how it benefits modern police departments.

4 Identify the differences between the police academy and field training as learning tools for recruits.

5 Describe the challenges facing women who choose law enforcement as a career.

6 Indicate some of the most important law enforcement agencies under the control of the Department of Homeland Security.

7 Identify the duties of the FBI.

8 Analyze the importance of private security today.

Throughout the chapter you will see each learning objective repeated in the margin next to the content it relates to. The chapter summary on pages 121 and 122 includes all of the learning objectives for review.

CHAPTER OUTLINE

- The Responsibilities of the Police
- A Short History of the American Police
- Recruitment and Training: Becoming a Police Officer
- Women and Minorities in Policing Today
- Public and Private Law Enforcement

LIFE ON THE TWEET

Sergeant Cynthia Schumann, a twenty-six-year police veteran, has been jotting down notes about her on-the-job experiences for most of her career. "People would not believe—you can't make it up—what we've seen," she said at a writing workshop sponsored by the Chicago Police Department for its officers in February 2012. "Every policeman has said more than once, 'We have got to write a book.'"

Thanks to social media technology, law enforcement agents no longer have to write a book to share their opinions and exploits with the public. Every day, thousands of police officers express themselves in 140-character bursts of insight via Twitter, providing a panorama of the policing life that goes beyond what any single novel or true-crime best seller has to offer. A random fifteen-minute visit to "Cops on the Tweet," a public list of U.S. law enforcement personnel tweets, reveals the personalities of a sheriff from Big Bend, Texas, who is fascinated by the Old West; a Youngstown, Ohio, patrolman telling Valentine's Day jokes; and a Los Angeles homicide detective weighing in on the death of pop singer Whitney Houston.

The freedom of expression provided by Twitter can be a double-edged sword. In 2011, Detective Pete Dwyer lost his job at the Albuquerque (New Mexico) Police Department thanks to a series of unfortunate tweets. One of the messages made an insensitive joke about Muslims, and another offered a link to a Web site that compared the administration of President Barack Obama to the Nazis. "We respect and value the right to free speech," said Albuquerque police chief Ray Schultz, "but comments that impair our officers' ability to perform their duties and bring discredit to the [department] will not be tolerated."

An Albuquerque, New Mexico, law enforcement official updates the city's public safety Twitter site.

AP Photo/Tim Korte

Not all of Pete Dwyer's colleagues felt that he should have been fired for his indiscretions. Joey Sigala, president of the Albuquerque Police Officer's Association, says that while department officials can dictate an officer's on-the-job behavior, "I don't believe they have the right to tell us what to do outside of that."[1] Nevertheless, many police departments across the country have instituted policies to regulate their employees' social media etiquette. These protocols recognize that police officers are "by far the most visible of all criminal justice institutions"[2] and must be held to a high standard of behavior.

Indeed, the men and women in blue symbolize the criminal justice system for many Americans who may never see the inside of a courtroom or a prison cell. The police are entrusted with immense power to serve and protect the public good: the power to use weapons and the power to arrest. But that same power alarms many citizens, who fear that it may be turned arbitrarily against them. The role of the police is constantly debated as well. Is their primary mission to fight crime, or should they also be concerned with the social conditions that presumably lead to crime?

This chapter will lay the foundation for our study of law enforcement agents and the work that they do. It includes a short history of policing, followed by a discussion of police recruitment and an examination of the many different agencies that make up the law enforcement system. We will also look at the issues facing members of minority groups and women who choose to follow careers in policing, as well as the subject of private security. We start, however, by answering a basic—though hardly simple—question: What do police do?

THE RESPONSIBILITIES OF THE POLICE

As we begin our examination of police and policing, you should understand that the realities of law enforcement rarely match the depiction of the profession in the popular media. For the most part, the incidents that make up a police officer's daily routine would not make it on to television dramas such as the *NCIS* series or *Hawaii Five-O*. Besides catching criminals, police spend a great deal of time on such mundane tasks as responding to noise complaints, confiscating firecrackers, and poring over paperwork. Sociologist Egon Bittner warned against the tendency to see the police primarily as agents of law enforcement and crime control. A more inclusive accounting of "what the police do," Bittner believed, would recognize that they provide "situationally justified force in society."[3] In other words, the function of the police is to solve any problem that may *possibly*, though not *necessarily*, require the use of force.

> "Every community gets the kind of law enforcement it insists on."
> —**Robert Kennedy,** U.S. attorney general (1964)

Within Bittner's rather broad definition of "what the police do," we can pinpoint four basic responsibilities of the police:

1. To enforce laws.
2. To provide services.
3. To prevent crime.
4. To preserve the peace.

As will become evident over the next two chapters, there is a great deal of debate among legal and other scholars and law enforcement officers over which responsibilities deserve the most police attention and what methods should be employed by the police in meeting those responsibilities.

Learning Objective 1 List the four basic responsibilities of the police.

ENFORCING LAWS

In the public mind, the primary role of the police is to enforce society's laws—hence, the term *law enforcement officer*. In their role as "crime fighters," police officers have a clear mandate to seek out and apprehend those who have violated the law. The crime-fighting responsibility is so dominant that all police activity—from the purchase of new automobiles to a plan to hire more minority officers—must often be justified in terms of its law enforcement value.[4]

Police officers also see themselves primarily as crime fighters, a perception that often leads people into what they believe will be an exciting career in law enforcement. Although the job certainly offers challenges unlike any other, police officers normally do not spend most of their time on law enforcement duties. After surveying a year's worth of dispatch data from the Wilmington (Delaware) Police Department, researchers Jack Greene and Carl Klockars found that officers spent only about half of their working hours enforcing the law or dealing with crimes. The rest of their time was spent on order maintenance, service provision, traffic patrol, and medical assistance.[5]

Furthermore, information provided by the Uniform Crime Report shows that most arrests are made for "crimes of disorder" or public annoyances rather than violent or property crimes.[6] In 2011, for example, police made 10.2 million arrests for drunkenness, liquor law violations, disorderly conduct, vagrancy, loitering, and other minor offenses, but only about 535,000 arrests for violent crimes.[7] (Sometimes, as the feature *You Be the Police Commissioner—Occupational Hazard* below shows, the decision to enforce criminal law is not easily made.)

PROVIDING SERVICES

The popular emphasis on crime fighting and law enforcement tends to overshadow the fact that a great deal of a police officer's time is spent providing services for the community. The motto "To Serve and Protect" has been adopted by thousands of local police departments, and the *Law Enforcement Code of Ethics* recognizes the duty "to serve the community" in its first sentence.[8] The services that police provide are numerous—a partial list would include directing traffic, performing emergency medical procedures, counseling those involved in domestic disputes, providing directions to tourists, and finding lost children.

Along with firefighters, police officers are among the first public servants called to conduct search and rescue operations. This particular duty adds considerably to the

YOU BE THE POLICE COMMISSIONER
Occupational Hazard

THE SITUATION Starting in September 2011, demonstrators protesting economic inequality "occupied" dozens of American cities, sometimes in numbers reaching the thousands. Some of these protests resulted in violent clashes with police, but the Occupy Boston movement has been, for the most part, peaceful. The Boston protesters agreed to limit their activities to a "safe area" in downtown's Dewey Square, thus avoiding confrontation with law enforcement.

One day in October, however, a group of protestors sought to block traffic on the North Washington Street Bridge. Then, that evening, about two hundred members of Occupy Boston moved into the Greenway—a city park that had been specifically forbidden to them by city officials. At about 1:20 A.M., Boston police officers surrounded the Greenway, and a police official, using a bullhorn, asked the demonstrators to disperse. They responded with chants of defiance. The police official gave what he promised was a final warning. The protestors refused to budge.

THE LAW A Boston ordinance gives police the legal authority to arrest anyone in the Greenway after 11 P.M. and charge him or her with trespassing and unlawful assembly.

YOUR DECISION Suppose you are the Boston police commissioner watching the events at the Greenway. Do you give the order for your officers to move in and arrest the protestors? What are the pros and cons of taking such an action? Although the demonstrators are technically breaking the law, they do not appear to be threatening any violence against persons or property. Furthermore, you are well aware of the public relations risks of a confrontation. The protestors are well armed with video-recording devices, and negative media coverage of seemingly heavy-handed police tactics would create a backlash against you and your department.

[To see how the Boston police commissioner reacted in this situation, go to Example 4.1 in Appendix B.]

dangers faced by law enforcement agents (discussed in more detail in Chapter 5). As we will also see in the next section, a majority of police departments have adopted a strategy called *community policing* that requires officers to provide assistance in areas that are not, at first glance, directly related to law enforcement.[9]

PREVENTING CRIME

Perhaps the most controversial responsibility of the police is to *prevent* crime. According to Jerome Skolnick, co-director of the Center for Research in Crime and Justice at the New York University School of Law, there are two predictable public responses when crime rates begin to rise in a community. The first is to punish convicted criminals with stricter laws and more severe penalties. The second is to demand that the police keep crimes from occurring in the first place. Is it, in fact, possible for the police to "prevent" crimes? The strongest response that Professor Skolnick is willing to give to this question is "maybe."[10]

A Los Angeles police officer oversees community efforts to clean up trash and graffiti. What are the benefits and drawbacks of having law enforcement agents provide services that do not directly involve preventing and solving crimes?

Monica Almeida/*New York Times*/Redux Pictures

On a limited basis, police can certainly prevent some crimes. If a rapist is dissuaded from attacking a solitary woman because a patrol car is cruising the area, then the police officer behind the wheel has prevented a crime. Furthermore, exemplary police work can have a measurable effect. "Quite simply, cops count," says William Bratton, who has directed police departments in Boston, Los Angeles, and New York. "[T]he quickest way to impact crime is with a well-led, managed, and appropriately resourced police force."[11] In general, however, the deterrent effects of police presence are unclear. Carl Klockars has written that the "war on crime" is a war that the police cannot win because they cannot control the factors—such as unemployment, poverty, immorality, inequality, political change, and lack of educational opportunities—that contribute to criminal behavior in the first place.[12]

PRESERVING THE PEACE

To a certain extent, the fourth responsibility of the police, that of preserving the peace, is related to preventing crime. Police have the legal authority to use the power of arrest, or even force, in situations in which no crime has yet occurred, but might occur in the immediate future.

> **"That's the only thing that made me feel safe last night when I came home from work."**
>
> —**Penny Baily,** resident of Indianapolis, commenting on the police car patrolling her neighborhood

In the words of James Q. Wilson, the police's peacekeeping role (which Wilson believed to be the most important role of law enforcement officers) often takes on a pattern of simply "handling the situation."[13] For example, when police officers arrive on the scene of a loud late-night house party, they may feel the need to disperse the party and even arrest some of the partygoers for disorderly conduct. By their actions, the officers have lessened the chances of serious and violent crimes taking place later in the evening. The same principle is often used when dealing with domestic disputes, which, if escalated, can lead to homicide. Such situations are in need of, to use Wilson's terminology again, "fixing up," and police can use the power of arrest, or threat, or coercion, or sympathy, to do just that.

The basis of Wilson and fellow criminologist George Kelling's zero-tolerance theory is similar: street disorder—such as public drunkenness, urination, and loitering—signals to both law-abiding citizens and criminals that the law is not being enforced and therefore leads to more violent crime. Hence, if police preserve the peace and "crack down" on the minor crimes that make up street disorder, they will in fact be preventing serious crimes that would otherwise occur in the future.[14]

SELFASSESSMENT
Fill in the blanks and check your answers on page 123.
Both the public and law enforcement officers themselves believe that the police's primary job is to _____ laws. A large and crucial part of policing, however, involves providing _____ such as directing traffic. The ability of the police to actually _____ crime is a matter of great debate, and some experts believe that the most important role of a police officer is to _____ the peace.

A SHORT HISTORY OF THE AMERICAN POLICE

Although modern society relies on law enforcement officers to control and prevent crime, in the early days of this country, police services had little to do with crime control. The policing efforts in the first American cities were directed toward controlling certain groups of people (mostly slaves and Native Americans), delivering goods, regulating activities such as buying and selling in the town market, maintaining health and sanitation, controlling gambling and vice, and managing livestock and other animals.[15] Furthermore, these police services were for the most part performed by volunteers, as a police force was an expensive proposition. Often, the volunteers were organized using the **night watch system,** brought over from England by colonists in the seventeenth century. Under this system, all physically fit males were required to offer their services to protect the community on a rotating nightly basis.[16]

Night Watch System An early form of American law enforcement in which volunteers patrolled their community from dusk to dawn to keep the peace.

THE EVOLUTION OF AMERICAN LAW ENFORCEMENT

The night watch system did not ask much of its volunteers, who were often required to do little more than loudly announce the time and the state of the weather. Furthermore, many citizens avoided their duties by hiring others to "go on watch" in their place, and those who did serve frequently spent their time on watch sleeping and drinking alcohol.[17] Eventually, as the populations of American cities grew in the late eighteenth and early nineteenth centuries, so did the need for public order and the willingness to devote public resources to the establishment of formal police forces. The night watch system was insufficient to meet these new demands, and its demise was inevitable.

EARLY POLICE DEPARTMENTS In 1833, Philadelphia became the first American city to employ both day and night watchmen. Five years later, working from a model established by British home secretary Sir Robert "Bobbie" Peel in London, Boston officials formed the first American organized police department, consisting of six full-time officers. In 1844, New York City laid the foundation for the modern police department by combining its day and night watches under the control of a single police chief. By the onset of the Civil War in 1861, a number of American cities, including Baltimore, Boston, Chicago, Cincinnati, New Orleans, and Philadelphia, had similarly consolidated police departments, modeled on the Metropolitan Police of London.[18]

THE POLITICAL ERA Like their modern counterparts, many early police officers were hard working, honest, and devoted to serving and protecting the public. On the whole, however, in the words of historian Samuel Walker, "The quality of American police service in the nineteenth century could hardly have been worse."[19] This poor quality can be attributed to the fact that the recruitment and promotion of police officers were intricately tied to the politics of the day. Police officers received their jobs as a result of political connections, not because of any particular skills or knowledge. Whichever political party was in power in a given city would hire its own cronies to run the police department. Consequently, the police were often more concerned with serving the interests of the political bosses than with protecting the citizens.[20]

Corruption was rampant during this *political era* of policing, which lasted roughly from 1840 to 1930. Police salaries were relatively low, and many police officers saw their positions as opportunities to make extra income through any number of illegal activities. Bribery was common, as police would use their close proximity to the people to request "favors," which went into the police officers' own pockets or into the coffers of the local political party as "contributions."[21] This was known as the **patronage system,** or the "spoils system," because to the political victors went the spoils.

THE REFORM ERA The abuses of the political era of policing did not go unnoticed. Led by August Vollmer, the police chief of Berkeley, California, from 1905 to 1932, advocates of dramatic changes in American law enforcement initiated the *reform era* in American policing.[22] Along with his protégé O. W. Wilson, Vollmer promoted a style of policing known as the **professional model.** Under the professional model, police chiefs, who had been little more than figureheads during the political era, took more control over their departments. A key to these efforts was the reorganization of police departments in many major cities. To improve their control over operations, police chiefs began to add midlevel positions to the force. These new officers, known as majors or assistant chiefs, could develop and implement crime-fighting strategies and more closely supervise individual officers. Police chiefs also tried to consolidate their power by bringing large areas of a city under their control so that no local ward, neighborhood, or politician could easily influence a single police department.

The professionalism trend benefited law enforcement agents in a number of ways. Salaries and working conditions improved, and for the first time, women and members of minority groups were given opportunities—albeit limited—to serve.[23] At the same time, police administrators controlled officers to a much greater extent than in the past, expecting them to meet targets for arrests and other numerical indicators that were seen as barometers of effectiveness.

Any contact with citizens that did not explicitly relate to law enforcement was considered "social work" and was discouraged.[24] As police expert Chris Braiden puts it, American police officers were expected to "park their brains at the door of the stationhouse" and simply "follow orders like a robot."[25] The isolation of officers from the public was made complete by an overreliance on the patrol car, a relatively new technological innovation at the time. In the political era, officers walked their beats, interacting with citizens. In the reform era, they were expected to stay inside their "rolling fortresses," driving from one call to the next without wasting time or resources on public relations.[26]

Learning Objective 2 Tell how the patronage system affected policing.

Patronage System A form of corruption in which the political party in power hires and promotes police officers, receiving job-related "favors" in return.

Professional Model A style of policing advocated by August Vollmer and O. W. Wilson that emphasizes centralized police organizations, increased use of technology, and a limitation of police discretion through regulations and guidelines.

A horse-drawn police wagon used by the New York City Police Department, circa 1886. Why might this new form of transportation have represented a "revolution" for early American police forces?

Corbis/Bettmann

Project 54: Dura Tech, USA Inc.

High-Tech Cop Cars

When patrol cars came into common use by police departments in the 1930s, they changed the face of American policing. Eight decades later, the technology associated with patrol cars continues to evolve. Project 54, a voice-recognition system developed at the University of New Hampshire, allows police officers to "multitask" without having to divert their attention from the road or take a hand off the wheel. The officer simply presses a button, and all the technological equipment in the car becomes voice activated. Four Andrea digital array microphones positioned in the cab of the automobile cancel all noise except the sound of the officer's voice. So, for example, if the officer witnesses a hit-and-run accident, he or she simply says the word "pursuit" to activate the automobile's siren and flashing lights. Then the officer can call for an ambulance and run a check on the suspect's license plate—all by voice command.

Other recent innovations include Automatic License Plate Recognition, a three-camera computer-operated system that performs a "20-millisecond" background check on every license plate it sees, and the StarChase launcher, a small, laser-guided cannon that shoots a small, sticky radio transmitter at a fleeing vehicle. Once the offending car has been "tagged" with this device, police can track the fugitive at a safe distance without the need for a dangerous, high-speed pursuit.

THINKING ABOUT POLICE AUTOMOBILE TECHNOLOGY:

Approximately 75 percent of all patrol cars in the United States are equipped with on-board computers. How might these computers pose a danger to the police officer driving the car and to other drivers or pedestrians? How does the University of New Hampshire's Project 54 help alleviate this danger?

THE COMMUNITY ERA The drawbacks of the professional model became evident in the 1960s, one of the most turbulent decades in American history. Unrest associated with the civil rights movement and protests against the Vietnam War (1964–1975) led to a series of clashes—often violent—between police and certain segments of society. By the early 1970s, many observers believed that poor policing was contributing to the national turmoil. The National Advisory Commission on Civil Disorders stated bluntly that poor relations between the police and African American communities were partly to blame for the violence that plagued many of those communities.[27] In striving for professionalism, the police appeared to have lost touch with the citizens they were supposed to be serving. To repair their damaged relations with a large segment of the population, police would have to rediscover their community roots.

The result of this rediscovery was the *community era* of American policing. Starting in the 1970s, most large-city police departments established entire units devoted to community relations, implementing programs that ranged from summer recreation activities for inner-city youths to "officer-friendly" referral operations that encouraged citizens to come to the police with their crime concerns.

At the same time, the country was hit by a crime wave. Thus, police administrators were forced to combine efforts to improve community relations with aggressive and innovative crime-fighting strategies. As we will see in Chapter 5 when we discuss these strategies in more depth, the police began to focus on stopping crimes before they occur, rather than concentrating only on solving crimes that have already been committed. A dedication to such proactive strategies led to widespread acceptance of *community policing* in the 1980s and 1990s. Community policing is based on the notion that meaningful interaction between officers and citizens will lead to a partnership in preventing and fighting crime. (See Figure 4.1 below for an overview of the three eras of policing described in this section.)

Intelligence-Led Policing
An approach that measures the risk of criminal behavior associated with certain individuals or locations so as to predict when and where such criminal behavior is most likely to occur in the future.

POLICING TODAY: INTELLIGENCE, TERRORISM, AND TECHNOLOGY

To effectively prevent crime using the community policing model, police administrators needed to better understand crime patterns. To better understand crime patterns, police administrators needed more information about those patterns. As a result, the process of collecting, analyzing, and mapping such crime data has become a hallmark of policing in the twenty-first century.

INTELLIGENCE-LED POLICING "Humans are not nearly as random as we think," says Jeff Brantingham, an anthropologist at the University of California, Los Angeles. "In a sense, crime is just a physical process, and if you can explain how offenders move and how they mix with their victims, you can understand an incredible amount."[28] Brantingham and his colleagues are working on computer programs that will be able to predict when and where crimes are likely to occur. This approach is known as predictive policing, or **intelligence-led policing,** because it relies on data—or intelligence—concerning past crime patterns to predict future crime patterns.

Learning Objective 3 Explain how intelligence-led policing works and how it benefits modern police departments.

FIGURE 4.1 The Three Eras of American Policing

George L. Kelling and Mark H. Moore have separated the history of policing in the United States from 1840 to 2000 into three distinct periods. Below is a brief summarization of these three eras.

1840 1850 1860 1870 1880 1890 1900 1910 1920 1930 1940 1950 1960 1970 1980 1990 2000

	The Political Era	The Reform Era	The Community Era
Time Period	1840 to 1930	1930 to 1980	1980 to 2000
Primary Function of Police	Provide range of social services to citizenry	Control crime	Continue to control crime while providing a broader range of social services
Organization	Decentralized	Centralized	Decentralized, with specialized units and task forces
Police-Community Relationship	Intimate	Professional and distant	Return to intimate
Tactics	Patrolling neighborhoods on foot	Patrolling neighborhoods in cars, rapid response to emergency calls for service (911 calls)	Foot patrolling, problem solving, and public relations
Strategic Goal	Satisfy the needs of citizens and political bosses	Control crime	Improve the quality of life of citizens
Strategic Weakness	Widespread police corruption and brutality	Lack of communication with citizens fostered mistrust and community violence (riots)	An overreliance on police officers to solve all of society's problems

Sources: Adapted from George L. Kelling and Mark H. Moore, "From Political to Reform to Community: The Evolving Strategy of Police," in *Community Policing: Rhetoric or Reality,* ed. Jack R. Greene and Stephen D. Mastrofski (New York: Praeger Publishers, 1991), 14–15, 22–23; plus authors' updates. Reproduced with permission of Greenwood Publishing Group, Inc., Westport, Connecticut.

For example, suppose that a city has been plagued by random gunfire each New Year's Eve. In any given year, police administrators could determine where such incidents had occurred in previous years and send more police officers to those areas. In theory, the police would then be better able to deter random gunfire and respond more quickly when shots were fired.[29] This kind of intelligence-led policing should also help police administrators do "more with less," an important consideration as police budgets shrink around the country.[30] Thus, in this example, instead of blanketing the city with officers on New Year's Eve, police administrators would only need to deploy a small force in the areas most likely to experience gunfire.

THE CHALLENGES OF ANTI-TERRORISM If the importance of intelligence-based policing was not evident before September 11, 2001, the tragic events of that day made it clear that the nation's law enforcement agencies could not simply react to the crime of terrorism. With such a high toll in human lives, such attacks needed to be prevented. Within two years of September 11, about 90 percent of the nation's local police departments and sheriffs' offices serving large cities (250,000 residents or more) had written plans to deal with terrorist attacks.[31] Today, a similar percentage of these agencies are also gathering intelligence related to terrorism,[32] a task that represents a significant shift for the local law enforcement community. All police officers in the country are now expected to prepare for a terrorist attack in their communities, and counterterrorism has become part of the day-to-day law enforcement routine. (See the feature *Anti-Terrorism in Action—Under Suspicion* below to learn about a particular aspect of these daily responsibilities.)

This transition has not always been smooth. Many local police departments have had to shift personnel from traditional crime units, such as antigang or white-collar crime, to counterterrorism. Limited funds are also an issue. Raymond Kelly, police com-

ANTI-TERRORISM IN ACTION

UNDER SUSPICION

First, the unidentified male walking around the harbor in Newport Beach, California, took several photographs of the Orange County Sheriff's Department's fireboat and the Balboa Ferry with his cell phone camera. Then he made a phone call, walked to his car, and returned five minutes later to take more pictures. Next, he met another person, with whom he watched boat traffic. Finally, another adult with two children joined the pair, and the group boarded the ferry.

Was this behavior suspicious? Apparently, it was suspicious enough to be noted by a local law enforcement officer and filed as Suspicious Activity Report (SAR) NO3821, to be passed along to the federal government. The goal of the SAR program is to have officers from every local police and sheriff's department provide tips about potential terrorism activity to one of seventy-two fusion centers across the United States. At these fusion centers,

federal terrorism experts examine the reports to determine if any actual threat exists. Such examinations rarely lead to further legal action. The first 161,000 recorded SARs resulted in only five arrests, none of which had to do with terrorism. "Ninety-nine percent don't pan out or lead to anything," said one Federal Bureau of Investigation (FBI) special agent of the information from local police officers. "But we're happy to wade through these things."

FOR CRITICAL ANALYSIS The federal government's definition of *suspicious activity* is "observed behavior reasonably indicative of pre-operational planning related to terrorism or other criminal activity." What is your opinion of this definition? Is it too broad? Why do you think the actions of the Newport Beach suspect described above resulted in an SAR? What potential for abuse, if any, do you see in the SAR program?

missioner of New York, has testified to the "huge expenses" of counterterrorism and intelligence actitivies.[33] Although the federal government provided $31 billion in grants to state and local governments for homeland security between 2003 and 2010, many law enforcement agencies continue to rely on already-stretched-thin city budgets to cover the extra costs of anti-terrorism activities.[34]

LAW ENFORCEMENT 2.0 Fortunately, just as more intelligence has become crucial to police work, the means available to gather such intelligence have also increased greatly. As you will see in Chapter 14, nearly every successful anti-terrorism investigation has relied on information gathered from the Internet. Furthermore, traditional criminals are now frequently getting caught on the Web. Police in South Charleston, West Virginia, arrested six young men who photographed themselves destroying a local hotel room and posted the incriminating pictures on various Twitter accounts. Utah police discovered material on a convicted sex offender's MySpace account that proved forbidden contact with two youths. Memphis detectives were able to apprehend two burglars who had stolen alcohol from a restaurant when one of them wrote on Facebook, "I'd like to collect some of the booty we liberated Sunday, if there's any left."

According to a recent poll, more than 60 percent of American law enforcement agencies use social networking sites during crime investigations. In addition, 40 percent employ social media such as Twitter for community outreach and to notify the public of crime problems.[35]

Some law enforcement veterans are concerned that the "art" of policing is being lost in an era of intelligence-led policing and increased reliance on social media technology. "If it becomes all about the science," says Los Angeles Police Department deputy chief Michael Downing, "I worry we'll lose the important nuances."[36] As the remainder of this chapter and the two that follow show, however, the human element continues to dominate all aspects of policing in America.

SELFASSESSMENT

Fill in the blanks and check your answers on page 123.

During the _____ era of American policing, which lasted roughly from 1840 to 1930, police officers used the _____ system to enrich themselves. The _____ era, which followed, saw the modernization of our nation's law enforcement system through innovations like Vollmer and Wilson's _____ model of policing. Following the national turmoil of the 1960s and early 1970s, _____ era strategies encouraged a partnership between citizens and the police. Today, _____-led policing efforts attempt to make law enforcement agencies more efficient and better able to prevent future _____ attacks.

RECRUITMENT AND TRAINING: BECOMING A POLICE OFFICER

In 1961, police expert James H. Chenoweth commented that the methods used to hire police officers had changed little since the days of the first American police forces.[37] The past half-century, however, has seen a number of improvements in the way that police administrators handle the task of **recruitment,** or the development of a pool of qualified applicants from which to select new officers. Efforts have been made to diversify police rolls, and recruits in most police departments undergo a substantial array of tests and screens—discussed on the next page—to determine their aptitude. Furthermore,

Recruitment The process by which law enforcement agencies develop a pool of qualified applicants from which to select new members.

annual starting salaries that can exceed $70,000, along with the opportunities offered by an interesting profession in the public service field, have attracted a wide variety of applicants to police work. (To learn what a police officer can expect to earn in his or her first year on the job, see Figure 4.2 below.)

BASIC REQUIREMENTS

The selection process involves a number of steps, and each police department has a different method of choosing candidates. Most agencies, however, require at a minimum that a police officer:

- Be a U.S. citizen.
- Not have been convicted of a felony.
- Have or be eligible to have a driver's license in the state where the department is located.
- Be at least twenty-one years of age.
- Meet weight and eyesight requirements.

In addition, few departments will accept candidates older than forty-five years of age.

BACKGROUND CHECKS AND TESTS Beyond these minimum requirements, police departments usually engage in extensive background checks, including (a) drug tests, (b) a review of the applicant's educational, military, and driving records, (c) credit checks, (d) interviews with spouses, acquaintances, and previous employers, (e) and a background search to determine whether the applicant has been convicted of any criminal acts.[38] Police agencies generally require certain physical attributes in applicants: normally, they must be able to pass a physical agility or fitness test. (For an example of one such test, see Figure 4.3 on the facing page.)

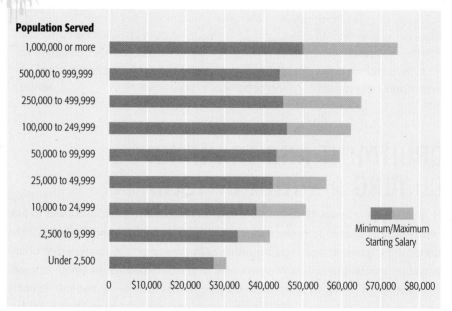

FIGURE 4.2 Average Annual Salary for Entry-Level Officers by Size of Population Served

Source: Bureau of Justice Statistics, *Local Police Departments, 2007* (Washington, D.C.: U.S. Department of Justice, December 2010), Table 7, page 12.

FIGURE 4.3 Physical Agility Exam for the Henrico County (Virginia) Division of Police

Those applying for the position of police officer must finish this physical agility exam within 3 minutes, 30 seconds. During the test, applicants are required to wear the equipment (with a total weight of between 9 and 13 pounds) worn by patrol officers, which includes the police uniform, leather gun belt, firearm, baton, portable radio, and ballistics vest.

1. Applicant begins test seated in a police vehicle, door closed, seat belt fastened.
2. Applicant must exit vehicle and jump or climb a six-foot barrier.
3. Applicant then completes a one-quarter-mile run or walk, making various turns along the way, to simulate a pursuit run.
4. Applicant must jump a simulated five-foot culvert/ditch.
5. Applicant must drag a "human simulator" (dummy) weighing 175 pounds a distance of 50 feet (to simulate a situation in which an officer is required to pull or carry an injured person to safety).
6. Applicant must draw his or her weapon and fire five rounds with the strong hand and five rounds with the weak hand.

EDUCATIONAL REQUIREMENTS One of the most dramatic differences between today's police recruits and those of several generations ago is their level of education. In the 1920s, when August Vollmer began promoting the need for higher education in police officers, few had attended college. Today, 82 percent of all local police departments require at least a high school diploma, and 9 percent require a degree from a two-year college.[39] Recruits with college or university experience are generally thought to have an advantage in hiring and promotion.

Not all police observers believe that education is a necessity for police officers, however. In the words of one police officer, "effective street cops learn their skills on the job, not in a classroom."[40] By emphasizing a college degree, say some, police departments discourage those who would make solid officers but lack the education necessary to apply for positions in law enforcement.

TRAINING

If an applicant successfully navigates the application process, he or she will be hired on a *probationary* basis. During this **probationary period,** which can last from six to eighteen months depending on the department, the recruit is in jeopardy of being fired without cause if he or she proves inadequate to the challenges of police work. Almost every state requires that police recruits pass through a training period while on probation. During this time, they are taught the basics of police work and are under constant supervision by superiors. The training period usually has two components: the police academy and field training. On average, local police departments serving populations of 250,000 or more require 1,648 hours of training—972 hours in the classroom and 676 hours in the field.[41]

ACADEMY TRAINING The *police academy,* run by either the state or a police agency, provides recruits with a controlled, militarized environment in which they receive their introduction to the world of the police officer. They are taught the laws of search, seizure, arrest, and interrogation; how and when to use weapons; the procedures of securing a crime scene and interviewing witnesses; first aid; self-defense; and other essentials of police work. Nine in ten police academies also provide terrorism-related training to teach recruits how to respond to terrorist incidents, including those involving weapons of mass destruction.[42] Academy instructors evaluate the recruits' performance and send intermittent progress reports to police administrators.

Probationary Period A period of time at the beginning of a police officer's career during which she or he may be fired without cause.

Learning Objective 4 Identify the differences between the police academy and field training as learning tools for recruits.

A recruit performs pushups under duress at the Cleveland Police Academy. Why are police academies an important part of the learning process for a potential police officer?

Marvin Fong/Cleveland Plain Dealer/Landov

IN THE FIELD **Field training** takes place outside the confines of the police academy. A recruit is paired with an experienced police officer known as a field training officer (FTO). The goal of field training is to help rookies apply the concepts they have learned in the academy "to the streets," with the FTO playing a supervisory role to make sure that nothing goes awry. While the academy introduces recruits to the formal rules of police work, field training gives the rookies their first taste of the informal rules. In fact, the initial advice to recruits from some FTOs is often along the lines of "O.K., kid. Forget everything you learned in the classroom. You're in the real world now." Nonetheless, the academy is a critical component in the learning process, as it provides rookies with a road map to the job.

SELFASSESSMENT

Fill in the blanks and check your answers on page 123.

Most police agencies require that recruits be at least _____-_____ years of age and have no prior _____ convictions. During the _____ period, which can last as long as eighteen months, a recruit will attend a _____ _____ to learn the rules of police work in an institutional setting. Then, she or he will leave the classroom and partner with an experienced officer for _____ _____.

WOMEN AND MINORITIES IN POLICING TODAY

Field Training The segment of a police recruit's training in which he or she is removed from the classroom and placed on the beat, under the supervision of a senior officer.

Discrimination The illegal use of characteristics such as gender or race by employers when making hiring or promotion decisions.

Affirmative Action A hiring or promotion policy favoring those groups, such as women, African Americans, or Hispanics, who have suffered from discrimination in the past or continue to suffer from discrimination.

For many years, the typical American police officer was white and male. As recently as 1968, African Americans represented only 5 percent of all sworn officers in the United States, and the percentage of "women in blue" was even lower.[43] Only within the past thirty years has this situation been addressed, and only within the past twenty years have many police departments actively tried to recruit women, African Americans, Hispanics, Asian Americans, and members of other minority groups. The result, as you will see, has been a steady though not spectacular increase in the diversity of the nation's police forces. When it comes to issues of gender, race, and ethnicity, however, mere statistics rarely tell the entire story.

ANTIDISCRIMINATION LAW AND AFFIRMATIVE ACTION

In large measure, external forces have driven law enforcement agencies to increase the number of female and minority recruits. The 1964 Civil Rights Act and its 1972 amendments guaranteed members of minority groups and women equal access to jobs in law enforcement. The Equal Employment Opportunity Commission (EEOC), established in 1965, ensures fairness in police hiring practices. The United States Supreme Court has also ruled on several occasions that **discrimination** by law enforcement agencies violates federal law.[44] In legal terms, discrimination occurs when hiring and promotion decisions are based on individual characteristics such as gender or race, and not on job-related factors.

Since the early 1970s, numerous law enforcement agencies have instituted **affirmative action** programs to increase the diversity of their employees. These programs are designed to give women and members of minority groups certain advantages in hiring and promotion to remedy the effects of past discrimination and prevent future discrimination. Often, affirmative action programs are established voluntarily. Sometimes, however, they are the result of lawsuits brought by employees or potential employees who believe that the employer has discriminated against them. In such instances, if the court finds that discrimination did occur, it will implement a *consent decree* to remedy the situation. Under a consent decree, the law enforcement agency often agrees to meet certain numerical goals in hiring women and members of minority groups. If it fails to meet these goals, it is punished with a fine or some other sanction.[45]

WORKING WOMEN: GENDER AND LAW ENFORCEMENT

Learning Objective 5 Describe the challenges facing women who choose law enforcement as a career.

In 1987, about 7.6 percent of all local police officers were women. Twenty years later, that percentage had risen to almost 12 percent.[46] That increase seems less impressive, however, when one considers that women make up more than half of the population of the United States, meaning that they are severely underrepresented in law enforcement.

ADDED SCRUTINY There are several reasons for the low levels of women serving as police officers. First, relatively few women hold leadership positions in American policing. More than half of this country's large police departments have no women in their highest ranks,[47] and fewer than 1 percent of the police chiefs in the United States are women.[48] Consequently, female police officers have few superiors who might be able to mentor them in what can be a hostile work environment. In addition to the dangers and pressures facing all law enforcement agents, which we will discuss in the next chapter, women must deal with an added layer of scrutiny. Many male police officers feel that their female counterparts are mentally soft, physically weak, and generally unsuited for the rigors of the job. At the same time, male officers often try to protect female officers by keeping them out of hazardous situations, thereby denying the women the opportunity to prove themselves.[49]

TOKENISM Women in law enforcement also face the problem of *tokenism*, or the belief that they have been hired or promoted to fulfill diversity requirements and have not earned their positions. Tokenism creates pressure to prove the stereotypes wrong. As one female officer told researcher Teresa Lynn Wertsch:

> The guys can view you as a sex object instead of a professional. It makes me try harder to put up more fronts and play more of the macho, boy role rather than accept that I am a female. . . . You can't be meek or mild, too quiet. You can't be too loud or boisterous because then you would be a dike, too masculine. I wish it didn't have to be this way, but you're either a bitch, a dike, or a slut.[50]

In fact, most of the negative attitudes toward women police officers are based on prejudice rather than actual experience. A number of studies have shown that there is very little difference between the performances of men and women in uniform.[51] (For more on this topic, see the feature *Myth versus Reality—Women Make Bad Cops* on the following page.)

MINORITY REPORT: RACE AND ETHNICITY IN LAW ENFORCEMENT

As Figure 4.4 on page 113 shows, like women, members of minority groups have been slowly increasing their presence in local police departments since the late 1980s. Specifically, African American officers make up about 12 percent of the nation's police officers; Hispanic officers, about 10 percent; and other minority groups such as Asians, American Indians, and Pacific Islanders, about 3 percent.[52] By some measures, members of minority groups are better

Since the formation of the earliest police departments in the nineteenth century, policing has been seen as "man's work." Only men were considered to have the physical strength necessary to deal with the dangers of the street.

THE MYTH The perception that women are not physically strong enough to be effective law enforcement officers prevails both in the public mind and within police forces themselves. Criminologist Susan Martin has found that policewomen are under "constant pressure to demonstrate their competence and effectiveness vis-à-vis their male counterparts." One female police officer describes her experience:

> I got a call. They send another male officer and then another male officer. The attitude is—get a guy. I'm there with the one male officer and when the other guy shows up, the first male officer says to the second, this is right in front of me—"I'm glad you came."

THE REALITY In fact, a number of studies have shown that policewomen can be as effective as men in most situations, and often more so. Citizens appear to prefer dealing with a female police officer rather than a male during service calls—especially those that involve domestic violence. In general, policewomen are less aggressive and more likely to reduce the potential for a violent situation by relying on verbal skills rather than their authority as law enforcement agents. According to a study conducted by the National Center for Women and Policing, payouts in lawsuits for

claims of brutality and misconduct involving male officers exceed those involving females by a ratio of 43 to 1. Furthermore, female police officers are certainly capable of acts of bravery and physical prowess—the names of more than 250 women are included on the National Law Enforcement Memorial in Washington, D.C.

FOR CRITICAL ANALYSIS Do you believe that female police officers can be just as effective as men in protecting citizens from criminal behavior? Why or why not?

A female member of the Los Angeles Police Department stands guard outside the county courthouse during a high-profile trial.
Kim Kulish/Corbis

represented than women in policing. Cities such as Detroit and Washington have local police departments that closely match their civilian populations in terms of diversity, and in recent years, a majority of police recruits in New York City have been members of minority groups. In other areas, such as promotion, minorities in law enforcement continue to seek parity.[53]

DOUBLE MARGINALITY According to Peter C. Moskos, a professor at the John Jay College of Criminal Justice in New York, "black and white police officers remain two distinct shades of blue, with distinct attitudes toward each other and the communities they serve."[54] While that may be true, minority officers generally report that they have good relationships with their white fellow officers.[55] Often, though, members of minority groups in law enforcement—particularly African Americans and Hispanics—do face the problem of **double marginality.** This term refers to a situation in which minority officers are viewed with suspicion under two sets of circumstances:

1. White police officers believe that minority officers will give members of their own race or ethnicity better treatment on the streets.
2. Those same minority officers face hostility from members of their own community who are under the impression that black and Hispanic officers are traitors to their race or ethnicity.

Double Marginality The double suspicion that minority law enforcement officers face from their white colleagues and from members of the minority community to which they belong.

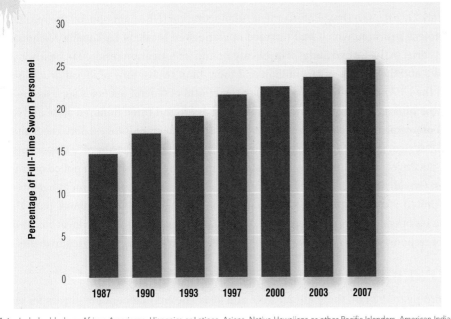

Note: Includes blacks or African Americans, Hispanics or Latinos, Asians, Native Hawaiians or other Pacific Islanders, American Indians, Alaska Natives, and persons identifying two or more races.
Source: Bureau of Justice Statistics, *Local Police Departments, 2007* (Washington, D.C.: U.S. Department of Justice, December 2010), Figure 9, page 14.

In response, minority officers may feel the need to act more harshly toward minority offenders to prove that they are not biased in favor of their own racial or ethnic group.[56]

THE BENEFITS OF A DIVERSE POLICE FORCE In 1986, Supreme Court justice John Paul Stevens spoke for many in the criminal justice system when he observed that "an integrated police force could develop a better relationship [with a racially diverse citizenry] and therefore do a more effective job of maintaining law and order than a force composed of white officers."[57] Indeed, despite the effects of double marginality, African American officers may have more credibility in a predominantly black neighborhood than white police officers, leading to better community-police relations and a greater ability to solve and prevent crimes.

Certainly, in the Mexican American communities typical of border states such as Arizona, California, and Texas, many Hispanic officers are able to gather information that would be very difficult for non-Spanish-speaking officers to collect. Finally, however, the best argument for a diverse police force is that members of minority groups represent a broad source of talent in this country, and such talent can only enhance the overall effectiveness of American law enforcement.

SELFASSESSMENT

Fill in the blanks and check your answers on page 123.

In the past, women and members of minority groups in law enforcement have suffered from _____, or hiring practices that exclude potential employees based on their gender, race, or ethnicity. To remedy this situation, many law enforcement agencies have instituted _____ _____ programs to diversify their workforces. In some instances, a court will issue a _____ _____, under which an agency agrees to reach certain numerical hiring goals or be penalized.

PUBLIC AND PRIVATE LAW ENFORCEMENT

On July 21, 2011, the Drug Enforcement Administration (DEA) announced the resolution of Project Delirium, which had targeted operations of Mexico's La Familia Michoacana drug cartel in the United States. The twenty-month investigation resulted in nearly 20,000 arrests and the seizure of $62 million and more than twelve tons of illegal drugs. Along with the DEA, Project Delirium relied on the efforts of federal agencies such as the FBI and the Internal Revenue Service (IRS), as well as around three hundred state and local law enforcement agencies, including the Texas Department of Public Safety, the Santa Fe (New Mexico) Police Department, and the El Paso County (Texas) Sheriff's Department.

As Project Delirium shows, Americans are served by a multitude of police organizations. Overall, there are about 18,000 public (government) law enforcement agencies in the United States, employing more than 1.1 million people.[58] For the most part, these agencies operate on three different levels: local, state, and federal. Each level has its own set of responsibilities, which we shall discuss starting with local police departments.

MUNICIPAL LAW ENFORCEMENT AGENCIES

According to the FBI, there are 2.9 state and local law enforcement employees for every 1,000 citizens in the United States.[59] This average somewhat masks the discrepancies between the police forces in urban and rural America. The majority of all police officers work in small and medium-sized police departments (see Figure 4.5 on the left). While the New York City Police Department employs about 36,000 police personnel, 50 percent of all local police departments have ten or fewer law enforcement officers.[60]

Of the three levels of law enforcement, municipal agencies have the broadest authority to apprehend criminal suspects, maintain order, and provide services to the community. Whether the local officer is part of a large force or the only law enforcement officer in the community, he or she is usually responsible for a wide spectrum of duties, from responding to noise complaints to investigating homicides.

SHERIFFS AND COUNTY LAW ENFORCEMENT

The **sheriff** is a very important figure in American law enforcement. Almost every one of the more than 3,000 counties in the United States (except those in Alaska) has a sheriff. In every state except Rhode Island and Hawaii, sheriffs are elected by members of the community for two- or four-year terms and are paid a salary set by the state legislature or county board. As elected officials who do not necessarily need a background in law enforcement, modern sheriffs resemble their counterparts from the political era of policing in many ways. Simply stated, the sheriff is also a politician.

SIZE AND RESPONSIBILITY OF SHERIFFS' DEPARTMENTS Like municipal police forces, sheriffs' departments vary in size. The largest is the Los Angeles County Sheriff's Department, with more than 9,400 deputies. Of the 3,063 sheriffs' departments in the country, thirteen employ more than 1,000 officers, while forty-five have only one.[61]

Most sheriffs' departments are assigned their duties by state law. These duties encompass a wide variety of criminal and civil matters. About 80 percent of all sheriffs' departments have the primary responsibility for investigating violent crimes in their jurisdictions. Other common responsibilities of a sheriff's department include the following:

- Investigating drug crimes.
- Maintaining the county jail.

Sheriff The primary law enforcement officer in a county, usually elected to the post by a popular vote.

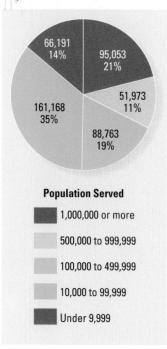

FIGURE 4.5 Full-Time Police Personnel, by Size of Population Served

66,191
14%

95,053
21%

51,973
11%

161,168
35%

88,763
19%

Population Served

- 1,000,000 or more
- 500,000 to 999,999
- 100,000 to 499,999
- 10,000 to 99,999
- Under 9,999

Source: Bureau of Justice Statistics, *Local Police Departments, 2007* (Washington, D.C.: U.S. Department of Justice, December 2010), Table 3, page 9.

- Carrying out civil and criminal processes within county lines, such as serving eviction notices and court summonses.
- Keeping order in the county courthouse.
- Collecting taxes.
- Enforcing orders of the court, such as overseeing the isolation of a jury during a trial.[62]

It is easy to confuse sheriffs' departments and local police departments. Both law enforcement agencies are responsible for many of the same tasks, including crime investigation and routine patrol. There are differences, however. Sheriffs' departments are more likely to be involved in county court and jail operations and to perform certain services such as search and rescue. Local police departments, for their part, are more likely to perform traffic-related functions than are sheriffs' departments.[63]

THE COUNTY CORONER Another elected official on the county level is the **coroner,** or medical examiner. Duties vary from county to county, but the coroner has a general mandate to investigate "all sudden, unexplained, unnatural, or suspicious deaths" reported to the office. The coroner is ultimately responsible for determining the cause of death in these cases. Coroners also perform autopsies and assist other law enforcement agencies in homicide investigations.[64] For example, after singer Whitney Houston died in February 2012, the Los Angeles County coroner needed to determine the cause of death. After a two-month investigation, the coroner confirmed that Houston drowned in her bathroom, with heart disease and cocaine use listed as contributing factors.

Coroner The medical examiner of a county, usually elected by popular vote.

STATE POLICE AND HIGHWAY PATROLS

The most visible state law enforcement agency is the state police or highway patrol agency. Historically, state police agencies were created for three reasons:

1. To assist local police agencies, which often did not have adequate resources or training to handle their law enforcement tasks.
2. To investigate criminal activities that crossed jurisdictional boundaries (such as when bank robbers committed a crime in one county and then fled to another part of the state).
3. To provide law enforcement in rural and other areas that did not have local or county police agencies.

Today, there are twenty-three state police agencies and twenty-six highway patrols in the United States. State police agencies have statewide jurisdiction and are authorized to perform a wide variety of law enforcement tasks. Thus, they provide the same services as city or county police departments and are restricted only by the boundaries of the state. In contrast, highway patrols have limited authority. Their duties are generally defined either by their jurisdiction or by the specific types of offenses they have the authority to control. As their name suggests, most highway patrols concentrate primarily on regulating traffic. Specifically, they enforce traffic laws and investigate traffic accidents. Furthermore, they usually limit their activity to patrolling state and federal highways.

A Connecticut State Police officer provides advice for a motorist stuck in a snowstorm on Interstate 84 in East Hartford. In what ways do state law enforcement officers supplement the efforts of local police officers?

AP Photo/Jessica Hill

FEDERAL LAW ENFORCEMENT AGENCIES

Statistically, employees of federal agencies do not make up a large part of the nation's law enforcement force. In fact, the New York City Police Department has about one-third as many employees as all of the federal law enforcement agencies combined. Nevertheless, the influence of these federal agencies is substantial.

Unlike local police departments, which must deal with all forms of crime, federal agencies have been authorized, usually by Congress, to enforce specific laws or attend to specific situations. The U.S. Coast Guard, for example, patrols the nation's coasts, while U.S. Postal Inspectors investigate and prosecute crimes perpetrated through the use of the U.S. mails. Here, you will learn the basic elements of the most important federal law enforcement agencies, which are grouped according to the federal department or bureau to which they report. (See Figure 4.6 below for the current federal law enforcement "lineup.")

THE DEPARTMENT OF HOMELAND SECURITY About thirteen months after the September 11, 2001, terrorist attacks, President George W. Bush signed the Homeland Security Act.[65] This legislation created the Department of Homeland Security (DHS), a new cabinet-level department designed to coordinate federal efforts to protect the United States against international and domestic terrorism. The department has no new agencies.

FIGURE 4.6 Federal Law Enforcement Agencies

A number of federal agencies employ law enforcement officers who are authorized to carry firearms and make arrests. The most prominent ones are under the control of the U.S. Department of Homeland Security, the U.S. Department of Justice, or the U.S. Department of the Treasury.

Department of Homeland Security

DEPARTMENT NAME	APPROXIMATE NUMBER OF OFFICERS	MAIN RESPONSIBILITIES
U.S. Customs and Border Protection (CBP)	21,000	• (1) Prevent the illegal flow of people and goods across America's international borders; (2) facilitate legal trade and travel
U.S. Immigration and Customs Enforcement (ICE)	11,000	• Uphold public safety and homeland security by enforcing the nation's immigration and customs laws
U.S. Secret Service	7,000	• (1) Protect the president, the president's family, and other high-ranking politicians; (2) combat currency counterfeiters

Department of Justice

DEPARTMENT NAME	APPROXIMATE NUMBER OF OFFICERS	MAIN RESPONSIBILITIES
Federal Bureau of Investigation (FBI)	14,000	• (1) Protect national security by fighting international and domestic terrorism; (2) enforce federal criminal laws such as those dealing with cyber crime, public corruption, and civil rights violations
Drug Enforcement Administration (DEA)	5,000	• Enforce the nation's laws regulating the sale and use of drugs
Bureau of Alcohol, Tobacco, Firearms and Explosives (ATF)	3,000	• (1) Combat the illegal use and trafficking of firearms and explosives; (2) investigate the illegal diversion of alcohol and tobacco products
U.S. Marshals Service	4,000	• (1) Provide security at federal courts; (2) protect government witnesses; (3) apprehend fugitives from the federal court or corrections system

Department of the Treasury

DEPARTMENT NAME	APPROXIMATE NUMBER OF OFFICERS	MAIN RESPONSIBILITIES
Internal Revenue Service (IRS)	4,100	• Investigate potential criminal violations of the nation's tax code

Sources: U.S. Department of Homeland Security, U.S. Department of Justice, and U.S. Department of the Treasury.

Instead, twenty-two existing agencies were shifted under the control of the secretary of homeland security, a post now held by Janet Napolitano. U.S. Customs and Border Protection, U.S. Immigration and Customs Enforcement, and the U.S. Secret Service are the three most visible agencies under the direction of the DHS.

U.S. Customs and Border Protection (CBP) One of the most important effects of the Homeland Security Act was the termination of the Immigration and Naturalization Service (INS), which had monitored and policed the flow of immigrants into the United States since 1933. Many of the INS's duties have been transferred to **U.S. Customs and Border Protection (CBP),** which polices the flow of goods and people across the United States' international borders. In general terms, this means that the agency has two primary goals: (1) to keep illegal immigrants, drugs, and drug traffickers from crossing our borders, and (2) to facilitate the smooth flow of legal trade and travel. Consequently, CBP officers are stationed at every port of entry and exit to the United States. The officers have widespread authority to investigate and search all international passengers, whether they arrive on airplanes, ships, or other forms of transportation.

The U.S. Border Patrol, a branch of the CBP, has the burden of policing both the Mexican and Canadian borders between official ports of entry. In 2011, Border Patrol agents caught about 340,000 people entering the country illegally and confiscated nearly five million pounds of narcotics.[66] Today, more than 21,000 Border Patrol agents guard 19,000 miles of land and sea borders, about double the number of ten years earlier.

U.S. Immigration and Customs Enforcement (ICE) The CBP shares responsibility for locating and apprehending those persons illegally in the United States with special agents from **U.S. Immigration and Customs Enforcement (ICE).** While the CBP focuses almost exclusively on the nation's borders, ICE has a broader mandate to investigate and to enforce our country's immigration and customs laws. Simply stated, the CBP covers the borders, and ICE covers everything else. The latter agency's duties include detaining illegal aliens and deporting (removing) them from the United States, ensuring that individuals without permission do not work or gain other benefits in this country, and disrupting human trafficking operations.

Recently, ICE has become more aggressive in its efforts to apprehend and remove illegal immigrants with criminal records. During a single week in September 2011, ICE agents arrested 2,900 criminal aliens, more than half of whom had been convicted of felonies. Overall, in 2011, ICE removed nearly 400,000 illegal immigrants from this country, the highest number ever recorded.[67]

The U.S. Secret Service When it was created in 1865, the **U.S. Secret Service** was primarily responsible for combating currency counterfeiters. In 1901, the agency was given the added responsibility of protecting the president of the United States, the president's family, the vice president, the president-elect, and former presidents. These duties have remained the cornerstone of the agency, with several expansions. After a number of threats against presidential candidates in the 1960s and early 1970s, including the shootings of Robert Kennedy of New York and Governor George Wallace of Alabama, in 1976 Secret Service agents became responsible for protecting those political figures as well.

In Douglas, Arizona, Border Patrol agents detain a man suspected of smuggling marijuana across the U.S. border from Mexico. What is the difference between U.S. Customs and Border Protection, which oversees the Border Patrol, and U.S. Immigration and Customs Enforcement?

Joshua Lott/*New York Times*/Redux Pictures

U.S. Customs and Border Protection (CBP) The federal agency responsible for protecting U.S. borders and facilitating legal trade and travel across those borders.

U.S. Immigration and Customs Enforcement (ICE) The federal agency that enforces the nation's immigration and customs laws.

U.S. Secret Service A federal law enforcement organization with the primary responsibility of protecting the president, the president's family, the vice president, and other important political figures.

In addition to its special plainclothes agents, the agency also directs two uniformed groups of law enforcement officers. The Secret Service Uniformed Division protects the grounds of the White House and its inhabitants, and the Treasury Police Force polices the Treasury Building in Washington, D.C. This responsibility includes investigating threats against presidents and those running for presidential office. To aid its battle against counterfeiters and forgers of government bonds, the agency has the use of a laboratory at the Bureau of Engraving and Printing in the nation's capital.

THE DEPARTMENT OF JUSTICE The U.S. Department of Justice, created in 1870, is still the primary federal law enforcement agency in the country. With the responsibility of enforcing criminal law and supervising the federal prisons, the Justice Department plays a leading role in the American criminal justice system. To carry out its responsibilities to prevent and control crime, the department has a number of law enforcement agencies, including the Federal Bureau of Investigation; the federal Drug Enforcement Administration; the Bureau of Alcohol, Tobacco, Firearms and Explosives; and the U.S. Marshals Service.

The Federal Bureau of Investigation (FBI) Initially created in 1908 as the Bureau of Investigation, this agency was renamed the **Federal Bureau of Investigation (FBI)** in 1935. The primary investigative agency of the federal government, the FBI has jurisdiction over nearly two hundred federal crimes, including white-collar crimes, espionage (spying), kidnapping, extortion, interstate transportation of stolen property, bank robbery, interstate gambling, and civil rights violations. With its network of agents across the country and the globe, the FBI is uniquely positioned to combat worldwide criminal activity such as terrorism and drug trafficking. The agency also provides valuable support to local and state law enforcement agencies.

The FBI's Identification Division maintains a large database of fingerprint information and offers assistance in finding missing persons and identifying the victims of fires, airplane crashes, and other disfiguring disasters. The services of the FBI Laboratory, the largest crime laboratory in the world, are available at no cost to other police agencies. Finally, the FBI's National Crime Information Center (NCIC) provides lists of stolen vehicles and firearms, missing license plates, vehicles used to commit crimes, and other information to local and state law enforcement officers who may access the NCIC database. The FBI employs about 35,500 people and has a budget of approximately $8 billion.

The Drug Enforcement Administration (DEA) With a $2 billion budget and about five thousand special agents, the **Drug Enforcement Administration (DEA)** is one of the most important law enforcement agencies in the country. The mission of the DEA is to enforce domestic drug laws and regulations and to assist other federal and foreign agencies in combating illegal drug manufacture and trade on an international level. The agency also enforces the provisions of the Controlled Substances Act, which governs the manufacture, distribution, and dispensing of legal drugs, such as prescription drugs.

The Bureau of Alcohol, Tobacco, Firearms and Explosives (ATF) As its name suggests, the Bureau of Alcohol, Tobacco, Firearms and Explosives (ATF) is primarily concerned with the illegal sale, possession, and use of firearms and the control of untaxed tobacco and liquor products. The Firearms Division of the agency has the responsibility of enforcing the Gun Control Act of 1968, which sets the circumstances under which firearms may be sold and used in this country. The bureau also regulates all gun trade

Learning Objective 7 Identify the duties of the FBI.

Federal Bureau of Investigation (FBI) The branch of the Department of Justice responsible for investigating violations of federal law.

Drug Enforcement Administration (DEA) The federal agency responsible for enforcing the nation's laws and regulations regarding narcotics and other controlled substances.

CAREERS IN CJ

ARNOLD E. BELL
FEDERAL BUREAU OF INVESTIGATION (FBI) AGENT

Photo Courtesy of FBI.gov

I came to the FBI from the U.S. Army, where I worked as a crewman on a UH-1 helicopter and subsequently as a special agent with the U.S. Army Criminal Investigation Command. My work experience in the U.S. Army and degree from St. Leo College (now University) provided the educational foundation that allowed entry into the FBI. After graduating from the FBI Academy in Quantico, Virginia, I was assigned to our Los Angeles division, where I spent the next twelve years. It was a particularly interesting time to be working in Los Angeles, which was experiencing a boom in bank robberies. During the most intense stretches, we were averaging between five and seven bank robberies a day! When I wasn't chasing down a bank robber, I had my hands full with hunting down fugitives, working against organized crime, and dealing with public corruption.

I am currently assigned to the FBI's cyber division as an assistant section chief. The primary mission of my division is to combat cyber-based terrorism and hostile-intelligence operations conducted via the Internet, and to address general cyber crime. Since September 11, 2001, our primary focus has shifted from criminal work to counterterrorism. This has been a difficult transformation for many of us "old-timers" because we grew up in the Bureau doing criminal work. We all recognize, however, the importance of this new challenge, and, despite the difficulties, I believe we have been successful in fulfilling both missions.

fbi.gov

Social Media Career Tip

Be aware of your e-mail address/screen name/login name and what it represents. Stay away from nicknames. Use a professional and unique name to represent yourself consistently across social media platforms. f Linked in. 🐦

FAST FACTS

FBI AGENT, JOB DESCRIPTION:

- Primary role is to oversee intelligence and investigate crimes.
- Special agent careers are divided into five career paths: intelligence, counterintelligence, counterterrorism, criminal, and cyber.

WHAT KIND OF TRAINING IS REQUIRED?

- Bachelor's and/or master's degree, plus three years of work experience. U.S. citizen, 23–36 years old.
- A written and oral examination, medical and physical examinations, a psychological assessment, and an exhaustive background investigation.

ANNUAL SALARY RANGE?

- $61,100–$69,900

---

between the United States and foreign nations and collects taxes on all firearm importers, manufacturers, and dealers. In keeping with these duties, the ATF is also responsible for policing the illegal use and possession of explosives. Furthermore, the ATF is charged with enforcing federal gambling laws.

The U.S. Marshals Service The oldest federal law enforcement agency is the U.S. Marshals Service. In 1789, President George Washington assigned thirteen U.S. marshals to protect his attorney general. That same year, Congress created the office of the U.S. Marshals and Deputy Marshals. Originally, the U.S. marshals acted as the main law enforcement officers in the western territories. Following the Civil War (1861–1865), when most of these territories had become states, these agents were assigned to work for the U.S. district courts, where federal crimes are tried. The relationship between the U.S. Marshals Service and the federal courts continues today and forms the basis for the officers' main duties, which include the following:

1. Providing security at federal courts for judges, jurors, and other courtroom participants.
2. Controlling property that has been ordered seized by federal courts.
3. Protecting government witnesses who put themselves in danger by testifying against the targets of federal criminal investigations. This protection is sometimes accomplished by relocating the witnesses and providing them with different identities.
4. Transporting federal prisoners to detention institutions.
5. Investigating violations of federal fugitive laws.[68]

THE DEPARTMENT OF THE TREASURY The Department of the Treasury, formed in 1789, is mainly responsible for all financial matters of the federal government. It pays all the federal government's bills, borrows funds, collects taxes, mints coins, and prints paper currency. The largest bureau of the Treasury Department, the Internal Revenue Service (IRS), is concerned with violations of tax laws and regulations. The bureau has three divisions, only one of which is involved in criminal investigations. The examination branch of the IRS audits the tax returns of corporations and individuals. The collection division attempts to collect taxes from corporations or citizens who have failed to pay the taxes they owe. Finally, the criminal investigation division investigates cases of tax evasion and tax fraud. Criminal investigation agents can make arrests.

The IRS has long played a role in policing criminal activities such as gambling and selling drugs for one simple reason: those who engage in such activities almost never report any illegally gained income on their tax returns. Therefore, the IRS is able to apprehend them for tax evasion. The most famous example took place in the early 1930s, when the IRS finally arrested famed crime boss Al Capone—responsible for numerous violent crimes—for not paying his taxes.

PRIVATE SECURITY

Even with hundreds of thousands of local, state, and federal law enforcement officers, the police do not have the ability to prevent every crime. Recognizing this, many businesses and citizens have decided to hire private guards for their properties and homes. In fact, according to the Freedonia Group, an industry-research firm, demand for **private security** generates revenues of nearly $50 billion a year.[69] More than 10,000 firms employing around 1.1 million people provide private security services in this country, compared with about 700,000 public law enforcement agents.

PRIVATIZING LAW ENFORCEMENT As there are no federal regulations regarding private security, each state has its own rules for employment as a security guard. In several states, including California and Florida, prospective guards must have at least forty hours of training. Ideally, a security guard—lacking the extensive training of a law enforcement agent—should only observe and report criminal activity unless use of force is needed to prevent a felony.[70]

Private Security The practice of private corporations or individuals offering services traditionally performed by police officers.

As a rule, private security is not designed to replace law enforcement. It is intended to deter crime rather than stop it.[71] A uniformed security guard patrolling a shopping mall parking lot or a bank lobby has one primary function—to convince a potential criminal to search out a shopping mall or bank that does not have private security. For the same reason, many citizens hire security personnel to drive marked cars through their neighborhoods, making them a less attractive target for burglaries, robberies, vandalism, and other crimes.

CONTINUED GROWTH IN THE INDUSTRY Indicators point to continued higher rates of growth for the private security industry. *The Hallcrest Report II,* a far-reaching overview of private security trends funded by the National Institute of Justice, identifies four factors driving this growth:

1. An increase in fear on the part of the public, triggered by media coverage of crime.
2. The problem of crime in the workplace. According to the University of Florida's National Retail Security Survey, American retailers lose about $34 billion a year because of shoplifting and employee theft.[72]
3. Budget cuts in states and municipalities that have forced reductions in the number of public police, thereby raising the demand for private ones.
4. A rising awareness of private security products (such as home burglar alarms) and services as cost-effective protective measures.[73]

A private security guard makes the rounds near the Food Court at Landmark Mall in Alexandria, Virginia. Why is being visible such an important aspect of many private security jobs?

Newhouse News Service/Landov

Another reason for the industry's continued health is terrorism. Private security is responsible for protecting more than three-fourths of the nation's likely terrorist targets, such as power plants, financial centers, dams, malls, oil refineries, and transportation hubs.

SELFASSESSMENT

Fill in the blanks and check your answers on page 123.

Municipal police departments and _____ departments are both considered "local" organizations and have many of the same responsibilities. On the state level, the authority of the _____ _____ is usually limited to enforcing traffic laws. Nationally, the _____ has jurisdiction over all federal crimes, while the _____ focuses on federal drug laws and the _____ regulates the illegal sale and possession of guns. Private security is designed to _____ crime rather than to stop it.

CHAPTER SUMMARY

Learning Objective 1 **List the four basic responsibilities of the police.** (a) To enforce laws, (b) to provide services, (c) to prevent crime, and (d) to preserve the peace.

Learning Objective 2 **Tell how the patronage system affected policing.** During the political era of policing (1840–1930), bribes paid by citizens and business owners often went into the coffers of the local political party. This became known as the patronage system.

Learning Objective 3 **Explain how intelligence-led policing works and how it benefits modern police departments.** Intelligence-led polic-

ing uses past crime patterns to predict when and where crime will occur in the future. In theory, intelligence-led policing allows police administrators to use fewer resources because it removes costly and time-consuming "guesswork" from the law enforcement equation.

Learning Objective 4 **Identify the differences between the police academy and field training as learning tools for recruits.** The police academy is a controlled environment where police recruits learn the basics of policing from instructors in classrooms. In contrast, field training takes place in the "real world": the recruit goes on patrol with an experienced police officer.

Learning Objective 5 **Describe the challenges facing women who choose law enforcement as a career.** Many male officers believe that their female counterparts are not physically or mentally strong enough for police work, which puts pressure on women officers to continually prove themselves. Female officers must also deal with tokenism, or the stigma that they were hired only to fulfill diversity requirements.

Learning Objective 6 **Indicate some of the most important law enforcement agencies under the control of the Department of Homeland Security.** (a) U.S. Customs and Border Protection, which polices the flow of goods and people across the United States' international borders and oversees the U.S. Border Patrol; (b) U.S. Immigration and Customs Enforcement, which investigates and enforces our nation's immigration and customs laws; and (c) the U.S. Secret Service, which protects high-ranking federal government officials and federal property.

Learning Objective 7 **Identify the duties of the FBI.** The FBI has jurisdiction to investigate hundreds of federal crimes, including white-collar crime, kidnapping, bank robbery, and civil rights violations. The FBI is also heavily involved in combating terrorism and drug-trafficking operations in the United States and around the world. Finally, the agency provides support to state and local law enforcement agencies through its crime laboratories and databases.

Learning Objective 8 **Analyze the importance of private security today.** In the United States, businesses and citizens spend billions of dollars each year on private security. Heightened fear of crime and increased crime in the workplace have fueled the growth in spending on private security.

QUESTIONS FOR CRITICAL ANALYSIS

1. Which of the four basic responsibilities of the police do you think is most important? Why?

2. Some law enforcement agencies have the same physical agility and fitness requirements for male and female applicants, while others do not hold women to the same physical standards as men. Which approach do you favor, and why?

3. Review the discussion of double marginality on pages 112–113. Why would members of a minority community think that police officers of the same race or ethnicity were "traitors"? What can police departments do to dispel this misperception?

4. One of the major differences between a local police chief and a sheriff is that the sheriff is elected, while the police chief is appointed. What are some of the possible problems with having a law enforcement official who, like any other politician, is responsible to voters? What are some of the possible benefits of this situation?

5. Twenty-nine states do not require any specific training for private security personnel. What are the arguments for and against requiring at least forty hours of training, as is the case in California and Florida?

KEY TERMS

affirmative action **110**
coroner **115**
discrimination **110**
double marginality **112**
Drug Enforcement Administration (DEA) **118**
Federal Bureau of Investigation (FBI) **118**

field training **110**
intelligence-led policing **105**
night watch system **102**
patronage system **103**
private security **120**
probationary period **109**
professional model **103**
recruitment **107**

sheriff **114**
U.S. Customs and Border Protection (CBP) **117**
U.S. Immigration and Customs Enforcement (ICE) **117**
U.S. Secret Service **117**

SELF ASSESSMENT ANSWER KEY

COURSEMATE

For online help and access to resources that accompany *Criminal Justice in Action: The Core*, go to **www.cengage-brain.com/shop/ISBN/978-1-285-06915-9**. Click "Access Now," where you will find flashcards, an online quiz, and other helpful study aids. If you have an access code for CourseMate, log in and go to the chapter of your choice for additional online study aids.

NOTES

1. Quoted in Erica Goode, "Police Lesson: Network Tools Have 2 Edges," *New York Times* (April 7, 2011), A1.

2. Steven Chermak and Alexander Weiss, "Maintaining Legitimacy Using External Communication Strategies: An Analysis of Police-Media Relations," *Journal of Criminal Justice* 33 (2005), 501.

3. Egon Bittner, *The Functions of Police in a Modern Society*, Public Health Service Publication No. 2059 (Chevy Chase, MD: National Institute of Mental Health, 1970), 38–44.

4. Carl Klockars, "The Rhetoric of Community Policing," in *Community Policing: Rhetoric or Reality*, ed. Jack Greene and Stephen Mastrofski (New York: Praeger Publishers, 1990), 244.

5. Jack R. Greene and Carl B. Klockars, "What Do Police Do?" in *Thinking about Police*, 2d ed., ed. Carl B. Klockars and Stephen D. Mastrofski (New York: McGraw-Hill, 1991), 273–284.

6. John S. Dempsey and Linda S. Forst, *An Introduction to Policing*, 6th ed. (Clifton Park, NY: Delmar Cengage Learning, 2012), 380–381.

7. Federal Bureau of Investigation, *Crime in the United States, 2011* (Washington, D.C.: U.S. Department of Justice, 2012), at **www.fbi.gov/about-us/cjis/ucr/crime-in-the-u.s/2011/crime-in-the-u.s.-2011/tables/table-29**.

8. Reprinted in *The Police Chief* (January 1990), 18.

9. Jeffrey M. Wilson, *Community Policing in America* (New York: Routledge, 2006), 7–16.

10. Jerome H. Skolnick, "Police: The New Professionals," *New Society* (September 5, 1986), 9–11.

11. Quoted in Nancy Ritter, ed., "LAPD Chief Bratton Speaks Out: What's Wrong with Criminal Justice Research—and How to Make It Right," *National Institute of Justice Journal* 257 (2007), 29.

12. Klockars, 250.

13. James Q. Wilson, *Varieties of Police Behavior: The Management of Law and Order in Eight Communities* (Cambridge, MA: Harvard University Press, 1968).

14. James Q. Wilson and George L. Kelling, "Broken Windows," *Atlantic Monthly* (March 1982), 29.

15. M. K. Nalla and G. R. Newman, "Is White-Collar Crime Policing, Policing?" *Policing and Society* 3 (1994), 304.

16. Mitchell P. Roth, *Crime and Punishment: A History of the Criminal Justice System*, 2d ed. (Belmont, CA: Wadsworth Cengage Learning, 2011), 65.

17. *Ibid.*

18. Mark H. Moore and George L. Kelling, "'To Serve and Protect': Learning from Police History," *Public Interest* 70 (1983), 53.

19. Samuel Walker, *The Police in America: An Introduction* (New York: McGraw-Hill, 1983), 7.

20. Moore and Kelling, 54.

21. Mark H. Haller, "Chicago Cops, 1890–1925," in *Thinking about Police*, ed. Carl Klockars and Stephen Mastrofski (New York: McGraw-Hill, 1991), 90.

22. Roger G. Dunham and Geoffrey P. Alpert, *Critical Issues in Policing: Contemporary Issues* (Prospect Heights, IL: Waveland Press, 1989).

23. Ken Peak and Emmanuel P. Barthe, "Community Policing and CompStat: Merged, or Mutually Exclusive?" *The Police Chief* (December 2009), 73.

24. *Ibid.*, 74.

25. Quoted in *ibid.*

26. Peter K. Manning, "The Police: Mandate, Strategies, and Appearances," in *Crime and Justice in American Society*, ed. Jack D. Douglas (Indianapolis, IN: Bobbs-Merrill, 1971), 149–163.

27. National Advisory Commission on Civil Disorder, *Report* (Washington, D.C.: U.S. Government Printing Office, 1968), 157–160.

28. Quoted in Joel Rubin, "Stopping Crime before It Starts," *Los Angeles Times* (August 21, 2010), A17.

29. Colleen McCue, Andre Parker, Paul J. McNulty, and David McCoy, "Doing More with Less: Data Mining in Police Deployment Decisions," *Violent Crime Newsletter* (Washington, D.C.: U.S. Department of Justice, Spring 2004), 4–5.

30. Office of Community Oriented Policing Services, *The Impact of the Economic Downturn on American Police Agencies* (Washington, D.C.: U.S. Department of Justice, October 2011), 26.

31. Bureau of Justice Statistics, *Local Police Departments, 2003* (Washington, D.C.: U.S. Department of Justice, May 2006), i; and Bureau of Justice Statistics, *Sheriffs' Offices, 2003* (Washington, D.C.: U.S. Department of Justice, May 2006), i.

32. Bureau of Justice Statistics, *Local Police Departments, 2007* (Washington, D.C.: U.S. Department of Justice, December 2010), Text table 4, page 32.

33. Raymond W. Kelly, "Homeland Security Preparedness in New York City," prepared statement before the U.S. House of Representatives, 2005.

34. Dana Priest and William M. Arkin, "Monitoring America," *Washington Post* (December 20, 2010), A1; and Lois M. Davis, et al., *Law Enforcement's Post-9/11 Focus on Counterterrorism and Homeland Security* (Santa Monica, CA: RAND Corporation, 2010), 8.

35. David J. Robert, "Technology's Impact on Law Enforcement—Community Interaction," *The Police Chief* (February 2011), 78.

36. Quoted in Rubin, A17.

37. James H. Chenoweth, "Situational Tests: A New Attempt at Assessing Police Candidates," *Journal of Criminal Law, Criminology and Police Science* 52 (1961), 232.

38. Bureau of Justice Statistics, *Local Police Departments, 2007*, 11.

39. *Ibid*, Table 5, page 11.

40. D. P. Hinkle, "College Degree: An Impractical Prerequisite for Police Work," *Law and Order* (July 1991), 105.

41. Bureau of Justice Statistics, *Local Police Departments, 2007*, 12.

42. Bureau of Justice Statistics, *State and Local Law Enforcement Training Academies, 2006* (Washington, D.C.: U.S. Department of Justice, February 2009), 7.

43. National Advisory Commission on Civil Disorder, *Report*, Chapter 11.

44. *Griggs v. Duke Power Co.*, 401 U.S. 424 (1971); and *Abermarle Paper Co. v. Moody*, 422 U.S. 405 (1975).

45. Gene L. Scaramella, Steven M. Cox, and William P. McCamey, *Introduction to Policing* (Thousand Oaks, CA: Sage Publications, 2011), 30–31.

46. Bureau of Justice Statistics, *Local Police Departments, 2007*, 14.

47. National Center for Women and Policing, *Equality Denied: The Status of Women in Policing: 2001* (Washington, D.C.: U.S. Government Printing Office, 2002), 4.

48. Jacqueline Mroz, "Female Police Chiefs: A Novelty No More," *New York Times* (April 6, 2008), 3.

49. Scaramella, Cox, and McCamey, 318.

50. Quoted in Teresa Lynn Wertsch, "Walking the Thin Blue Line: Policewomen and Tokenism Today," *Women and Criminal Justice* (1998), 35–36.

51. Katherine Stuart van Wormer and Clemens Bartollas, *Women and the Criminal Justice System*, 3d ed. (Upper Saddle River, NJ: Pearson Education, 2011), 318–319.

52. Bureau of Justice Statistics, *Local Police Departments, 2007*, 14.

53. David Alan Sklansky, "Not Your Father's Police Department: Making Sense of the New Demographics of Law Enforcement," *Journal of Criminal Law and Criminology* (Spring 2006), 1209–1243.

54. Peter C. Moskos, "Two Shades of Blue: Black and White in the Blue Brotherhood," *Law Enforcement Executive Forum* (2008), 57.

55. Scaramella, Cox, and McCamey, 324.

56. Dempsey and Forst, 183.

57. *Wygant v. Jackson Board of Education*, 476 U.S. 314 (1986).

58. Bureau of Justice Statistics, *Census of State and Local Law Enforcement Agencies, 2008* (Washington, D.C.: U.S. Department of Justice, July 2011), 2.

59. *Crime in the United States, 2011*, at **www.fbi.gov/about-us/cjis/ucr/crime-in-the-u.s/2011/crime-in-the-u.s.-2011/tables/table_70_full-time_law_enforcement_employees_by_region_and_geographic_division_by_population_group_number_and_rate_per_1000_inhabitants_2011.xls**.

60. Bureau of Justice Statistics, *Local Police Departments, 2007*, Table 3, page 9.

61. Bureau of Justice Statistics, *Census of State and Local Law Enforcement Agencies, 2008*, Table 4, page 5.

62. Bureau of Justice Statistics, *Sheriffs' Offices, 2003*, 15–18.

63. Bureau of Justice Statistics, *Sheriffs' Departments, 1997* (Washington, D.C.: U.S. Department of Justice, February 2000), 14.

64. Bureau of Justice Statistics, *Medical Examiners and Coroners' Offices, 2004* (Washington, D.C.: U.S. Department of Justice, June 2007), 1.

65. Pub. L. No. 107-296, 116 Stat. 2135.

66. "CBP's 2011 Fiscal Year in Review," at **www.cbp.gov/xp/cgov/newsroom/news_releases/national/2011_news_archive/12122011.xml**.

67. Laura Wides-Munoz, "ICE Deports Record Number of Immigrants in Year," *Associated Press* (October 18, 2011).

68. United States Marshals Service, "Fact Sheet," at **www.justice.gov/marshals/duties/factsheets/general-1209.html**.

69. *Private Security Services to 2014* (Cleveland, OH: Freedonia Group, November 2010), 15.

70. John B. Owens, "Westec Story: Gated Communities and the Fourth Amendment," *American Criminal Law Review* (Spring 1997), 1138.

71. Bruce L. Benson, "Guns, Crime, and Safety," *Journal of Law and Economics* (October 2001), 725.

72. National Retail Federation, "Retail Fraud, Shoplifting Rates Decrease, According to National Retail Security Survey," at **www.nrf.com/modules.php?name=News&op=viewlive&sp_id=945**.

73. William C. Cunningham, John J. Strauchs, and Clifford W. Van Meter, *The Hallcrest Report II: Private Security Trends, 1970 to 2000* (Boston: Butterworth-Heinemann, 1990), 236.

CHAPTER

5

Problems and Solutions in Modern Policing

Joshua Lott/Reuters/Landov

LEARNING OBJECTIVES

After reading this chapter, you should be able to...

1 List the three primary purposes of police patrol.

2 Indicate some investigation strategies that are considered aggressive.

3 Describe how forensic experts use DNA fingerprinting to solve crimes.

4 Explain why differential response strategies enable police departments to respond efficiently to 911 calls.

5 Explain community policing and its contribution to the concept of problem-oriented policing.

6 Determine when police officers are justified in using deadly force.

7 Identify the three traditional forms of police corruption.

8 Explain what an ethical dilemma is and name four categories of ethical dilemmas that a police officer typically may face.

Throughout the chapter you will see each learning objective repeated in the margin next to the content it relates to. The chapter summary on pages 153 and 154 includes all of the learning objectives for review.

CHAPTER OUTLINE

- Police Organization and Field Operations
- Police Strategies: What Works
- "Us versus Them": Issues in Modern Policing
- Police Misconduct and Ethics

TEXAS TRAGEDY

On January 4, 2012, thirteen-year-old Jaime Gonzalez walked into a first-period class at Cummings Middle School in Brownsville, Texas, and, for no apparent reason, punched another student in the face. As school administrators tried to calm an agitated Gonzalez in the hallway, their puzzlement turned to alarm—the eighth grader had a gun tucked into his pants. Within minutes, the school was in lockdown and two local police officers had arrived on the scene. They shouted at Gonzalez to "Put the gun down! Put it on the floor!" Disregarding these orders, Gonzalez raised his weapon. The officers fired three times and hit the teenager twice, once in the chest and once in the abdomen. "Subject shot," one of the officers said as he called for emergency medical aid.

After Gonzalez died from his wounds in a local hospital, an already-shaken community learned one more piece of disturbing news. Although the weapon Gonzalez had been brandishing looked like a black Glock semiautomatic pistol, it was actually a relatively harmless .177-caliber BB gun, available on the Internet for $60. As might be expected, this development opened the Brownsville police to a great deal of criticism. "Why was so much excess force used on

a minor?" asked Gonzalez's father, Jaime Sr. "What happened was an injustice," insisted Noralva, the boy's mother.

Brownsville interim police chief Orlando Rodriguez defended his officers' decision making. He stressed that, as far as the two men knew, they were dealing with an armed suspect roaming the halls of a school with more than seven hundred students and about seventy-five staff. "When I looked at that gun, there is no doubt [that] from a distance it's absolutely real," agreed Carl A. Montoya, a school official. "I think the officers responded, obviously, from their training. From that perspective, it was a real gun."

Jaime and Noralva Gonzalez embrace at the funeral of their son, Jaime, who was fatally shot by Brownsville, Texas, police after brandishing what appeared to be a handgun at his school.

AP Photo/Brownsville Herald, Yvette Vela

Jaime Gonzalez's death was hardly an isolated incident. In recent years, law enforcement agents in a number of states, including California, Florida, and Maryland, have shot dozens of children and adults armed with BB guns or other types of air pistols that appeared to be deadly weapons.[1] Following these episodes, the police officers involved often are blamed for not waiting to determine the full extent of the threat posed by the shooter. As you will see later in the chapter, however, police officers have the right to use force—including deadly force—when it is reasonable to do so.[2] In the Brownsville case, was it reasonable of the officers to assume that Gonzalez's gun was real?

Judging by the facts, the answer to the question is yes, though this may be cold comfort to Gonzalez's parents and, indeed, to the officers who shot him. Many law enforcement agents suffer symptoms of postshooting trauma, such as nightmares and social withdrawal, following the use of lethal force, particularly when the victim is a minor.[3] Indeed, most Americans cannot imagine the on-the-job situations that the average law enforcement agent faces, or the pressures involved in dealing with these situations.

For the topic of this chapter, we turn to the many challenges of law enforcement. As one-time police officer and later professor James Fyfe has explained, by telling police officers that we expect them to eradicate crime, we are putting them in a "no win war."[4] In the pages that follow, we will examine the strategies employed by law enforcement agencies to gain victories, both large and small, in the struggle against crime. We will also scrutinize what Fyfe described as the inevitable atrocities of his "no win war," including police misconduct such as brutality and corruption. Our look inside the world of the law enforcement agent begins with an overview of how police departments are organized and operated.

POLICE ORGANIZATION AND FIELD OPERATIONS

Brownsville police administrators placed the two officers involved in Jamie Gonzalez's death on *administrative leave* pending an investigation into the incident. In other words, the officers were temporarily relieved of their duties, with pay. This step does not imply that they were suspected of wrongdoing. Most law enforcement agencies react similarly when a firearm is fired in the line of duty, both to allow for a full investigation of the event and to give the officer a chance to recover from what can be a traumatic experience.

Administrative leave is a *bureaucratic* response to an officer-involved shooting. In a **bureaucracy,** formal rules govern an individual's actions and relationships with co-employees. The ultimate goal of any bureaucracy is to reach its maximum efficiency—in the case of a police department, to provide the best service for the community within the confines of limited resources such as staff and budget. Although some police departments are experimenting with alternative structures based on a partnership between management and the officers in the field,[5] most continue to rely on the hierarchical structure described below.

THE STRUCTURE OF THE POLICE DEPARTMENT

Each police department is organized according to its environment: the size of its jurisdiction, the type of crimes it must deal with, and the demographics of the population under its protection. A police department in a racially diverse city often faces different challenges than a department in a homogeneous one. Geographic location also influences police organization. The makeup of the police department in Miami, Florida, for example, is partially determined by the fact that the city is a gateway for illegal drugs smuggled from Central and South America. Consequently, the department directs a high percentage of its resources to special drug-fighting units. It has also formed cooperative partnerships with federal agencies such as the FBI and U.S. Customs and Border Protection in an effort to stop the flow of narcotics and weapons into the South Florida area.

CHAIN OF COMMAND Whatever the size or location of a police department, it needs a clear rank structure and strict accountability to function properly. One of the goals of the police reformers, especially beginning in the 1950s, was to lessen the corrupting influence of politicians. The result was a move toward a militaristic organization of police.[6] As you can see in Figure 5.1 on the following page, a typical police department is based on a chain of command that leads from the police chief down through the various levels of the department. In this formalized structure, all persons are aware of their place in the chain and of their duties and responsibilities within the organization.

Delegation of authority is a critical component of the chain of command, especially in larger departments. The chief of police delegates authority to assistant or division chiefs, who delegate authority to commanders, and on down through the organization. This structure creates a situation in which nearly every member of a police department

Bureaucracy A hierarchically structured administrative organization that carries out specific functions.

Delegation of Authority The principles of command on which most police departments are based, in which personnel take orders from and are responsible to those in positions of power directly above them.

FIGURE 5.1 The Command Chain of the Cincinnati (Ohio) Police Department

The Cincinnati Police Department is made up of more than 1,000 sworn law enforcement officers and about 120 civilians. As this figure shows, the chain of command runs from the chief of police through four main bureau chiefs down to a wide variety of sections, squads, and units.

**Police Chief
James E. Craig**

**Patrol Bureau
Assistant Chief
James L. Whalen**

- Street patrol
- Marine patrol
- Mounted patrol
- Traffic
- Community-oriented policing

**Resource Bureau
Assistant Chief
Cindy M. Combs**

- Evidence/property management
- Personnel/finance management
- Training

**Investigations Bureau
Assistant Chief
Vincent Demasi**

- Central vice control
- Criminal investigations Intelligence

**Administration Bureau
Assistant Chief
Richard Janke**

- Internal investigations
- Planning and resources
- Inspections

Source: Cincinnati Police Department.

is directly accountable to a superior. As was the original goal of police reformers, these links encourage discipline and control and lessen the possibility that any individual police employee will have the unsupervised freedom to abuse her or his position.[7]

ORGANIZING BY AREA AND TIME In most metropolitan areas, police responsibilities are divided according to zones known as *beats* and *precincts.* A beat is the smallest stretch that a police officer or a group of police officers regularly patrol. A precinct—also known as a *district* or a *station*—is a collection of beats. A precinct commander, or captain, is held responsible by his or her superiors at police headquarters for the performance of the officers in that particular precinct.[8]

Police administrators must also organize their personnel by time. Most departments separate each twenty-four-hour day into three eight-hour *shifts,* also called *tours* or *platoons.* The night shift generally lasts from midnight to 8 A.M., the day shift from 8 A.M. to 4 P.M., and the evening shift from 4 P.M. to midnight. Officers either vary their hours by, say, working days one month and nights the next, or they have fixed tours in which they consistently take day, night, or evening shifts.[9]

LAW ENFORCEMENT IN THE FIELD To a large extent, the main goal of any police department is the most efficient organization of its *field services.* Also known as "operations" or "line services," field services include patrol activities, investigations, and special operations. According to Henry M. Wrobleski and Karen M. Hess, most police departments are "generalists." Thus, police officers are assigned to general areas and perform all field service functions within the boundaries of their beats. Larger departments may be more specialized, with personnel assigned to specific types of crime, such as homicide, vice (dealing with illegal drugs, prostitution, and gambling), or white-collar crime, rather than geographic locations. Smaller departments, which make up the bulk of local law enforcement agencies, rely almost exclusively on general patrol.[10]

POLICE ON PATROL:
THE BACKBONE OF THE DEPARTMENT

Every police department has a patrol unit, and patrol is usually the largest division in the department. More than two-thirds of the **sworn officers,** or those officers authorized to make arrests and use force, in local police departments in the United States have patrol duties.[11]

> "Life on the street" is not easy. Patrol officers must be able to handle any number of difficult situations, and experience is often the best and, despite training programs, the only teacher. As one patrol officer commented:

> You never stop learning. You never get your street degree. The person who says . . . they've learned it all is the person that's going to wind up dead or in a very compromising position. They've closed their minds.[12]

It may take a patrol officer years to learn when a gang is "false flagging" (trying to trick rival gang members into the open) or what to look for in a suspect's eyes to sense if he or she is concealing a weapon. This learning process is the backdrop to a number of different general functions that a patrol officer performs on a daily basis.

THE PURPOSE OF PATROL In general, patrol officers do not spend most of their shifts chasing, catching, and handcuffing suspected criminals. The vast majority of patrol shifts are completed without a single arrest.[13] Officers spend a great deal of time meeting with other officers, completing paperwork, and patrolling with the goal of preventing crime in general rather than focusing on any specific crime or criminal activity.

> As police accountability expert Samuel Walker has noted, the basic purposes of police patrol have changed very little since 1829, when Sir Robert Peel founded the modern police department. These purposes include the following:

1. The deterrence of crime by maintaining a visible police presence.
2. The maintenance of public order and a sense of security in the community.
3. The twenty-four-hour provision of services that are not crime related.[14]

> The first two goals—deterring crime and keeping order—are generally accepted as legitimate police functions. The third, however, has been more controversial. As noted in Chapter 4, the community era saw a resurgence of the patrol officer as a provider of community services, many of which have little to do with crime. The extent to which noncrime incidents dominate patrol officers' time is evident in the Police Services Study, a survey of 26,000 calls to police in sixty different neighborhoods. The study found that only one out of every five calls involved the report of criminal activity.[15] (See Figure 5.2 on the following page for the results of another survey of crime calls.)

PATROL ACTIVITIES To recap, the purposes of police patrols are to prevent and deter crime and also to provide social services. How can the police best accomplish these goals? Of course, each department has its own methods and strategies, but William Gay, Theodore Schell, and Stephen Schack are able to divide routine patrol activity into four general categories:

Sworn Officer A law enforcement agent who has been authorized to make arrests and use force, including deadly force, against civilians.

Learning Objective 1 — List the three primary purposes of police patrol.

Given that most patrol shifts end without an officer making a single arrest, what activities take up most of a patrol officer's time?
David Turnley/Corbis

FIGURE 5.2 Calls for Service

Over a period of two years, the Project on Policing Neighborhoods gathered information on calls for service in Indianapolis, Indiana, and St. Petersburg, Florida. As you can see, the largest portion of these calls involved disputes in which no violence or threat of violence existed. (Be aware also that nearly two-thirds of the nonviolent dispute calls and nearly half of the assault calls answered by police dealt with domestic confrontations.)

Description of Violation	Percentage of Total Calls
NONSERIOUS CRIME CALLS	
Nonviolent disputes	42
Public disorder (examples: drunk, disorderly, begging, prostitution)	11
Assistance (examples: missing persons, traffic accident, damaged property)	10
Minor violations (examples: shoplifting, trespassing, traffic/parking offense, refusal to pay)	4
SERIOUS CRIME CALLS	
Assaults (examples: using violence against a person, kidnapping, child abuse)	26
Serious theft (examples: motor vehicle theft, burglary, purse snatching)	5
General disorder (examples: illicit drugs, fleeing police, leaving the scene of an accident)	2

Source: Adapted from: Stephen D. Mastrofski, Jeffrey B. Snipes, Roger B. Parks, and Christopher D. Maxwell, "The Helping Hand of the Law: Police Control of Citizens on Request," *Criminology* 38 (May 2000), Table 5, page 328.

Eldad Carin/iStockphoto

1. *Preventive patrol.* By maintaining a presence in a community, either in a car or on foot, patrol officers attempt to prevent crime from occurring. This strategy, which O. W. Wilson called "omnipresence," was a cornerstone of early policing philosophy and still takes up roughly 40 percent of patrol time.

2. *Calls for service.* Patrol officers spend nearly a quarter of their time responding to 911 calls for emergency service or other citizen problems and complaints.

3. *Administrative duties.* Paperwork takes up nearly 20 percent of patrol time.

4. *Officer-initiated activities.* Incidents in which the patrol officer initiates contact with citizens, such as stopping motorists and pedestrians and questioning them, account for 15 percent of patrol time.[16]

The category estimates made by Gay, Schell, and Schack are not universally accepted. Professor of law enforcement Gary W. Cordner argues that administrative duties account for the largest percentage of patrol officers' time. According to Cordner, when officers are not consumed with paperwork and meetings, they are either answering calls for service (which takes up 67 percent of the officers' time on the street) or initiating activities themselves (the remaining 33 percent).[17]

"NOISE, BOOZE, AND VIOLENCE" There are dozens of academic studies that purport to answer the question of how patrol officers spend their days and nights. Perhaps it is only fair, then, to give a police officer the chance to describe the duties patrol officers perform. In the words of Anthony Bouza, a former police chief:

> [Patrol officers] hurry from call to call, bound to their crackling radios, which offer no relief—especially on summer weekend nights. . . . The cops jump from crisis to crisis, rarely having time to do more than tamp one down sufficiently and leave for the next. Gaps of boredom and inactivity fill the interims, although there aren't many of these in the hot months. Periods of boredom get increasingly longer as the nights wear on and the weather gets colder.[18]

Bouza paints a picture of a routine beat as filled with "noise, booze, violence, drugs, illness, blaring TVs, and human misery." This may describe the situation in high-crime neighborhoods, but it certainly does not represent the reality for the majority of patrol officers in the United States. Duties that all patrol officers have in common, whether they work in Bouza's rather nightmarish city streets or in the quieter environment of rural America, include controlling traffic, conducting preliminary investigations, making arrests, and patrolling public events.

POLICE INVESTIGATIONS

Investigation is the second main function of police, along with patrol. Whereas patrol is primarily preventive, investigation is reactive. After a crime has been committed and the patrol officer has gathered the preliminary information from the crime scene, the responsibility of finding "who dunnit" is delegated to the investigator, generally known as the **detective.** The most common way for someone to become a detective is to be promoted from patrol officer. Detectives have not been the focus of nearly as much reform attention as their patrol counterparts, mainly because the scope of the detective's job is limited to law enforcement, with less emphasis given to social services or order maintenance.

The detective's job is not quite as glamorous as it is sometimes portrayed by the media. Detectives spend much of their time investigating common crimes such as burglaries and are more likely to be tracking down stolen property than a murderer. They must also prepare cases for trial, which involves a great deal of time-consuming paperwork. Furthermore, a landmark Rand Corporation study estimated that more than 97 percent of cases that are "solved" can be attributed to a patrol officer making an arrest at the scene, witnesses or victims identifying the perpetrator, or detectives undertaking routine investigative procedures that could easily be performed by clerical personnel.[19]

For example, even though a task force of up to thirty-five Los Angeles detectives worked around the clock for a week on the January 2012 murder of seventeen-year-old Francisco Rodriguez, it was an informant's tip that finally directed police to two suspects in the killing. "There is no Sherlock Holmes," said one investigator. "The good detective on the street is the one who knows all the weasels and one of the weasels will tell him who did it."[20]

AGGRESSIVE INVESTIGATION STRATEGIES

Detective bureaus also have the option of implementing more aggressive strategies. Perhaps the most dangerous and controversial operation a law enforcement agent can undertake is to go *undercover,* or to assume a false identity in order to obtain information concerning illegal activities. Though each department has its own guidelines on when undercover operations are necessary, all that is generally required is the suspicion that illegal activity is taking place. (As you may recall from the discussion of entrapment in Chapter 3, police officers are limited in what they can do to convince the target of an undercover operation to participate in the illegal activity.) Today, undercover officers are most commonly used to infiltrate large-scale narcotics operations or those run by organized crime.

In some situations, a detective bureau may not want to take the risk of exposing an officer to undercover work or may believe that an outsider cannot infiltrate a crime

Two undercover U.S. Fish and Wildlife Service agents pose as hunters to combat the illegal poaching of protected animals in Louisiana. What sort of training might be required for this dangerous work?

Gary Moore/realworldimage.com

Detective The primary police investigator of crimes.

Learning Objective **2** Indicate some investigation strategies that are considered aggressive.

network. When the police need access and information, they have the option of turning to a **confidential informant (CI)**. A CI is a person who is involved in criminal activity and gives information about that activity and those who engage in it to the police. The United States Supreme Court, in *Rovario v. United States* (1957),[21] held that the state has a confidential informant privilege. This means that government agents are not required to disclose the identity of an informant unless a court finds that such information is needed to determine the guilt or innocence of a suspect.

CLEARANCE RATES AND COLD CASES

The ultimate goal of all law enforcement activity is to *clear* a crime, or secure the arrest and prosecution of the offender. Even a cursory glance at **clearance rates,** which show the percentage of reported crimes that have been cleared, reveals that investigations succeed only part of the time. In 2011, just 65 percent of homicides and 48 percent of total violent crimes were solved, while police cleared only 19 percent of property crimes.[22] For the most part, the different clearance rates for different crimes reflect the resources that a law enforcement agency expends on each type of crime. The police generally investigate a murder or a rape more vigorously than the theft of an automobile or an iPad.

As a result of low clearance rates, police departments are often saddled with a number of **cold cases,** or criminal investigations that are not cleared after a certain amount of time. More than 80 percent of large-city police departments have cold case squads dedicated to unsolved crimes.[23] (The length of time before a case becomes "cold" varies from department to department. In general, a cold case must be "somewhat old" but not "so old that there can be no hope of ever solving it."[24])

FORENSIC INVESTIGATIONS AND DNA

Although the crime scene typically offers a wealth of evidence, some of it is incomprehensible to a patrol officer or detective without assistance. For that aid, law enforcement officers rely on experts in **forensics,** or the practice of using science and technology to investigate crimes. Forensic experts apply their knowledge to items found at the crime scene to determine crucial facts such as the following:

- The cause of death or injury.
- The time of death or injury.
- The type of weapon or weapons used.
- The identity of the crime victim, if that information is unavailable.
- The identity of the offender (in the best-case scenario).[25]

To assist forensic experts, many police departments operate or are affiliated with crime laboratories. As noted in the previous chapter, the FBI also offers the services of its crime lab, the largest in the world, to agencies with limited resources. These services can be crucial, as recent research shows that forensic evidence greatly increases the chances of case clearances, particularly with regard to sexual assaults, robberies, and burglaries.[26]

CRIME SCENE FORENSICS The first law enforcement agent to reach a crime scene has the important task of protecting any **trace evidence** from contamination. Trace evidence is generally very small—often invisible to the naked human eye—and often requires technological aid for detection. Hairs, fibers, blood, fingerprints, broken glass, and footprints are all examples of trace evidence. A study released by the National Institute of Justice in 2010 confirmed that when police are able to link such evidence to a suspect, the likelihood of a conviction rises dramatically.[27] Police will also search a crime scene for bullets and spent cartridge casings. These items can provide clues as to how far the shooter was from the target. They can also be compared with information stored in national firearms databases to determine, under some circumstances, the gun used and its most recent owner. The study of firearms and its application to solving crimes goes under the general term **ballistics.**

THE HUMAN FINGERPRINT For more than a century, the most important piece of trace evidence has been the human fingerprint. Because no two fingerprints are alike, they are considered reliable sources of identification. Forensic scientists compare a fingerprint lifted from a crime scene with that of a suspect and declare a match if there are between eight and sixteen "points of similarity." This method of identification is not infallible, however. It is often difficult to lift a suitable print from a crime scene, and researchers have uncovered numerous cases in which innocent persons were convicted based on evidence obtained through faulty fingerprinting procedures.[28]

THE DNA REVOLUTION The technique of **DNA fingerprinting,** or using a suspect's DNA to match the suspect to a crime, emerged in the mid-1990s and has now all but replaced fingerprint evidence in many types of criminal investigations. The shift has been a boon to crime fighters: one law enforcement agent likened DNA fingerprinting to "the finger of God pointing down" at a guilty suspect.[29]

DNA, which is the same in each cell of a person's body, provides a "genetic blueprint" or "code" for every living organism. DNA fingerprinting is useful in criminal investigations because no two people, save for identical twins, have the same genetic code. Therefore, lab technicians can compare certain characteristics of a DNA sample from a suspect to the evidence found at the crime scene. If the match is negative, it is certain that the two samples did not come from the same source. If enough characteristics of the DNA sample have a positive match, the lab will determine the odds that the DNA sample could have come from someone other than the suspect. Those odds are so low—sometimes reaching 30 billion to one—that a match is practically conclusive.[30]

The process begins when forensic technicians gather blood, semen, skin, saliva, or hair from the scene of a crime. Blood cells and sperm are rich in DNA, making them particularly useful in murder and rape cases, but DNA has also been extracted from sweat on dirty laundry, skin cells on eyeglasses, and saliva on used envelope seals. Once a suspect is identified, her or his DNA can be used to determine whether she or he can be placed at the crime scene. In 2011, for example, investigators connected Aaron Thomas, the "East Coast Rapist," to a series of sexual assaults that took place from Rhode Island to Virginia by obtaining Thomas's DNA sample from a discarded cigarette.

DNA IN ACTION The ability to "dust" for genetic information on such a wide variety of evidence, as well as that evidence's longevity and accuracy, greatly increases the chances that a crime will be solved. Indeed, police no longer need a witness or even a suspect in custody to solve crimes. What they do need is a piece of evidence and a database. In 2012, for example, William Payne was arrested for murdering Nikolaus Crumbley in San Francisco's McLaren Park on November 16, 1983. Semen found on Crumbley's corpse had been collected at the time of the crime, but police could not identify a suspect. Three decades later, this evidence was matched to a sample of Payne's DNA, taken when he was arrested for an unrelated felony and his DNA pattern stored in a California Department of Justice database.

Databases and Cold Hits The identification of William Payne is an example of what police call a **cold hit.** Such "hits" occur when law enforcement finds a suspect "out of nowhere" by comparing DNA evidence from a crime scene against the contents of a

Ballistics The study of firearms, including the firing of the weapon and the flight of the bullet.

DNA Fingerprinting The identification of a person based on a sample of her or his DNA, the genetic material found in the cells of all living things.

Cold Hit The establishment of a connection between a suspect and a crime, often through the use of DNA evidence, in the absence of an ongoing criminal investigation.

Learning Objective **3** Describe how forensic experts use DNA fingerprinting to solve crimes.

CAREERS IN CJ

MARTHA BLAKE
FORENSIC SCIENTIST

In high school, I was interested in science, but didn't want to end up being a technician doing the same thing every day. I was looking in college catalogues and came across criminalistics at U.C. Berkeley. The coursework included such courses as microscopy, instrumental analysis, trace evidence, criminal law, and statistics, and it sounded fascinating. I decided in my senior year of high school to become a forensic scientist.

As quality assurance manager at the San Francisco Police Department's crime lab, I am often called to criminal court to testify about evidence that has passed through our lab. I am always nervous when I testify, and I think it is healthy to be a little nervous. As an expert witness, the most challenging part of my testimony is describing my findings to a jury of primarily nonscientists in a way that will make my testimony understandable and credible. I've found that juries tend to understand evidence that is part of their lives. Everyone can identify the writing of a family member or spouse, so describing how handwriting is identified is not too hard. Explaining how DNA analysis works is more difficult.

Social Media Career Tip

When people Google you, they won't click past the first page. Check to see where your material appears on a regular basis. **f** **Linked in**

FAST FACTS

FORENSIC SCIENTIST, JOB DESCRIPTION:

- Examine, test, and analyze tissue samples, chemical substances, physical materials, and ballistics evidence collected at a crime scene.

WHAT KIND OF TRAINING IS REQUIRED?

- Bachelor's degree in science, particularly chemistry, biology, biochemistry, or physics.

- Certification programs (usually 2 years' additional study) can help prospective applicants specialize as forensic consultants, fingerprint technicians, forensic investigators, laboratory technicians, and fingerprint examiners.

ANNUAL SALARY RANGE?

- $25,100 – $65,000

---

database. The largest and most important database is the National Combined DNA Index System (CODIS). Operated by the FBI since 1998, CODIS gives local and state law enforcement agencies access to the DNA profiles of those who have been convicted of various crimes. CODIS contains DNA records of 9.7 million people, and as of June 2012, the database had produced 182,200 cold hits nationwide.[31]

New Developments The investigative uses of DNA fingerprinting are expanding rapidly. Taking advantage of a new technique known as "touch DNA," investigators can collect evidence from surfaces that are not marked by obvious clues such as bloodstains or well-preserved fingerprints. With this technique, forensic scientists can gather enough microscopic cells to test for the presence of DNA by scraping a piece of food or an article of clothing. In addition, although CODIS was designed to help police solve murders and rapes, it is becoming increasingly useful in identifying suspects in burglaries and other property crimes. A recent study funded by the National Institute of Justice found that twice as many suspects were arrested when DNA fingerprinting was added to property crime investigations.[32]

Because relatives have similar DNA, law enforcement agents are now conducting "familial searches" of parents, siblings, and other relatives to gain more information about suspects. One such search led to the 2010 arrest of Los Angeles's "Grim Sleeper"—so called because there was a fourteen-year gap between the murders he committed in the 1980s and those in the first decade of the 2000s. Investigators were able to narrow their focus to Lonnie Franklin, Jr., after DNA evidence from various Grim Sleeper crime scenes exhibited similarities to the DNA of Lonnie's son Christopher, who had recently been convicted on a weapons charge (see the photo alongside).

Forensic experts are also raising the possibility that DNA will be able to act as a "genetic witness." That is, a DNA sample taken from a crime scene soon may be able to provide law enforcement with a physical description of a suspect, including her or his eye, skin, and hair color and age.[33]

How did "familial DNA" lead investigators to Lonnie Franklin, Jr., left, shown here in a Los Angeles courtroom? Why might privacy advocates criticize this method of using DNA to identify criminal suspects?

AP Photo/Irfan Khan, Pool

SELFASSESSMENT

Fill in the blanks and check your answers on page 154.

_____ officers make up the backbone of a police department. One of their primary functions is to _____ crime by maintaining a visible _____ in the community. _____, in contrast, investigate crimes that have already occurred. In the past two decades, _____, or the science of crime investigation, has been revolutionized by the technique of _____ _____, in which crime labs use samples of a person's genetic material to match suspects to crimes.

POLICE STRATEGIES: WHAT WORKS

No matter how "miraculous" DNA fingerprinting may appear, the technology does have its limitations. Forensic evidence, including DNA fingerprinting, is the primary factor in only about 30 percent of solved cold cases.[34] Furthermore, any evidence, forensic or otherwise, can only help police solve a crime that has already taken place. It does little to prevent crime that has yet to occur. Finally, law enforcement's ability to take advantage of DNA fingerprinting is being hampered by extensive budget cuts. The state crime lab in Kansas, for example, is facing a backlog of nearly one thousand cases, while the state has reduced the number of technicians who work there by one-fifth.[35]

Police departments are facing the same financial pressures. Across the nation, many are being forced to reduce staff to levels not seen since the 1980s. The results can be disheartening: two months after Camden, New Jersey, laid off more than 160 officers in January 2011, violent crime in the city rose 19 percent, and aggravated assaults with firearms increased by 259 percent.[36] Some departments have taken drastic steps in the face of budget cuts. After losing three hundred officers, the Fresno (California) Police Department began utilizing volunteers to perform duties such as collecting evidence and interviewing witnesses.[37] For the most part, however, police administrators are refocusing on two bulwarks of police crime prevention—responding to calls for service and providing effective patrols.

Learning Objective **4** Explain why differential response strategies enable police departments to respond efficiently to 911 calls.

RESPONSE TIME TO 911 CALLS

Even though law enforcement officers do not like to think of themselves as being at the "beck and call" of citizens, that is the operational basis of much police work. All police departments practice **incident-driven policing,** in which calls for service are the primary instigators of action. Between 40 and 60 percent of police activity is the result of 911 calls or other citizen requests, which means that police officers in the field initiate only about half of such activity.[38]

RESPONSE TIME AND EFFICIENCY The speed with which the police respond to calls for service has traditionally been seen as a crucial aspect of crime fighting and crime prevention. In incident-driven policing, the ideal scenario is as follows: a citizen sees a person committing a crime and calls 911, and the police arrive quickly and catch the perpetrator in the act. Alternatively, a citizen who is the victim of a crime, such as a mugging, calls 911 as soon as possible, and the police arrive to catch the mugger before she or he can flee the immediate area of the crime. Although such scenarios are quite rare in real life, **response time,** or the time elapsed between the instant a call for service is received and the instant the police arrive on the scene, has become a benchmark for police efficiency.

IMPROVING RESPONSE TIME EFFICIENCY Many police departments have come to realize that overall response time is not as critical as response time for the most important calls. For this reason, since the mid-1990s, a number of metropolitan areas have introduced 311 nonemergency call systems to reduce the strain on 911 operations.[39] Another popular method of improving performance in this area is a **differential response** strategy, in which the police distinguish among different calls for service so that they can respond more quickly to the most serious incidents.

Suppose, for example, that a police department receives two calls for service at the same time. The first caller reports that a burglar is in her house, and the second says that he has returned home from work to find his automobile missing. If the department employs differential response, the burglary in progress—a "hot" crime—will receive immediate attention. The missing automobile—a "cold" crime that could have been committed several hours earlier—will receive attention "as time permits," and the caller may even be asked to make an appointment to come to the police station to formally report the theft.

AN OUTDATED SYSTEM The most pressing shortcomings of America's 911 services are not organizational, but rather technological. These systems were developed more than forty years ago, when copper-wire landlines ran between telephones and a central switch. Today, more than 70 percent of emergency calls for service come from mobile phones, and increasing numbers of consumers are taking advantage of VoIP (voice-over-Internet protocol) technology to turn their computers into telephones. By 2011, a quarter of American households were wireless only—a percentage that is certain to increase in the near future.[40]

This situation presents a problem for law enforcement. Standard 911 systems cannot pinpoint the exact location of a mobile phone or a computer. If a caller is unable to provide that information, then, it can prove very difficult for police officers to determine the site of the emergency. To resolve this issue, various government agencies and private businesses are planning a new nationwide intelligence network that should be able to locate all calls, read texts, and even watch streaming video. The network will not be fully operational, however, until 2016.[41]

PATROL STRATEGIES

Earlier in this chapter, we noted that the majority of police officers are assigned to patrol duties. Most of these officers work **general patrol,** making the rounds of a specific area with the purpose of carrying out the various patrol functions. Every police department in the United States patrols its jurisdiction using automobiles. In addition, 53 percent utilize foot patrols; 32 percent, bicycle patrols; 16 percent, motorcycle patrols; 4 percent, boat patrols; and 1 percent, horse patrols.[42]

General patrols are *random* because the officers spend a substantial amount of their shifts hoping to notice any crimes that may be occurring. In contrast, **directed patrols** are specifically designed to deal with crimes that commonly occur in certain locations and under circumstances that provide police with opportunity for preparation. The Pittsburgh (Pennsylvania) Police Department's recent decision to set up weekend traffic checkpoints and send undercover detectives into "nuisance" bars in some of the city's high-violence neighborhoods is a good example of a directed patrol.

A communications supervisor monitors 911 calls and police dispatches for the Boynton Beach, Florida, police department. What are some reasons that a 911 caller might not be able to relate her or his exact location and the nature of the emergency? Mark Randall/MCT/Landov

TESTING GENERAL PATROL THEORIES IN KANSAS CITY Some observers have compared a patrol officer to a scarecrow because of the hope that the officer's presence alone will deter any would-be criminals from attempting a crime.[43] This theory was tested in the Kansas City Preventive Patrol Experiment of 1972 and 1973. With the cooperation of the local police department, a team of researchers chose three areas, each comprising five beats with similar crime statistics. Over the course of twelve months, the police applied different patrol strategies to each designated area:

- On the *control* beats, normal preventive measures were taken, meaning that a single automobile drove the streets when not answering a call for service.
- On the *proactive* beats, the level of preventive measures was increased, with automobile patrols being doubled or tripled.
- On the *reactive* beats, preventive patrol was eliminated entirely, and patrol cars only answered calls for service.

Before, during, and after the experiments, the researchers also interviewed residents of the three designated areas to determine their opinion of police service and fear of crime.

The results of the Kansas City experiment were somewhat shocking. Researchers found that increasing or decreasing preventive patrol had little or no impact on crimes, public opinion, the effectiveness of the police, police response time, traffic accidents, or reports of crime to police.[44]

General Patrol A patrol strategy that relies on police officers monitoring a certain area with the goal of detecting crimes in progress or preventing crime by their presence.

Directed Patrol A patrol strategy that is designed to focus on a specific type of criminal activity at a specific time.

PREDICTIVE POLICING AND CRIME MAPPING

In the previous chapter, we discussed how predictive, or intelligence-led, policing strategies help law enforcement agencies anticipate patterns of criminal activity, allowing them to respond to, or even prevent, crime more effectively. Predictive policing is increasingly attractive to police administrators because, in theory, it requires fewer resources than traditional policing. "We're facing a situation where we have

"Why aren't we thinking more about 'wheredunit' rather than 'whodunit'?"

—Lawrence Sherman, American criminologist

thirty percent more calls for service but twenty percent less staff than in the year 2000," said Zach Friend, a crime analyst for the Santa Cruz (California) Police Department. "So, we have to deploy our resources in a more effective way."[45] Friend and his colleagues are doing so by using computer models for predicting aftershocks from earthquakes to generate projections about where property crimes are most likely to take place.

FINDING "HOT SPOTS" Predictive policing strategies are strongly linked with directed patrols, which seek to improve on general patrols by targeting specific high-crime areas already known to law enforcement. The target areas for directed patrols are often called **hot spots** because they contain greater numbers of criminals and have higher-than-average levels of victimization. Needless to say, police administrators are not sticking pins in maps to determine where hot spots exist. Rather, police departments are using **crime mapping** technology to locate and identify hot spots and "cool" them down. Crime mapping uses geographic information systems (GIS) to track criminal acts as they occur in time and space. Once sufficient information has been gathered, it is analyzed to predict future crime patterns.

Researchers are using GIS technology and hot spot policing techniques to reassess the results of the Kansas City experiment detailed on the previous page. Following that undertaking, professor James Q. Wilson noted that it proved nothing about the capabilities of foot patrols, as it focused on police officers in marked automobiles.[46] Several years ago, a group of criminologists used GIS techniques to study foot patrols in sixty violent crime hot spots in Philadelphia. The results, released in 2011, showed that levels of violent crime in the proactive beats were 23 percent lower than those in the control beats. These findings suggests that directed foot patrols can make neighborhoods safer, particularly neighborhoods marked by high levels of crime.[47]

THE RISE OF COMPSTAT Computerized crime mapping was popularized when the New York Police Department launched CompStat in the mid-1990s. Still in use, CompStat starts with police officers reporting the exact location of crime and other crime-related information to department officials. These reports are then fed into a computer, which prepares grids of a particular city or neighborhood and highlights areas with a high incidence of serious offenses. (See Figure 5.3 on the facing page for an example of a GIS crime map.)

In New York and many other cities, the police department holds "Crime Control Strategy Meetings," during which precinct commanders are held accountable for CompStat's data-based reports in their districts. In theory, this system provides the police with accurate information about patterns of crime and gives them the ability to flood hot spots with officers at short notice. About two-thirds of large departments now employ some form of computerized crime mapping,[48] and Wesley Skogan, a criminologist at Northwestern University, believes that CompStat and similar technologies are the most likely cause of recent declines in big-city crime.[49]

ARREST STRATEGIES

Like patrol strategies, arrest strategies can be broken into two categories that reflect the intent of police administrators. **Reactive arrests** are those arrests made by police officers, usually on general patrol, who observe a criminal act or respond to a call for service. **Proactive arrests** occur when the police take the initiative to target a particular type of criminal or behavior. Proactive arrests are often associated with directed patrols of hot spots, and thus are believed by many experts to have a greater influence on an area's crime rates.[50]

The popularity of proactive theories was solidified by a magazine article that James Q. Wilson and George L. Kelling wrote in 1982.[51] In their piece, entitled "Broken

Hot Spots Concentrated areas of high criminal activity that draw a directed police response.

Crime Mapping Technology that allows crime analysts to identify trends and patterns of criminal behavior within a given area.

Reactive Arrests Arrests that come about as part of the ordinary routine of police patrol and responses to calls for service.

Proactive Arrests Arrests that occur because of concerted efforts by law enforcement agencies to respond to a particular type of criminal or criminal behavior.

FIGURE 5.3 A GIS Crime Map for a Neighborhood in New Orleans

This crime map shows the incidence of various crimes during a two-week period in a neighborhood near downtown New Orleans.

The Omega Group/crimemapping.com

Windows," Wilson and Kelling argued that reform-era policing strategies focused on violent crime to the detriment of the vital police role of promoting the quality of life in neighborhoods. As a result, many communities, particularly in large cities, had fallen into a state of disorder and disrepute, with two very important consequences. First, these neighborhoods—with their broken windows, dilapidated buildings, and lawless behavior by residents—send out "signals" that criminal activity is tolerated. Second, this disorder spreads fear among law-abiding citizens, dissuading them from leaving their homes or attempting to improve their surroundings.

Thus, the **broken windows theory** is based on "order maintenance" of neighborhoods by cracking down on "quality-of-life" crimes such as panhandling, public drinking and urinating, loitering, and graffiti painting. Only by encouraging directed arrest strategies with regard to these quality-of-life crimes, the two professors argued, could American cities be rescued from rising crime rates.

COMMUNITY POLICING AND PROBLEM SOLVING

In "Broken Windows," Wilson and Kelling insisted that to reduce fear and crime in high-risk neighborhoods, police had to rely on the cooperation of citizens. For all its drawbacks, the political era of policing (see Chapter 4) did have characteristics that observers such as Wilson and Kelling have come to see as advantageous. During the nineteenth century, the police were much more involved in the community than they were after the reforms. Officers performed many duties that today are associated with social services, such as operating soup kitchens and providing lodging for homeless people. They also played a more direct role in keeping public order by "running in" drunks and intervening in minor disturbances.[52] In many aspects, **community policing** advocates a return to this understanding of the police mission.

Broken Windows Theory
Wilson and Kelling's theory that a neighborhood in disrepair signals that criminal activity is tolerated in the area. By cracking down on quality-of-life crimes, police can reclaim the neighborhood and encourage law-abiding citizens to live there.

Community Policing
A policing philosophy that emphasizes community support for and cooperation with the police in preventing crime.

Learning Objective **5** Explain community policing and its contribution to the concept of problem-oriented policing.

Two Washington, D.C., police officers offer suggestions to a six-year-old during the annual "Shop with a Cop" event in the nation's capital. How can establishing friendly relations with citizens help law enforcement agencies reduce crime?

Andrew Harnik/*Washington Times*/Landov

RETURN TO THE COMMUNITY Community policing can be defined as an approach that promotes community-police partnerships, proactive problem solving, and community engagement to address issues such as fear of crime and the causes of such fear in a particular area.[53] During the reform era, police were more detached from the community. They did their jobs to the best of their ability but were more concerned with making arrests or speedily answering calls for service than learning about the problems or concerns of the citizenry. In their efforts to eliminate police corruption, administrators put more emphasis on segregating the police from the public than on cooperatively working with citizens to resolve community problems. Under community policing, patrol officers have much more freedom to improvise. They are expected to develop personal relationships with residents and to encourage those residents to become involved in making the community a safer place.

The Quiet Revolution The strategy of increasing police presence in the community has been part of, in the words of George Kelling, a "quiet revolution" in American law enforcement.[54] Today, nearly two-thirds of police departments mention community policing in their mission statements, and a majority of the departments in large cities offer community policing training for employees.[55] Furthermore, the idea seems to be popular among law enforcement agents. A 2011 survey of more than 1,200 officers in eleven police departments found that between 60 and 95 percent agreed with the idea that "police officers should try to solve non-crime problems on their beat."[56] A majority of the officers also reported having positive relations with members of the public, who they felt generally appreciated community policing efforts.[57]

Criticisms of Community Policing Nevertheless, despite, or maybe because of, its "feel-good" associations, community policing has been the target of several criticisms. First, more than half of the police chiefs and sheriffs in a survey conducted by the National Institute of Justice were unclear about the actual meaning of "community policing,"[58] leading one observer to joke that Professor Kelling's revolution is even quieter than expected.[59] Second, since its inception, community policing has been criticized—not the least by police officials—as having more to do with public relations than with actual crime fighting.[60] Finally, a number of experts feel that American law enforcement's new emphasis on homeland security, which relies on implementing technology and gathering intelligence, is incompatible with the tenets of community policing.[61]

PROBLEM-ORIENTED POLICING A drawback inherent in most police strategies can be summed up with the truism, "Catch a thief, there will always be another one to take his or her place." In other words, common street criminals such as burglars, auto thieves, and shoplifters are so numerous that arresting one seems to have little or no impact.[62] By itself, community policing may not offer much hope for solving this dilemma. But having law enforcement establish a cooperative presence in the community is a crucial part of a strategy that focuses on long-term crime prevention. Introduced by Herman Goldstein of the Police Executive Research Forum in the 1970s, **problem-oriented policing** is based on the premise that police depart-

Problem-Oriented Policing A policing philosophy that requires police to identify potential criminal activity and develop strategies to prevent or respond to that activity.

FIGURE 5.4 Operation Heat Wave

In 2011, the Dallas Police Department combined aspects of crime mapping, community policing, and problem-oriented policing in an effort to reduce burglaries and auto thefts during the summer. The initiative, called Operation Heat Wave, required two steps.

Step One—Create TAAGs

Using GIS technology (see page 140), Dallas crime experts have determined which parts of the city are most likely to see high rates of victimization and criminal behavior. The resulting Target Area Action Grids (TAAGs) indicated which areas will be provided with directed police patrols. To determine the most vulnerable neighborhoods, Dallas police looked at the following indicators:

Event-Based Indicators	Place-Based Indicators
1. Arrests for drugs, prostitution and weapons.	1. Gang members' home addresses.
2. Calls for service (see page 132).	2. The home addresses of persons arrested for burglary, robbery, and auto theft.
3. Part I offenses (see page 36 in Chapter 2 to review these crimes).	3. The home addresses of persons on parole (covered in Chapter 12).

Step Two—Go Door to Door

The event- and place-based indicators identified twenty-seven at-risk areas, covering about 7 percent of the city. Over the course of the summer, each detective within the department spent thirty-two to forty hours in these neighborhoods, in uniform, going door to door to engage the residents. The detectives tried to obtain information about offenses committed nearby and encouraged attendance at community crime-watch meetings.

Source: Brigitte Gassaway, Steven Armon, and Dana Perez, "Engaging the Community: Operation Heat Wave," *Geography and Public Safety* (October 2011), 8–9.

ments devote too many of their resources to reacting to calls for service and too few to "acting on their own initiative to prevent or reduce community problems."[63] To rectify this situation, problem-oriented policing moves beyond simply responding to incidents and attempts instead to control or even solve the root causes of criminal behavior.

Goldstein's theory encourages police officers to stop looking at their work as a day-to-day proposition. Rather, they should try to shift the patterns of criminal behavior in a positive direction. For example, instead of responding to a 911 call concerning illegal drug use by simply arresting the offender—a short-term response—the patrol officers should also look at the long-term implications of the situation. They should analyze the pattern of similar arrests in the area and interview the arrestee to determine the reasons, if any, that the site was selected for drug activity. Then additional police action should be taken to prevent further drug sales at the identified location. (For an example of problem-oriented policing in action, see Figure 5.4 above.)

SELFASSESSMENT

Fill in the blanks and check your answers on page 154.
Without exception, modern police departments practice _____-driven policing, in which officers respond to calls for _____, such as 911 phone calls after a crime has occurred. Along the same lines, most patrol officers work _____ patrols, in which they cover designated areas and react to the incidents they encounter. _____ patrols, which often focus on "hot spots" of crime, and _____ arrest policies, which target a particular type of criminal behavior, have both been shown to be very effective.

"US VERSUS THEM": ISSUES IN MODERN POLICING

The night after two police officers shot and killed Jaime Gonzalez, described in the opening to this chapter, the Brownsville police received several death threats. Apparently, some members of the community were unconvinced by the argument that the officers' actions were justified because Gonzalez appeared to be in possession of an actual handgun. Indeed, there seems to be a public perception, fueled by heavy coverage of police shootings, that American law enforcement agents are "trigger happy" when it comes to using lethal force. The reality is that such fatal shootings are quite rare.[64] According to one estimate, the average New York City police officer would have to work 694 years to shoot and kill someone, and the likelihood is more remote in most other cities.[65]

The question of when to use lethal force is one of many on-the-job issues that make law enforcement such a challenging and often difficult career. When faced with a scenario such as the one in the halls of Brownsville's Cummings Middle School, sometimes police officers make the right decisions, and sometimes they make the wrong ones. Often, it is difficult to tell the two apart.

POLICE SUBCULTURE

As a rule, police officers do not appreciate being second-guessed when it comes to their split-second shooting decisions. To officers, it often seems that civilians believe that suspects with weapons should be given a "free shot" before being fired at by law enforcement.[66] Feelings of frustration and mistrust toward the public are hallmarks of **police subculture.** This broad term is used to describe the basic assumptions and values that permeate law enforcement agencies and are taught to new members of a law enforcement agency as the proper way to think, perceive, and act. Every organization has a subculture, with values shaped by the particular aspects and pressures of that organization. In the police subculture, those values are formed in an environment characterized by danger, stress, boredom, and violence.

From the first day on the job, rookies begin the process of **socialization,** in which they are taught the values and rules of police work. This process is aided by a number of rituals that are common to the law enforcement experience. Police theorist Harry J. Mullins believes that the following events are critical to the police officer's acceptance, and even embrace, of police subculture:

- Attending a police academy.
- Working with a senior officer, who passes on the lessons of police work and life to the younger officer.
- Making the initial felony arrest.
- Using force to make an arrest for the first time.
- Using or witnessing deadly force for the first time.
- Witnessing a major, traumatic incident for the first time.[67]

Each of these rituals makes it clear to the police officer that this is not a "normal" job. The only other people who can understand the stresses of police work are fellow officers, and consequently, law enforcement officers tend to insulate themselves from civilians. Eventually, the insulation breeds mistrust, and the police officer develops an "us versus them" outlook toward those outside the force. In turn, this outlook creates what sociologist William Westly called the **blue curtain,** also known as the "blue wall of silence" or simply "the code."[68] This curtain separates the police from the civilians they are meant to protect.

THE PHYSICAL DANGERS OF POLICE WORK

On December 9, 2011, police sergeant David Enzbrenner was serving a nuisance order in Atchison, Kansas, when a gunman "came out of nowhere" and fatally shot him in the back of the head. According to the Officer Down Memorial Page, Enzbrenner was one of

Police Subculture The values and perceptions that are shared by members of a police department and, to a certain extent, by all law enforcement agents.

Socialization The process through which a police officer is taught the values and expected behavior of the police subculture.

Blue Curtain A metaphorical term used to refer to the value placed on secrecy and the general mistrust of the outside world shared by many police officers.

170 law enforcement agents who died in the line of duty in 2011, and one of sixty-seven who were killed by hostile gunfire.[69] In addition, about 53,000 assaults are committed against police officers annually, with a quarter of these assaults resulting in an injury.[70] These numbers are hardly surprising. As police experts John S. Dempsey and Linda S. Forst point out, police "deal constantly with what may be the most dangerous species on this planet—the human being."[71] At the same time, Dempsey and Forst note that according to data compiled by the federal government, citizens and the police come into contact about 40 million times a year.[72] Given this figure, the police have relatively low death and injury rates.

A fellow officer pays his respects during the funeral of Chattachoochee Hills, Georgia, police officer Mike Vogt, who was shot and killed while on patrol. Besides physical violence, what are some of the other occupational threats that police officers face on a daily basis?

AP Photo/Brant Sanderlin

STRESS AND THE MENTAL DANGERS OF POLICE WORK

In addition to physical dangers, police work entails considerable mental pressure and stress. Professor John Violanti and his colleagues at the University of Buffalo have determined that police officers experience unusually high levels of *cortisol*, otherwise known as the "stress hormone." Cortisol is associated with serious health problems such as diabetes and heart disease.[73] "Intervention is necessary to help officers deal with this difficult and stressful occupation," says Violanti. "[Police officers] need to learn how to relax, how to think differently about things they experience as a cop."[74]

POLICE STRESSORS The conditions that cause stress—such as worries over finances or relationships—are known as **stressors.** Each profession has its own set of stressors, but police are particularly vulnerable to occupational pressures and stress factors such as the following:

- The constant fear of being a victim of violent crime.
- Exposure to violent crime and its victims.
- The need to comply with the law in nearly every job action.
- Lack of community support.
- Negative media coverage.

Stressors The aspects of police work and life that lead to feelings of stress.

Burnout A mental state that occurs when a person suffers from exhaustion and has difficulty functioning normally as a result of overwork and stress.

Police face a number of internal pressures as well, including limited opportunities for career advancement, excessive paperwork, and low wages and benefits. The unconventional hours of shift work can also interfere with an officer's private life and contribute to lack of sleep. Each of these is a primary stressor associated with police work.[75]

THE CONSEQUENCES OF POLICE STRESS Police stress can manifest itself in different ways. The University of Buffalo study cited above found that the stresses of law enforcement often lead to high blood pressure and heart problems.[76] Other research shows that police officers are three times more likely to suffer from alcoholism than the average American.[77] If stress becomes overwhelming, an officer may suffer from **burnout,** becoming listless and ineffective as a result of mental and physical exhaustion. Another problem related to stress is *post-traumatic* *stress disorder (PTSD).* Often recognized in war veterans and rape victims, PTSD is a reaction to a stressor that evokes significant stress. For police officers, such stressors might include the death of a fellow agent or the shooting of a civilian. An officer suffering from PTSD will:

1. Re-experience the traumatic event through nightmares and flashbacks.
2. Become less and less involved in the outside world by withdrawing from others and refusing to participate in normal social interactions.
3. Experience "survival guilt," which may lead to loss of sleep and memory impairment.[78]

The effects of stress can be seen most tragically in the high rate of suicide among law enforcement officers—three times higher than in the general population.[79]

AUTHORITY AND THE USE OF FORCE

Learning Objective 6 Determine when police officers are justified in using deadly force.

If the police subculture is shaped by the dangers of the job, it often finds expression through authority. The various symbols of authority that decorate a police officer—including the uniform, badge, nightstick, and firearm—establish the power she or he holds over civilians. For better or for worse, both police officers and civilians tend to equate terms such as *authority* and *respect* with the ability to use force.

Near the beginning of the twentieth century, a police officer stated that his job was to "protect the good people and treat the crooks rough."[80] Implicit in the officer's statement is the idea that to do the protecting, he had to do some roughing up as well. This attitude toward the use of force is still with us today. Indeed, it is generally accepted that not only is police use of force inevitable, but that police officers who are unwilling to use force in certain circumstances cannot do their jobs effectively.

THE "MISUSE" OF FORCE In general, the use of physical force by law enforcement personnel is very rare, occurring in only about 1.4 percent of the 40 million annual police-public encounters mentioned earlier. Still, the Department of Justice estimates that law enforcement officers threaten to use force or do use force in encounters with 770,000 Americans a year, and nearly 14 percent of those incidents result in a complaint against the officer.[81] Federal authorities also report that about 690 civilian deaths occur in the process of an arrest on an annual basis.[82] Of course, police officers are often justified in using force to protect themselves and other citizens. As noted earlier, police officers are the targets of tens of thousands of assaults each year.

At the same time, few observers would be naïve enough to believe that the police are *always* justified in the use of force. A recent survey of emergency room physicians found that 98 percent believed that they had treated patients who were victims of excessive police force.[83] How, then, is "misuse" of force to be defined? One attempt to define excessive force that has been lauded by legal scholars, if not necessarily by police officers, was offered by the Christopher Commission. Established in Los Angeles in 1991 after the beating of African American motorist Rodney King, the commission advised that "an officer may resort to force only where he or she faces a credible threat, and then may only use the minimum amount necessary to control the subject."[84]

To provide guidance for officers in this tricky area, nearly every law enforcement agency designs a *use of force matrix.* As the example in Figure 5.5 on the facing page shows, such a matrix presents officers with the proper force options for different levels of contact with a civilian. Note that there are two examples of *less-lethal weapons* referenced in the figure: chemical spray and the Taser. In general, less-lethal weapons are designed to subdue but not seriously harm their targets. The most common chemical spray is oleoresin capsicum, an organic substance that causes a sensation similar to hav-

FIGURE 5.5 The Orlando (Florida) Police Department's Use of Force Matrix

Like most local law enforcement agencies, the Orlando Police Department has a policy to guide its officers' use of force. These policies instruct an officer on how to react to an escalating series of confrontations with a civilian and are often expressed visually, as shown here.

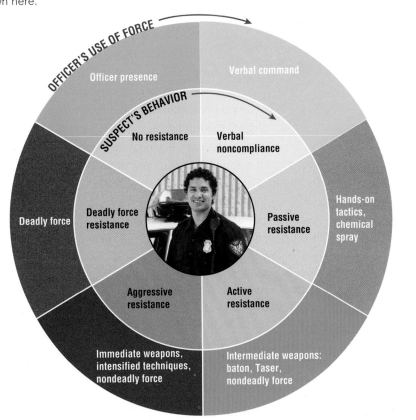

OFFICER'S USE OF FORCE

SUSPECT'S BEHAVIOR

- Officer presence
- Verbal command
- No resistance
- Verbal noncompliance
- Deadly force
- Deadly force resistance
- Passive resistance
- Hands-on tactics, chemical spray
- Aggressive resistance
- Active resistance
- Immediate weapons, intensified techniques, nondeadly force
- Intermediate weapons: baton, Taser, nondeadly force

Mie Ahmt/iStockphoto

Source: Michael E. Miller, "Taser Use and the Use-of-Force Continuum," *Police Chief* (September 2010), 72.

ing sand or needles in the eyes when sprayed in a suspect's face. The Taser is a handheld electrical stun gun that fires blunt darts up to a range of about twenty-one feet. On contact, these darts deliver 50,000 volts for about five seconds.

TYPES OF FORCE To comply with the various, and not always consistent, laws concerning the use of force, a police officer must understand that there are two kinds of force: *nondeadly force* and *deadly force*. Most force used by law enforcement is nondeadly force. In most states, the use of nondeadly force is regulated by the concept of **reasonable force,** which allows the use of nondeadly force when a reasonable person would assume that such force was necessary. In contrast, **deadly force** is force that an objective police officer realizes will place the subject in direct threat of serious injury or death.

THE UNITED STATES SUPREME COURT AND USE OF FORCE The United States Supreme Court set the limits for the use of deadly force by law enforcement officers in *Tennessee v. Garner* (1985).[85] The case involved an incident in which Memphis police officer Elton Hymon shot and killed a suspect who was trying to climb over a fence after stealing ten dollars from a residence. Hymon testified that he had been trained to shoot to keep a suspect from escaping, and indeed Tennessee law at the time allowed police officers to apprehend fleeing suspects in this manner.

In reviewing the case, the Court focused not on Hymon's action but on the Tennessee statute itself, ultimately finding it unconstitutional:

Reasonable Force The degree of force that is appropriate to protect the police officer or other citizens and is not excessive.

Deadly Force Force applied by a police officer that is likely or intended to cause death.

When the suspect poses no immediate threat to the officer and no threat to others, the use of deadly force is unjustified.... It is not better that all felony suspects die than that they escape.[86]

The Court's decision forced twenty-three states to change their fleeing felon rules, but it did not completely eliminate police discretion in such situations. Police officers still may use deadly force if they have probable cause to believe that the fleeing suspect poses a threat of serious injury or death to the officers or others. (We will discuss the concept of probable cause in the next chapter.) In essence, the Court recognized that police officers must be able to make split-second decisions without worrying about the legal ramifications.

Four years after the *Garner* case, the Court tried to clarify this concept in *Graham v. Connor* (1989), stating that the use of any force should be judged by the "reasonableness of the moment."[87] In 2004, the Court modified this rule by suggesting that an officer's use of force could be "reasonable" even if, by objective measures, the force was not needed to protect the officer or others in the area.[88] (See the feature *You Be the Sheriff's Deputy—Threat Level* below.)

SELFASSESSMENT
Fill in the blanks and check your answers on page 154.

Like any organization, a police department has a _____ that determines the values of its employees. In law enforcement, these values are shaped by the _____ dangers, such as assault, and mental dangers, such as high levels of _____, that officers face every day. Laws regulating police use of force rely on two concepts: _____ force, which is the amount of force that a rational person would consider necessary in a given situation, and _____ force, which is a level of force that will place the subject in grave bodily danger.

YOU BE THE SHERIFF'S DEPUTY
Threat Level

THE SITUATION You receive a call from dispatch telling you that Lee Dylan, a mentally unstable man, has just escaped from a local jail where he was being held on suspicion of committing a nonviolent felony. Driving toward the jail, you see a man matching Dylan's description running down a back alley. Jumping out of your car, you and your partner follow on foot. Eventually, you and your partner corner the man, who is indeed Dylan, in a construction site. Dylan, who is of average height and build, grabs a loose brick and makes threatening motions with it. You pull your gun and, along with your partner, move toward Dylan. You yell, "Drop the brick!" He screams, "You're going to have to kill me!" and rushes at you.

THE LAW The use of force by a law enforcement agent—even deadly force—is based on the concept of reasonableness. In other words, would a reasonable police officer in this officer's shoes have been justified in using force?

YOUR DECISION Does Dylan pose a threat of serious bodily harm to you or your partner? How you answer this question will determine the type of force you use against him. Keep in mind that almost all police officers experience an adrenaline rush in stressful situations, and this may influence your reaction.

[To see how a law enforcement officer in Cincinnati reacted in similar circumstances, go to Example 5.1 in Appendix B.]

POLICE MISCONDUCT AND ETHICS

As the two deadly force cases highlighted at the end of the previous section show, American courts generally will uphold a police officer's freedom to decide "what law to enforce, how much to enforce it, against whom, and on what occasions."[89] This judicial support of police discretion is based on the following factors:

- Police officers are generally considered trustworthy and are therefore assumed to make honest decisions, regardless of contradictory testimony by a suspect.
- Experience and training give officers the ability to determine whether certain activity poses a threat to society, and to take any reasonable action necessary to investigate or prevent such activity.
- Due to the nature of their jobs, police officers are extremely knowledgeable in human, and by extension criminal, behavior.
- Police officers may find themselves in danger of personal, physical harm and must be allowed to take reasonable and necessary steps to protect themselves.[90]

At the same time, as we noted during our discussion of discretion in Chapter 1, freedom to make decisions can mean freedom to make the wrong decisions. Too often, the enormous amount of discretion afforded to police officers, when mixed with the temptations inherent in the law enforcement working environment, can lead to excessive force and other forms of police misconduct, which we will address in this section.

POLICE CORRUPTION

Police *corruption* has been a concern since the first organized American police departments. As you recall from Chapter 4, a desire to eradicate, or at least limit, corruption was one of the motivating factors behind the reform movement of policing. For general purposes, **police corruption** can be defined as the misuse of authority by a law enforcement officer in a manner designed to produce personal gain.

Police Corruption The abuse of authority by a law enforcement officer for personal gain.

TYPES OF CORRUPTION The Knapp Commission, set up to investigate the behavior of "dirty cops" in New York City in the 1970s, identified three basic, traditional types of police corruption:

Learning Objective **7** Identify the three traditional forms of police corruption.

1. *Bribery,* in which the police officer accepts money or other forms of payment in exchange for "favors," which may include allowing a certain criminal activity to continue or misplacing a key piece of evidence before a trial. Related to bribery are *payoffs,* in which an officer demands payment from an individual or a business in return for certain services.
2. *Shakedowns,* in which an officer attempts to coerce money or goods from a citizen or criminal.
3. *Mooching,* in which the police officer accepts free "gifts" such as cigarettes, liquor, or services in return for favorable treatment of the gift giver.[91]

Additionally, corrupt police officers have many opportunities to engage in theft or burglary by taking money or property in the course of their duties. Vice investigations, for example, often uncover temptingly large amounts of illegal drugs and cash. In May 2011, a Wake County (North Carolina) sheriff's deputy was arrested after she improperly "confiscated" a package of marijuana and $6,435 in cash seized during a drug bust. Another scenario involves police misconduct that becomes pervasive, infecting a group of officers. In December 2011, the federal government accused several members of the East Haven (Connecticut) Police Department of a pattern of harassment toward that

In January 2012, East Haven, Connecticut, police chief Leonard Gallo, left, resigned after federal agents arrested four of his officers. How does the kind of misconduct that allegedly occurred in East Haven undermine public confidence in the police?

Courtesy of Julie Weisberg, Patch.com

Internal Affairs Unit (IAU) A division within a police department that receives and investigates complaints of wrongdoing by police officers.

Citizen Oversight The process by which citizens review complaints brought against individual police officers or police departments.

city's Hispanic community and of trying to cover up their behavior by arresting eyewitnesses and destroying security videotapes (see photo alongside).[92]

CORRUPTION IN POLICE SUBCULTURE There is no single reason why police misconduct occurs. Certain types of officers do, however, seem more likely to engage in corruption—the young, the relatively uneducated (lacking a college degree), those with records of prior criminality and citizens' complaints, and those unlikely to be promoted.[93] Lawrence Sherman has identified several stages in the moral decline of these "bad cops."[94]

In the first stage, the officers accept minor gratuities, such as the occasional free meal from a restaurant on their beat. These gratuities gradually evolve into outright bribes, in which the officers receive the gratuity for overlooking some violation. For example, a law officer may accept pay from a bar owner to ensure that the establishment is not investigated for serving alcohol to minors. In the final stage, officers no longer passively accept bribes but actively seek them out. The officers may even force the other party to pay for unwanted police services. This stage often involves large amounts of money and may entail protection of or involvement in drug, gambling, or prostitution organizations.

POLICE ACCOUNTABILITY

Given the seeming inevitability of excessive force, corruption, and other misconduct among a small number of law enforcement agents, the question becomes—*who shall police the police?* The mechanism for such investigations within a police department is the **internal affairs unit (IAU).** In many smaller police departments, the police chief conducts internal affairs investigations, while midsized and large departments have a team of internal affairs officers. The New York Police Department's IAU has an annual budget of nearly $62 million and consists of 650 officers.

As much as police officers may resent internal affairs units, many realize that it is preferable to settle disciplinary matters in house. The alternatives may be worse. Police officers are criminally liable for any crimes they might commit, and city and state governments can be held civilly liable for wrongdoing by their police officers. The taxpayers of Pennsylvania, for example, have paid nearly $13 million to settle several civil claims against a single state trooper. In 2011, this same officer was a defendant in two more lawsuits, stemming from incidents in which he allegedly beat one civilian following a traffic stop and fatally shot another during a car chase.

Many communities also rely on an external procedure for handling citizen complaints, known as **citizen oversight.** In this process, citizens—people who are not sworn officers and, by inference, not biased in favor of law enforcement officers—review allegations of police misconduct or brutality. According to data gathered by police accountability expert Samuel Walker, nearly one hundred cities now operate some kind of review procedure by an independent body.[95] For the most part, citizen review boards can only recommend action to the police chief or other executive. They do not have the power to discipline officers directly. Police officers generally resent this intrusion by civilians, and most studies have shown that civilian review boards are not widely successful in their efforts to convince police chiefs to take action against their subordinate officers.[96]

CJ&TECHNOLOGY

Self-Surveillance

One form of citizen oversight that has been highly successful in curbing police misconduct is cheap digital video. Every week, it seems, video taken by citizens using a handheld camera, smartphone, or some other device goes "viral" online, flooding the Internet with examples of police brutality or some other form of misbehavior. "All of our people should be conducting themselves like they are being recorded all the time," says Robin Larson of the Broward County (Florida) Sheriff's Department.

Indeed, law enforcement agents may soon be under constant surveillance—by their own superiors. Police departments in Aberdeen (South Dakota), Cincinnati, Fort Smith (Arkansas), and San Jose are conducting an experiment in which officers wear tiny cameras near their ears. The device sees everything the officer sees, and records it. Police administrators hope that this system will help protect officers against unfounded charges of misconduct. "In this job we're frequently accused of things we haven't done, or things that [were] kind of embellished," says Bainbridge Island (Washington) police officer Ben Sias. "And the cameras show a pretty unbiased opinion of what actually did happen."

Korhan Hasim Isik/iStockphoto

THINKING ABOUT SELF-SURVEILLANCE: Dennis Kenney, a professor at New York's John Jay College of Criminal Justice, warns that this technology "raises tremendous privacy concerns." What might be some of those concerns?

ETHICS IN LAW ENFORCEMENT

Police corruption is intricately connected with the ethics of law enforcement officers. Given the significant power that police officers hold, society expects very high standards of ethical behavior from them. These expectations are summed up in the *Police Code of Conduct*, which was developed by the International Association of Chiefs of Police in 1989.

In some aspects, the *Police Code of Conduct* is self-evident: "A police officer will not engage in acts of corruption or bribery." In others, it is idealistic, perhaps unreasonably so: "Officers will never allow personal feelings, animosities, or friendships to influence official conduct." The police working environment—rife with lying, cheating, lawbreaking, and violence—often does not allow for such ethical absolutes.

ETHICAL DILEMMAS Some police actions are obviously unethical, such as the behavior of a Pennsylvania officer who paid a woman he was dating $500 to pretend to be an eyewitness in a murder trial. The majority of ethical dilemmas that a police officer will face are not so clear cut. Criminologists Joycelyn M. Pollock and Ronald F. Becker define an ethical dilemma as a situation in which law enforcement officers:

- Do not know the right course of action;
- Have difficulty doing what they consider to be right; and/or
- Find the wrong choice very tempting.[97]

Because of the many rules that govern policing—the subject of the next chapter—police officers often find themselves tempted by a phenomenon called **noble cause corruption.** This type of corruption occurs when, in the words of John P. Crank and Michael A. Caldero,

> **Learning Objective 8** Explain what an ethical dilemma is and name four categories of ethical dilemmas that a police officer typically may face.

> **Noble Cause Corruption** Knowing misconduct by a police officer with the goal of attaining what the officer believes is a "just" result.

"officers do bad things because they believe the outcomes will be good."[98] Examples include planting evidence or lying in court to help convict someone the officer knows to be guilty and the situation discussed in the feature *A Question of Ethics—The "Dirty Harry" Problem* below.

ELEMENTS OF ETHICS Pollock and Becker, both of whom have extensive experience as ethics instructors for police departments, further identify four categories of ethical dilemmas, involving discretion, duty, honesty, and loyalty.[99]

- *Discretion.* The law provides rigid guidelines for how police officers must act and how they cannot act, but it does not offer guidelines for how officers *should* act in many circumstances. As mentioned at the beginning of this section, police officers often use discretion to determine how they should act, and ethics plays an important role in guiding discretionary actions.

- *Duty.* The concept of discretion is linked with **duty,** or the obligation to act in a certain manner. Society, by passing laws, can make a police officer's duty clearer and, in the process, help eliminate discretion from the decision-making process. But an officer's duty will not always be obvious, and ethical considerations can often supplement "the rules" of being a law enforcement agent.

- *Honesty.* Of course, honesty is a critical attribute for an ethical police officer. A law enforcement agent must make hundreds of decisions in a day, and most of them require him or her to be honest to properly do the job.

- *Loyalty.* What should a police officer do if she or he witnesses a partner using excessive force on a suspect? The choice often sets loyalty against ethics, especially if the officer does not condone the violence.

Duty The moral sense of a police officer that she or he should behave in a certain manner.

A QUESTION OF **ETHICS:** *The "Dirty Harry" Problem*

THE SITUATION A young girl has been kidnapped by a psychotic killer named Scorpio. Demanding a $200,000 ransom, Scorpio has buried the girl alive, leaving her with just enough oxygen to survive for a few hours. Detective Harry Callahan manages to find Scorpio, but the kidnapper stubbornly refuses to reveal the location of the girl. Callahan comes to the conclusion that the only way he can get this information from Scorpio in time is to beat it out of him.

THE ETHICAL DILEMMA The U.S. Constitution, as interpreted by the United States Supreme Court, forbids the torture of criminal suspects. Following proper procedure, Callahan should arrest Scorpio and advise him of his constitutional rights. If Scorpio requests an attorney, Callahan must comply. If the attorney then advises Scorpio to remain silent, there is nothing Callahan can do. Of course, after all this time, the girl will certainly be dead.*

WHAT IS THE SOLUTION? What should Detective Callahan do? According to the late Carl B. Klockars of the University of Delaware, "Each time a police officer considers deceiving a suspect into confessing by telling him that his [or her] fingerprints were found at the scene or that a conspirator has already confessed, each time a police officer considers adding some untrue details to his [or her] account of a probable cause to legitimate a crucial stop or search, [that police officer] faces" the same problem as Detective Callahan. Are police ever justified in using unlawful methods, no matter what good may ultimately be achieved?

*This scenario is taken from *Dirty Harry* (1971), one of the most popular police dramas of all time. In the film, Detective Callahan, played by Clint Eastwood, shoots Scorpio and then tortures him. Although Callahan eventually gets the information he needs, it is too late to save the girl.

Although an individual's ethical makeup is determined by a multitude of personal factors, police departments can create an atmosphere that is conducive to professionalism. Brandon V. Zuidema and H. Wayne Duff, both captains with the Lynchburg (Virginia) Police Department, believe that law enforcement administrators can encourage ethical policing by doing the following:

1. Incorporating ethics into the department's mission statement.
2. Conducting internal training sessions in ethics.
3. Accepting "honest mistakes" and helping the officer learn from those mistakes.
4. Adopting a zero-tolerance policy toward unethical decisions when the mistakes are not so honest.[100]

SELFASSESSMENT

Fill in the blanks and check your answers on page 154.

Misconduct such as accepting bribes or shaking down citizens is known as _____, and such behavior is investigated by _____ _____ units within police departments. In matters of ethics, a police officer is often guided by his or her sense of _____, or the obligation to act in a certain manner, and feelings of _____ toward fellow officers.

CHAPTER SUMMARY

Learning Objective 1 **List the three primary purposes of police patrol.** (a) The deterrence of crime, (b) the maintenance of public order, and (c) the provision of services that are not related to crime.

Learning Objective 2 **Indicate some investigation strategies that are considered aggressive.** Using undercover officers is considered an aggressive (and often dangerous) investigative technique. The use of informants is also aggressive, but involves danger for those who inform.

Learning Objective 3 **Describe how forensic experts use DNA fingerprinting to solve crimes.** Law enforcement agents gather trace evidence such as blood, semen, skin, or hair from the crime scene. Because these items are rich in DNA, which provides a unique genetic blueprint for every living organism, crime labs can create a DNA profile of the suspect and test it against other such profiles of known criminals stored in databases. If the profiles match, then law enforcement agents have found a strong suspect for the crime.

Learning Objective 4 **Explain why differential response strategies enable police departments to respond efficiently to 911 calls.** A differential response strategy allows a police department to distinguish among calls for service so that officers may respond to important calls more quickly. Therefore, a "hot" crime, such as a burglary in progress, will receive more immediate attention than a "cold" crime, such as a missing automobile that disappeared several days earlier.

Learning Objective 5 **Explain community policing and its contribution to the concept of problem-oriented policing.** Community policing involves proactive problem solving and a community-police partnership in which the community engages itself along with the police to address crime and the fear of crime in a particular geographic area. By establishing a cooperative presence in a community, police officers are better able to recognize the root causes of criminal behavior there and apply problem-oriented policing methods when necessary.

Learning Objective 6 **Determine when police officers are justified in using deadly force.** Police officers must make a reasonable judgment in determining when to use force that will place the suspect in threat of injury or death. That is, given the circumstances, the officer must reasonably assume that the use of such force is necessary to avoid serious injury or death to the officer or someone else.

Learning Objective 7 **Identify the three traditional forms of police corruption.** The three traditional forms are bribery, shakedowns, and mooching.

Learning Objective 8 **Explain what an ethical dilemma is and name four categories of ethical dilemmas that a police officer typically may face.** An ethical dilemma is a situation in which police officers (a) do not know the right course of action, (b) have difficulty doing what they consider to be right, and/or (c) find the wrong choice very tempting. The four types of ethical dilemmas involve (a) discretion, (b) duty, (c) honesty, and (d) loyalty.

QUESTIONS FOR CRITICAL ANALYSIS

1. In most states, DNA samples are routinely collected from those persons who have been *convicted* of felonies. Eighteen states, however, collect DNA from persons who have only been *arrested* for committing a crime. Why might civil libertarians frown on such policies?

2. According to the late University of Delaware professor Carl Klockars, "It makes about as much sense to have police patrol routinely in cars to fight crime as it does to have firemen patrol routinely in fire trucks to fight fire." What point do you think Professor Klockars was trying to make? Explain why you agree or disagree with his statement.

3. Research has shown that levels of violence increase in areas with high concentrations of bars, restaurants, and other establishments that serve liquor for consumption on site. How might this information be used as part of a predictive policing strategy (see pages 139–140)?

4. Relate the concept of "broken windows" to high-crime neighborhoods and potential ways to combat crime in such neighborhoods.

5. Nearly every police department in the country has a policy that limits its officers' discretion to engage in high-speed automobile pursuits of fleeing suspects. Why do you think such policies are so popular among police administrators?

KEY TERMS

ballistics **135**
blue curtain **144**
broken windows theory **141**
bureaucracy **129**
burnout **145**
citizen oversight **150**
clearance rate **134**
cold case **134**
cold hit **135**
community policing **141**
confidential informant (CI) **134**
crime mapping **140**

deadly force **147**
delegation of authority **129**
detective **133**
differential response **138**
directed patrol **139**
DNA fingerprinting **135**
duty **152**
forensics **134**
general patrol **139**
hot spots **140**
incident-driven policing **138**
internal affairs unit (IAU) **150**

noble cause corruption **151**
police corruption **149**
police subculture **144**
proactive arrests **140**
problem-oriented policing **142**
reactive arrests **140**
reasonable force **147**
response time **138**
socialization **144**
stressors **145**
sworn officer **131**
trace evidence **134**

SELF ASSESSMENT ANSWER KEY

Page 137 i. Patrol; **ii.** deter; **iii.** presence; **iv.** Detectives; **v.** forensics; **vi.** DNA fingerprinting

Page 143: i. incident; **ii.** service; **iii.** general; **iv.** Directed; **v.** proactive

Page 148: i. subculture; **ii.** physical; **iii.** stress; **iv.** reasonable; **v.** deadly

Page 153: i. corruption; **ii.** internal affairs; **iii.** duty; **iv.** loyalty

COURSEMATE

For online help and access to resources that accompany *Criminal Justice in Action: The Core*, go to **www.cengage-brain.com/shop/ISBN/978-1-285-06915-9**. Click "Access Now," where you will find flashcards, an online quiz, and other helpful study aids. If you have an access code for CourseMate, log in and go to the chapter of your choice for additional online study aids.

NOTES

1. Manny Fernandez, "Texas Death Offers Grim Reminder That Replicas Can Fool Police," *New York Times* (January 9, 2012), A8.

2. J. Pete Blair, Joycelyn Pollock, Don Montague, et al., "Reasonableness and Reaction Time," *Police Quarterly* (December 2011), 327.

3. Rogers L. Ken, *Post Traumatic Stress Disorder: A Police Officer's Report* (Livonia, MI: First Page, 2000), 13–24.

4. Quoted in Gordon Witkin, "When the Bad Guys Are Cops," *U.S. News and World Report* (September 11, 1995), 22.

5. H. Nees, "Policing 2001," *Law and Order* (January 1990), 257–264.

6. Samuel Walker, *The Police in America: An Introduction*, 2d ed. (New York: McGraw-Hill, 1992), 16.

7. George L. Kelling and Mark H. Moore, "From Political to Reform to Community: The Evolving Strategy of Police," in *Community Policing: Rhetoric or Reality*, ed. Jack Greene and Stephen Mastrofski (New York: Praeger Publishers, 1988), 13.

8. John S. Dempsey and Linda S. Forst, An *Introduction to Policing*, 6th ed. (Clifton Park, NY: Delmar Cengage Learning, 2011), 84.

9. *Ibid.*, 86–87.

10. Henry M. Wrobleski and Karen M. Hess, *Introduction to Law Enforcement and Criminal Justice*, 7th ed. (Belmont, CA: Wadsworth/Thomson Learning, 2003), 119.

11. Bureau of Justice Statistics, *Local Police Departments, 2007* (Washington, D.C.: U.S. Department of Justice, December 2010), 6.

12. Connie Fletcher, "What Cops Know," *On Patrol* (Summer 1996), 44–45.

13. David H. Bayley, *Police for the Future* (New York: Oxford University Press, 1994), 20.

14. Walker, 103.

15. Eric J. Scott, *Calls for Service: Citizens Demand an Initial Police Response* (Washington, D.C.: National Institute of Justice, 1981), 28–30.

16. William G. Gay, Theodore H. Schell, and Stephen Schack, *Routine Patrol: Improving Patrol Productivity*, vol. 1 (Washington, D.C.: National Institute of Justice, 1977), 3–6.

17. Gary W. Cordner, "The Police on Patrol," in *Police and Policing: Contemporary Issues*, ed. Dennis Jay Kenney (New York: Praeger Publishers, 1989), 60–71.

18. Anthony V. Bouza, *The Police Mystique: An Insider's Look at Cops, Crime, and the Criminal Justice System* (New York: Plenum Press, 1990), 27.

19. Peter W. Greenwood and Joan Petersilia, *The Criminal Investigation Process: Summary and Policy Implications* (Santa Monica, CA: Rand Corporation, 1975).

20. Fletcher, 46.

21. 353 U.S. 53 (1957).

22. Federal Bureau of Investigation, *Crime in the United States, 2011* (Washington, D.C.: U.S. Department of Justice, 2012), at **www.fbi.gov/about-us/cjis/ucr/crime-in-the-u.s/2011/crime-in-the-u.s.-2011/tables/table_25.**

23. James M. Cronin, Gerard R. Murphy, Lisa L. Spahr, Jessica I. Toliver, and Richard E. Weger, *Promoting Effective Homicide Investigations* (Washington, D.C.: Police Executive Research Forum, August 2007), 102–103.

24. Timothy G. Keel, "Homicide Investigations: Identifying Best Practices," *FBI Law Enforcement Bulletin* (February 2008), 5.

25. Ronald F. Becker, *Criminal Investigations*, 2d ed. (Sudbury, MA: Jones & Bartlett, 2004), 7.

26. Tom McEwen, *The Role and Impact of Forensic Evidence in the Criminal Justice System: Executive Summary* (Alexandria, VA: Institute for Law and Justice, December 2010), 4.

27. Joseph Peterson, Ira Sommers, Deborah Baskin, and Donald Johnson, *The Role and Impact of Forensic Evidence in the Criminal Justice Process* (Washington, D.C.: National Institute of Justice, September 2010), 8–9.

28. Simon A. Cole, "More Than Zero: Accounting for Error in Latent Fingerprinting Identification," *Journal of Criminal Law and Criminology* (Spring 2005), 985–1078.

29. Quoted in "New DNA Database Helps Crack 1979 N.Y. Murder Case," *Miami Herald* (March 14, 2000), 18A.

30. Judith E. Lewter, "The Use of Forensic DNA in Criminal Cases in Kentucky as Compared with Other Selected States," *Kentucky Law Journal* (1997–1998), 223.

31. "CODIS—NDIS Statistics," at **www.fbi.gov/about-us/lab/codis/ndis-statistics**.

32. Nancy Ritter, "DNA Solves Property Crimes (But Are We Ready for That?)," *NIJ Journal* (October 2008), 2–12.

33. Evan Pellegrino, "UA Team Adds Precision to DNA Forensics," *Arizona Daily Star* (March 3, 2009), A1; and Gautam Naik, "To Sketch a Thief: Genes Draw Likeness of Suspects," *Wall Street Journal* (March 29, 2009), A9.

34. Karen Hawkins, "More Are Getting Away with Murder," *Associated Press* (December 8, 2008).

35. Alex Johnson, "Already under Fire, Crime Labs Cut to the Bone" (February 23, 2010), at **www.msnbc.msn.com/id/35319938/ns/us_news-crime_and_courts**.

36. Barbara Boyer and Darran Simon, "Statistics Say Crime Is Up in Camden since Police Layoffs," *Philadelphia Inquirer* (March 3, 2011), B1.

37. Jesse McKinley, "Police Departments Turn to Volunteers," *New York Times* (March 2, 2011), A13.

38. Wrobleski and Hess, 173.

39. National Institute of Justice, *Managing Calls to the Police with 911/311 Systems* (Washington, D.C.: U.S. Department of Justice, February 5, 2005).

40. Christopher Curran, "Help Is on the Way," *Law Enforcement Technology* (July 2011), 10–13.

41. Christine Kenneally, "How to Fix 911," *Time* (April 11, 2011), 38.

42. Bureau of Justice Statistics, *Local Police Departments, 2007*, Table 12, page 15.

43. Dale O. Cloninger, "Enforcement Risks and Deterrence: A Reexamination," *Journal of Socio-Economics* 23 (1994), 273.

44. George L. Kelling, Tony Pate, Duane Dieckman, and Charles Brown, *The Kansas City Preventive Patrol Experiment: A Summary Report* (Washington, D.C.: The Police Foundation, 1974), 3–4.

45. Quoted in Erica Goode, "Sending the Police Before There's a Crime," *New York Times* (August 16, 2011), A11.

46. James Q. Wilson, *Thinking about Crime* (New York: Basic Books, 1983), 65–66.

47. Jerry H. Ratcliffe, Travis Taniguchi, Elizabeth R. Groff, and Jennifer D. Wood, "The Philadelphia Foot Patrol Experiment: A Randomized Controlled Trial of Police

Patrol Effectiveness in Violent Crime Hotspots," *Criminology* (August 2011), 796–823.

48. David Weisburd and Cynthia Lum, "The Diffusion of Computerized Crime Mapping in Policing: Linking Research and Practice," *Police Practice and Research* 6 (2005), 419–434.

49. Quoted in "New Model Police," *Economist* (June 9, 2007), 29.

50. Lawrence W. Sherman, "Policing for Crime Prevention," in *Contemporary Policing: Controversies, Challenges, and Solutions*, ed. Quint C. Thurman and Jihong Zhao (Los Angeles: Roxbury Publishing, 2004), 62.

51. Ibid., 65.

52. Mark H. Moore and George L. Kelling, "'To Serve and Protect': Learning from Police History," *Public Interest* (Winter 1983), 54–57.

53. A. Steven Deitz, "Evaluating Community Policing: Quality Police Service and Fear of Crime," *Policing: An International Journal of Police Strategies and Management* 20 (1997), 83–100.

54. George Kelling, "Police and Community: The Quiet Revolution," in *Perspectives in Policing* (Washington, D.C.: National Institute of Justice, 1988).

55. Bureau of Justice Statistics, *Local Police Departments, 2003*, (Washington, D.C.: U.S. Department of Justice, 2007), 19.

56. Wesley K. Skogan and Megan Alderden, *Police and the Community* (Washington, D.C.: National Police Research Platform, February 2011), 4.

57. Ibid., 5–6.

58. National Institute of Justice Preview, *Community Policing Strategies* (Washington, D.C.: Office of Justice Programs, November 1995), 1.

59. Jihong Zhao and Quint C. Thurman, "Community Policing: Where Are We Now?" *Crime and Delinquency* (July 1997), 345–357.

60. Robert C. Trojanowicz and David Carter, "The Philosophy and Role of Community Policing," at **www.cj.msu.edu/~people/cp/cpphil.html**.

61. Jason Vaughn Lee, "Policing after 9/11: Community Policing in an Age of Homeland Security," *Police Quarterly* (December 2010), 351.

62. Tom Casady, "Beyond Arrest: Using Crime Analysis to Prevent Crime," *The Police Chief* (September 2008), 24.

63. Herman Goldstein, "Improving Policing: A Problem-Oriented Approach," *Crime and Delinquency* 25 (1979), 236–258.

64. Blair, Pollock, and Montague, 324.

65. William A. Geller and Michael S. Scott, *Deadly Force: What We Know* (Washington, D.C.: Police Executive Research Forum, 1992).

66. Blair, Pollock, and Montague, 329.

67. Harry J. Mullins, "Myth, Tradition, and Ritual," *Law and Order* (September 1995), 197.

68. William Westly, *Violence and the Police: A Sociological Study of Law, Custom, and Morality* (Cambridge, MA: MIT Press, 1970).

69. The Officer Down Memorial Page, "Honoring Officers Killed in the Year 2011," at **www.odmp.org/year.php?year=2011**.

70. Federal Bureau of Investigation, *Law Enforcement Officers Killed and Assaulted, 2010* (Washington, D.C.: U.S. Department of Justice, 2011), at **www.fbi.gov/about-us/cjis/ucr/leoka/leoka-2010/officers-assaulted/officers-assaulted**.

71. Dempsey and Forst, 170.

72. Bureau of Justice Statistics, *Contacts between Police and the Public, 2008* (Washington, D.C.: U.S. Department of Justice, October 2011), 1.

73. University of Buffalo, "Impact of Stress on Police Officers' Physical and Mental Health," *Science Daily* (September 29, 2008), at **www.sciencedaily.com/releases/2008/09/080926105029.htm**.

74. Quoted in *ibid.*

75. J. L. O'Neil and M. A. Cushing, *The Impact of Shift Work on Police Officers* (Washington, D.C.: Police Executive Research Forum, 1991), 1.

76. University of Buffalo.

77. James Hibberd, "Police Psychology," *On Patrol* (Fall 1996), 26.

78. M. J. Horowitz, N. Wilner, N. B. Kaltreider, and W. Alvarez, "Signs and Symptoms of Post Traumatic Stress Disorder," *Archives of General Psychiatry* 37 (1980), 85–92.

79. Laurence Miller, "Practical Strategies for Preventing Officer Suicide," *Law and Order* 3 (2006), 90–92.

80. Lawrence M. Friedman, *Crime and Punishment in American History* (New York: Basic Books, 1993), 362.

81. Bureau of Justice Statistics, *Contacts between Police and the Public, 2008*, 14.

82. Bureau of Justice Statistics, *Arrest-Related Deaths, 2003–2009, Statistical Tables* (Washington, D.C.: U.S. Department of Justice, November 2011), 1.

83. H. Range Hutson, Deirdre Anglin, Phillip Rice, Demetrious N. Kyriacou, Michael Guirguis, and Jared Strote, "Excessive Use of Force by Police: A Survey of Academic Emergency Physicians," *Emergency Medicine Journal* (January 2009), 20–22.

84. Independent Commission on the Los Angeles Police Department, *Report of the Independent Commission on the Los Angeles Police Department* (1991), ix.

85. 471 U.S. 1 (1985).

86. 471 U.S. 1, 11 (1985).

87. 490 U.S. 386 (1989).

88. *Brosseau v. Haugen*, 543 U.S. 194 (2004).

89. Kenneth Culp David, *Police Discretion* (St. Paul, MN: West Publishing, 1975).

90. C. E. Pratt, "Police Discretion," *Law and Order* (March 1992), 99–100.

91. Knapp Commission, *Report on Police Corruption* (New York: Brazilier, 1973).

92. Susan Haigh, "Police Bias Found in E. Haven," *(Meriden, CT) Record-Journal* (December 20, 2011), 11.

93. Robert J. Kane and Michael D. White, "Bad Cops: A Study of Career-Ending Misconduct among New York City Police Officers," *Criminology & Public Policy* (November 2009), 764.

94. Lawrence W. Sherman, "Becoming Bent: Moral Careers of Corrupt Policemen," in *Police Corruption: A Sociological Perspective*, ed. Lawrence W. Sherman (Garden City, NY: Doubleday, 1974), 191–208.

95. "Roster of Civilian Oversight Agencies in the U.S.," National Association for Civilian Oversight of Law Enforcement, at **www.nacole.org**.

96. Hazel Glenn Beh, "Municipal Liability for Failure to Investigate Citizen Complaints against Police," *Fordham Urban Law Journal* 23 (Winter 1998), 209.

97. Joycelyn M. Pollock and Ronald F. Becker, "Ethics Training Using Officers' Dilemmas," *FBI Law Enforcement Bulletin* (November 1996), 20–28.

98. Quoted in Thomas J. Martinelli, "Dodging the Pitfalls of Noble Cause Corruption and the Intelligence Unit," *The Police Chief* (October 2009), 124.

99. Pollock and Becker.

100. Brandon V. Zuidema and H. Wayne Duff, "Organizational Ethics through Effective Leadership," *Law Enforcement Bulletin* (March 2009), 8–9.

CHAPTER

6

Police and the Constitution

The Rules of Law Enforcement

LEARNING OBJECTIVES

After reading this chapter, you should be able to...

1 Outline the four major sources that may provide probable cause.

2 Explain the exclusionary rule and the exceptions to it.

3 Distinguish between a stop and a frisk, and indicate the importance of the case *Terry v. Ohio*.

4 List the four elements that must be present for an arrest to take place.

5 List the four categories of items that can be seized by use of a search warrant.

6 Explain when searches can be made without a warrant.

7 Describe the plain view doctrine and indicate one of its limitations.

8 Indicate situations in which a *Miranda* warning is unnecessary.

Throughout the chapter you will see each learning objective repeated in the margin next to the content it relates to. The chapter summary on page 183 includes all of the learning objectives for review.

CHAPTER OUTLINE

- The Fourth Admendment
- Stops and Frisks
- Arrests
- Lawful Searches and Seizures
- The Interrogation Process and *Miranda*

WHAT'S THAT SMELL?

For the three Lexington-Fayette (Kentucky) narcotics officers, the odds of making the correct decision seemed fifty-fifty. They had just followed a suspected drug dealer into the breezeway of an apartment complex and saw two doors, one on the left and one on the right. They knew the suspect had entered one of the apartments, but they had no way of determining which one. Then the officers smelled marijuana smoke coming from the apartment on the left. They immediately started banging on that door, yelling, "This is the police!" After hearing suspicious movements inside, the officers forced themselves into the apartment.

They did not find their suspect. Instead, the officers discovered Hollis King and two friends sitting on his sofa, smoking marijuana. A quick search of the apartment uncovered a stash of marijuana, powder and crack cocaine, and cash. King was arrested, convicted of several drug-related offenses, and sentenced to eleven years in prison. He appealed the conviction, claiming that the narcotics officers had improperly burst into and searched his apartment.

Generally, law enforcement agents cannot enter any sort of dwelling without written permission from a judge, called a *warrant*. As you will learn later in the chapter, however, the warrant requirement does not apply under certain "exigent," or urgent, circumstances. In this case, the narcotics officers believed that the suspicious noises they heard were made by someone destroying evidence, thus creating an exigent circumstance. In May 2011, the United States Supreme Court ruled in favor of the officers, holding that their warrantless entry into King's apartment was justified even though, as it turned out, the original suspect was elsewhere.

Through its decisions, the United States Supreme Court determines the guidelines law enforcement agents must follow when forcibly entering a dwelling.

AP Photo/Columbian via Clark Skamania Drug Task Force

The Supreme Court's decision in *Kentucky v. King* puzzled many legal experts. Didn't the Lexington-Fayette narcotics officers mistakenly create the exigent circumstances that they were relying on to avoid the warrant requirement? If the officers had not knocked on Hollis King's door, then they would not have heard the "suspicious noises" that allowed them to enter the apartment.[1] In the Court's view, the Kentucky law enforcement agents had good reason—erroneous though it may have been—to force their way into King's apartment. Consequently, as Justice Samuel Alito stated, their "warrantless entry to prevent the destruction of evidence is reasonable and thus allowed."[2]

In the previous chapter, we discussed the importance of discretion in the criminal justice system. Certainly, as in this case, police officers have a great deal of discretion to make the decisions they feel are necessary to enforce criminal law. This discretion is not absolute, however. For the most part, a law enforcement agent's actions are determined by the rules for policing set down in the U.S. Constitution and enforced by the courts. In this chapter, we will examine the extent to which police behavior is controlled by the law, starting with a discussion of the constitutional principles on which such control is grounded.

THE FOURTH AMENDMENT

In *Kentucky v. King*, the Supreme Court did not address whether Hollis King was guilty or innocent of the charges against him. That was for the trial court to decide. Rather, the Court ruled that the Lexington-Fayette narcotics officers had not overstepped the boundaries of their authority in entering and searching King's apartment. To understand these boundaries, law enforcement officers must understand the Fourth Amendment, which reads as follows:

> The right of the people to be secure in their persons, houses, papers, and effects, against unreasonable searches and seizures, shall not be violated, and no Warrants shall issue, but upon probable cause, supported by Oath or affirmation, and particularly describing the place to be searched, and the persons or things to be seized.

This amendment contains two critical legal concepts: a prohibition against *unreasonable* **searches and seizures** and the requirement of **probable cause** to issue a warrant.

REASONABLENESS

Law enforcement personnel use searches and seizures to look for and collect the evidence they need to convict individuals suspected of crimes. As you have just read, when police are conducting a search or seizure, they must act reasonably. Although courts have spent innumerable hours scrutinizing the word, no specific meaning for *reasonable* exists. A thesaurus can provide useful synonyms—logical, practical, sensible, intelligent, plausible—but because each case is different, those terms are relative.

In the *King* case, the Supreme Court rejected the argument that the search had been so unreasonable as to violate the Fourth Amendment's prohibition against unreasonable searches and seizures. That does not mean that the police officers' actions would have been reasonable under any circumstances. What if the narcotics officers, after having lost the trail of their suspected drug dealer, had begun randomly kicking down doors in the apartment complex, eventually discovering Hollis King and his illegal drug stash? Under those circumstances, their conduct would almost certainly have been considered unreasonable.

Indeed, one Supreme Court justice, Ruth Bader Ginsberg, did believe that the officers in the *King* case had acted unreasonably. The Court's decision, she warned, "arms the police with a way routinely to dishonor the Fourth Amendment's warrant requirement."[3] For example, she noted, law enforcement agents can now simply roam the hallways of apartment buildings, knock whenever they smell marijuana, and make a forced entry if they think they hear something suspicious.[4]

PROBABLE CAUSE

The concept of reasonableness is linked to probable cause. The Supreme Court has ruled, for example, that any arrest or seizure is unreasonable unless it is supported by probable cause.[5] The burden of probable cause requires more than mere suspicion on a police officer's part. The officer must know of facts and circumstances that would reasonably lead to "the belief that an offense has been or is being committed."[6]

SOURCES OF PROBABLE CAUSE
If no probable cause existed when a police officer took a certain action, it cannot be retroactively applied. If, for example, a police officer stops a person for jaywalking and then (without the help of a drug-sniffing dog) finds several ounces of marijuana in that person's pocket, the arrest for marijuana possession would probably be disallowed. Remember, suspicion does not equal probable cause. If, however,

Searches and Seizures The legal term, as found in the Fourth Amendment to the U.S. Constitution, that generally refers to the searching for and the confiscating of evidence by law enforcement agents.

Probable Cause Reasonable grounds to believe the existence of facts warranting certain actions, such as the search or arrest of a person.

CAREERS IN CJ

WILLIAM HOWE
POLICE DETECTIVE

Each crime scene, each major accident, each time you are called to investigate, you are presented with a puzzle with various pieces missing. When you discover and interpret the interlocking missing pieces together in a successful prosecution, there is no better feeling. The payoff is when you get the opportunity to show off your completed "puzzle" to the jury and they agree that the pieces fit. When I once thrilled at the chase of the bad guy through the alleys and neighborhoods, I now enjoy even more pursuing them with the mental skills I have developed— accident reconstruction, fingerprint identification, and the interpretation of crime scenes. This can be every bit as rewarding as the foot pursuit, not to mention ever so much easier on the body.

Having been in police work for thirty-five years, I have been assaulted only four times on the job (two of which were at gunpoint). This confirmed for me, once and for all, the importance of being able to use your mind rather than your size to, first, talk your way out of trouble and, second, talk the bad guys into going along with your plans for them.

Social Media Career Tip

For your profile photo, stick with a close-up, business-appropriate photo in which you are smiling and wearing something you would wear as a potential employee. Avoid symbols, party photos, long-distance shots, or baby pictures. **f Linked in** ⌄

FAST FACTS

POLICE DETECTIVE, JOB DESCRIPTION:

- Collect evidence and obtain facts pertaining to criminal cases.
- Conduct interviews, observe suspects, examine records, and help with raids and busts.

WHAT KIND OF TRAINING IS REQUIRED?

- 2–5 years' experience as a police patrol officer is required before testing to become a detective.
- Larger departments require 60 units of college credit or an associate's degree.

ANNUAL SALARY RANGE?

- $43,920–$76,350

---

an informant had tipped the officer off that the person was a drug dealer, probable cause might exist and the arrest could be valid. Informants are one of several sources that may provide probable cause. Other sources include the following:

Learning Objective 1 Outline the four major sources that may provide probable cause.

1. *Personal observation.* Police officers may use their personal training, experience, and expertise to infer probable cause from situations that may not be obviously criminal. If, for example, a police officer observes several people in a car slowly circling a certain building in a high-crime area, that officer may infer that the people are "casing" the building in preparation for a burglary. Probable cause could be established for detaining the suspects.

2. *Information.* Law enforcement officers receive information from victims, eyewitnesses, informants, and official sources such as police bulletins or broadcasts. Such information, as long as it is believed to be reliable, is a basis for probable cause.

3. *Evidence.* In certain circumstances, which will be examined later in this chapter, police have probable cause for a search or seizure based on evidence—such as a shotgun—in plain view.

4. *Association.* Under certain circumstances, if the police see a person with a known criminal background in a high-crime neighborhood, they have probable cause to stop that person. Generally, however, association is not adequate to establish probable cause.[7]

THE PROBABLE CAUSE FRAMEWORK In a sense, the concept of probable cause allows police officers to do their job effectively. Most arrests are made without a warrant, because most arrests are the result of quick police reaction to the commission of a crime. Indeed, it would not be practical to expect a police officer to obtain a warrant before making an arrest on the street. Thus, probable cause provides a framework that limits the situations in which police officers can make arrests, but also gives officers the freedom to act within that framework. In 2003, the Supreme Court reaffirmed this freedom by ruling that Baltimore (Maryland) police officers acted properly when they arrested all three passengers of a car in which cocaine had been hidden in the back seat. "A reasonable officer," wrote Chief Justice William H. Rehnquist, "could conclude that there was probable cause to believe" that the defendant, who had been sitting in the front seat, was in "possession" of the illicit drug despite his protestations to the contrary.[8]

Once an arrest is made, the arresting officer must prove to a judge that probable cause existed. In *County of Riverside v. McLaughlin* (1991),[9] the Supreme Court ruled that this judicial determination of probable cause must be made within forty-eight hours after the arrest, even if this two-day period includes a weekend or holiday. (The *Comparative Criminal Justice—Extending a Firm Hand* feature on the following page describes one country's elastic interpretation of probable cause in response to a vicious crime wave.)

THE EXCLUSIONARY RULE

Learning Objective 2 Explain the exclusionary rule and the exceptions to it.

Historically, the courts have looked to the Fourth Amendment for guidance in regulating the activity of law enforcement officers, as the language of the Constitution does not expressly do so. The courts' most potent legal tool in this endeavor is the **exclusionary rule,** which prohibits the use of illegally seized evidence. According to this rule, any evidence obtained by an unreasonable search or seizure is inadmissible (may not be used) against a defendant in a criminal trial.[10] Even highly incriminating evidence, such as a knife stained with the victim's blood, usually cannot be introduced at a trial if illegally obtained.

Furthermore, any physical or verbal evidence police are able to acquire by using illegally obtained evidence is known as the **fruit of the poisoned tree** and is also inadmissible. In *Kentucky v. King,* the case that opened this chapter, if a court had found that the narcotics officers had improperly entered Hollis King's apartment, the illegal drugs found there would have been considered "poisoned" evidence and inadmissible. The main implication of the exclusionary rule is that it forces police to gather evidence properly. If they follow appropriate procedures, they are more likely to be rewarded with a conviction. If they are careless or abuse the rights of the suspect, they are less likely to get a conviction. A strict application of the exclusionary rule, therefore, will permit guilty people to go free because of police carelessness, errors, or improper tactics.

Exclusionary Rule A rule under which any evidence that is obtained in violation of the accused's rights, as well as any evidence derived from illegally obtained evidence, will not be admissible in criminal court.

Fruit of the Poisoned Tree Evidence that is acquired through the use of illegally obtained evidence and is therefore inadmissible in court.

THE "INEVITABLE DISCOVERY" EXCEPTION Critics of the exclusionary rule have long maintained that the costs to society of losing critical evidence are higher than the benefits of deterring police misconduct. Several Supreme Court decisions have mirrored this view and

COMPARATIVE CRIMINAL JUSTICE

EXTENDING A FIRM HAND

Mara Salvatrucha (MS-13) is one of the most powerful and fastest-growing street gangs in the world. In the United States, where MS-13 has about 10,000 members and a presence in forty-two states, the Federal Bureau of Investigation (FBI) has set up a task force to deal exclusively with the gang. U.S. immigration officials routinely deport members back to their home countries in Central America. One of these countries, El Salvador, has responded to the resulting influx of violent gang members with strict antigang legislation.

Over the past decade, Salvadoran politicians passed a series of *mano dura*, or "firm hand," laws designed to crack down on criminal gang activity. These laws made it easier for police to detain suspects who exhibited certain characteristics such as having gang tattoos or loitering in known gang areas. Still, several years ago, MS-13 members fired on two crowded buses in San Salvador, the country's capital, killing seventeen people and intensifying public outrage over gang violence. Three months later, in response, Salvadoran president Muaricio Funes signed the country's harshest antigang legislation to date. Under the new law, merely belonging to a gang is punishable by four to six years in prison, even if no other criminal activity is proved.

FOR CRITICAL ANALYSIS At times, Salvadoran police officers have been permitted to use gang tattoos as proof of gang membership, and thus grounds for immediate arrest. How does the Fourth Amendment's probable cause requirement prohibit this sort of action by American law enforcement agents?

Gang tattoos cover the face and body of a prisoner incarcerated in El Salvador's Izalco penitentiary.
Reuters/Ulises Rodriguez/Landov

"Inevitable Discovery" Exception The legal principle that illegally obtained evidence can be admissible in court if police using lawful means would have "inevitably" discovered it.

provided exceptions to the exclusionary rule. The **"inevitable discovery" exception** was established in the wake of the disappearance of ten-year-old Pamela Powers of Des Moines, Iowa, on Christmas Eve, 1968.

The primary suspect in the case, a religious fanatic named Robert Williams, was tricked by a detective into leading police to the site where he had buried Powers. The detective convinced Williams that if he did not lead police to the body, he would soon forget where it was buried. This would deny his victim a "Christian burial." Initially, in *Brewer v. Williams* (1977),[11] the Court ruled that the evidence (Powers's body) had been obtained illegally because Williams's attorney had not been present during the interrogation that led to his admission. Several years later, in *Nix v. Williams* (1984),[12] the Court reversed itself, ruling that the evidence was admissible because the body would have eventually ("inevitably") been found by lawful means.

THE "GOOD FAITH" EXCEPTION The scope of the exclusionary rule has been further diminished by two cases involving faulty warrants. In the first, *United States v. Leon* (1984),[13] the police seized evidence on authority of a search warrant that had been improperly issued by a judge. In the second, *Herring v. United States* (2009),[14] due to a computer error, police officers detained a man on the mistaken belief that he was subject to an arrest warrant. As a result, they found that the suspect was carrying illegal drugs and an unregistered firearm.

In both cases, the Court allowed the evidence to stand under a **"good faith" exception** to the exclusionary rule. Under this exception, evidence acquired by a police officer using a technically invalid warrant is admissible during trial if the officer was unaware of the error. In these two cases, the Court said that the officers acted in "good faith." By the same token, if police officers use a search warrant that they know to be technically incorrect, the good faith exception does not apply, and the evidence can be suppressed.

SELFASSESSMENT

Fill in the blanks and check your answers on page 184.

The Fourth Amendment contains two critically important restrictions on police authority: a prohibition against _____ searches and seizures and a requirement of _____ _____ that a crime has been committed before a warrant for a search or seizure can be issued. Judges rely on the _____ rule to keep _____ that has been improperly obtained by the police out of criminal courts.

STOPS AND FRISKS

In February 2011, an Indianapolis (Indiana) police officer was patrolling a high-crime neighborhood when he saw a bicycle sitting next to a car in a gas station parking lot. The officer watched as Michael Woodson got out of the car, put on a backpack, and began to cycle away. After stopping Woodson, the officer searched the backpack, finding more than thirty contraband DVDs. Woodson challenged his eventual conviction on two charges of fraud, claiming that the police officer had no good reason to stop him in the first place.

A three-judge Indiana appeals panel agreed and overturned Woodson's conviction. The panel rejected the argument that, given the setting and Woodson's behavior, the police officer was justified in thinking that a drug deal was taking place. That is, no *reasonable suspicion* existed that a crime had been committed in the gas station parking lot.[15] When such reasonable suspicion does exist, police officers are well within their rights to *stop and frisk* a suspect. In a stop and frisk, law enforcement officers (1) briefly detain a person they reasonably believe to be suspicious and, (2) if they believe the person to be armed, proceed to pat down, or "frisk," that person's outer clothing.[16]

THE ELUSIVE DEFINITION OF REASONABLE SUSPICION

The precedent for the ever-elusive definition of a "reasonable" suspicion in stop-and-frisk situations was established in *Terry v. Ohio* (1968).[17] In that case, a detective named McFadden observed two men (one of whom was Terry) acting strangely in downtown Cleveland. The men would walk past a certain store, peer into the window, and then stop at a street corner and confer. While they were talking, another man joined the conversation and then left quickly. Several minutes later the three men met again at another corner a few blocks away. Detective McFadden believed the trio was planning to break into the store. He approached them, told them who he was, and asked for identification. After receiving a mumbled response, the detective frisked the three men and found handguns on two of them, who were tried and convicted of carrying concealed weapons.

The Supreme Court upheld the conviction, ruling that Detective McFadden had reasonable cause to believe that the men were armed and dangerous and that swift action was necessary to protect himself and other citizens in the area.[18] The Court accepted McFadden's interpretation of the unfolding scene as based on objective facts

Learning Objective 3 Distinguish between a stop and a frisk, and indicate the importance of the case *Terry v. Ohio*.

and practical conclusions. It therefore concluded that the detective's suspicion was reasonable. In contrast, in the case just described, the Indianapolis police officer's grounds for stopping Michael Woodson—activity that looked like an illegal drug deal in a part of town where such activity is common—were not seen by the Indiana appeals court as reasonable.

THE "TOTALITY OF THE CIRCUMSTANCES" TEST For the most part, the judicial system has refrained from placing restrictions on police officers' ability to make stops. In the *Terry* case, the Supreme Court did say that an officer must have "specific and articulable facts" to support the decision to make a stop, but added that the facts may be "taken together with rational inferences."[19] The Court has consistently ruled that because of their practical experience, law enforcement agents are in a unique position to make such inferences and should be given a good deal of freedom in doing so.

In the years since the *Terry* case was decided, the Court has settled on a "totality of the circumstances" test to determine whether a stop is based on reasonable suspicion.[20] In 2002, for example, the Court ruled that a U.S. Border Patrol agent's stop of a minivan in Arizona was reasonable.[21] On being approached by the Border Patrol car, the driver had stiffened, slowed down his van, and avoided making eye contact with the agent. Furthermore, the children in the van waved at the officer in a mechanical manner, as if ordered to do so. The agent pulled over the van and found 128 pounds of marijuana.

In his opinion, Chief Justice William Rehnquist pointed out that such conduct might have been unremarkable on a busy city highway, but on an unpaved road thirty miles from the Mexican border it was enough to reasonably arouse the agent's suspicion.[22] The justices also made clear that the need to prevent terrorist attacks is part of the "totality of the circumstances," and therefore, law enforcement agents will have more leeway to make stops near U.S. borders.

RACE AND REASONABLE SUSPICION In general, a person's race or ethnicity alone cannot provide reasonable suspicion for stops and frisks. Some statistical measures, however, seem to show that these factors do, at times, play a troubling role in this area of policing. African Americans and Hispanics represented 87 percent of the nearly 700,000 stops made by New York City police officers in 2011, even though these two groups constitute a relatively small percentage of the city's population.[23] That same year, just four Shelbyville (Tennessee) police officers made nearly two-thirds of all arrests of Hispanics for traffic violations in Bedford County, Tennessee.[24]

These and other similar data are seen as proof that police sometimes use **racial profiling** in deciding which suspects to stop. Racial profiling occurs when a police action is based on the race, ethnicity, or national origin of the suspect rather than any reasonable suspicion that he or she has broken the law. The issue of racial profiling gained national attention in 2010, when Arizona passed a law aimed at policing its large number of undocumented immigrants. The legislation, known as S.B. 1070, requires state and local police officers, "when practicable," to check the immigration status of someone they have a "reasonable suspicion" is in the country illegally.[25]

The language of Arizona's law does prohibit officers from using a suspect's race or ethnicity as the sole consideration in determining reasonable suspicion. The law's critics, however, believe that police will have no choice but to focus

Racial Profiling The practice of targeting people for police action based solely on their race, ethnicity, or national origin.

Under a new state law, Arizona law enforcement agents such as this Tucson police officer would be required to detain anyone they suspected of being an "unauthorized alien." Why do critics of this law believe that it requires racial profiling on the part of police officers? Do you agree with this criticism? Why or why not?

Photo by Scott Olson/Getty Images

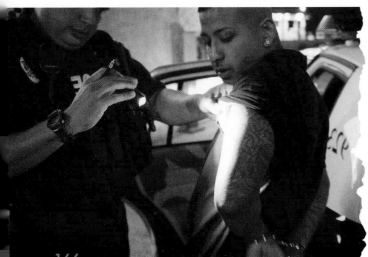

on Arizona's Hispanic population, as determined primarily by skin color. In 2012, the U.S. Supreme Court upheld the "show me your papers" provision of S.B. 1070. At the same time, the Court suggested that it would revisit the issue should evidence show that the statute indeed leads to racial profiling in Arizona.[26]

A STOP

The terms *stop* and *frisk* are often used in concert, but they describe two separate acts. A **stop** takes place when a law enforcement officer has reasonable suspicion that a criminal activity is about to take place. Because an investigatory stop is not an arrest, there are limits to the extent police can detain someone who has been stopped. For example, in one situation an airline traveler and his luggage were restrained for ninety minutes while the police waited for a drug-sniffing dog to arrive. The Supreme Court ruled that the initial stop of the passenger was constitutional, but that the ninety-minute wait was excessive.[27]

In 2004, the Court held that police officers could require suspects to identify themselves during a stop that is otherwise valid under the *Terry* ruling.[28] The case involved a Nevada rancher who was fined $250 for refusing to give his name to a police officer investigating a possible assault. The defendant argued that such requests force citizens to incriminate themselves against their will, which is prohibited, as we shall see later in the chapter, by the Fifth Amendment. Justice Anthony Kennedy wrote, however, that "asking questions is an essential part of police investigations" that would be made much more difficult if officers could not determine the identity of a suspect.[29] The ruling validated "stop-and-identify" laws in twenty states and numerous cities and towns.

A FRISK

The Supreme Court has stated that a **frisk** should be a protective measure. Police officers cannot conduct a frisk as a "fishing expedition" simply to try to find items besides weapons, such as illegal narcotics, on a suspect.[30] A frisk does not necessarily follow a stop and in fact may occur only when the officer is justified in thinking that the safety of police officers or other citizens may be endangered.

Again, the question of reasonable suspicion is at the heart of determining the legality of frisks. In the *Terry* case, the Court accepted that Detective McFadden reasonably believed that the three suspects posed a threat. The suspects' refusal to answer McFadden's questions, though within their rights because they had not been arrested, provided the detective with sufficient motive for the frisk. In 2009, the Court extended the "stop and frisk" authority by ruling that a police officer could order a passenger in a car that had been pulled over for a traffic violation to submit to a pat-down.[31] To do so, the officer must have a reasonable suspicion that the suspect may be armed and dangerous.

Stop A brief detention of a person by law enforcement agents for questioning.

Frisk A pat-down or minimal search by police to discover weapons.

A police officer frisks a suspect in San Francisco, California. What is the main purpose behind a frisk? When are police justified in frisking someone?

Mark Richards/PhotoEdit

SELFASSESSMENT

Fill in the blanks and check your answers on page 184.

A police officer can make a _____ , which is not the same as an arrest, if she or he has a _____ suspicion that a criminal act is taking place or is about to take place. Then, the officer has the ability to _____ the suspect for weapons as a protective measure.

ARRESTS

Arrest To take into custody a person suspected of criminal activity.

As in the *Terry* case, a stop and frisk may lead to an **arrest.** An arrest is the taking into custody of a citizen for the purpose of detaining her or him on a criminal charge. It is important to understand the difference between a stop and an arrest. In the eyes of the law, a stop is a relatively brief intrusion on a citizen's rights, whereas an arrest—which involves a deprivation of liberty—is deserving of a full range of constitutional protections, which we shall discuss throughout the chapter (see *Mastering Concepts—The Difference between a Stop and an Arrest* below). Consequently, while a stop can be made based on reasonable suspicion, a law enforcement officer needs probable cause, as defined earlier, to make an arrest.[32]

ELEMENTS OF AN ARREST

Learning Objective 4 List the four elements that must be present for an arrest to take place.

When is somebody under arrest? The easy—and incorrect—answer would be whenever the police officer says so. In fact, the state of being under arrest is dependent not only on the actions of the law enforcement officers but also on the perception of the suspect. Suppose Mr. Jones is stopped by plainclothes detectives, driven to the police station, and detained for three hours for questioning. During this time, the police never tell Mr. Jones he is under arrest, and in fact, he is free to leave at any time. But if Mr. Jones or any other reasonable person *believes* he or she is not free to leave, then, according to the Supreme Court, that person is in fact under arrest and must receive the necessary constitutional protections.[33]

Criminal justice professor Rolando V. del Carmen of Sam Houston State University has identified four elements that must be present for an arrest to take place:

1. The *intent* to arrest. In a stop, though it may entail slight inconvenience and a short detention period, there is no intent on the part of the law enforcement officer to take the person into custody. Therefore, there is no arrest. As *intent* is a subjective term, it is sometimes difficult to determine whether the police officer intended to arrest. In situations when the intent is unclear, courts often rely—as in our hypothetical case of Mr. Jones—on the perception of the arrestee.[34]

MASTERINGCONCEPTS

THE DIFFERENCE BETWEEN A STOP AND AN ARREST

During a stop, police can interrogate the person and frisk his or her outer clothing. If a "probable cause" event occurs during the stop, such as the discovery of an illegal weapon, then officers may arrest the person. **If an arrest is made,** the suspect is now in police custody and is protected by the U.S. Constitution in a number of ways that will be discussed later in the chapter.

	STOP	ARREST
Justification	Reasonable suspicion only	Probable cause
Warrant	None	Required in some, but not all, situations
Intent of Officer	To investigate suspicious activity	To make a formal charge against the suspect
Search	May frisk, or "pat down," for weapons	May conduct a full search for weapons or evidence
Scope of Search	Outer clothing only	Area within the suspect's immediate control or "reach"

2. The *authority* to arrest. State laws give police officers the authority to place citizens under custodial arrest, or take them into custody. Like other state laws, the authorization to arrest varies among the fifty states. Some states, for example, allow off-duty police officers to make arrests, while others do not.

3. *Seizure or detention.* A necessary part of an arrest is the detention of the subject. Detention is considered to have occurred as soon as the arrested individual submits to the control of the officer, whether peacefully or under the threat or use of force.

4. The *understanding* of the person that she or he has been arrested. Through either words—such as "you are now under arrest"—or actions, the person taken into custody must understand that an arrest has taken place. When a suspect has been forcibly subdued by the police, handcuffed, and placed in a patrol car, he or she is believed to understand that an arrest has been made. This understanding may be lacking if the person is intoxicated, insane, or unconscious.[35]

ARRESTS WITH A WARRANT

When law enforcement officers have established probable cause to arrest an individual who is not in police custody, they obtain an **arrest warrant** for that person. An arrest warrant contains information such as the name of the person suspected and the crime she or he is suspected of having committed. (See Figure 6.1 below for an example of an arrest warrant.) Judges or magistrates issue arrest warrants after first determining that the law enforcement officers have indeed established probable cause of criminal activity.

ENTERING A DWELLING There is a perception that an arrest warrant gives law enforcement officers the authority to enter a dwelling without first announcing themselves. This is not accurate. In *Wilson v. Arkansas* (1995),[36] the Supreme Court reiterated the common law requirement that police officers must knock and announce their identity and purpose before entering a dwelling. As you may recall from the opening of this chapter, under certain conditions, known as **exigent circumstances,** law enforcement officers need not announce themselves. These circumstances include situations in which the officers have a reasonable belief of any of the following:

- The suspect is armed and poses a strong threat of violence to the officers or others inside the dwelling.
- Persons inside the dwelling are in the process of destroying evidence or escaping because of the presence of the police.
- A felony is being committed at the time the officers enter.[37]

THE WAITING PERIOD The Supreme Court severely weakened the practical impact of the "knock and announce" rule with its decision in *Hudson v. Michigan* (2006).[38] In that case, Detroit

Arrest Warrant A written order, based on probable cause and issued by a judge or magistrate, commanding that the person named on the warrant be arrested by the police.

Exigent Circumstances Situations that require extralegal or exceptional actions by the police.

FIGURE 6.1 Example of an Arrest Warrant

United States District Court
DISTRICT OF

UNITED STATES OF AMERICA
V.

WARRANT FOR ARREST

CASE NUMBER:

To: The United States Marshal
and any Authorized United States Officer

YOU ARE HEREBY COMMANDED to arrest _____
name

and bring him or her forthwith to the nearest magistrate to answer a(n)

☐ Indictment ☐ Information ☐ Complaint ☐ Order of Court ☐ Violation Notice ☐ Probation Violation Petition

charging him or her with (brief description of offense)

in violation of Title _____ United States Code, Section(s) _____

Name of Issuing Officer   Title of Issuing Officer

Signature of Issuing Officer   Date and Location

Bail fixed at $ _____   by _____
                                    Name of Judicial Officer

RETURN
This warrant was received and executed with the arrest of the above-named defendant at _____

DATE RECEIVED   NAME AND TITLE OF ARRESTING OFFICER   SIGNATURE OF ARRESTING OFFICER

DATE OF ARREST

police did not knock before entering the defendant's home with a warrant. Instead, they announced themselves and then waited only three to five seconds before making their entrance, not the fifteen to twenty seconds suggested by a prior Court ruling.[39] Hudson argued that the drugs found during the subsequent search were inadmissible because the law enforcement agents did not follow proper procedure.

The Court disagreed. In his majority opinion, Justice Antonin Scalia stated that an improper "knock and announce" is not unreasonable enough to provide defendants with a "get-out-of-jail-free card" by disqualifying evidence uncovered on the basis of a valid search warrant.[40] Thus, the exclusionary rule, discussed earlier in this chapter, would no longer apply under such circumstances. Legal experts still advise, however, that police observe a reasonable waiting period after knocking and announcing to be certain that any evidence found during the subsequent search will be allowed in court.[41]

ARRESTS WITHOUT A WARRANT

Arrest warrants are not always required, and in fact, most arrests are made on the scene without a warrant.[42] A law enforcement officer may make a **warrantless arrest** if:

1. The offense is committed in the presence of the officer; or
2. The officer has knowledge that a crime has been committed and probable cause to believe the crime was committed by a particular suspect.[43]

The type of crime also comes to bear in questions of arrests without a warrant. As a general rule, officers can make a warrantless arrest for a crime they did not see if they have probable cause to believe that a felony has been committed. For misdemeanors, the crime must have been committed in the presence of the officer for a warrantless arrest to be valid.

In certain situations, warrantless arrests are unlawful even though a police officer can establish probable cause. In *Payton v. New York* (1980),[44] for example, the Supreme Court held that when exigent circumstances do not exist and the suspect does not give consent to enter a dwelling, law enforcement officers cannot force themselves in for the purpose of making a warrantless arrest. The *Payton* ruling was expanded to cover the homes of third parties in *Steagald v. United States* (1981).[45] That case saw the Court rule that if the police wish to arrest a criminal suspect in another person's home, they cannot enter that home to arrest the suspect without first obtaining a search warrant, a process we will discuss in the following section.

Warrantless Arrest An arrest made without first seeking a warrant for the action.

SELFASSESSMENT

Fill in the blanks and check your answers on page 184.

An arrest occurs when a law enforcement agent takes a suspect into _____ on a criminal charge. If the officer has prior knowledge of the suspect's criminal activity, she or he must obtain a _____ from a judge or magistrate before making the arrest. Officers can, however, make _____ arrests if an offense is committed in their presence or they have _____ _____ to believe that a crime was committed by the particular subject.

LAWFUL SEARCHES AND SEIZURES

How far can law enforcement agents go in searching and seizing private property? Consider the steps taken by Jenny Stracner, an investigator with the Laguna Beach (California) Police Department. After receiving information that a suspect, Greenwood, was engaged in drug trafficking, Stracner enlisted the aid of the local trash collector in procuring evidence. Instead of taking Greenwood's trash bags to be incinerated, the collector agreed to give them to Stracner. The officer found enough drug paraphernalia in the garbage to obtain a warrant to search the suspect's home. Subsequently, Greenwood was arrested and convicted on narcotics charges.[46]

Remember, the Fourth Amendment is quite specific in forbidding unreasonable searches and seizures. Were Stracner's search of Greenwood's garbage and her seizure of its contents "reasonable"? The Supreme Court thought so, holding that Greenwood's garbage was not protected by the Fourth Amendment.[47]

THE ROLE OF PRIVACY IN SEARCHES

A crucial concept in understanding search and seizure law is *privacy*. By definition, a **search** is a governmental intrusion on a citizen's reasonable expectation of privacy. The recognized standard for a "reasonable expectation of privacy" was established in *Katz v. United States* (1967).[48] The case dealt with the question of whether the defendant was justified in his expectation of privacy in the calls he made from a public phone booth. The Supreme Court held that "the Fourth Amendment protects people, not places," and Katz prevailed.

In his concurring opinion, Justice John Harlan, Jr., set a two-pronged test for a person's expectation of privacy:

1. The individual must prove that she or he expected privacy, and
2. Society must recognize that expectation as reasonable.[49]

Accordingly, the Court agreed with Katz's claim that he had a reasonable right to privacy in a public phone booth. (Remember, however, that the *Terry* case allows for conditions under which a person's privacy rights are overcome by a reasonable suspicion on the part of a law enforcement officer that a threat to public safety exists.)

In contrast, in *California v. Greenwood* (1988),[50] described above, the Court did not believe that the suspect had a reasonable expectation of privacy when it came to his garbage bags. The Court noted that when we place our trash on a curb, we expose it to any number of intrusions by "animals, children, scavengers, snoops, and other members of the public."[51] In other words, if Greenwood had truly intended for the contents of his garbage bags to remain private, he would not have left them on the side of the road. To give another example, the Court also upheld the search in a case in which a drug-sniffing dog was used to detect marijuana in the trunk of a car after the driver was stopped for speeding. The Court ruled that no one has a legitimate privacy interest in possessing illegal drugs or other contraband such as explosives in the trunk of his or her car.[52]

SEARCH AND SEIZURE WARRANTS

To protect against charges that they have unreasonably infringed on privacy rights during a search, law enforcement officers can obtain a **search warrant**. (See Figure 6.2 on the following page for an example of a search warrant.) Similar to an arrest warrant, a search warrant is a court order that authorizes police to search a certain area. Before a judge or magistrate will issue a search warrant, law enforcement officers must provide the following:

- Information showing probable cause that a crime has been or will be committed.
- Specific information on the premises to be searched, the suspects to be found and the illegal activities taking place at those premises, and the items to be seized.

Search The process by which police examine a person or property to find evidence that will be used to prove guilt in a criminal trial.

Search Warrant A written order, based on probable cause and issued by a judge or magistrate, commanding that police officers or criminal investigators search a specific person, place, or property to obtain evidence.

FIGURE 6.2 Example of a Search Warrant

United States District Court

_____DISTRICT OF_____

In the Matter of the Search of

(Name, address or brief description of person or property to be searched)

SEARCH WARRANT

CASE NUMBER:

TO:_____ and any Authorized Officer of the United States

Affidavit(s) having been made before me by_____ who has reason to

Affiant

believe that ☐ on the person of or ☐ on the premises known as (name, description and/or location)

in the_____District of_____there is now

concealed a certain person or property, namely (describe the person or property)

I am satisfied that the affidavit(s) and any recorded testimony establish probable cause to believe that the person or property so described is now concealed on the person or premises above-described and establish grounds for the issuance of this warrant.

YOU ARE HEREBY COMMANDED to search on or before_____

Date

(not to exceed 10 days) the person or place named above for the person or property specified, serving this warrant and making the search (in the daytime — 6:00 A.M. to 10:00 P.M.) (at any time in the day or night as I find reasonable cause has been established) and if the person or property be found there to seize same, leaving a copy of this warrant and receipt for the person or property taken, and prepare a written inventory of the person or property seized and promptly return this warrant to_____

as required by law.

U.S. Judge or Magistrate

Date and Time Issued_____ at _____ City and State

Name and Title of Judicial Officer_____ Signature of Judicial Officer

Learning Objective **5** List the four categories of items that can be seized by use of a search warrant.

Affidavit A written statement of facts, confirmed by the oath or affirmation of the party making it and made before a person having the authority to administer the oath or affirmation.

Seizure The forcible taking of a person or property in response to a violation of the law.

The purpose of a search warrant is to establish, before the search takes place, that a *probable cause to search* justifies infringing on the suspect's reasonable expectation of privacy.

PARTICULARITY OF SEARCH WARRANTS The members of the First Congress specifically did not want law enforcement officers to have the freedom to make "general, exploratory" searches through a person's belongings.[53] Consequently, the Fourth Amendment requires that a warrant describe with "particularity" the place to be searched and the things—either people or objects—to be seized.

This "particularity" requirement places a heavy burden on law enforcement officers. Before going to a judge to ask for a search warrant, they must prepare an **affidavit** in which they provide specific, written information on the property that they wish to search and seize. They must know the specific address of any place they wish to search. General addresses of apartment buildings or office complexes are not sufficient. Furthermore, courts generally frown on vague descriptions of goods to be seized. "Stolen goods" would most likely be considered unacceptably imprecise, while "1 MacBook Pro laptop computer" would be preferred.

A **seizure** is the act of taking possession of a person or property by the government because of a (suspected) violation of the law. In general, four categories of items can be seized by use of a search warrant:

1. Items resulting from the crime, such as stolen goods.
2. Items that are inherently illegal for anybody to possess (with certain exceptions), such as narcotics and counterfeit currency.
3. Items that can be called "evidence" of the crime, such as a bloodstained sneaker or a ski mask.
4. Items used in committing the crime, such as an ice pick or a printing press used to make counterfeit bills.[54]

REASONABLENESS DURING A SEARCH AND SEIZURE No matter how "particular" a warrant is, it cannot provide for all the conditions that are bound to come up during its service. Consequently, the law gives law enforcement officers the ability to act "reasonably" during a search and seizure in the event of unforeseeable circumstances. For example, if a police officer is searching an apartment for a stolen MacBook Pro laptop computer and notices a vial of crack cocaine sitting on the suspect's bed, that contraband is considered to be in "plain view" and can be seized.

Note that if law enforcement officers have a search warrant that authorizes them to search for a stolen laptop computer, they would not be justified in opening small drawers. Because a computer could not fit in a small drawer, an officer would not have a basis for reasonably searching one. Hence, officers are restricted in terms of where they can look by the items they are searching for.

SEARCHES AND SEIZURES WITHOUT A WARRANT

Although the Supreme Court has established the principle that searches conducted without warrants are *per se* (by definition) unreasonable, it has set "specifically established" exceptions to the rule.[55] In fact, most searches, like most arrests, take place in the absence of a judicial order. Warrantless searches and seizures can be lawful when police are in "hot pursuit" of a subject or when they search bags of trash left at the curb for regular collection. Because of the magnitude of smuggling activities in "border areas" such as airports, seaports, and international boundaries, a warrant normally is not needed to search property in those places. Furthermore, in 2006 the Court held unanimously that police officers do not need a warrant to enter a private home in an emergency, such as when they reasonably fear for the safety of the inhabitants.[56] The two most important circumstances in which a warrant is not needed, though, are (1) searches incidental to an arrest and (2) consent searches.

Learning Objective **6** Explain when searches can be made without a warrant.

SEARCHES INCIDENTAL TO AN ARREST The most frequent exception to the warrant requirement involves **searches incidental to arrests,** so called because nearly every time police officers make an arrest, they also search the suspect. As long as the original arrest was based on probable cause, these searches are valid for two reasons, established by the Supreme Court in *United States v. Robinson* (1973):

1. The need for a police officer to find and confiscate any weapons a suspect may be carrying.
2. The need to protect any evidence on the suspect's person from being destroyed.[57]

Searches Incidental to Arrests Searches for weapons and evidence that are conducted on persons who have just been arrested.

Consent Searches Searches by police that are made after the subject of the search has agreed to the action. In these situations, consent, if given of free will, validates a warrantless search.

Law enforcement officers are, however, limited in the searches they may make during an arrest. These limits were established by the Supreme Court in *Chimel v. California* (1969).[58] In that case, police arrived at Chimel's home with an arrest warrant but not a search warrant. Even though Chimel refused their request to "look around," the officers searched the entire three-bedroom house for nearly an hour, finding stolen coins in the process. Chimel was convicted of burglary and appealed, arguing that the evidence of the coins should have been suppressed.

The Supreme Court held that the search was unreasonable. In doing so, the Court established guidelines as to the acceptable extent of searches incidental to an arrest. Primarily, the Court ruled that police may search any area within the suspect's "immediate control" to confiscate any weapons or evidence that the suspect could destroy. The Court found, however, that there was no justification

> for routinely searching rooms other than that in which the arrest occurs—or, for that matter, for searching through all desk drawers or other closed or concealed areas in that room itself. Such searches, in the absence of well-recognized exceptions, may be made only under the authority of a search warrant.[59]

The exact interpretation of the "area within immediate control" has been left to individual courts, but in general it has been taken to mean the area within the reach of the arrested person. Thus, the Court is said to have established the "arm's reach doctrine" in its *Chimel* decision.

SEARCHES WITH CONSENT **Consent searches,** the second most common type of warrantless searches, take place when individuals voluntarily give law enforcement officers permission to search their persons, homes, or belongings. The most relevant factors in determining whether consent is voluntary are the following:

1. The age, intelligence, and physical condition of the consenting suspect.
2. Any coercive behavior by the police, such as the language used to request consent.
3. The length of the questioning and its location.[60]

If a court finds that a person has been physically threatened or otherwise coerced into giving consent, the search is invalid.[61] Furthermore, the search consented to must be reasonable. Several years ago, the North Carolina Supreme Court invalidated a consent search that turned up a packet of cocaine. As part of this search, the police had pulled down the suspect's underwear and shone a flashlight on his groin. The court ruled that a reasonable person in the defendant's position would not consent to such an intrusive examination.[62]

The standard for consent searches was set in *Schneckcloth v. Bustamonte* (1973),[63] in which, after being asked, the defendant told police officers to "go ahead" and search his car. A packet of stolen checks found in the trunk was ruled valid evidence because the driver consented to the search. Numerous court decisions have also supported the "knock and talk" strategy, in which the law enforcement agent simply walks up to the door of a residence, knocks, and asks to come in and talk to the resident.[64] The officer does not need reasonable suspicion or probable cause that a crime has taken place in this situation, because the decision to cooperate rests with the civilian. (For an overview of the circumstances under which warrantless searches are allowed, see Figure 6.3 below.)

SEARCHES OF AUTOMOBILES

In *Carroll v. United States* (1925),[65] the Supreme Court ruled that the law would distinguish among automobiles, homes, and persons in questions involving police searches. In the years since its *Carroll* decision, the Court has established that the Fourth Amendment does not require police to obtain a warrant to search automobiles or other movable vehicles when the police have probable cause to believe that a vehicle contains contraband or evidence of criminal activity.[66] The reasoning behind such leniency is straightforward: requiring a warrant to search an automobile places too heavy a burden on police officers. By the time the officers could communicate with a judge and obtain the warrant, the suspects could have driven away and destroyed any evidence. Consequently, the Court has consistently held that someone in a vehicle does not have the same reasonable expectation of privacy as someone at home or even in a phone booth.

WARRANTLESS SEARCHES OF AUTOMOBILES For nearly three decades, police officers believed that if they lawfully arrested the driver of a car, they could legally make a warrantless search of the car's entire front and back compartments. This understanding was based on the Supreme Court's ruling in *New York v. Benton* (1981),[67] which seemed

FIGURE 6.3 Exceptions to the Requirement that Officers Have a Search Warrant

In many instances, it would be impractical for police officers to leave a crime scene, go to a judge, and obtain a search warrant before conducting a search. Therefore, under the following circumstances, a search warrant is not required.

INCIDENT TO LAWFUL ARREST
Police officers may search the area within immediate control of a person after they have arrested him or her.

CONSENT
Police officers may search a person without a warrant if that person voluntarily agrees to be searched and has the legal authority to authorize the search.

STOP AND FRISK
Police officers may frisk, or "pat down," a person if they suspect that the person may be involved in criminal activity or pose a danger to those in the immediate area.

HOT PURSUIT
If police officers are in "hot pursuit," or chasing a person they have probable cause to believe committed a crime, and that person enters a building, the officers may search the building without a warrant.

AUTOMOBILE EXCEPTION
If police officers have probable cause to believe that an automobile contains evidence of a crime, they may, in most instances, search the vehicle without a warrant.

PLAIN VIEW
If police officers are legally engaged in police work and happen to see evidence of a crime in "plain view," they may seize it without a warrant.

ABANDONED PROPERTY
Any property, such as a hotel room that has been vacated or contraband that has been discarded, may be searched and seized by police officers without a warrant.

BORDER SEARCHES
Law enforcement officers on border patrol do not need a warrant to search vehicles crossing the border.

to allow this expansive interpretation of the "area within immediate control" with regard to automobiles.

In *Arizona v. Gant* (2009), however, the Court announced that its *Benton* decision had been misinterpreted. Such warrantless searches are allowed only if (1) the person being arrested is close enough to the car to grab or destroy evidence or a weapon inside the car or (2) the arresting officer reasonably believes that the car contains evidence pertinent to the same crime for which the arrest took place.[68] So, for example, police will no longer be able to search an automobile for contraband if the driver has been arrested for failing to pay previous speeding tickets—unless the officer reasonably believes the suspect has the ability to reach and destroy any such contraband.

SIGNIFICANT POWERS As you can imagine, the law enforcement community reacted negatively to the new restrictions outlined in the *Gant* decision.[69] Police officers, however, still can conduct a warrantless search of an automobile based on circumstances other than the incidental-to-an-arrest doctrine. These circumstances include probable cause of criminal activity, consent of the driver, and "protective searches" to search for weapons if police officers have a reasonable suspicion that such weapons exist.[70]

In addition, officers have a great deal of leeway in making automobile stops and searches. Crucially, as long as an officer has probable cause to believe that a traffic law has been broken, her or his "true" motivation for making the stop is irrelevant.[71] Even if the officer pulls over a car based on the driver's race, for example, if that person was indeed speeding or his or her car had a broken taillight, the stop is valid. To learn more about such "pretextual stops," see the feature *You Be the Judge—A Valid Pretext?* on the following page.

Ohio State Highway Patrol troopers talk with motorists at a sobriety checkpoint designed to deter drivers who drink or use drugs. What argument could be made that these sobriety checkpoints—which allow police to stop all drivers on a certain road—constitute unreasonable searches and seizures?

AP Photo/David Kohl

THE PLAIN VIEW DOCTRINE

The Constitution, as interpreted by our courts, provides very little protection to contraband *in plain view*. For example, suppose a traffic officer pulls over a person for speeding, looks in the driver's side window, and clearly sees what appears to be a bag of heroin resting on the passenger seat. In this instance, under the **plain view doctrine,** the officer would be justified in seizing the drugs without a warrant.

The plain view doctrine was first enunciated by the Supreme Court in *Coolidge v. New Hampshire* (1971).[72] The Court ruled that law enforcement officers may make a warrantless seizure of an item if four criteria are met:

1. The item is positioned so as to be detected easily by an officer's sight or some other sense.
2. The officer is legally in a position to notice the item in question.
3. The discovery of the item is inadvertent. That is, the officer had not intended to find the item.
4. The officer immediately recognizes the illegal nature of the item. No interrogation or further investigation is allowed under the plain view doctrine.

Advances in technology that allow law enforcement agents to "see" beyond normal human capabilities have raised new issues in regard to plain view principles. *Thermal imagers,* for example, measure otherwise invisible levels of infrared radiation. These

Learning Objective 7 Describe the plain view doctrine and indicate one of its limitations.

Plain View Doctrine The legal principle that objects in plain view of a law enforcement agent who has the right to be in a position to have that view may be seized without a warrant.

devices are particularly effective in detecting marijuana plants grown indoors because of the heat thrown off by the "grow lights" that the plants need to survive. The question for the courts has been whether a warrantless search of a dwelling through its walls by means of a thermal imager violates Fourth Amendment protections of privacy. According to the Supreme Court, an item is not in plain view if law enforcement agents need the aid of technology to "see" it.[73] Thus, information from a thermal imager is not by itself justification for a warrantless search.

ELECTRONIC SURVEILLANCE

During the course of a criminal investigation, law enforcement officers may decide to use **electronic surveillance,** or electronic devices such as wiretaps or hidden microphones ("bugs"), to monitor and record conversations, observe movements, and trace or record telephone calls.

BASIC RULES: CONSENT AND PROBABLE CAUSE Given the invasiveness of electronic surveillance, the Supreme Court has generally held that the practice is prohibited by the Fourth Amendment. In *Burger v. New York* (1967),[74] however, the Court ruled that it was permissible under certain circumstances. That same year, *Katz v. United States* (discussed on page 171) established that recorded conversations are inadmissible as evidence unless certain procedures are followed.

Electronic Surveillance
The use of electronic equipment by law enforcement agents to record private conversations or observe conduct that is meant to be private.

YOU BE THE JUDGE

A Valid Pretext?

THE SITUATION Six months ago, Lieutenant Collier, a drug task force agent, arrested Hector Ramirez after Collier found five hundred grams of heroin in Ramirez's late-model Ford. In his postarrest report, written two days after the stop, Collier described clocking Ramirez at seventy-nine miles per hour (mph) in a seventy mph zone before pulling him over and finding the illegal drugs. Evidence from the dashboard camera in Collier's own automobile, however, contradicts his version of events. The recording shows that Ramirez had been driving the speed limit at the time of the stop. Furthermore, in court, Collier has changed his story, saying that he had pulled over the defendant because he thought he saw a suspicious object—that turned out to be a pink child's car seat—in the back of the Ford.

THE LAW As far as the Fourth Amendment is concerned, any subjective reasons that a police officer might have for stopping a suspect, including any motives based on racial stereotyping or bias, are irrelevant. As long as the officer has objective probable cause to believe a traffic violation or other wrongdoing has occurred, the stop is valid.

YOUR DECISION No one disputes that Ramirez was in possession of the illegal drugs. The important question is, Did Collier have a valid, objective reason to stop Ramirez and search his car? If not, then the search was unconstitutional, and the heroin cannot be used against Ramirez in court. If you were the judge in the case, how would you rule?

[To see what a federal district judge in Tennessee did in a similar situation, go to Example 6.1 in Appendix B.]

Rasmus Rasmusson/iStockphoto/iStockphoto/Photodisc/Shutterstock/James Stadl/iStockphoto

In general, law enforcement officers can use electronic surveillance only if consent is given by one of the parties to be monitored, or, in the absence of such consent, with a warrant.[75] For the warrant to be valid, it must:

1. Detail with "particularity" the conversations that are to be overheard.
2. Name the suspects and the places that will be under surveillance.
3. Show probable cause to believe that a specific crime has been or will be committed.[76]

Once the specific information has been gathered, the law enforcement officers must end the electronic surveillance immediately.[77] In any case, the surveillance cannot last more than thirty days without a judicial extension.

FORCE MULTIPLYING More pervasive forms of electronic surveillance are allowed under the theory that people who are in public places have no reasonable expectation of privacy.[78] For example, many Americans would be surprised to learn how often they are under the watchful eye of law enforcement via closed-circuit television (CCTV) cameras. CCTV surveillance relies on strategically placed video cameras to record and transmit all activity in a targeted area, such as on a public street or in a government building. The images are monitored in real time so that law enforcement personnel can investigate any suspicious or criminal activity captured by cameras.

The growing use of traffic cameras has also been a boon to law enforcement. Police in Red Bank, Tennessee, were recently able to catch four suspects in a violent home invasion by reviewing video of the suspects' car captured by a nearby red-light camera. CCTV and traffic cameras are examples of *force multipliers,* so called because these forms of electronic surveillance allow law enforcement agencies to expand their capabilities without a significant increase in personnel. Speaking of CCTV, Brian Harvey, a deputy chief with the Dallas Police Department, says, "One camera operator can cover a lot more area than field officers can."[79]

CJ& TECHNOLOGY

Automatic License Plate Recognition

An increasingly popular force multiplier involves computerized infrared cameras that take digital photos of license plates. Usually mounted on police cars, these automatic license-plate recognition (ALPR) devices convert the images to text. Then the numbers are instantly checked against databases that contain records of the license plates of stolen cars and other vehicles driven by a wide variety of targets, from wanted felons to citizens with unpaid parking tickets. In heavy-traffic areas, ALPR units can check thousands of license plates each hour. After adding ALPR technology to its patrol cars in December 2011, the Gloucester Township (New Jersey) police used the system to arrest twenty wanted criminals in just under a month.

THINKING ABOUT AUTOMATIC LICENSE PLATE RECOGNITION: How might law enforcement use ALPR not only to identify "hot" license plates but also as part of ongoing criminal investigations? For example, how might narcotics officers on a stakeout of a suspected drug dealer's house take advantage of ALPR technology?

Monica Almeida/New York Times/Redux Pictures

CONSTITUTIONAL CONCERNS Critics of CCTV cameras, ALPR, and other forms of high-tech surveillance contend that these technologies infringe on individual privacy, allowing law enforcement to create "digital dossiers" on people without probable cause.[80] As long as the periods of public surveillance are relatively short, however, courts have ruled that such tracking of a person or a vehicle on public streets does not constitute a Fourth Amendment search, because no reasonable expectation of privacy exists in such situations.[81]

That outlook changes when the period of surveillance in question is much longer. Consider the case of suspected Washington, D.C., drug kingpin Antoine Jones. Without first getting a warrant, police placed a Global Positioning System (GPS) device on Jones's Grand Jeep Cherokee, allowing them to track his movements for a month using satellite technology. With this information, prosecutors were able to convict Jones of conspiring to sell cocaine, and he was sentenced to life in prison. In 2012, the Supreme Court overturned the conviction, holding that the installation of the GPS device constituted a search and the police's failure to obtain a warrant rendered much of the evidence against Jones invalid.[82]

SOCIAL MEDIA SEARCHES

As we saw in Chapter 4, law enforcement agents now routinely use social networking sites such as Facebook and Twitter to investigate criminal behavior. Given that the widespread use of these sites is a relatively new phenomenon, the law governing such investigations has yet to settle. From 2008 to 2011, federal law enforcement agents did obtain at least two dozen warrants to search individuals' Facebook accounts, following the procedure for electronic surveillance detailed on pages 176–177.[83] At the same time, Facebook receives up to twenty police requests for information a day and often complies with such requests. In such instances, neither the government nor the social networking company is required to inform the suspect of law enforcement's interest in her or his personal profile.[84]

Furthermore, even though most social networking sites forbid individuals from using fake identities, police officers routinely do so when investigating criminal activity. On a number of occasions, law enforcement agents have gone "friending undercover" online to apprehend sex offenders, thwart drug deals, find missing persons, and monitor juvenile misconduct. As of yet, no court decision or law prohibits such behavior. When the issue does arise, it will inevitably focus on whether people have a reasonable expectation of privacy when it comes to posting information about themselves online.[85]

SELFASSESSMENT

Fill in the blanks and check your answers on page 184.

A search is a governmental intrusion on the _____ of an individual. To protect these rights, law enforcement agents must procure a _____ _____ before examining a suspect's home or personal possessions. During a properly executed search, officers may _____ any items that may be used as evidence or that are inherently illegal to possess. Law enforcement agents do not need a judge's prior approval to conduct a search incidental to an _____ or when the subject of the search gives his or her _____.

THE INTERROGATION PROCESS AND *MIRANDA*

After the Pledge of Allegiance, there is perhaps no recitation that comes more readily to the American mind than the *Miranda* warning:

You have the right to remain silent. If you give up that right, anything you say can and will be used against you in a court of law. You have the right to speak with an attorney and to have the attorney present during questioning. If you so desire and cannot afford one, an attorney will be appointed for you without charge before questioning.

The *Miranda* warning is not a mere prop. It strongly affects one of the most important aspects of any criminal investigation—the **interrogation,** or questioning of a suspect from whom the police want to get information concerning a crime, and perhaps a confession.

THE LEGAL BASIS FOR *MIRANDA*

The Fifth Amendment guarantees protection against self-incrimination. In other words, as we shall see again in Chapter 8, a defendant cannot be required to provide information about his or her own criminal activity. A defendant's choice *not* to incriminate himself or herself cannot be interpreted as a sign of guilt by a jury in a criminal trial. A confession, or admission of guilt, is by definition a statement of self-incrimination. How, then, to reconcile the Fifth Amendment with the critical need of law enforcement officers to gain confessions? The answer lies in the concept of **coercion,** or the use of physical or psychological duress to obtain a confession.

When torture or brutality is involved, it is relatively easy to determine that a confession was improperly coerced and is therefore invalid. When the Supreme Court handed down its decision in *Miranda v. Arizona* (1966),[86] establishing the *Miranda* **rights,** it was more concerned with the possibility of what Columbia University law professor H. Richard Uviller called *inherent coercion.* This terms refers to the assumption that even if a police officer does not lay a hand on a suspect, the general atmosphere of an interrogation is in and of itself coercive.[87]

Although the *Miranda* case is best remembered for the procedural requirement it spurred, at the time the Supreme Court was more concerned about the treatment of suspects during interrogation. (See the feature *Landmark Cases*—Miranda v. Arizona on the following page.) The Court found that routine police interrogation strategies, such as leaving suspects alone in a room for several hours before questioning them, were inherently coercive. Therefore, the Court reasoned, every suspect needed protection from coercion, not just those who had been physically abused. The *Miranda* warning is a result of this need. In theory, if the warning is not given to a suspect before an interrogation, the fruits of that interrogation, including a confession, are invalid.

WHEN A *MIRANDA* WARNING IS REQUIRED

As we shall see, a *Miranda* warning is not necessary under several conditions, such as when no questions are asked of the suspect. Generally, *Miranda* requirements apply only when a suspect is in **custody.** In a series of rulings since *Miranda,* the Supreme Court has defined custody as an arrest or a situation in which a reasonable person would not feel free to leave.[88] Consequently, a **custodial interrogation** occurs when a suspect is under arrest or is deprived of her or his freedom in a significant manner. Remember, a *Miranda* warning is only required before a custodial interrogation takes place. For example, if four police officers enter a suspect's bedroom at 4:00 A.M., wake him, and form a circle around him, then they must give him a *Miranda* warning before questioning. Even though the suspect has not been arrested, he will "not feel free to go where he please[s]."[89]

Interrogation The direct questioning of a suspect to gather evidence of criminal activity and to try to gain a confession.

Coercion The use of physical force or mental intimidation to compel a person to do something—such as confess to committing a crime—against her or his will.

***Miranda* Rights** The constitutional rights of accused persons taken into custody by law enforcement officials, such as the right to remain silent and the right to counsel.

Custody The forceful detention of a person, or the perception that a person is not free to leave the immediate vicinity.

Custodial Interrogation The questioning of a suspect after that person has been taken into custody. In this situation, the suspect must be read his or her *Miranda* rights before interrogation can begin.

What aspects of the situation shown in this photo indicate that the Aspen (Colorado) police officer is required to "Mirandize" the suspect before asking him any questions, even if he never formally places the suspect under arrest?

Photo by Chris Hondros/Getty Images

LANDMARK CASES: *Miranda v. Arizona*

AP/Wide World

Ernesto Miranda

In 1963, a rape and kidnapping victim identified produce worker Ernesto Miranda as her assailant in a lineup. Detectives questioned Miranda for two hours concerning the crime, at no time informing him that he had a right to have an attorney present. When the police emerged from the session, they had a signed statement by Miranda confessing to the crimes. He was subsequently convicted and sentenced to twenty to thirty years in prison. After the conviction was confirmed by the Arizona Supreme Court, Miranda appealed to the United States Supreme Court, claiming that he had not been warned that any statement he made could be used against him, and that he had a right to counsel during the interrogation. The *Miranda* case was one of four examined by the Court that dealt with the question of coercive questioning.

Miranda v. Arizona
United States Supreme Court
384 U.S. 436 (1966)
laws.findlaw.com/US/384/436.html

IN THE WORDS OF THE COURT...
CHIEF JUSTICE WARREN, MAJORITY OPINION
* * * *

The cases before us raise questions which go to the roots of our concepts of American criminal jurisprudence: the restraints society must observe consistent with the Federal Constitution in prosecuting individuals for crime. More specifically, we deal with the admissibility of statements obtained from an individual who is subjected to custodial police interrogation and the necessity for procedures which assure that the individual is accorded his privilege under the Fifth Amendment to the Constitution not to be compelled to incriminate himself.
* * * *

It is obvious that such an interrogation environment is created for no purpose other than to subjugate the individual to the will of his examiner. This atmosphere carries its own badge of intimidation. To be sure, this is not physical intimidation, but it is equally destructive of human dignity. The current practice of incommunicado interrogation is at odds with one of our Nation's most cherished principles— that the individual may not be compelled to incriminate himself. Unless adequate protective devices are employed to dispel the compulsion inherent in custodial surroundings, no statement obtained from the defendant can truly be the product of his free choice.

Decision
The Court overturned Miranda's conviction, stating that police interrogations are, by their very nature, coercive and therefore deny suspects their constitutional right against self-incrimination by "forcing" them to confess. Consequently, any person who has been arrested and placed in custody must be informed of his or her right to be free from self-incrimination and to be represented by counsel during any interrogation. In other words, suspects must be told that they *do not have to* answer police questions. To accomplish this, the Court established the *Miranda* warning.

FOR CRITICAL ANALYSIS
What is meant by the phrase "coercion can be mental as well as physical"? What role does the concept of "mental coercion" play in Chief Justice Warren's opinion?

WHEN A *MIRANDA* WARNING IS NOT REQUIRED
A *Miranda* warning is not necessary in a number of situations:

Learning Objective 8 Indicate situations in which a *Miranda* warning is unnecessary.

1. When the police do not ask the suspect any questions that are *testimonial* in nature. Such questions are designed to elicit information that may be used against the suspect in court. Note that "routine booking questions," such as the suspect's name, address, height, and eye color, do not require a *Miranda* warning. Even though answering these questions may provide incriminating evidence (especially if the person answering is a prime suspect), the Supreme Court has held that they

are absolutely necessary if the police are to do their jobs.[90] (Imagine the officer not being able to ask a suspect her or his name.)

2. When the police have not focused on a suspect and are questioning witnesses at the scene of a crime.
3. When a person volunteers information before the police have asked a question.
4. When the suspect has given a private statement to a friend or some other acquaintance. *Miranda* does not apply to these statements so long as the government did not orchestrate the situation.
5. During a stop and frisk, when no arrest has been made.
6. During a traffic stop.[91]

A Los Angeles police officer reads a handcuffed "suspect" his *Miranda* rights during a training exercise. Does a police officer need to take this action every time he or she arrests a suspect? If not, under what circumstances must an officer administer the *Miranda* warning?
Kim Kulish/Corbis

Suspects can *waive* their Fifth Amendment rights and speak to a police officer, but only if the waiver is made voluntarily. Silence on the part of a suspect does not mean that his or her *Miranda* protections have been relinquished. To waive their rights, suspects must state—either in writing or orally—that they understand those rights and that they will voluntarily answer questions without the presence of counsel.

To ensure that the suspect's rights are upheld, prosecutors are required to prove by a preponderance of the evidence that the suspect "knowing and intelligently" waived his or her *Miranda* rights.[92] To make the waiver perfectly clear, police will ask suspects two questions in addition to giving the *Miranda* warning:

1. Do you understand your rights as I have read them to you?
2. Knowing your rights, are you willing to talk to another law enforcement officer or me?

If the suspect indicates that she or he does not want to speak to the officer, thereby invoking her or his right to silence, the officer must *immediately* stop any questioning.[93] Similarly, if the suspect requests a lawyer, the police can ask no further questions until an attorney is present.[94]

THE FUTURE OF *MIRANDA*

"*Miranda* has become embedded in routine police practice to the point where the warnings have become part of our national culture," wrote then chief justice William Rehnquist over a decade ago.[95] This may be so, but at the same time, many legal scholars believe that a series of Supreme Court rulings have eroded *Miranda's* protections. "It's death by a thousand cuts," says Jeffrey L. Fisher of the National Association of Criminal Defense Lawyers, who believes the Court is "doing everything it can to ease the admissibility of confessions that police wriggle out of suspects."[96]

VOLUNTARY STATEMENTS One such exception, created by the Supreme Court in 2004, is crucial to understanding the status of the *Miranda* rights in current criminal law. The case involved a Colorado defendant who voluntarily told the police the location of his gun (which, being an ex-felon, he was not allowed to possess) without being read his rights.[97] The Court upheld the conviction, finding that the *Miranda* warning is merely *prophylactic*. In other words, it is only intended to prevent violations of the Fifth Amendment. Because only the gun, and not the defendant's testimony, was presented at trial, the police had not violated the defendant's constitutional rights. In essence,

FIGURE 6.4 Supreme Court Decisions Eroding *Miranda* Rights

New York v. Quarles (467 U.S. 649 [1984]). **This case established the "public-safety" exception to the *Miranda* rule.** It concerned a police officer who, after feeling an empty shoulder holster on a man he had just arrested, asked the suspect the location of the gun without informing him of his *Miranda* rights. The Court ruled that the gun was admissible as evidence and that the need for police officers to protect the public is more important than a suspect's *Miranda* rights.

Moran v. Burbine (475 U.S. 412 [1986]). **This case established that police officers are not required to tell suspects undergoing custodial interrogation that their attorney is trying to reach them.** The Court ruled that events that the suspect could have no way of knowing about have no bearing on his ability to waive his *Miranda* rights.

Arizona v. Fulminante (499 U.S. 279 [1991]). **In this very important ruling, the Court held that a conviction is not automatically overturned if the suspect was coerced into making a confession.** If the other evidence introduced at the trial is strong enough to justify a conviction without the confession, then the fact that the confession was illegally gained can be, for all intents and purposes, ignored.

Texas v. Cobb (532 U.S. 162 [2001]). When a suspect refuses to waive his or her *Miranda* rights, a police officer cannot lawfully continue the interrogation until the suspect's attorney arrives on the scene. In this case, however, **the Court held that a suspect may be questioned without having a lawyer present if the interrogation does not focus on the crime for which he or she was arrested,** even though it does touch on another, closely related, offense.

Florida v. Powell (559 U.S. ___ [2010]). Florida's version of the *Miranda* warning informs suspects that they have a right "to talk with an attorney" but does not clearly inform them of the right to a lawyer during any police interrogation. The Court upheld Florida's warning, **ruling that different jurisdictions may use whatever version of the *Miranda* warning they please, as long as it reasonably conveys the essential information about a suspect's rights.**

Howes v. Fields (556 U.S. ___ [2012]) The Court ruled that a Michigan jail inmate who was questioned by sheriff's deputies in a conference room for five to seven hours was not improperly coerced into confessing to a sex crime. In general, **people already in prison and jail are not in "custody" for purposes of determining custodial interrogation, and therefore a *Miranda* warning is not required before questioning them.**

the Court was ruling that the "fruit of the poisoned tree" doctrine, discussed earlier in this chapter, does not bar the admission of physical evidence that is discovered based on voluntary statements by a suspect who has not been "Mirandized."[98] (See Figure 6.4 above for a rundown of other significant Court rulings that have weakened the *Miranda* requirements over the past two decades.)

RECORDING CONFESSIONS *Miranda* may eventually find itself obsolete regardless of any decisions made in the courts. A relatively new trend in law enforcement has been for agencies to record interrogations and confessions digitally. Several states now require that all interrogations of suspects of serious felonies be recorded, and hundreds of law enforcement agencies voluntarily engage in the practice. Some scholars have suggested that recording all custodial interrogations would satisfy the Fifth Amendment's prohibition against coercion and thus render the *Miranda* warning unnecessary.

SELFASSESSMENT

Fill in the blanks and check your answers on page 184.

Miranda requirements apply only when law enforcement agents have the suspect in _____. The *Miranda* warning is only required _____ a custodial interrogation takes place. A suspect can _____ his or her *Miranda* rights, but this must be done "knowingly and intentionally." If the suspect indicates that he or she does not wish to speak, the police officer must _____ stop any questioning. The suspect can also end questioning any time by requesting the presence of an _____.

CHAPTER SUMMARY

Learning Objective 1 **Outline the four major sources that may provide probable cause.** (a) Personal observation, usually due to an officer's personal training, experience, and expertise; (b) information, gathered from informants, eyewitnesses, victims, police bulletins, and other sources; (c) evidence, which often has to be in plain view; and (d) association, which generally must involve a person with a known criminal background who is seen in a place where criminal activity is openly taking place.

Learning Objective 2 **Explain the exclusionary rule and the exceptions to it.** This rule prohibits illegally seized evidence, or evidence obtained by an unreasonable search and seizure in an inadmissible way, from being used against the accused in criminal court. Exceptions to the exclusionary rule are the "inevitable discovery" exception established in *Nix v. Williams* and the "good faith" exception established in *United States v. Leon* and *Herring v. United States*.

Learning Objective 3 **Distinguish between a stop and a frisk, and indicate the importance of the case *Terry v. Ohio*.** Although the terms *stop* and *frisk* are often used in concert, a stop is the separate act of detaining a suspect when an officer reasonably believes that a criminal activity is about to take place. A frisk is the physical pat-down of a suspect. In *Terry v. Ohio,* the Supreme Court ruled that an officer must have "specific and articulable facts" before making a stop, but those facts may be "taken together with rational inferences."

Learning Objective 4 **List the four elements that must be present for an arrest to take place.** (a) Intent, (b) authority, (c) seizure or detention, and (d) the understanding of the person that he or she has been arrested.

Learning Objective 5 **List the four categories of items that can be seized by use of a search warrant.** (a) Items resulting from a crime, such as stolen goods; (b) inherently illegal items; (c) evidence of the crime; and (d) items used in committing the crime.

Learning Objective 6 **Explain when searches can be made without a warrant.** Searches and seizures can be made without a warrant if they are incidental to an arrest (but they must be reasonable); when they are made with voluntary consent; when they involve the "movable vehicle" exception; when property has been abandoned; and when items are in plain view, under certain restricted circumstances (see *Coolidge v. New Hampshire*).

Learning Objective 7 **Describe the plain view doctrine and indicate one of its limitations.** Under the plain view doctrine, police officers are justified in seizing an item if (a) the item is easily seen by an officer who is legally in a position to notice it; (b) the discovery of the item is unintended; and (c) the officer, without further investigation, immediately recognizes the illegal nature of the item. An item is not in plain view if the law enforcement agent needs to use technology such as a thermal imager to "see" it.

Learning Objective 8 **Indicate situations in which a *Miranda* warning is unnecessary.** (a) When no questions that are testimonial in nature are asked of the suspect; (b) when there is no suspect and witnesses in general are being questioned at the scene of a crime; (c) when a person volunteers information before the police ask anything; (d) when a suspect has given a private statement to a friend without the government orchestrating it; (e) during a stop and frisk when no arrests have been made; and (f) during a traffic stop.

QUESTIONS FOR CRITICAL ANALYSIS

1. What are the two most significant legal concepts contained in the Fourth Amendment, and why are they important?

2. Suppose that a police officer stops a person who "looks funny." The person acts strangely, so the police officer decides to frisk him. The officer feels a bulge in the suspect's coat pocket, which turns out to be a bag of cocaine. Would the arrest for cocaine possession hold up in court? Why or why not?

3. What if, in the case that opens this chapter, the Kentucky police officers had not smelled marijuana and had simply knocked on Hollis King's door and asked to talk with him? What would have been King's options in that situation?

4. Should law enforcement agents be required to get a search warrant before accessing records that reveal a cell phone user's location? Those who think a warrant

is unnecessary in this situation argue that once users turn their phones on, they have decided to waive their expectations of privacy by "voluntarily" transmitting their location. What is your opinion of this argument?

5. Do you think it is unethical for police officers to use fake profiles in online social networking sites to "friend" suspects or crime victims as part of a criminal investigation? Why or why not?

KEY TERMS

affidavit **172**

arrest **168**

arrest warrant **169**

coercion **179**

consent searches **173**

custodial interrogation **179**

custody **179**

electronic surveillance **176**

exclusionary rule **163**

exigent circumstances **169**

frisk **167**

fruit of the poisoned tree **163**

"good faith" exception **165**

"inevitable discovery" exception **164**

interrogation **179**

Miranda rights **179**

plain view doctrine **175**

probable cause **161**

racial profiling **166**

search **171**

search warrant **171**

searches and seizures **161**

searches incidental to arrests **173**

seizure **172**

stop **167**

warrantless arrest **170**

SELF ASSESSMENT ANSWER KEY

Page 165: **i.** unreasonable; **ii.** probable cause; **iii.** exclusionary; **iv.** evidence

Page 167: **i.** stop; **ii.** reasonable; **iii.** frisk

Page 170: **i.** custody; **ii.** warrant; **iii.** warrantless; **iv.** probable cause

Page 178: **i.** privacy; **ii.** search warrant; **iii.** seize; **iv.** arrest; **v.** consent

Page 182: **i.** custody; **ii.** before; **iii.** waive; **iv.** immediately; **v.** attorney

COURSEMATE

For online help and access to resources that accompany *Criminal Justice in Action: The Core*, go to **www.cengagebrain.com/shop/ISBN/978-1-285-06915-9**. Click "Access Now," where you will find flashcards, an online quiz, and other helpful study aids. If you have an access code for CourseMate, log in and go to the chapter of your choice for additional online study aids.

NOTES

1. Orin Kerr, "Police-Created Exigent Circumstances in *Kentucky v. King*," January 5, 2011, at **www.scotusblog.com/?p=111396**.

2. *Kentucky v. King*, 131 S.Ct. 1849, 1858 (2011).

3. *Ibid.*, 1869.

4. Adam Liptak, "Justices Look Again at How Police May Search Homes," *New York Times* (January 13, 2011), A18.

5. *Michigan v. Summers*, 452 U.S. 692 (1981).

6. *Brinegar v. United States*, 338 U.S. 160 (1949).

7. Rolando V. del Carmen, *Criminal Procedure for Law Enforcement Personnel* (Monterey, CA: Brooks/Cole Publishing Co., 1987), 63–64.

8. *Maryland v. Pringle*, 540 U.S. 366 (2003).

9. 500 U.S. 44 (1991).

10. *United States v. Leon*, 468 U.S. 897 (1984).

11. 430 U.S. 387 (1977).

12. 467 U.S. 431 (1984).

13. 468 U.S. 897 (1984).

14. 555 U.S. 135 (2009).

15. *Woodson v. Indiana*, No. 49A05-1106-CR-306 (2011).

16. Karen M. Hess and Henry M. Wrobleski, *Police Operation: Theory and Practice* (St. Paul, MN: West Publishing Co., 1997), 122.

17. 392 U.S. 1 (1968).

18. *Ibid.*, 20.

19. *Ibid.*, 21.

20. See *United States v. Cortez*, 449 U.S. 411 (1981); and *United States v. Sokolow*, 490 U.S. 1 (1989).

21. *United States v. Arvizu*, 534 U.S. 266 (2002).

22. *Ibid.*, 270.

23. Center for Constitutional Rights, "2011 Data Reveals Record Number of Stop-and-Frisks with No Change in Racial Disparities," February 14, 2012, at **ccrjustice.org/**

newsroom/press-releases/2011-data-reveals-record-number-of-stop-and-frisks-no-change-racial-disparities.

24. Sarah White and Salmun Kazerounian, *The Forgotten Constitution: Racial Profiling and Immigration Enforcement in Bedford County, Tennessee* (Nashville, TN: Tennessee Immigrant and Refugee Rights Coalition, 2011), 7.

25. Arizona Revised Statutes Sections 11-1051(B), 13-1509, 13-2929(C).

26. *Arizona v. United States,* 567 U.S. ____ (2012).

27. *United States v. Place,* 462 U.S. 696 (1983).

28. *Hibel v. Sixth Judicial District Court,* 542 U.S. 177 (2004).

29. *Ibid.,* 182.

30. *Minnesota v. Dickerson,* 508 U.S. 366 (1993).

31. *Arizona v. Johnson,* 555 U.S. 323 (2009).

32. Rolando V. del Carmen and Jeffrey T. Walker, *Briefs of Leading Cases in Law Enforcement,* 2d ed. (Cincinnati, OH: Anderson, 1995), 38–40.

33. *Florida v. Royer,* 460 U.S. 491 (1983).

34. See also *United States v. Mendenhall,* 446 U.S. 544 (1980).

35. del Carmen, 97–98.

36. 514 U.S. 927 (1995).

37. Linda J. Collier and Deborah D. Rosenbloom, *American Jurisprudence,* 2d ed. (Rochester, NY: Lawyers Cooperative Publishing, 1995), 122.

38. 547 U.S. 586 (2006).

39. *United States v. Banks,* 540 U.S. 31, 41 (2003).

40. *Hudson v. Michigan,* 547 U.S. 586, 593 (2006).

41. Tom Van Dorn, "Violation of Knock-and-Announce Rule Does Not Require Suppression of All Evidence Found in Search," *The Police Chief* (October 2006), 10.

42. Wayne R. LeFave and Jerold H. Israel, *Criminal Procedure* (St. Paul, MN: West Publishing Co., 1985), 141–144.

43. David Orlin, Jacob Thiessen, Kelli C. McTaggart, Lisa Toporek, and James Pearl, "Warrantless Searches and Seizures," in "Twenty-Sixth Annual Review of Criminal Procedure," *Georgetown Law Journal* 85 (April 1997), 847.

44. 445 U.S. 573 (1980).

45. 451 U.S. 204 (1981).

46. *California v. Greenwood,* 486 U.S. 35 (1988).

47. *Ibid.*

48. 389 U.S. 347 (1967).

49. *Ibid.,* 361.

50. 486 U.S. 35 (1988).

51. *Ibid.*

52. *Illinois v. Caballes,* 543 U.S. 405 (2005).

53. *Coolidge v. New Hampshire,* 403 U.S. 443, 467 (1971).

54. del Carmen, 158.

55. *Katz v. United States,* 389 U.S. 347, 357 (1967).

56. *Brigham City v. Stuart,* 547 U.S. 398 (2006).

57. 414 U.S. 234–235 (1973).

58. 395 U.S. 752 (1969).

59. *Ibid.,* 763.

60. Carl A. Benoit, "Questioning 'Authority': Fourth Amendment Consent Searches," *FBI Law Enforcement Bulletin* (July 2008), 24.

61. *Bumper v. North Carolina,* 391 U.S. 543 (1968).

62. *State v. Stone,* 362 N.C. 50, 653 S.E.2d 414 (2007).

63. 412 U.S. 218 (1973).

64. Jayme W. Holcomb, "Knock and Talks," *FBI Law Enforcement Bulletin* (August 2006), 22–32.

65. 267 U.S. 132 (1925).

66. *United States v. Ross,* 456 U.S. 798, 804–809 (1982); and *Chambers v. Maroney,* 399 U.S. 42, 44, 52 (1970).

67. 453 U.S. 454 (1981).

68. *Arizona v. Gant,* 556 U.S. 332 (2009).

69. Adam Liptak, "Justices Significantly Cut Back Officers' Searches of Cars of People They Arrest," *New York Times* (April 22, 2009), A12.

70. Dale Anderson and Dave Cole, "Search and Seizure after *Arizona v. Gant,*" *Arizona Attorney* (October 2009), 15.

71. *Whren v. United States,* 517 U.S. 806 (1996).

72. 403 U.S. 443 (1971).

73. *Kyollo v. United States,* 533 U.S. 27 (2001).

74. 388 U.S. 42 (1967).

75. 18 U.S.C. Sections 2510(7), 2518(1)(a), 2516 (1994).

76. Christopher K. Murphy, "Electronic Surveillance," in "Twenty-Sixth Annual Review of Criminal Procedure," *Georgetown Law Journal* 85 (April 1997), 920.

77. *United States v. Nguyen,* 46 F.3d 781, 783 (8th Cir. 1995).

78. Joseph Siprut, "Privacy Through Anonymity: An Economic Argument for Expanding the Right of Privacy in Public Places," *Pepperdine Law Review* 33 (2006), 311, 320.

79. Quoted in Rebecca Kanable, "Dallas' First Year with CCTV," *Law Enforcement Technology* (February 2008), 35.

80. Sharon B. Franklin, "Watching the Watchers: Establishing Limits on Public Video Surveillance," *Champion* (April 2008), 40.

81. *United States v. Knotts,* 460 U.S. 276 (1983).

82. *United States v. Jones,* 565 U.S. ____ (2012).

83. Reuters, "Facebook Fishing: Officials Using Sites to Crack Cases—Without Telling Users," *Chicago Tribune* (July 13, 2011), 6.

84. Shirin Chahal, "Balancing the Scales of Justice: Undercover Investigations on Social Networking Sites," *Journal on Telecommunications and High Technology Law* (Winter 2011), 293–298.

85. Edward M. Marsico, "Social Networking Websites: Are MySpace and Facebook the Fingerprints of the Twenty-First Century?" *Widener Law Journal* 19 (2010), 967–976.

86. *Miranda v. Arizona,* 384 U.S. 436 (1966).

87. H. Richard Uviller, *Tempered Zeal* (Chicago: Contemporary Books, 1988), 188–198.

88. *Orozco v. Texas,* 394 U.S. 324 (1969); *Oregon v. Mathiason,* 429 U.S. 492 (1977); and *California v. Beheler,* 463 U.S. 1121 (1983).

89. *Orozco,* 325.

90. *Pennsylvania v. Muniz,* 496 U.S. 582 (1990).

91. del Carmen, 267–268.

92. *Moran v. Burbine,* 475 U.S. 412 (1986).

93. *Michigan v. Mosley,* 423 U.S. 96 (1975).

94. *Fare v. Michael C.,* 442 U.S. 707, 723–724 (1979).

95. *Dickerson v. United States,* 530 U.S. 443 (2000).

96. Quoted in Jesse J. Holland, "High Court Trims *Miranda* Warning Rights Bit by Bit," *Associated Press* (August 2, 2010).

97. *United States v. Patane,* 542 U.S. 630 (2004).

98. *Ibid.,* 640.

CHAPTER 7

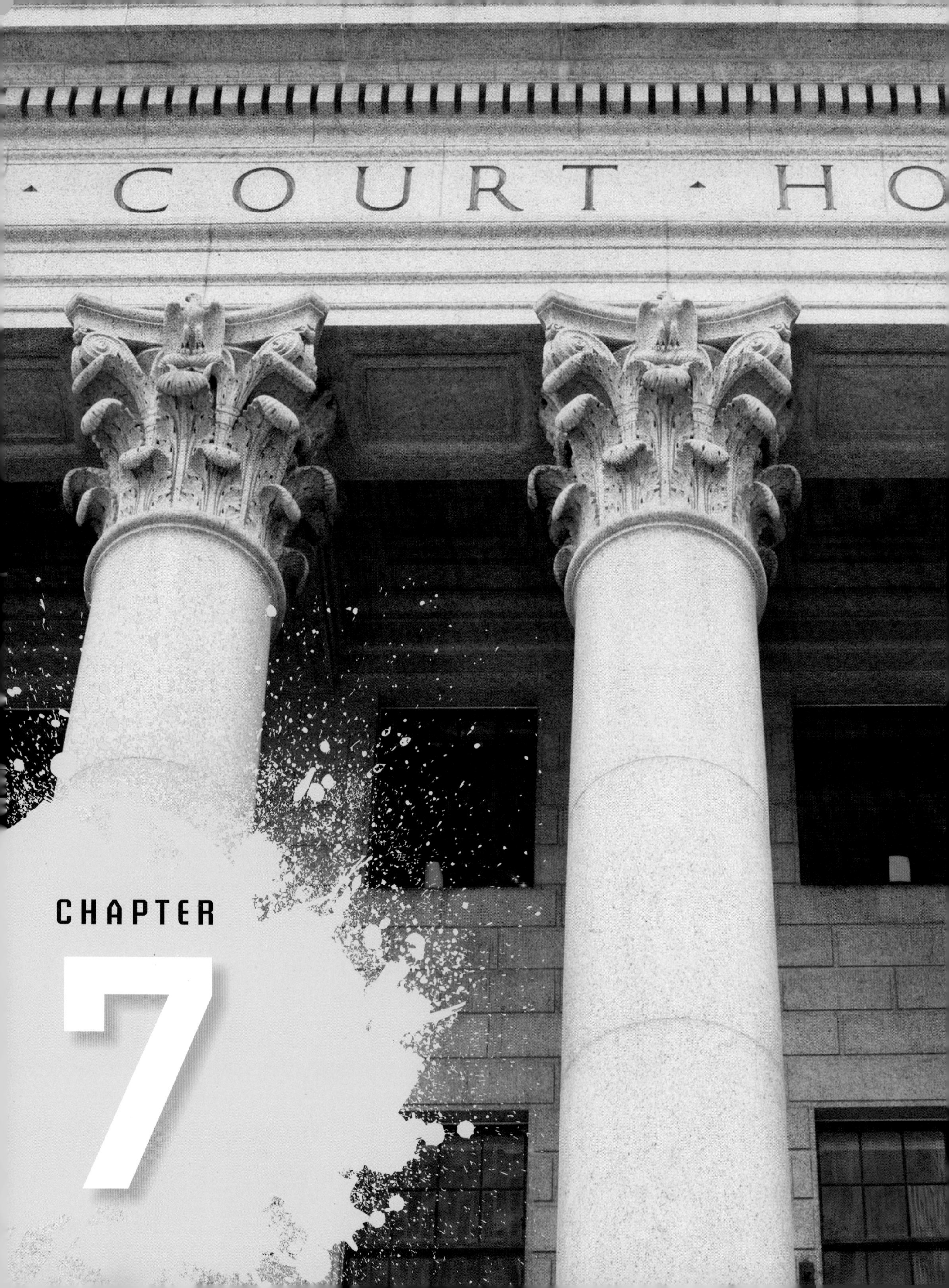

Courts and the Quest for Justice

PierreDesrosiers/Shutterstock

LEARNING OBJECTIVES

After reading this chapter, you should be able to...

1 Define *jurisdiction* and contrast geographic and subject-matter jurisdiction.

2 Explain the difference between trial and appellate courts.

3 Outline the several levels of a typical state court system.

4 Outline the federal court system.

5 Explain briefly how a case is brought to the Supreme Court.

6 List and describe the members of the courtroom work group.

7 List the different names given to public prosecutors and indicate the general powers that they have.

8 Delineate the responsibilities of defense attorneys.

Throughout the chapter you will see each learning objective repeated in the margin next to the content it relates to. The chapter summary on page 211 includes all of the learning objectives for review.

CHAPTER OUTLINE

• Functions of the Courts

• The Basic Principles of the American Judicial System

• State Court Systems

• The Federal Court System

• Judges in the Court System

• The Courtroom Work Group

A PRANK OR A CRIME?

Clearly, there was one reason—and one reason only—why Dharun Ravi found himself facing criminal charges in a New Brunswick, New Jersey, courtroom, on February 24, 2012: his role in Tyler Clementi's death. Eighteen months earlier, Ravi and Clementi had been freshman roommates at Rutgers University, when Ravi set up a hidden webcam in their dorm room. Ravi then joined Molly Wei, another Rutgers student, in her room, and the pair briefly watched a live stream of Clementi embracing another man. "I saw him making out with a dude. Yay," Ravi tweeted soon thereafter. Two days later, Ravi attempted to set up another viewing of his roommate's romantic activities. One day after that, Clementi took a train to nearby New York City and jumped to his death from the George Washington Bridge.

Despite these troubling circumstances, Clementi's suicide was not mentioned once during Ravi's three-week trial. Legally, his death was irrelevant to the proceedings. Instead, prosecutors had charged Ravi with invasion of privacy for observing Clementi engaged in sexual contact. (Despite reports to the contrary, Ravi never recorded the footage or uploaded it onto the Internet.) In addition, Ravi was charged with "bias intimidation," with prosecutors alleging that he had harassed his roommate because of Clementi's homosexuality. Due to the nature of hate crime law, which we discussed in Chapter 3, Ravi faced a maximum sentence of ten years behind bars for what is normally a relatively minor offense.

On the first day of Ravi's trial, prosecutor Julie McClure told jurors that the defendant deliberately planned to deprive Clement of his dignity. Earlier, she called Ravi's actions "malicious, purposeful, and criminal." In contrast, Ravi's defense attorneys characterized his behavior as that of an immature eighteen-year-old boy. It was a "kid's prank that went wrong," contended one supporter. For his part, James Clementi, Tyler's father, had only one request of the court: "[T]hat justice will be found."

Former Rutgers University student Dharun Ravi looks back at family members during his trial in Middlesex County, New Jersey, for invasion of privacy and bias intimidation.

Lucas Jackson/Reuters/Landov

"Frankly, I think Dharun Ravi should be charged with more than just invasion of privacy, which is essentially calling him a 'Peeping Tom,'" said Steven Goldstein of Garden State Equality, a gay rights group. "In my view, he should be charged with manslaughter."[1] Although it would have been practically impossible to prove that Ravi's actions reached the level of manslaughter (defined on page 74), Goldstein's words reflected widespread frustration with the criminal justice system's response to Tyler Clementi's suicide. "Sometimes the laws don't adequately address the situation," admitted one New Jersey official.[2]

On March 16, 2012, the New Jersey jury found Ravi guilty on multiple counts of invasion of privacy and bias intimidation. The jurors felt that, even though Ravi did not intend to harass or intimidate Clementi, such was the actual effect of his actions. Many observers disagreed with the verdict, given the lack of a violent, underlying crime. Even within the gay rights community, Ravi's conviction drew a mixed reception. According to one activist, the verdict demonstrated that "bias crimes do not require physical weapons like a knife in one's hands."[3] Another said, "I would hesitate to use the word 'justice' here. It was a difficult case."[4] In May 2012, a judge sentenced the defendant to spend thirty days in jail and three years on probation.

In the end, was Dharun Ravi treated fairly by the court system? Famed jurist Roscoe Pound characterized "justice" as society's demand "that serious offenders be convicted and punished," while at the same time "the innocent and unfortunate are not oppressed."[5] We can expand on this noble, if idealistic, definition. Citizens expect their courts to discipline the guilty, provide deterrents for illegal activities, protect civil liberties, and rehabilitate criminals—all simultaneously. Over the course of the next three chapters, we shall examine these lofty goals and the extent to which they can be reached. We start with a discussion of how courts in the United States work.

FUNCTIONS OF THE COURTS

Simply stated, a court is a place where arguments are settled. The argument may be between the federal government and a corporation accused of violating environmental regulations, between business partners, between a criminal and the state, or between any number of other parties. The court provides an environment in which the basis of the argument can be decided through the application of the law.

Courts have extensive powers in our criminal justice system: they can bring the authority of the state to seize property and to restrict individual liberty. Given that the rights to own property and to enjoy personal freedom are enshrined in the U.S. Constitution, a court's *legitimacy* in taking such measures must be unquestioned by society. This legitimacy is based on two factors: impartiality and independence.[6] In theory, each party involved in a courtroom dispute must have an equal chance to present its case and must be secure in the belief that no outside factors are going to influence the decision rendered by the court. In reality, as we shall see over the next three chapters, it does not always work that way.

DUE PROCESS AND CRIME CONTROL IN THE COURTS

As mentioned in Chapter 1, the criminal justice system has two sets of underlying values: due process and crime control. Due process values focus on protecting the rights of the individual, whereas crime control values stress the punishment and repression of criminal conduct. The competing nature of these two value systems is often evident in the nation's courts.

THE DUE PROCESS FUNCTION
The due process function of the courts is to protect individuals from the unfair advantages that the government—with its immense resources—automatically enjoys in legal battles. Seen in this light, constitutional guarantees such as the right to counsel, the right to a jury trial, the right to confront one's accusers, and protection from self-incrimination are equalizers in the "contest" between the state and the individual. The idea that the two sides in a courtroom dispute are adversaries is, as we shall discuss later in the chapter, fundamental in American courts.

THE CRIME CONTROL FUNCTION
Advocates of crime control distinguish between the court's obligation to be fair to the accused and its obligation to be fair to society.[7] The crime control function of the courts emphasizes punishment and retribution—criminals must suffer for the harm done to society, and it is the courts' responsibility to see that they do so. Given this responsibility to protect the public, deter criminal behavior, and "get criminals off the streets," the courts should not be concerned solely with giving the accused a fair chance. Rather than using due process rules as "equalizers," the courts should use them as protection against blatantly unconstitutional acts. For example, a

Three trial lawyers confer as the judge waits at the Sedgwick County Courthouse in Wichita, Kansas. What role do bureaucratic requirements play in the functioning of a typical criminal court?

Jaime Oppenheimer/MCT/Landov

detective who beats a suspect with a tire iron to get a confession has obviously infringed on the suspect's constitutional rights. If, however, the detective uses trickery to gain a confession, the court should allow the confession to stand because it is not in society's interest that law enforcement agents be deterred from outwitting criminals.

THE REHABILITATION FUNCTION

A third view of the court's responsibility is based on the "medical model" of the criminal justice system. In this model, criminals are analogous to patients, and the courts perform the role of physicians who dispense "treatment."[8] The criminal is seen as sick, not evil, and therefore treatment is morally justified. Of course, treatment varies from case to case, and some criminals require harsh penalties such as incarceration. In other cases, however, it may not be in society's best interest for the criminal to be punished according to the formal rules of the justice system. Perhaps the criminal can be rehabilitated to become a productive member of society and thus save taxpayers the costs of incarceration or further punishment.

THE BUREAUCRATIC FUNCTION

In many ways, the crime control, due process, and rehabilitation functions of a court are secondary to its bureaucratic function. A court may have the general goal of protecting society or protecting the rights of the individual, but on a day-to-day basis that court has the more pressing task of dealing with the cases brought before it.

Like any bureaucracy, a court is concerned with speed and efficiency, and loftier concepts such as justice can be secondary to a judge's need to wrap up a particular case before six o'clock so that administrative deadlines can be met. Indeed, many observers feel that the primary adversarial relationship in the courts is not between the two parties involved but between the ideal of justice and the reality of bureaucratic limitations.[9]

SELFASSESSMENT

Fill in the blanks and check your answers on page 212.

The _____ _____ function of American courts is to protect _____ from the unfair advantages that the government enjoys during legal proceedings. In contrast, the _____ _____ function of the courts emphasizes punishment—criminals must suffer for the harm they do to _____. A third view of the court system focuses on the need to _____ a criminal, in much the same way as a doctor would treat a patient.

THE BASIC PRINCIPLES OF THE AMERICAN JUDICIAL SYSTEM

One of the most often cited limitations of the American judicial system is its complex nature. In truth, the United States does not have a single judicial system, but fifty-two different systems—one for each state, the District of Columbia, and the federal government. As each state has its own unique judiciary with its own set of rules, some of which may be in conflict with the federal judiciary, it is helpful at this point to discuss some basics—jurisdiction, trial and appellate courts, and the dual court system.

JURISDICTION

In Latin, *juris* means "law," and *diction* means "to speak." Thus, **jurisdiction** literally refers to the power "to speak the law." Before any court can hear a case, it must have jurisdiction over the persons involved in the case or its subject matter. The jurisdiction of every court, even the United States Supreme Court, is limited in some way.

Learning Objective 1 Define *jurisdiction* and contrast geographic and subject-matter jurisdiction.

GEOGRAPHIC JURISDICTION One limitation is geographic. Generally, a court can exercise its authority only over residents of a certain area. A state trial court, for example, normally has jurisdictional authority over crimes committed in a particular area of the state, such as a county or a district. A state's highest court (often called the state supreme court) has jurisdictional authority over the entire state, and the United States Supreme Court has jurisdiction over the entire country.

For the most part, criminal jurisdiction is determined by legislation. The U.S. Congress or a state legislature can determine what acts are illegal within the geographic boundaries it controls, thus giving federal or state courts jurisdiction over those crimes. One interesting geographic jurisdictional situation involves the 310 Native American reservations in the United States. Under federal law, tribal courts do have jurisdiction to prosecute tribal members for crimes committed on reservation land.[10] These courts, however, cannot sentence most convicted defendants to more than three years in prison. Consequently, tribal leaders often ask the U.S. Department of Justice to prosecute serious crimes such as murder and rape in federal courts.

Jurisdiction The authority of a court to hear and decide cases within an area of the law or a geographic territory.

Extradition The process by which one jurisdiction surrenders a person accused or convicted of violating another jurisdiction's criminal law to the second jurisdiction.

INTERNATIONAL JURISDICTION Under international law, each country has the right to create and enact criminal law for its territory. Therefore, the notion that a nation has jurisdiction over any crimes committed within its borders is well established. The situation becomes more delicate when one nation feels the need to go outside its own territory to enforce its criminal law. International precedent does, however, provide several bases for expanding jurisdiction across international borders.

For example, either through treaty-based agreements or case-by-case negotiations, one country may decide to *extradite* a criminal suspect to another country. **Extradition** is the formal process in which one legal authority, such as a state or a nation, transfers a fugitive or a suspect to another country that has a valid claim on that person. In 2011, for example, The Netherlands extradited Mohamud Said Omar to the United States. American officials believe that Omar, a citizen of Somalia, recruited about twenty young men from Minnesota to join the terrorist group al-Shabaab in that African country.

For legal and political reasons, some countries will not expedite criminal suspects to the United States. Nevertheless, American authorities have been able to assert authority in such cases, particularly regarding possible terrorists. They have relied on the principle that our government has jurisdiction over persons who commit crimes against U.S. citizens even when these suspects live in a foreign country. This principle was cited after the drone attack that killed Anwar al-Awlaki in Yemen, an event discussed in Chapter 3 (see page 90). Yemeni officials had resolutely refused to extradite Awlaki to the United States.[11] Furthermore, some behavior, such as piracy and genocide,

In February 2011, Somali pirates killed Scott and Jean Adam, the American couple shown here, off the coast of Oman in the Arabian Sea. Why do American law enforcement authorities have the power to arrest the pirates, even though they are foreign citizens and the alleged crime took place far from the United States?

Splash News/SvQuest/Newscom

is considered a crime against all nations collectively and, according to the principles of *universal jurisdiction,* can be prosecuted by any nation with custody of the wrongdoer (see the photo alongside).

SUBJECT-MATTER JURISDICTION Jurisdiction over subject matter also acts as a limitation on the types of cases a court can hear. State court systems include courts of *general* (unlimited) *jurisdiction* and courts of *limited jurisdiction.* Courts of general jurisdiction have no restrictions on the subject matter they may address, and therefore deal with the most serious felonies and civil cases. Courts of limited jurisdiction, also known as lower courts, handle misdemeanors and civil matters under a certain amount, usually $1,000.

As we will discuss later in the chapter, many states have created special subject-matter courts that only dispose of cases involving a specific crime. For example, a number of jurisdictions have established drug courts to handle an overload of illicit narcotics arrests. Furthermore, under the Uniform Code of Military Justice, the U.S. military has jurisdiction over active personnel who commit crimes, even if those crimes occur outside the course of duty.[12] In such cases, military officials can either attempt to court-martial the suspect in military court or allow civilian prosecutors to handle the case in state or federal court.

TRIAL AND APPELLATE COURTS

Another distinction is between courts of original jurisdiction and courts of appellate, or review, jurisdiction. Courts having *original jurisdiction* are courts of the first instance, or **trial courts.** Almost every case begins in a trial court. It is in this court that a trial (or a guilty plea) takes place, and the judge imposes a sentence if the defendant is found guilty. Trial courts are primarily concerned with *questions of fact.* They are designed to determine exactly what events occurred that are relevant to questions of the defendant's guilt or innocence.

Courts having *appellate jurisdiction* act as reviewing courts, or **appellate courts.** In general, cases can be brought before appellate courts only on appeal by one of the parties in the trial court. (Note that because of constitutional protections against being tried twice for the same crime, prosecutors who lose in criminal trial court *cannot* appeal the verdict.) An appellate court does not use juries or witnesses to reach its decision. Instead, its judges make a decision on whether the case should be *reversed* and *remanded,* or sent back to the court of original jurisdiction for a new trial. Appellate judges present written explanations for their decisions, and these **opinions** of the court are the basis for a great deal of the precedent in the criminal justice system.

It is important to understand that appellate courts do not determine the defendant's guilt or innocence—they only make judgments on questions of procedure. In other words, they are concerned with *questions of law* and normally accept the facts as established by the trial court. Only rarely will an appeals court question a jury's decision. Instead, the appellate judges will review the manner in which the facts and evidence were provided to the jury and rule on whether errors were made in the process.

Learning Objective 2 Explain the difference between trial and appellate courts.

Trial Courts Courts in which most cases usually begin and in which questions of fact are examined.

Appellate Courts Courts that review decisions made by lower courts, such as trial courts.

Opinions Written statements by the judges expressing the reasons for the court's decision in a case.

FIGURE 7.1 The Dual Court System

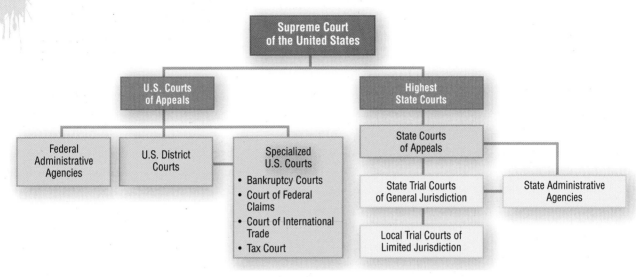

THE DUAL COURT SYSTEM

As we saw in Chapter 1, America's system of federalism allows both the federal government and the governments of the fifty states a measure of authority over the law. As a result, the federal government and each of the fifty states, as well as the District of Columbia, have their own separate court systems. Because of the split between the federal courts and the state courts, this is known as the **dual court system.** (See Figure 7.1 above to get a better idea of how federal and state courts operate as distinct yet parallel entities.)

Federal and state courts both have limited jurisdiction. Generally, federal courts preside over cases involving violations of federal law, and state courts preside over cases involving violations of state law. The distinction is not always clear, however. Federal courts have jurisdiction over more than four thousand crimes, many of which also exist in state criminal codes. Thus, **concurrent jurisdiction,** which occurs when two different court systems have simultaneous jurisdiction over the same case, is quite common. Most often in these situations, federal and state officials will decide which of the two systems is best equipped to handle the case.

In rare, high-profile instances, a defendant will receive two trials for the same criminal activity, one in federal court and one in state court. For example, in 2008, professional football player Michael Vick faced state dogfighting charges in a Surry County, Virginia, courtroom after having being found guilty of similar charges in federal court.

Dual Court System The separate but interrelated court system of the United States, made up of the courts on the national level and the courts on the state level.

Concurrent Jurisdiction The situation that occurs when two or more courts have the authority to preside over the same criminal case.

SELFASSESSMENT

Fill in the blanks and check your answers on page 212.

Before any court can hear a case, it must have _____ over the persons involved or the _____ _____ of the dispute. Almost every case begins in a _____ court, which is primarily concerned with determining the facts of the dispute. After this first trial, the participants can, under some circumstances, ask an _____ court to review the proceedings for errors in applying the law. The American court system is called a _____ court system because _____ courts address violations of federal law and _____ courts address violations of state law.

Learning
Objective **3** Outline the
several levels
of a typical
state court
system.

STATE COURT SYSTEMS

Typically, a state court system includes several levels, or tiers, of courts. State courts may include (1) lower courts, or courts of limited jurisdiction, (2) trial courts of general jurisdiction, (3) appellate courts, and (4) the state's highest court. As previously mentioned, each state has a different judicial structure, in which different courts have different jurisdictions, but there are enough similarities to allow for a general discussion. Figure 7.2 below shows a typical state court system.

COURTS OF LIMITED JURISDICTION

Most states have local trial courts that are limited to trying cases involving minor criminal matters, such as traffic violations, prostitution, and drunk and disorderly conduct. Although these minor courts usually keep no written record of the trial proceedings and cases are decided by a judge rather than a jury, defendants have the same rights as those in other trial courts. The majority of all minor criminal cases are decided in these lower courts. Courts of limited jurisdiction can also be responsible for the preliminary stages of felony cases. Arraignments, bail hearings, and preliminary hearings, all discussed in the next chapter, often take place in these lower courts.

FIGURE 7.2 A Typical State Court System

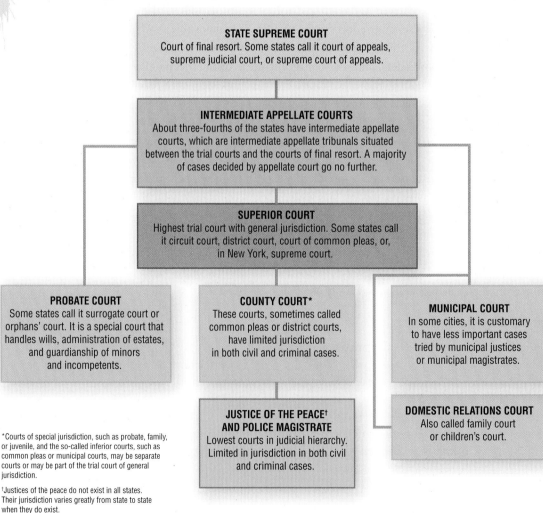

STATE SUPREME COURT
Court of final resort. Some states call it court of appeals, supreme judicial court, or supreme court of appeals.

INTERMEDIATE APPELLATE COURTS
About three-fourths of the states have intermediate appellate courts, which are intermediate appellate tribunals situated between the trial courts and the courts of final resort. A majority of cases decided by appellate court go no further.

SUPERIOR COURT
Highest trial court with general jurisdiction. Some states call it circuit court, district court, court of common pleas, or, in New York, supreme court.

PROBATE COURT
Some states call it surrogate court or orphans' court. It is a special court that handles wills, administration of estates, and guardianship of minors and incompetents.

COUNTY COURT*
These courts, sometimes called common pleas or district courts, have limited jurisdiction in both civil and criminal cases.

MUNICIPAL COURT
In some cities, it is customary to have less important cases tried by municipal justices or municipal magistrates.

**JUSTICE OF THE PEACE†
AND POLICE MAGISTRATE**
Lowest courts in judicial hierarchy. Limited in jurisdiction in both civil and criminal cases.

DOMESTIC RELATIONS COURT
Also called family court or children's court.

*Courts of special jurisdiction, such as probate, family, or juvenile, and the so-called inferior courts, such as common pleas or municipal courts, may be separate courts or may be part of the trial court of general jurisdiction.

†Justices of the peace do not exist in all states. Their jurisdiction varies greatly from state to state when they do exist.

Magistrates, or, in some states, municipal court judges, preside over courts whose jurisdiction is limited to disputes between private individuals and to crimes punishable by small fines or short jail terms. Magistrate courts have the same limited jurisdiction as do justice courts in rural settings. In most jurisdictions, magistrates are responsible for providing law enforcement agents with search and seizure warrants, discussed in Chapter 6.

As mentioned earlier, many states have created **specialty courts** that have jurisdiction over very narrowly defined areas of criminal justice. Not only do these courts remove many cases from the existing court system, but they also allow court personnel to become experts in a particular subject. Specialty courts include the following:

1. Drug courts, which deal only with illegal substance crimes.
2. Gun courts, which have jurisdiction over crimes that involve the illegal use of firearms.
3. Juvenile courts, which specialize in crimes committed by minors. (We will discuss juvenile courts in more detail in Chapter 13.)
4. Domestic courts, which deal with crimes of domestic violence, such as child and spousal abuse.
5. Mental health courts, which focus primarily on the treatment and rehabilitation of offenders with mental health problems.

As we will see in Chapter 10, many state and local governments are searching for cheaper alternatives to locking up nonviolent offenders in prison or jail. Because specialty courts offer a range of treatment options for wrongdoers, these courts are becoming increasingly popular in today's more budget-conscious criminal justice system. For example, about 2,500 drug courts are now operating in the United States, a number that is expected to increase as the financial benefits of diverting drug law violators from correctional facilities become more attractive to politicians.

Judge Sarah Smith, left, talks with an offender at her drug court in downtown Tulsa, Oklahoma. What are some of the benefits of drugs courts and other specialty courts?
Photo by Adam Wisneski/Tulsa World

Magistrate A public civil officer or official with limited judicial authority within a particular geographic area, such as the authority to issue an arrest warrant.

Specialty Courts Lower courts that have jurisdiction over one specific area of criminal activity, such as illegal drugs or domestic violence.

TRIAL COURTS OF GENERAL JURISDICTION

State trial courts that have general jurisdiction may be called county courts, district courts, superior courts, or circuit courts. In Ohio, the name is the court of common pleas and in Massachusetts, the trial court. (The name sometimes does not correspond with the court's functions. For example, in New York the trial court is called the supreme court, whereas in most states the supreme court is the state's highest court.) Courts of general jurisdiction have the authority to hear and decide cases involving many types of subject matter, and they are the setting for criminal trials.

STATE COURTS OF APPEALS

Every state has at least one court of appeals (known as an appellate, or reviewing, court), which may be an intermediate appellate court or the state's highest court. About three-fourths of the states have intermediate appellate courts. The highest appellate court in a state is usually called the supreme court, but in both New York and Maryland, the highest state court is called the court of appeals. The decisions of each state's highest court on all questions of state law are final. Only when issues pertaining to federal law or the

Constitution are involved can the United States Supreme Court overrule a decision made by a state's highest court.

SELFASSESSMENT
Fill in the blanks and check your answers on page 212.

State court systems include several levels of courts. Lower courts, or courts of _____ jurisdiction, hear only cases involving minor criminal matters or narrowly defined areas of crime such as domestic violence. Trial courts of _____ jurisdiction hear cases involving many different subject matters. The state courts of _____ make the final decisions on all questions of state law.

Learning Objective 4 Outline the federal court system.

THE FEDERAL COURT SYSTEM

The federal court system is basically a three-tiered structure consisting of (1) U.S. district courts (trial courts of general jurisdiction) and various courts of limited jurisdiction, (2) U.S. courts of appeals (intermediate courts of appeals), and (3) the United States Supreme Court.

Unlike state court judges, who are usually elected, federal court judges—including the justices of the Supreme Court—are appointed by the president of the United States, subject to the approval of the Senate. All federal judges receive lifetime appointments (because under Article III of the Constitution they "hold their offices during Good Behavior").

U.S. DISTRICT COURTS

On the lowest tier of the federal court system are the U.S. district courts, or federal trial courts. These are the courts in which cases involving federal laws begin, and a judge or jury decides the case (if it is a jury trial). Every state has at least one federal district court, and there is one in the District of Columbia. The number of judicial districts varies over time, primarily owing to population changes and corresponding caseloads. At the present time, there are ninety-four judicial districts. The federal system also includes other trial courts of limited jurisdiction, such as the Tax Court and the Court of International Trade.

U.S. COURTS OF APPEALS

In the federal court system, there are thirteen U.S. courts of appeals—also referred to as U.S. circuit courts of appeals. The federal courts of appeals for twelve of the circuits hear appeals from the district courts located within their respective judicial circuits (see Figure 7.3 on the facing page). The Court of Appeals for the Thirteenth Circuit, called the Federal Circuit, has national appellate jurisdiction over certain types of cases, such as cases in which the U.S. government is a defendant. The decisions of the circuit courts of appeals are final unless a further appeal is pursued and granted. In that case, the matter is brought before the United States Supreme Court.

THE UNITED STATES SUPREME COURT

Although it reviews a minuscule percentage of the cases decided in this country each year, the rulings of the United States Supreme Court profoundly affect American society. The impact of Court decisions on the criminal justice system is equally far reaching: *Gideon v. Wainwright* (1963)[13] established every American's right to be represented by counsel in a criminal trial; *Miranda v. Arizona* (1966)[14] transformed pretrial interroga-

FIGURE 7.3 Geographic Boundaries of the Federal Circuit Courts of Appeals

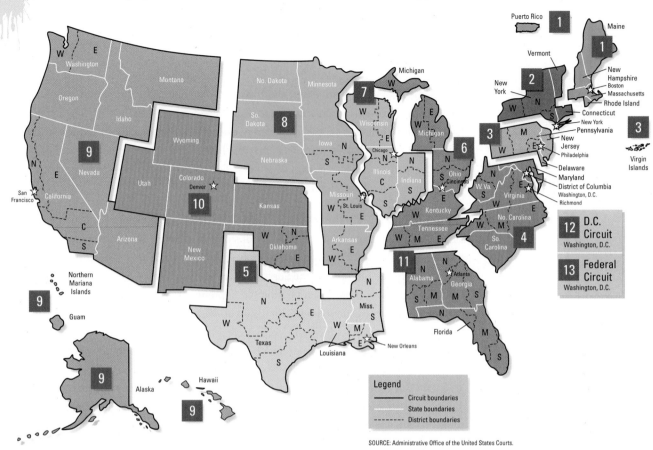

Legend
— Circuit boundaries
— State boundaries
---- District boundaries

SOURCE: Administrative Office of the United States Courts.

tions; *Furman v. Georgia* (1972)[15] ruled that the death penalty was unconstitutional; and *Gregg v. Georgia* (1976)[16] spelled out the conditions under which the death penalty could be allowed. As you have no doubt noticed from references in this textbook, the Court has addressed nearly every important facet of criminal law.

INTERPRETING AND APPLYING THE LAW The Supreme Court "makes" criminal justice policy in two important ways: through *judicial review* and through its authority to interpret the law. **Judicial review** refers to the power of the Court to determine whether a law or action by the other branches of the government is constitutional. For example, in the late 1990s, Congress passed a law restricting Internet sales of "crush" videos, which showed women crushing small animals to death with their bare feet or high heels.[17] The wording of the statute prohibited the sale of videos showing any form of graphic violence against animals. Several years after the law's passage, Robert Stevens of Pittsville, Virginia, was sentenced to three years in prison for distributing videos that featured pit bull fights. In 2010, the Supreme Court overturned Stevens's conviction and invalidated the federal law as unconstitutional on the ground that it violated the First Amendment's protections of freedom of expression.[18]

As the final interpreter of the Constitution, the Supreme Court must also determine the meaning of certain statutory provisions when applied to specific situations. In the previous chapter, you learned that a law enforcement officer must immediately stop questioning a suspect who invokes her or his *Miranda* rights (see page 180). In *Maryland v. Shatzer* (2010),[19] the Court considered a situation in which a sexual abuse suspect invoked his *Miranda* rights, spent more than two years in prison (for an unrelated

Judicial Review The power of a court—particularly the United States Supreme Court—to review the actions of the executive and legislative branches and, if necessary, declare those actions unconstitutional.

Learning Objective **5** Explain briefly how a case is brought to the Supreme Court.

John G. Roberts, Jr., pictured here, is the seventeenth chief justice of the United States Supreme Court. What does it mean to say that Roberts and the eight associate members of the Court "make criminal justice policy"?

AP Photo/Lawrence Jackson, File

crime), and then waived his *Miranda* rights. The Court rejected the suspect's claim that due to his much earlier action, the later waiver, although made willingly, "did not count." Instead, the Court decided on a new rule: a *Miranda* invocation is good for only fourteen days. After that, a suspect must clearly reestablish his or her right to silence.

JURISDICTION OF THE SUPREME COURT The United States Supreme Court consists of nine justices—a chief justice and eight associate justices. The Supreme Court has original, or trial, jurisdiction only in rare instances (set forth in Article III, Section 2, of the Constitution). In other words, only rarely does a case originate at the Supreme Court level. Most of the Court's work is as an appellate court. It has appellate authority over cases decided by the U.S. courts of appeals, as well as over some cases decided in the state courts when federal questions are at issue.

WHICH CASES REACH THE SUPREME COURT? There is no absolute right to appeal to the United States Supreme Court. Although thousands of cases are filed with the Supreme Court each year, in 2011–2012 the Court heard only seventy-seven. With a **writ of *certiorari*** (pronounced sur-shee-uh-*rah*-ree), the Supreme Court orders a lower court to send it the record of a case for review. A party can petition the Supreme Court to issue a writ of *certiorari*, but whether the Court will do so is entirely within its discretion. More than 90 percent of the petitions for writs of *certiorari* (or "certs," as they are popularly called) are denied. A denial is not a decision on the merits of a case, nor does it indicate agreement with the lower court's opinion. Therefore, the denial of the writ has no value as a precedent.

The Court will not issue a writ unless at least four justices approve of it. This is called the **rule of four.** Although the justices are not required to give their reasons for refusing to hear a case, the discretionary decision generally is based on whether the legal issue involves a "substantial federal question." Often, such questions arise when lower courts split on a particular issue. For example, in recent years different federal and state courts have produced varying opinions on the question of whether police officers can search the stored digital contents of cell phones incident to an arrest.[20] To clear up confusion on this increasingly important matter, the Court will likely hear a case involving cell phone searches in the near future. Practical considerations aside, if the justices feel that a case does not address an important federal law or constitutional issue, they will vote to deny the writ of *certiorari*.

SUPREME COURT DECISIONS Like all appellate courts, the Supreme Court normally does not hear any evidence. The Court's decision in a particular case is based on the written record of the case and the written arguments (briefs) that the attorneys submit. The attorneys also present **oral arguments**—arguments presented in person rather than on paper—to the Court, after which the justices discuss the case in *conference*. The conference is strictly private—only the justices are allowed in the room.

When the Court has reached a decision, the chief justice, if in the majority, assigns the task of writing the Court's opinion to one of the justices. When the chief justice is not in the majority, the most senior justice voting with the majority assigns the writing of the Court's opinion. The opinion outlines the reasons for the Court's decision, the rules of law that apply, and the decision.

Often, one or more justices who agree with the Court's decision may do so for different reasons than those outlined in the majority opinion. These justices may write **concurring opinions** setting forth their own legal reasoning on the issue. Frequently, one or more justices disagree with the Court's conclusion. These justices may write **dissenting opinions** outlining the reasons why they feel the majority erred. Although a dissenting opinion does not affect the outcome of the case before the Court, it may be important later. In a subsequent case concerning the same issue, a justice or attorney may use the legal reasoning in the dissenting opinion as the basis for an argument to reverse the previous decision and establish a new precedent.

SELFASSESSMENT

Fill in the blanks and check your answers on page 212.

The lowest tier of the federal court system contains U.S. _____ courts, also known as federal trial courts. Appeals from this lower tier are heard in the thirteen U.S. _____ courts of appeals. A decision handed down by a court in this second tier is final unless the United States _____ Court issues a writ of _____, indicating that it has agreed to review the case.

Concurring Opinions
Separate opinions prepared by judges who support the decision of the majority of the court but who want to make or clarify a particular point or to voice disapproval of the grounds on which the decision was made.

Dissenting Opinions
Separate opinions in which judges disagree with the conclusion reached by the majority of the court and expand on their own views about the case.

JUDGES IN THE COURT SYSTEM

Supreme Court justices are the most visible and best-known American jurists, but in many ways they are unrepresentative of the profession as a whole. Few judges enjoy three-room office suites fitted with a fireplace and a private bath, as do the Supreme Court justices. Few judges have four clerks to assist them. Few judges get a yearly vacation that stretches from July through September. Most judges, in fact, work at the lowest level of the system, in criminal trial courts, where they are burdened with overflowing caseloads and must deal daily with the pettiest of criminals.

One attribute a Supreme Court justice and a criminal trial judge in any small American city do have in common is the expectation that they will be just. Of all the participants in the criminal justice system, no single person is held to the same high standards as the judge. From her or his lofty perch in the courtroom, the judge is counted on to be "above the fray" of the bickering defense attorneys and prosecutors. When the other courtroom contestants rise at the entrance of the judge, they are placing the burden of justice squarely on the judge's shoulders.

THE ROLES AND RESPONSIBILITIES OF TRIAL JUDGES

One of the reasons that judicial integrity is considered so important is the amount of discretionary power a judge has over the court proceedings. Nearly every stage of the trial process includes a decision or action to be taken by the presiding judge.

BEFORE THE TRIAL A great deal of the work done by a judge takes place before the trial even starts, free from public scrutiny. These duties, some of which you have seen from a different point of view in the section on law enforcement agents, include determining the following:

1. Whether there is sufficient probable cause to issue a search or arrest warrant.
2. Whether there is sufficient probable cause to authorize electronic surveillance of a suspect.

3. Whether enough evidence exists to justify the temporary incarceration of a suspect.
4. Whether a defendant should be released on bail, and if so, the amount of the bail.
5. Whether to accept pretrial motions by prosecutors and defense attorneys.
6. Whether to accept a plea bargain.

During these pretrial activities, the judge takes on the role of the *negotiator*.[21] As most cases are decided through plea bargains rather than through trial proceedings, the judge often offers his or her services as a negotiator to help the prosecution and the defense "make a deal." The amount at which bail is set is often negotiated as well. Throughout the trial process, the judge usually spends a great deal of time in his or her *chambers*, or office, negotiating with the prosecutors and defense attorneys.

DURING THE TRIAL When the trial starts, the judge takes on the role of *referee*. In this role, she or he is responsible for seeing that the trial unfolds according to the dictates of the law and that the participants in the trial do not overstep any legal or ethical bounds. While doing so, the judge is expected to be neutral, determining the admissibility of testimony and evidence on a completely objective basis. The judge also acts as a *teacher* during the trial, explaining points of law to the jury. If the trial is not a jury trial, then the judge must also make decisions concerning the guilt or innocence of the defendant.

At the close of the trial, if the defendant is found guilty, the judge must decide on the length of the sentence and the type of sentence. (Different types of sentences, such as incarceration, probation, and other forms of community-based corrections, will be discussed in Chapters 9 and 10.) The sentencing phase also gives the judge a chance to make personal comments about the proceedings, if he or she wishes. While sentencing Dr. Conrad Murray to the maximum four years behind bars for the involuntary manslaughter of pop singer Michael Jackson on November 28, 2011, Los Angeles County Superior Court judge Michael Pastor delivered a thirty-minute scolding. Pastor chastised the defendant for being motivated by a desire for "money, fame, and prestige" and criticized Murray for suggesting, in a documentary film, that Jackson was responsible for his own death. "Yikes," said Pastor at the hearing. "Talk about blaming the victim!"[22]

CJ&TECHNOLOGY

Andrey Prokhorov/iStockphoto

New Fingerprinting Techniques

Despite the widespread use of DNA evidence testing, old-fashioned fingerprint matching is still the favored forensic method for determining who was at a crime scene. (Both techniques were described in Chapter 5). Just over a decade ago, however, federal judge Louis H. Pollak, in his role as referee of a trial, became the first judge to question the scientific reliability of fingerprint matches. In the years since then, additional questions have been raised. An internal audit by the Federal Bureau of Investigation found an error rate of nearly 1 percent for its fingerprint matches. A National Academy of Sciences report found little basis for claims that the process is infallible. Most recently, in 2011, *Psychological Science* magazine published the results of an experiment that found that thirty-seven qualified fingerprint experts mistakenly matched 0.68 percent of fingerprints to innocent persons.

Some of these imperfect matches can be attributed to human error. But it is also clear that there are flaws in the predominant method of fingerprint identification, known as ACE-V (Analysis Comparison Evaluation Verification). ACE-V usually relies on infrared or X-ray imaging of secretions from the body, which may be incomplete or in some way damaged, to produce fingerprint matches. One new method, developed by forensic scientists at Penn State University, reads the shape of the fingerprint without the damaging use of chemicals. Another, created by researchers in Australia and Illinois, uses gold nanoparticles to give a clearer image of the body chemicals that make up each fingerprint. This process can even "read" old and dry fingerprints, potentially allowing for "cold hits" in cases where only fingerprint evidence remains.

THINKING ABOUT NEW FINGERPRINT TECHNIQUES: The vast majority of judges still accept fingerprint evidence without hesitation. Given the studies noted above, what would be the pros and cons of judges telling juries that ACE-V fingerprint matching is not 100 percent reliable? What role, if any, should judges play in improving fingerprinting methods?

THE ADMINISTRATIVE ROLE Judges are also *administrators* and are responsible for the day-to-day functioning of their courts. A primary administrative task of a judge is scheduling. Each courtroom has a **docket,** or calendar of cases, and it is the judge's responsibility to keep the docket current. This entails not only scheduling the trial but also setting pretrial motion dates and deciding whether to grant attorneys' requests for *continuances,* or additional time to prepare for the trial. Judges must also keep track of the immense paperwork generated by each case and manage the various employees of the court. In 1939, Congress, recognizing the burden of such tasks, created the Administrative Office of the United States Courts to provide administrative assistance for federal court judges.[23] Most state court judges, however, do not have the luxury of similar aid, though they are supported by a court staff.

SELECTION OF JUDGES

In the federal court system, all judges are appointed by the president and confirmed by the Senate. It is difficult to make a general statement about how judges are selected in state court systems, however, because the procedure varies widely from state to state. In some states, such as New Jersey, all judges are appointed by the governor and confirmed by the upper chamber of the state legislature. In other states, such as Alabama, **partisan elections** are used to choose judges. In these elections, a judicial candidate declares allegiance to a political party, usually the Democrats or the Republicans, before the election. States such as Kentucky that conduct **nonpartisan elections** do not require a candidate to affiliate herself or himself with a political party in this manner.

In 1940, Missouri became the first state to combine appointment and election in a single process. When all jurisdiction levels are counted, nineteen states and the District of Columbia now utilize the **Missouri Plan,** as this process has been labeled. The Missouri Plan consists of three basic steps:

- When a vacancy on the bench arises, candidates are nominated by a nonpartisan committee of citizens.
- The names of the three most qualified candidates are sent to the governor or executive of the state judicial system, and that person chooses who will be the judge.

Docket The list of cases entered on a court's calendar and thus scheduled to be heard by the court.

Partisan Elections Elections in which candidates are affiliated with and receive support from political parties.

Nonpartisan Elections Elections in which candidates are presented on the ballot without any party affiliation.

Missouri Plan A method of selecting judges that combines appointment and election.

- A year after the new judge has been installed, a "retention election" is held so that voters can decide whether the judge deserves to keep the post.[24]

The goal of the Missouri Plan is to eliminate partisan politics from the selection procedure, while at the same time giving the citizens a voice in the process. (See the feature *Comparative Criminal Justice—Back to School* below to learn about the French alternative to choosing judges through elections.)

DIVERSITY ON THE BENCH

One criticism of the Missouri plan is that the members of the selection committee, who are mostly white, upper-class attorneys, nominate mostly white, upper-class attorneys.[25] In South Carolina, which uses this method to select most members of the judiciary, only 16 of the state's 186 judges are African American, and only 5 of its 46 circuit court judges are women. "There's a perception that [the selection process] is tied to the good-old-boys network rather than picking the best person for the seat," says one observer.[26] The lack of diversity is particularly striking given that almost 30 percent of South Carolina's population is black, a pattern that is repeated in other states. Arizona's population, for example, is 40 percent nonwhite, but the state has no minority supreme court justices, and minorities hold less than 20 percent of other state judgeships.[27]

FEDERAL DIVERSITY The federal judiciary shows a similar pattern. Of the nearly 1,300 federal judges in this country, 8 percent are African American, 5 percent are Hispanic, and less than 1 percent are Asian American. Furthermore, only 15 percent are women.[28]

COMPARATIVE CRIMINAL JUSTICE

BACK TO SCHOOL

Elections for judges are extremely rare outside the United States. Indeed, only two nations—Japan and Switzerland—engage in the practice, and then only in very limited situations. For the rest of the world, according to one expert, "American adherence to judicial elections is as incomprehensible as our rejection of the metric system." Much more common, for example, is the French system, crafted to provide extensive training for potential judges.

French judicial candidates must pass two exams. The first, open to law school graduates only, combines oral and written sections and lasts at least four days. In some years, only 5 percent of the applicants overcome this hurdle. Not surprisingly, the pressure is intense. "It gives you nightmares for years afterwards," says Jean-Marc Baissus, a judge in Toulouse. "You come out of [the exam] completely shattered." Those who do survive the first test enter a two-year program at the École Nationale de la Magistrature, a judicial training academy. This school is similar to a police training academy in the United States, in that candidates spend half of their time in the classroom and the other half in the courtroom.

At the end of this program, judicial candidates are subject to a second examination. Only those who pass the exam may become judges. The result, in the words of Mitchell Lasser, a law professor at Cornell University, is that French judges "actually know what the hell they are doing. They've spent years in school taking practical and theoretical courses on how to be a judge." The French also pride themselves on creating judges who are free from the kind of political pressures faced by American judges who must go before the voters.

FOR CRITICAL ANALYSIS Do you think that the French system of training judges is superior to the American system of electing them? Before explaining your answer, consider that French judges lack the practical courtroom experience of American judges, the majority of whom served as lawyers earlier in their careers.

Of the 111 justices who have served on the United States Supreme Court, two have been African American: Thurgood Marshall (1970–1991) and Clarence Thomas (1991–present). In 2009, Sonia Sotomayor became the first Hispanic appointed to the Court and the third woman, following Sandra Day O'Connor (1981–2006) and Ruth Bader Ginsburg (1993–present). A year later, Elena Kagan became the fourth woman appointed to the Court.

THE IMPACT OF PAST DISCRIMINATION Edward Chen, a federal judge for the Northern District of California, identifies a number of reasons for the low minority representation on the bench. Past discrimination in law schools has limited the pool of experienced minority attorneys who have the political ties, access to "old boy" networks, and career opportunities that lead to judgeships.[29] Only recently, as increased numbers of minorities have graduated from law schools, have rates of minority judges begun to creep slowly upward. Traditionally, efforts to diversify American judges by race, ethnicity, and gender have been met with resistance from those who argue that because judges must be impartial, it makes no difference whether a judge is black, Asian, Hispanic, or white.[30]

Sherrilyn A. Ifill of the University of Maryland School of Law rejects this argument. She believes that "diversity on the bench" can only enrich our judiciary by introducing a variety of voices and perspectives into what are perhaps the most powerful positions in the criminal justice system. By the same token, Ifill credits the lack of diversity in many trial and appeals courts with a number of harmful consequences, such as more severe sentences for minority youths than for white youths who have committed similar crimes, disproportionate denial of bail to minority defendants, and the disproportionate imposition of the death penalty on minority defendants accused of killing white victims.[31]

Before his appointment, New Jersey Superior Court judge Sohail Mohammed, a native of India, represented nearly three dozen suspects detained following the 9/11 terrorist attacks. He has also trained more than 7,000 law enforcement agents to better understand the Muslim American community. What are the benefits of having judges with a wide range of cultural experiences on the bench?
New Jersey Governor's Office/Tim Larsen

SELFASSESSMENT

Fill in the blanks and check your answers on page 212.

In the federal court system, judges are appointed by the _____ and confirmed by the _____. In state court systems, however, the selection process varies. Some states mirror the federal system, with the _____ making judicial appointments with the approval of the legislature. Others conduct either _____ elections, in which political parties openly support judicial candidates, or _____ elections, in which the candidate is not affiliated with any political group. Finally, a number of states rely on _____ selection, which combines appointment and election.

THE COURTROOM WORK GROUP

Television dramas often depict the courtroom as a battlefield, with prosecutors and defense attorneys spitting fire at each other over the loud and insistent protestations of a frustrated judge. Consequently, many people are somewhat disappointed when they witness a real courtroom at work. Rarely does anyone raise his or her voice, and the courtroom professionals appear—to a great extent—to be cooperating with each other. In Chapter 5, we discussed the existence of a police subculture, based on the shared values of law enforcement agents. A courtroom subculture exists as well, centered on the **courtroom work group.**

Courtroom Work Group The social organization consisting of the judge, prosecutor, defense attorney, and other court workers.

CAREERS IN CJ

SHAWN DAVIS

BAILIFF

Basically, there are two kinds of bailiffs: administrative bailiffs and criminal bailiffs. An administrative bailiff will handle paperwork, set up court dates, and answer questions about filings that the attorneys may have. A criminal bailiff is responsible for bringing the court to session, directing jurors, and overseeing court security, which involves keeping everybody—judges, attorneys, jurors, spectators, witnesses, and defendants—safe. In my case, I do double duty as an administrative and criminal bailiff.

Violence in the courtroom is rare. Most inmates are on their best behavior in front of the judge. It can flare up in an instant, however, and you have to be constantly on guard. One time, an inmate under my control made a run for it as we were transporting him back to the jail from his court appearance. His leg shackles broke, giving him a short-lived sense of freedom. We were able to tackle him in front of the courthouse just before he could jump into a waiting convertible. We later learned that the accomplice—the inmate's brother—was supposed to bring a handgun and shoot us as part of the escape plan. Another time, a defendant started taking off his shirt and tried to attack the victim, who had just given testimony. He was quickly tackled, cuffed, and carted off to jail.

Social Media Career Tip

Networking is crucial. Develop as many useful social media contacts as possible, and cultivate those contacts. Also, reciprocate. If you help others establish online contacts, they are likely to remember you and return the favor. **f** **Linked in**. 🐦

FAST FACTS

**BAILIFF
JOB DESCRIPTION:**

- Maintain order and provide security in the courtroom during trials.
- Open and close court, call cases, call witnesses, and the like.
- Escort and guard juries, prevent juries from having contact with the public.

WHAT KIND OF TRAINING IS REQUIRED?

- At a minimum, a high school diploma or GED.

ANNUAL SALARY RANGE?

- $30,000–$38,000

The most important feature of any work group is that it is a *cooperative* unit, whose members establish shared values and methods that help the group efficiently reach its goals. Although cooperation is not a concept usually associated with criminal courts, it is in fact crucial to the adjudication process.

Learning Objective 6 List and describe the members of the courtroom work group.

MEMBERS OF THE COURTROOM WORK GROUP

The courtroom work group is made up of those individuals who are involved with the defendant from the time she or he is arrested until sentencing. Its most prominent members are the judge, the prosecutor, and the defense attorney (you will be introduced to the latter two shortly). Three other important courtroom participants complete the work group:

1. The *bailiff of the court* is responsible for maintaining security and order in the judge's chambers and the courtroom. Bailiffs lead the defendant in and out of the

courtroom and attend to the needs of the jurors during the trial. A bailiff, often a member of the local sheriff's department but sometimes an employee of the court, also delivers summonses in some jurisdictions.

2. The *clerk of the court* has an exhausting list of responsibilities. Any plea, motion, or other matter to be acted on by the judge must go through this court employee. The large amount of paperwork generated during a trial, including transcripts, photographs, evidence, and any other records, is maintained by the clerk. She or he also issues subpoenas for jury duty and coordinates the jury selection process. In the federal court system, judges select clerks, while state clerks are either appointed or, in nearly a third of the states, elected.

3. *Court reporters* record every word that is said during the course of the trial. They also record any *depositions*, or pretrial question-and-answer sessions in which a party or a witness answers an attorney's questions under oath.

THE JUDGE IN THE COURTROOM WORK GROUP

The judge is the dominant figure in the courtroom and therefore exerts the most influence over the values and norms of the work group. A judge who runs a "tight ship" follows procedure and restricts the freedom of attorneys to deviate from regulations, while a "*laissez-faire*" judge allows more leeway to members of the work group. A judge's personal philosophy also affects the court proceedings. If a judge has a reputation for being "tough on crime," both prosecutors and defense attorneys will alter their strategies accordingly.

Although preeminent in the work group, a judge must still rely on other members of the group. Ideally, the judge should be the least informed member of the trio. Like a juror, the judge generally learns the facts of the case as they are presented by the attorneys. If the attorneys do not properly present the facts, then the judge is hampered in making rulings.

> "A judge is not supposed to know anything about the facts . . . until they have been presented in evidence and explained to him at least three times."
>
> **—Lord Chief Justice Parker,** British judge (1961)

THE PROSECUTION

If the judge is, as we suggested on page 200, the referee of the courtroom, then the prosecutor and the defense attorney are its two main combatants. On the side of the government, acting in the name of "the people," the **public prosecutor** tries cases against criminal defendants. The public prosecutor in federal criminal cases is called a U.S. attorney. In cases tried in state or local courts, the public prosecutor may be referred to as a *state's attorney, state prosecutor, district attorney, county attorney,* or *city attorney.* Given their great autonomy, prosecutors are generally considered the most dominant figures in the American criminal justice system. In some jurisdictions, the district attorney is the chief law enforcement officer, with broad powers over police operations.

Prosecutors have the power to bring the resources of the state against the individual, and they hold the legal keys to meting out or withholding punishment.[32] Ideally, this power is balanced by a duty of fairness and a recognition that the prosecutor's ultimate goal is not to win cases, but to see that justice is done. In *Berger v. United States* (1935), Justice George Sutherland called the prosecutor

in a peculiar and very definite sense the servant of the law, the twofold aim of which is that guilt shall not escape or innocence suffer. He may prosecute with earnestness and vigor— indeed, he should do so. But, while he may strike hard blows, he is not at liberty to strike

Learning Objective 7 List the different names given to public prosecutors and indicate the general powers that they have.

Public Prosecutor An individual, acting as a trial lawyer, who initiates and conducts cases in the government's name and on behalf of the people.

foul ones. It is as much his duty to refrain from improper methods calculated to produce a wrongful conviction as it is to use every legitimate means to bring about a just one.[33]

In part to lessen the opportunity for "foul" behavior by prosecutors, they are not permitted to keep from the defendant evidence that may be useful in showing his or her innocence.[34] For example, in 1995, Juan Smith was convicted of five murders at a party in New Orleans and eventually sentenced to death. The only eyewitness to the crime gave conflicting comments to police, including that he could not "ID anyone because [he] couldn't see faces."[35] Obviously, Smith's defense attorneys could have used such statements to create doubt in the jurors' minds concerning their client's guilt. Because prosecutors never provided them with this evidence, in 2012 the Supreme Court overturned Smith's conviction and ordered a new trial.[36]

THE OFFICE OF THE PROSECUTOR As we have just seen, when he or she is acting as an *officer of the law* during a criminal trial, there are limits on the prosecutor's conduct. During the pretrial process, however, prosecutors have a great deal of discretion in making the following important decisions:

1. Whether an individual who has been arrested by the police will be charged with a crime.
2. The level of the charges to be brought against the suspect.
3. If and when to stop the prosecution.[37]

There are more than eight thousand prosecutor's offices around the country, serving state, county, and municipal jurisdictions. Even though the **attorney general** is the chief law enforcement officer in any state, she or he has limited (and in some states, no) control over prosecutors within the state's boundaries.

Each jurisdiction has a chief prosecutor, who is sometimes appointed but more often elected. As an elected official, he or she typically serves a four-year term, though in some states, such as Alabama, the term is six years. In smaller jurisdictions, the chief prosecutor has several assistants, and they work closely together. In larger ones, the chief prosecutor may have numerous *assistant prosecutors,* many of whom she or he rarely meets. Assistant prosecutors—for the most part, young attorneys recently graduated from law school—may be assigned to particular sections of the organization, such as criminal prosecutions in general or areas of *special prosecution,* such as narcotics or gang crimes. (See Figure 7.4 on the facing page for the structure of a typical prosecutor's office.)

THE PROSECUTOR AS ELECTED OFFICIAL The chief prosecutor's autonomy is not absolute. As an elected official, she or he must answer to the voters. (There are exceptions: U.S. attorneys are nominated by the president and approved by the Senate, and chief prosecutors in Alaska, Connecticut, New Jersey, Rhode Island, and the District of Columbia are either appointed or hired as members of the attorney general's office.) The prosecutor may be part of the political machine. In many jurisdictions, the prosecutor must declare a party affiliation and is expected to reward fellow party members with positions in the district attorney's office if elected.

The post is often seen as a "stepping-stone" to higher political office, and many prosecutors have gone on to serve in legislatures or as judges. Sonia Sotomayor (see the photo on the facing page), the first Hispanic member of the United States Supreme Court, started her legal career in 1979 as an assistant district attorney in New York City. While at that job, she first came to public attention by helping to prosecute the

Attorney General The chief law officer of a state; also, the chief law officer of the nation.

Social Media and CJ
Like police departments, many prosecutors' offices have set up Facebook pages to keep the communities they serve in touch with local crime news. To access the **Cuyahoga County (Ohio) Prosecutor's Office** Facebook page, visit the *Criminal Justice CourseMate* at cengagebrain.com and select the *Web Links* for this chapter.

FIGURE 7.4 The Baltimore City State's Attorney's Office

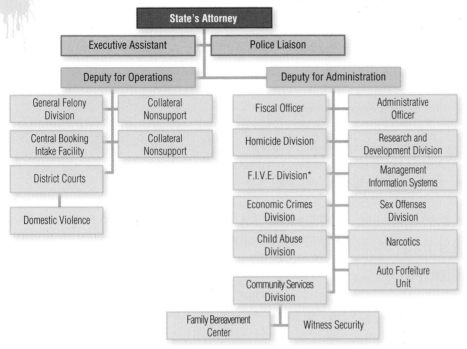

*F.I.V.E. is an acronym for "Firearms Investigation Violence Enforcement."

Source: Baltimore City State's Attorney's Office.

"Tarzan Murderer," an athletic criminal responsible for at least twenty burglaries and four killings.

Like judges, who are the other elected members of the courtroom work group, prosecutors are subject to community pressures. Following Tyler Clementi's suicide, described in the opening of this chapter, prosecutors initially seemed disinclined to bring any charges against Dharun Ravi. Nonetheless, according to a former New Jersey prosecutor, because of pressure from antibullying groups and gay rights groups, as well as global media attention, the case was "one that had to be prosecuted."[38] Furthermore, when prosecutorial misconduct leads to wrongful convictions of innocent defendants, that misconduct is often explained—though not excused—as being the result of public demands that prosecutors be "tough on crime."

THE DEFENSE ATTORNEY

The media provide most people's perception of defense counsel: the idealistic public defender who nobly serves the poor, the "ambulance chaser," or the celebrity attorney in the $3,000 suit. These stereotypes, though not entirely fictional, tend to obscure the crucial role that the **defense attorney** plays in the criminal justice system. Most persons charged with crimes have little or no knowledge of criminal procedure. Without assistance, they would be helpless in court. By acting as a staunch advocate for her or his client, the defense attorney (ideally) ensures that the government proves every point against that client beyond a reasonable doubt, even for cases that do not go to trial. In sum, the defense attorney provides a counterweight against the state in our criminal justice system.

THE RESPONSIBILITIES OF THE DEFENSE ATTORNEY The Sixth Amendment right to counsel is not limited to the actual criminal trial. In a number of instances, the United States Supreme Court has held that defendants are entitled to representation as soon as their rights may be denied, which includes, as we

Defense Attorney The lawyer representing the defendant.

Give several reasons why experience as a prosecutor would make someone such as United States Supreme Court justice Sonia Sotomayor a more effective judge.

AP Photo/Pablo Martinez Monsivais

have seen, the custodial interrogation and various identification procedures.[39] Therefore, an important responsibility of the defense attorney is to represent the defendant at the various stages of the custodial process, such as arrest, interrogation, lineup, and arraignment. Other responsibilities include the following:

Learning Objective 8 Delineate the responsibilities of defense attorneys.

- Investigating the incident for which the defendant has been charged.
- Communicating with the prosecutor, which includes negotiating plea bargains.
- Preparing the case for trial.
- Submitting defense motions, including motions to suppress evidence.
- Representing the defendant at trial.
- Negotiating a sentence, if the client has been convicted.
- Determining whether to appeal a guilty verdict.[40]

> **"Look at the stakes. In civil law, if you screw up, it's just money. Here, it's the client— his life, his time in jail."**
>
> **—Stacey Richman**
> Criminal defense attorney

DEFENDING THE GUILTY At one time or another in their careers, all defense attorneys will face a difficult question: Must I defend a client whom I know to be guilty? According to the American Bar Association's code of legal ethics, the answer is almost always, "yes."[41] The most important responsibility of the criminal defense attorney is to be an advocate for his or her client. As such, the attorney is obligated to use all ethical and legal means to achieve the client's desired goal, which is usually to avoid or lessen punishment for the charged crime.

As Supreme Court justice Byron White once noted, defense counsel has no "obligation to ascertain or present the truth." Rather, our criminal justice system insists that the defense attorney "defend the client whether he is innocent or guilty."[42] Indeed, if defense attorneys refused to represent clients whom they believed to be guilty, the Sixth Amendment guarantee of a criminal trial for all accused persons would be rendered meaningless. (To learn more about the difficult situations that can arise with a guilty defendant, see the feature *A Question of Ethics—The Right Decision?* on the facing page.)

THE PUBLIC DEFENDER Generally speaking, there are two different types of defense attorneys: (1) private attorneys, who are hired by individuals, and (2) **public defenders,** who work for the government. The distinction is not absolute, as many private attorneys accept employment as public defenders, too.

Public Defenders Court-appointed attorneys who are paid by the state to represent defendants who are unable to hire private counsel.

The modern role of the public defender was established by the Supreme Court's interpretation of the Sixth Amendment in *Gideon v. Wainwright* (1963).[43] In that case, the Court ruled that no defendant can be "assured a fair trial unless counsel is provided for him," and therefore the state must provide a public defender to those who cannot afford to hire an attorney for themselves. Subsequently, the Court extended this protection to juveniles in *In re Gault* (1967)[44] and to those faced with imprisonment for committing misdemeanors in *Argersinger v. Hamlin* (1972).[45] The impact of these decisions has been substantial: about 90 percent of all criminal defendants in the United States are represented by public defenders or other appointed counsel.[46]

Eligibility Issues Although the Supreme Court's *Gideon* decision obligated the government to provide attorneys for poor defendants, it offered no guidance on just how poor the defendant needs to be to qualify for a public defender. In theory, counsel should be provided for those who are unable to hire an attorney themselves without "substantial hardship."[47] In reality, each jurisdiction has its own guidelines, and a defendant refused counsel in one area might be entitled to it in another. A judge in Kittitas County,

Washington, to give an extreme example, frequently denies public counsel for college student defendants. This judge believes that any person who chooses to go to school rather than work automatically falls outside the *Gideon* case's definition of indigence.[48]

Effectiveness of Public Defenders Under the U.S. Constitution, a defendant who is paying for her or his defense attorney has a right to choose that attorney without interference from the court.[49] This right of choice does not extend to indigent defendants. According to the United States Supreme Court, "a defendant may not insist on an attorney he cannot afford."[50] In other words, an indigent defendant must accept the public defender provided by the court system. (Note that unless the presiding judge rules otherwise, a person can waive his or her Sixth Amendment rights and act as his or her own defense attorney.)

This lack of control contributes to the widespread belief that public defenders do not provide an acceptable level of defense to indigents. Statistics show, however, that conviction rates of defendants with private counsel and those represented by publicly funded attorneys are generally the same. The difference comes during sentencing, when a higher percentage of defendants with public defenders are sent to prison.[51]

ATTORNEY-CLIENT PRIVILEGE To defend a client effectively, a defense attorney must have access to all the facts concerning the case, even those that may be harmful to the defendant. To promote the unrestrained flow of information between the two parties,

A QUESTION OF ETHICS: *The Right Decision?*

THE SITUATION Gerard Marrone is the defense attorney for Levi Aron, charged with kidnapping, murdering, and dismembering eight-year-old Leiby Kletzky in Brooklyn, New York. There is little question of Aron's guilt, as he provided the police with a signed confession and has no alibi for his whereabouts at the time of the crime. Marrone is uncertain about whether he wants to continue representing this "horrific" client. "You can't look at your kids and then look at yourself in the mirror, knowing that a little boy, who's close in age to my eldest son, was murdered so brutally," Marrone said about his conflicting feelings.

THE ETHICAL DILEMMA The criminal justice system would not be able to function if lawyers refused to represent clients they knew to be guilty. At the same time, a lawyer must be guided by his or her own conscience. If a client is so repugnant to the lawyer as to impair the quality of representation, then perhaps the lawyer should drop the case.

WHAT IS THE SOLUTION? What would you do in Marrone's shoes? In July 2011, he decided that his conscience prevented him from representing Aron, and he withdrew from the case. His

replacement, Jennifer McCann, criticized Marrone's actions. "To sit there and say, 'This is a hard case, I don't want to take it,'" McCann said. "That's for somebody else, that's not who I am." She added, "It's not about defending [Aron's] actions. It's about defending his rights."

Defense attorneys Pierre Bazile, right, and Jennifer McCann appear with their client Levi Aron at the State Supreme Court in Brooklyn in New York on August 4, 2011.

Jesse Ward via *New York Times*/Redux Pictures

Defense attorney John Amabile makes a point on behalf of his client in a Woburn, Massachusetts, courtroom. Why are the rules of attorney-client privilege necessary for a defense attorney to properly do his or her job?

ZUMA Press/Newscom

Attorney-Client Privilege A rule of evidence requiring that communications between a client and his or her attorney be kept confidential, unless the client consents to disclosure.

legislatures and lawyers themselves have constructed rules of **attorney-client privilege.** These rules require that communications between a client and his or her attorney be kept confidential, unless the client consents to the disclosure.

The Privilege and Confessions Attorney-client privilege does not stop short of confessions.[52] Indeed, if, on hearing any statement that points toward guilt, the defense attorney could alert the prosecution or try to resign from the case, attorney-client privilege would be rendered meaningless. Even if the client says, "I have just killed seventeen women. I selected only pregnant women so I could torture them and kill two people at once. I did it. I liked it. I enjoyed it," the defense attorney must continue to do her or his utmost to serve that client.[53]

Without attorney-client privilege, observes legal expert John Kaplan, lawyers would be forced to give their clients the equivalent of the *Miranda* warning before representing them.[54] In other words, lawyers would have to make clear what clients could or could not say in the course of preparing for trial, because any incriminating statement might be used against the client in court. Such a development would have serious ramifications for the criminal justice system.

The Exception to the Privilege The scope of attorney-client privilege is not all encompassing. In *United States v. Zolin* (1989),[55] the Supreme Court ruled that lawyers may disclose the contents of a conversation with a client if the client has provided information concerning a crime that has yet to be committed. This exception applies only to communications involving a crime that is ongoing or will occur in the future. If the client reveals a past crime, the privilege is still in effect, and the attorney may not reveal any details of that particular criminal act.

SELFASSESSMENT

Fill in the blanks and check your answers on page 212.

If the courtroom work group can be said to have a dominant figure, it is the _____. Public _____ are employed by the government and try cases on behalf of "the people." There are two types of defense attorneys: (1) _____ attorneys hired by individuals and (2) _____ defenders, provided to _____ defendants by the government.

CHAPTER SUMMARY

Learning Objective 1 **Define *jurisdiction* and contrast geographic and subject-matter jurisdiction.** Jurisdiction relates to the power of a court to hear a particular case. Courts are typically limited in geographic jurisdiction—for example, to a particular state. Some courts are restricted in subject matter, such as a small claims court, which can hear only cases involving civil matters under a certain monetary limit.

Learning Objective 2 **Explain the difference between trial and appellate courts.** Trial courts are courts of the first instance, where a case is first heard. Appellate courts review the proceedings of a lower court. Appellate courts do not have juries.

Learning Objective 3 **Outline the several levels of a typical state court system.** (a) At the lowest level are courts of limited jurisdiction, (b) next are trial courts of general jurisdiction, (c) then appellate courts, and (d) finally, the state's highest court.

Learning Objective 4 **Outline the federal court system.** (a) At the lowest level are the U.S. district courts, in which trials are held, as well as various minor federal courts of limited jurisdiction; (b) next are the U.S. courts of appeals, otherwise known as circuit courts of appeals; and (c) finally, the United States Supreme Court.

Learning Objective 5 **Explain briefly how a case is brought to the Supreme Court.** Cases decided in U.S. courts of appeals, as well as cases decided in the highest state courts (when federal questions arise), can be appealed to the Supreme Court. If at least four justices approve of a case filed with the Supreme Court, the Court will issue a writ of *certiorari,* ordering the lower court to send the Supreme Court the record of the case for review.

Learning Objective 6 **List and describe the members of the courtroom work group.** (a) The judge; (b) the prosecutor, who brings charges in the name of the people (the state) against the accused; (c) the defense attorney; (d) the bailiff, who is responsible for maintaining security and order in the judge's chambers and the courtroom; (e) the clerk, who accepts all pleas, motions, and other matters to be acted on by the judge; and (f) court reporters, who record what is said during a trial, as well as at depositions.

Learning Objective 7 **List the different names given to public prosecutors and indicate the general powers that they have.** At the federal level, the prosecutor is called the *U.S. attorney.* In state and local courts, the prosecutor may be referred to as the *state's attorney, state prosecutor, district attorney, county attorney,* or *city attorney.* Prosecutors in general have the power to decide when and how the state will pursue an individual suspected of criminal wrongdoing. In some jurisdictions, the district attorney is also the chief law enforcement officer, holding broad powers over police operations.

Learning Objective 8 **Delineate the responsibilities of defense attorneys.** (a) Representation of the defendant during the custodial process, (b) investigation of the supposed criminal incident, (c) communication with the prosecutor (including plea bargaining), (d) preparation of the case for trial, (e) submission of defense motions, (f) representation of the defendant at trial, (g) negotiation of a sentence after conviction, and (h) appeal of a guilty verdict.

QUESTIONS FOR CRITICAL ANALYSIS

1. In 2010, authorities in Thailand extradited Russian citizen and alleged international arms dealer Viktor Bout to the United States. The evidence against Bout included an audio recording of a conversation he had with American agents posing as Colombian rebels. During this conversation, Bout agreed to furnish the "revolutionaries" with weapons for the purpose of killing American pilots. How does this evidence give the United States jurisdiction over Bout?

2. Several years ago, the United States Supreme Court "denied cert" in the case of Yasin Muhammed Basardh, a Yemeni citizen still in the custody of the U.S. military even though he had been ruled innocent of terrorism charges by a U.S. court. What does it mean for the Court to "deny cert"? In this instance, what might be some of the reasons for the Court's refusal to consider Basardh's case?

3. The United States Supreme Court does not allow its proceedings to be televised. Do you think that doing so would increase or diminish public confidence in the Court? Why or why not?

4. Prosecutors cannot face civil lawsuits for misconduct, even if they have deliberately sent an innocent person to prison. In practical terms, why do you think prosecutors are protected in this manner? Do you agree with a policy of blanket immunity for prosecutors? Why or why not?

5. Government agencies can charge fees for "free" legal counsel when the fees will not impose a "significant legal hardship" on the defendant. Why might this practice go against the Supreme Court's ruling in *Gideon v. Wainwright* (see page 208)?

KEY TERMS

appellate courts   **192**
attorney-client privilege   **210**
attorney general   **206**
concurrent jurisdiction   **193**
concurring opinions   **199**
courtroom work group   **203**
defense attorney   **207**
dissenting opinions   **199**
docket   **201**

dual court system   **193**
extradition   **191**
judicial review   **197**
jurisdiction   **191**
magistrate   **195**
Missouri Plan   **201**
nonpartisan elections   **201**
opinions   **192**

oral arguments   **198**
partisan elections   **201**
public defenders   **208**
public prosecutor   **205**
rule of four   **198**
specialty courts   **195**
trial courts   **192**
writ of *certiorari*   **198**

SELF ASSESSMENT ANSWER KEY

Page 190: i. due process; **ii.** individuals; **iii.** crime control; **iv.** society; **v.** rehabilitate

Page 193: i. jurisdiction; **ii.** subject matter; **iii.** trial; **iv.** appellate; **v.** dual; **vi.** federal; **vii.** state

Page 196: i. limited; **ii.** general; **iii.** appeals

Page 199: i. district; **ii.** circuit; **iii.** Supreme; **iv.** *certiorari*

Page 203: i. president; **ii.** Senate; **iii.** governor; **iv.** partisan; **v.** nonpartisan; **vi.** merit

Page 210: i. judge; **ii.** prosecutors; **iii.** private; **iv.** public; **v.** poor/indigent

COURSEMATE

For online help and access to resources that accompany *Criminal Justice in Action: The Core*, go to **www.cengage-brain.com/shop/ISBN/978-1-285-06915-9**. Click "Access Now," where you will find flashcards, an online quiz, and other helpful study aids. If you have an access code for CourseMate, log in and go to the chapter of your choice for additional online study aids.

NOTES

1. Quoted in Kerry Sanders, "Rutgers Suicide Trial: This Isn't an Open and Shut Case," *U.S. News on msnbc.com* (February 21, 2012), at **usnews.msnbc.msn.com/_news /2012/02/21/10470351-rutgers-suicide -trial-this-isnt-an-open-and-shut-case**.

2. Quoted in Ian Parker, "The Story of a Suicide," *New Yorker* (February 6, 2012), 51.

3. Quoted in George Anastasia, "Rutgers Student Lost His Dice Roll," *Philadelphia Inquirer* (March 18, 2012), B1.

4. *Ibid.*

5. Roscoe Pound, "The Administration of Justice in American Cities," *Harvard Law Review* 12 (1912).

6. Russell Wheeler and Howard Whitcomb, *Judicial Administration: Text and Readings* (Englewood Cliffs, NJ: Prentice Hall, 1977), 3.

7. Herbert Packer, "The Courts, the Police and the Rest of Us," *Criminal Law, Criminology & Political Science* 57 (1966), 238–239.

8. Larry J. Siegel, *Criminology: Instructor's Manual*, 6th ed. (Belmont, CA: West/Wadsworth Publishing Co., 1998), 440.

9. Gerald F. Velman, "Federal Sentencing Guidelines: A Cure Worse Than the Disease," *American Criminal Law Review* 29 (Spring 1992), 904.

10. Pub. L. No. 111-211, 124 Stat. 2258, 2279 (2010).

11. Eli Lake, "Yemen Refuses to Let U.S. Try Cleric," *Washington Times* (May 12, 2010), A1.

12. 18 U.S.C. Section 3231; and *Solorio v. United States*, 483 U.S. 435 (1987).

13. 372 U.S. 335 (1963).

14. 384 U.S. 436 (1966).

15. 408 U.S. 238 (1972).

16. 428 U.S. 153 (1976).

17. 18 U.S.C. Section 48 (1999).

18. *United States v. Stevens*, 559 U.S. _____ (2010).

19. 559 U.S. _____ (2010).

20. Carl Milazzo, "Searching Cell Phones Incident to Arrest: 2009," *The Police Chief* (May 2009), 12.

21. Barry R. Schaller, *A Vision of American Law: Judging Law, Literature, and the Stories We Tell* (Westport, CT: Praeger, 1997).

22. Quoted in Linda Deutsch, "Murray Gets 4-Year Sentence, Tongue-Lashing from Judge," *Associated Press* (November 29, 2011).

23. Pub. L. No. 76-299, 53 Stat. 1223, codified as amended at 28 U.S.C. Sections 601–610 (1988 & Supp. V 1993).

24. James E. Lozier, "The Missouri Plan a.k.a. Merit Selection Is the Best Solution for Selecting Michigan's Judges," *Michigan Bar Journal* 75 (September 1996), 918.

25. Richard A. Watson and Rondal G. Downing, *The Politics of the Bench and Bar: Judicial Selection under the Missouri Nonpartisan Court Plan* (New York: John Wiley & Sons, 1969).

26. Quoted in Robert Hehre, "League Looks to Diversify Courts," *The Post and Courier* (Charleston, SC) (October 4, 2010), at **www.postandcourier.com/news/2010/oct/04/league-looks-to-diversify-courts**.

27. Ciara Torres-Spelliscy, Monique Chase, and Emma Greenman, *Improving Judicial Diversity*, 2d ed. (New York: Brennan Center for Justice, 2010), 1.

28. Russell Wheeler, *The Changing Face of the Federal Judiciary* (Washington, D.C.: The Brookings Institution, August 2009), Appendix table 1, page 11.

29. Edward M. Chen, "The Judiciary, Diversity, and Justice for All," *California Law Review* (July 2003), 1109.

30. Theresa B. Beiner, "The Elusive (but Worthwhile) Quest for a Diverse Bench in the New Millennium," *University of California at Davis Law Review* (February 2003), 599.

31. Sherrilyn A. Ifill, "Racial Diversity on the Bench: Beyond Role Models and Public Confidence," *Washington and Lee Law Review* (Spring 2000), 405.

32. Bennett L. Gershman, "Abuse of Power in the Prosecutor's Office," in *Criminal Justice 92/93*, ed. John J. Sullivan and Joseph L. Victor (Guilford, CT: Dushkin Publishing Group, 1991), 117–123.

33. 295 U.S. 78 (1935).

34. *Brady v. Maryland*, 373 U.S. (1963).

35. *Smith v. Cain*, 132 S.Ct. 627 (2012).

36. *Ibid.*

37. Celesta Albonetti, "Prosecutorial Discretion: The Effects of Uncertainty," *Law and Society Review* 21 (1987), 291–313.

38. Quoted in Michael Koenigs and Ian Shern, "Tyler Clementi Cyberbullying Trial Begins Today," *Good Morning America/Yahoo! News* (February 20, 2012), at **gma.yahoo.com/tyler-clementi-cyberbullying-trial-begins-today-182111675-abc-news.html**.

39. *Gideon v. Wainwright*, 372 U.S. 335 (1963); *Massiah v. United States*, 377 U.S. 201 (1964); *United States v. Wade*, 388 U.S. 218 (1967); *Argersinger v. Hamlin*, 407 U.S. 25 (1972); and *Brewer v. Williams*, 430 U.S. 387 (1977).

40. Larry Siegel, *Criminology*, 6th ed. (Belmont, CA: West/Wadsworth Publishing Co., 1998), 487–488.

41. Center for Professional Responsibility, *Model Rules of Professional Conduct* (Washington, D.C.: American Bar Association, 2003), Rules 1.6 and 3.1.

42. *United States v. Wade*, 388 U.S. 218, 256–258 (1967).

43. 372 U.S. 335 (1963).

44. 387 U.S. 1 (1967).

45. 407 U.S. 25 (1972).

46. Peter A. Joy and Kevin C. McMunigal, "Client Autonomy and Choice of Counsel," *Criminal Justice* (Fall 2006), 57.

47. American Bar Association, "Providing Defense Services," Standard 5-7.1, at **www.abanet.org/crimjust/standards/defsvcs_blk.html#7.1**.

48. Robert C. Boruchowitz, "The Right to Counsel: Every Accused Person's Right," *Washington State Bar Association Bar News* (January 2004), at **www.wsba.org/media/publications/barnews/2004/jan-04-boruchowitz.htm**.

49. *United States v. Gonzalez-Lopez*, 548 U.S. 140 (2006).

50. *Wheat v. United States*, 486 U.S. 153, 159 (1988).

51. Bureau of Justice Statistics, *Defense Counsel in Criminal Cases* (Washington, D.C.: U.S. Department of Justice, 2000), 3.

52. *Model Rules of Professional Conduct*, Rule 1.2(c)–(d).

53. Randolph Braccialarghe, "Why Were Perry Mason's Clients Always Innocent?" *Valparaiso University Law Review* (Fall 2004), 65.

54. John Kaplan, "Defending Guilty People," *University of Bridgeport Law Review* (1986), 223.

55. 491 U.S. 554 (1989).

Pretrial Procedures and the Criminal Trial

LEARNING OBJECTIVES

After reading this chapter, you should be able to...

1 Identify the steps involved in the pretrial criminal process.

2 Explain how a prosecutor screens potential cases.

3 Indicate why prosecutors, defense attorneys, and defendants often agree to plea bargains.

4 Identify the basic protections enjoyed by criminal defendants in the United States.

5 Explain what "taking the Fifth" really means.

6 Contrast challenges for cause and peremptory challenges during *voir dire*.

7 Explain the difference between testimony and real evidence, between lay witnesses and expert witnesses, and between direct and circumstantial evidence.

8 List the five basic steps of an appeal.

Throughout the chapter you will see each learning objective repeated in the margin next to the content it relates to. The chapter summary on page 246 includes all of the learning objectives for review.

Deborah Cheramie/iStockphoto

CHAPTER OUTLINE

- Pretrial Detention
- Establishing Probable Cause
- The Prosecutorial Screening Process
- Pleading Guilty
- Special Features of Criminal Trials
- Jury Selection
- The Trial
- The Final Steps of the Trial and Postconviction Procedures

215

NO EXCUSES

By the time University of Virginia senior George Huguely got to Yeardley Love's off-campus apartment just after midnight, he was quite drunk. When Love, also a senior at the school, refused to open the door, Huguely kicked his way in. Later, speaking to the Charlottesville police, Huguely admitted grabbing Love, his ex-girlfriend, by the neck and wrestling her to the floor. He also admitted that when he left, Love was suffering from a "nosebleed" as a result of their altercation. Several hours later, Love's roommate found her face down in a pool of blood on a pillow, dead. "I should not have gone over there when I was drinking," Huguely told the detectives who quickly arrested him.

During Huguely's February 2012 trial, prosecutors portrayed the defendant as a violent time bomb. District attorney Warner Chapman read an e-mail to the jury in which Huguely had written to Love, "I should have killed you," after learning that she was seeing someone else. Witnesses testified to a previous incident in which he had choked her at a party. According to the government lawyers, Love died of blunt-force trauma to the head, and they charged Huguely with premeditated, first degree murder. If convicted of this crime, the defendant faced a lifetime in prison.

In contrast, Huguely's lawyers painted their client as an immature "boy athlete" who made a bad decision under the influence of alcohol. He had no intention of harming Love on the night of her death, they argued, and had left the apartment thinking that she was not seriously injured. They presented evidence that Love suffocated to death on her wet, blood-stained pillow and therefore reasoned that Huguely was guilty of the lesser crime of involuntary manslaughter. "George's drinking was out of control," defense attorney Rhonda Quagliana told the jury. "It's not an excuse, it's not a justification. It's just a fact."

George Huguely, center, is escorted to court in Charlottesville, Virginia, during the trial for the death of his former girlfriend, Yeardley Love.

Andrew Shurtleff/ZUMA Press/Newscom

Given the options of first degree murder and involuntary manslaughter, the jury in George Huguely's trial chose neither. Instead, the jurors decided that although Huguely had acted maliciously, he had not intended to kill Yeardley Love. So, on February 22, 2012, the jurors found Huguely guilty of second degree murder and sentenced him to twenty-six years behind bars. In the end, the competing theories of how Love died held little interest for the jurors. Of more importance was a video of Huguely's interview with police in which the defendant reacted with shock and anguish at the news of Love's death. "I was emotionally shredded inside" by the sight of Huguely crying on the video, said one juror. "I absolutely feel for the guy."[1]

Not surprisingly, given the youth and attractiveness of Huguely and Love—both lacrosse players from privileged backgrounds—the trial drew nationwide attention. According to the *"wedding cake" model*, those who followed the proceedings may have gotten a skewed version of how the criminal justice system works.[2] This model suggests that only the top, and smallest, "layer" of trials comes close to meeting our standards of justice. In these celebrity trials, such as Huguely's, committed (and expensive) attorneys argue minute technicalities for days, and numerous expert (and expensive) witnesses take the stand for both sides.

On the bottom, largest layer of the wedding cake, the vast majority of defendants are dealt with informally, and the end goal seems to be speed rather than justice. Indeed, as you will see in this chapter, trial by jury is quite rare. The fate of most criminal suspects in this country is decided during pretrial procedures, which start almost as soon as the police have identified a suspect.

PRETRIAL DETENTION

Learning Objective 1 Identify the steps involved in the pretrial criminal process.

After an arrest has been made, the first step toward determining the suspect's guilt or innocence is the **initial appearance.** (For an overview of the entire process, see Figure 8.1 on the following page.) During this brief proceeding, a magistrate (see Chapter 7) informs the defendant of the charges that have been brought against him or her and explains his or her constitutional rights—particularly, the right to remain silent (under the Fifth Amendment) and the right to be represented by counsel (under the Sixth Amendment).

At this point, if the defendant cannot afford to hire a private attorney, a public defender may be appointed, or private counsel may be hired by the state to represent the defendant. As the U.S. Constitution does not specify how soon a defendant must be brought before a magistrate after arrest, it has been left to the judicial branch to determine the timing of the initial appearance. The Supreme Court has held that the initial appearance must occur "promptly," which in most cases means within forty-eight hours of booking.[3]

In misdemeanor cases, a defendant may decide to plead guilty and be sentenced during the initial appearance. Otherwise, the magistrate will usually release those charged with misdemeanors on their promise to return at a later date for further proceedings. For felony cases, however, the defendant is not permitted to make a plea at the initial appearance because a magistrate's court does not have jurisdiction to decide felonies. Furthermore, in most cases the defendant will be released only if she or he posts **bail**—an amount paid by the defendant to the court and retained by the court until the defendant returns for further proceedings. In theory, then, bail ensures that the defendant will not flee the jurisdiction of the court before her or his trial.

Initial Appearance An accused's first appearance before a judge or magistrate following arrest.

Bail The dollar amount or conditions set by the court to ensure that an individual accused of a crime will appear for further criminal proceedings.

THE PURPOSE OF BAIL

Bail is provided for under the Eighth Amendment. The amendment does not, however, guarantee the right to bail. Instead, it states that "excessive bail shall not be required." This has come to mean that in all cases except those involving a capital crime (where bail is prohibited), the amount of bail required must be reasonable compared with the seriousness of the wrongdoing. It does *not* mean that the amount of bail must be within the defendant's ability to pay.

SETTING BAIL There is no uniform system that governs pretrial detention. Each jurisdiction has its own *bail tariffs,* or general guidelines concerning the proper amount of bail. For misdemeanors, the police usually follow a preapproved bail schedule created by local judicial authorities. In felony cases, the primary responsibility to set bail lies with the judge, with the bail tariff acting as a loose guideline. Figure 8.2 on page 219 shows the typical bail amounts for violent offenses.

Defendants who cannot afford bail are generally kept in a local jail or lockup until the date of their trial, though many jurisdictions are searching for alternatives to this practice because of overcrowded incarceration facilities. Government statistics show that 62 percent of felony defendants are released before their trials.[4]

FIGURE 8.1 The Steps Leading to a Trial

Booking   After arrest, at the police station, the suspect is searched, photographed, fingerprinted, and allowed at least one telephone call. After the booking, charges are reviewed, and if they are not dropped, a complaint is filed and a judge or magistrate examines the case for probable cause.

Initial Appearance   The suspect appears before the judge, who informs the suspect of the charges and of her or his rights. If the suspect requests a lawyer, one is appointed. The judge sets bail (monetary conditions under which a suspect can obtain release pending disposition of the case).

Grand Jury   A grand jury determines whether there is probable cause to believe that the defendant committed the crime. The federal government and about one-third of the states require grand jury indictments for at least some felonies.

Preliminary Hearing   A preliminary hearing is a court proceeding in which the prosecutor presents evidence and the judge determines whether there is probable cause to hold the defendant over for trial.

Indictment   An indictment is the charging instrument issued by the grand jury.

Information   An information is the charging instrument issued by the prosecutor.

Arraignment   The suspect is brought before the trial court, informed of the charges, and asked to enter a plea.

Plea Bargain   A plea bargain is a prosecutor's promise of concessions (or promise to seek concessions) in return for the defendant's guilty plea. Concessions include a reduced charge and/or a lesser sentence.

Guilty Plea   In most jurisdictions, the majority of cases that reach the arraignment stage do not go to trial but are resolved by a guilty plea, often as the result of a plea bargain.

Trial   If the defendant refuses to plead guilty, he or she proceeds to either a jury trial (in most instances) or a bench trial.

PREVENTIVE DETENTION The vagueness of the Eighth Amendment has encouraged a second purpose of bail: to protect the community by preventing the defendant from committing another crime before trial. To achieve this purpose, a judge can set bail at a level the suspect cannot possibly afford. In January 2012, for example, a Los Angeles superior court judge set the bail for indigent defendant Harry Burkhart, accused of setting dozens of fires across the city over the New Year's weekend, at $2.85 million.

Alternatively, more than thirty states and the federal government have passed **preventive detention** legislation to the same effect. These laws allow judges to act "in the best interests of the community" by denying bail to arrestees with prior records of violence, thus keeping them in custody prior to trial.

GAINING PRETRIAL RELEASE

One of the most popular alternatives to bail is **release on recognizance (ROR).** This is used when the judge, based on the advice of trained personnel, decides that the defendant is not at risk to "jump" bail and does not pose a threat to the community. The defendant is then released at no cost with the understanding that he or she will return at the time of the trial. The Vera Institute, a nonprofit organization in New York City, introduced the concept of ROR as part of the Manhattan Bail Project in the 1960s, and such programs are now found in nearly every jurisdiction. When properly administered, ROR programs seem to be successful, with less than 5 percent of the participants failing to show for trial.[5]

POSTING BAIL Those suspected of committing a felony are rarely released on recognizance. These defendants may post, or pay, the full amount of the bail to the court in cash. The money will be returned when the suspect appears for trial. Given the large amount of funds required, and the relative lack of wealth of many criminal defendants, a defendant can rarely post bail in cash. Another option is to use real property, such as a house, instead of cash as collateral. These **property bonds** are also rare, because most courts require property valued at double the bail amount. Thus, if bail is set at $20,000, the defendant (or the defendant's family and friends) will have to produce property valued at $40,000.

BAIL BOND AGENTS If unable to post bail with cash or property, a defendant may arrange for a **bail bond agent** to post a bail bond on the defendant's behalf. The bond agent, in effect, promises the court that she or he will turn over to the court the full amount of bail if the defendant fails to return for further proceedings. The defendant usually must give the bond agent a certain percentage of the bail (frequently 10 percent) in cash. This amount, which is often not returned to the defendant later, is considered payment for the bond agent's assistance and assumption of risk. Depending on the amount of the bail bond, the defendant may also be required to sign over to the bond agent rights to certain property as security for the bond. Such property can be a car, a watch, or some other valuable asset.

SELFASSESSMENT

Fill in the blanks and check your answers on page 247.

During the _____ _____, a magistrate informs the defendant of the charges brought against her or him and explains her or his _____ rights. Following this proceeding, the defendant will be detained until trial unless he or she can post _____, the amount of which is determined by the _____. Even if the defendant can afford to pay this amount, he or she may be kept in jail until trial under a _____ detention statute if the court decides that he or she poses a risk to the community.

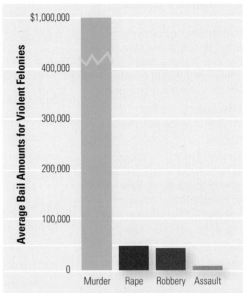

FIGURE 8.2 **Average Bail Amounts for Violent Felonies**
These figures represent the mean bail amounts for the seventy-five largest counties in the nation.

Source: Adapted from Bureau of Justice Statistics, *Felony Defendants in Large Urban Counties, 2006* (Washington, D.C.: U.S. Department of Justice, May 2010), Table 7, page 7.

Preventive Detention The retention of an accused person in custody due to fears that she or he will commit a crime if released before trial.

Release on Recognizance (ROR) A judge's order that releases an accused from jail with the understanding that he or she will return for further proceedings of his or her own will.

Property Bond An alternative to posting bail in cash, in which the defendant gains pretrial release by providing the court with property valued at the bail amount as assurance that she or he will return for trial.

Bail Bond Agent A businessperson who agrees, for a fee, to pay the bail amount if the accused fails to appear in court as ordered.

ESTABLISHING PROBABLE CAUSE

Once the initial appearance has been completed and bail has been set, the prosecutor must establish *probable cause*. In other words, the prosecutor must show that a crime was committed and link the defendant to that crime. There are two formal procedures for establishing probable cause at this stage of the pretrial process: preliminary hearings and grand juries.

THE PRELIMINARY HEARING

During the **preliminary hearing,** the defendant appears before a judge or magistrate who decides whether the evidence presented is sufficient for the case to proceed to trial. Normally, every person arrested has a right to this hearing within a reasonable amount of time after her or his initial arrest[6]—usually, no later than ten days if the defendant is in custody or within thirty days if he or she has gained pretrial release.

THE PRELIMINARY HEARING PROCESS The preliminary hearing is conducted in the manner of a mini-trial. Typically, a police report of the arrest is presented by a law enforcement officer, supplemented with evidence provided by the prosecutor. Because the burden of proving probable cause is relatively light (compared with proving guilt beyond a reasonable doubt), prosecutors rarely call witnesses during the preliminary hearing, saving them for the trial.

During this hearing, the defendant has a right to be represented by counsel, who may cross-examine witnesses and challenge any evidence offered by the prosecutor. In most states, defense attorneys can take advantage of the preliminary hearing to begin the process of **discovery,** in which they are entitled to have access to any evidence in the possession of the prosecution relating to the case. Discovery makes trial proceedings fairer by allowing each side access to all relevant information the other side may have concerning the details of the case.

WAIVING THE HEARING The preliminary hearing often seems rather perfunctory, although in some jurisdictions it replaces grand jury proceedings. It usually lasts no longer than five minutes, and the judge or magistrate rarely finds that probable cause does not exist. For this reason, defense attorneys commonly advise their clients to waive their right to a preliminary hearing. Once a judge has ruled affirmatively, in many jurisdictions the defendant is bound over to the **grand jury,** a group of citizens called to decide whether probable cause exists. In other jurisdictions, the prosecutor issues an **information,** which replaces the police complaint as the formal charge against the defendant for the purposes of a trial.

THE GRAND JURY

The federal government and about one-third of the states require a grand jury to make the decision as to whether a case should go to trial. Grand juries are *impaneled,* or created, for a period of time usually not exceeding three months. During that time, the grand jury sits in closed (secret) session and hears only evidence presented by the prosecutor—the defendant cannot present evidence at this hearing. The prosecutor can introduce key aspects of his or her case against the defendant, including

---

Preliminary Hearing An initial hearing in which a magistrate decides whether there is probable cause to believe that the defendant committed the crime with which he or she is charged.

Discovery Formal investigation by each side prior to trial.

Grand Jury The group of citizens called to decide whether probable cause exists to believe that a suspect committed the crime with which she or he has been charged.

Information The formal charge against the accused issued by the prosecutor after a preliminary hearing has found probable cause.

While trial juries decide the defendant's guilt or innocence, a grand jury decides only whether the prosecutor has enough evidence to charge the defendant with a crime. Practically, why does the prosecution hold a major advantage during grand jury proceedings?

Johnny Hanson/Houston Chronicle

photographs, documents, tangible objects, the testimony of witnesses, and other items. If the grand jury finds that probable cause exists, it issues an **indictment** (pronounced in-*dyte*-ment) against the defendant. Like an information in a preliminary hearing, the indictment becomes the formal charge against the defendant.

SELFASSESSMENT

Fill in the blanks and check your answers on page 247.

If a case is to proceed to trial, the prosecutor must establish _____ _____ that the defendant committed the crime in question. One way of doing this involves a _____ hearing, in which a judge or magistrate rules whether the prosecutor has met this burden. In the other method, the decision rests with a group of citizens called a _____ _____, who will hand down an _____ if they believe the evidence is sufficient to support the charges.

THE PROSECUTORIAL SCREENING PROCESS

Some see the high government success rates in pretrial proceedings as proof that prosecutors successfully screen out weak cases before they get to a grand jury or preliminary hearing. Others, however, point out that procedural rules at this stage favor the prosecution and that grand juries rarely, if ever, fail to indict defendants set before them. That being the case, what is to keep prosecutors from using their charging powers indiscriminately? Nothing, say many observers. Once the police have initially charged a defendant with committing a crime, the prosecutor can prosecute the case as it stands, reduce or increase the initial charge, file additional charges, or dismiss the case.

In a system of government and law that relies on checks and balances, asked legal expert Kenneth Culp Davis, why should the prosecutor be "immune to review by other officials and immune to review by the courts?"[7] Although American prosecutors have far-ranging discretionary charging powers, it is not entirely correct to say that they are unrestricted. Controls are indirect and informal, but they do exist.

CASE ATTRITION

Prosecutorial discretion includes the power *not* to prosecute cases. For example, federal prosecutors decline to bring charges in nearly three out of every four computer fraud cases referred to them by investigators.[8] Figure 8.3 on the following page depicts the average outcomes of one hundred felony arrests in the United States. As you can see, of the sixty-five adult arrestees brought before the district attorney, only thirty-five are prosecuted, and only eighteen of these prosecutions lead to incarceration. Consequently, fewer than one in three adults arrested for a felony sees the inside of a prison or jail cell. This phenomenon is known as **case attrition,** and it is explained in part by prosecutorial discretion.

About half of those adult felony cases brought to prosecutors by police are dismissed through a *nolle prosequi* (Latin for "unwilling to pursue"). Why are these cases "nolled," or not prosecuted by the district attorney? In the section on law enforcement, you learned that the police do not have the resources to arrest every lawbreaker in the nation. Similarly, district attorneys do not have the resources to prosecute every arrest. They must choose how to distribute their scarce resources. Several years ago, for example, Contra Costa County (California)

> "You can paint pictures and get people indicted for just about anything."
>
> **—Alfonse D'Amato**
> Former U.S. senator from New York

FIGURE 8.3 Following One Hundred Felony Arrests: The Criminal Justice Funnel

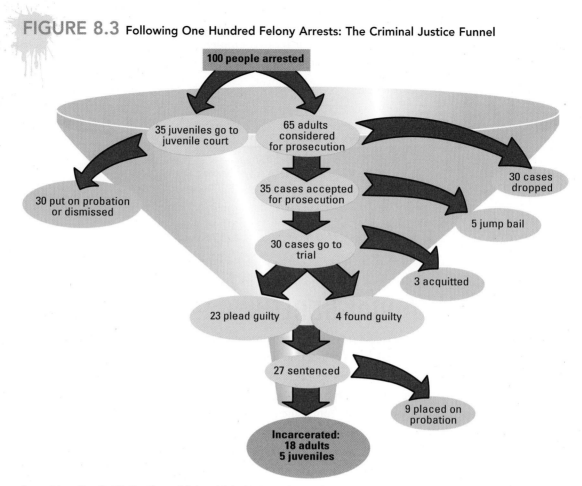

Source: Adapted from Todd R. Clear, George F. Cole, and Michael D. Reisig, *American Corrections,* 9th ed. (Belmont, CA: Wadsworth, 2011), 134.

district attorney Robert Kochly announced that due to budget shortfalls, his office would no longer prosecute anyone caught with less than a gram of methamphetamine or cocaine, less than half a gram of heroin, and fewer than five pills of Ecstasy.[9]

In some cases, the decision is made for prosecutors, such as when police break procedural law and negate important evidence. This happens rarely—less than 1 percent of felony arrests are dropped because of the exclusionary rule (see pages 163–165) and almost all of these dismissals are the result of illegal drug searches.[10]

SCREENING FACTORS

Learning Objective 2 Explain how a prosecutor screens potential cases.

Most prosecutors have a *screening* process for deciding when to prosecute and when to "noll." This process varies a bit from jurisdiction to jurisdiction, but most prosecutors consider several factors in making the decision:

- The most important factor in deciding whether to prosecute is not the prosecutor's belief in the guilt of the suspect, but whether there is *sufficient evidence for conviction.*[11] If prosecutors have strong physical evidence and a number of reliable and believable witnesses, they are quite likely to prosecute.

- Prosecutors also tend to establish *case priorities.* In other words, everything else being equal, a district attorney will prosecute a rapist instead of a jaywalker, because the former presents a greater threat to society than does the latter. A prosecutor will also be more likely to prosecute someone with an extensive record of wrongdoing than a first-time offender. Often, in coordination with the police, a district attorney's office will target a single area of crime, such as illegal drug use or drunk driving.

- Sometimes a case is dropped even when it involves a serious crime and a wealth of evidence exists against the suspect. These situations usually involve *uncooperative victims*. Domestic violence cases are particularly difficult to prosecute because the victims may want to keep the matter private, fear reprisals, or have a strong desire to protect their abuser.[12] In some jurisdictions, as many as 80 percent of domestic violence victims refuse to cooperate with the prosecution.[13]

- A prosecutor may be willing to drop a case or reduce the charges against *a defendant who is willing to testify against other offenders*. Federal law encourages this kind of behavior by offering sentencing reductions to defendants who provide "substantial assistance in the investigation or prosecution of another person who has committed an offense."[14]

The unreliability of a victim can also affect prosecutorial screening decisions. In 2011, for example, Manhattan prosecutors gathered significant physical evidence suggesting that Dominique Strauss-Kahn, a prominent French politician, had "engaged in a hurried sexual encounter" with a housekeeper in the Sofitel New York hotel. None of the evidence clearly indicated a lack of consent, however, so the case hinged on the housekeeper's testimony that she had been sexually assaulted.

Although prosecutors initially believed the victim to be truthful, they eventually learned that she had lied previously about being gang-raped by soldiers in her native Guinea in order to gain immigration benefits in the United States. Also, she had been less than forthcoming about her desire to benefit financially from Strauss-Kahn's alleged sexual assault. Finally, prosecutors asked the presiding judge to drop all charges. "If we do not believe her beyond a reasonable doubt," the prosecutors said in a statement, "we cannot ask a jury to do so."[15] (To learn about one country's especially prosecutor-friendly system, see the feature *Comparative Criminal Justice—Japan's All-Powerful Prosecutors* on the following page.)

SELFASSESSMENT

Fill in the blanks and check your answers on page 247.

On average, of sixty-five adult arrestees, a district attorney will prosecute only thirty-five. This process, which is known as case _____, requires that the prosecutor _____ all potential cases and dismiss the ones where the likelihood of _____ is weakest. The most important factor in this decision is whether there is sufficient _____ to find the defendant guilty.

PLEADING GUILTY

Based on the information (delivered during the preliminary hearing) or indictment (handed down by the grand jury), the prosecutor submits a motion to the court to order the defendant to appear before the trial court for an **arraignment.** Due process of law, as guaranteed by the Fifth Amendment, requires that a criminal defendant be informed of the charges brought against her or him and be offered an opportunity to respond to those charges. The arraignment is one of the ways in which due process requirements are satisfied by criminal procedure law.

At the arraignment, the defendant is informed of the charges and must respond by pleading not guilty or guilty. In some but not all states, the defendant may also enter

Arraignment A court proceeding in which the suspect is formally charged with the criminal offense stated in the indictment.

COMPARATIVE CRIMINAL JUSTICE

JAPAN'S ALL-POWERFUL PROSECUTORS

Prosecutors in the United States are generally believed to have a great deal of charging discretion. The discretionary power of American prosecutors, however, does not equal that of their Japanese counterparts. With the ability to "cherry pick" their cases, prosecutors in Japan routinely have annual conviction rates of over 99.9 percent.

The "Confession Mill"

One observer described the Japanese courts as a "confession mill." Unlike the American system, Japan has no arraignment procedure during which the accused can plead guilty or innocent. Instead, the focus of the Japanese criminal justice system is on extracting confessions of guilt: police can hold and question suspects for up to twenty-three days without pressing charges. Furthermore, the suspect has no absolute right to counsel during the interrogation, and police are often able to get confessions that make for open-and-shut convictions. The prosecutor also has the "benevolent" discretion to drop the case altogether if the suspect expresses remorse.

In addition, the extraordinarily high conviction rate is a product of Japanese culture. To fail in an attempt to convict results in a loss of face, not only for the individual prosecutor but also for the court system as a whole. The Japanese Justice Ministry estimates that, to avoid the risk of losing, prosecutors decline to press charges against 35 percent of indictable suspects each year. Japanese judges—there are almost no juries—contribute to the high conviction rate by rarely questioning the manner in which prosecutors obtain confessions.

No Plea Bargaining

Interestingly, given the amount of prosecutorial discretion, the Japanese criminal justice system does not allow for plea bargaining. The Japanese see the practice of "trading" a guilty plea for a lesser sentence as counterproductive, as a defendant may be tempted to confess to crimes she or he did not commit if the prosecution has a strong case. For the Japanese, a confession extracted after, say, twenty-three days of interrogation may be "voluntary," but a confession gained through a promise of leniency is "forced" and therefore in conflict with the system's goals of truth seeking and accuracy.

FOR CRITICAL ANALYSIS Explain the fundamental differences between the American and Japanese criminal justice systems. Do you think the power wielded by Japan's prosecutors weakens or strengthens the Japanese system in comparison with the American one?

Nolo Contendere Latin for "I will not contest it." A criminal defendant's plea, in which she or he chooses not to challenge, or contest, the charges brought by the government.

Plea Bargaining The process by which the accused and the prosecutor work out a mutually satisfactory conclusion to the case, subject to court approval.

a plea of **nolo contendere,** which is Latin for "I will not contest it." The plea of *nolo contendere* is neither an admission nor a denial of guilt. (The consequences for someone who pleads guilty and for someone who pleads *nolo contendere* are the same in a criminal trial, but the latter plea cannot be used in a subsequent civil trial as an admission of guilt.) Most frequently, the defendant pleads guilty to the initial charge or to a lesser charge that has been agreed on through *plea bargaining* between the prosecutor and the defendant. If the defendant pleads guilty, no trial is necessary, and the defendant is sentenced based on the crime he or she has admitted committing.

PLEA BARGAINING IN THE CRIMINAL JUSTICE SYSTEM

Plea bargaining most often takes place after the arraignment and before the beginning of the trial. In its simplest terms, it is a process by which the accused, represented by the defense counsel, and the prosecutor work out a mutually satisfactory disposition of the case, subject to court approval. Usually, plea bargaining involves the defendant's pleading guilty to the charges against her or him in return for a lighter sentence, but other variations are possible as well. The defendant can agree to plead guilty in exchange for having the charge against her or him reduced from, say, felony burglary to the lesser offense of breaking and entering. Or a person charged with multiple counts may agree to plead guilty if the prosecutor agrees to drop one or more of the counts. Whatever the particulars, the results of a plea bargain are generally the same: the prosecutor gets a conviction, and the defendant a lesser punishment.

In *Santobello v. New York* (1971),[16] the Supreme Court held that plea bargaining "is not only an essential part of the process but a highly desirable part for many reasons." Some observers would agree, but with ambivalence. They understand that plea bargaining offers the practical benefit of saving court resources, but they question whether it is the best way to achieve justice.[17]

MOTIVATIONS FOR PLEA BARGAINING

Learning Objective 3 — Indicate why prosecutors, defense attorneys, and defendants often agree to plea bargains.

Sometimes, it is difficult to perceive criminal court proceedings as anything other than a sort of a contest in which the prosecution and the defense treat each other as adversaries, with a verdict of guilty or not guilty as the "prize" to be won at the conclusion. In many instances, this *adversarial system* begins in earnest when the two sides try to work out a plea bargain. Still, given the extremely high rate of plea bargaining—accounting for about 97 percent of criminal convictions in state courts[18]—it follows that the defendant, prosecutor, and defense attorney each have strong reasons to engage in the practice.

DEFENDANTS AND PLEA BARGAINING The plea bargain allows the defendant a measure of control over his or her fate. Several years ago, for example, John Albert Gardner was convicted of killing fourteen-year-old Amber Dubois and seventeen-year old Chelsea King (see the photo below). Despite the violent nature of the crimes, San Diego County prosecutors agreed not to seek the death penalty if Gardner pleaded guilty to both murders. He did so, and a judge sentenced him to life in prison without parole. As Figure 8.4 on the following page shows, defendants who plea bargain receive significantly lighter sentences on average than those who are found guilty at trial.

PROSECUTORS AND PLEA BARGAINING In most cases, a prosecutor has a single goal after charging a defendant with a crime: conviction. If a case goes to trial, no matter how certain a prosecutor may be that the defendant is guilty, there is always a chance that a jury or judge will disagree. Plea bargaining removes this risk. Furthermore, the prosecutorial screening process described earlier in the chapter is not infallible. Sometimes, a prosecutor will find that the evidence against the accused is weaker than first thought or will uncover new information that changes the complexion of the case. In these situations, the prosecutor may decide to drop the charges or, if he or she still feels that the defendant is guilty, turn to plea bargaining to "save" a questionable case.

The prosecutor's role as an administrator also comes into play. She or he may be interested in the quickest, most efficient manner to dispose of caseloads, and plea bargains reduce the time and money spent on each case. Personal philosophy can affect the proceedings as well. A prosecutor who feels that a mandatory minimum sentence for a particular crime, such as marijuana possession, is too strict may plea bargain in order to lessen the penalty. Similarly, some prosecutors will consider plea bargaining only in certain instances—for burglary and theft, for example, but not for more serious felonies such as rape and murder.[19]

DEFENSE ATTORNEYS AND PLEA BARGAINING Political scientist Milton Heumann has said that the most important lesson that a defense attorney learns is that "most of his

Why did John Albert Gardner agree to plead guilty to murdering two teenagers? What incentives might the San Diego prosecutors have had for accepting Gardner's guilty plea and declining to seek his execution?

AP Photo/*San Diego Union-Tribune*, Nelvin C. Cepeda, Pool

FIGURE 8.4 Sentencing Outcomes for Guilty Pleas

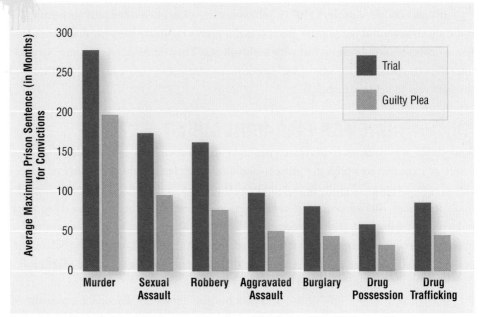

Source: Bureau of Justice Statistics, *Felony Sentences in State Courts, 2006—Statistical Tables* (Washington, D.C.: U.S. Department of Justice, December 2009), Table 4.3.

[or her] clients are guilty."[20] Given this stark reality, favorable plea bargains are often the best a defense attorney can do for clients, aside from helping them to gain acquittals. Some have suggested that defense attorneys have other, less savory motives for convincing a client to plead guilty, such as a desire to increase profit margins by quickly disposing of cases[21] or a wish to ingratiate themselves with the other members of the courtroom work group by showing their "reasonableness."[22]

PROTECTING THE DEFENDANT Often, the defendant plays only a minor role in the plea-bargaining process, which is dominated by give-and-take between the prosecutor and the defense attorney. The Supreme Court is aware of the potential for taking advantage of the defendant in plea bargaining and has taken steps to protect the accused. Until *Boykin v. Alabama* (1969),[23] judges would often accept the defense counsel's word that the defendant wanted to plead guilty. In *Boykin,* the Court held that the defendant must make a clear statement that he or she accepts the plea bargain. As a result, many jurisdictions now ask the accused to sign a *Boykin* **form** waiving her or his right to a trial.

PLEADING NOT GUILTY Despite the large number of defendants who eventually plead guilty, the plea of not guilty is fairly common at the arraignment. This is true even when the facts of the case seem stacked against the defendant. Generally, a not-guilty plea in the face of strong evidence is part of a strategy to (1) gain a more favorable plea bargain, (2) challenge a crucial part of the evidence on constitutional grounds, or (3) submit one of the affirmative defenses discussed in Chapter 3.

Of course, if either side is confident in the strength of its arguments and evidence, it will obviously be less likely to accept a plea bargain. Also, both prosecutors and defense attorneys may favor a trial to gain publicity, and sometimes public pressure will force a chief prosecutor (who is, remember, normally an elected official) to take a weak case to trial. Finally, a defendant may be convinced of her or his innocence, regardless of any

Boykin **Form** A form that must be completed by a defendant who pleads guilty. The defendant states that she or he has done so voluntarily and with full comprehension of the consequences.

other factors. Dharun Ravi, whose invasion of privacy charges we discussed at the beginning of Chapter 7, twice refused plea bargains that would have allowed him to avoid incarceration and thus risked the possibility of a ten-year sentence at trial. In the remainder of this chapter, we examine what happens to the roughly 3 percent of defendants who do, for one reason or another, find themselves in criminal court.

SELFASSESSMENT

Fill in the blanks and check your answers on page 247.

A _____ _____ occurs when the prosecution and the defense work out an agreement that resolves the case. Generally, a defendant will plead guilty in exchange for a reduction of the _____ against him or her or a lighter _____, or both. To ensure that the defendant understands the terms of the plea, she or he must sign a _____ form waiving her or his right to a _____.

SPECIAL FEATURES OF CRIMINAL TRIALS

Criminal trial procedures reflect the need to protect criminal defendants against the power of the state by providing them with a number of rights. Many of the significant rights of the accused are spelled out in the Sixth Amendment, which reads, in part, as follows:

Learning Objective 4 Identify the basic protections enjoyed by criminal defendants in the United States.

> In all criminal prosecutions, the accused shall enjoy the right to a speedy and public trial, by an impartial jury of the State and the district wherein the crime shall have been committed, . . . and to be informed of the nature and cause of the accusation; to be confronted with the witnesses against him; to have compulsory process for obtaining witnesses in his favor; and to have the Assistance of Counsel for his defense.

In the last chapter, we discussed the Sixth Amendment's guarantee of the right to counsel. Here, we will examine the other important aspects of the criminal trial, beginning with two protections explicitly stated in the Sixth Amendment: the right to a speedy trial by an impartial jury.

A "SPEEDY" TRIAL

As you have just read, the Sixth Amendment requires a speedy trial for those accused of a criminal act. The reason for this requirement is obvious: depending on various factors, the defendant may lose his or her right to move freely and may be incarcerated prior to trial. Also, the accusation that a person has committed a crime jeopardizes that person's reputation in the community. If the defendant is innocent, the sooner the trial is held, the sooner his or her innocence can be established in the eyes of the court and the public.

THE DEFINITION OF A SPEEDY TRIAL The Sixth Amendment does not specify what is meant by the term *speedy*. The United States Supreme Court has refused to measure "speedy" as well, ruling instead in *Barker v. Wingo* (1972)[24] that only in situations in which the delay is unwarranted and proved to be prejudicial can the accused claim a violation of Sixth Amendment rights.

SPEEDY-TRIAL LAWS To meet constitutional requiements, all fifty states have their own speedy-trial statutes. For example, the Illinois Speedy Trial Act holds that a defendant must be tried within 120 days of arrest unless both the prosecution and the defense agree otherwise.[25] Keep in mind, however, that a defendant does not automatically go free if her or his trial is not "speedy" enough. There must be judicial action, which is rare but does occur from time to time. In 2012, for example, Ernest Burnett spent 106 days in the Schenectady County (New York) jail—sixteen days more than allowed under state law—while prosecutors failed to start his trial process. As a result of this oversight, a county judge was forced to release Burnett, who had been arrested for kidnapping and trying to kill an ex-girlfriend.

Nearly half of all criminal trials in state courts are settled within three months of the defendant's arrest. About 12 percent take more than a year to adjudicate.[26] At the national level, the Speedy Trial Act of 1974[27] (amended in 1979) specifies the following time limits for those in the federal court system:

1. No more than thirty days between arrest and indictment.
2. No more than ten days between indictment and arraignment.
3. No more than seventy days between arraignment and trial.

Federal law allows extra time for hearings on pretrial motions, mental competency examinations, and other procedural actions.

STATUTES OF LIMITATIONS Note that the Sixth Amendment's guarantee of a speedy trial does not apply until a person has been accused of a crime. Citizens are protected against unreasonable delays before accusation by **statutes of limitations.** These legislative time limits require prosecutors to charge a defendant with a crime within a certain amount of time after the illegal act took place. If the statute of limitations on a particular crime is ten years, and the police do not identify a suspect until ten years and one day after the criminal act occurred, then that suspect cannot be charged with that particular offense.

In general, prosecutions for murder and other offenses that carry the death penalty do not have a statute of limitations. This exception provides police with the ability to conduct cold case investigations (see page 134) that last for decades. In 2011, for example, Sycamore (Illinois) police arrested Jack Daniel McCullough for the abduction and murder of a seven-year-old girl in 1957. The long-awaited break in this case came when investigators were finally able to disprove McCullough's alibi that he had been on a train at the time of the crime. The problem with prosecuting such cases, of course, is that so much time has passed since the criminal act that witnesses may be missing or dead, memories may be unreliable, and other evidence may have been lost.

Statute of Limitations A law limiting the amount of time prosecutors have to bring criminal charges against a suspect after the crime has occurred.

Jury Trial A trial before a judge and a jury.

Bench Trial A trial conducted without a jury, in which a judge determines the defendant's guilt or innocence.

In 2011, New York prosecutors gathered "credible" evidence that former Syracuse University assistant basketball coach Bernie Fine, right, had sexually abused a minor eight years earlier. Because the statute of limitations for the crime had expired, however, authorities could not charge Fine with any wrongdoing. What are the arguments for and against statutes of limitations in sexual abuse cases?

Jim McIsaac/Getty Images

THE ROLE OF THE JURY

The Sixth Amendment also states that anyone accused of a crime shall be judged by "an impartial jury." In *Duncan v. Louisiana* (1968),[28] the Supreme Court solidified this right by ruling that in all felony cases, the defendant is entitled to a **jury trial.** The Court has, however, left it to the individual states to decide whether juries are required for misdemeanor cases.[29] If the defendant waives her or his right to trial by jury, a **bench trial** takes place, in which a judge decides questions of legality and fact, and no jury is involved.

The typical American jury consists of twelve persons. About a dozen states do, under varying circumstances, allow for juries with fewer than twelve members for felony cases. In federal courts, defendants are entitled to have the case heard by a twelve-member jury unless both parties agree in writing to a smaller jury.

In most jurisdictions, jury verdicts in criminal cases must be *unanimous* for **acquittal**— a declaration of innocence—or conviction. In other words, all twelve jurors must agree on the defendant's fate. The Supreme Court has held that unanimity is not a rigid requirement. It declared that jury verdicts must be unanimous in federal criminal trials, but has given states leeway to set their own rules.[30] As a result, Louisiana and Oregon continue to require only ten votes for conviction in criminal cases.

Acquittal A declaration following a trial that the individual accused of the crime is innocent in the eyes of the law and thus is absolved of the charges.

THE PRIVILEGE AGAINST SELF-INCRIMINATION

In addition to the Sixth Amendment, which specifies the protections we have just discussed, the Fifth Amendment to the Constitution also provides important safeguards for the defendant. The Fifth Amendment states that no person "shall be compelled in any criminal case to be a witness against himself." Therefore, a defendant has the right not to testify at a trial if to do so would implicate him or her in the crime.

Witnesses may also refuse to testify on this ground. For example, if a witness, while testifying, is asked a question and the answer would reveal his or her own criminal wrongdoing, the witness may "take the Fifth." In other words, she or he can refuse to testify on the ground that such testimony may be self-incriminating. Such a refusal rarely occurs, however, as witnesses are often granted *immunity* before testifying, meaning that no information they disclose can be used to bring criminal charges against them. Witnesses who have been granted immunity cannot refuse to answer questions on the basis of self-incrimination.

Learning Objective **5** Explain what "taking the Fifth" really means.

It is important to note that not only does the defendant have the right to "take the Fifth," but also that the decision to do so should not prejudice the jury in the prosecution's favor. The Supreme Court came to this controversial decision while reviewing *Adamson v. California* (1947),[31] a case involving the convictions of two defendants who had declined to testify in their own defense against charges of robbery, kidnapping, and murder. The prosecutor in the *Adamson* proceedings frequently and insistently brought this silence to the notice of the jury in his closing argument, insinuating that if the pair had been innocent, they would not have been afraid to testify. The Court ruled that such tactics effectively invalidated the Fifth Amendment by using the defendants' refusal to testify as a sign of their guilt. Now judges are required to inform the jury that an accused's decision to remain silent cannot be held against him or her.

THE PRESUMPTION OF A DEFENDANT'S INNOCENCE

The presumption in criminal law is that a defendant is innocent until proved guilty. The burden of proving guilt falls on the state (the public prosecutor). Even if a defendant did in fact commit the crime, she or he will be "innocent" in the eyes of the law unless the prosecutor can support the charge with sufficient evidence to convince a jury (or judge in a bench trial) of the defendant's guilt.[32]

Sometimes, especially when a case involves a high-profile violent crime, pretrial publicity may have convinced many members of the community—including potential jurors—that a defendant is guilty. In these instances, a judge has the authority to change the venue of the trial to ensure an unbiased jury. In 2012, defense attorneys for Thayne Ormsby successfully requested a change of venue for their client's trial for the brutal murders of two men and a ten-year-old boy in Houlton, Maine. Given the size of Houlton—population 6,123—and the case's local notoriety, Ormsby's lawyers argued that the trial should be moved to Caribou, sixty miles to the north.

A STRICT STANDARD OF PROOF

In a criminal trial, the defendant is not required to prove his or her innocence. As mentioned earlier, the burden of proving the defendant's guilt lies entirely with the state. Furthermore, the state must prove the defendant's guilt *beyond a reasonable doubt*. In other words, the prosecution must show that, based on all the evidence, the defendant's guilt is clear and unquestionable. In *In re Winship* (1970),[33] a case involving the due process rights of juveniles, the Supreme Court concluded that the reasonable doubt standard is a Constitutional requirement. As such, according to the Court, it reduces the risks of convicting innocent people and therefore reassures Americans of the law's moral force and legitimacy.

This high standard of proof in criminal cases reflects a fundamental social value—the belief that it is worse to convict an innocent individual than to let a guilty one go free. The consequences to the life, liberty, and reputation of an accused person from an erroneous conviction for a crime are substantial, and this idea has been factored into the process. Placing a high standard of proof on the prosecutor reduces the margin of error in criminal cases (at least in one direction). This strict standard of proof is one of the few protections enjoyed by defendants in military tribunals. The *Anti-Terrorism in Action—Trying Times* feature below addresses these tribunals, the once and future venue

ANTI-TERRORISM IN ACTION

TRYING TIMES

According to federal prosecutors, Ahmed Khalfan Ghailani, a citizen of Tanzania, was an integral member of a 1998 al Qaeda plot that led to the bombing of two American embassies in East Africa. In 2011, a federal jury in New York convicted Ghailani of one count of conspiracy to destroy government buildings and property, and Judge Lewis A. Kaplan sentenced him to life in prison. At the same time, however, Ghailani was acquitted of more than 280 counts of conspiracy and murder, partially because Kaplan disallowed damning evidence that had been improperly obtained by a coerced interrogation.

To a certain degree, the Ghailani trial was a test of President Barack Obama's strategy of trying terrorism suspects in civilian criminal courts. Given the suppression of important evidence and Ghailani's acquittal on almost all the charges, many observers felt it was a test that failed. According to Republican senator Mitch McConnell of Kentucky, the Ghailani verdict was "all the proof we need that the administration's approach to prosecuting terrorists has been deeply misguided and indeed potentially harmful as a matter of national security."

POLICY CHANGE

The Obama administration seems to have taken this criticism to heart. In April 2011, federal officials announced

that Khalid Shaikh Mohammed and four other defendants would be tried by military tribunals, rather than by civilian courts as originally intended. Mohammed and the others were accused of plotting the September 11, 2001, terrorist attacks. In these tribunals, defendants do not have the right to a trial by jury, as guaranteed by the Sixth Amendment. Instead, a panel of at least five military officials acts in place of the judge and jury and decides questions of both "fact and law."

Only two-thirds of the panel members need to agree for a conviction, in contrast to the unanimous jury required in criminal trials. Furthermore, evidence that would be inadmissible in criminal court is allowed before these tribunals. In response to complaints that Obama had "flip-flopped" on military tribunals, a White House spokesperson replied, "First and foremost, the president does what is in the best security interests of the United States."

FOR CRITICAL ANALYSIS Do you think that foreigners suspected of terrorist acts should be given the same protections as defendants in U.S. criminal courts? Why or why not?

for judging terrorist suspects, most of whom were captured during military operations in Iraq and Afghanistan.

JURY SELECTION

The initial step in a criminal trial involves choosing the jury. The main goal of jury selection is to produce a representative cross section of the population of the jurisdiction where the crime was committed. Besides having to live in the jurisdiction where the case is being tried, there are very few restrictions on eligibility to serve on a jury. State legislatures generally set the requirements, and they are similar in most states. For the most part, jurors must be

1. Citizens of the United States.
2. Over eighteen years of age.
3. Free of felony convictions.
4. Healthy enough to function in a jury setting.
5. Sufficiently intelligent to understand the issues of a trial.
6. Able to read, write, and comprehend the English language (with one exception— New Mexico does not allow non-English-speaking citizens to be eliminated from jury lists simply because of their lack of English-language skills).

The **master jury list,** sometimes called the *jury pool,* is made up of all the eligible jurors in a community. This list is usually drawn from voter-registration lists or driver's license rolls, which have the benefit of being easily available and timely.

The next step in gathering a jury is to draw together the **venire** (Latin for "to come"). The *venire* is composed of all those people who are notified by the clerk of the court that they have been selected for jury duty. Those selected to be part of the *venire* are ordered to report to the courthouse on the date specified by the notice.

Master Jury List The list of citizens in a court's district from which a jury can be selected; compiled from voter-registration lists, driver's license lists, and other sources.

Venire The group of citizens from which the jury is selected.

During the 2012 murder trial of Shanterrica Madden in Murfreesboro, Tennessee, jurors were allowed to question witnesses directly from the jury box. What is your opinion of this practice, which is rarely permitted? Do you agree with Madden's attorneys, who felt that it was unfair to their client?

AP Photo/*Daily News Journal*, Jim Davis

VOIR DIRE

At the courthouse, prospective jurors are gathered, and the process of selecting those who will actually hear the case begins. This selection process is not haphazard. The court ultimately seeks jurors who are free of any biases that may affect their willingness to listen to the facts of the case impartially. To this end, both the prosecutor and the defense attorney have some input into the ultimate makeup of the jury. Each attorney questions prospective jurors in a proceeding known as *voir dire* (French for "to speak the truth"). During *voir dire*, jurors are required to provide the court with a significant amount of personal information, including home address, marital status, employment status, arrest record, and life experiences.

The *voir dire* process involves both written and oral questioning of potential jurors. Attorneys fashion their inquiries in such a manner as to uncover any biases on the parts of prospective jurors and to find persons who might identify with the plights of their respective sides. As one attorney noted, though a lawyer will have many chances to talk to a jury as a whole, *voir dire* is his or her only chance to talk with the individual jurors. (To better understand the specific kinds of questions asked during this process, see Figure 8.5 on the facing page.) Increasingly, attorneys are also conducting virtual *voir dires* on the Internet, using social networking sites such as Facebook to learn valuable information about potential jurors.

CHALLENGING POTENTIAL JURORS During *voir dire*, the attorney for each side may exercise a certain number of challenges to prevent particular persons from serving on the jury. Both sides can exercise two types of challenges: challenges "for cause" and peremptory challenges.

> "A jury consists of twelve persons chosen to decide who has the better lawyer."
>
> **—Robert Frost,**
> American poet
> (1874–1963)

Challenges for Cause If a defense attorney or prosecutor concludes that a prospective juror is unfit to serve, the attorney may exercise a **challenge for cause** and request that that person not be included on the jury. Attorneys must provide the court with a sound, legally justifiable reason for why potential jurors are "unfit" to serve. For example, jurors can be challenged for cause if they are mentally incompetent, do not understand English, or are proved to have a prior link—be it personal or financial—with the defendant or victim.

Peremptory Challenges Each attorney may also exercise a limited number of **peremptory challenges.** These challenges are based solely on an attorney's subjective reasoning, and the attorney usually is not required to give any legally justifiable reason for wanting to exclude a particular person from the jury. Because of the rather random nature of peremptory challenges, each state limits the number that an attorney may utilize: between five and ten for felony trials (depending on the state) and between ten and twenty for trials that could possibly result in the death penalty (also depending on the state). Once an attorney's peremptory challenges are used up, he or she must accept forthcoming jurors, unless a challenge for cause can be used.

RACE AND GENDER ISSUES IN JURY SELECTION

For many years, prosecutors used their peremptory challenges as an instrument of segregation in jury selection. Prosecutors were able to keep African Americans off juries in cases in which an African American was the defendant. The argument that African Americans—or members of any other racial or ethnic group—would be partial toward one of their own was tacitly supported by the Supreme Court. Despite its own assertion, made in *Swain v. Alabama* (1965),[34] that blacks have the same right to appear on a jury as whites, the Court mirrored the apparent racism of society as a whole by protecting the questionable actions of many prosecutors.

THE *BATSON* REVERSAL The Supreme Court reversed this policy in 1986 with *Batson v. Kentucky.*[35] In that case, the Court declared that the Constitution prohibits prosecutors

FIGURE 8.5 Sample Juror Questionnaire

Several years ago, Brian David Mitchell went on trial in Salt Lake City, Utah, for kidnapping fourteen-year-old Elizabeth Smart and keeping her in captivity for "nine months of hell." Mitchell held a number of extreme religious views, including the belief that he was a godlike figure who would play a prominent role in the coming "end of the world." As Mitchell's religion would play a significant part in the criminal proceedings, both the prosecution and the defense were interested in the religious beliefs of potential jurors, as this excerpt from the juror questionnaire shows.

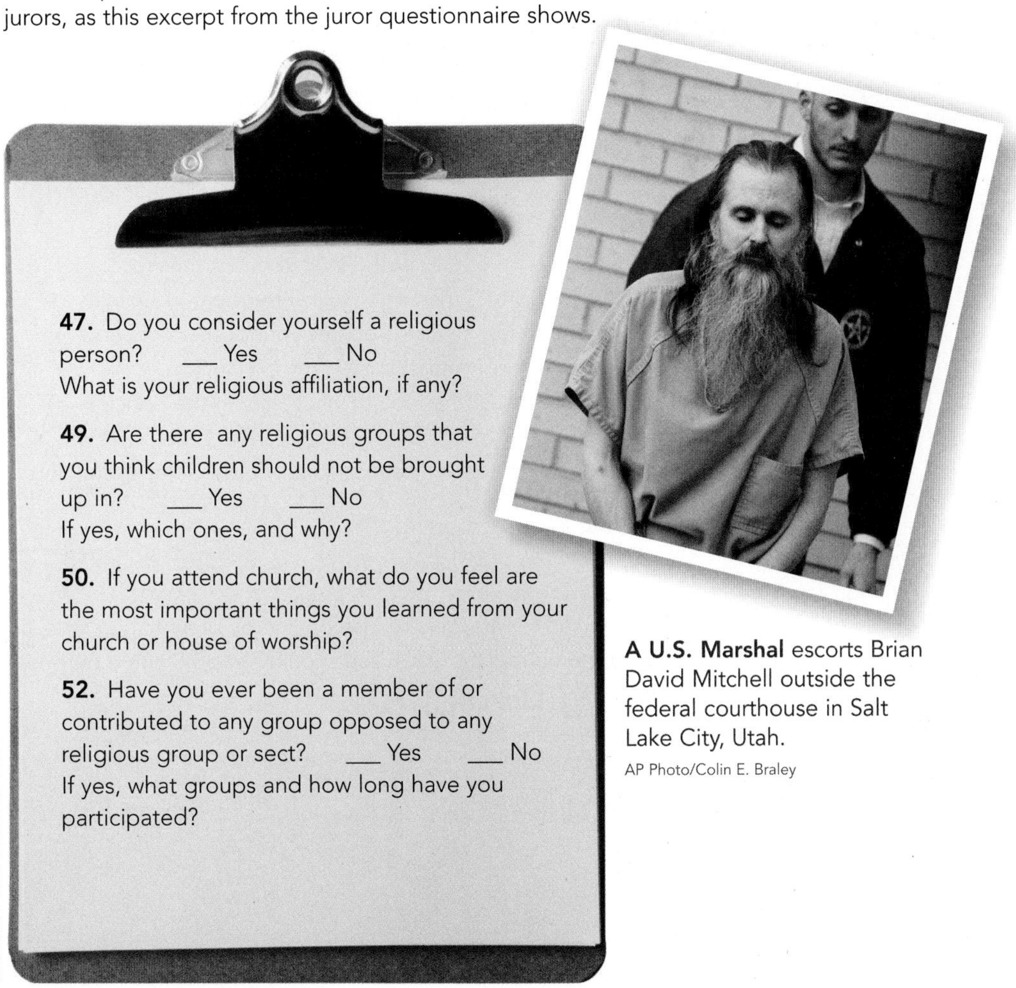

47. Do you consider yourself a religious person?   ___ Yes   ___ No
What is your religious affiliation, if any?

49. Are there any religious groups that you think children should not be brought up in?   ___ Yes   ___ No
If yes, which ones, and why?

50. If you attend church, what do you feel are the most important things you learned from your church or house of worship?

52. Have you ever been a member of or contributed to any group opposed to any religious group or sect?   ___ Yes   ___ No
If yes, what groups and how long have you participated?

Paul-Andre Belle-Isle/Shutterstock

A U.S. Marshal escorts Brian David Mitchell outside the federal courthouse in Salt Lake City, Utah.

AP Photo/Colin E. Braley

from using peremptory challenges to strike possible jurors on the basis of race. Under the *Batson* ruling, the defendant must prove that the prosecution's use of a peremptory challenge was racially motivated. Doing so requires a number of legal steps:[36]

1. First, the defendant must make a *prima facie* case that there has been discrimination during *venire*. (*Prima facie* is Latin for "at first sight." Legally, it refers to a fact that is presumed to be true unless contradicted by evidence.)
2. To do so, the defendant must show that she or he is a member of a recognizable racial group and that the prosecutor has used peremptory challenges to remove members of this group from the jury pool.
3. Then, the defendant must show that these facts and other relevant circumstances raise the possibility that the prosecutor removed the prospective jurors solely because of their race.
4. If the court accepts the defendant's charges, the burden shifts to the prosecution to prove that its peremptory challenges were race neutral. If the court finds against the prosecution, it rules that a *Batson* violation has occurred.

CAREERS IN CJ

ANNIKA CARLSTEN
PUBLIC DEFENDER

My very first day on the job, I watched another attorney conduct *voir dire* (see page 232) on a domestic violence assault. I wondered if I would ever be that comfortable and confident in court. Many years later, the cases have started to blur in my memory. That said, I will always remember my very first "not guilty" verdict. I was utterly convinced of my client's innocence, and very emotionally invested in winning the case for him. At the other end of the spectrum, I will never forget having to explain court proceedings to a man only hours after he accidentally shot and killed his child. Nothing in law school prepares you for that conversation. Nothing in life prepares you for that conversation.

Most of all, I believe passionately in the idea of what I do, in the principle of equal justice for everyone, regardless of money or circumstance. On a good day, I see that ideal fulfilled. On a great day, I feel like I personally have done something to make it so.

Social Media Career Tip
You need to differentiate yourself from everyone else on line by providing unique, relevant, high-quality content on a regular basis. You should network with a purpose, not just to share fun things. [f] Linked[in]. [y]

Photo Courtesy of Annika Carlsten

FAST FACTS

PUBLIC DEFENDER, JOB DESCRIPTION:

- Interview low-income applicants for legal services; advise and counsel individuals and groups regarding their legal rights; handle a reasonable caseload; and, where necessary, engage in the negotiation, trial, and/or appeal of legal issues that have a substantial impact on the rights of eligible clients.

WHAT KIND OF TRAINING IS REQUIRED?

- A law degree and membership in the relevant state bar association.

ANNUAL SALARY RANGE?

- $44,000–$92,000

The Court has revisited the issue of race a number of times in the years since its *Batson* decision. In *Powers v. Ohio* (1991),[37] it ruled that a defendant may contest race-based peremptory challenges even if the defendant is not of the same race as the excluded jurors. In *Georgia v. McCollum* (1992),[38] the Court placed defense attorneys under the same restrictions as prosecutors when making race-based peremptory challenges.

Finally, in 2008, the Court, reaffirming its *Batson* decision of twenty-two years earlier, overturned the conviction of an African American death row inmate because a Louisiana prosecutor improperly picked an all-white jury for his murder trial.[39] These rulings do not mean that a black defendant can never be judged by a jury made up entirely of whites. Rather, they indicate that attorneys cannot use peremptory challenges to reject a prospective juror because of her or his race.

WOMEN ON THE JURY In *J.E.B. v. Alabama ex rel. T.B.* (1994),[40] the Supreme Court extended the principles of the *Batson* ruling to cover gender bias in jury selection. The case was a civil suit for paternity and child support brought by the state of Alabama. Prosecutors used nine of their ten challenges to remove men from the jury, while the defense made similar efforts to remove women. When challenged, the state defended its actions by referring to what it called the rational belief that men and women might have different views on the issues of paternity and child support. The Court disagreed and held this approach to be unconstitutional.

SELFASSESSMENT

Fill in the blanks and check your answers on page 247.

The _____ is composed of all those people who have been identified as potential jurors for a particular trial. These people are then gathered for the process of _____ _____, in which the prosecution and defense choose the actual members of the jury. Both sides can remove jurors in two ways: (1) through unlimited challenges for _____, which require the attorney to give a reason for the removal, and (2) through a limited number of _____ challenges, for which no reason is necessary. According to the United States Supreme Court, potential jurors cannot be removed for reasons of _____ or _____.

Social Media and CJ
The Center for Court Innovation is a New York-based nonprofit organization dedicated to improving the public's trust in the court system. To access its Twitter page, visit the *Criminal Justice CourseMate* at **cengagebrain.com** and select the *Web Links* for this chapter.

THE TRIAL

Once the jury members have been selected, the judge swears them in and the trial itself can begin. A rather pessimistic truism among attorneys is that every case "has been won or lost when the jury is sworn." This reflects the belief that a juror's values are the major, if not dominant, factor in the decision of guilt or innocence.[41]

In actuality, it is difficult to predict how a jury will go about reaching a decision. Despite a number of studies on the question, researchers have not been able to identify any definitive consistent patterns of jury behavior. Sometimes, jurors in a criminal trial will follow instructions to find a defendant guilty unless there is a reasonable doubt, and sometimes they seem to follow instinct or prejudice and apply the law any way they choose.[42]

OPENING STATEMENTS

Attorneys may choose to open the trial with a statement to the jury, though they are not required to do so. In these **opening statements,** the attorneys give a brief version of the facts and the supporting evidence that they will present during the trial. Because some trials can drag on for weeks or even months, it is extremely helpful for jurors to hear a summary of what will unfold. In short, the opening statement is a kind of "road map" that describes the destination that each attorney hopes to reach and outlines how he or she plans to reach it. The danger for attorneys is that they will offer evidence during the trial that might contradict an assertion made during the opening statement. This may cause jurors to disregard the evidence or shift their own thinking further away from the narrative being offered by the attorney.[43] (For an example of an opening statement, see Figure 8.6 on the following page.)

THE ROLE OF EVIDENCE

Once the opening statements have been made, the prosecutor begins the trial proceedings by presenting the state's evidence against the defendant. Courts have complex rules about what types of evidence may be presented and how the evidence may be brought out during the trial. **Evidence** is anything that is used to prove the existence or nonexistence of a fact. For the most part, evidence can be broken down into two categories: testimony and real evidence. **Testimony** consists of statements by competent witnesses. **Real evidence,**

Opening Statements The attorneys' statements to the jury at the beginning of the trial.

Evidence Anything that is used to prove the existence or nonexistence of a fact.

Testimony Verbal evidence given by witnesses under oath.

Real Evidence Evidence that is brought into court and seen by the jury, as opposed to evidence that is described for a jury.

FIGURE 8.6 The Opening Statement

Mazoltuv Borukhova was charged with hiring her cousin, Mikhail Mallayev, to kill her husband. In his opening statement, New York prosecutor Brad Leventhal asked the jury why Mallayev would commit such a murder, given that he did not know the victim. The prosecutor proceeded to answer his own question:

"Because he was hired to do it. He was paid to do it. He's an assassin. A paid assassin. An executioner. A hit man. For who? Who would hire this man, this defendant, to murder in cold blood an innocent victim in the presence of his own daughter? Who could have such strong feelings toward Daniel Malekov that they would hire an assassin to end his life. Who?"

Leventhal then pointed his finger at Borukhova and said,

"Her."

Mazoltuv Borukhova was sentenced to life in prison after being found guilty of hiring a hit man to murder her husband.

Photo Courtesy the Queens District Attorney's office

Source: Janet Malcolm, "Iphigenia in Forest Hills," *New Yorker* (May 3, 2010), 36.

Learning Objective **7** Explain the difference between testimony and real evidence, between lay witnesses and expert witnesses, and between direct and circumstantial evidence.

Lay Witness A witness who can truthfully and accurately testify on a fact in question without having specialized training or knowledge.

Expert Witness A witness with professional training or substantial experience qualifying her or him to testify on a certain subject.

Direct Evidence Evidence that establishes the existence of a fact that is in question without relying on inference.

presented to the court in the form of exhibits, includes any physical items—such as the murder weapon or a bloodstained piece of clothing—that affect the case.

Rules of evidence are designed to ensure that testimony and exhibits presented to the jury are relevant, reliable, and not unfairly prejudicial against the defendant. One of the tasks of the defense attorney is to challenge evidence presented by the prosecution by establishing that the evidence is not reliable. Of course, the prosecutor also tries to demonstrate the irrelevance or unreliability of evidence presented by the defense. The final decision on whether evidence is allowed before the jury rests with the judge, in keeping with his or her role as the "referee" of the adversary system.

TESTIMONIAL EVIDENCE A person who is called to testify on factual matters that would be understood by the average citizen is referred to as a **lay witness.** If asked about the condition of a victim of an assault, for example, a lay witness could relate certain facts, such as "she was bleeding from her forehead" or "she was unconscious on the ground for several minutes."

A lay witness could not, however, give information about the medical extent of the victim's injuries, such as whether she suffered from a fractured skull or internal bleeding. Coming from a lay witness, such testimony would be inadmissible. When the matter in question requires scientific, medical, or technical skill beyond the scope of the average person, prosecutors and defense attorneys may call an **expert witness** to the stand. The expert witness is an individual who has professional training, advanced knowledge, or substantial experience in a specialized area, such as medicine, computer technology, or ballistics.

DIRECT VERSUS CIRCUMSTANTIAL EVIDENCE Two types of testimonial evidence may be brought into court: direct evidence and circumstantial evidence. **Direct evidence** is evidence that has been witnessed by the person giving testimony. "I saw Bill shoot Chris" is an example of direct evidence. **Circumstantial evidence** is indirect evidence that, even if believed, does not establish the fact in question but only the degree of likelihood of the fact. In other words, circumstantial evidence can create an inference that a fact exists.

Suppose, for example, that the defendant owns a gun that shoots bullets of the type found in the victim's body. This circumstantial evidence, by itself, does not establish that the defendant committed the crime. Combined with other circumstantial evidence, however, it may do just that. For instance, if other circumstantial evidence indicates that the defendant had a motive for harming the victim and was at the scene of the crime when the shooting occurred, the jury might conclude that the defendant committed the crime.

THE "CSI EFFECT." When possible, defense attorneys will almost always make the argument that the state has failed to present any evidence other than circumstantial evidence against their client. Recently, this tactic has been aided by a phenomenon known as the "CSI effect," taking its name from the popular television series *CSI: Crime Scene Investigation* and its spin-offs. According to many prosecutors, these shows have fostered unrealistic notions among jurors as to what high-tech forensic science can accomplish as part of a criminal investigation. In reality, the kind of physical evidence used to solve crimes on *CSI* is often not available to the prosecution, which must rely instead on witnesses and circumstantial evidence.

Several years ago, researchers surveyed more than one thousand jurors in Washtenaw County, Michigan, and found that nearly half "expected the prosecutor to present scientific evidence in every criminal case." This expectation was particularly strong in rape trials and trials lacking direct evidence of a crime.[44] Indeed, some observers believe the CSI effect was responsible for Casey Anthony's acquittal of charges that she murdered her two-year old daughter, discussed in Chapter 1. In that 2011 trial, prosecutors could provide only circumstantial evidence of Anthony's guilt, and even that evidence sometimes worked against them. For example, Anthony's attorneys were able to convince jurors that DNA traces found on the duct tape used to suffocate the child could not be matched to their client (see photo alongside).[45]

RELEVANCE Evidence will not be admitted in court unless it is relevant to the case being considered. **Relevant evidence** is evidence that tends to prove or disprove a fact in question. Forensic proof that the bullets found in a victim's body were fired from a gun discovered in the suspect's pocket at the time of arrest, for example, is certainly relevant. The suspect's prior record, showing a conviction for armed robbery ten years earlier, is, as we shall soon see, irrelevant to the case at hand and in most instances will be ruled inadmissible by the judge.

PREJUDICIAL EVIDENCE Evidence may be excluded if it would tend to distract the jury from the main issues of the case, mislead the jury, or cause jurors to decide the issue on an emotional basis. In practice, this rule often precludes prosecutors from using

Circumstantial Evidence
Indirect evidence that is offered to establish, by inference, the likelihood of a fact that is in question.

Relevant Evidence
Evidence tending to make a fact in question more or less probable than it would be without the evidence. Only relevant evidence is admissible in court.

Jennifer Welch, a crime scene investigator with the Orange County (Florida) Sheriff's Office, holds up duct tape found on Caylee Anthony's body. How did Casey Anthony's defense attorney use this duct tape to create reasonable doubt that their client bound and killed her daughter?

Joe Burbank/MCT/Landov

prior purported criminal activities or actual convictions to show that the defendant has criminal propensities or an "evil character."[46] This concept is codified in the Federal Rules of Evidence, which state that evidence of "other crimes, wrongs, or acts is not admissible to prove the character of a person in order to show action in conformity therewith." Such evidence is allowed only when it does not apply to character construction and focuses instead on "motive, opportunity, intent, preparation, plan, knowledge, identity, or absence of mistake or accident."[47]

Although this legal concept has come under a great deal of criticism, it is consistent with the presumption-of-innocence standards discussed earlier. Arguably, if a prosecutor is allowed to establish that the defendant has shown antisocial or even violent character traits in the past, this will prejudice the jury against the defendant in the present trial. Even if the judge instructs jurors that this prior evidence is irrelevant, human nature dictates that it will probably have a "warping influence" on the jurors' perception of the defendant.[48] Therefore, whenever possible, defense attorneys will keep such evidence from the jury.

THE PROSECUTION'S CASE

Because the burden of proof is on the state, the prosecution is generally considered to have a more difficult task than the defense. The prosecutor attempts to establish guilt beyond a reasonable doubt by presenting the *corpus delicti* ("body of the offense" in Latin) of the crime to the jury. The *corpus delicti* is simply a legal term that refers to the substantial facts that show a crime has been committed. By establishing such facts through the presentation of relevant and nonprejudicial evidence, the prosecutor hopes to convince the jury of the defendant's guilt.

DIRECT EXAMINATION OF WITNESSES Witnesses are crucial to establishing the prosecutor's case against the defendant. The prosecutor will call witnesses to the stand and ask them questions pertaining to the sequence of events that the trial is addressing. This form of questioning is known as **direct examination.** During direct examination, the prosecutor will usually not be allowed to ask *leading questions*—questions that might suggest to the witness a particular desired response.

A leading question might be something like "So, Mrs. Williams, you noticed the defendant threatening the victim with a broken beer bottle?" If Mrs. Williams answers "yes" to this question, she has, in effect, been "led" to the conclusion that the defendant was, in fact, threatening with a broken beer bottle. The fundamental purpose behind testimony is to establish what actually happened, not what the trial attorneys would like the jury to believe happened. (A properly worded query would be, "Mrs. Williams, please describe the defendant's manner toward the victim during the incident.")

HEARSAY When interviewing a witness, both the prosecutor and the defense attorney will make sure that the witness's statements are based on the witness's own knowledge and not hearsay. **Hearsay** can be defined as any testimony given in court about a statement made by someone else. Literally, it is what someone heard someone else say. For the most part, hearsay is not admissible as evidence. It is excluded because the listener may have misunderstood what the other person said, and without the opportunity of cross-examining the originator of the statement, the misconception cannot be challenged.

For example, prosecutors in the trial of Dharun Ravi, discussed in the previous chapter, tried to introduce a dorm room change application on which Tyler Clementi had written "Roommate with webcam spying on me." The judge did not allow the state-

Direct Examination The examination of a witness by the attorney who calls the witness to the stand to testify.

Hearsay An oral or written statement made by an out-of-court speaker that is later offered in court by a witness (not the speaker) concerning a matter before the court. Hearsay usually is not admissible as evidence.

ment in court, ruling that it was hearsay because Clementi was not available to attest to its authenticity.[49]

CROSS-EXAMINATION

After the prosecutor has directly examined her or his witnesses, the defense attorney is given the chance to question the same witnesses. The Sixth Amendment states, "In all criminal prosecutions, the accused shall enjoy the right . . . to be confronted with witnesses against him." This **confrontation clause** gives the accused, through his or her attorneys, the right to cross-examine witnesses. **Cross-examination** refers to the questioning of an opposing witness during trial, and both sides of a case are allowed to do so.

Cross-examination allows the attorneys to test the truthfulness of opposing witnesses and usually entails efforts to create doubt in the jurors' minds that the witness is reliable. Cross-examination is also linked to the problems presented by hearsay evidence. When a witness offers hearsay, the person making the original remarks is not in the court and therefore cannot be cross-examined. If such testimony were allowed, the defendant's Sixth Amendment right to confront witnesses against him or her would be violated.

After the defense has cross-examined a prosecution witness, the prosecutor may want to reestablish any reliability that might have been lost. The prosecutor can do so by again questioning the witness, a process known as *redirect examination*. Following the redirect examination, the defense attorney will be given the opportunity to ask further questions of prosecution witnesses, or recross-examination. Thus, each side has two opportunities to question a witness. The attorneys need not do so, but only after each side has been offered the opportunity will the trial move on to the next witness or the next stage.

Confrontation Clause The part of the Sixth Amendment that guarantees all defendants the right to confront witnesses testifying against them during the criminal trial.

Cross-Examination The questioning of an opposing witness during trial.

THE DEFENDANT'S CASE

After the prosecution has finished presenting its evidence, the defense has the option to offer the defendant's case. Because the burden is on the state to prove the accused's guilt, the defense is not required to offer any case at all. It can simply "rest" without calling any witnesses or producing any real evidence and ask the jury to decide the merits of the case on what it has seen and heard from the prosecution.

CREATING A REASONABLE DOUBT Defense lawyers most commonly defend their clients by attempting to expose weaknesses in the prosecutor's case. Remember that if the defense attorney can create reasonable doubt concerning the client's guilt in the mind of just a single juror, the defendant has a good chance of gaining an acquittal or at least a *hung jury,* a circumstance explained later in the chapter.

Even if the prosecution can present seemingly strong evidence, a defense attorney may succeed by creating reasonable doubt. In an illustrative case, Jason Korey bragged to his friends that he had shot and killed Joseph Brucker in Pittsburgh, Pennsylvania, and a great deal of circumstantial evidence linked Korey to the killing. The police, however, could find no direct evidence: they could not link Korey to the murder weapon, nor could they match his footprints to those found at the crime scene. Michael Foglia, Korey's defense attorney, explained his client's bragging as an attempt to gain attention, not a true statement. Although this explanation may strike some as unlikely, in the absence of physical evidence it did create doubt in the jurors' minds, and Korey was acquitted. (For a better idea of how this strategy works in court, see the feature *You Be the Defense Attorney—A Gang Murder* on the following page.)

YOU BE THE DEFENSE ATTORNEY

A Gang Murder

THE SITUATION Your client is Daniel, a twenty-three-year-old member of a violent Los Angeles street gang. Daniel is charged with the first degree murder of Christopher, his best friend and fellow gang member. Christopher was killed because other gang members believed he had "snitched" about their criminal activity. According to prosecutors, Daniel lured Christopher to a garage, where other gang members hit him in the head with a shotgun and then stabbed him more than sixty times. During the trial, José, the prosecution's main witness, who admitted taking part in the stabbing while high on methamphetamine, testified that Daniel kicked Christopher's dead body. In her opening argument, the prosecutor told the jury that even though your client did not stab Christopher, he was just as guilty of murder as those who did.

THE LAW To find a defendant guilty (in this jurisdiction), a jury must find *beyond a reasonable doubt* that he or she committed the crime. For Daniel to be guilty of first degree murder, the prosecution must prove that he acted with "malice aforethought" in luring Christopher to his death in the garage.

YOUR DECISION As a defense attorney, your job is to create reasonable doubt in the jurors' minds about Daniel's intent to lure Christopher to his death. Besides the facts presented above, other important details about this case include the following: (1) José, the prosecution's main witness, was allowed to plead guilty to a lesser charge of voluntary manslaughter in return for his testimony, and (2) José was dating Christopher's sister at the time of the murder. What argument will you make before the jury to create reasonable doubt?

[To see how a Los Angeles defense attorney argued in a case with similar facts, go to Example 8.1 in Appendix B.]

OTHER DEFENSE STRATEGIES The defense can choose among a number of strategies to generate reasonable doubt in the jurors' minds. It can present an *alibi defense,* by submitting evidence that the accused was not at or near the scene of the crime at the time the crime was committed. Another option is to attempt an *affirmative defense,* by presenting additional facts to the ones offered by the prosecution. Possible affirmative defenses, which we discussed in detail in Chapter 3, include the following:

1. Self-defense   2. Insanity   3. Duress   4. Entrapment

With an affirmative defense strategy, the defense attempts to prove that the defendant should be found not guilty because of certain circumstances surrounding the crime. An affirmative strategy can be difficult to carry out because it forces the defense to prove the reliability of its own evidence, not simply disprove the evidence offered by the prosecution.

The defense is often willing to admit that a certain criminal act took place, especially if the defendant has already confessed. When this happens, the primary question of the trial becomes not whether the defendant is guilty, but what the defendant is guilty of. In these situations, the defense strategy focuses on obtaining the lightest possible penalty for the defendant. As we saw earlier, this strategy is responsible for the high percentage of proceedings that end in plea bargains.

REBUTTAL AND SURREBUTTAL

After the defense closes its case, the prosecution is permitted to bring new evidence forward that was not used during its initial presentation to the jury. This is called the **rebuttal** stage of the trial. When the rebuttal stage is finished, the defense is given the opportunity to cross-examine the prosecution's new witnesses and introduce new witnesses of its own. This final act is part of the *surrebuttal.* After these stages have been completed, the defense may file a request called a *motion for a directed verdict,* asking the judge to find in the defendant's favor. If this motion is rejected—and it almost always is—the trial continues, and the opposing sides offer their closing arguments.

CLOSING ARGUMENTS

In their **closing arguments,** the attorneys summarize their presentations and argue one final time for their respective cases. In most states, the defense attorney goes first, and then the prosecutor. (In Colorado, Kentucky, and Missouri, the order is reversed.) An effective closing argument includes all of the major points that support the defense's or the government's case. It also emphasizes the shortcomings of the opposing party's case.

Jurors will view a closing argument with some skepticism if it merely recites the central points of a party's claim or defense without also responding to the unfavorable facts or issues raised by the other side. Of course, neither attorney wants to focus too much on the other side's position, but the elements of the opposing position do need to be acknowledged and their flaws highlighted. (For an example of opposing closing arguments, see Figure 8.7 below.) Once both attorneys have completed their remarks,

Rebuttal Evidence given to counteract or disprove evidence presented by the opposing party.

Closing Arguments Arguments made by each side's attorney after the cases for the prosecution and the defense have been presented.

FIGURE 8.7 Closing Arguments

Defense attorneys for Keith Kidwell, charged with murdering a convenience store worker in Bull City, North Carolina, argued that the case against their client was "flawed to the core." In her closing argument, district attorney Tracey Cline focused on one particular piece of evidence to contradict this assertion:

> Inside that [store] that morning, there were footprints, shoe impressions. All the ones that were in blood—and I'm not talking about what the kids put on their face at Halloween. Real blood. Blood that had once run warm inside a body. But all of the shoe prints in blood can be traced to Mr. Kidwell's shoes. Outside sole design, same physical size, general wear, similar features. Scientific words. You, each of you, had in your hands the picture of that bloody shoe print on Mr. Nelms' back and matched it up—I said matched—with his shoe. Coincidence?

Renee Keith/iStockphoto

The jury found Kidwell guilty of first degree murder, and he was sentenced to life in prison without the possibility of parole.

Source: For a complete transcript of Cline's closing argument, go to **media2.newsobserver.com/smedia/2011/09/05/09/47/ qSaKF.So.156.pdf.**

the case is submitted to the jury, and the attorneys' role in the trial is, for the moment, complete.

SELFASSESSMENT

Fill in the blanks and check your answers on page 247.

Evidence is any object or spoken _____ that can be used in a criminal trial to prove or disprove a _____ related to the crime. Evidence will not be admitted into the trial unless it is _____ and does not unfairly _____ the jury against the defendant by appealing to emotion rather than fact. The prosecution will usually try to build its case through _____ examination of its witnesses, which the defense will counter with a _____ -examination of its own. The defense's main goal is to create _____ _____ concerning the defendant's guilt in the minds of as many jurors as possible.

THE FINAL STEPS OF THE TRIAL AND POSTCONVICTION PROCEDURES

Charge The judge's instructions to the jury following the attorneys' closing arguments.

After closing arguments, the outcome of the trial is in the hands of the jury. Before the jurors begin their deliberations, the judge gives the jury a **charge,** summing up the case and instructing the jurors on the rules of law that apply to the issues in the case. These charges, also called jury instructions, are usually prepared during a special *charging conference* involving the judge and the trial attorneys. In this conference, the attorneys suggest the instructions they would like to see be sent to the jurors, but the judge makes the final decision as to the charges submitted. If the defense attorney disagrees with the charges sent to the jury, he or she can enter an objection, thereby setting the stage for a possible appeal.

JURY DELIBERATION

After receiving the charge, the jury begins its deliberations. Jury deliberation is a somewhat mysterious process, as it takes place in complete seclusion. Most of what is known about how a jury deliberates comes from mock trials or interviews with jurors after the verdict has been reached. A general picture of the deliberation process constructed from this research shows that the romantic notion of jurors with high-minded ideals of justice making eloquent speeches is, for the most part, not the reality. In approximately three out of every ten cases, the initial vote by the jury led to a unanimous decision. In 90 percent of the remaining cases, the majority eventually dictated the decision.[50]

One of the most important instructions that a judge normally gives the jurors is that they should seek no outside information during deliberation. The idea is that jurors should base their verdict *only* on the evidence that the judge has deemed admissible. In extreme cases, the judge will order that the jury be *sequestered,* or isolated from the public, during the trial and deliberation stages of the proceedings. Sequestration is used when deliberations are expected to be lengthy, or the trial is attracting a high amount of interest and the judge wants to keep the jury from being unduly influenced. Juries are usually sequestered in hotels and kept under the watch and guard of officers of the court.

CJ&TECHNOLOGY

Wireless Devices in the Courtroom

One former juror, fresh from trial, complained that the members of the courtroom work group had not provided the jury with enough information to render a fair verdict. "We felt deeply frustrated at our inability to fill those gaps in our knowledge," he added. Until recently, frustrated jury members have lacked the means to carry out their own investigations in court. Today, however, jurors with smartphones have news stories and online research tools at their fingertips. With wireless devices, they can look up legal terms, blog and tweet about their experiences, and sometimes even try to contact other participants in the trial through "friend" requests on social media Web sites.

This access can cause serious problems for judges, whose responsibility it is to ensure that no outside information taints the jury's decision. During deliberations at the end of one recent trial in Florida concerning illegal Internet drug sales, the judge found that nine of the twelve jurors had conducted Google research about the case. One jury member even discovered that the defendant had previously prescribed drugs later used in a double suicide—information that the defense had successfully argued should be kept out of court. The judge had no choice but to declare a *mistrial*, requiring that the proceedings start again with a different jury.

Alina Solovyova-Vincent/iStockphoto

THINKING ABOUT WIRELESS DEVICES IN THE COURTROOM:

The Sixth Amendment guarantees the accused the right to trial by an "impartial jury." How does the use of wireless devices in the courtroom threaten this right?

THE VERDICT

Once it has reached a decision, the jury issues a **verdict.** The most common verdicts are guilty and not guilty, though juries may signify different degrees of guilt if instructed to do so by the judge. Following the announcement of a guilty or not guilty verdict and, in some instances we will discuss in the next chapter, the sentencing phase, the jurors are discharged, and the jury trial proceedings are finished.

When a jury in a criminal trial is unable to agree on a unanimous verdict—or a majority of the jurors in certain states—it returns with no decision. This is known as a **hung jury.** Following a hung jury, the judge will declare a mistrial, and the case will be tried again in front of a different jury if the prosecution decides to pursue the matter a second time. A judge can do little to reverse a hung jury, considering that "no decision" is just as legitimate a verdict as guilty or not guilty.

In some states, if there are only a few dissenters to the majority view, a judge can send the jury back to the jury room under a set of rules set forth more than a century ago by the Supreme Court in *Allen v. United States* (1896).[51] The **Allen Charge,** as this instruction is called, asks the jurors in the minority to reconsider the majority opinion. Many jurisdictions do not allow *Allen* Charges on the ground that they improperly coerce jurors with the minority opinion to change their minds.[52]

Verdict A formal decision made by the jury.

Hung Jury A jury whose members are so irreconcilably divided in their opinions that they cannot reach a verdict.

***Allen* Charge** An instruction by a judge to a deadlocked jury with only a few dissenters that asks the jurors in the minority to reconsider the majority opinion.

In 2009, the murder trial of John Katehis, left, for stabbing New York radio reporter George Weber fifty times ended in a hung jury. Following a second trial in 2011, Katehis was convicted and sentenced to twenty-five years to life in prison. Why should trials that end in a hung jury not "count" for purposes of double jeopardy?

AP Photo/Robert Mecea

Appeal The process of seeking a higher court's review of a lower court's decision for the purpose of correcting or changing this decision.

Double Jeopardy To twice place at risk (jeopardize) a person's life or liberty. The Fifth Amendment to the U.S. Constitution prohibits a second prosecution in the same court for the same criminal offense.

Habeas Corpus An order that requires corrections officials to bring an inmate before a court or a judge and explain why she or he is being held in prison.

Learning Objective **8** List the five basic steps of an appeal.

APPEALS

Even if a defendant is found guilty, the trial process is not necessarily over. In our criminal justice system, a person convicted of a crime has a right to appeal. An **appeal** is the process of seeking a higher court's review of a lower court's decision for the purpose of correcting or changing the lower court's judgment. A defendant who loses a case in a trial court cannot automatically appeal the conviction. The defendant normally must first be able to show that the trial court acted improperly on a question of law. Common reasons for appeals include the introduction of tainted evidence by the prosecution or faulty jury instructions delivered by the trial judge. In federal courts, about 17 percent of criminal convictions are appealed.[53]

DOUBLE JEOPARDY The appeals process is available only to the defense. If a jury finds the accused not guilty, the prosecution cannot appeal to have the decision reversed. To do so would infringe on the defendant's Fifth Amendment rights against multiple trials for the same offense. This guarantee against being tried a second time for the same crime is known as protection from **double jeopardy.** The prohibition against double jeopardy means that once a criminal defendant is found not guilty of a particular crime, the government may not reindict the person and retry him or her for the same crime.

There are several nuances to this rule, however. First, a state's prosecution does not prevent a separate federal prosecution of the same crime, and vice versa. Second, acquitted defendants can be sued in *civil* court for circumstances arising from the alleged wrongdoing on the theory that they are not being tried for the same *crime* twice. Third, a hung jury is *not* an acquittal for purposes of double jeopardy. So, if a jury is deadlocked, the government is free to seek a new trial.

THE APPEAL PROCESS There are two basic reasons for the appeal process. The first is to correct an error made during the initial trial. The second is to review policy. Because of this second function, the appellate courts are an important part of the flexible nature of the criminal justice system. When existing law has ceased to be effective or no longer reflects the values of society, an appellate court can effectively change the law through its decisions and the precedents that it sets.[54] A classic example was the *Miranda v. Arizona* decision (see page 180), which, although it failed to change the fate of the defendant (he was found guilty on retrial), had a far-reaching impact on custodial interrogation of suspects.

It is also important to understand that once the appeal process begins, the defendant is no longer presumed innocent. The burden of proof has shifted, and the defendant is obligated to prove that her or his conviction should be overturned. The method of filing an appeal differs slightly among the fifty states and the federal government, but the five basic steps are similar enough for summarization in Figure 8.8 on the facing page. For the most part, defendants are not required to exercise their right to appeal. The one exception involves the death sentence. Given the seriousness of capital punishment, the defendant is required to appeal the case, regardless of his or her wishes.

HABEAS CORPUS Even after the appeals process is exhausted, a convict may have access to one final procedure, known as **habeas corpus** (Latin for "you have the body"). *Habeas corpus* is a judicial order that commands a corrections official to bring a prisoner before

FIGURE 8.8 The Steps of an Appeal

1. The defendant, or *appellant*, files a **notice of appeal**—a short written statement outlining the basis of the appeal.

2. The appellant transfers the trial court record to the appellate court. This record contains items such as evidence and a transcript of the testimony.

3. Both parties file **briefs**. A brief is a written document that presents the party's legal arguments.

4. Attorneys from both sides present **oral arguments** before the appellate court.

5. Having heard from both sides, the judges of the appellate court retire to deliberate the case and make their decision. As described in Chapter 7, this decision is issued as a **written opinion.** Appellate courts generally do one of the following:
   - **Uphold** the decision of the lower court.
   - **Modify** the lower court's decision by changing only a part of it.
   - **Reverse** the decision of the lower court.
   - **Reverse and remand** the case, meaning that the matter is sent back to the lower court for further proceedings.

a federal court so that the court can hear the convict's claim that he or she is being held illegally. A writ of *habeas corpus* differs from an appeal in that it can be filed only by someone who is imprisoned.

WRONGFUL CONVICTIONS

The appeals process is primarily concerned with "legal innocence." That is, appeals courts focus on how the law was applied in a case, rather than on the facts of the case. But what if a defendant who is factually innocent has been found guilty at trial? For the most part, such **wrongful convictions** can be righted only with the aid of new evidence suggesting the defendant's innocence. When such new evidence is uncovered, a prosecutor's office can choose to reopen the case in order to acquit. Or, the defendant's attorneys can use the *habeas corpus* procedure described above to restart court proceedings.

Wrongful Conviction The conviction, either by verdict or by guilty plea, of a person who is factually innocent of the charges.

In Chapter 5, we saw how DNA fingerprinting has been a boon for law enforcement. According to the Innocence Project, a New York–based legal group, as of August 2012, the procedure has also led to the exoneration of 297 convicts in the United States.[55] For example, in 1986, Michael Morton was wrongly convicted of murdering his wife in Williamson County, Texas. Morton subsequently spent twenty-five years in prison before tests of DNA on a bloody blue bandana found near the murder scene showed his wife's blood mingled with the blood of another suspect. Acting on this new evidence, on October 4, 2011, a district judge set Morton free.

SELFASSESSMENT

Fill in the blanks and check your answers on page 247.

Once both the prosecution and the defense have completed their closing arguments, the judge will give the jury a _____ summing up the case and providing instructions on how to proceed. After the jury has _____ and reached a decision, it will announce a _____ of guilty or not guilty. If the jury cannot do so, a _____ jury occurs, and the judge will call a mistrial. If a defendant is convicted, he or she has the option of _____ this outcome based on a showing that the trial court acted improperly on a question of _____, not fact, during the proceedings.

CHAPTER SUMMARY

Learning Objective 1 **Identify the steps involved in the pre-trial criminal process.** (a) Suspect taken into custody or arrested; (b) initial appearance before a magistrate, at which time the defendant is informed of his or her constitutional rights and a public defender may be appointed or private counsel may be hired by the state to represent the defendant; (c) the posting of bail or release on recognizance; (d) preventive detention (if deemed necessary to ensure the safety of other persons or the community) or regular detention (if the defendant is unable to post bail); (e) preliminary hearing (mini-trial), at which the judge rules on whether there is probable cause and the prosecutor issues an information; or, alternatively, (f) grand jury hearings, after which an indictment is issued against the defendant if the grand jury finds probable cause; (g) arraignment, in which the defendant is informed of the charges and must respond by pleading not guilty or guilty (or in some cases *nolo contendere*); and (h) plea bargaining.

Learning Objective 2 **Explain how a prosecutor screens potential cases.** (a) Is there sufficient evidence for conviction? (b) What is the priority of the case? The more serious the alleged crime, the higher the priority. The more extensive the defendant's criminal record, the higher the priority. (c) Are the victims cooperative? Violence against family members often yields uncooperative victims, so these cases are rarely prosecuted. (d) Might the defendant be willing to testify against other offenders? (e) Are the victims reliable?

Learning Objective 3 **Indicate why prosecutors, defense attorneys, and defendants often agree to plea bargains.** For prosecutors, a plea bargain removes the risk of losing the case at trial, particularly if the evidence against the defendant is weak. For defense attorneys, the plea bargain may be the best deal possible for a potentially guilty client. For defendants, plea bargains give a measure of control over a highly uncertain future.

Learning Objective 4 **Identify the basic protections enjoyed by criminal defendants in the United States.** According to the Sixth Amendment, a criminal defendant has the right to a speedy and public trial by an impartial jury in the physical location where the crime was committed. Additionally, a person accused of a crime must be informed of the nature of the crime and be confronted with the witnesses against him or her. Further, the accused must be able to summon witnesses in her or his favor and have the assistance of counsel.

Learning Objective 5 **Explain what "taking the Fifth" really means.** The Fifth Amendment states that no person "shall be compelled in any criminal case to be a witness against himself." Thus, defendants do not have to testify if their testimony would implicate them in the crime. Witnesses may refuse to testify on this same ground. (Witnesses, though, are often granted immunity and thereafter can no longer take the Fifth.) In the United States, silence on the part of a defendant cannot be used by the jury in forming its opinion about guilt or innocence.

Learning Objective 6 **Contrast challenges for cause and peremptory challenges during *voir dire*.** A challenge for cause occurs when an attorney provides the court with a legally justifiable reason why a potential juror should be excluded—for example, the juror does not understand English. In contrast, peremptory challenges do not require any justification by the attorney and are usually limited to a small number. They cannot, however, be based, even implicitly, on race or gender.

Learning Objective 7 **Explain the difference between testimony and real evidence, between lay witnesses and expert witnesses, and between direct and circumstantial evidence.** Testimony consists of statements by competent witnesses, whereas real evidence includes physical items that affect the case. A lay witness is an "average person," whereas an expert witness speaks with the authority of one who has professional training, advanced knowledge, or substantial experience in a specialized area. Direct evidence is evidence presented by witnesses; circumstantial evidence can create an inference that a fact exists, but it does not directly establish the fact.

Learning Objective 8 **List the five basic steps of an appeal.** (a) The filing of a notice of appeal; (b) the transfer of the trial court record to the appellate court; (c) the filing of briefs; (d) the presentation of oral arguments; and (e) the issuance of a written opinion by the appellate judges, upholding the decision of the lower court, modifying part of the decision, reversing the decision, or reversing and remanding the case to the trial court.

QUESTIONS FOR CRITICAL ANALYSIS

1. Suppose that a billionaire investment adviser is arrested for defrauding her clients out of millions of dollars. Should she be released on recognizance, released on bail, or denied bail before her trial? Why? How do bail issues for white-collar criminals differ from those for violent criminals?

2. Do you think that a prosecutor should offer a favorable plea bargain to a defendant who provides helpful information concerning a different defendant? What are the pros and cons of this practice?

3. How might the "CSI effect" (see page 237) have a positive impact on criminal trials from the standpoint of both prosecutor preparation and juror interest?

4. Police find a critically wounded man lying in the parking lot of a gas station. When they ask him what happened, he indicates that the defendant shot him. Then, the man dies. Should the dead man's identification of his killer be allowed in court? Before answering, review the concepts of hearsay (page 238) and the confrontation clause (page 239). (To see how the United States Supreme Court ruled in a similar case, go to **www.scotusblog .com/case-files/cases/michigan-v-bryant**.)

5. Why is the appeals process so important to the American criminal justice system? What would be some of the consequences if criminal defendants did not have the ability to appeal questionable convictions?

KEY TERMS

acquittal **229**

Allen Charge **243**

appeal **244**

arraignment **223**

bail **217**

bail bond agent **219**

bench trial **228**

Boykin form **226**

case attrition **221**

challenge for cause **232**

charge **242**

circumstantial evidence **237**

closing arguments **241**

confrontation clause **239**

cross-examination **239**

direct evidence **236**

direct examination **238**

discovery **220**

double jeopardy **244**

evidence **235**

expert witness **236**

grand jury **220**

habeas corpus **244**

hearsay **238**

hung jury **243**

indictment **221**

information **220**

initial appearance **217**

jury trial **228**

lay witness **236**

master jury list **231**

nolo contendere **224**

opening statements **235**

peremptory challenges **232**

plea bargaining **224**

preliminary hearing **220**

preventive detention **219**

property bond **219**

real evidence **235**

rebuttal **241**

release on recognizance (ROR) **219**

relevant evidence **237**

statute of limitations **228**

testimony **235**

venire **231**

verdict **243**

voir dire **232**

wrongful conviction **245**

SELF ASSESSMENT ANSWER KEY

Page 219: i. initial appearance; **ii.** constitutional; **iii.** bail; **iv.** judge; **v.** preventive

Page 221: i. probable cause; **ii.** preliminary; **iii.** grand jury; **iv.** indictment

Page 223: i. attrition; **ii.** screen; **iii.** conviction; **iv.** evidence

Page 227: i. plea bargain; **ii.** charges; **iii.** sentence; **iv.** *Boykin;* **v.** trial

Page 231: i. jury; **ii.** bench; **iii.** judge; **iv.** self-incrimination; **v.** innocent; **vi.** guilty; **vii.** state/prosecutor; **viii.** reasonable doubt

Page 235: i. *venire;* **ii.** *voir dire;* **iii.** cause; **iv.** peremptory; **v.** race; **vi.** gender

Page 242: i. testimony; **ii.** fact; **iii.** relevant; **iv.** prejudice; **v.** direct; **vi.** cross; **vii.** reasonable doubt

Page 245: i. charge; **ii.** deliberated; **iii.** verdict; **iv.** hung; **v.** appealing; **vi.** law

COURSEMATE

For online help and access to resources that accompany *Criminal Justice in Action: The Core*, go to **www.cengage-brain.com/shop/ISBN/978-1-285-06915-9**. Click "Access Now," where you will find flashcards, an online quiz, and other helpful study aids. If you have an access code for CourseMate, log in and go to the chapter of your choice for additional online study aids.

NOTES

1. Quoted in Jenna Johnson and Mary Pat Flaherty, "Juror: Jury Split over Huguely's Intent," *Winchester (Virginia) Star* (February 27, 2012), A3.

2. Lawrence M. Friedman and Robert V. Percival, *The Roots of Justice* (Chapel Hill, NC: University of North Carolina Press, 1981).

3. *Riverside County, California v. McLaughlin*, 500 U.S. 44 (1991).

4. Bureau of Justice Statistics, *Pretrial Release of Felony Defendants in State Courts* (Washington, D.C.: U.S. Department of Justice, November 2007), 2.

5. Todd R. Clear, George F. Cole, and Michael D. Reisig, *American Corrections*, 10th ed. (Belmont, CA: Wadsworth, 2013), 173.

6. *Gerstein v. Pugh*, 420 U.S. 103 (1975).

7. Kenneth C. Davis, *Discretionary Justice: A Preliminary Inquiry* (Baton Rouge, LA: Louisiana State University Press, 1969), 189.

8. Ryan Blitstein, "Online Crooks Often Escape Prosecution," *San Jose Mercury News* (November 18, 2007), 1A.

9. Henry K. Lee, "D.A. Cuts Efforts on Lesser Crimes," *San Francisco Chronicle* (April 22, 2009), B1.

10. Milton Hirsh and David Oscar Markus, "Fourth Amendment Forum," *Champion* (December 2002), 42.

11. Barbara Boland, Paul Mahanna, and Ronald Scones, *The Prosecution of Felony Arrests, 1988* (Washington, D.C.: Bureau of Justice Statistics, 1992).

12. Richard Felson and Paul-Philippe Pare, *The Reporting of Domestic Violence and Sexual Assault by Nonstrangers to the Police* (Washington, D.C.: U.S. Department of Justice, March 2005), 6.

13. Tom Lininger, "Evidentiary Issues in Federal Prosecutions of Violence against Women," *Indiana Law Review* 36 (2003), 709.

14. 18 U.S.C. Section 3553(e) (2006).

15. William K. Rashbaum and John Elgion, "District Attorney Asks Judge to Drop Strauss-Kahn Case," *New York Times* (August 23, 2011), A1.

16. 404 U.S. 257 (1971).

17. Fred C. Zacharias, "Justice in Plea Bargaining," *William and Mary Law Review* 39 (March 1998), 1121.

18. Bureau of Justice Statistics, *Prosecutors in State Courts, 2007—Statistical Tables* (Washington, D.C.: U.S. Department of Justice, December 2011), 2.

19. Albert W. Alschuler, "The Prosecutor's Role in Plea Bargaining," *University of Chicago Law Review* 36 (1968), 52.

20. Milton Heumann, *Plea Bargaining: The Experiences of Prosecutors, Judges, and Defense Attorneys* (Chicago: University of Chicago Press, 1978), 58.

21. Albert W. Alschuler, "The Defense Attorney's Role in Plea Bargaining," *Yale Law Journal* 84 (1975), 1200.

22. Stephen J. Schulhofer, "Plea Bargaining as Disaster," *Yale Law Journal* 101 (1992), 1987.

23. 395 U.S. 238 (1969).

24. 407 U.S. 514 (1972).

25. 725 Illinois Compiled Statutes Section 5/103-5 (1992).

26. Bureau of Justice Statistics, *Felony Defendants in Large Urban Counties, 2006* (Washington, D.C.: U.S. Department of Justice, May 2010), Table 10, page 10.

27. 18 U.S.C. Section 3161.

28. 391 U.S. 145 (1968).

29. *Blanton v. Las Vegas*, 489 U.S. 538 (1989).

30. *Apodaca v. Oregon*, 406 U.S. 404 (1972); and *Lee v. Louisiana*, No. 07-1523 (2008).

31. 332 U.S. 46 (1947).

32. Barton L. Ingraham, "The Right of Silence, the Presumption of Innocence, the Burden of Proof, and a Modest Proposal," *Journal of Criminal Law and Criminology* 85 (1994), 559–595.

33. 397 U.S. 358 (1970).

34. 380 U.S. 224 (1965).

35. 476 U.S. 79 (1986).

36. Eric L. Muller, "Solving the *Batson* Paradox: Harmless Error, Jury Representation, and the Sixth Amendment," *Yale Law Journal* 106 (October 1996), 93.

37. 499 U.S. 400 (1991).

38. 502 U.S. 1056 (1992).

39. *Snyder v. Louisiana*, 552 U.S. 472 (2008).

40. 511 U.S. 127 (1994).

41. Harry Kalven and Hans Zeisel, *The American Jury* (Boston: Little, Brown, 1966), 163–167.

42. Douglas D. Koski, "Testing the Story Model of Juror Decision Making," *Sex Offender Law* (June/July 2003), 53–58.

43. Nancy Pennington and Reid Hastie, "The Story Model for Juror Decision Making," in *Inside the Juror: The Psychology of Juror Decision Making* (Cambridge, MA: Harvard University Press, 1983), 192, 194–195.

44. Donald E. Shelton, "Juror Expectations for Scientific Evidence in Criminal Cases: Perceptions and Reality about the 'CSI Effect' Myth," *Thomas M. Cooley Law Review* 27 (2010), at **lawreview.tmc.cooley.edu/ Resources/Documents/1_27-1%20 Shelton%20Article.pdf**.

45. Kyle Hightower, "Defense Focuses on DNA in Anthony Trial," *Associated Press* (June 16, 2011).

46. Thomas J. Reed, "Trial by Propensity: Admission of Other Criminal Acts Evidenced in Federal Criminal Trials," *University of Cincinnati Law Review* 50 (1981), 713.

47. *Ibid.*

48. *People v. Zackowitz*, 254 N.Y. 192 (1930).

49. Colleen Cury, "Rutgers Trial: Jury Won't Hear Why Tyler Clementi Wanted Room Change," *ABC News* (February 27, 2012).

50. David W. Broeder, "The University of Chicago Jury Project," *Nebraska Law Review* 38 (1959), 744–760.

51. 164 U.S. 492 (1896).

52. *United States v. Fioravanti*, 412 F.2d 407 (3d Cir. 1969).

53. Bureau of Justice Statistics, *Federal Justice Statistics, 2008—Statistical Tables* (Washington, D.C.: U.S. Department of Justice, November 2010), Table 5.2 and Table 6.1.

54. David W. Neubauer, *America's Courts and the Criminal Justice System*, 5th ed. (Belmont, CA: Wadsworth, 1996), 254.

55. The Innocence Project, "Innocence Project Case Files," at **www.innocenceproject.org/ know**.

CHAPTER

9

Punishment and Sentencing

AP Photo/John O'Boyle, Pool

CHAPTER OUTLINE

- The Purpose of Sentencing
- The Structure of Sentencing
- Inconsistencies in Sentencing
- Sentencing Reform
- Capital Punishment—The Ultimate Sentence

LEARNING OBJECTIVES

After reading this chapter, you should be able to...

1 List and contrast the four basic philosophical reasons for sentencing criminals.

2 Contrast indeterminate with determinate sentencing.

3 List the four primary forms of punishment available to the judge.

4 State who has input into the sentencing decision and list the factors that determine a sentence.

5 Explain some of the reasons why sentencing reform has occurred.

6 Identify the arguments for and against the use of victim impact statements during sentencing hearings.

7 Identify the two stages that make up the bifurcated process of death penalty sentencing.

8 Describe the main issues of the death penalty debate.

Throughout the chapter you will see each learning objective repeated in the margin next to the content it relates to. The chapter summary on page 279 includes all of the learning objectives for review.

A LIFETIME FOR LOOKING

Daniel Vilca's conviction for possession of child pornography came as no great surprise. After all, Collier County, Florida, sheriff's investigators had found plenty of evidence. A computer in the twenty-six-year-old's East Naples apartment contained about three hundred photos and thirty taped hours of sexually explicit content involving children. Vilca's case gained nationwide attention, however, when, on November 3, 2011, a circuit county judge sentenced Vilca to life in prison without parole for his crimes.

Does a child pornographer deserve the same punishment as someone found guilty of first degree murder? Technically, yes. Under Florida law, possession of child pornography is a third degree felony, punishable by as many as five years behind bars. Because Vilca was charged with 454 counts of possession—one for each image found on his computer—the judge had little choice but to impose a lengthy sentence. Regardless, many questioned the fairness of Vilca's fate. Lee Hollander, Vilca's defense attorney, said, "Life in prison for looking at images, even child images, is beyond comprehension."

Within the criminal justice system, opinions about the proper punishment for child pornography–related crimes vary widely. A recent poll of federal judges found that 70 percent believe the sentencing requirements for child pornography defendants are too harsh. Ingrid Cronin, a federal public defender, points out that defendants such as Vilca often receive longer prison terms than those who are caught "actually having sex with a child." Florida assistant state attorney Steve Marseca, who prosecuted Vilca, counters that real children are harmed in the production of these images. "Too many people look at this as a victimless crime, and that's not true," he said. "These children are victimized, and when the images are shown over and over again, they're victimized over and over again."

Daniel Vilca, shown here in a Collier County (Florida) courtroom, was sentenced to life in prison without parole for possessing a large cache of child pornography.

Greg Kahn/Naples Daily News

One problem with child pornography laws, say critics, is that they were written under the assumption that it takes time and effort to obtain sexually explicit images of children. Taking such time and effort, it was assumed, indicated a particularly dangerous form of deviance. While this might once have been the case, with the advent of the Internet, hundreds or even thousands of explicit images can be downloaded in a short time. When each image represents a single criminal count, the resulting punishment can be quite severe, as was the case with Daniel Vilca.[1]

Furthermore, there is considerable debate concerning the link between child pornography and child molestation. On the one hand, some research identifies child pornographers as generally passive viewers of illicit images who rarely engage in the sexual assault of children.[2] On the other hand, a recent study conducted at a North Carolina prison found that 85 percent of those convicted of possessing child pornography had also engaged in at least one "hands-on" sexual offense against a minor.[3] This finding would suggest that a harsher approach is justified to deter potential sexual abusers. The authors of that study, however, cautioned against a one-size-fits-all approach, pointing out that "we know less about online child pornographers than many other types of offenders."[4]

As you can see, punishment and sentencing present some of the most complex issues of the criminal justice system. One scholar has even asserted:

There is no such thing as "accurate" sentencing; there are only sentences that are more or less just, more or less effective. Nothing in the recent or distant history of sentencing reform suggests that anything approaching perfection is attainable.[5]

In this chapter, we will discuss the various attempts to "perfect" the practice of sentencing over the past century. We will particularly focus on recent national and state efforts to limit judicial discretion in this area, a trend that has had the overall effect of producing harsher sentences for many offenders. In addition, we will examine the issues surrounding the death penalty, a controversial subject that forces us to confront the basic truth of sentencing: the way we punish criminals says a great deal about the kind of people we are.

THE PURPOSE OF SENTENCING

Learning Objective 1 List and contrast the four basic philosophical reasons for sentencing criminals.

Professor Herbert Packer of Stanford University said that punishing criminals serves two ultimate purposes: the "deserved infliction of suffering on evil doers" and "the prevention of crime."[6] Even this straightforward assessment raises several questions. How does one determine the sort of punishment that is "deserved"? How can we be sure that certain penalties "prevent" crime? Should criminals be punished solely for the good of society, or should their well-being also be taken into consideration? Sentencing laws indicate how any given group of people has answered these questions, but do not tell us why they were answered in that manner. To understand why, we must first consider the four basic philosophical reasons for sentencing—retribution, deterrence, incapacitation, and rehabilitation. (For an introduction to these concepts, see Figure 9.1 below.)

RETRIBUTION

The oldest and most common justification for punishing someone is that he or she "deserved it"—as the Old Testament states, "an eye for an eye and a tooth for a tooth." Under a system of justice that favors **retribution,** a wrongdoer who has freely chosen to violate society's rules must be punished for the infraction. Retribution relies on the principle of **just deserts,** which holds that the severity of the punishment must be in proportion to the severity of the crime. Retributive justice is not the same as *revenge*. Whereas revenge implies that the wrongdoer is punished only with the aim of satisfying a victim or victims, retribution is more concerned with the needs of society as a whole.

Retribution The philosophy that those who commit criminal acts should be punished based on the severity of the crime and that no other factors need be considered.

Just Deserts A sanctioning philosophy based on the assertion that criminals deserve to be punished for breaking society's rules.

FIGURE 9.1 Sentencing Philosophies

Recently, a judge sentenced Eric Stefanski to a five-year prison term for shoplifting $622 worth of clothing from a Macy's department store in Kahului, Hawaii. Although the sentence may seem harsh, Stefanski was a repeat offender participating in a drug court program at the time of his arrest. Thus, his punishment was in keeping with the four main philosophies of sentencing.

Retribution	Punishment is society's means of expressing condemnation of illegal acts such as shoplifting. Repeat offenders should be punished more harshly because of their continuing criminal behavior.
Deterrence	Harsh sentences for shoplifting may convince others not to engage in that behavior. Also, when Stefanski has completed his sentence, he will avoid repeating his crimes because he will want to avoid returning to prison.
Incapacitation	While he is in prison, Stefanski will be unable to commit more crimes.
Rehabilitation	Stefanski's shoplifting may be connected to his substance abuse. While in prison, he can participate in drug treatment programs to address this problem.

> ## "Men are not hanged for stealing horses, but that horses may not be stolen."
>
> —**Marquis de Halifax,**
> *Political Thoughts and Reflections* (1750)

One problem with retributive ideas of justice lies in proportionality. Whether or not one agrees with the death penalty, the principle behind it is easy to fathom: the punishment (death) often fits the crime (murder). But what about the theft of an automobile? How does one fairly determine the amount of time the thief must spend in prison for that crime? Should the type of car or the wealth of the car owner matter? Theories of retribution often have a difficult time providing answers to such questions.[7]

DETERRENCE

Deterrence The strategy of preventing crime through the threat of punishment.

Incapacitation A strategy for preventing crime by detaining wrongdoers in prison, thereby separating them from the community and reducing criminal opportunities.

The concept of **deterrence** (as well as incapacitation and rehabilitation) takes a different approach than does retribution. That is, rather than seeking only to punish the wrongdoer, the goal of sentencing should be to prevent future crimes. By "setting an example," society is sending a message to potential criminals that certain actions will not be tolerated. Deterrence can take two forms: general and specific. The basic idea of *general deterrence* is that by punishing one person, others will be discouraged from committing a similar crime. *Specific deterrence* assumes that an individual, after being punished once for a certain act, will be less likely to repeat that act because she or he does not want to be punished again.[8]

Both forms of deterrence have proved problematic in practice. General deterrence assumes that a person commits a crime only after a rational decision-making process, in which he or she implicitly weighs the benefits of the crime against the possible costs of the punishment. This is not necessarily the case, especially for young offenders who tend to value the immediate rewards of crime over the possible future consequences. The argument for specific deterrence is somewhat weakened by the fact that a relatively small number of habitual offenders are responsible for the majority of certain criminal acts.

INCAPACITATION

In a Santa Ana, California, courtroom, Andrew Gallo reacts to his sentence of fifty-one years in prison for killing three people in a drunk driving automobile accident. How do theories of deterrence and incapacitation justify Gallo's punishment?

AP Photo/Mark Rightmire, Pool

"Wicked people exist," said James Q. Wilson. "Nothing avails except to set them apart from innocent people."[9] Wilson's blunt statement summarizes the justification for **incapacitation** as a form of punishment. As a purely practical matter, incarcerating criminals guarantees that they will not be a danger to society, at least for the length of their prison terms. At some level, the death penalty can also be justified in terms of incapacitation, as it prevents the offender from committing any future crimes.

Several studies do support incapacitation's efficacy as a crime-fighting tool. Criminologist Isaac Ehrlich of the University of Buffalo estimated that a 1 percent increase in sentence length will produce a 1 percent decrease in the crime rate.[10] University of Chicago professor Steven Levitt has noticed a trend that further supports incapacitation. He found that violent crime rates rise in communities where inmate litigation over prison overcrowding has forced the early release of some inmates and a subsequent drop in the prison population.[11] More recently, Avinash

Singh Bhati of the Urban Institute in Washington, D.C., found that higher levels of incarceration lead to fewer violent crimes but have little impact on property crime rates.[12]

Incapacitation as a theory of punishment does suffer from several weaknesses. Unlike retribution, it offers no proportionality with regard to a particular crime. Giving a burglar a life sentence would certainly ensure that she or he would not commit another burglary. Does that justify such a severe penalty? Furthermore, incarceration protects society only until the criminal is freed. Many studies have shown that, on release, offenders may actually be more likely to commit crimes than before they were imprisoned.[13] In that case, incapacitation may increase the likelihood of crime, rather than diminish it.

REHABILITATION

For most of the past century, **rehabilitation** has been seen as the most "humane" goal of punishment. This line of thinking reflects the view that crime is a "social phenomenon" caused not by the inherent criminality of a person but by factors in that person's surroundings. By removing wrongdoers from their environment and intervening to change their values and personalities, the rehabilitative model suggests, criminals can be "treated" and possibly even "cured" of their proclivities toward crime.[14]

Although studies of the effectiveness of rehabilitation are too varied to be easily summarized, it does appear that, under certain circumstances, criminals who receive treatment are less likely to reoffend than those who do not. (See the feature *Comparative Criminal Justice—The Norwegian Way* below to learn about a country where a national commitment to rehabilitation shapes sentencing practices.)

Rehabilitation The philosophy that society is best served when wrongdoers are provided the resources needed to eliminate criminality from their behavioral pattern.

COMPARATIVE CRIMINAL JUSTICE

THE NORWEGIAN WAY

On July 22, 2011, thirty-three-year-old Anders Behring Breivik fatally shot sixty-nine people on Utoya Island off the coast of Norway. He also claimed responsibility for a bomb attack that killed another eight people in the capital city of Oslo. After a seven-month investigation, Norwegian prosecutors charged Breivik with committing a terrorist act. In the United States, Breivik would almost certainly face the death penalty for his multiple, violent offenses.

In Norway, however, a terror charge carries a maximum sentence of twenty-one years in prison. Indeed, the maximum sentence for most crimes in Norway, including premeditated murder, is twenty-one years. Like all European countries, Norway prohibits the death penalty, and it has also abolished the life sentence as a possible form of punishment. This reflects the Norwegian criminal justice system's focus on rehabilitation rather than retribution or incapacitation. The goal in Norway is to return offenders to—rather than separate them from—society.

Extended Stay

In August 2012, as expected, Breivik received the maximum twenty-one year prison sentence. Theoretically, he could remain incarcerated for the rest of his life. Norwegian law allows prison terms to be extended for periods of five years at a time if the offender remains a threat to society. Still, the incident seems to have shaken the country's confidence in its system of punishment, which sees few offenders spending more than fourteen years behind bars. In a poll conducted six days after Breivik's attacks, 65 percent of Norwegians said that the penalties for serious crimes in their country were "too low."

FOR CRITICAL ANALYSIS Norway's murder rate is minuscule—about 0.7 murders per 100,000 people. By comparison, the murder rate in the United States is 4.8 per 100,000. Similarly, violent crime is much more common in the United States than in Norway. How do you think these differences shape the two nations' divergent sentencing philosophies?

RESTORATIVE JUSTICE

Despite the emergence of victim impact statements, which we will discuss later in the chapter, victims have historically been restricted from participating in the punishment process. Such restrictions are supported by the general assumption that victims are focused on vengeance rather than justice. According to criminologists Heather Strang of Australia's Center for Restorative Justice and Lawrence W. Sherman of the University of Pennsylvania, however, this is not always the case. After the initial shock of the crime has worn off, Strang and Sherman have found, victims are more interested in three things that have little to do with revenge: (1) an opportunity to participate in the process, (2) financial reparations, and (3) an apology.[15]

Restorative justice strategies focus on these concerns by attempting to repair the damage that a crime does to the victim, the victim's family, and society as a whole. This outlook relies on the efforts of the offender to "undo" the harm caused by the criminal act through an apology and **restitution,** or monetary compensation for losses suffered by the victim or victims.

The amount of restitution is sometimes determined through *victim-offender mediation,* a process that involves a face-to-face meeting between the two parties of the crime. Usually only available when the underlying offense is a property crime or minor assault, this form of intercession allows the victim to speak directly to the offender about the criminal incident, and for the offender to apologize directly to the victim. Although victim-offender mediation services are not universally available, research suggests that the experience is often satisfying for both parties.[16]

Restorative Justice An approach to punishment designed to repair the harm done to the victim and the community by the offender's criminal act.

Restitution Monetary compensation for damages done to the victim by the offender's criminal act.

Indeterminate Sentencing An indeterminate term of incarceration in which a judge decides the minimum and maximum terms of imprisonment.

SELFASSESSMENT

Fill in the blanks and check your answers on page 280.

The saying "an eye for an eye and a tooth for a tooth" reflects the concept of _____ as a justification for punishment. The goal of _____ is to prevent future crimes by "setting an example," while _____ purports to prevent crime by keeping offenders behind bars. Models of _____ suggest that criminals can be "treated" and possibly even "cured."

THE STRUCTURE OF SENTENCING

Philosophy not only is integral to explaining *why* we punish criminals, but also influences *how* we do so. The history of criminal sentencing in the United States has been characterized by shifts in institutional power among the three branches of the government. When public opinion moves toward more severe strategies of retribution, deterrence, and incapacitation, legislatures have responded by asserting their power over determining sentencing guidelines. In contrast, periods of rehabilitative justice are marked by a transfer of this power to judges.

Learning Objective 2 Contrast indeterminate with determinate sentencing.

LEGISLATIVE SENTENCING AUTHORITY

Because legislatures are responsible for making laws, these bodies are also initially responsible for passing the criminal codes that determine the length of sentences.

INDETERMINATE SENTENCING For a good part of the twentieth century, goals of rehabilitation dominated the criminal justice system, and legislatures were more likely to enact **indeterminate sentencing** policies. Penal codes with indeterminate sentences set a minimum and maximum amount of time that a person must spend in prison. For example, the indeterminate sentence for aggravated assault can be three to nine years, or six to twelve years, or twenty years to life. Within these parameters, a judge can prescribe a particular term, after which an administrative body known as the *parole board* decides at what point the offender is to be released. A prisoner is aware that he or she is eligible for *parole* as soon as the minimum time has been served and that good behavior can further shorten the sentence.

DETERMINATE SENTENCING Disillusionment with the ideals of rehabilitation has led to **determinate sentencing,** or fixed sentencing. As the name implies, in determinate sentencing an offender serves exactly the amount of time to which she or he is sentenced (minus "good time," described below). For example, if the legislature deems that the punishment for a first-time armed robber is ten years, then the judge has no choice but to impose a sentence of ten years, and the criminal will serve ten years minus good time before being freed.

"GOOD TIME" AND TRUTH IN SENTENCING Often, the amount of time prescribed by a judge bears little relation to the amount of time the offender actually spends behind bars. In states with indeterminate sentencing, parole boards have broad powers to release prisoners once they have served the minimum portion of their sentence. Furthermore, all but four states offer prisoners the opportunity to reduce their sentences by doing **"good time"**—or behaving well—as determined by prison administrators. (See Figure 9.2 below for an idea of the effects of good-time regulations and other early-release programs on state prison sentences.)

Sentence-reduction programs promote discipline within a correctional institution and reduce overcrowding, so many prison officials welcome them. The public, however, may react negatively to news that a violent criminal has served a shorter term than ordered by a judge and pressure elected officials to "do something." In Illinois, for example, some inmates were serving less than half their sentences by receiving a one-day reduction in their term for each day of "good time." Under pressure from victims' groups, the state legislature passed a **truth-in-sentencing law** in 1995 that requires murderers and others

Determinate Sentencing
A period of incarceration that is fixed by a sentencing authority and cannot be reduced by judges or other corrections officials.

"Good Time" A reduction in time served by prisoners based on good conduct, conformity to rules, and other positive behavior.

Truth-in-Sentencing Laws
Legislative attempts to ensure that convicts will serve approximately the terms to which they were initially sentenced.

FIGURE 9.2 Average Sentence Length and Estimated Time to Be Served in State Prison

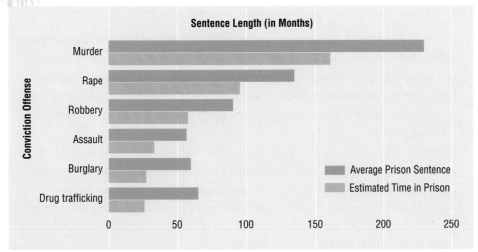

Source: Bureau of Justice Statistics, *National Corrections Reporting Program: Sentence Length of State Prisoners, by Offense, Admission Type, Sex, and Race* (January 20, 2011), "Table 9: First Releases from State Prison, 2008," at bjs.ojp.usdoj.gov/index.cfm?ty=pbdetail&iid=2056.

Judge Dee Anna Farnell of the Pinellas County (Florida) Drug Court tells a drug offender that if she keeps shooting heroin, she's "going to die." What are some of the arguments for giving judges the discretion to make sentencing decisions?
ZUMA Press/Newscom

convicted of serious crimes to complete at least 85 percent of their sentences with no time off for good behavior.[17]

As their name suggests, the primary goal of these truth-in-sentencing laws is to provide the public with more accurate information about the actual amount of time an offender will spend behind bars. They have also found support with those who believe that keeping offenders incapacitated for longer periods of time will reduce crime.[18] Today, forty states have instituted some form of truth-in-sentencing laws, though the future viability of such statutes is somewhat in doubt due to the pressure of overflowing prisons.

JUDICIAL SENTENCING AUTHORITY

During the pretrial procedures and the trial itself, the judge's role is somewhat passive and reactive. She or he is primarily a "procedural watchdog," ensuring that the rights of the defendant are not infringed while the prosecutor and defense attorney dictate the course of action. At a traditional sentencing hearing, however, the judge is no longer an arbiter between the parties. He or she is now called on to exercise the ultimate authority of the state in determining the defendant's fate.

From the 1930s to the 1970s, when theories of rehabilitation held sway over the criminal justice system, indeterminate sentencing practices were guided by the theory of "individualized justice." Just as a physician gives specific treatment to individual patients depending on their particular health needs, the hypothesis goes, a judge needs to consider the specific circumstances of each individual offender in choosing the best form of punishment. Taking the analogy one step further, just as the diagnosis of a qualified physician should not be questioned, a qualified judge should have absolute discretion in making the sentencing decision. *Judicial discretion* rests on the assumption that a judge should be given ample leeway in determining punishments that fit both the crime and the criminal.[19] As we shall see later in the chapter, the growth of determinate sentencing has severely restricted judicial discretion in many jurisdictions.

Learning Objective 3 List the four primary forms of punishment available to the judge.

JUDICIAL DISPOSITIONS Within whatever legislative restrictions apply, the sentencing judge has a number of options when it comes to choosing the proper form of punishment. These sentences, or *dispositions,* include the following:

1. *Capital punishment.* Reserved normally for those who commit first degree murder—that is, a premeditated killing—capital punishment, or the death penalty, is a sentencing option in thirty-three states. It is also an option in federal court, where a defendant can be put to death for murder, as well as for trafficking in a large amount of illegal drugs, *espionage* (spying), and *treason* (betraying the United States).

2. *Imprisonment.* Whether for the purpose of retribution, deterrence, incapacitation, or rehabilitation, a common form of punishment in American history has been imprisonment. In fact, it is used so commonly today that judges—and legislators—are having to take factors such as prison overcrowding into consideration when making sentencing decisions. The issues surrounding imprisonment will be discussed in Chapters 11 and 12.

3. *Probation.* One of the effects of prison overcrowding has been a sharp rise in the use of probation, in which an offender is permitted to live in the community under

supervision and is not incarcerated. (Probation is covered in Chapter 10.) *Alternative sanctions* (also discussed in Chapter 10) combine probation with other dispositions such as electronic monitoring, house arrest, boot camps, and shock incarceration.

4. *Fines.* Fines can be levied by judges in addition to incarceration and probation or independently of other forms of punishment. When a fine is the only punishment, it usually reflects the judge's belief that the offender is not a threat to the community and does not need to be imprisoned or supervised. In some instances, mostly involving drug offenders, a judge can order the seizure of an offender's property, such as his or her home.

After Jason Householder, left, and John Stockum were convicted of criminal damaging for throwing beer bottles at a car, municipal court judge David Hostetler of Coshocton, Ohio, gave them a choice: jail time or a walk down Main Street in women's clothing. As you can see, they chose the dresses. What reasons might a judge have for handing down this sort of "creative" sentence?

AP Photo/Dante Smith/*Coshocton Tribune*

OTHER FORMS OF PUNISHMENT Whereas fines are payable to the government, restitution and *community service* are seen as reparations to the injured party or to the community. Restitution (see page 256) is a direct payment to the victim or victims of a crime. Community service consists of "good works"—such as cleaning up highway litter or tutoring disadvantaged youths—that benefit the entire community. As we saw earlier in this chapter, when the offender has committed a less serious crime, many judges are turning to restorative justice to provide a remedy. At the heart of restorative justice is the apology. So, for example, a judge in Texas required a teenager who had vandalized thirteen schools to go to each school and apologize to the students and faculty.

In some jurisdictions, judges have a great deal of discretionary power and can impose sentences that do not fall into any predetermined category. This "creative sentencing," as it is sometimes called, has produced some interesting results. Teenagers who violate noise ordinances in Fort Lupton, Colorado, have been required to spend Friday nights in a courtroom listening to Barry Manilow, opera, and the "Barney" theme song. A judge in Painesville, Ohio, ordered a man who had stolen from a Salvation Army kettle to pass twenty-four hours as a homeless person. In Broward County, Florida, a man who shoved his wife was sentenced to "take her to Red Lobster," go bowling with her, and then undergo marriage counseling.[20] Though these types of punishments are often ridiculed, many judges see them as a viable alternative to incarceration for less dangerous offenders.

THE SENTENCING PROCESS

The decision of how to punish a wrongdoer is the end result of what Yale Law School professor Kate Stith and federal appeals court judge José A. Cabranes call the "sentencing ritual."[21] The two main participants in this ritual are the judge and the defendant, but prosecutors, defense attorneys, and probation officers also play a role in the proceedings. Individualized justice requires that the judge consider all the relevant circumstances in making sentencing decisions. Therefore, judicial discretion is often tantamount to *informed* discretion—without the aid of the other members of the courtroom work group, the judge would not have sufficient information to make the proper sentencing choice.

THE PRESENTENCE INVESTIGATIVE REPORT For judges operating under various states' indeterminate sentencing guidelines, information in the **presentence investigative report** is a valuable component of the sentencing ritual. Compiled by a probation officer, the report

Presentence Investigative Report An investigative report on an offender's background that assists a judge in determining the proper sentence.

describes the crime in question, notes the suffering of any victims, and lists the defendant's prior offenses (as well as any alleged but uncharged criminal activity). The report also contains a range of personal data such as family background, work history, education, and community activities—information that is not admissible as evidence during trial. In putting together the presentence investigative report, the probation officer is supposed to gain a "feel" for the defendant and communicate these impressions of the offender to the judge.

The report also includes a sentencing recommendation. In the past, this aspect has been criticized as giving probation officers too much power in the sentencing process, because less diligent judges would simply rely on the recommendation in determining punishment.[22] Consequently, many jurisdictions have moved to limit the influence of the presentence investigative report.

THE PROSECUTOR AND DEFENSE ATTORNEY To a certain extent, the adversary process does not end when the guilt of the defendant has been established. Both the prosecutor and the defense attorney are interviewed in the process of preparing the presentence investigative report, and both will try to present a version of the facts consistent with their own sentencing goals. The defense attorney in particular has a duty to make sure that the information contained in the report is accurate and not prejudicial toward his or her client. Depending on the norms of any particular courtroom work group, prosecutors and defense attorneys may petition the judge directly for certain sentences.

Note that this process is not always adversarial. In some instances the prosecutor will advocate leniency and may join the defense attorney in requesting a short term of imprisonment, probation, or some form of intermediate sanction.[23]

SENTENCING AND THE JURY Juries also play an important role in the sentencing process. As we will see later in the chapter, it is the jury, and not the judge, who generally decides whether a convict eligible for the death penalty will in fact be executed. Additionally, six states—Arkansas, Kentucky, Missouri, Oklahoma, Texas, and Virginia—allow juries, rather than judges, to make the sentencing decision even when the death penalty is not an option. In these states, the judge gives the jury instructions on the range of penalties available, and then the jury makes the final decision.[24]

Juries have traditionally been assigned a relatively small role in felony sentencing, largely out of concern that jurors' lack of experience and legal expertise leaves them unprepared for the task. When sentencing by juries is allowed, the practice is popular with prosecutors because jurors are more likely than judges to give harsh sentences, particularly for drug crimes, sexual assault, and theft.[25]

FACTORS OF SENTENCING

The sentencing ritual strongly lends itself to the concept of individualized justice. With inputs—sometimes conflicting—from the prosecutor, attorney, and probation officer, the judge can be reasonably sure of getting the "full picture" of the crime and the criminal. In making the final decision, however, most judges consider two factors above all others: the seriousness of the crime and any mitigating or aggravating circumstances.

THE SERIOUSNESS OF THE CRIME As would be expected, the gravity of the crime is the primary factor in a judge's sentencing decision. The more serious the crime, the harsher the punishment—society demands no less. Each judge has her or his own methods of determining the seriousness of the offense. Many judges simply consider the "conviction offense," basing their sentence on the crime for which the defendant was convicted.

Other judges—some mandated by statute—focus instead on the **"real offense"** in determining the punishment. The "real offense" is based on the actual behavior of the defendant, regardless of the official conviction. For example, through a plea bargain, a defendant may plead guilty to simple assault when in fact he hit his victim in the face with a baseball bat. A judge, after reading the presentence investigative report, could decide to sentence the defendant as if he had committed aggravated assault, which is the "real" offense. Although many prosecutors and defense attorneys are opposed to "real offense" procedures, which can render a plea bargain meaningless, there is a growing belief in criminal justice circles that they bring a measure of fairness to the sentencing decision.[26]

MITIGATING AND AGGRAVATING CIRCUMSTANCES When deciding the severity of punishment, judges and juries are often required to evaluate the *mitigating* and *aggravating circumstances* surrounding the case. **Mitigating circumstances** are those circumstances, such as the fact that the defendant was coerced into committing the crime, that allow a lighter sentence to be handed down. In contrast, **aggravating circumstances,** such as a prior record, blatant disregard for the safety of others, or the use of a weapon, can lead a judge or jury to inflict a harsher penalty than might otherwise be warranted. (See Figure 9.3 below for a list of common aggravating and mitigating circumstances.)

In 2011, for example, twenty-year-old Colton Harris-Moore pleaded guilty to thirty-three charges ranging from burglary to identity theft in a Coupeville, Washington, court. In providing mitigating circumstances for their client's behavior, Harris-Moore's defense attorneys focused on his troubled upbringing by a cruel, alcoholic mother who went for long stretches without feeding her son. Also, a psychiatrist for the defense testified that Harris-Moore's mother drank heavily while pregnant, probably affecting his mental development. Judge Vicki Churchill sentenced Harris-Moore to seven years and three months in prison, well below the punishment requested by prosecutors. "We cannot excuse people because of their upbringing," said Churchill, "but we can recognize that that upbringing has some effect."[27]

"Real Offense" The actual offense committed, as opposed to the charge levied by a prosecutor as the result of a plea bargain.

Mitigating Circumstances Any circumstances accompanying the commission of a crime that may justify a lighter sentence.

Aggravating Circumstances Any circumstances accompanying the commission of a crime that may justify a harsher sentence.

FIGURE 9.3 Aggravating and Mitigating Circumstances

Aggravating Circumstances	Mitigating Circumstances
• An offense involved multiple participants, and the offender was the leader of the group.	• An offender acted under strong provocation, or other circumstances in the relationship between the offender and the victim make the offender's behavior less serious and therefore less deserving of punishment.
• A victim was particularly vulnerable.	• An offender played a minor or passive role in the offense or participated under circumstances of coercion or duress.
• A victim was treated with particular cruelty for which an offender should be held responsible.	• An offender, because of youth or physical impairment, lacked substantial capacity for judgment when the offense was committed.
• The offense involved injury or threatened violence to others and was committed to gratify an offender's desire for pleasure or excitement.	
• The degree of bodily harm caused, attempted, threatened, or foreseen by an offender was substantially greater than average for the given offense.	
• The degree of economic harm caused, attempted, threatened, or foreseen by an offender was substantially greater than average for the given offense.	
• The amount of contraband materials possessed by the offender or under the offender's control was substantially greater than average for the given offense.	

Photodisc

Source: American Bar Association.

JUDICIAL PHILOSOPHY Most states spell out mitigating and aggravating circumstances in statutes, but there is room for judicial discretion in applying the law to particular cases. Judges are not uniform, or even consistent, in their opinions of which circumstances are mitigating or aggravating. One judge may believe that a fourteen-year-old is not fully responsible for her or his actions, while another may believe that teenagers should be treated as adults by criminal courts. Those judges who support rehabilitative theories of criminal justice have been found to give more lenient sentences than those who subscribe to theories of deterrence and incapacitation.[28] Furthermore, judges can have different philosophies with regard to different crimes, handing down, for example, harsh penalties for domestic abusers while showing leniency toward drug offenders.

SELFASSESSMENT

Fill in the blanks and check your answers on page 280.

_____ sentences set a minimum and a maximum amount of time a convict must spend in prison, whereas _____ sentences reflect the exact length of incapacitation, minus reductions for _____ _____, or behaving well. Judges often rely on information contained in the _____ _____ report when making sentencing decisions. The primary factor in the sentencing process is the _____ of the crime for which the defendant was convicted. _____ circumstances allow a lighter sentence to be handed down, while _____ circumstances can lead to the imposition of a harsher penalty.

Learning Objective 5 Explain some of the reasons why sentencing reform has occurred.

INCONSISTENCIES IN SENTENCING

For some, the natural differences in judicial philosophies, when combined with a lack of institutional control, raise important questions. Why should a bank robber in South Carolina and a bank robber in Michigan receive different sentences? Even federal indeterminate sentencing guidelines seem overly vague: a bank robber can receive a prison term from one day to twenty years, depending almost entirely on the judge.[29] Furthermore, if judges have freedom to use their discretion, do they not also have the freedom to misuse it?

Purported improper judicial discretion is often the first reason given for two phenomena that plague the criminal justice system: *sentencing disparity* and *sentencing discrimination*. Although the two terms are often used interchangeably, they describe different statistical occurrences—the causes of which are open to debate.

SENTENCING DISPARITY

Justice would seem to demand that those who commit similar crimes should receive similar punishments. **Sentencing disparity** occurs when this expectation is not met in one of three ways:

1. Criminals receive similar sentences for different crimes of unequal seriousness.
2. Criminals receive different sentences for similar crimes.
3. Mitigating or aggravating circumstances have a disproportionate effect on sentences. Prosecutors, for example, reward drug dealers who inform on their associates with lesser sentences. As a result, low-level drug sellers, who have no information to trade for reduced sentences, often spend more time in prison than their better-informed bosses.[30]

Most of the blame for sentencing disparities is placed at the feet of the judicial profession. Even with the restrictive presence of the sentencing reforms we will discuss

Sentencing Disparity A situation in which those convicted of similar crimes do not receive similar sentences.

shortly, judges have a great deal of influence over the sentencing outcome, whether they are making the decision themselves or instructing the jury on how to do so. Like other members of the criminal justice system, judges are individuals, and their discretionary sentencing decisions reflect that individuality.

For wrongdoers, the amount of time spent in prison often depends as much on where the crime was committed as on the crime itself. A comparison of the sentences for drug trafficking reveals that someone convicted of the crime in the Northern District of California faces an average of 79 months in prison, whereas a similar offender in northern Iowa can expect an average of 148 months.[31]

The average sentences imposed in the Fourth Circuit, which includes North Carolina, South Carolina, Virginia, and West Virginia, are consistently harsher than those in the Ninth Circuit, comprising most of the western states: 57 months longer for firearms violations and 28 months longer for all offenses.[32] Such disparities can be attributed to a number of different factors, including local attitudes toward crime and available financial resources to cover the expenses of incarceration. Also, because of different sentencing guidelines, which we will discuss later in the chapter, the punishment for the same crime in federal and state courts can be dramatically different. Figure 9.4 below shows the sentencing disparities for certain crimes in the two systems.

SENTENCING DISCRIMINATION

Sentencing discrimination occurs when disparities can be attributed to extralegal variables such as the defendant's gender, race, or economic standing.

RACE AND SENTENCING At first glance, racial discrimination would seem to be rampant in sentencing practices. Research by Cassia Spohn of Arizona State University and David Holleran of the College of New Jersey suggests that minorities pay a "punishment penalty" when it comes to sentencing.[33] In Chicago, Spohn and Holleran

Sentencing Discrimination
A situation in which the length of a sentence appears to be influenced by a defendant's race, gender, economic status, or other factor not directly related to the crime he or she committed.

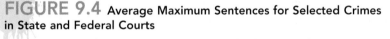

FIGURE 9.4 Average Maximum Sentences for Selected Crimes in State and Federal Courts

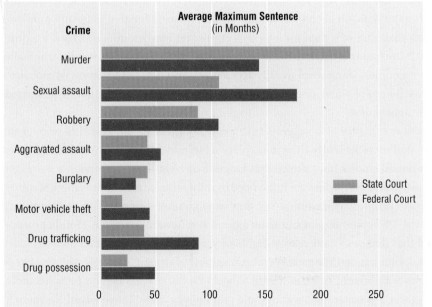

Source: Bureau of Justice Statistics, *Felony Sentences in State Courts, 2006—Statistical Tables* (Washington, D.C.: U.S. Department of Justice, December 2009), Table 1.6, page 9.

Antwain Black, shown here celebrating with his mother, was one of thousands of federal inmates serving time for crack cocaine–related crimes given an early release in 2011. Because about 80 percent of federal crack defendants are African American, the harsh mandatory sentences from crimes involving that drug were widely criticized for being unfair. How does the appearance of discrimination— whether intended or not—harm the legitimacy of the criminal justice system?

AP Photo/Seth Perlman

found that convicted African Americans were 12.1 percent and convicted Hispanics were 15.3 percent more likely to go to prison than convicted whites. In Miami, Hispanics were 10.3 percent more likely to be imprisoned than either blacks or whites.[34] Nationwide, about 43 percent of all inmates in state and federal prisons are African American,[35] even though members of that minority group make up only about 13 percent of the country's population and represent approximately 28 percent of those arrested.[36]

Interestingly, Spohn and Holleran found that the rate of imprisonment rose significantly for minorities who were young and unemployed. This led them to conclude that the disparities between races were not the result of "conscious" discrimination on the part of the sentencing judges. Rather, faced with limited time to make decisions and limited information about the offenders, the judges would resort to stereotypes, considering not just race, but age and unemployment as well.[37] Another study found that older judges and judges who were members of minority groups in Pennsylvania were less likely to send offenders to prison, regardless of their race.[38] Such research findings have been used to support the argument in favor of diversity among judges, discussed in Chapter 7.

WOMEN AND SENTENCING Few would argue that race or ethnicity should be a factor in sentencing decisions—the system should be "color-blind." Does the same principle apply to women? In other words, should the system be "gender-blind" as well—at least on a policy level? Congress answered that question in the Sentencing Reform Act of 1984, which emphasized the ideal of gender-neutral sentencing.[39] In practice, however, this has not occurred. Women who are convicted of crimes are less likely to go to prison than men, and those who are incarcerated tend to serve shorter sentences. According to government data, on average, a woman receives a sentence that is twenty-nine months shorter than that of a man for a violent crime and nine months shorter for a property crime.[40] One study attributes these differences to the elements of female criminality: in property crimes, women are usually accessories, and in violent crimes, women are usually reacting to physical abuse. In both situations, the mitigating circumstances lead to lesser punishment.[41]

Other evidence also suggests that a *chivalry effect,* or the idea that women should be treated more leniently than men, plays a large role in sentencing decisions. Several self-reported studies have shown that judges may treat female defendants more "gently" than males and that judges are influenced by mitigating factors such as marital status and family background with women that they would ignore with men.[42] In certain situations, however, a woman's gender can work against her. Several years ago, Florida prosecutors asked that Emose Oceant receive eighteen years in prison for a child abuse conviction. Instead, circuit judge Margaret Steinbeck sentenced Oceant, who had whipped her seven children with boards, belts, and wire hangers, to thirty years behind bars. According to Keith Crew, a professor of sociology and criminology at the University of Northern Iowa, defendants who are seen as bad mothers often "get the hammer" from judges and juries.[43]

SELFASSESSMENT

Fill in the blanks and check your answers on page 280.

Sentencing _____ occurs when similar crimes are punished with dissimilar sentences, while sentencing _____ is the result of judicial consideration of extralegal variables such as the defendant's race or gender.

SENTENCING REFORM

Judicial discretion, then, appears to be a double-edged sword. Although it allows judges to impose a wide variety of sentences to fit specific criminal situations, it appears to fail to rein in a judge's subjective biases, which can lead to disparity and perhaps discrimination. Critics of judicial discretion believe that its costs (the lack of equality) outweigh its benefits (providing individualized justice). As Columbia law professor John C. Coffee noted:

> If we wish the sentencing judge to treat "like cases alike," a more inappropriate technique for the presentation could hardly be found than one that stresses a novelistic portrayal of each offender and thereby overloads the decisionmaker in a welter of detail.[44]

In other words, Professor Coffee feels that judges are given too much information in the sentencing process, making it impossible for them to be consistent in their decisions. It follows that limiting judicial discretion would not only simplify the process but also lessen the opportunity for disparity or discrimination. Since the 1970s, this attitude has spread through state and federal legislatures, causing more extensive changes in sentencing procedures than in almost any other area of the American criminal justice system over that time period.

SENTENCING GUIDELINES

In an effort to eliminate the inequities of disparity by removing judicial bias from the sentencing process, many states and the federal government have turned to **sentencing guidelines,** which require judges to dispense legislatively determined sentences based on factors such as the seriousness of the crime and the offender's prior record.

Sentencing Guidelines
Legislatively determined guidelines that judges are required to follow when sentencing those convicted of specific crimes.

STATE SENTENCING GUIDELINES In 1978, Minnesota became the first state to create a Sentencing Guidelines Commission with a mandate to construct and monitor the use of a determinate sentencing structure. The Minnesota Commission left no doubt as to the philosophical justification for the new sentencing statutes, stating unconditionally that retribution was its primary goal.[45] Today, about twenty states employ some form of sentencing guidelines with similar goals.

In general, these guidelines remove discretionary power from state judges by turning sentencing into a mathematical exercise. Members of the courtroom work group are guided by a *grid,* which helps them determine the proper sentence. Figure 9.5 on the following page shows a portion of the grid established by the Massachusetts sentencing commission. As in the grids used by most states, one axis ranks the type of crime, while the other refers to the offender's criminal history. In the grid for Massachusetts, the red boxes indicate the "incarceration zone." A prison sentence is required for crimes in this zone. The yellow boxes delineate a "discretionary zone," in which the judge can decide between incarceration or intermediate sanctions, which you will learn about in the next chapter.[46]

FEDERAL SENTENCING GUIDELINES In 1984, Congress passed the Sentencing Reform Act (SRA),[47] paving the way for federal sentencing guidelines that went into effect three

FIGURE 9.5 A Portion of Massachusetts Sentencing Guidelines

Sentencing Guidelines Grid

Level	Illustrative Offenses	Sentence Range				
6	Manslaughter (Involuntary) Armed Robbery (No Gun) A&B DW* (Significant Injury)	40–60 Months	45–67 Months	50–75 Months	60–90 Months	80–120 Months
5	Unarmed Robbery Unarmed Burglary Stalking in Violation of Order Larceny ($50,000 and over)	12–36 Months IS-IV IS-III IS-II	24–36 Months IS-IV IS-III IS-II	36–54 Months	48–72 Months	60–90 Months
	Criminal History Scale	A No/Minor Record	B Moderate Record	C Serious Record	D Violent/Repetitive	E Serious Violent

Intermediate Sanction Levels

IS-IV	24-Hour Restriction
IS-III	Daily Accountability
IS-II	Standard Supervision

*A&B DW = Assault and Battery, Dangerous Weapon

The numbers in each cell represent the range from which the judge selects the maximum sentence (Not More Than). The minimum sentence (Not Less Than) is two-thirds of the maximum sentence and constitutes the initial parole eligibility date.

www.mass.gov/courts/formsandguidelines/sentencing/grid.html

years later. Similar in many respects to the state guidelines, the SRA also eliminated parole for federal prisoners and severely limited early release from prison due to good behavior.[48] The impact of the SRA and the state guidelines has been dramatic. Sentences have become harsher—by the middle of the first decade of the 2000s, the average federal prison sentence was fifty months, more than twice as long as in 1984.[49] Furthermore, much of the discretion in sentencing has shifted from the judge to the prosecutor.

Because the prosecutor chooses the criminal charge, she or he can, in effect, present the judge with the range of sentences. Defendants and their defense attorneys realize this and are more likely to agree to a plea bargain, which is, after all, a "deal" with the prosecutor.[50]

JUDICIAL DEPARTURES Even in their haste to limit a judge's power, legislators realized that sentencing guidelines could not be expected to cover every possible criminal situation. Therefore, both state and federal sentencing guidelines allow an "escape hatch" of limited judicial discretion known as a **departure.**

Departure A stipulation in many federal and state sentencing guidelines that allows a judge to adjust his or her sentencing decision based on the special circumstances of a particular case.

Department Downward Judges in Massachusetts can "depart" from the above grid if a case involves mitigating or aggravating circumstances.[51] Furthermore, the United States Supreme Court has upheld federal judges' freedom to similarly deviate from the federal guidelines.[52] So, for example, federal judge Jack Weinstein acted properly when, in 2010, he overturned a twenty-year sentence for child pornography, ruling that "unless applied with care," the federal requirements "can lead to unreasonable sentences."[53] As we noted in the opening to this chapter, federal judges often react this way to child pornography punishments. Indeed, they depart downward about 40 percent of the time in child pornography cases—more often than in cases involving any other offense.[54]

Increasing Inconsistency Much to the regret of supporters of sentencing reform, a series of Supreme Court decisions handed down midway though the first decade of the 2000s held that federal sentencing guidelines were advisory only.[55] It appears that federal judges have taken advantage of the freedom to deviate from those guidelines. A 2012 study by the Transactional Records Access Clearinghouse found widespread sentencing disparities in federal courts, particularly in drug, weapons, and white-collar cases.[56] Furthermore, the U.S. Sentencing Commission reports that racial disparity in federal courts is again on the rise, with African American male defendants receiving sentences of about 20 percent greater length than white males who have been convicted of similar offenses.[57]

MANDATORY SENTENCING GUIDELINES

In an attempt to close even the limited loophole of judicial discretion offered by departures, politicians (often urged on by their constituents) have passed sentencing laws even more contrary to the idea of individualized justice. These **mandatory** (minimum) **sentencing guidelines** further limit a judge's power to deviate from determinate sentencing laws by setting firm standards for certain crimes. Forty-six states have mandatory sentencing laws for crimes such as selling illegal drugs, driving under the influence of alcohol, and committing any crime with a dangerous weapon. In Alabama, for example, any person caught selling illegal drugs must spend at least two years in prison, with five years added to the sentence if the sale takes place within three miles of a school or public housing.[58] Similarly, Congress has set mandatory minimum sentences for more than one hundred crimes, mostly drug offenses.

As might be expected, such laws are often unpopular with judges. After being forced to send a defendant to prison for fifty-five years for selling marijuana and illegally possessing a handgun, U.S. district judge Paul Cassell called the sentence "unjust, cruel, and irrational."[59]

HABITUAL OFFENDERS **Habitual offender laws** are a form of mandatory sentencing that has become increasingly popular over the past several decades. Also known as "three-strikes-and-you're-out" laws, these statutes require that any person convicted of a third felony must serve a lengthy prison sentence. The crime does not have to be of a violent or dangerous nature. Under Washington's habitual offender law, for example, a "persistent offender" is automatically sentenced to life even if the third felony offense happens to be "vehicular assault" (an automobile accident that causes injury), unarmed robbery, or attempted arson, among other lesser felonies.[60] Today, twenty-six states and the federal government employ "three-strikes" statutes, with varying degrees of severity.

"THREE STRIKES" IN COURT The United States Supreme Court paved the way for these three-strikes laws when it ruled in *Rummel v. Estelle* (1980)[61] that Texas's habitual offender statute did not constitute "cruel and unusual punishment" under the Eighth Amendment. Basically, the Court gave each state the freedom to legislate such laws in the manner that it deems proper.

Twenty-three years later, in *Lockyer v. Andrade* (2003),[62] the Court upheld California's three-strikes law. The California statute allows prosecutors to seek penalties up to life imprisonment without parole on conviction of *any* third felony, including for nonviolent crimes. Leandro Andrade received

Mandatory Sentencing Guidelines Statutorily determined punishments that must be applied to those who are convicted of specific crimes.

Habitual Offender Laws Statutes that require lengthy prison sentences for those who are convicted of multiple felonies.

On August 16, 2010, Gregory Taylor, right, wipes away tears following a judge's decision that he be set free after spending thirteen years in prison. Taylor was serving a potential life sentence for stealing food from a Los Angeles church—his "third strike" under California law. Why might prosecutors seek such a harsh sentence for a seemingly minor crime?

AP Photo/Anne Cusack, Pool

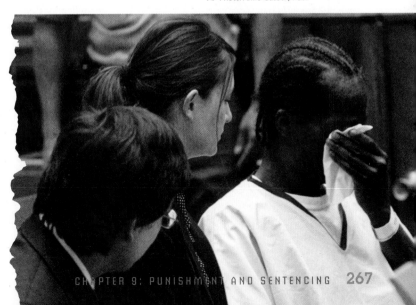

fifty years in prison for stealing $153 worth of videotapes, his fourth felony conviction. A federal appeals court overturned the sentence, agreeing with Andrade's attorneys that it met the definition of cruel and unusual punishment.[63]

In a bitterly divided 5–4 decision, the Supreme Court reversed. Justice Sandra Day O'Connor, writing for the majority, stated that the sentence was not so "objectively" unreasonable that it violated the Constitution.[64] In his dissent, Justice David H. Souter countered that "[i]f Andrade's sentence is not grossly disproportionate, the principle has no meaning."[65] Basically, the justices who upheld the law said that if the California legislature—and by extension the California voters—felt that the law was reasonable, then the judicial branch was in no position to disagree.

VICTIM IMPACT EVIDENCE

The final piece of the sentencing puzzle involves victims and victims' families. As was mentioned in Chapter 2, crime victims traditionally were banished to the peripheries of the criminal justice system. This situation has changed dramatically with the emergence of the victims' rights movement over the past few decades. Victims are now given the opportunity to testify—in person or through written testimony—during sentencing hearings about the suffering they experienced as the result of the crime. These **victim impact statements (VISs)** have proved extremely controversial, however, and even the Supreme Court has had a difficult time determining whether they cause more harm than good.

BALANCING THE PROCESS Every state and federal government has some form of victim impact legislation. In general, these laws allow a victim (or victims) to tell his or her "side of the story" to the sentencing body, be it a judge, jury, or parole officer. In nonhomicide cases, the victim can personally describe the physical, financial, and emotional impact of the crime. When the charge is murder or manslaughter, relatives or friends can give personal details about the victim and describe the effects of her or his death. In almost all instances, the goal of the VIS is to increase the harshness of the sentence.

Most of the debate surrounding VISs centers on their use in the sentencing phases of death penalty cases. Supporters point out that the defendant has always been allowed to present character evidence in the hopes of dissuading a judge or jury from capital punishment. According to some, a VIS balances the equation by giving survivors a voice in the process. Presenting a VIS is also said to have psychological benefits for victims, who are no longer forced to sit in silence as decisions that affect their lives are made by others.[66] Finally, on a purely practical level, a VIS may help judges and juries make informed sentencing decisions by providing them with an understanding of all of the consequences of the crime.

THE RISKS OF VICTIM EVIDENCE Opponents of the use of VISs claim that they interject dangerously prejudicial evidence into the sentencing process, which should be governed by reason, not emotion. The inflammatory nature of VISs, they say, may distract judges and juries from the facts of the case—the only proper basis for a sentence.[67] In fact, research has shown that hearing victim impact evidence makes jurors more likely to impose the death penalty.[68] The Supreme Court, however, has given its approval to the use of VISs, allowing judges to decide whether the statements are admissible on a case-by-case basis just as they do with any other type of evidence.[69]

Victim Impact Statement (VIS) A statement to the sentencing body (judge, jury, or parole board) in which the victim is given the opportunity to describe how the crime has affected her or him.

Learning Objective **6** Identify the arguments for and against the use of victim impact statements during sentencing hearings.

SELFASSESSMENT

Fill in the blanks and check your answers on page 280.

With the aim of limiting judicial discretion, many states and the federal government have enacted sentencing _____. These laws have greatly _____ the length of prison sentences in the United States. The trend toward longer prison terms has also been influenced by _____ - _____ laws, a form of mandatory sentencing that requires increased punishment for a person convicted of multiple felonies.

CAPITAL PUNISHMENT— THE ULTIMATE SENTENCE

"You do not know how hard it is to let a human being die," Abraham Lincoln (1809–1865) once said, "when you feel that a stroke of your pen will save him." Despite these misgivings, during his four years in office Lincoln approved the execution of 267 soldiers, including those who had slept at their posts.[70] Our sixteenth president's ambivalence toward **capital punishment** is reflected in America's continuing struggle to reconcile the penalty of death with the morals and values of society. Capital punishment has played a role in sentencing since the earliest days of the Republic and—having survived a brief period of abolition between 1972 and 1976—continues to garner public support.

Capital Punishment The use of the death penalty to punish wrongdoers for certain crimes.

Still, few topics in the criminal justice system inspire such heated debate. Death penalty opponents such as legal expert Stephen Bright wonder whether "there comes a time when a society gets beyond some of the more primitive forms of punishment."[71] Critics point out that only twenty-three of the world's countries still employ the death penalty, and that the United States is the only Western democracy that continues the practice. Critics also claim that a process whose subjects are chosen by "luck and money and race" cannot serve the interests of justice.[72] Proponents believe that the death penalty serves as the ultimate deterrent for violent criminal behavior and that the criminals who are put to death are the "worst of the worst" and deserve their fate.

Today, about 3,200 convicts are living on "death row" in American prisons, meaning they have been sentenced to death and are awaiting execution. In the 1940s, as many as two hundred people were put to death in the United States in one year. As Figure 9.6 on page 271 shows, the most recent high-water mark was ninety-eight in 1999. Despite declines since then, states and the federal government are still executing convicts at a rate not seen in six decades. Consequently, the questions that surround the death penalty—Is it fair? Is it humane? Does it deter crime?—will continue to mobilize both its supporters and its detractors.

METHODS OF EXECUTION

In its early years, when the United States adopted the practice of capital punishment from England, it also adopted English methods, which included drawing and quartering and boiling the convict alive. By the nineteenth century, these techniques had been deemed "barbaric" and were replaced by hanging. Indeed, the history of capital punishment in America is marked by attempts to make the act more humane. The 1890s saw the introduction of electrocution as a less painful method of execution than hanging, and in 1890 in Auburn Prison, New York, William Kemmler became the first American to die in an electric chair.

CAREERS IN CJ

ANNE SEYMOUR
NATIONAL VICTIM ADVOCATE

The aspect of my job that I enjoy the most is my direct work with crime victims and survivors. These are people who have been severely traumatized by pain and suffering and loss, and I consider it a true honor to be able to assist them. I'll never forget the day I met a young survivor who had been abducted, beaten within an inch of her life, raped, and then left to die in the forest. This young woman became one of my closest friends, and I helped her to speak out in her state and at the national level. Every time she does so, she has a powerful impact on our society. So my help in turning a victim/survivor into a stellar victim advocate/ activist began on the day I met her, and it continues.

THE NATIONAL CENTER FOR Victims of Crime

Victim advocacy is one of the most exciting and rewarding careers you could ever embark on, though it is not one that you should get into because of the money. (Few victim advocates become rich doing this work!) Every day is unique and different, reflecting the people I assist and the colleagues with whom I interact. I am never, ever bored and never will be. AND I go to bed every single day knowing that I have done at least one thing—and often many more than one!—to promote social justice and to help someone who is hurting. It's an amazing feeling!

Social Media Career Tip

Social media technologies are about connecting and sharing information—which means privacy is an important issue. Make sure you understand who can see the material you post and how you can control it. Facebook has numerous privacy settings, for example, as does Google+. **f** **Linked in**.

FAST FACTS

NATIONAL VICTIM ADVOCATE, JOB DESCRIPTION:

- Provide direct support, advocacy, and short-term crisis counseling to crime victims.

WHAT KIND OF TRAINING IS REQUIRED?

- Bachelor's degree in criminal justice, social work/psychology, or related field.
- A minimum of two years' experience in the criminal justice system, one year of which must have involved direct services with victims

ANNUAL SALARY RANGE?

- $29,000 – $44,000

The "chair" remained the primary form of execution until 1977, when Oklahoma became the first state to adopt lethal injection. Today, this method dominates executions in all thirty-three states that employ the death penalty. In the lethal injection process, the condemned convict is given a sedative, followed by a combination of deadly drugs administered intravenously. Sixteen states authorize at least two different methods of execution, meaning that electrocution (nine states), lethal gas (three states), hanging (three states), and the firing squad (two states) are still used on rare occasions.[73]

THE DEATH PENALTY AND THE SUPREME COURT

The United States Supreme Court's attitude toward the death penalty has been shaped by two decisions made more than a century ago. First, in 1890, the Court established that as long as they are not carried out in an "inhuman" or "barbarous" fashion, executions are not forbidden by the Eighth Amendment.[74] Since that case, the Court has never ruled that any *method* of execution is unconstitutionally "cruel and unusual."

FIGURE 9.6 Executions in the United States, 1976 to 2011

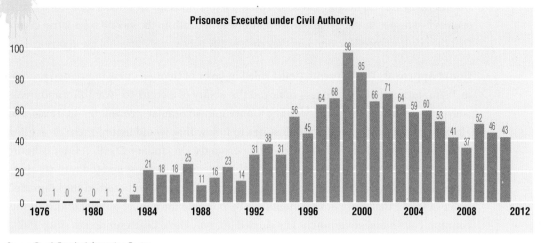

Prisoners Executed under Civil Authority

Source: Death Penalty Information Center.

Then, in *Weems v. United States* (1910),[75] the Supreme Court made a ruling that further clarified the meaning of "cruel and unusual" as defined by the Eighth Amendment, though the facts of the case did not involve capital punishment. The defendant had been sentenced to fifteen years of hard labor, a heavy fine, and a number of other penalties for the relatively minor crime of falsifying official records. The Court overturned the sentence, ruling that the penalty was too harsh considering the nature of the offense. Ultimately, in the *Weems* decision, the Court set three important precedents concerning sentencing:

1. Cruel and unusual punishment is defined by the changing norms and standards of society and therefore is not based on historical interpretations.
2. Courts may decide whether a punishment is unnecessarily cruel with regard to physical pain.
3. Courts may decide whether a punishment is unnecessarily cruel with regard to psychological pain.[76]

REFORMING THE DEATH PENALTY In the 1960s, the Supreme Court became increasingly concerned about what it saw as serious flaws in the way the states administered capital punishment. Finally, in 1967, the Court put a moratorium on executions until it could "clean up" the process. The chance to do so came with the *Furman v. Georgia* case, decided in 1972.[77]

The Bifurcated Process In its *Furman* decision, by a 5–4 margin, the Supreme Court essentially held that the death penalty, as administered by the states, violated the Eighth Amendment. Justice Potter Stewart was particularly eloquent in his concurring opinion, stating that the sentence of death was so arbitrary as to be comparable to "being struck by lightning."[78] Although the *Furman* ruling invalidated the death penalty for more than six hundred offenders on death row at the time, it also provided the states with a window to make the process less arbitrary, therefore bringing their death penalty statutes up to constitutional standards.

The result was a two-stage, or *bifurcated,* procedure for capital cases. In the first stage, a jury determines the guilt or innocence of the defendant for a crime that has, by state statute, been determined to be punishable by death. If the defendant is found guilty, the jury reconvenes in the second stage and considers all aggravating and mitigating factors to decide

Learning Objective 7 Identify the two stages that make up the bifurcated process of death penalty sentencing.

whether the death sentence is in fact warranted. (See *Mastering Concepts—The Bifurcated Death Penalty Process* below.) Therefore, even if a jury finds the defendant guilty of a crime, such as first degree murder, that *may be* punishable by death, in the second stage it can decide that the circumstances surrounding the crime justify only a punishment of life in prison.

Court Approval The Supreme Court ruled in favor of Georgia's new bifurcated process in 1976, stating that the process removed the ability of a court to "wantonly and freakishly impose the death penalty."[79] The Court upheld similar procedures in Texas and Florida, establishing a model for all states to follow that would assure them protection from lawsuits based on Eighth Amendment grounds. On January 17, 1977, Gary Gilmore became the first American executed (by Utah) under the new laws, and today thirty-three states and the federal government have capital punishment laws based on the bifurcated process. (Note that state governments are responsible for almost all executions in this country. The federal government has carried out only three death sentences since 1963.)

THE JURY'S ROLE The Supreme Court reaffirmed the important role of the jury in death penalties in *Ring v. Arizona* (2002).[80] The case involved Arizona's bifurcated process: after

MASTERINGCONCEPTS
THE BIFURCATED DEATH PENALTY PROCESS

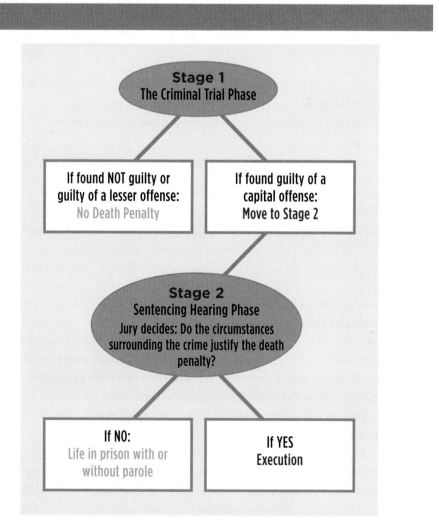

the jury determined a defendant's guilt or innocence, it would be dismissed, and the judge alone would decide whether execution was warranted. The Court found that this procedure violated the defendant's Sixth Amendment right to a jury trial, ruling that juries must be involved in *both* stages of the bifurcated process. The decision invalidated death penalty laws in Arizona, Colorado, Idaho, Montana, and Nebraska, forcing legislatures in those states to hastily revamp their procedures.

Some states still allow for a measure of judicial discretion in capital punishment decisions. In Alabama, Delaware, and Florida, the jury only recommends a sentence of death or life in prison. If the judge feels that the sentence is unreasonable, he or she can override the jury. In 2011, for example, an Alabama jury voted unanimously that Iraq War veteran Courtney Lockhart should spend his life in prison for kidnapping and murdering college freshman Lauren Burk. Nonetheless, Lee County circuit judge Jacob Walker, noting that the jury was unaware of the defendant's extensive criminal history, overrode its recommendation and sentenced Lockhart to death.

MITIGATING CIRCUMSTANCES Several mitigating circumstances will prevent a defendant found guilty of first degree murder from receiving the death penalty. In 1986, the United States Supreme Court held that the Constitution prohibits the execution of a person who is insane.[81] Sixteen years later, in *Atkins v. Virginia* (2002),[82] the Court similarly ended the death penalty for mentally handicapped defendants. This later decision underscored the continuing importance of the *Weems* test (see page 271). In 1989, the Court had rejected the arguments that the execution of a mentally handicapped person was "cruel and unusual" under the Eighth Amendment.[83] At the time, only two states barred execution of the mentally handicapped. Thirteen years later, eighteen states had such laws, and the Court decided that this increased number reflected "changing norms and standards of society."

Following the *Atkins* case, many observers, including four Supreme Court justices, hoped that the same reasoning would be applied to the question of whether convicts who committed the relevant crime when they were juveniles may be executed. These hopes were realized in 2005 when the Court issued its *Roper v. Simmons* decision, which effectively ended the execution of those who committed crimes as juveniles.[84] As in the *Atkins* case, the Court relied on the "evolving standards of decency" test, noting that a majority of the states, as well as every other civilized nation, prohibited the execution of offenders who committed their crimes before the age of eighteen. The *Roper* ruling required that seventy-two convicted murderers in twelve states be resentenced and took the death penalty "off the table" for dozens of pending cases in which prosecutors were seeking capital punishment for juvenile criminal acts.

STILL CRUEL AND UNUSUAL?

As noted earlier, lethal injection is the dominant form of execution in this country. Most states employ the same three-drug process. First, the sedative sodium thiopental is administered to deaden pain. Then pancuronium bromide, a paralytic, immobilizes the prisoner. Finally, a dose of potassium chloride stops the heart. Members of the law enforcement and medical communities have long claimed that, if performed correctly, this procedure kills the individual quickly and painlessly. Many others, however, contend that the second drug—the

In January 2012, sixteen-year-old Robert C. Richardson was charged with fatally shooting his father at their home in Harford County, Maryland. Why did the U.S. Supreme Court make juvenile murder defendants such as Richardson ineligible for the death penalty?

Harford County Sheriff's Office

paralytic—masks any outward signs of distress and thus keeps observers from knowing whether the inmate suffers extreme pain before death.[85]

In 2007, two convicted murderers in Kentucky asked the United States Supreme Court to invalidate the state's lethal injection procedure because of the possibility that it inflicted undetectable suffering. Nearly all of the scheduled executions in the United States were placed on hold while the Court deliberated this issue. In 2008, the Court ruled in *Baze v. Rees* that the mere possibility of pain "does not establish the sort of 'objectively intolerable risk of harm' that qualifies as cruel and unusual" punishment.[86] (See the feature *Landmark Cases*—Baze v. Rees on the facing page.) Although executions resumed shortly after the *Baze* decision, the states that employ the death penalty faced another challenge when the only American producer of sodium thiopental—the first drug used in the cocktail—stopped its production.

By 2011, ten of these states had replaced sodium thiopental in their three-step processes with a similar sedative called pentobarbital, commonly used in this country to euthanize animals. In addition, Ohio now uses a single, very strong dose of pentobarbital to carry out the death penalty.

Learning Objective **8** Describe the main issues of the death penalty debate.

DEBATING THE SENTENCE OF DEATH

Of the topics covered in this textbook, few inspire such passionate argument as the death penalty. Many advocates believe that execution is "just deserts" for those who commit heinous crimes. In the words of sociologist Ernest van den Haag, death is the "only fitting retribution for murder that I can think of."[87] Opponents worry that retribution is simply another word for vengeance and that "the use of the death penalty by the state will increase the acceptance of revenge in our society and will give official sanction to a climate of violence."[88] As the debate over capital punishment continues, it tends to focus on several key issues: deterrence, fallibility, arbitrariness, and discrimination.

DETERRENCE Those advocates of the death penalty who wish to show that the practice benefits society often turn to the idea of deterrence. In other words, they believe that by executing convicted criminals, the criminal justice system discourages potential criminals from committing similar violent acts. Several reports released in the 2000s claim that each convict executed deters between three and eighteen future homicides.[89] "I oppose the death penalty," says Naci Mocan, an economics professor at Louisiana State University. "But my results show that the death penalty [has a deterrent effect]—what am I going to do, hide them?"[90]

The main problem with studies that support the death penalty, say its critics, is that there are too few executions carried out in the United States each year to adequately determine their impact.[91] Furthermore, each study that "proves" the deterrent effect of the death penalty seems be matched by one that "disproves" the same premise.[92] In the end, the deterrence debate follows a familiar pattern. Opponents of the death penalty claim that murderers rarely consider the consequences of their act, and therefore it makes no difference whether capital punishment exists or not. Proponents counter that this proves the death penalty's deterrent value, because if the murderers *had* considered the possibility of execution, they would not have committed their crimes.

FALLIBILITY In a sense, capital punishment acts as the ultimate deterrent by rendering those executed incapable of committing further crimes. Incapacitation as a justification

Social Media and CJ The Web sites of the **Death Penalty Information Center** and **Pro Death Penalty** provide opposing views on capital punishment. To access their Facebook pages, visit the *Criminal Justice CourseMate* at **cengagebrain.com** and select the *Web Links* for this chapter.

for the death penalty, though, rests on two debatable assumptions: (1) every convicted murderer is likely to recidivate, and (2) the criminal justice system is *infallible*. In other words, the system never convicts someone who is actually not guilty.

As of yet, conclusive evidence that an innocent person has been executed in the United States has not been accepted by any American court. According to the Death Penalty Information Center, however, between 1973, when the Supreme Court had temporarily suspended capital punishment, and August 2012, 140 American men and women who had been convicted of capital crimes and sentenced to death—though not executed—were later found to be innocent. Over that same time period, about 1,300 executions took place, meaning that for every nine convicts put to death during that period, about one death row inmate has been found innocent.[93]

LANDMARK CASES: *Baze v. Rees*

Ralph Baze shot and killed two Powell County sheriff's deputies. Ralph Bowling murdered Tina and Eddie Earley in Lexington. For their crimes, the state of Kentucky decided that the two men would be put to death. Baze's and Bowling's lawyers, however, challenged their clients' executions on the ground that Kentucky's method of lethal injection—the three-drug "cocktail" described on page 273—was unreliable and inflicted "unnecessary pain." After the Kentucky Supreme Court rejected this argument, the United States Supreme Court agreed to hear the inmates' appeal. The Court's decision was eagerly awaited, as state governments and courts had placed more than forty executions by lethal injection on hold pending the ruling.

Baze v. Rees
United States Supreme Court
553 U.S. 35 (2008)
www.scotusblog.com/case-files/cases/baze-v-rees

IN THE WORDS OF THE COURT...
CHIEF JUSTICE ROBERTS, MAJORITY OPINION

* * * *

We begin with the principle, settled by *Gregg*, that capital punishment is constitutional. It necessarily follows that there must be a means of carrying it out. Some risk of pain is inherent in any method of execution—no matter how humane.

Our cases recognize that subjecting individuals to a risk of future harm—not simply actually inflicting pain—can qualify as cruel and unusual punishment. To establish that such exposure violates the Eighth Amendment, however,

the conditions presenting the risk must be "sure or very likely to cause serious illness and needless suffering," and give rise to "sufficiently imminent dangers."

* * * *

In applying these standards to the facts of this case, we note at the outset that it is difficult to regard a practice as "objectively intolerable" when it is in fact widely tolerated. Thirty-six States that sanction capital punishment have adopted lethal injection as the preferred method of execution. * * * This broad consensus goes not just to the method of execution, but also to the specific three-drug combination used by Kentucky. Thirty States, as well as the Federal Government, use a series of sodium thiopental, pancuronium bromide, and potassium chloride, in varying amounts.

Decision

The Court found that the pain caused by any mode of execution, be it accidental or "an inescapable cause of death," does not trigger Eighth Amendment protections against "cruel and unusual punishment." In essence, the Court said that this form of lethal injection, though perhaps not perfect, was acceptable. It therefore upheld the decision of the Kentucky Supreme Court.

FOR CRITICAL ANALYSIS

Do you agree that it would be unreasonable to expect corrections officials to provide death row inmates with a completely painless mode of execution? If a less painful alternative to the three-drug "cocktail" becomes readily available, should the Court require states to use it? Explain your answers.

ARBITRARINESS As noted earlier, one of the reasons it is so difficult to determine the deterrent effect of the death penalty is that it is rarely meted out. Despite the bifurcated process required by the Supreme Court's *Furman* ruling (see pages 271–272), a significant amount of arbitrariness appears to remain in the system. Only 2 percent of all defendants convicted of murder are sentenced to death, and, as we have seen, relatively few of those on death row are ever executed.[94]

The chances of a defendant in a capital trial being sentenced to death seem to depend heavily on, as we have seen, the quality of the defense counsel and the jurisdiction where the crime was committed. As Figure 9.7 below shows, a convict's likelihood of being executed is strongly influenced by geography. Five states (Florida, Missouri, Oklahoma, Texas, and Virginia) account for about two-thirds of all executions, while seventeen states and the District of Columbia do not provide for capital punishment within their borders. Thus, a person on trial for first degree murder in Idaho has a much better chance of avoiding execution than someone who has committed the same crime in Texas.

DISCRIMINATORY EFFECT Whether or not capital punishment is imposed arbitrarily, some observers claim that it is not done without bias. A disproportionate number of those executed since 1976—just over one-third—have been African American, and today 42 percent of all inmates on death row are black.[95] Another set of statistics also continues to be problematic: in 252 cases involving interracial murders in which the defendant was executed between 1976 and March 2012, the defendant was African American and the victim was white. Over that same time period, only 18 cases involved a white defendant and a black victim.[96]

FIGURE 9.7 **Executions by State, 1976–2011**

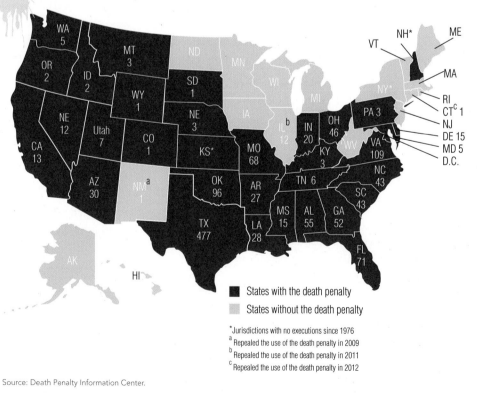

States with the death penalty

States without the death penalty

[*] Jurisdictions with no executions since 1976
[a] Repealed the use of the death penalty in 2009
[b] Repealed the use of the death penalty in 2011
[c] Repealed the use of the death penalty in 2012

Source: Death Penalty Information Center.

In **September 2011,** the state of Georgia executed Troy Davis for murdering an off-duty police officer twenty-two years earlier. Many people, including these protestors at Davis's funeral in Savannah, doubted that Davis was guilty of the crime. Why is the question of whether an innocent defendant has ever been executed so important for the death penalty debate?

AP Photo/Stephen Morton

Practically, these numbers have had little impact on the mechanics of the death penalty. In *McCleskey v. Kemp* (1987),[97] the Supreme Court made it very difficult to prove discriminatory intent in capital punishment based on statistics alone. Several years ago, however, North Carolina did pass the Racial Justice Act, which allows death row inmates to challenge their sentences on the ground that their race played a significant role in the proceedings.[98] In 2012, Marcus Robinson became the first death row inmate to take advantage of the new law by successfully claiming that state prosecutors discriminated against blacks in selecting the jury for his capital trial. A state judge changed Robinson's sentence to life in prison without parole.

THE IMMEDIATE FUTURE OF THE DEATH PENALTY

As Figure 9.6 on page 271 made clear, the number of executions carried out each year in the United States has decreased dramatically since 1999. Other statistics also indicate a decline in death penalty activity. In 2011, only 78 people were sentenced to death, compared with 277 in 1999.[99]

REASONS FOR THE DECLINE IN EXECUTIONS We have already addressed some of the reasons for the diminishing presence of executions in the criminal justice system. With its earlier decisions in the *Atkins* (2002) and *Roper* (2005) cases, the United States Supreme Court removed the possibility that hundreds of mentally handicapped and juvenile offenders could be sentenced to death. Furthermore, nearly all of the states that allow for the death penalty now permit juries to impose a sentence of life in prison without parole as an alternative to death. In Texas, the number of death sentences imposed each year dropped by about 50 percent after jurors were given the life-without-parole option in 2005, a trend that has been mirrored throughout the United States.[100]

Financial considerations are also starting to color the capital punishment picture. Because of the costs of intensive investigations, extensive *voir dire* (see pages 231–232), and lengthy appellate reviews, pursuing the death penalty can be very expensive for state taxpayers. A recent study by the Urban Institute found that the average death penalty trial costs a state $2 million more than a murder trial in which capital punishment is not sought.[101] Taking all of the system's costs into account, Florida spends $24 million per execution, and California spends an extraordinary $250 million per execution.[102] As state budgets come under increased pressure, officials are looking at capital punishment as an area of potential savings.

CONTINUED SUPPORT FOR THE DEATH PENALTY In November 2011, Governor John Kitzhaber of Oregon called his state's capital punishment system "compromised and inequitable" and announced that no more executions would take place as long as he was in office.[103] Earlier that year, Illinois became the third state since 2007 to end capital punishment, along with New Jersey and New Mexico. Then, in 2012, Connecticut followed suit. Does this mean society's "standards of decency" are changing to the point where the death sentence is in danger of being completely abolished in the United States? Probably not. Despite its decisions in the 2000s, the Supreme Court has shown no interest in holding that the death penalty itself is unconstitutional. In addition to its *Baze* decision (see page 275), in 2007 the Court made it easier for prosecutors to seek the death penalty by allowing them to remove potential jurors who express reservations about the practice.[104]

Although public support for the death penalty has been steadily dropping since the mid-1990s, one poll taken in 2011 showed that 61 percent of Americans still favor the practice.[105] (That percentage does, however, drop to about 50 percent when the choice is between execution and a sentence of life in prison without parole.)[106] Another poll found that 58 percent of the respondents favored an official moratorium on executions nationwide to consider the problem of wrongful death sentences.[107] In the 2000s, then, Americans seem more interested in making the sentence of death fairer than in doing away with it altogether.

SELFASSESSMENT

Fill in the blanks and check your answers on page 280.

By a large margin, _____ _____ is the most widespread method of execution in the United States today. According to the United States Supreme Court's *Weems* decision, "cruel and unusual punishment" under the Eighth Amendment is determined by the changing _____ _____ _____ of society. Following the *Weems* guidelines, in 2002 the Court barred the execution of the _____ _____, and in 2005 it prohibited the execution of persons who were _____ at the time of their crime.

CHAPTER SUMMARY

Learning Objective 1 **List and contrast the four basic philosophical reasons for sentencing criminals.** (a) Retribution, (b) deterrence, (c) incapacitation, and (d) rehabilitation. Under the principle of retributive justice, the severity of the punishment is in proportion to the severity of the crime. Punishment is an end in itself. In contrast, the deterrence approach seeks to prevent future crimes by setting an example. Such punishment is based on its deterrent value and not necessarily on the severity of the crime. The incapacitation theory of punishment simply argues that a criminal in prison cannot inflict further harm on society. In contrast, the rehabilitation theory believes that criminals can be rehabilitated in the appropriate prison environment.

Learning Objective 2 **Contrast indeterminate with determinate sentencing.** Indeterminate sentencing follows from legislative penal codes that set minimum and maximum amounts of incarceration time. Determinate sentencing carries a fixed amount of time, although this may be reduced for "good time."

Learning Objective 3 **List the four primary forms of punishment available to the judge.** (a) Capital (death sentence), (b) imprisonment, (c) probation, and (d) fines.

Learning Objective 4 **State who has input into the sentencing decision and list the factors that determine a sentence.** The prosecutor, defense attorney, probation officer, and judge provide inputs. The factors considered in sentencing are (a) the seriousness of the crime, (b) mitigating circumstances, (c) aggravating circumstances, and (d) judicial philosophy.

Learning Objective 5 **Explain some of the reasons why sentencing reform has occurred.** One reason is sentencing disparity, which is indicative of a situation in which those convicted of similar crimes receive dissimilar sentences (often due to a particular judge's sentencing philosophy). Sentencing discrimination has also occurred on the basis of defendants' gender, race, or economic standing.

Learning Objective 6 **Identify the arguments for and against the use of victim impact statements during sentencing hearings.** Proponents of victim impact statements believe that they allow victims to provide character evidence in the same manner as defendants have always been allowed to do and that they give victims a therapeutic "voice" in the sentencing process. Opponents argue that the statements bring unacceptable levels of emotion into the courtroom and unfairly prejudice juries against defendants.

Learning Objective 7 **Identify the two stages that make up the bifurcated process of death penalty sentencing.** The first stage of the bifurcated process requires a jury to find the defendant guilty or not guilty of a crime that is punishable by execution. If the defendant is found guilty, then, in the second stage, the jury reconvenes to decide whether the death sentence is warranted.

Learning Objective 8 **Describe the main issues of the death penalty debate.** Many of those who favor capital punishment believe that it is "just deserts" for the most violent of criminals. Those who oppose it see the act as little more than revenge. There is also disagreement over whether the death penalty acts as a deterrent. The relatively high number of death row inmates who have been found innocent has raised questions about the fallibility of the process, while certain statistics seem to show that execution is rather arbitrary. Finally, many observers contend that capital punishment is administered unfairly with regard to members of minority groups.

QUESTIONS FOR CRITICAL ANALYSIS

1. Suppose that the U.S. Congress passed a new law that punished shoplifting with a mandatory eighty-five-year prison term. What would be the impact of the new law on shoplifting nationwide? Would such a harsh law be justified by its deterrent effect? What about imposing a similarly extreme punishment on a more serious crime— a mandatory sentence of life in prison for, say, drunk driving? Would such a law be in society's best interest? Why or why not?

2. Why are truth-in-sentencing laws generally popular among victims' rights advocates? Why might these laws

not be so popular with prison administrators or government officials charged with balancing a state budget?

3. One judge complained that thanks to sentencing guidelines, his role in the sentencing process was like "following an elaborate cookbook." Why would proponents of sentencing reform argue that this sort of restriction on judicial discretion is a positive development?

4. In Alabama, Delaware, and Florida, judges can override death penalty sentencing decisions made by juries.

What are the arguments for and against giving judges this power? How might these three states be in conflict with the United States Supreme Court's *Ring* decision, described on pages 272–273?

5. Some observers believe that by abolishing the death penalty, officials in states such as Connecticut and Illinois have taken away an important bargaining chip for prosecutors to use during plea bargaining. Why might this be the case?

KEY TERMS

aggravating circumstances **261**

capital punishment **269**

departure **266**

determinate sentencing **257**

deterrence **254**

"good time" **257**

habitual offender laws **267**

incapacitation **254**

indeterminate sentencing **256**

just deserts **253**

mandatory sentencing guidelines **267**

mitigating circumstances **261**

presentence investigative report **259**

"real offense" **261**

rehabilitation **255**

restitution **256**

restorative justice **256**

retribution **253**

sentencing discrimination **263**

sentencing disparity **262**

sentencing guidelines **265**

truth-in-sentencing laws **257**

victim impact statement (VIS) **268**

SELF ASSESSMENT ANSWER KEY

Page 256: **i.** retribution; **ii.** deterrence; **iii.** incapacitation; **iv.** rehabilitation

Page 262: **i.** Indeterminate; **ii.** determinate; **iii.** good time; **iv.** presentence investigative; **v.** seriousness; **vi.** Mitigating; **vii.** aggravating

Page 265: **i.** disparity; **ii.** discrimination

Page 269: **i.** guidelines; **ii.** increased; **iii.** three-strikes/ habitual offender

Page 278: **i.** lethal injection; **ii.** norms and standards; **iii.** mentally handicapped; **iv.** juveniles/minors

COURSEMATE

For online help and access to resources that accompany *Criminal Justice in Action: The Core*, go to **www.cengagebrain.com/shop/ISBN/978-1-285-06915-9**. Click "Access Now," where you will find flashcards, an online

quiz, and other helpful study aids. If you have an access code for CourseMate, log in and go to the chapter of your choice for additional online study aids.

NOTES

1. Erica Goode, "Life Sentence for Possession of Child Pornography Spurs Debate over Severity," *New York Times* (November 5, 2011), A9.

2. Philip Jenkins, *Beyond Tolerance: Child Pornography on the Internet* (New York: New York University Press, 2001); and Max Taylor and Ethel Quayle, *Child Pornography:* *An Internet Crime* (New York: Brunner-Routledge, 2003).

3. Michael L. Bourke and Andres E. Hernandez, "The 'Butner Study' Redux: A Report on the

Incidence of Hands-On Child Victimization by Child Pornography Offenders," *Journal of Family Violence* (2009), 183–191.

4. *Ibid.*, 188.

5. David Yellen, "Just Deserts and Lenient Prosecutors: The Flawed Case for Real Offense Sentencing," *Northwestern University Law Review* 91 (Summer 1997), 1434.

6. Herbert L. Packer, "Justification for Criminal Punishment," in *The Limits of Criminal Sanction* (Palo Alto, CA: Stanford University Press, 1968), 36–37.

7. Harold Pepinsky and Paul Jesilow, *Myths That Cause Crime* (Cabin John, MD: Seven Locks Press, 1984).

8. Brian Forst, "Prosecution and Sentencing," in *Crime,* ed. James Q. Wilson and Joan Petersilia (San Francisco: ICS Press, 1995), 376.

9. James Q. Wilson, *Thinking about Crime* (New York: Basic Books, 1975), 235.

10. Isaac Ehrlich, "Participation in Illegitimate Activities: A Theoretical and Empirical Investigation," *Journal of Political Economy* 81 (May/June 1973), 521–564.

11. Steven Levitt, "The Effect of Prison Population Size on Crime Rates," *Quarterly Journal of Economics* 111 (May 1996), 319.

12. Avinash Singh Bhati, *An Information Theoretic Method for Estimating the Number of Crimes Averted by Incapacitation* (Washington, D.C.: Urban Institute, July 2007), 18–33.

13. Todd Clear, *Harm in Punishment* (Boston: Northeastern University Press, 1980).

14. Robert J. Meadows and Julie Kuehnel, *Evil Minds: Understanding and Responding to Violent Predators* (Upper Saddle River, NJ: Pearson Prentice Hall, 2005), 256–258.

15. Heather Strang and Lawrence W. Sherman, "Repairing the Harm: Victims and Restorative Justice," *Utah Law Review* (2003), 15, 18, 20–25.

16. Russell E. Farbiarz, "Victim-Offender Mediation," *Michigan State University Journal of Medicine & Law* (Summer 2008), 367.

17. Gregory W. O'Reilly, "Truth-in-Sentencing: Illinois Adds Yet Another Layer of 'Reform' to Its Complicated Code of Corrections," *Loyola University of Chicago Law Journal* (Summer 1996), 986, 999–1000.

18. Marc Mauer, "The Truth about Truth-in-Sentencing," *Corrections Today* (February 1, 1996), 1–8.

19. Paul W. Keve, *Crime Control and Justice in America: Searching for Facts and Answers* (Chicago: American Library Association, 1995), 77.

20. Danielle A. Alvarez, "Flowers, Dinner, Bowling—and Counseling—Ordered by Broward Judge in Domestic Case," *Sunsentinel.com* (February 7, 2012), at **articles.sun-sentinel.com/2012-02-07/news/ fl-flowers-food-bowling-20120207_1_ red-lobster-broward-judge-judge-john-jay-hurley.**

21. Kate Stith and José A. Cabranes, "Judging under the Federal Sentencing Guidelines," *Northwestern University Law Review* 91 (Summer 1997), 1247.

22. Mark M. Lanier and Claud H. Miller III, "Attitudes and Practices of Federal Probation Officers towards Pre-Plea/Trial Investigative Report Policy," *Crime & Delinquency* 41 (July 1995), 365–366.

23. Stith and Cabranes, 1247.

24. Nancy J. King and Rosevelt L. Noble, "Felony Jury Sentencing in Practice: A Three-State Study," *Vanderbilt Law Review* (2004), 1986.

25. Jena Iontcheva, "Jury Sentencing as Democratic Practice," *Virginia Law Review* (April 2003), 325.

26. Julie R. O'Sullivan, "In Defense of the U.S. Sentencing Guidelines Modified Real-Offense System," *Northwestern University Law Review* 91 (1997), 1342.

27. Quoted in Isolde Raftery, "'Barefoot Bandit' Gets Prison for Stealing from Neighbors," *New York Times* (December 17, 2011), A12.

28. Brian Forst and Charles Wellford, "Punishment and Sentencing: Developing Sentencing Guidelines Empirically from Principles of Punishment," *Rutgers Law Review* 33 (1981).

29. 18 U.S.C. Section 2113(a) (1994).

30. Bob Barr and Eric Sterling, "The War on Drugs: Fighting Crime or Wasting Time?" *American Criminal Law Review* (Fall 2001), 1545.

31. United States Sentencing Commission, "Statistical Information Packet, Fiscal Year 2009, Northern District of California," Table 7, at **www.ussc.gov/Data_and_Statistics/ Federal_Sentencing_Statistics/State_ District_Circuit/JP2009.htm**; and "Statistical Information Packet, Fiscal Year 2009, Northern District of Iowa," Table 7, at **www.ussc.gov/ Data_and_Statistics/Federal_Sentencing_ Statistics/State_District_Circuit/2009/ ian09.pdf**.

32. United States Sentencing Commission, "Statistical Information Packet, Fiscal Year 2009, Fourth Circuit," Table 7, at **www.ussc.gov/Data_and_Statistics/ Federal_Sentencing_Statistics/State_ District_Circuit/2009/4c09.pdf**; and "Statistical Information Packet, Fiscal Year 2009, Ninth Circuit," Table 7, at **www. ussc.gov/Data_and_Statistics/Federal_ Sentencing_Statistics/State_District_ Circuit/2009/9c09.pdf**.

33. Cassia Spohn and David Holleran, "The Imprisonment Penalty Paid by Young, Unemployed Black and Hispanic Male Offenders," *Criminology* 35 (2000), 281.

34. *Ibid.*, 297.

35. Bureau of Justice Statistics, *Prison Inmates at Midyear 2009—Statistical Tables* (Washington, D.C.: U.S. Department of Justice, June 2010), Table 16, page 19.

36. Federal Bureau of Investigation, *Crime in the United States, 2011* (Washington, D.C.: U.S. Department of Justice, 2012), at **www.fbi.gov/ about-us/cjis/ucr/crime-in-the-u.s/2011/ crime-in-the-u.s.-2011/tables/table-43**.

37. Spohn and Holleran, 301.

38. Brian Johnson, "The Multilevel Context of Criminal Sentencing: Integrating Judge- and County-Level Influences," *Criminology* (May 2006), 259–298.

39. 28 U.S.C. Section 991 (1984).

40. Bureau of Justice Statistics, *Felony Sentences in State Courts, 2006—Statistical Tables* (Washington, D.C.: U.S. Department of Justice, December 2009), Table 3.5, page 20.

41. Clarice Feinman, *Women in the Criminal Justice System*, 3d ed. (Westport, CT: Praeger, 1994), 35.

42. Darrell Steffensmeier, John Kramer, and Cathy Streifel, "Gender and Imprisonment Decisions," *Criminology* 31 (1993), 411.

43. Quoted in Kareem Fahim and Karen Zraick, "Seeing Failure of Mother as Factor in Sentencing," *New York Times* (November 17, 2008), A24.

44. John C. Coffee, "Repressed Issues of Sentencing," *Georgetown Law Journal* 66 (1978), 987.

45. J. S. Bainbridge, Jr., "The Return of Retribution," *ABA Journal* (May 1985), 63.

46. The Massachusetts Court System, "Introduction: Sentencing Guidelines," at **www.mass.gov/courts/formsandguide lines/sentencing/step1.html#step1**.

47. Pub. L. No. 98-473, 98 Stat. 1987, codified as amended at 18 U.S.C. Sections 3551–3742 and 28 U.S.C. Sections 991–998 (1988).

48. Julia L. Black, "The Constitutionality of Federal Sentences Imposed under the Sentencing Reform Act of 1984 after *Mistretta v. United States,*" *Iowa Law Review* 75 (March 1990), 767.

49. *Fifteen Years of Guidelines Sentencing: An Assessment of How Well the Federal Criminal Justice System Is Achieving the Goals of Sentencing Reform* (Washington, D.C.: U.S. Sentencing Commission, November 2004), 46.

50. Todd R. Clear, George F. Cole, and Michael D. Reisig, *American Corrections,* 7th ed. (Belmont, CA: Thomson Wadsworth, 2006), 86.

51. Neal B. Kauder and Brian J. Ostrom, *State Sentencing Guidelines: Profiles and Continuum* (Williamsburg, VA: National Center for State Courts, 2008), 15.

52. *United States v. Booker,* 543 U.S. 220 (2005); *Gall v. United States,* 552 U.S. 38 (2007); and *Kimbrough v. United States,* 552 U.S. 85 (2007).

53. Quoted in A. G. Sulzberger, "Defiant Judge Takes on Child Pornography Laws," *New York Times* (May 22, 2010), A1.

54. Tim McGlone, "Leniency Often Granted in Child Porn Cases," *Virginian-Pilot* (Norfolk, VA) (January 16, 2011), at **hamptonroads. com/2011/01/leniency-often-granted-porn-cases**.

55. *Blakely v. Washington,* 542 U.S. 296 (2004); *United States v. Booker,* 543 U.S. 220 (2005); and *Gall v. United States,* 552 U.S. 38 (2007).

56. Transactional Records Access Clearinghouse, "Wide Variations Seen in Federal Sentencing" (March 5, 2012), at **trac.syr.edu/whatsnew/email.120305.html.**

57. *Demographic Differences in Federal Sentencing Practices: An Update of the Booker Report's Multivariate Regression Analysis* (Washington, D.C.: U.S. Sentencing Commission, March 2010), C-3.

58. Alabama Code 1975 Section 20–2–79.

59. Quoted in Melinda Rogers, "Reluctant Utah Judge Orders Man to 57 Years in Prison for Gang Robberies," *Salt Lake Tribune* (December 15, 2011), at **www.sltrib.com/sltrib/mobile/53124012-90/maumau-prison-angelos-court.html.csp.**

60. Washington Revised Code Annotated Section 9.94A.030.

61. 445 U.S. 263 (1980).

62. 538 U.S. 63 (2003).

63. *Lockyer v. Andrade,* 270 F.3d 743 (9th Cir. 2001).

64. *Lockyer v. Andrade,* 538 U.S. 63, 76 (2003).

65. *Ibid.,* 83.

66. Edna Erez, "Victim Voice, Impact Statements, and Sentencing: Integrating Restorative Justice and Therapeutic Jurisprudence Principles in Adversarial Proceedings," *Criminal Law Bulletin* (September/October 2004), 495.

67. Bryan Myers and Edith Greene, "Prejudicial Nature of Impact Statements," *Psychology, Public Policy, and Law* (December 2004), 493.

68. Ray Paternoster and Jerome Deise, "A Heavy Thumb on the Scale: The Effect of Victim Impact Evidence on Capital Decision Making," *Criminology* (February 2011), 129–161.

69. *Payne v. Tennessee,* 501 U.S. 808 (1991).

70. Walter Berns, "Abraham Lincoln (Book Review)," *Commentary* (January 1, 1996), 70.

71. Comments made at the Georgetown Law Center, "The Modern View of Capital Punishment," *American Criminal Law Review* 34 (Summer 1997), 1353.

72. David Bruck, quoted in Bill Rankin, "Fairness of the Death Penalty Is Still on Trial," *Atlanta Constitution-Journal* (July 29, 1997), A13.

73. Bureau of Justice Statistics, *Capital Punishment, 2010* (Washington, D.C.: U.S. Department of Justice, December 2011), 2.

74. *In re Kemmler,* 136 U.S. 447 (1890).

75. 217 U.S. 349 (1910).

76. Pamela S. Nagy, "Hang by the Neck until Dead: The Resurgence of Cruel and Unusual Punishment in the 1990s," *Pacific Law Journal* 26 (October 1994), 85.

77. 408 U.S. 238 (1972).

78. 408 U.S. 309 (1972) (Stewart, concurring).

79. *Gregg v. Georgia,* 428 U.S. 153 (1976).

80. 536 U.S. 584 (2002).

81. *Ford v. Wainwright,* 477 U.S. 399, 422 (1986).

82. 536 U.S. 304 (2002).

83. *Penry v. Lynaugh,* 492 U.S. 302 (1989).

84. 543 U.S. 551 (2005).

85. *Baze v. Rees,* 217 S.W.3d 207 (Ky. 2006).

86. 553 U.S. 35 (2008).

87. Ernest van den Haag, "The Ultimate Punishment: A Defense," *Harvard Law Review* 99 (1986), 1669.

88. *The Death Penalty: The Religious Community Calls for Abolition* (pamphlet published by the National Coalition to Abolish the Death Penalty and the National Interreligious Task Force on Criminal Justice, 1988), 48.

89. Hashem Dezhbakhsh, Paul H. Rubin, and Joanna M. Shepherd, "Does Capital Punishment Have a Deterrent Effect? New Evidence from Postmoratorium Panel Data," *American Law and Economics Review* 5 (2003), 344–376; H. Naci Mocan and R. Kaj Gittings, "Getting Off Death Row: Commuted Sentences and the Deterrent Effect of Capital Punishment," *Journal of Law and Economics* 46 (2003), 453–478; Joanna M. Shepherd, "Deterrence versus Brutalization: Capital Punishment's Differing Impact among States," *Michigan Law Review* 104 (2005), 203–255; and Paul R. Zimmerman, "State Executions, Deterrence, and the Incidence of Murder," *Journal of Applied Economics* 7 (2005), 163–193.

90. Quoted in Robert Tanner, "Studies Say Death Penalty Deters Crime," *Associated Press* (June 10, 2007).

91. Richard Berk, "Can't Tell: Comments on 'Does the Death Penalty Save Lives?'" *Criminology and Public Policy* (November 2009), 845–851.

92. John J. Donohue and Justin Wolfers, "Uses and Abuses of Empirical Evidence in the Death Penalty Debate," *Stanford Law Review* 58 (2005), 791–845.

93. Death Penalty Information Center, "Innocence and the Death Penalty," at **www.deathpenaltyinfo.org/innocence-and-death-penalty.**

94. Adam Liptak, "Geography and the Machinery of Death," *New York Times* (February 5, 2007), A10.

95. Bureau of Justice Statistics, *Capital Punishment, 2010—Statistical Tables* (Washington, D.C.: U.S. Department of Justice, December 2011), Table 4, page 8, and Table 13, page 17.

96. Death Penalty Information Center, "National Statistics on the Death Penalty and Race," at **www.deathpenaltyinfo.org/race-death-row-inmates-executed-1976#defend.**

97. 481 U.S. 279 (1987).

98. North Carolina General Statute Section 15A-2010 (2009).

99. Death Penalty Information Center, "The Death Penalty in 2011: Year End Report," at **www.deathpenaltyinfo.org/documents/2011_Year_End.pdf.**

100. David McCord, "What's Messing with Texas Death Sentences?" *Texas Tech Law Review* (Winter 2011), 601–608.

101. Cited in "Saving Lives and Money," *The Economist* (March 14, 2009), 32.

102. Mary Kate Cary, "The Case against the Death Penalty," *U.S. News Weekly* (March 25, 2011), 13.

103. Jonathan J. Cooper, "Oregon Governor Bans Death Penalty," *Chicago Sun-Times* (November 24, 2011), 27.

104. *Uttecht v. Brown,* 551 U.S. 1 (2007).

105. Gallup, "In U.S., Support for Death Penalty Falls to 39-Year Low" (October 13, 2011), at **www.gallup.com/poll/150089/Support-Death-Penalty-Falls-Year-Low.aspx.**

106. Gallup, "In U.S. 64% Support Death Penalty in Cases of Murder" (November 8, 2010), at **www.gallup.com/poll/144284/support-death-penalty-cases-murder.aspx.**

107. Richard C. Dieter, *A Crisis of Confidence: Americans' Doubts about the Death Penalty* (Washington, D.C.: Death Penalty Information Center, June 2007), 5, 9.

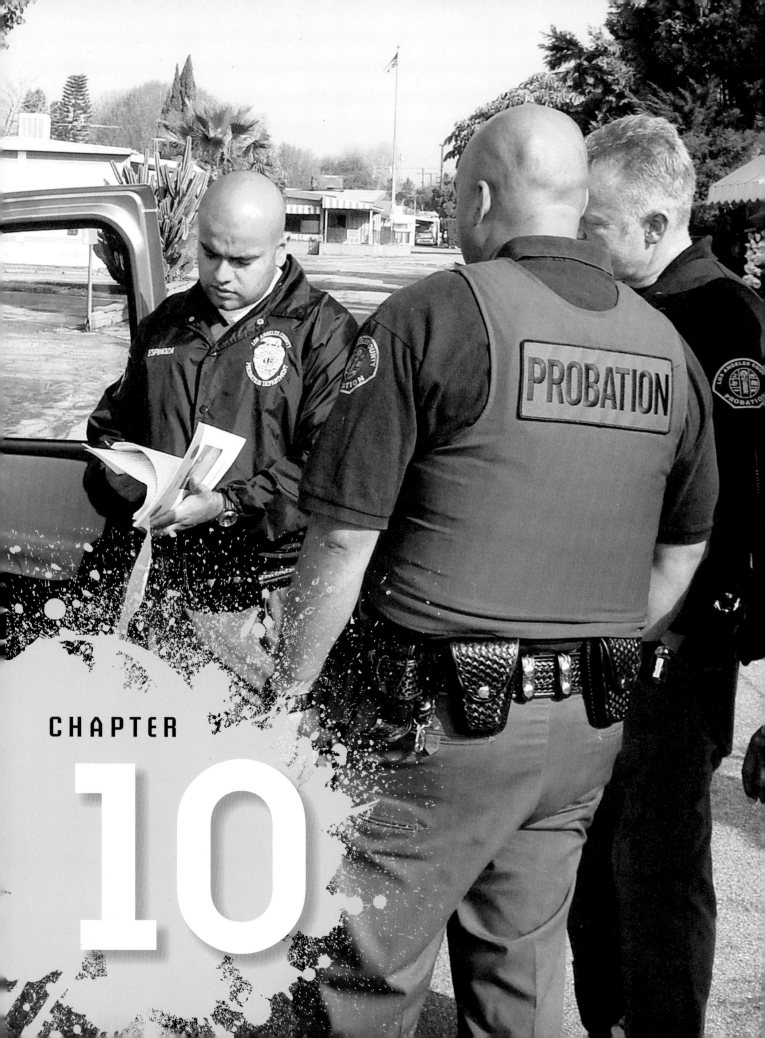

Los Angeles County Probation Department

Probation
and
Intermediate Sanctions

CHAPTER OUTLINE

- The Justification for Community Corrections
- Probation: Doing Time in the Community
- Intermediate Sanctions
- The Paradox of Community Corrections

A TRIAL OF FAITH

When two-year-old Kent Schaible came down with what seemed to be a bad cold, his parents did not take the boy to the doctor. Instead, Herbert and Catherine followed the teachings of their fundamentalist church, which instructs its members to avoid traditional medicine and place their faith in the healing power of God. For nearly two weeks, as Kent suffered from chest congestion, a sore throat, and diarrhea, the Schaibles prayed fervently for their son's recovery. After the young boy died, Herbert told a Philadelphia social worker, "We tried to fight the devil, but in the end the devil won."

Others saw the situation in a different light. A medical examiner ruled Kent's death a homicide, noting that the bacterial pneumonia from which he was suffering could have been alleviated with basic medical care. Prosecutors charged Herbert and Catherine with involuntary manslaughter and child endangerment. "You have to take care of your children. It's not enough to pray for them," said Philadelphia assistant district attorney Joanne Pescatore during the Schaibles' criminal trial. "You also have to give them care when they need it." A jury agreed and found the couple guilty of causing Kent's death.

Under Pennsylvania law, common pleas court judge Carolyn Engel Temin could have sentenced both Herbert and Catherine to a maximum of seventeen years behind bars for their crimes. In February 2011, however, taking into account the Schaibles' lack of criminal records and the fact that they still had seven other children to care for, the judge decided against incarceration. Instead, she sentenced the couple to ten years of probation each, during which time they would be required to set up regular medical exams for each of their children and consult a doctor at any sign of sickness. Should the Schaibles violate these conditions, they could be sent to prison.

Herbert and Catherine Schaible were sentenced to probation after being found guilty of causing their son's death.

AP Photo/Philadelphia Police Department

Mythri Jayarman, Catherine Schaible's defense attorney, was satisfied with the outcome of her client's trial. "I think it was a fair sentence," she said. "The most important thing is the safety of the [Schaibles'] children."[1] Prosecutor Joanne Pescatore agreed: "Like the judge said, they are not criminals, they don't have records, they have seven kids to take care of."[2] In this case, then, the members of the courtroom work group felt that imprisonment made little sense, given that the Schaibles were not hardened criminals and their children would have suffered greatly by their parents' absence.

In such situations, the criminal justice system often relies on **community corrections** as a punishment option. Community corrections cover a wide variety of alternative sentences in which offenders are allowed to serve their terms under supervision without going to jail or prison. *Probation* is not only the most common form of community supervision in the United States but also the country's most common sentence. Along with Herbert and Catherine Schaible, about 4 million American adults are presently on probation.[3]

In this chapter, we will discuss the strengths and weaknesses of probation and of other forms of community corrections called *intermediate sanctions,* which include intensive probation, boot camps, day reporting centers, and home confinement. Given the growing scarcity of resources for prisons and jails, policy decisions made today con-

Community Corrections The correctional supervision of offenders in the community as an alternative to sending them to prison or jail.

cerning these alternative punishments will affect the criminal justice system for decades to come.

THE JUSTIFICATION FOR COMMUNITY CORRECTIONS

In the court of popular opinion, retribution and crime control take precedence over community-based correctional programs. America, says University of Minnesota law professor Michael Tonry, is preoccupied with the "absolute severity of punishment" and the "widespread view that only imprisonment counts."[4] Mandatory sentencing guidelines and "three-strikes" laws are theoretically the opposite of community-based corrections.[5] To a certain degree, correctional programs that are administered in the community are considered a less severe, and therefore a less worthy, alternative to imprisonment.

Learning Objective 1 Explain the justifications for community-based corrections programs.

REINTEGRATION

Supporters of probation and intermediate sanctions reject such views as not only shortsighted but also contradictory to the aims of the corrections system. A very small percentage of all convicted offenders have committed crimes that warrant life imprisonment or capital punishment. At some point, most will return to the community. Consequently, according to one group of experts, the task of the corrections system

> includes building or rebuilding solid ties between the offender and the community, integrating or reintegrating the offender into community life—restoring family ties, obtaining employment and an education, securing in the larger sense a place for the offender in the routine functioning of society.[6]

Some studies have shown higher recidivism rates for offenders who are subjected to prison culture, and a frequent justification of community-based corrections is that they help to reintegrate the offender into society.

Reintegration has a strong theoretical basis in rehabilitative theories of punishment. An offender is generally considered to be "rehabilitated" when he or she no longer represents a threat to other members of the community and therefore is believed to be fit to live in that community. In the context of this chapter and the two that follow, it will also be helpful to see reintegration as a process through which corrections officials such as probation and parole officers provide the offender with incentives to follow the rules of society. These incentives can be positive, such as enrolling the offender in a drug treatment program. They can also be negative—in particular, the threat of return to prison or jail for failure to comply.

In all instances, corrections system professionals must carefully balance the needs of the individual offender against the rights of law-abiding members of the community.

Reintegration A goal of corrections that focuses on preparing the offender for a return to the community unmarred by further criminal behavior.

Diversion In the context of corrections, a strategy to divert those offenders who qualify away from prison and jail and toward community-based sanctions.

DIVERSION

Another justification for community-based corrections, based on practical considerations, is **diversion.** As you are already aware, many criminal offenses fall into the category of "petty," and it is well-nigh impossible, as well as unnecessary, to imprison every offender for every offense. Community-based corrections are an important means of diverting criminals to alternative modes of punishment so that scarce incarceration resources are consumed by only the most dangerous criminals. In his "strainer" analogy, corrections expert Paul H. Hahn likens this process to the workings of a kitchen strainer. With each "shake" of the corrections "strainer," the less serious offenders are diverted

In Dallas, street prostitutes such as the two shown here are often treated as crime victims and offered access to treatment and rehabilitation programs. How might society benefit if such offenders are kept out of jail or prison through these kinds of diversion programs?

AP Photo/LM Otero, File

from incarceration. At the end, only the most serious convicts remain to be sent to prison.[7]

The diversionary role of community-based punishments has become more pronounced as prisons and jails have filled up over the past three decades. In fact, probationers now account for about 60 percent of all adults in the American corrections system. According to the U.S. Department of Justice, on any single day, almost 2 percent of all adults in this country are under probation supervision.[8]

THE "LOW-COST ALTERNATIVE"

Not all of the recent expansion of community corrections can be attributed to acceptance of its theoretical underpinnings. Many politicians and criminal justice officials who do not look favorably on ideas such as reintegration and diversion have embraced programs to keep nonviolent offenders out of prison. The reason is simple: economics. The cost of constructing and maintaining prisons and jails, as well as housing and caring for inmates, has placed a great deal of pressure on corrections budgets across the country. Indeed, to cut incarceration costs, state prisons are taking such steps as installing windmills and solar panels to save energy and using medical students rather than physicians to provide less costly health care.[9]

Community corrections offer an enticing financial alternative to imprisonment. Data compiled by the Center for Economic and Policy Research suggest that for each nonviolent offender shifted from incarceration to community supervision, the federal government saves about $22,7000, and state governments save about $23,200.[10] It is not surprising that the majority of states have passed community corrections legislation aimed at moving offenders from their cells into the community.[11] In Texas, corrections officials estimate that programs designed to increase the use of probation and intermediate sanctions have saved the state nearly $450 million in prison costs.[12] Officials can also require community-based criminals to pay the bill for their own supervision. In Oklahoma, probationers pay a $40 monthly fee to cover part of the costs of their supervision.[13]

SELFASSESSMENT

Fill in the blanks and check your answers on page 305.

The three basic justifications for community corrections are (1) _____ , which focuses on building or rebuilding the offender's ties with the community; (2) _____ , a strategy that attempts to allocate scarce jail and prison space to only the most dangerous criminals; and (3) _____ considerations, as community corrections are generally _____ expensive than incarceration.

PROBATION: DOING TIME IN THE COMMUNITY

Not everyone was satisfied with the sentences given to Herbert and Catherine Schaible, described at the opening of this chapter. Critics pointed out that "faith-based neglect" is not a recognized defense for criminal behavior, and parents who involuntarily injure or kill their children for nonreligious reasons are often punished with prison terms.[14] Still,

Judge Carolyn Engel Temin hardly broke new ground by choosing *probation* for the Schaibles. A system that initially provided judges with the discretion to show leniency to first-time, minor offenders increasingly allows those who have committed serious crimes to avoid incarceration. Fifty percent of probationers in this country have been convicted of a felony, and about 770,000 have been found guilty of a violent crime such as assault or rape.[15]

As Figure 10.1 alongside shows, **probation** is the most common form of punishment in the United States. Although it is administered differently in various jurisdictions, probation can be generally defined as

> the legal status of an offender who, after being convicted of a crime, has been directed by the sentencing court to remain in the community under the supervision of a probation service for a designated period of time and subject to certain conditions imposed by the court or by law.[16]

(As you read this chapter, keep in mind the distinction between *probation* and *parole*. Although they sound similar and both involve community supervision of offenders, there are differences. Probation is a sentence handed down by a judge following conviction and usually does not include incarceration. Parole, as will be explained in detail in Chapter 12, is a form of conditional release from prison.)

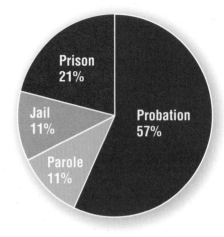

FIGURE 10.1 **Probation in American Corrections**
As you can see, the majority of convicts under the control of the American corrections system are on probation.

Source: Bureau of Justice Statistics, *Correctional Population in the United States, 2010* (Washington, D.C.: U.S. Department of Justice, December 2011), Table 1, page 3.

SENTENCING CHOICES AND PROBATION

Probation is basically an arrangement between sentencing authorities and the offender. In traditional probation, the offender agrees to comply with certain terms for a specified amount of time in return for serving the sentence in the community. One of the primary benefits for the offender, besides not getting sent to a correctional facility, is that the length of the probationary period is usually considerably shorter than the length of a prison term (see Figure 10.2 on the following page).

The traditional form of probation is not the only arrangement that can be made. A judge can hand down a **suspended sentence**, under which a defendant who has been convicted and sentenced to be incarcerated is not required to serve the sentence. Instead, the judge puts the offender on notice, keeping open the option of reinstating the original sentence and sending the offender to prison or jail if he or she reoffends. In practice, suspended sentences are quite similar to probation.

Learning Objective 2 Explain several alternative sentencing arrangements that combine probation with incarceration.

ALTERNATIVE SENTENCING ARRANGEMENTS Judges can also combine probation with incarceration. Such sentencing arrangements include the following:

- *Split sentences.* In **split sentence probation,** also known as *shock probation,* the offender is sentenced to a specific amount of time in prison or jail, to be followed by a period of probation.
- *Shock incarceration.* In this arrangement, an offender is sentenced to prison or jail with the understanding that after a period of time, she or he may petition the court to be released on probation. (Shock incarceration is discussed more fully later in the chapter.)
- *Intermittent incarceration.* With intermittent incarceration, the offender spends a certain amount of time each week, usually during the weekend, in a jail, workhouse, or other government institution.

Split sentences are popular with judges, as they combine the "treatment" aspects of probation with the "punishment" aspects of incarceration. According to the U.S.

Probation A criminal sanction in which a convict is allowed to remain in the community rather than be imprisoned.

Suspended Sentence A judicially imposed condition in which an offender is sentenced after being convicted of a crime, but is not required to begin serving the sentence immediately.

Split Sentence Probation A sentence that consists of incarceration in a prison or jail, followed by a probationary period in the community.

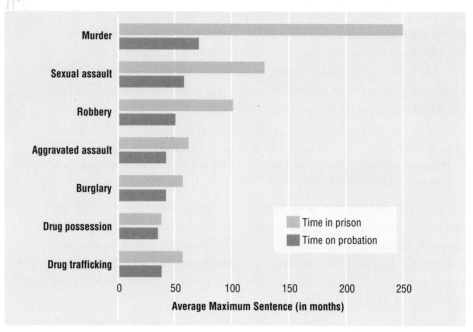

FIGURE 10.2 Average Length of Sentence: Prison versus Probation

As you can see, the average probation sentence is shorter than the average prison sentence for most crimes.

Source: Bureau of Justice Statistics, *Felony Sentences in State Courts, 2006—Statistical Tables* (Washington, D.C.: U.S. Department of Justice, December 2009), Table 1.3.

Department of Justice, about a fifth of all probationers are also sentenced to some form of incarceration.[17]

Learning Objective 3 Specify the conditions under which an offender is most likely to be denied probation.

ELIGIBILITY FOR PROBATION Not every offender is eligible for probation. In Bell County, Texas, for example, juries can recommend probation only for assessed prison sentences of ten years or less. Generally, research has shown that offenders are most likely to be denied probation if they:

- Are convicted on multiple charges.
- Were on probation or parole at the time of the arrest.
- Have two or more prior convictions.
- Are addicted to narcotics.
- Seriously injured the victim of the crime.
- Used a weapon during the commission of the crime.[18]

As noted earlier, about half of all probationers have been found guilty of a misdemeanor, and about half have been found guilty of a felony.[19] As might be expected, the chances of a felon being sentenced to probation are highly dependent on the seriousness of the crime he or she has committed. Only one in five felons on probation has been convicted of a violent crime.[20]

CONDITIONS OF PROBATION

A judge may decide to impose certain conditions as part of a probation sentence. These conditions represent a "contract" between the judge and the offender, in which the latter agrees that if she or he does not follow certain rules, probation may be revoked (see Figure 10.3 on the facing page). The probation officer usually recommends the conditions of probation, but judges also have the power to set any terms they believe to be necessary. As we saw at the beginning of this chapter, Judge Carolyn Engel Temin imposed several conditions on the Schaibles, requiring that the couple make their seven children available to physicians on a regular basis.

PRINCIPLES OF PROBATION A judge's personal philosophy is often reflected in the probation conditions that he or she creates for probationers. In *In re Quirk* (1997),[21] for example, the Louisiana Supreme Court upheld the ability of a trial judge to impose church attendance as a condition of probation. Although judges have a great deal of discretion in setting the conditions of probation, they do operate under several guiding principles. First, the conditions must be related to the dual purposes of probation, which most federal and state courts define as (1) the rehabilitation of the probationer and (2) the protection of the community. Second, the conditions must not violate the U.S. Constitution, as probationers are generally entitled to the same constitutional rights as other prisoners.[22]

Of course, probationers do give up certain constitutional rights when they consent to the terms of probation. Most probationers, for example, agree to spot checks of their homes for contraband such as drugs or weapons, and they therefore have a diminished expectation of privacy.

In *United States v. Knights* (2001),[23] the United States Supreme Court upheld the actions of deputy sheriffs in Napa County, California, who searched a probationer's home without a warrant or probable cause. The unanimous decision was based on the premise that because those on probation are more likely to commit crimes, law enforcement agents "may therefore justifiably focus on probationers in a way that [they do] not on the ordinary citizen."[24]

TYPES OF CONDITIONS Obviously, probationers who break the law are very likely to have their probation revoked. Other, less serious infractions may also result in revocation. The conditions placed on a probationer fall into three general categories:

- *Standard conditions,* which are imposed on all probationers. These include reporting regularly to the probation officer, notifying the agency of any change of address, not leaving the jurisdiction without permission, and remaining employed.
- *Punitive conditions,* which usually reflect the seriousness of the offense and are intended to increase the punishment of the offender. Such conditions include

FIGURE 10.3 Conditions of Probation

UNITED STATES DISTRICT COURT
FOR THE
DISTRICT OF COLUMBIA

To: _____ No. 84-417

Address: 1440 N St., N.W., #10, Wash., D.C.

In accordance with authority conferred by the United States Probation Law, you have been placed on probation this date, January 25, 2013, for a period of one year by the Hon. Thomas F. Hogan United States District Judge, sitting in and for this District Court at Washington, D.C.

CONDITIONS OF PROBATION

It is the order of the Court that you shall comply with the following conditions of probation:

(1)-You shall refrain from violation of any law (federal, state, and local). You shall get in touch immediately with your probation officer if arrested or questioned by a law enforcement officer.

(2)-You shall associate only with law-abiding persons and maintain reasonable hours.

(3)-You shall work regularly at a lawful occupation and support your legal dependents, if any, to the best of your ability. When out of work you shall notify your probation officer at once. You shall consult him prior to job changes.

(4)-You shall not leave the judicial district without permission of the probation officer.

(5)-You shall notify your probation officer immediately of any change in your place of residence.

(6)-You shall follow the probation officer's instructions.

(7)-You shall report to the probation officer as directed.

(8)-You shall not possess a firearm (handgun or rifle) for any reason.

The special conditions ordered by the Court are as follows:

   Imposition of sentence suspended, one year probation, Fine of $75 on each count.

I understand that the Court may change the conditions of probation, reduce or extend the period of probation, and at any time during the probation period or within the maximum probation period of 5 years permitted by law, may issue a warrant and revoke probation for a violation occurring during the probation period.

I have read or had read to me the above conditions of probation. I fully understand them and I will abide by them.

_____ Date _____
Probationer

You will report as follows: _____ as directed by your Probation Officer

_____ Date _____
U.S. Probation Officer

fines, community service, restitution, drug testing, and home confinement (discussed later).

• *Treatment conditions,* which are imposed to reverse patterns of self-destructive behavior. Data show that more than 40 percent of probationers were required to undergo drug or alcohol treatment as part of their sentences, and an additional 18 percent were ordered to seek other kinds of treatment, such as anger-control therapy.[25]

Some observers feel that judges often impose overly restrictive probation conditions that no person, much less one who has exhibited antisocial tendencies, could meet. Citing prohibitions on drinking liquor, gambling, and associating with "undesirables," as well as requirements such as meeting early curfews, the late University of Delaware professor Carl Klockars claimed that if probation rules were taken seriously, "very few probationers would complete their terms without violation."[26]

As more than six out of ten federal probationers do complete their terms successfully, Klockars's statement suggests one of two scenarios. Either probation officers are unable to determine that violations are taking place, or they routinely decide not to report minor probation violations. Perhaps the officers realize that violating probationers for every single "slip-up" is unrealistic and would add to the already significant problem of prison overcrowding.

> "I try to get in the field two to three nights a week to see my offenders. It's really the only way to stop trouble before it happens. Otherwise, it's a free-for-all."
>
> **—Kevin Dudley,**
> Salt Lake City probation officer

Social Media and CJ **Probation Officers** provides constant tweeting news about probation officers and probation departments. To access this Twitter page online, visit the *Criminal Justice CourseMate* at **cengagebrain.com** and select the *Web Links* for this chapter.

THE SUPERVISORY ROLE OF THE PROBATION OFFICER

The probation officer has two basic roles. The first is investigative and consists of compiling the presentence investigative report, which was discussed in Chapter 9. The second is supervisory and begins as soon as the offender has been sentenced to probation. In smaller probation agencies, individual officers perform both tasks. In larger jurisdictions, the trend has been toward separating the responsibilities, with *investigating officers* handling the presentence investigation and *line officers* concentrating on supervision.

Supervisory policies vary and are often a reflection of whether the authority to administer probation services is *decentralized* (under local, judicial control) or *centralized* (under state, administrative control). In any circumstance, however, certain basic principles of supervision apply. Starting with a preliminary interview, the probation officer establishes a relationship with the offender. This relationship is based on the mutual goal of both parties: the successful completion of the probationary period. Just because the line officer and the offender have the same goal, however, does not necessarily mean that cooperation will be a feature of probation.

THE USE OF AUTHORITY The ideal probation officer–offender relationship is based on trust. In reality, this trust often does not exist. Any incentive an offender might have to be completely truthful with a line officer is marred by one simple fact: self-reported wrongdoing can be used to revoke probation. Even probation officers whose primary mission is to rehabilitate are under institutional pressure to punish their clients for violating conditions of probation. One officer deals with this situation by telling his clients

> that I'm here to help them, to get them a job, and whatever else I can do. But I tell them too that I have a family to support and that if they get too far off track, I can't afford to put my job on the line for them. I'm going to have to violate them.[27]

In the absence of trust, most probation officers rely on their **authority** to guide an offender successfully through the sentence. An officer's authority, or ability to influence a person's actions without resorting to force, is based partially on her or his power to revoke probation. It also reflects her or his ability to impose a number of lesser sanctions. For example, if a probationer fails to attend a required alcohol treatment program, the officer can send him or her to a "lockup," or detention center, overnight. To be successful, a probation officer must establish this authority early in the relationship, because it is the primary tool for persuading the probationer to behave in a manner acceptable to the community.[28]

A Washington, D.C., probation officer makes phone curfew checks while her partner watches. Why is trust so often difficult to achieve between probation officers and offenders?

Mark Gail/*Washington Post*/Getty Images

THE CASELOAD DILEMMA Even the most balanced, "firm but fair" approach to probation can be defeated by the problem of excessive *caseloads*. A **caseload** is the number of clients a probation officer is responsible for at any one time. Heavy probation caseloads seem inevitable: unlike a prison cell, a probation officer can always take "just one more" client. Furthermore, the ideal caseload size is very difficult to determine because different offenders require different levels of supervision.[29]

The consequences of disproportionate probation officer–probationer ratios are self-evident, however. When burdened with large caseloads, probation officers find it practically impossible to rigorously enforce the conditions imposed on their clients. Lack of surveillance leads to lack of control, which can undermine the very basis of a probationary system. Chicago sex offender Acurie Collier violated the terms of his probation at least forty times before sexually assaulting a thirteen-year-old girl several years ago. The Chicago probation department's sex offender unit had four probation officers overseeing 130 cases at the time—considered a low workload by city standards.[30]

REVOCATION OF PROBATION

The probation period can end in one of two ways. Either the probationer successfully fulfills the conditions of the sentence, or the probationer misbehaves and probation is revoked, resulting in a prison or jail term. The decision of whether to revoke after a **technical violation**—such as failing to report a change of address or testing positive for drug use—is often a judgment call by the probation officer and therefore the focus of controversy. (See the feature *You Be the Probation Officer—A Judgment Call* on the following page to learn more about the issues surrounding revocation.)

As we have seen, probationers do not always enjoy the same protections under the U.S. Constitution as other members of society. The United States Supreme Court has not stripped these offenders of all rights, however. In *Mempa v. Rhay* (1967),[31] the Court ruled that probationers were entitled to an attorney during the revocation process. Then, in *Morrissey v. Brewer* (1972) and *Gagnon v. Scarpelli* (1973),[32] the Court established a three-stage procedure by which the "limited" due process rights of probationers must be protected in potential revocation situations:

- *Preliminary hearing.* In this court appearance, the facts of the violation or arrest are presented, and a "disinterested person" (often a judge) determines whether

Authority The power designated to an agent of the law over a person who has broken the law.

Caseload The number of individual probationers or parolees under the supervision of a probation or parole officer.

Technical Violation An action taken by a probationer that, although not criminal, breaks the terms of probation as designated by the court.

Learning Objective **5** Explain the three stages of probation revocation.

probable cause for revoking probation exists. This hearing can be waived by the probationer.

- *Revocation hearing.* During this hearing, the probation agency presents evidence to support its claim of violation, and the probationer can attempt to refute this evidence. The probationer has the right to know the charges being brought against him or her. Furthermore, probationers can testify on their own behalf and present witnesses in their favor, as well as confront and cross-examine adverse witnesses. A "neutral and detached" body must hear the evidence and rule on the validity of the proposed revocation.

- *Revocation sentencing.* If the presiding body rules against the probationer, then the judge must decide whether to impose incarceration and for what length of time. In a revocation hearing dealing with technical violations, the judge will often reimpose probation with stricter terms or intermediate sanctions.

In effect, this is a "bare-bones" approach to due process. Most of the rules of evidence that govern regular trials do not apply to revocation hearings. Probation officers are not, for example, required to read offenders their *Miranda* rights before questioning them about crimes they may have committed during probation. In *Minnesota v. Murphy* (1984),[33] the Supreme Court ruled that a meeting between probation officer

YOU BE THE PROBATION OFFICER
A Judgment Call

THE FACTS Your client, Alain, was convicted of selling drugs and given a split sentence—three years in prison and three years on probation. You meet Alain for the first time two days after his release, and you are immediately concerned about his mental health. His mother confirms your worries, telling you that Alain needs help. You refer him to a psychiatric hospital, but the officials there determine that he "does not require mental health treatment at this time." Several weeks later, Alain's mother tells you that he is staying out late at night and "hanging out with the wrong crowd," both violations of his probation agreement. After he tests positive for marijuana, you warn Alain that after one more violation, you will revoke his probation and send him back to prison. He tells you that he is "feeling agitated" and "having intermittent rage." You refer him to a substance abuse and mental health treatment facility, where he tests positive for marijuana once again.

THE LAW For any number of reasons, but particularly for the failed drug tests, you can start revocation proceedings against Alain. These proceedings will almost certainly conclude with his return to prison.

YOUR DECISION On the one hand, Alain has violated the terms of his probation agreement numerous times. On the other hand, he has been convicted of only one crime—a drug violation—and you have no evidence that he is behaving violently or poses a danger to himself or others. Furthermore, Alain has strong family support and is willing to enter treatment for his drug problems. Do Alain's technical violations cause you to begin the revocation process? Why or why not?

[To see how a Fairfield County, Connecticut, probation officer dealt with a similar situation, go to Example 10.1 in Appendix B.]

and client does not equal custody and, therefore, the Fifth Amendment protection against self-incrimination does not apply, either.

NEW MODELS OF PROBATION

In their efforts to cut the costs and caseloads associated with corrections, a number of jurisdictions are experimenting with new models of probation. Hawaii's Office of the Attorney General, for example, operates Hawaii's Opportunity Probation with Enforcement (HOPE) program under the "swift and certain" principle. The rules of HOPE are simple. Each substance abuse probationer must call the courthouse every day to learn if she or he is required to come in for urine tests for drugs, or *urinalysis*. If drugs are found in the probationer's system during one of these frequent tests, a short jail term— one to two weeks—is automatically served. HOPE has resulted in large reductions in positive drugs tests by probationers, and its 1,500 participants are significantly less likely to be rearrested than those not in the program.[34]

In 2000, with the approval of a ballot initiative, California embarked on an even more ambitious undertaking. The Substance Abuse and Crime Prevention Act changed the state penal code to mandate probation for any first- or second-time drug offender arrested for a crime involving personal use.[35] As a condition of probation, the offender must complete a yearlong drug treatment program followed by six months of aftercare. A study by researchers at the University of California at Los Angeles found that, in the five years following the law's passage, the number of drug possession–related prison admissions in California decreased by 30 percent. During that same period, the state saved nearly $3,000 per year for each probationer in treatment rather than behind bars.[36]

SELFASSESSMENT

Fill in the blanks and check your answers on page 305.

Offenders sentenced to probation serve their sentence in the _____ under the supervision of a _____ _____. If a probationer commits a _____ _____ by failing to follow the _____ of his or her probation, it may be revoked. If revocation occurs, the offender will be sent to _____.

INTERMEDIATE SANCTIONS

Many observers feel that the most widely used sentencing options—imprisonment and probation—fail to reflect the immense diversity of crimes and criminals. **Intermediate sanctions** provide a number of additional sentencing options for those wrongdoers who require stricter supervision than that supplied by probation, but for whom imprisonment would be unduly harsh and counterproductive.[37] The intermediate sanctions discussed in this section are designed to match the specific punishment and treatment of an individual offender with a corrections program that reflects that offender's situation.

Intermediate Sanctions Sanctions that are more restrictive than probation and less restrictive than imprisonment.

Dozens of different variations of intermediate sanctions are handed down each year. To cover the spectrum succinctly, two general categories of such sanctions will be discussed in this section: those administered primarily by the courts and those administered primarily by corrections departments, including day reporting centers, intensive supervision probation, shock incarceration, and home confinement. Remember that none of these sanctions are exclusive. They are often combined with imprisonment and probation, and with each other.

CAREERS IN CJ

PEGGY McCARTHY
LEAD PROBATION OFFICER

Courtesy Peggy McCarthy

The best thing about my job is that every day is different. I may be in court first thing in the morning, and then in my office meeting with defendants or developing case plans. In the afternoon, I may be at the jail taking statements for court reports or out in the field seeing my defendants. If I work a late shift, I may be visiting counseling agencies or talking to collateral sources or doing surveillance. I may be organizing a search on a defendant's home or making an arrest. I may be working with the police to solve crimes or locate absconders. Or I may simply be completing administrative duties like filing or returning phone calls to defendants and/or their family members. Anything can happen at any time, and I have to be ready to respond. If a probation officer gets bored, something is wrong.

I take a great deal of pride in assisting defendants with the difficult task of making positive change in their lives. The rewards may be few and far between, but when a defendant with a history of substance abuse stays clean and sober for a year, when a gang-affiliated defendant secures a job and no longer associates with negative peers, or when a defendant who admittedly never liked school obtains a GED or diploma, that is when I realize that what I'm doing day in and day out is 100 percent worthwhile.

Social Media Career Tip

Manage your online reputation—or someone else will do it for you. Monitor your profile using tools such as iSearch, Pipl, and ZabaSearch. Check BoardTracker, BoardReader, and Omgili for information on what people are saying about you on message boards. f **Linked** in. ⬤

FAST FACTS

LEAD PROBATION OFFICER, JOB DESCRIPTION:

- Work with offenders or clients who have been sentenced to probation.
- Work with the courts. Investigate backgrounds, write presentence reports, and recommend sentences.

WHAT KIND OF TRAINING IS REQUIRED?

- Bachelor's degree in criminal justice, social work/psychology, or related field.
- Must be at least 21 years of age, have no felony convictions, and have strong writing and interview skills. Experience in multicultural outreach a plus.

ANNUAL SALARY RANGE?

- $31,500 – $51,500

JUDICIALLY ADMINISTERED SANCTIONS

The lack of sentencing options is most frustrating for the person who, in the majority of cases, does the sentencing—the judge. Consequently, when judges are given the discretion to "color" a punishment with intermediate sanctions, they will often do so. In addition to imprisonment and probation, a judge has five sentencing options:

Learning Objective 6 List the five sentencing options for a judge besides imprisonment and probation.

1. Fines.
2. Community service.
3. Restitution.
4. Pretrial diversion programs.
5. Forfeiture.

Fines, community service, and restitution were discussed in Chapter 9. In the context of intermediate sanctions, it is important to remember that these punishments are generally combined with incarceration or probation. For that reason, some critics feel the retributive or deterrent impact of such punishments is severely limited. Many European countries, in contrast, rely heavily on fines as the sole sanctions for a variety of crimes. (See the feature *Comparative Criminal Justice—Swedish Day-Fines* on the following page.)

PRETRIAL DIVERSION PROGRAMS Not every criminal violation requires the courtroom process. Consequently, some judges have the discretion to order an offender into a **pretrial diversion program** during the preliminary hearing. (Prosecutors can also offer an offender the opportunity to join such a program in return for reducing or dropping the initial charges.) These programs represent an "interruption" of the criminal proceedings and are generally reserved for young or first-time offenders who have been arrested on charges of illegal drug use, child or spousal abuse, or sexual misconduct. Pretrial diversion programs usually include extensive counseling, often in a treatment center. If the offender successfully follows the conditions of the program, the criminal charges are dropped.

Pretrial Diversion Program
An alternative to trial offered by a judge or prosecutor, in which the offender agrees to participate in a specified counseling or treatment program in return for withdrawal of the charges.

PROBLEM-SOLVING COURTS In many instances, judges have found opportunities to divert low-level offenders by presiding over *problem-solving courts*. In these comparatively informal courtrooms, judges attempt to address problems such as drug addiction, mental illness, and homelessness that often lead to the eventual rearrest of the offender.[38]

Drug Courts About three thousand problem-solving courts are operating in the United States. Although these specialized courts cover a wide variety of subjects, from domestic violence to juvenile crime to mental illness, the most common problem-solving courts are *drug courts*. Although the specific procedures of drug courts vary widely from jurisdiction to jurisdiction, most follow a general pattern. Either after arrest or on conviction, the offender is given the option of entering a drug court program or continuing through the standard courtroom process. Those who choose the former come under the supervision of a judge who will oversee a mixture of treatment and sanctions designed to cure their addiction. When offenders successfully complete the program, the drug court rewards them by dropping all charges against them. Drug courts operate on the assumption that when a criminal addict's drug use is reduced, his or her drug-fueled criminal activity will also decline.

Growing Influence Research shows that drug courts reduce the probably of continued drug abuse and, consequently, lead to a significant reduction in recidivism rates of participants when compared with nonparticipants.[39] As a result of this kind of success, problem-solving principles are moving beyond specialty courts into mainstream criminal courts, allowing judges to insert principles of restorative justice, which we discussed in Chapter 9, into their diversion efforts.

For example, more judges are taking advantage of *community dispute resolution centers* to move certain misdemeanors and minor criminal matters out of the court system completely. At these centers, specialists help the parties engaged in a dispute—such as one involving vandalism or noise complaints—by *mediating,* or negotiating, a satisfactory outcome for both sides. In 2011, New York judges, prosecutors, and police officers referred more than 3,100 criminal cases to community dispute resolution centers, thus diverting the participants from the formal court system.[40]

FORFEITURE In 1970, Congress passed the Racketeer Influenced and Corrupt Organizations Act (RICO) in an attempt to prevent the use of legitimate business enterprises as shields for organized crime.[41] As amended, RICO and other statutes give judges

COMPARATIVE CRIMINAL JUSTICE

SWEDISH DAY-FINES

Few ideals are cherished as highly in our criminal justice system as is equality. Most Americans take it for granted that individuals guilty of identical crimes should face identical punishments. From an economic perspective, however, this emphasis on equality renders our system decidedly unequal. Take two citizens, one a millionaire investment banker and the other a checkout clerk earning the minimum wage. Driving home from work one afternoon, each is caught by a traffic officer doing 80 miles per hour in a 55-mile-per-hour zone. The fine for this offense is $150. This amount, though equal for both, has different consequences: it represents mere pocket change for the investment banker, but a significant chunk out of the checkout clerk's weekly paycheck.

Restricted by a "tariff system" that sets specific amounts for specific crimes, regardless of the financial situation of the convict, American judges often refrain from using fines as a primary sanction. They either assume that poor offenders cannot pay the fine or worry that a fine will allow wealthier offenders to "buy" their way out of a punishment.

Paying for Crime

In searching for a way to make fines more effective sanctions, many reformers have seized on the concept of the "day-fine," as practiced in Sweden and several other European countries. In this system, which was established nearly a century ago, the fine amount is linked to the monetary value of the offender's daily income. Depending on the seriousness of the crime, a Swedish offender will be sentenced to 1 to 120 day-fines or, as combined punishment for multiple crimes, up to 200 day-fines.

For each day-fine unit assessed, the offender is required to pay one-thousandth of her or his annual gross income (minus a deduction for basic living expenses, as determined by the Prosecutor General's Office) to the court. Consequently, the day-fine system not only reflects the degree of the crime but also ensures that the economic burden will be equal for those with different incomes.

Swedish police and prosecutors can levy day-fines without court involvement. As a result, plea bargaining is nonexistent, and more than 80 percent of all offenders are sentenced to intermediate sanctions without a trial. The remaining cases receive full trials, with an acquittal rate of only 6 percent, compared with roughly 32 percent in the United States.

FOR CRITICAL ANALYSIS Do you think a day-fine system would be feasible in the United States? Why might it be difficult to implement in this country?

Forfeiture The process by which the government seizes private property attached to criminal activity.

the ability to implement forfeiture proceedings in certain criminal cases. **Forfeiture** is a process by which the government seizes property gained from or used in criminal activity. For example, if a person is convicted for smuggling cocaine into the United States from South America, a judge can order the seizure of not only the narcotics but also the speedboat the offender used to deliver the drugs to a pickup point off the coast of South Florida. In *Bennis v. Michigan* (1996),[42] the Supreme Court ruled that a person's home or car could be forfeited even though the owner was unaware that the property was connected to illegal activity.

Once property is forfeited, the government has several options. It can sell the property, with the proceeds going to the state and/or federal law enforcement agencies involved in the seizure. Alternatively, the government agency can use the property directly in further crime-fighting efforts or award it to a third party, such as an informant. Forfeiture is financially rewarding—the U.S. Marshals Service manages nearly $4 billion worth of contraband and property impounded from alleged criminals. Each year, the agency shares about $580 million of these funds with state and local law enforcement agencies, with an additional $345 million going to crime victims.[43]

DAY REPORTING CENTERS

First used in Great Britain, **day reporting centers (DRCs)** are mainly tools to reduce jail and prison overcrowding. Although the offenders are allowed to live in the community rather than jail or prison, they must spend all or part of each day at a reporting center. In general, being sentenced to a DRC is an extreme form of supervision. With offenders under a single roof, they are much more easily monitored and controlled.

DRCs are instruments of rehabilitation as well. They often feature treatment programs for drug and alcohol abusers and provide counseling for a number of psychological problems, such as depression and anger management. Many of those found guilty in the Roanoke (Virginia) Drug Court, for example, are ordered to participate in a yearlong day reporting program. At the center, offenders meet with probation officers, submit to urine tests, and attend counseling and education programs, such as parenting and life-skills classes. After the year has passed, if the offender has completed the program to the satisfaction of the judge and has found employment, the charges will be dropped.[44]

INTENSIVE SUPERVISION PROBATION

Over the past several decades, a number of jurisdictions have turned to **intensive supervision probation (ISP)** to solve the problems associated with burdensome caseloads we discussed earlier in the chapter. ISP offers a more restrictive alternative to regular probation, with higher levels of face-to-face contact between offenders and officers and frequent modes of control such as urine tests for drugs. In New Jersey, for example, ISP officers have caseloads of only 20 offenders (compared with 115 for other probation officers in the state) and are provided with additional resources to help them keep tabs on their charges.[45] Different jurisdictions have different methods of determining who is eligible for ISP, but a majority of states limit ISP to offenders who do not have prior probation violations.

The main goal of ISP is to provide prisonlike control of offenders while keeping them out of prison. Critics of ISP believe that it "causes" high failure rates, as more supervision increases the chances that an offender will be caught breaking conditions of probation.[46] A recent comparison of ISP with DRCs, however, found the intensive supervision of ISP to be more effective. In the six months following termination of the program, DRC participants were more likely to be convicted for a new offense and to test positive for drugs than their ISP counterparts. The study suggests that when combined with services such as outpatient drug treatment and educational training, ISP can be effective in producing low rates of recidivism.[47]

SHOCK INCARCERATION

As the name suggests, **shock incarceration** is designed to "shock" criminals into compliance with the law. Following conviction, the offender is first sentenced to a prison or jail term. Then, usually within ninety days, he or she is released and resentenced to probation. The theory behind shock incarceration is that by getting a taste of the brutalities of the daily prison grind, the offender will be shocked into a crime-free existence.

In the past, shock incarceration was targeted primarily toward youthful, first-time offenders who were thought to be more likely to be "scared straight" by a short stint behind bars. Recent data show, however, that 20 percent of all adults sentenced to probation spend some time in jail or prison before being released into the community.[48] Critics of shock incarceration are dismayed by this trend. They argue that the practice needlessly disrupts

Day Reporting Center (DRC) A community-based corrections center to which offenders report on a daily basis for treatment, education, and rehabilitation.

Intensive Supervision Probation (ISP) A punishment-oriented form of probation in which the offender is placed under stricter and more frequent surveillance and control than in conventional probation by probation officers with limited caseloads.

Shock Incarceration A short period of incarceration that is designed to deter further criminal activity by "shocking" the offender with the hardships of imprisonment.

Learning Objective **7** Contrast day reporting centers with intensive supervision probation.

Inmates engage in morning calisthenics at the Impact Incarceration Program in Illinois. In theory, why would boot camps like this one benefit first-time nonviolent offenders more than a jail or prison sentence?

Journal Courier/The Image Works Image

the lives of low-level offenders who would not otherwise be eligible for incarceration and exposes them to the mental and physical hardships of prison life (which we will discuss in Chapter 12).[49] Furthermore, there is little evidence that shock probationers fare any better than regular probationers when it comes to recidivism rates.[50]

The *boot camp* is a variation on traditional shock incarceration. Instead of spending the "shock" period of incarceration in prison or jail, offenders are sent to a boot camp. Modeled on military basic training, these camps are generally located within prisons and jails, though some can be found in the community. The programs emphasize strict discipline, manual labor, and physical training. They are designed to instill self-responsibility and self-respect in participants, thereby lessening the chances that they will return to a life of crime. More recently, boot camps have also emphasized rehabilitation, incorporating such components as drug and alcohol treatment programs, anger-management courses, and vocational training.[51]

HOME CONFINEMENT AND ELECTRONIC MONITORING

Home Confinement A community-based sanction in which offenders serve their terms of incarceration in their homes.

Electronic Monitoring A technique of probation supervision in which the offender's whereabouts are kept under surveillance by an electronic device.

Various forms of **home confinement**—in which offenders serve their sentences not in a government institution but at home—have existed for centuries. Home confinement has often served, and continues to serve, as a method of political control used by totalitarian regimes to isolate and silence dissidents. For purposes of general law enforcement, home confinement was impractical until relatively recently. After all, one could not expect offenders to keep their promises to stay at home, and the personnel costs of guarding them were prohibitive. In the 1980s, however, with the advent of **electronic monitoring,** or using technology to guard the prisoner, home confinement became more viable. Today, all fifty states and the federal government have home monitoring programs with about 130,000 offenders participating at any one time.[52]

THE LEVELS OF HOME MONITORING Home monitoring has three general levels of restriction:

1. *Curfew,* which requires offenders to be in their homes at specific hours each day, usually at night.
2. *Home detention,* which requires that offenders remain home at all times, with exceptions being made for education, employment, counseling, or other specified activities such as the purchase of food or, in some instances, attendance at religious ceremonies.
3. *Home incarceration,* which requires the offender to remain home at all times, save for medical emergencies.

Under ideal circumstances, home confinement serves many of the goals of intermediate sanctions. It protects the community. It saves public funds and space in correctional

Learning Objective 8 List the three levels of home monitoring.

facilities by keeping convicts out of institutional incarceration. It meets public expectations of punishment for criminals. Uniquely, home confinement also recognizes that convicts, despite their crimes, play important roles in the community, and it allows them to continue in those roles. An offender, for example, may be given permission to leave confinement to care for elderly parents.

Home confinement is also lauded for giving sentencing officials the freedom to match the punishment with the needs of the offender. In Missouri, for instance, the conditions of detention for a musician required him to remain at home during the day, but allowed him to continue his career at night. In addition, he was obligated to make antidrug statements before each performance, to be verified by the manager at the club where he appeared.

Offenders who are confined to their homes are often monitored by electronic devices like this one, which fits around the ankle. What are some of the benefits of electronic monitoring as an intermediate sanction?

Damon Higgins/ZUMA Press/Newscom

TYPES OF ELECTRONIC MONITORING According to some reports, the inspiration for electronic monitoring was a *Spider-Man* comic book in which the hero was trailed by the use of an electronic device on his arm. In 1979, a New Mexico judge named Jack Love, having read the comic, convinced an executive at Honeywell, Inc., to begin developing similar technology to supervise convicts.[53]

Two major types of electronic monitoring have grown out of Love's initial concept. The first is a "programmed contact" program, in which the offender is contacted periodically by telephone or beeper to verify his or her whereabouts. Verification is obtained via a computer that uses voice or visual identification techniques or by requiring the offender to enter a code in an electronic box when called. The second is a "continuously signaling" device, worn around the convict's wrist, ankle, or neck. A transmitter in the device sends out a continuous signal to a "receiver-dialer" device located in the offender's dwelling. If the receiver device does not detect a signal from the transmitter, it informs a central computer, and the police are notified.[54]

CJ&**TECHNOLOGY**

Global Positioning System (GPS)

After Henry L. Murray committed a series of robberies in the Gainesville, Florida, area, he fled north into Georgia. Murray may have felt he was beyond the reach of the law, but Georgia authorities soon found him, thanks in large part to the global positioning system (GPS) device strapped to his ankle. GPS technology is a form of tracking technology that relies on twenty-four military satellites orbiting thousands of miles above the earth. The satellites transmit signals to each other and to a receiver on the ground, allowing a monitoring station to determine the location of a receiving device to within a few feet. GPS provides a much more precise level of supervision than regular electronic monitoring. A probationer like Murray wears a transmitter, similar to a traditional electronic monitor, around her or his ankle or wrist. This transmitter communicates with a portable tracking device, a small box that uses the military satellites to determine the probationer's movements.

AP Photo/Suchat Pederson

(Continued)

GPS technology can be used either "actively" to constantly monitor the subject's whereabouts, or "passively" to ensure that the offender remains within the confines of a limited area determined by a judge or probation officer. Inclusion and exclusion zones are also important to GPS supervision. Inclusion zones are areas, such as a home or workplace, where the offender is expected to be at certain times. Exclusion zones are areas such as parks, playgrounds, and schools, where the offender is not permitted to go. GPS-linked computers can alert officials immediately when an exclusion zone has been breached and can create a computerized record of the probationer's movements for review at a later time. Despite the benefits of this technology, it is rarely implemented. According to the Bureau of Justice Statistics, only about eight thousand offenders are currently being tracked by GPS.

THINKING ABOUT GPS: How could GPS technology be used to ensure that a convicted sex offender complies with a judge's order to stay away from areas where large numbers of children are present?

WIDENING THE NET

As mentioned above, most of the convicts chosen for intermediate sanctions are low-risk offenders. From the point of view of the corrections official doing the choosing, this makes sense. Such offenders are less likely to commit crimes and attract negative publicity. This selection strategy, however, appears to invalidate one of the primary reasons intermediate sanctions exist: to reduce prison and jail populations. If most of the offenders in intermediate sanctions programs would otherwise have received probation, then the effect on these populations is nullified. Indeed, studies have shown this to be the case.[55]

At the same time, intermediate sanctions broaden the reach of the corrections system. In other words, they increase rather than decrease the amount of control the state exerts over the individual. Suppose a person is arrested for a misdemeanor such as shoplifting and, under normal circumstances, would receive probation. With access to intermediate sanctions, the judge may add a period of home confinement to the sentence. Critics contend that such practices **widen the net** of the corrections system by augmenting the number of citizens who are under the control and surveillance of the state and also *strengthen the net* by increasing the government's power to intervene in the lives of its citizens.[56] Technological advances—such as the GPS devices mentioned above—will only accelerate the trend.

Widen the Net The criticism that intermediate sanctions designed to divert offenders from prison actually increase the number of citizens who are under the control and surveillance of the American corrections system.

SELFASSESSMENT
Fill in the blanks and check your answers on page 305.
Judicially administered sanctions include fines, restitution, and _____, a process in which the government seizes property connected to illegal activity. Offenders may also be sentenced to spend part of their time at _____ _____ _____, where they receive treatment and are more easily _____ by corrections officials. _____ _____, or militaristic programs designed to instill self-responsibility, are a form of _____ incarceration. Home confinement, another intermediate sanction, has become more effective in recent years thanks to technology known as _____ _____.

THE PARADOX OF COMMUNITY CORRECTIONS

Community-based corrections programs provide benefits, including cost savings, treatment options, and the ability to divert hundreds of thousands of nonviolent wrongdoers from prisons and jails. Still, this aspect of American corrections does suffer from a basic paradox: the more effectively offenders are controlled, the more likely they are to be caught violating the terms of their release. As you may have noticed, the community supervision programs discussed in this chapter are evaluated according to rates of recidivism and revocation, with low levels of each reflecting a successful program. Increased control and surveillance, however, will necessarily raise the level of violations, thus increasing the probability that any single violation will be discovered. Therefore, as factors such as the number of conditions placed on probationers and the technological proficiency of electronic monitoring devices increase, so, too, will the number of offenders who fail to meet the conditions of their community-based punishment.

One observer calls this the "quicksand" effect of increased surveillance. Instead of helping offenders leave the corrections system, increased surveillance pulls them more deeply into it.[57] According to researchers Barbara Sims of Penn State University–Harrisburg and Mark Jones of East Carolina University, the quicksand effect can be quite strong. In a study of North Carolina corrections data, Sims and Jones found that 26 percent of the probationers whose probation terms were revoked had been guilty of violations such as failing a single drug test. The researchers believe this strategy is overly punitive—anybody who has tried to quit smoking is aware of the difficulties of breaking an addiction.[58]

Ryan LeVin, center, surrenders to authorities in Crest Hill, Illinois, on June 13, 2011, after pleading guilty in the hit-and-run deaths of two British businessmen. For his crimes, a judge sentenced LeVin to two years of house arrest, ten years of probation, and 1,000 hours of community service. Do you think community corrections are appropriate for crimes that involve serious injury or loss of life? Why or why not?
Zbigniew Bzdak/MCT/Landov

CHAPTER SUMMARY

Learning Objective 1 **Explain the justifications for community-based corrections programs.** One justification involves reintegration of the offender into society. Reintegration restores family ties, encourages employment and education, and secures a place for the offender in the routine functioning of society. Other justifications involve diversion and cost savings. By diverting criminals to alternative modes of punishment, further overcrowding of jail and prison facilities can be avoided, as can the costs of incarcerating the offenders.

Learning Objective 2 **Explain several alternative sentencing arrangements that combine probation with incarceration.** With a suspended sentence, a convicted offender is not required to serve the sentence, but the judge has the option of reinstating the sentence if the person reoffends. In addition, there are three other general types of sentencing arrangements: (a) split sentence probation, in which the judge specifies a certain time in jail or prison followed by a certain time on probation; (b) shock incarceration, in which a judge sentences an offender to be incarcerated but allows that person to petition the court to be released on probation; and (c) intermittent incarceration, in which an offender spends a certain amount of time each week in jail or in a halfway house or another government institution.

Learning Objective 3 **Specify the conditions under which an offender is most likely to be denied probation.** The offender (a) has been convicted of multiple charges, (b) was on probation or parole when arrested, (c) has two or more prior convictions, (d) is addicted to narcotics, (e) seriously injured the victim of the crime, or (f) used a weapon while committing the crime.

Learning Objective 4 Describe the three general categories of conditions placed on a probationer. (a) Standard conditions, such as requiring that the probationer notify the agency of a change of address, not leave the jurisdiction without permission, and remain employed; (b) punitive conditions, such as restitution, community service, and home confinement; and (c) treatment conditions, such as required drug or alcohol treatment.

Learning Objective 5 Explain the three stages of probation revocation. (a) The preliminary hearing, usually before a judge, during which the facts of the probation violation are presented; (b) the revocation hearing, during which the probation agency presents its claims of violation and the probationer has an opportunity to refute them; and (c) revocation sentencing, during which a judge decides what to do with the probationer convicted of violating the terms of probation.

Learning Objective 6 List the five sentencing options for a judge besides imprisonment and probation. (a) Fines, (b) community service, (c) restitution, (d) pretrial diversion programs, and (e) forfeiture.

Learning Objective 7 Contrast day reporting centers with intensive supervision probation. In a day reporting center, the offender is allowed to remain in the community, but must spend all or part of each day at the reporting center. While at the center, offenders meet with probation officers, submit to drug tests, and attend counseling and education programs. With intensive supervision probation (ISP), more restrictions are imposed, and there is more face-to-face contact between offenders and probation officers.

Learning Objective 8 List the three levels of home monitoring. (a) Curfew, which requires that the offender be at home during specified hours; (b) home detention, which requires that the offender be at home except for education, employment, and counseling; and (c) home incarceration, which requires that the offender be at home at all times except for medical emergencies.

QUESTIONS FOR CRITICAL ANALYSIS

1. What are the dual purposes of probation (see page 291)? Which is more important? Why?

2. Review our discussion of Hawaii's Opportunity Probation with Enforcement (HOPE) program on page 295. What might explain why second violations of the urine tests are rare?

3. Review our discussion of California's Substance Abuse and Crime Prevention Act on page 295. The program has had one unintended consequence: in its first four years, drug arrests in California increased significantly.

Before 2000, these rates had been falling. How might the new law have contributed to this increase in drug crime?

4. Why might probationers or those subjected to intermediate sanctions want to limit their social media activity? Give an example of a circumstance in which a Facebook posting could cause probation to be revoked.

5. In your own words, explain what the phrase "widening the net" means. What might be some of the unintended consequences of increasing the number of offenders who are supervised by corrections officers in the community?

KEY TERMS

authority **293**
caseload **293**
community corrections **286**
day reporting center (DRC) **299**
diversion **287**
electronic monitoring **300**
forfeiture **298**

home confinement **300**
intensive supervision probation (ISP) **299**
intermediate sanctions **295**
pretrial diversion program **297**
probation **289**

reintegration **287**
shock incarceration **299**
split sentence probation **289**
suspended sentence **289**
technical violation **293**
widen the net **302**

SELF ASSESSMENT ANSWER KEY

Page 288: **i.** reintegration; **ii.** diversion; **iii.** cost; **iv.** less

Page 295: **i.** community; **ii.** probation officer; **iii.** technical violation; **iv.** conditions; **v.** prison/jail

Page 302: **i.** forfeiture; **ii.** day reporting centers; **iii.** supervised; **iv.** Boot camps; **v.** shock; **vi.** electronic monitoring

COURSEMATE

For online help and access to resources that accompany *Criminal Justice in Action: The Core*, go to **www.cengage-brain.com/shop/ISBN/978-1-285-06915-9**. Click "Access Now," where you will find flashcards, an online quiz, and other helpful study aids. If you have an access code for CourseMate, log in and go to the chapter of your choice for additional online study aids.

NOTES

1. Quoted in Mensah M. Dean, "Parents Get Probation for Using Prayer to Cure Ill Son, 2, Who Died," *Philadelphia Daily News* (February 3, 2011), 4.

2. *Ibid.*

3. Bureau of Justice Statistics, *Probation and Parole in the United States, 2010* (Washington, D.C.: U.S. Department of Justice, December 2011), 1.

4. Michael Tonry, *Sentencing Matters* (New York: Oxford Press, 1996), 28.

5. Todd Clear and Anthony Braga, "Community Corrections," in *Crime*, ed. James Q. Wilson and Joan Petersilia (San Francisco: ICS Press, 1995), 444.

6. Corrections Task Force of the President's Commission on Law Enforcement and Administration of Justice (1967).

7. Paul H. Hahn, *Emerging Criminal Justice: Three Pillars for a Proactive Justice System* (Thousand Oaks, CA: Sage Publications, 1998), 106–108.

8. Bureau of Justice Statistics, *Probation and Parole in the United States, 2010*, Table 1, page 3.

9. "Cutting Costs: How States Are Addressing Corrections Budget Shortfalls," *Corrections Directions* (December 2008), 6.

10. John Schmitt, Kris Warner, and Sarika Gupta, *The High Budgetary Cost of Incarceration* (Washington, D.C.: Center for Economic and Policy Research, June 2010), Table 4, page 11.

11. Mary Shilton, "Community Corrections Acts by State," at **centerforcommunitycorrections.org/?page_id=78**.

12. Lisa Falkenberg, "Austin Deserves Credit Here," *Houston Chronicle* (April 14, 2011), B1.

13. Nathan Koppel, "Probation Pays Bills for Prosecutors," *Wall Street Journal* (February 12, 2012), A2.

14. Jonathan Turley, "No Justice: Suffer the Little Children," *Tulsa World* (November 22, 2009), G3.

15. Bureau of Justice Statistics, *Probation and Parole in the United States, 2010*, Appendix table 5, page 33.

16. Paul W. Keve, *Crime Control and Justice in America* (Chicago: American Library Association, 1995), 183.

17. Bureau of Justice Statistics, *Probation and Parole in the United States, 2010*, Appendix table 3, page 31.

18. Joan Petersilia and Susan Turner, *Prison versus Probation in California: Implications for Crime and Offender Recidivism* (Santa Monica, CA: RAND Corporation, 1986).

19. Bureau of Justice Statistics, *Probation and Parole in the United States, 2010*, Appendix table 5, page 33.

20. *Ibid.*

21. 705 So.2d 172 (La. 1997).

22. Neil P. Cohen and James J. Gobert, *The Law of Probation and Parole* (Colorado Springs, CO: Shepard's/McGraw-Hill, 1983), Section 5.01, 183–184; Section 5.03, 191–192.

23. 534 U.S. 112 (2001).

24. *Ibid.*, 113.

25. Bureau of Justice Statistics, *Substance Abuse and Treatment for Adults on Probation, 1995* (Washington, D.C.: U.S. Department of Justice, March 1998), 11.

26. Carl B. Klockars, Jr., "A Theory of Probation Supervision," *Journal of Criminal Law, Criminology, and Police Science* 63 (1972), 550–557.

27. *Ibid.*, 551.

28. Hahn, 116–118.

29. Matthew T. DeMichele, *Probation and Parole's Growing Caseloads and Workload Allocation: Strategies for Managerial Decision Making* (Lexington, KY: American Probation and Parole Association, May 2007).

30. Jason Meisner, "Probation Officer Sued in Rape Case," *Chicago Tribune* (January 27, 2011), 7.

31. 389 U.S. 128 (1967).

32. *Morrissey v. Brewer*, 408 U.S. 471 (1972); and *Gagnon v. Scarpelli*, 411 U.S. 778 (1973).

33. 465 U.S. 420 (1984).

34. Angela Hawkins and Mark Kleiman, *Managing Drug Involved Probationers and Swift and Certain Sanctions: Evaluating Hawaii's HOPE* (Washington, D.C.: U.S. Department of Justice, December 2009), 4.

35. California Penal Code Sections 1210, 1210.1 (West Supp. 2004); and California Health and Safety Code Sections 11999.4–11999.13 (West Supp. 2004).

36. Douglas Longshore, Angela Hawken, Darren Urada, and M. Douglas Anglin, *Evaluation of the Substance Abuse and Crime Prevention Act: SACPA Cost-Analysis Report (First and Second Years)* (Los Angeles: UCLA Integrated Substance Abuse Programs, 2006), 5.

37. Norval Morris and Michael Tonry, *Between Prison and Probation: Intermediate Punishments in a Rational Sentencing System* (Oxford: Oxford University Press, 1990).

38. Robert V. Wolf, *Principles of Problem Solving Justice* (New York: Center for Court Innovation, 2007), 1.

39. Shelli B. Rossman et al., *The Multi-Site Adult Drug Court Evaluation: Executive Summary* (Washington, D.C.: Urban Institute, November 2011), 5; and *Studies Show Courts Reduce Recidivism, but DOJ Could Enhance Future Performance Measure Revision Efforts* (Washington, D.C.: U.S. Government Accounting Office, December 2011), 19–24.

40. *Community Dispute Resolution Centers Program: Annual Report 2010–2011* (New York: New York State Unified Court System, February 2012), 14.

41. 18 U.S.C. Sections 1961–1968.

42. 516 U.S. 442 (1996).

43. David Ashenfelter, "Police Gain Millions from Forfeited Assets," *Detroit Free Press* (February 27, 2012), A3.

44. Model State Drug Court Legislation Committee, *Model State Drug Court Legislation: Model Drug Offender Accountability and Treatment Act* (Alexandria, VA: National Drug Court Institute, May 2004), 42.

45. Kate Coscarelli, "A Model Program for Model Prisoners," *(Newark) Star Ledger* (February 24, 2004), 25.

46. Joan Petersilia and Susan Turner, "Intensive Probation and Parole," *Crime and Justice* 17 (1993), 281–335.

47. Douglas J. Boyle et al., *Outcomes of a Randomized Trial of an Intensive Community Corrections Program—Day Reporting Center—for Parolees,* final report for the National Institute of Justice (October 2011), 3–4.

48. Bureau of Justice Statistics, *Probation and Parole in the United States, 2010,* Appendix table 3, page 31.

49. Todd R. Clear, George F. Cole, and Michael D. Reisig, *American Corrections,* 7th ed. (Belmont, CA: Thomson Wadsworth, 2006).

50. Ted Palmer, "Programmatic and Non-programmatic Aspects of Successful Intervention: New Directions for Research," *Crime and Delinquency* (1995), 100–131.

51. Dale Parent, *Correctional Boot Camps: Lessons from a Decade of Research* (Washington, D.C.: U.S. Department of Justice, June 2003), 6.

52. Robert S. Gable, "Left to Their Own Devices: Should Manufacturers of Offender Monitoring Equipment Be Liable for Design Defect?" *University of Illinois Journal of Law, Technology, and Policy* (Fall 2009), 334.

53. Josh Kurtz, "New Growth in a Captive Market," *New York Times* (December 31, 1989), 12.

54. Edna Erez, Peter R. Ibarra, and Norman A. Lurie, "Electronic Monitoring of Domestic Violence Cases—A Study of Two Bilateral Programs," *Federal Probation* (June 2004), 15–20.

55. Michael Tonry and Mary Lynch, "Intermediate Sanctions," in *Crime and Justice,* vol. 20, ed. Michael Tonry (Chicago: University of Chicago Press, 1996), 99.

56. Dennis Palumbo, Mary Clifford, and Zoann K. Snyder-Joy, "From Net Widening to Intermediate Sanctions: The Transformation of Alternatives to Incarceration from Benevolence to Malevolence," in *Smart Sentencing: The Emergence of Intermediate Sanctions,* ed. James M. Byrne, Arthur Lurigio, and Joan Petersilia (Newbury Park, CA: Sage, 1992), 231.

57. Keve, 207.

58. Barbara Sims and Mark Jones, "Predicting Success or Failure on Probation: Factors Associated with Felony Probation Outcomes," *Crime and Delinquency* (July 1997), 314–327.

CHAPTER

11

Prisons and Jails

David Madison/Getty Images

LEARNING OBJECTIVES

After reading this chapter, you should be able to...

1. Contrast the Pennsylvania and the New York penitentiary theories of the 1800s.

2. List the factors that have caused the prison population to grow dramatically in the last several decades.

3. Describe the formal prison management system.

4. List and briefly explain the four types of prisons.

5. List the reasons why private prisons can often be run more cheaply than public ones.

6. Summarize the distinction between jails and prisons, and indicate the importance of jails in the American corrections system.

7. Explain how jails are administered.

8. Indicate some of the consequences of our high rates of incarceration.

Throughout the chapter you will see each learning objective repeated in the margin next to the content it relates to. The chapter summary on page 331 includes all of the learning objectives for review.

CHAPTER OUTLINE

- A Short History of American Prisons
- Inmate Population Trends
- Prison Organization and Management
- The Emergence of Private Prisons
- Jails
- The Consequences of Our High Rates of Incarceration

THE WAKE-UP CALL

California correctional authorities called the bunks—often stacked three high and jammed into day rooms, gyms, and any other available spaces—"nontraditional beds." Inmates had another name for their sleeping berths, crammed together so that there was no room to stand between them: "bad beds." Whatever the terminology, images of these tight living quarters have become a symbol of overcrowding in the California prison system, which, at its worst, had 162,000 inmates living in facilities designed to hold 80,000. "It's an unacceptable working environment for everyone," said a former state corrections official. "It leads to greater violence, more staff overtime, and a total inability to deal with health care and mental illness issues."

In May 2011, the United States Supreme Court agreed, ordering California to reduce its prison population by more than 30,000 inmates. Columnist Cal Thomas hailed the Court's decision as a "wake up call" for a "broken" American prison system. Besides California, a number of other states have heard the alarm. A month after the Court's ruling, New York announced plans to close seven prisons, eliminating 3,800 unused beds and saving state taxpayers nearly $200 million. Michigan had already shuttered five prisons, and numerous jurisdictions have taken steps to remove nonviolent inmates from their corrections systems.

As a consequence of these types of policies, in 2010, the total U.S. prison population declined for the first time in nearly four decades. To be sure, this decline was very small—about 0.6 percent—and does little to threaten America's title as "the globe's leading incarcerator." Still, the fact that many state politicians are willing to accept policies that reduce the number of people in prison represents a sea change in the nation's corrections strategy. According to Georgia governor Nathan Day, "We're at a point in time where the necessity for doing something has gotten so big that to . . . pretend the problem does not exist is not responsible government."

Overcrowding at California prisons such as the Institution for Men in Chino resulted in a U.S. Supreme Court order to reduce state inmate populations.

Monica Almeida/New York Times/Redux

Plans to "do something" aside, the American corrections system remains a colossal institution. Besides the nearly 5 million people under community supervision discussed in the last chapter, our prisons and jails hold nearly 2.3 million inmates—about one of every hundred adults.[1] The United States locks up six times as many of its citizens as Canada does, and seven times as many as most European democracies.

Throughout this textbook, we have discussed many of the social and political factors that help explain this situation, often referred to as "mass incarceration." In this chapter and the next, we turn our attention to the incarceration system itself. This chapter focuses on the history and organizational structures of prisons (which generally hold those who have committed serious felonies and are serving long sentences) and jails (which generally hold, for short periods of time, those who have committed less serious felonies and misdemeanors, and those awaiting trial). Although the two terms are often used interchangeably, they refer to two very different institutions, each with its own place in the criminal justice system and its own set of problems and challenges.

A SHORT HISTORY OF AMERICAN PRISONS

Today, we view prisons as instruments of punishment. The loss of freedom imposed on inmates is society's retribution for the crimes they have committed. This has not always been the function of incarceration. The prisons of eighteenth-century England, known as "bridewells" after London's Bridewell Palace, actually had little to do with punishment. These facilities were mainly used to hold debtors or those awaiting trial, execution, or banishment from the community. (In many ways, as will be made clear, these facilities resembled the modern jail.) English courts generally imposed one of two sanctions on convicted felons: they turned them loose, or they executed them.[2] To be sure, most felons were released, pardoned either by the court or the clergy after receiving a whipping or a branding.

The correctional system in the American colonies differed very little from that of the motherland. If anything, colonial administrators were more likely to use corporal punishment than their English counterparts, and the death penalty was not uncommon in early America. The one dissenter was William Penn, who adopted the "Great Law" in Pennsylvania in 1682. Based on Quaker ideals of humanity and rehabilitation, this criminal code forbade the use of torture and mutilation as forms of punishment.

Instead, felons were ordered to pay restitution of property or goods to their victims. If the offenders did not have sufficient property to make restitution, they were placed in a prison, which was primarily a "workhouse."[3] The death penalty was still allowed under the "Great Law," but only in cases of premeditated murder. Penn proved to be an exception, however, and the path to reform was much slower in the colonies than in England.

WALNUT STREET PRISON: THE FIRST PENITENTIARY

On William Penn's death in 1718, the "Great Law" was rescinded in favor of a harsher criminal code, similar to those of the other colonies. At the time of the American Revolution, however, the Quakers were instrumental in the first broad swing of the incarceration pendulum from punishment to rehabilitation. In 1776, Pennsylvania passed legislation ordering that offenders be reformed through treatment and discipline rather than simply beaten or executed.[4] Several states, including Massachusetts and New York, quickly followed Pennsylvania's example.

Pennsylvania continued its reformist ways by opening the country's first **penitentiary** in a wing of Philadelphia's Walnut Street Jail in 1790. The penitentiary operated on the assumption that silence and labor provided the best hope of rehabilitating the criminal spirit. Remaining silent would force the prisoners to think about their crimes, and eventually the weight of conscience would lead to repentance. At the same time, enforced labor would attack the problem of idleness—regarded as the main cause of crime by experts of the time.[5] Consequently, inmates at Walnut Street were isolated from one another in solitary rooms and kept busy with constant menial chores.

Penitentiary An early form of correctional facility that emphasized separating inmates from society and from each other.

Eventually, the penitentiary at Walnut Street succumbed to the same problems that continue to plague institutions of confinement: overcrowding and excessive costs. As an influx of inmates forced more than one person to be housed in a room, maintaining silence became nearly impossible. By the early 1800s, officials could not find work for all of the convicts, so many were left idle.

THE GREAT PENITENTIARY RIVALRY: PENNSYLVANIA VERSUS NEW YORK

Learning Objective 1 Contrast the Pennsylvania and the New York penitentiary theories of the 1800s.

The apparent lack of success at Walnut Street did little to dampen enthusiasm for the penitentiary concept. Throughout the first half of the nineteenth century, a number of states reacted to prison overcrowding by constructing new penitentiaries. Each state tended to have its own peculiar twist on the roles of silence and labor, and two such systems—those of Pennsylvania and New York—emerged to shape the debate over the most effective way to run a prison.

THE PENNSYLVANIA SYSTEM After the failure of Walnut Street, Pennsylvania constructed two new prisons: the Western Penitentiary near Pittsburgh (opened in 1826) and the Eastern Penitentiary in Cherry Hill, near Philadelphia (1829). The Pennsylvania system took the concept of silence as a virtue to new extremes. Based on the idea of **separate confinement,** these penitentiaries were constructed with back-to-back cells facing outward from the center. (See Figure 11.1 below for the layout of the original Eastern Penitentiary.) To protect each inmate from the corrupting influence of the others, prisoners worked, slept, and ate alone in their cells. Their only contact with other human beings came in the form of religious instruction from a visiting clergyman or prison official.[6]

THE NEW YORK SYSTEM If Pennsylvania's prisons were designed to transform wrongdoers into honest citizens, those in New York focused on obedience. When New York's Newgate Prison (built in 1791) became overcrowded, the state authorized the construction of Auburn Prison, which opened in 1816. Auburn initially operated under many of the same assumptions that guided the penitentiary at Walnut Street. Solitary confinement, however, seemed to lead to an inordinate amount of sickness, insanity, and even suicide among inmates, and it was abandoned in 1822. Nine years later, Elam Lynds became warden at Auburn and instilled the **congregate system,** also known as the Auburn system. Like Pennsylvania's separate confinement system, the congregate system was based on silence and labor. At Auburn, however, inmates worked and ate together, with silence enforced by prison guards.[7]

If either state can be said to have "won" the debate, it was New York. The Auburn system proved more popular, and a majority of the new prisons built in the United States in the 1800s followed New York's lead, though mainly for economic reasons rather than philosophical ones. New York's penitentiaries were cheaper to build because they did not require so much space. Furthermore, inmates in New York were employed in workshops, whereas those in Pennsylvania toiled alone in their cells. Consequently, the Auburn system was better positioned to exploit prison labor in the early years of widespread factory production.

THE REFORMERS AND THE PROGRESSIVES

The Auburn system did not go unchallenged. In the 1870s, a group of reformers argued that fixed sentences, imposed silence, and isolation did nothing to improve prisoners. These critics proposed that penal institutions should offer the promise of early release as a prime tool for rehabilitation. Echoing the views of the Quakers a century earlier, the reformers presented an ideology that would heavily influence American corrections for the next century.

This "new penology" was put into practice at New York's Elmira Reformatory in 1876 (see the photo on facing page). At

Separate Confinement A nineteenth-century penitentiary system in which inmates were kept separate from one another at all times, with daily activities taking place in individual cells.

Congregate System A nineteenth-century penitentiary system in which inmates were kept in separate cells during the night but worked together in the daytime under a code of enforced silence.

FIGURE 11.1 **The Eastern Penintentiary**

As you can see, the Eastern Penitentiary was designed in the form of a "wagon wheel," known today as the radial style. The back-to-back cells in each "spoke" of the wheel faced outward from the center to limit contact between inmates. What was the primary goal of this design?

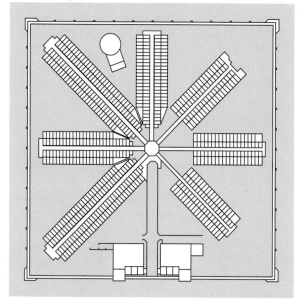

Elmira, good behavior was rewarded by early release, and misbehavior was punished with extended time under a three-grade system of classification. On entering the institution, the offender was assigned a grade of 2. If the inmate followed the rules and completed work and school assignments, after six months he was moved up to grade 1, the necessary grade for release. If, however, the inmate broke institutional rules, he was lowered to grade 3. A grade 3 inmate needed to behave properly for three months before he could return to grade 2 and begin to work back toward grade 1 and eventual release.[8]

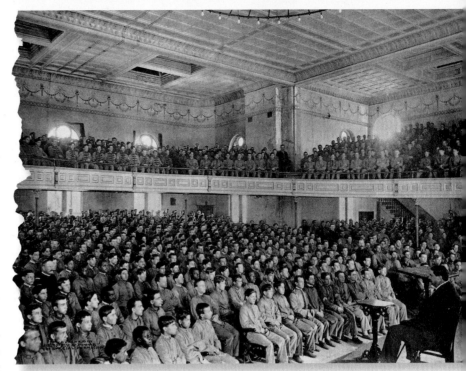

Inmates of the Elmira Reformatory in New York attend a presentation at the prison auditorium. To what extent do you believe that treatment should be a part of the incarceration of criminals?
Corbis

Although other penal institutions did not adopt the Elmira model, its theories came into prominence in the early part of the twentieth century thanks to the efforts of reformers who allied themselves with the burgeoning Progressive movement in American politics. The Progressives believed that criminal behavior was caused by social, economic, and biological factors and, therefore, a corrections system should have a goal of treatment, not punishment. Consequently, they trumpeted a **medical model** for prisons, which held that institutions should offer a variety of programs and therapies to cure inmates of their "ills," whatever the root causes. The Progressives were largely responsible for the spread of indeterminate sentences (Chapter 9), probation (Chapter 10), intermediate sanctions (Chapter 10), and parole (Chapter 12) in state corrections systems from 1900–1950.

THE REASSERTION OF PUNISHMENT

Even though the Progressives had a great influence on the corrections system as a whole, their theories had little impact on the prisons themselves. Many of these facilities had been constructed in the 1800s and were impervious to change. More important, prison administrators usually did not agree with the Progressives and their followers, so the day-to-day lives of most inmates varied little from the congregate system of Auburn Prison.

Medical Model A model of corrections in which the psychological and biological roots of an inmate's criminal behavior are identified and treated.

Academic attitudes began to shift toward the prison administrators in the mid-1960s. Then, in 1974, the publication of Robert Martinson's famous "What Works?" essay provided opponents of the medical model with statistical evidence that rehabilitation efforts did nothing to lower recidivism rates.[9] This is not to say that Martinson's findings went unchallenged. A number of critics argued that rehabilitative programs could be successful.[10] In fact, Martinson himself retracted most of his claims in a little-noticed article published five years after his initial report.[11] Attempts by Martinson and others to "set the record straight" went largely unnoticed, however, as crime rose sharply in the early 1970s. This trend led many criminologists and politicians to champion "get tough" measures to deal with criminals they now considered "incurable."

By the end of the 1980s, the legislative, judicial, and administrative strategies that we have discussed throughout this text had positioned the United States for an explosion in inmate populations and prison construction unparalleled in the nation's history.

INMATE POPULATION TRENDS

The number of Americans in prison or jail has more than tripled since 1985 (see Figure 11.2 below). To a large degree, this dramatic growth is a consequence of the *penal harm movement*.[12] Characterized by "get tough" ideologies in sentencing and punishment, this movement has been particularly influential when it comes to the "war" on drugs. Indeed, much of the growth in the number of Americans behind bars can be attributed to the enhancement and stricter enforcement of the nation's drug laws.

FACTORS IN PRISON POPULATION GROWTH

There are more people in prison and jail for drug offenses today than there were for *all* offenses in the early 1970s.[13] In 1980, about 19,000 drug offenders were incarcerated in state prisons and 4,800 drug offenders were in federal prisons. Thirty years later, state prisons held about 256,000 inmates who had been arrested for drug offenses, and the number of drug offenders in federal prisons had risen to more than 97,400 (representing just over half of all inmates in federal facilities).[14]

FIGURE 11.2 **The Inmate Population of the United States**
The total number of inmates in the United States rose from 744,208 in 1985 to about 2.24 million in 2011.

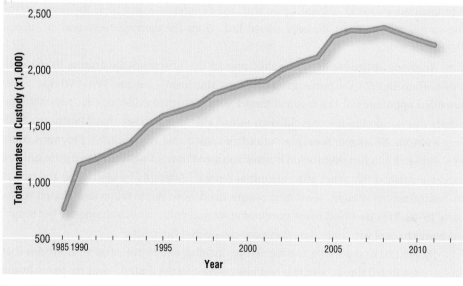

Source: U.S. Department of Justice.

Other reasons for the growth in incarcerated populations include the following:

- *Increased probability of incarceration.* Simply stated, the chance of someone who is arrested going to prison today is much greater than it was thirty years ago. Most of this growth took place in the 1980s, when the likelihood of incarceration in a state prison after arrest increased fivefold for drug offenses, threefold for weapons offenses, and twofold for crimes such as sexual assault, burglary, auto theft, and larceny.[15] For federal crimes, the proportion of convicted defendants being sent to prison rose from 64 percent in 1980 to 86 percent in 2011.[16]

- *Inmates serving more time for each crime.* In Chapter 9, we discussed a number of "get tough" sentencing laws passed in reaction to the crime wave of the 1970s and 1980s. These measures, including sentencing guidelines (see page 265), mandatory minimum sentences (see page 267), and truth-in-sentencing laws (see page 257), have significantly increased the length of prison terms in the United States.[17] In California, for example, before the Supreme Court's ruling discussed in the opening of this chapter,[18] a quarter of the inmate population had been sentenced under the state's "three-strikes" law, and these inmates' terms were nine years longer because of that legislation.[19] Furthermore, 140,000 prisoners—roughly one in eleven—are sentenced to life in American prisons with no chance of release.[20]

- *Federal prison growth.* Thanks in part to federal sentencing policy, the federal prison system is now the largest in the country, with nearly 210,000 inmates. In fact, since 1995 the federal prison population has more than doubled, whereas state prison populations have grown by "only" 24 percent.[21] Besides the increase in federal drug offenders already mentioned, this growth can be attributed to efforts by Presidents Bill Clinton and George W. Bush to federalize gun possession crimes. From 1995 to 2003, the number of inmates sent to federal prisons for weapons violations jumped by 120 percent.[22] Furthermore, between 1995 and 2010, immigration law offenders behind bars increased by nearly 600 percent (3,612 to 21,377).[23] As a result of this trend, a third of all federal inmates are now Hispanic.[24]

- *Rising incarceration rates of women.* In 1981, 14,000 women were prisoners in federal and state institutions. By 2010, the number had grown to about 113,000. Women still account for only 7 percent of all prisoners nationwide, but their rates of imprisonment are growing more rapidly than those of men.[25]

Learning Objective 2 List the factors that have caused the prison population to grow dramatically in the last several decades.

Several Hispanic inmates await health screening at the Val Verde Correctional Facility in Del Rio, Texas. What factor is most responsible for the surge in the number of Hispanics incarcerated by the federal government?

Tom Pennington/MCT/Newscom

THE COSTS OF INCARCERATION

The escalation in the U.S. prison population has been accompanied by increased costs. Today, the states together spend nearly $40 billion a year to operate their corrections systems—up from $12 billion in 1987. Twelve states allocate in excess of $1 billion a year for corrections-related services, often spending more on prisons than on education or health care.[26] Regardless of the Supreme Court's order to California to reduce its inmate population discussed earlier in the chapter, the state has had no choice but to cut corrections costs. Several years ago, it had a $20 billion budget deficit and was spending $10 billion a year on its prisons.[27] Arizona, which faces a similar problem, has decided to charge $25 for family and friend visits to inmates in its prison system to help make up its $1.6 billion budget deficit.[28]

DECARCERATION

For most states looking to cut corrections costs, the focus has been on *decarceration*, or the reduction of inmate populations. As recently as 2007, one expert lamented the unwillingness of corrections authorities to decarcerate, calling the strategy "practically virgin territory."[29] This is no longer the case, as the high cost of imprisonment has caused policymakers to consider a number of different methods to reduce the number of people in prison.

In general, decarceration relies on three strategies:

1. Decreasing the probability that nonviolent offenders will be sentenced to prison.
2. Increasing the rate of release of nonviolent offenders from prison.
3. Decreasing the rate of imprisonment for probation and parole violators.[30]

Many states have adopted one or more of these approaches. For instance, several years ago, Texas decided not to expand its corrections system in response to projected inmate overcrowding. Instead, state officials diverted nonviolent offenders into drug treatment and expanded *reentry* programs (discussed in the next chapter) designed to keep recently released inmates from recidivating. By 2011, the state prison system was operating sufficiently under capacity that, for the first time in its history, Texas closed a prison.[31]

Overall, in 2010, state prison releases exceeded prison admissions, with half of the states reducing their prison populations.[32] (To better understand the possible consequences of decarceration on crime rates, see the feature *Myth versus Reality—Does Putting Criminals in Prison Reduce Crime?* on the facing page.)

SELFASSESSMENT
Fill in the blanks and check your answers on page 332.
Of all the factors in the growth of the prison population in the last several decades, stricter enforcement of the nation's _____ laws has had the greatest impact. Other factors contributing to this growth include (1) increased probability of _____, (2) increased _____ of time served in prison, (3) the growth of the _____ prison system, and (4) rising incarceration rates of _____.

PRISON ORGANIZATION AND MANAGEMENT

The United States has a dual prison system that parallels its dual court system, which we discussed in Chapter 7. The Federal Bureau of Prisons (BOP) currently operates about one hundred confinement facilities, ranging from prisons to immigration detention centers to community corrections institutions.[33] In the federal corrections system, a national director, appointed by the president, oversees six regional directors and a staff of over 35,000 employees. All fifty states also operate state prisons, which number over 1,700 and make up more than 90 percent of the country's correctional facilities.[34] Governors are responsible for the organization and operation of state corrections systems, which vary widely based on each state's geography, *demographics* (population characteristics), and political culture.

Generally, those offenders sentenced in federal court for breaking federal law serve their time in federal prisons, and those offenders sentenced in state court for breaking

Since the early 1990s, violent crime rates in the United States have been stable or declining. Yet, during the same period, as Figure 11.2 on page 314 shows, the rate at which Americans are imprisoned has climbed precipitously. The correlation between these two trends is the subject of much discussion among crime experts.

THE MYTH Crime falls when the prison population rises. This can be attributed to the effects of deterrence and incapacitation, theories of punishment we discussed in Chapter 9. First, the threat of prison deters would-be criminals from committing crimes. Second, a prison inmate is incapable of committing crimes because he or she has been separated from the community.

THE REALITY Numerous statistical examples discredit a direct, sustained link between decreased crime rates and increased prison populations. Canada, for example, experienced a decline in crime rates similar to the United States in the 1990s without *any* national increase in incarceration levels. Furthermore, by one measurement, New York City has seen crime decrease by a remarkable 80 percent since the early 1990s. Yet, during the 2000s, the city has been locking up fewer people than it was at the height of its late-1980s crime wave.

According to one theory, massive incarceration accounted for about a quarter of the crime drop of the 1990s, as many of the most violent offenders were removed from society and remain behind bars. Since then, however, a large percentage of new prison admissions have been drug law offenders and probation/parole violators. The data tell us that removing these sorts of criminals from the community has a relatively limited effect on violent and property crime rates. In fact, their absence from their homes may even contribute to criminal activity. As we discussed in Chapter 2, many criminologists believe that widespread family disruption greatly increases the incidence of crime in a community.

Additionally, some experts believe that prisons are "schools of crime" that "teach" low-level offenders to be habitual criminals. If this is true, many inmates are more likely to commit crimes after their release from prison than they would have been if they had never been incarcerated in the first place.

FOR CRITICAL ANALYSIS How might the new trend of decarceration give criminologists a chance to test theories regarding the correlation between incarceration levels and crime rates?

---

state law serve their time in state prisons. As you can see in Figure 11.3 on the following page, federal prisons hold relatively few violent felons, because relatively few federal laws involve violent crime. At the same time, federal prisons are much more likely to hold public order offenders, a group that includes violators of federal immigration law.

PRISON ADMINISTRATION

Whether the federal government or a state government operates a prison, its administrators have the same general goals, summarized by sociologist Charles Logan as follows:

> The mission of a prison is to keep prisoners—to keep them in, keep them safe, keep them in line, keep them healthy, and keep them busy—and to do it with fairness, without undue suffering and as efficiently as possible.[35]

Considering the environment of a prison—an enclosed world inhabited by people who are generally violent and angry and would rather be anywhere else—Logan's mission statement is somewhat unrealistic. A prison staff must supervise the daily routines of hundreds or thousands of inmates, a duty that includes providing them with meals, education, vocational programs, and different forms of leisure. The smooth operation of this supervision is made more difficult—if not, at times, impossible—by budgetary restrictions, overcrowding, and continual inmate turnover.

FIGURE 11.3 Types of Offenses of Federal and State Prison Inmates

As the comparison below shows, state prisoners are most likely to have been convicted of violent crimes, while federal prisoners are most likely to have been convicted of drug and public order offenses.

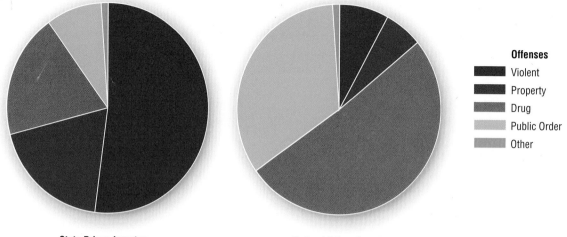

Offenses
- Violent
- Property
- Drug
- Public Order
- Other

State Prison Inmates   Federal Prison Inmates

Source: Bureau of Justice Statistics, *Prisoners in 2010* (Washington, D.C.: U.S. Department of Justice, December 2011), Appendix table 16a, page 28; and Appendix table 18, page 30.

FORMAL PRISON MANAGEMENT In some respects, the management structure of a prison is similar to that of a police department, as discussed in Chapter 4. Both systems rely on a hierarchical (top-down) *chain of command* to increase personal responsibility. Both assign different employees to specific tasks, though prison managers have much more direct control over their subordinates than do police managers. The main difference is that police departments have a *continuity of purpose* that is sometimes lacking in prison organizations. All members of a police force are, at least theoretically, working to reduce crime and apprehend criminals. In a prison, this continuity is less evident. An employee in the prison laundry service and one who works in the visiting center have little in common. In some instances, employees may even have cross-purposes: a prison guard may want to punish an inmate, while a counselor in the treatment center may want to rehabilitate her or him.

Learning Objective 3 Describe the formal prison management system.

Consequently, a strong hierarchy is crucial for any prison management team that hopes to meet Charles Logan's expectations. As Figure 11.4 on the facing page shows, the **warden** (also known as a superintendent) is ultimately responsible for the operation of a prison. He or she oversees deputy wardens, who in turn manage the various organizational lines of the institution. The custodial employees, who deal directly with the inmates and make up more than half of a prison's staff, operate under a militaristic hierarchy, with a line of command passing from the deputy warden to the captain to the correctional officer.

Warden The prison official who is ultimately responsible for the organization and performance of a correctional facility.

GOVERNING PRISONS The implications of prison mismanagement can be severe. While studying a series of prison riots, sociologists Bert Useem and Peter Kimball found that breakdown in managerial control commonly preceded such acts of mass violence.[36] During the 1970s, for example, conditions at the State Penitentiary in New Mexico deteriorated significantly. Inmates were increasingly the targets of random and harsh treatment at the hands of the prison staff, while at the same time a reduction in structured activities left prison life "painfully boring."[37] The result, in 1980, was one of the most violent prison riots in the nation's history.

FIGURE 11.4 Organizational Chart for a Typical Correctional Facility

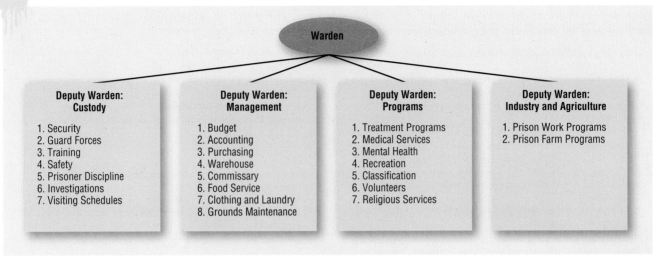

Warden

Deputy Warden: Custody
1. Security
2. Guard Forces
3. Training
4. Safety
5. Prisoner Discipline
6. Investigations
7. Visiting Schedules

Deputy Warden: Management
1. Budget
2. Accounting
3. Purchasing
4. Warehouse
5. Commissary
6. Food Service
7. Clothing and Laundry
8. Grounds Maintenance

Deputy Warden: Programs
1. Treatment Programs
2. Medical Services
3. Mental Health
4. Recreation
5. Classification
6. Volunteers
7. Religious Services

Deputy Warden: Industry and Agriculture
1. Prison Work Programs
2. Prison Farm Programs

TYPES OF PRISONS

One of the most important aspects of prison administration occurs soon after a defendant has been convicted of a crime. In this **classification** process, administrators determine what sort of correctional facility provides the best "fit" for each individual convict. In general, prison administrators rely on three criteria for classification purposes:

1. The seriousness of the crime committed.
2. The risk of future criminal or violent conduct.
3. The need for treatment and rehabilitation programs.[38]

In the federal prison system, this need to classify—and separate—different kinds of offenders has led to six different levels of correctional facilities. Inmates in level 1 facilities are usually nonviolent and require the least amount of security, while inmates in level 6 facilities are the most dangerous and require the harshest security measures. (Many states also use the six-level system, an example of which can be seen in Figure 11.5 on the following page.) To simplify matters, most observers refer to correctional facilities as being one of three levels—minimum, medium, or maximum. A fourth level—the supermaximum-security prison, known as the "supermax"—is relatively rare and extremely controversial due to its hyperharsh methods of punishing and controlling the most dangerous prisoners.

MAXIMUM-SECURITY PRISONS In a certain sense, the classification of prisoners today owes a debt to the three-grade system developed at the Elmira Reformatory, discussed earlier in the chapter. Once wrongdoers enter a corrections facility, they are constantly graded on behavior. Those who serve "good time," as we have seen, are often rewarded with early release. Those who compile extensive misconduct records are usually housed, along with violent and repeat offenders, in **maximum-security prisons.** The names of these institutions—Folsom, San Quentin, Sing Sing, Attica—conjure up foreboding images of concrete and steel jungles, with good reason.

Maximum-security prisons are designed with full attention to security and surveillance. In these institutions, inmates' lives are strictly controlled and programmed to keep them from escaping or from harming themselves or the prison staff. About a quarter of the prisons in the United States are classified as maximum security, and these institutions house about a third of the country's prisoners.

Learning Objective 4 List and briefly explain the four types of prisons.

Classification The process through which prison officials determine which correctional facility is best suited to the individual offender.

Maximum-Security Prison A correctional institution designed and organized to control and discipline dangerous felons, as well as prevent escape.

FIGURE 11.5 Security Levels of Correctional Facilities in Virginia

The security levels of correctional facilities in Virginia are graded from level 1 to level 6. As you can see, level 1 facilities are for those inmates who pose the least amount of risk to fellow inmates, staff members, and themselves. Level 6 facilities are for those who are considered the most dangerous by the Virginia Department of Corrections.

LEVEL 1 - LOW
No first or second degree murder, robbery, sex-related crime, kidnapping/abduction, felonious assault (current or prior), flight/escape history, carjacking, or malicious wounding. No disruptive behavior.

LEVEL 1 - HIGH
No first or second degree murder, robbery, sex-related crime, kidnapping/abduction, felonious assault (current or prior), flight/escape history. No disruptive behavior for at least past 24 months.

LEVEL 2
For initial assignment only. No escape history for past 5 years. No disruptive behavior for at least past 24 months prior to transfer to any less secure facility.

LEVEL 3
Single, multiple, and life+ sentences.* Must have served 20 consecutive years on sentence. No disruptive behavior for at least past 24 months prior to transfer to any less secure facility.

LEVEL 4
Single, multiple, and life+ sentences. No disruptive behavior for at least past 24 months prior to transfer to any less secure facility.

LEVEL 5
Same as level 4 except with fewer opportunities to participate in programs and jobs, fewer visitation and phone access privileges, and less freedom of movement within the facility. No disruptive behavior for at least past 24 months prior to transfer to any less secure facility.

LEVEL 6
Single, multiple, and life+ sentences. Profile of inmates: disruptive, assaultive, severe behavior problems, predatory-type behavior, escape risk. No disruptive behavior for at least past 24 months prior to transfer to any less secure facility.

* "Life +" means a life sentence plus extra years in case of an early release.

Source: Virginia Department of Corrections.

The Design Maximum-security prisons tend to be large—holding more than a thousand inmates—and they have similar features. The entire operation is usually surrounded by concrete walls that stand twenty to thirty feet high and have also been sunk deep into the ground to deter tunnel escapes. Fences reinforced with razor-ribbon barbed wire that can be electrically charged may supplement these barriers. The prison walls are studded with watchtowers, from which guards armed with shotguns and rifles survey the movement of prisoners below. Inmates live in cells, most of them with similar dimensions to those found in the I-Max maximum-security prison for women in Topeka, Kansas: eight feet by fourteen feet with cinder block walls.[39] The space contains bunks, a toilet, a sink, and possibly a cabinet or closet.

Cells are located in rows of *cell blocks,* each of which forms its own security unit, set off by a series of gates and bars. Most prisons, whether they were built using the radial design (see page 312) or other designs that resemble large courtyards or telephone poles, have cell blocks that open into sprawling prison exercise yards. The "prison of the future," however, rejects this layout. Instead, it relies on a podular design, as evident at the Two Rivers Correctional Institution in Umatilla, Oregon.

At Two Rivers, which opened in 2007, fourteen housing pods contain ninety-six inmates each. Each unit has its own yard, so inmates rarely, if ever, interact with members of other pods. This design gives administrators the flexibility to, for example, place violent criminals in pod A and white-collar criminals in pod B without worrying about mixing the two different security levels.[40]

Security Measures Within maximum-security prisons, inmates' lives are dominated by security measures. Whenever they move from one area of the prison to another, they do so in groups and under the watchful eye of armed correctional officers. Television surveillance cameras may be used to monitor their every move, even when sleeping, showering, or using the toilet. They are subject to frequent pat-downs or strip searches at the guards' discretion. Constant "head counts" ensure that every inmate is where he or she should be. Tower guards—many of whom have orders to shoot to kill in the case of a disturbance or escape attempt—constantly look down on the inmates as they move around outdoor areas of the facility.

What security measures can you identify from this photo of a cell block at Arizona State Prison in Florence?

AP Photo/Matt York

SUPERMAX PRISONS About thirty states and the federal BOP operate **supermax** (short for supermaximum-security) **prisons,** which are supposedly reserved for the "worst of the worst" of America's corrections population. Most of the inmates in these facilities are deemed high risks to commit murder behind bars—about a quarter of the occupants of the BOP's U.S. Penitentiary Administrative Maximum (ADX) in Florence, Colorado, have killed other prisoners or assaulted correctional officers elsewhere. In addition, a growing number are either high-profile individuals who would be at constant risk of attack in a general prison population or convicted terrorists. For instance, supermax prisons are presently housing Faisal Shahzad, who attempted to detonate a bomb in New York City's Times Square in 2010, Ted "the Unabomber" Kaczynski, and Terry Nichols, who was involved in the bombing of a federal office building in Oklahoma City in 1995.

The main purpose of a supermax prison is to strictly control the inmates' movement, thereby limiting (or eliminating) situations that could lead to breakdowns in discipline. The conditions at California's Security Housing Unit (SHU) at Pelican Bay State Prison are representative of most supermax institutions. Prisoners are confined to their one-person cells for twenty-two and a half hours each day under video camera surveillance. They receive meals through a slot in the door. The cells measure eight by ten feet in size and are windowless. No decorations of any kind are permitted on the walls.[41] For the most part, supermax prisons operate in a state of perpetual **lockdown,** in which all inmates are confined to their cells and social activities such as meals, recreational sports, and treatment programs are nonexistent.

MEDIUM- AND MINIMUM-SECURITY PRISONS Medium-security prisons hold about 45 percent of the prison population and minimum-security prisons 20 percent. Inmates at **medium-security prisons** have for the most part committed less serious crimes than those housed in maximum-security prisons and are not considered high risks for escaping or causing harm. Consequently, medium-security institutions are not designed for control to the same extent as maximum-security prisons and have a more relaxed atmosphere. These facilities also offer more educational and treatment programs and allow for more contact between inmates. Medium-security prisons are rarely walled, relying instead on high fences. Prisoners have more freedom of movement within the structures, and the levels of surveillance are much lower. Living quarters are less restrictive as well—many of the newer medium-security prisons provide dormitory housing.

A **minimum-security prison** seems at first glance to be more like a college campus than an incarceration facility. Most of the inmates at these institutions are first-time offenders who are nonviolent and well behaved. A high percentage are white-collar criminals. Indeed, inmates are often transferred to minimum-security prisons

Supermax Prison A correctional facility reserved for those inmates who have extensive records of misconduct in maximum-security prisons.

Lockdown A disciplinary action taken by prison officials in which all inmates are ordered to their quarters and nonessential prison activities are suspended.

Medium-Security Prison A correctional institution that houses less dangerous inmates and therefore uses less restrictive measures to prevent violence and escapes.

Minimum-Security Prison A correctional institution designed to allow inmates, most of whom pose low security risks, a great deal of freedom of movement and contact with the outside world.

as a reward for good behavior in other facilities. Therefore, security measures are lax compared with even medium-security prisons. Unlike medium-security institutions, minimum-security prisons do not have armed guards. Prisoners are provided with amenities such as television sets and computers in their rooms. They also enjoy freedom of movement and are allowed off prison grounds for educational or employment purposes to a much greater extent than those held in more restrictive facilities.

Some critics have likened minimum-security prisons to "country clubs," but in the corrections system, everything is relative. A minimum-security prison may seem like a vacation spot when compared with the horrors of Sing Sing, but it still represents a restriction of personal freedom and separates the inmate from the outside world.

SELFASSESSMENT
Fill in the blanks and check your answers on page 332.

The management of a prison is hierarchical, with the _____ (also known as a superintendent) at the top of the power structure. _____ is a crucial component of prison management, as it determines the security requirements needed to safely incarcerate each individual offender. Those offenders who have been convicted of violent crimes and repeat offenders are most likely to be sent to _____-security prisons. If a prisoner assaults another inmate or a correctional officer, prison officials may decide to transfer him or her to a _____ prison.

THE EMERGENCE OF PRIVATE PRISONS

In addition to all the other pressures placed on wardens and other prison administrators, these individuals must operate within a budget assigned to them by an overseeing governmental agency. Today, the great majority of all prisons are under the control of federal and state governments, but government-run prisons have not always been the rule. In the 1800s, a number of correctional facilities existed outside the purview of the state. In fact, the entire Texas prison system was privately operated from 1872 to the late 1880s. For most of the twentieth century, however, **private prisons,** or prisons run by private business firms to make a profit, could not be found in the United States.

That is certainly not the case today. With corrections exhibiting all appearances of, in the words of one observer, "a recession-proof industry," the American business community has eagerly entered the market. Fourteen private corrections firms operate more than two hundred facilities across the United States. The two largest corrections companies, Corrections Corporation of America (CCA) and the GEO Group, Inc., have contracted with both state governments and the federal BOP to supervise more than 100,000 inmates. By 2010, private penal institutions housed nearly 130,000 inmates, representing 8 percent of all prisoners in the state and federal corrections systems.[42]

WHY PRIVATIZE?

It would be a mistake to automatically assume that private prisons are less expensive to run than public ones. Nevertheless, the incentive to privatize is primarily financial.

COST EFFICIENCY In the 1980s and 1990s, a number of states and cities reduced operating costs by transferring government-run services such as garbage collection and road maintenance to the private sector. Similarly, private prisons can often be run more cheaply and efficiently than public ones for the following reasons:

Private Prisons Correctional facilities operated by private corporations instead of the government and, therefore, reliant on profits for survival.

Learning Objective 5 List the reasons why private prisons can often be run more cheaply than public ones.

CAREERS IN CJ

BERRY LARSON
PRISON WARDEN

Photo Courtesy of Berry Larson

Before I began my career as a correctional officer for the Arizona Department of Corrections, I had several people question my desire to work inside a prison. Why would I want to stick myself somewhere so unpleasant and stressful? While at the training academy, however, we were taught that "approach determines response." I found that to be very true during my time as a correctional officer. It is all about the way you carry yourself and the way you relate to the inmates. An inmate can tell if you are trying to be someone you are not. They can also tell if you are afraid. I never had to use physical force once in all the time I was a correctional officer—officer presence and nonverbal/verbal communication is usually sufficient to handle any situation, as long as you keep control of your emotions.

As warden of the Arizona State Prison Complex–Lewis, my duties include touring the units; attending special events such as inmate graduations for GED and vocational programs; managing emergency situations such as power outages, fights and assaults, and staff injuries; and eradicating all criminal activity from the facility. Many, if not most, of our inmates came to us in pretty bad shape—little or no education, a substance abuse history, or mental health or behavioral issues. These young men have spent their lives watching television and playing video games and simply do not have the skills to be successful in life. We try to remedy the situation by providing them with educational and vocational programs and "life-skills" classes that promote civil and productive behavior.

Social Media Career Tip

Regularly reevaluate your social media tools and the methods you use to keep up to date in your fields of interest. If you are still using the same tools as a year ago, you probably aren't keeping up with the latest developments in Internet technology.

- *Labor costs.* The wages of public employees account for nearly two-thirds of a government-run prison's operating expenses. Although private corrections firms pay base salaries comparable to those enjoyed by public prison employees, their nonunionized staffs receive lower levels of overtime pay, workers' compensation claims, sick leave, and health-care insurance.
- *Competitive bidding.* Because of the profit motive, private corrections firms have an incentive to buy goods and services at the lowest possible price.
- *Less red tape.* Private corrections firms are not part of the government bureaucracy and therefore do not have to contend with the massive amount of paperwork that can clog government organizations.[43]

In 2005, the National Institute of Justice released the results of a five-year study comparing low-security public and private prisons in California. The government agency

The Saguaro Correctional
Facility in Eloy, Arizona—
privately operated by the
Corrections Corporation of
America—has been criticized
for only accepting inmates who
are in relatively good health. If
true, why would this strategy
make financial sense for private
prisons?

Monica Almeida/*New York Times*/Redux
Pictures

found that private facilities cost taxpayers between 6 and 10 percent less than public ones.[44] More recent research conducted at Vanderbilt University found that each state saved about $15 million annually when they supplemented their corrections systems with privately managed institutions.[45]

OVERCROWDING AND OUTSOURCING Private prisons are becoming increasingly attractive to state governments faced with the competing pressures of tight budgets and overcrowded corrections facilities. Lacking the funds to alleviate overcrowding by building more prisons, state officials are turning to the private institutions for help. Often, the private prison is out of state, which leads to the "outsourcing" of inmates. Hawaii, for example, sends about one-third of its 6,000 inmates to private prisons in Arizona.[46] Over the past several years, California has alleviated its chronic overcrowding problems by sending more than 10,000 inmates to private institutions in Arizona, Colorado, Michigan, Minnesota, Missouri, Montana, and Oklahoma.[47]

THE ARGUMENT AGAINST PRIVATE PRISONS

The assertion that private prisons offer economic benefits is not universally accepted. A number of studies have found that private prisons are no more cost-effective than public ones.[48] Furthermore, opponents of private prisons worry that despite the assurances of corporate executives, private corrections companies will "cut corners" to save costs, denying inmates important security guarantees in the process.

SAFETY CONCERNS Criticism of private prisons might be justified by the anecdotal evidence. Certainly, these institutions have been the setting for a number of violent incidents over the past several years. In 2010, Hanni Elabed was severely beaten by another inmate at the Idaho Correctional Center (ICC), operated by CCA. Eight minutes passed before guards finally intervened to save Elabed, who was left permanently brain damaged. As part of the resulting lawsuit, a former employee said, "It is clear to me that ICC was more interested in making a profit than reducing prisoner violence."[49] In 2012, another CCA facility experienced a riot that ended with the death of a correctional officer and twenty other injuries. During this disturbance at the Adams County Correctional Center in Natchez, Mississippi, three hundred inmates used broomsticks and other homemade weapons to control the facility for nearly eight hours.[50]

Apart from anecdotal evidence, various studies have also uncovered patterns of misbehavior at private prisons. For example, officials from the BOP discovered higher levels of serious inmate violence and drug abuse at California's Taft Correctional Institute, operated by the GEO Group, than at three similar government-run prisons.[51] In addition, research conducted by Curtis R. Blakely of the University of South Alabama and Vic W. Bumphus of the University of Tennessee at Chattanooga found that a prisoner in a private correctional facility was twice as likely to be assaulted by a fellow inmate as a prisoner in a public one.[52]

PHILOSOPHICAL CONCERNS Other critics see private prisons as inherently unjust, even if they do save tax dollars or provide enhanced services. These observers believe that corrections is not simply another industry, like garbage collection or road maintenance, and that only the government has the authority to punish wrongdoers. In the words of John DiIulio:

> It is precisely because corrections involves the deprivation of liberty, precisely because it involves the legally sanctioned exercise of coercion by some citizens over others, that it must remain wholly within public hands.[53]

Critics of private correctional facilities also believe that private prisons are constitutionally problematic, offering Article I of the U.S. Constitution as support. That passage states that "legislative powers herein granted shall be vested in a Congress of the United States." These powers include the authority to define penal codes and to determine the punishments that will be handed out for breaking federal law. Therefore, a strict interpretation of the Constitution appears to prohibit the passing of this authority from the federal government to a private company.[54]

THE FUTURE OF PRIVATIZATION IN THE CORRECTIONS INDUSTRY

In February 2012, Florida's senate narrowly defeated a bill that would have privatized the state's entire corrections system.[55] The vote seemed to bode ill for what was once considered a recession-proof industry. Indeed, with more states reducing their prison populations, as we noted earlier, the growth of private prisons has stagnated. In an effort to find new avenues of business, CCA recently sent a letter to forty-eight states in which the company offered to purchase unwanted public prisons. So far, only one state has taken this step: in 2011, Ohio sold the Lake Erie Correctional Institution to CCA for nearly $73 million.[56]

Still, most experts see continued profitability for private prisons, for two reasons. First, as we have noted, shrinking budgets have forced states to look for less costly alternatives to housing inmates in public prisons. Second, as the number of federal prisoners increases, the BOP has turned to private prisons to expand its capacity. Between 2000 and 2010, the number of federal inmates in private prisons more than doubled, from about 15,500 to about 34,000.[57] The current emphasis on imprisoning violators of immigration law seems likely to ensure that this trend will continue.

SELFASSESSMENT

Fill in the blanks and check your answers on page 332.

The incentive for using private prisons is primarily _____. Prison officials also feel pressure to send inmates to private prisons to alleviate _____ of public correctional facilities. Critics of private prisons claim that as a result of their cost-cutting measures, inmates are denied important _____ guarantees and thus may be put in physical danger. The industry's future seems assured, however, largely because of increased demand for prison beds for immigration law violators on the part of the _____ government.

Learning Objective 6 Summarize the distinction between jails and prisons, and indicate the importance of jails in the American corrections system.

JAILS

Although prisons and prison issues dominate the public discourse on corrections, there is an argument to be made that jails are the dominant penal institutions in the United States. In general, a prison is a facility designed to house people convicted of felonies for lengthy

Jail A facility, usually operated by the county government, used to hold persons awaiting trial or those who have been found guilty of misdemeanors.

Pretrial Detainees
Individuals who cannot post bail after arrest and are therefore forced to spend the time prior to their trial incarcerated in jail.

periods of time, while a **jail** is authorized to hold pretrial detainees and offenders who have committed misdemeanors. On any given day, about 750,000 inmates are in jail in this country, and jails admit almost 13 million persons over the course of an entire year.[58] Nevertheless, jail funding is often a low priority for budget-conscious local governments, leading to severe overcrowding and other dismal conditions.

Many observers see this negligence as having far-reaching consequences for criminal justice. Jail is often the first contact that citizens have with the corrections system. It is at this point that treatment and counseling have the best chance to deter future criminal behavior.[59] By failing to take advantage of this opportunity, says Professor Franklin Zimring of the University of California at Berkeley School of Law, corrections officials have created a situation in which "today's jail folk are tomorrow's prisoners."[60] (To better understand the role that these two correctional institutions play in the criminal justice system, see *Mastering Concepts—The Main Differences between Prisons and Jails* below.)

THE JAIL POPULATION

Like those making up state prison populations, jail inmates are overwhelmingly young male adults. About 45 percent of jail inmates are white, 38 percent are African American, and 16 percent are Hispanic. The main difference between state prison and jail inmates involves their criminal activity.[61] As Figure 11.6 on the facing page shows, jail inmates are more likely to have been convicted of nonviolent crimes than their counterparts in state prison.

PRETRIAL DETAINEES A significant number of those detained in jails technically are not prisoners. They are **pretrial detainees** who have been arrested by the police and, for a variety of reasons that we discussed in Chapter 8, are unable to post bail.

Pretrial detainees are, in many ways, walking legal contradictions. According to the U.S. Constitution, they are innocent until proved guilty. At the same time, by being incarcerated while awaiting trial, they are denied a number of personal freedoms and are subjected to the poor conditions of many jails. In *Bell v. Wolfish* (1979), the Supreme Court rejected the notion that this situation is inherently unfair by refusing to give pretrial detainees greater legal protections than sentenced jail inmates have.[62] In essence, the Court recognized that treating pretrial detainees differently from convicted jail inmates would place too much of a burden on corrections officials and was therefore impractical.[63]

MASTERINGCONCEPTS
THE MAIN DIFFERENCES BETWEEN PRISONS AND JAILS

	Prisons	Jails
1.	. . . are operated by the federal and state governments.	. . . are operated by county and city governments.
2.	. . . hold inmates who may have lived quite far away before being arrested.	. . . hold mostly inmates from the local community.
3.	. . . house only those who have been convicted of a crime.	. . . house those who are awaiting trial or have recently been arrested, in addition to convicts.
4.	. . . generally hold inmates who have been found guilty of serious crimes and received sentences of longer than one year.	. . . generally hold inmates who have been found guilty of minor crimes and are serving sentences of less than a year.
5.	. . . often offer a wide variety of rehabilitation and educational programs for long-term prisoners.	. . . due to smaller budgets, tend to focus only on the necessities of safety, food, and clothing.

FIGURE 11.6 Types of Offenses of Prison and Jail Inmates

As the comparison below shows, jail inmates are more likely to have been convicted of nonviolent crimes than state prisoners. This underscores the main function of jails: to house less serious offenders for a relatively short period of time.

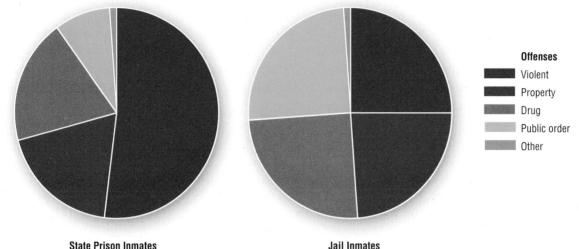

State Prison Inmates   Jail Inmates

Offenses
- Violent
- Property
- Drug
- Public order
- Other

Source: Bureau of Justice Statistics, *Prisoners in 2010* (Washington, D.C.: U.S. Department of Justice, December 2011), Appendix table 16a, page 28; and Bureau of Justice Statistics, *Profile of Jail Inmates, 2002* (Washington, D.C.: U.S. Department of Justice, July 2004), 1.

SENTENCED JAIL INMATES According to the U.S. Department of Justice, about 40 percent of those in jail have been convicted of their current charges.[64] In other words, they have been found guilty of a crime, usually a misdemeanor, and sentenced to time in jail. The typical jail term lasts between thirty and ninety days, and rarely does a prisoner spend more than one year in jail for any single crime. Often, a judge will credit the length of time the convict has spent in detention waiting for trial—known as **time served**—toward his or her sentence. This practice acknowledges two realities of jails:

1. Terms are generally too short to allow the prisoner to gain any benefit (that is, rehabilitation) from the jail's often limited or nonexistent treatment facilities. Therefore, the jail term can serve no purpose except to punish the wrongdoer. (Judges who believe jail time can serve purposes of deterrence and incapacitation may not agree with this line of reasoning.)
2. Jails are chronically overcrowded, and judges need to clear space for new offenders.

OTHER JAIL INMATES Pretrial detainees and those convicted of misdemeanors make up the majority of the jail population. Jail inmates also include probation and parole violators, the mentally ill, juveniles awaiting transfer to juvenile authorities, and immigration law violators being held for the federal government. Increasingly, jails are also called on to handle the overflow from state prisons. To comply with the Supreme Court's order to reduce its prison population, California corrections officials plan to divert an estimated 75,000 inmates from its prisons to its jails by 2015.[65]

THE SOCIOLOGY OF JAIL According to sociologist John Irwin, the unofficial purpose of a jail is to manage society's "rabble," so called because

> [they] are not well integrated into conventional society, they are not members of conventional social organizations, they have few ties to conventional social networks, and they are carriers of unconventional values and beliefs.[66]

In Irwin's opinion, rabble who act violently are arrested and sent to prison. The jail is reserved for merely offensive rabble, whose primary threat to society lies in their failure to conform to its behavioral norms. Nearly seven out of ten jail inmates, for example, are

Time Served The period of time a person denied bail (or unable to pay it) has spent in jail prior to her or his trial.

Social Media and CJ
The **Los Angeles County Sheriff's Department** operates the largest jail in the United States. To access its Facebook page, visit the *Criminal Justice CourseMate* at cengagebrain.com and select the *Web Links* for this chapter.

dependent on or abuse alcohol or drugs.[67] This concept of rabble has been used by some critics of American corrections to explain the disproportionate number of poor and minority groups who may be found in the nation's jails at any time.

JAIL ADMINISTRATION

Learning Objective 7 Explain how jails are administered.

Of the nearly 3,370 jails in the United States, more than 2,700 are operated on a county level by an elected sheriff. Most of the remainder are under the control of municipalities, although six state governments (Alaska, Connecticut, Delaware, Hawaii, Rhode Island, and Vermont) manage jails. The capacity of jails varies widely. The Los Angeles County Men's Central Jail holds nearly 7,000 people, but jails that large are the exception rather than the rule. Almost two-thirds of all jails in this country house fewer than 50 inmates.[68]

With their more complex and diverse populations, jails are often more difficult to manage than prisons. Jails hold people who have never been incarcerated before, people under the influence of drugs or alcohol at the time of their arrival, the mentally ill, and people who exhibit a range of violent behavior—from nonexistent to extreme—that only adds to the unpredictable atmosphere.[69] Still, as troublesome as they may be, jails can be politically useful for sheriffs. A sheriff has the power to appoint a jail administrator, or deputy sheriff, to oversee the day-to-day operations of the facility. The sheriff can also hire other staff members, such as deputy jailers.

The sheriff may award these jobs to people who helped her or him get elected, and in return, jail staffers can prove helpful to the sheriff in future elections. Furthermore, as the feature *A Question of Ethics—Canvas Incarceration* below shows, jail management can provide an important platform for a sheriff with a particular political agenda.

NEW-GENERATION JAILS

For most of the nation's history, the architecture of a jail was secondary to its purpose of keeping inmates safely locked away. Consequently, most jails in the

A QUESTION OF **ETHICS:** *Canvas Incarceration*

THE SITUATION Like many newly elected sheriffs, Joe Arpaio had a problem. The Maricopa County (Arizona) Jail, now his responsibility, was severely overcrowded. At the same time, he did not have the funds to construct a new jail. To create space, Arpaio came up with a novel, and controversial, solution. He built a "tent city" about five miles southwest of downtown Phoenix and placed a thousand inmates in it.

Lacking air conditioning, the tented jail quickly drew attention for its sweltering heat, particularly during the summer, when desert temperatures routinely reach 110 degrees. Arpaio has taken other steps to make his canvas incarceration compound particularly uncomfortable. The average meal there costs less than 40 cents and features items such as green bologna. Cigarettes, soft drinks, and coffee are prohibited. Almost no entertainment is available, save for the Disney Channel and the Weather Channel. For clothing, Arpaio provides striped uniforms and pink underwear.

THE ETHICAL DILEMMA As far as "Sheriff Joe" is concerned, there is no ethical dilemma concerning his treatment of the inmates in the tent jail. "Most wardens just run the jails. I use them to fight crime," he says. "I want to make it so tough nobody will come back."

WHAT IS THE SOLUTION? Arpaio's methods have been widely criticized as inhumane and, at times, unconstitutional. During Arpaio's two decades as sheriff, Maricopa County taxpayers have paid at least $30 million as a result of lawsuits brought because of inmate mistreatment. In 2012, he and his office faced charges in federal court for unfairly targeting Latinos for stops, questioning, and detention.

What do you think of Arpaio's approach to jail management? Is it unethical to make life so unpleasant for these offenders? As you answer, remember that most jail inmates are low-level criminals serving short sentences, probation violators, or individuals awaiting trial.

United States continue to resemble those from the days of the Walnut Street Jail in Philadelphia. In this *traditional*, or *linear*, *design*, jail cells are located along a corridor. To supervise the inmates while they are in their cells, custodial officers must walk up and down the corridor, so the number of prisoners they can see at any one time is severely limited. With this limited supervision, inmates can more easily break institutional rules.

PODULAR DESIGN In the 1970s, planners at the Bureau of Federal Prisons decided to upgrade the traditional jail design with the goal of improving conditions for both the staff and the inmates. The result was the **new-generation jail,** which differs significantly from its predecessors.[70] The layout of the new facilities makes it easier for the staff to monitor cell-confined inmates. The basic structure of the new-generation jail is based on a podular design. Each "pod" contains "living units" for individual prisoners. These units, instead of lining up along a straight corridor, are often situated in a triangle so that a staff member in the center of the triangle has visual access to nearly all the cells.

Daily activities such as eating and showering take place in the pod, which also has an outdoor exercise area. Treatment facilities are also located in the pod, allowing greater access for the inmates. During the day, inmates stay out in the open and are allowed back in their cells only when given permission. The officer locks the door to the cells from his or her control terminal.

DIRECT SUPERVISION APPROACH The podular design also enables a new-generation jail to be managed using a **direct supervision approach.**[71] One or more jail officers are stationed in the living area of the pod and are therefore in constant interaction with all prisoners in that particular pod. Some new-generation jails even provide a desk in the center of the living area, which sends a very different message to the prisoners than the traditional control booth (see the photo below). Theoretically, jail officials who have constant contact with inmates will be able to stem misconduct quickly and efficiently and will also be able to recognize "danger signs" from individual inmates and stop outbursts before they occur. (As noted earlier in the chapter, corrections officials are using aspects of podular design when building new prisons, for many of the same reasons that the trend has been popular in jails.)

New-Generation Jail A jail that is distinguished architecturally by a design that encourages interaction between inmates and jailers and that offers greater opportunities for treatment.

Direct Supervision Approach A process of prison and jail administration in which correctional officers are in continuous physical contact with inmates during the day.

How does the layout of this direct supervision jail differ from that of the maximum security prison pictured on page 321? What do these differences tell you about the security precautions needed for jail inmates as opposed to prison inmates?

Photo courtesy Bergen County Sheriff's Office, Bergen, NJ

SELFASSESSMENT

Fill in the blanks and check your answers on page 332.

A significant number of the people in jail are not prisoners, but rather _____ _____ who are unable to post bail and await trial. About 40 percent have been _____ of their current charges, meaning that the jail sentence is punishment for a crime—usually a _____ and not a felony. Most jails are operated on a local level by the county _____.

Learning
Objective 8 Indicate
some of the
consequences
of our high
rates of
incarceration.

THE CONSEQUENCES OF OUR HIGH RATES OF INCARCERATION

For many observers, especially those who support the crime control theory of criminal justice, America's high rate of incarceration has contributed significantly to the drop in the country's crime rates.[72] At the heart of this belief is the fact, which we discussed in Chapter 2, that most crimes are committed by a relatively small group of repeat offenders. Several studies have tried to corroborate this viewpoint, with varying results—estimates of the number of crimes committed each year by habitual offenders range from 3 to 187.[73] If one accepts the higher estimate, each year a repeat offender spends in prison prevents a significant number of criminal acts.

Criminologists, however, note the negative consequences of America's immense prison and jail population. For one, incarceration can have severe social consequences for communities and the families that make up those communities. About 1.7 million minor children—one in 43—have a parent in prison, putting them at greater risk of suffering financial hardship and reduced supervision and discipline.[74] As a result of the deterioration of the family structure, children of inmates are at a higher risk than their peers for antisocial behavior and mental health problems.[75]

Our high rates of incarceration also deny one of the basic rights of American democracy—the right to vote—to about 5.3 million Americans with criminal records.[76] A number of states and the federal government *disenfranchise,* or take the ability to vote away from, those convicted of felonies. This has a disproportionate impact on minority groups, weakening their voice in the democratic debate. Today, African American males are incarcerated at a rate seven times that of white males and almost three times that of Hispanic males.[77] With more black men behind bars than enrolled in the nation's colleges and universities, Marc Mauer of the Sentencing Project believes that the "ripple effect on their communities and on the next generation of kids, growing up with their fathers in prison, will certainly be with us for at least a generation."[78]

Whether our incarceration situation is "good" or "bad" depends to a large extent on one's personal philosophy. In the end, it is difficult to do a definitive cost-benefit analysis for each person incarcerated, weighing the benefits of preventing crimes that might (or might not) have been committed by an inmate against the costs to the convict's family and society. One thing that can be stated with some certainty is that even with the growing interest in decarceration described earlier in the chapter, the American prison system will remain one of the largest in the world for the foreseeable future.

A mother and child wait outside the Donald W. W. Wyatt Detention Facility in Central Falls, Rhode Island. What are the possible consequences of having a parent behind bars for the affected children and for American society as a whole?

Suzanne DeChillo/*New York Times*/Redux

CHAPTER SUMMARY

Learning Objective 1 **Contrast the Pennsylvania and the New York penitentiary theories of the 1800s.** Basically, the Pennsylvania system imposed total silence on its prisoners. Based on the concept of separate confinement, penitentiaries were constructed with back-to-back cells facing both outward and inward. Prisoners worked, slept, and ate alone in their cells. In contrast, New York used the congregate system: silence was imposed, but inmates worked and ate together.

Learning Objective 2 **List the factors that have caused the prison population to grow dramatically in the last several decades.** (a) The enhancement and stricter enforcement of the nation's drug laws; (b) increased probability of incarceration; (c) inmates serving more time for each crime; (d) federal prison growth; and (e) rising incarceration rates for women.

Learning Objective 3 **Describe the formal prison management system.** A formal system is militaristic, with a hierarchical (top-down) chain of command; the warden (or superintendent) is on top, then deputy wardens, and last, custodial employees.

Learning Objective 4 **List and briefly explain the four types of prisons.** (a) Maximum-security prisons, which are designed mainly with security and surveillance in mind. Such prisons are usually large and consist of cell blocks, each of which is set off by a series of gates and bars. (b) Medium-security prisons, which offer considerably more educational and treatment programs and allow more contact between inmates. Such prisons are usually surrounded by high fences rather than by walls. (c) Minimum-security prisons, which permit prisoners to have television sets and computers and often allow prisoners to leave the grounds for educational and employment purposes. (d) Supermaximum-security (supermax) prisons, in which prisoners are confined to one-person cells for up to twenty-two and a half hours per day under constant video camera surveillance.

Learning Objective 5 **List the reasons why private prisons can often be run more cheaply than public ones.** (a) Labor costs are lower because private prison employees are nonunionized and receive lower levels of overtime pay, sick leave, and health care. (b) Competitive bidding allows the operators of private prisons to buy goods and services at the lowest possible prices. (c) There is less red tape in a private prison facility.

Learning Objective 6 **Summarize the distinction between jails and prisons, and indicate the importance of jails in the American corrections system.** Generally, a prison is for those convicted of felonies who will serve lengthy periods of incarceration, whereas a jail is for those who have been convicted of misdemeanors and will serve less than a year of incarceration. Jails also hold individuals awaiting trial, juveniles awaiting transfer to juvenile authorities, probation and parole violators, and the mentally ill. In any given year, approximately 13 million people are admitted to jails, and therefore jails often provide the best chance for treatment or counseling that may deter future criminal behavior by these low-level offenders.

Learning Objective 7 **Explain how jails are administered.** Most jails are operated at the county level by an elected sheriff, although about 20 percent are under the control of municipalities and six states manage jails themselves. Sheriffs appoint jail administrators (deputy sheriffs), as well as deputy jailers.

Learning Objective 8 **Indicate some of the consequences of our high rates of incarceration.** Some people believe that the reduction in the country's crime rate is a direct result of increased incarceration rates. Others believe that high incarceration rates are having increasingly negative social consequences, such as financial hardships, reduced supervision and discipline of children, and a general deterioration of the family structure when one parent is in prison.

QUESTIONS FOR CRITICAL ANALYSIS

1. What might be some of the negative consequences of widespread decarceration in the United States?

2. Supermax prisons operate in a state of perpetual lockdown (see page 321). Why might a warden institute a lockdown in a maximum-security prison?

3. Do you agree with the argument that private prisons are inherently injust, no matter what costs they may save taxpayers? Why or why not?

4. Why have pretrial detainees (see page 326) been called "walking legal contradictions"? What are the

practical reasons why pretrial detainees will continue to be housed in jails prior to trial, regardless of whether their incarceration presents any constitutional irregularities?

5. What are the arguments for and against taking away the ability to vote from those Americans convicted of committing a crime? What is your opinion of this form of disenfranchisement?

KEY TERMS

classification **319**

congregate system **312**

direct supervision approach **329**

jail **326**

lockdown **321**

maximum-security prison **319**

medical model **313**

medium-security prison **321**

minimum-security prison **321**

new-generation jails **329**

penitentiary **311**

pretrial detainees **326**

private prisons **322**

separate confinement **312**

supermax prison **321**

time served **327**

warden **318**

SELF ASSESSMENT ANSWER KEY

Page 314: i. separate; **ii.** congregate; **iii.** silence; **iv.** cheaper; **v.** labor; **vi.** medical

Page 316: i. drug; **ii.** incarceration/imprisonment; **iii.** length; **iv.** federal; **v.** women

Page 322: i. warden; **ii.** Classification; **iii.** maximum; **iv.** supermax

Page 325: i. financial; **ii.** overcrowding; **iii.** security/safety; **iv.** federal

Page 329: i. pretrial detainees; **ii.** convicted; **iii.** misdemeanor; **iv.** sheriff

COURSEMATE

For online help and access to resources that accompany *Criminal Justice in Action: The Core*, go to **www.cengagebrain.com/shop/ISBN/978-1-285-06915-9**. Click "Access Now," where you will find flashcards, an online quiz, and other helpful study aids. If you have an access code for CourseMate, log in and go to the chapter of your choice for additional online study aids.

NOTES

1. Bureau of Justice Statistics, *Correctional Population in the United States, 2010* (Washington, D.C.: U.S. Department of Justice, December 2011), 1–3.

2. James M. Beattie, *Crime and the Courts in England, 1660–1800* (Princeton, NJ: Princeton University Press, 1986), 506–507.

3. Samuel Walker, *Popular Justice* (New York: Oxford University Press, 1980), 11.

4. Michael Meranze, *Laboratories of Virtue: Punishment, Revolution, and Authority in Philadelphia, 1760–1835* (Chapel Hill, NC: University of North Carolina Press, 1996), 55.

5. Negley K. Teeters, *The Cradle of the Penitentiary: The Walnut Street Jail at Philadelphia, 1773–1835* (Philadelphia: Pennsylvania Prison Society, 1955), 30.

6. Negley K. Teeters and John D. Shearer, *The Prison at Philadelphia's Cherry Hill* (New York: Columbia University Press, 1957), 142–143.

7. Henry Calvin Mohler, "Convict Labor Policies," *Journal of the American Institute of Criminal Law and Criminology* 15 (1925), 556–557.

8. Zebulon Brockway, *Fifty Years of Prison Service* (Montclair, NJ: Patterson Smith, 1969), 400–401.

9. Robert Martinson, "What Works? Questions and Answers about Prison Reform," *Public Interest* 35 (Spring 1974), 22.

10. See Ted Palmer, "Martinson Revisited," *Journal of Research on Crime and Delinquency* (1975), 133; and Paul Gendreau and Bob Ross, "Effective Correctional Treatment: Bibliotherapy for Cynics," *Crime & Delinquency* 25 (1979), 499.

11. Robert Martinson, "New Findings, New Views: A Note of Caution Regarding Sentencing Reform," *Hofstra Law Review* 7 (1979), 243.

12. Cheryl L. Jonson, Francis T. Cullen, and Edward J. Latessa, "Cracks in the Penal Harm Movement: Evidence from the Field," *Criminology & Public Policy* (August 2008), 423.

13. Steven D. Levitt, "Understanding Why Crime Fell in the 1990s: Four Factors That Explain the Decline and Six That Do Not," *Journal of Economic Perspectives* (Winter 2004), 177.

14. Bureau of Justice Statistics, *Prisoners in 2010* (Washington, D.C.: U.S. Department of Justice, December 2011), Appendix table 16a, page 28; and Appendix table 18, page 30.

15. Allen J. Beck, "Growth, Change, and Stability in the U.S. Prison Population, 1980–1995," *Corrections Management Quarterly* (Spring 1997), 9–10.

16. Bureau of Justice Statistics, "Criminal Defendants Sentenced in U.S. District Courts," *Sourcebook of Criminal Justice Statistics Online*, Table 5.23.10, at **www.albany.edu/sourcebook/pdf/t52322010.pdf**; and United States Courts, "U.S. District Courts—Criminal

Defendants Sentenced after Conviction, by Offense, during the 12-Month Period Ending September 30, 2011," at **www.uscourts.gov/ uscourts/Statistics/JudicialBusiness/2011/ appendices/D05Sep11.wwwwww**.

17. Joan Petersilia, "Beyond the Prison Bubble," *Wilson Quarterly* (Winter 2011), 27.

18. *Brown v. Plata*, 563 U.S. ____ (2011).

19. California State Auditor, *Inmates Sentenced under the Three Strikes Law and a Small Number of Inmates Receiving Specialty Care Represent Significant Costs* (Sacramento, CA: Bureau of State Audits, May 2011), 1.

20. Marc Mauer and David Cole, "Five Myths about Americans in Prison," *Washington Post* (June 17, 2011), at **www.washingtonpost. com/opinions/five-myths-about-incarcer- ation/2011/06/13/AGfIWvYH_story.html**.

21. Bureau of Justice Statistics, *Prison and Jail Inmates, 1995* (Washington, D.C.: U.S. Department of Justice, August 1996), 1; and Bureau of Justice Statistics, *Prisoners in 2010*, Appendix table 1, page 14.

22. Bureau of Justice Statistics, *Prisoners in 2005* (Washington, D.C.: U.S. Department of Justice, November 2006), Table 14, page 10.

23. Bureau of Justice Statistics, *Prisoners in 2010*, Appendix table 18, page 30.

24. Federal Bureau of Prisons, "Quick Facts about the Bureau of Prisons" (February, 2012), at **www.bop.gov/news/quick.jsp**.

25. Bureau of Justice Statistics, *Prisoners in 2010*, Appendix table 5, page 20; and Appendix table 7, page 22.

26. Christian Henrichson and Ruth Delaney, *The Price of Prisons: What Incarceration Costs Taxpayers* (New York: Center for Sentencing and Corrections, January 2012), 6, 8.

27. Rosemary Gartner, Anthony N. Doob, Franklin E. Zimring, "The Past as Prologue? Decarceration in California Then and Now," *Criminology & Public Policy* (May 2011), 292.

28. Erica Goode, "Inmate Visits Now Carry Added Cost in Arizona," *New York Times* (September 5, 2011), A10.

29. James B. Jacobs, "Finding Alternatives to the Carceral State," *Social Research* (Summer 2007), 695.

30. Gartner, Doob, and Zimring, 294–296.

31. Charlie Savage, "Trend to Lighten Harsh Sentences Catches on in Conservative States," *New York Times* (August 13, 2011), A12.

32. Bureau of Justice Statistics, "U.S. Correctional Population Declined for Second Consecutive Year," December 15, 2011, at **bjs.ojp.usdoj. gov/content/pub/press/p10cpus10pr.cfm**.

33. Bureau of Justice Statistics, *Census of State and Federal Correctional Facilities, 2005* (Washington, D.C.: U.S. Department of Justice, October 2008), 2.

34. *Ibid.*

35. Charles H. Logan, "Well Kept: Comparing Quality of Confinement in a Public and Private Prison," *Journal of Criminal Law and Criminology* 83 (1992), 580.

36. Bert Useem and Peter Kimball, *Stages of Siege: U.S. Prison Riots, 1971–1986* (New York: Oxford University Press, 1989).

37. Bert Useem, "Disorganization and the New Mexico Prison Riot of 1980," *American Sociology Review* 50 (1985), 685.

38. Todd R. Clear, George F. Cole, and Michael D. Reisig, *American Corrections*, 9th ed. (Belmont, CA: Wadsworth Cengage Learning, 2010), 162.

39. Tony Izzo, "I-Max Awaits Green," *Kansas City Star* (May 26, 1996), A1.

40. Douglas Page, "The Prison of the Future," *Law Enforcement Technology* (January 2012), 11–13.

41. Charles A. Pettigrew, "Technology and the Eighth Amendment: The Problem of Supermax Prisons," *North Carolina Journal of Law and Technology* (Fall 2002), 195.

42. Bureau of Justice Statistics, *Prisoners in 2010*, 7.

43. "A Tale of Two Systems: Cost, Quality, and Accountability in Private Prisons," *Harvard Law Review* (May 2002), 1872.

44. Douglas C. McDonald and Kenneth Carlson, *Contracting for Imprisonment in the Federal Prison System: Cost and Performance of the Privately Operated Taft Correctional Institution* (Cambridge, MA: Abt Associates, Inc., October 2005), vii.

45. Vanderbilt University Law School, "New Study Shows Benefits of Having Privately and Publicly Managed Prisons in the Same State" (November 25, 2008), at **law.vanderbilt.edu/article- search/article-detail/index.aspx?nid=213**.

46. Nelson Daranciang, "Isle Inmates Brought Home," *Honolulu Star-Advertiser* (January 28, 2011), A3.

47. John Tunison, "Baldwin Prisoners Will Be Classified Medium Security," *Grand Rapids (MI) Press* (December 11, 2010), A4.

48. "Behind the Bars: Experts Question Benefits of Private Prisons," *Kentucky Courier Journal* (July 5, 2010), at **www.courier-journal. com/article/20100705/NEWS01/7050312/ Behind-Bars-Experts-question-benefits- private-prisons**.

49. Quoted in Scott Cohn, "Private Prison Industry Grows Despite Critics," *cnbc.com* (October 18, 2011), at **today.msnbc.msn.com/ id/44936562/ns/today-today_news/t/ private-prison-industry-grows-despite- critics/#.T3DqUHheGll**.

50. Robbie Brown, "Mississippi Prison on Lockdown after Guard Dies," *New York Times* (May 23, 2012), A12.

51. Harley G. Lappin et al., *Evaluation of the Taft Demonstration Project: Performance of a Private-Sector Prison and the BOP* (Washington, D.C.: Federal Bureau of Prisons, 2005), 57–59.

52. Curtis R. Blakely and Vic W. Bumphus, "Private and Public Sector Prisons," *Federal Probation* (June 2004), 27.

53. John DiIulio, "Prisons, Profits, and the Public Good: The Privatization of Corrections," in *Criminal Justice Center Bulletin* (Huntsville, TX: Sam Houston State University, 1986).

54. Ira P. Robbins, "Privatization of Prisons, Privatization of Corrections: Defining the Issues," *Vanderbilt Law Review* 40 (1987), 823.

55. Steve Bousquet, "Nine Defectors Sink Private Prison Plan," *Tampa Bay Times* (February 15, 2012), 1A.

56. Chris Kirkham, "Private Prison Corporation Offers Cash in Exchange for State Prisons," *Huffington Post* (February 14, 2012), at **www. huffingtonpost.com/2012/02/14/private- prisons-buying-state-prisons_n_1272143. html**.

57. Bureau of Justice Statistics, *Prisoners in 2010*, Appendix table 19, page 30.

58. Bureau of Justice Statistics, *Jail Inmates at Midyear 2010—Statistical Tables* (Washington, D.C.: U.S. Department of Justice, April 2011), 1–2.

59. Arthur Wallenstein, "Jail Crowding: Bringing the Issue to the Corrections Center Stage," *Corrections Today* (December 1996), 76–81.

60. Quoted in Fox Butterfield, "'Defying Gravity,' Inmate Population Climbs," *New York Times* (January 19, 1998), A10.

61. Bureau of Justice Statistics, *Jail Inmates at Midyear 2010—Statistical Tables*, Table 6, page 7.

62. 441 U.S. 520 (1979).

63. *Ibid.*, at 546.

64. Bureau of Justice Statistics, *Jail Inmates at Midyear 2010—Statistical Tables*, Table 7, page 8.

65. Vauhini Vara and Bobby White, "County Jails Prepare for Extra Guests," *Wall Street Journal* (August 10, 2011), A4.

66. John Irwin, *The Jail: Managing the Underclass in American Society* (Berkeley, CA: University of California Press, 1985), 2.

67. Bureau of Justice Statistics, *Substance Dependence, Abuse, and Treatment of Jail Inmates, 2002* (Washington, D.C.: U.S. Department of Justice, July 2005), 1.

68. Bureau of Justice Statistics, *Bulletin* (Washington, D.C.: U.S. Department of Justice, May 2004), 10.

69. Philip L. Reichel, *Corrections: Philosophies, Practices, and Procedures*, 2d ed. (Boston: Allyn & Bacon, 2001), 283.

70. R. L. Miller, "New Generation Justice Facilities: The Case for Direct Supervision," *Architectural Technology* 12 (1985), 6–7.

71. David Bogard, Virginia A. Hutchinson, and Vicci Persons, *Direct Supervision Jails: The Role of the Administrator* (Washington, D.C.: National Institute of Corrections, February 2010), 1–2.

72. Dan Seligman, "Lock 'Em Up," *Forbes* (May 23, 2005), 216–217.

73. Franklin E. Zimring and Gordon Hawkins, *Incapacitation: Penal Confinement and the Restraint of Crime* (New York: Oxford University Press, 1995), 38, 40, 145.

74. Sarah Schirmer, Ashley Nellis, and Marc Mauer, *Incarcerated Parents and Their Children* (The Sentencing Project, February 2009), 2.

75. Sara Wakefield and Christopher Wildeman, "Mass Imprisonment and Racial Disparities in Childhood Behavioral Problems," *Criminology and Public Policy* (August 2011), 803–808.

76. The Sentencing Project, "Felony Dis- enfranchisement," at **www.sentencing project.org/IssueAreaHome.aspx?IssueID=4**.

77. Bureau of Justice Statistics, *Prisoners in 2010*, Appendix table 14, page 27.

78. Quoted in Fox Butterfield, "Study Finds 2.6% Increase in U.S. Prison Population," *New York Times* (July 28, 2003), A8.

CHAPTER

12

Behind Bars

The Life of an Inmate

LEARNING OBJECTIVES

After reading this chapter, you should be able to...

1 Explain the concept of prison as a total institution.

2 Indicate some of the reasons for violent behavior in prisons.

3 List and briefly explain the six general job categories among correctional officers.

4 Describe the hands-off doctrine of prisoner law and indicate two standards used to determine if prisoners' rights have been violated.

5 Contrast probation, parole, expiration release, pardon, and furlough.

6 Describe typical conditions of parole.

7 Explain the goal of prisoner reentry programs.

8 Indicate typical conditions for release for a paroled child molester.

Throughout the chapter you will see each learning objective repeated in the margin next to the content it relates to. The chapter summary on pages 360 and 361 includes all of the learning objectives for review.

CHAPTER OUTLINE

- Prison Culture
- Correctional Officers and Discipline
- Inside a Women's Prison
- Parole and Release from Prison
- Reentry into Society

TRIPLE FRAY

On December 7, 2011, a riot involving about 150 maximum-security inmates broke out in the exercise yard of C-Facility at California State Prison near Sacramento, also known as New Folsom. After pepper spray and rubber bullets failed to stop the brawl, correctional officers fired actual bullets into the mass of convicts, ten of whom were eventually sent to the hospital. Although such outbreaks are relatively rare in most American prisons, New Folsom and its nearby counterpart—"old" Folsom State Prison— recently have been plagued by mass violence. In May 2011, six New Folsom inmates were injured during a riot in the exercise yard of B-Facility. Then, on March 6, 2012, a battle broke out among seventy inmates at old Folsom.

Coincidentally, the first New Folsom disturbance took place just two days after the United States Supreme Court ordered California corrections officials to reduce overcrowding in state prisons, as discussed in the previous chapter. At the time of the incident, New Folsom housed more than 2,800 inmates even though it was designed to hold only 1,800.

According to one old Folsom inmate, the daily frustrations born of such congestion are the main reason for eruptions of violence. "Imagine you have to wait in line to relieve yourself or take a shower," he says, and "then watching someone crowd his way in." Adding to the discomfort is a "no frills" movement in public policy and prison management that has succeeded in removing all amenities from inmates' lives. Many state prisons ban weightlifting, televisions, radios, adult magazines, and conjugal visits. All states and the federal government have limited smoking in their correctional facilities, and some institutions feed their inmates an unpleasant concoction of nondairy cheese, powdered milk, tomato paste, and dehydrated potato flakes known as *nutraloaf.* As one observer puts it, today's penal institutions are often characterized by "grindingly dull routine interrupted by occasional flashes of violence and brutality."

To stop a December 2011 riot at the California State Prison near Sacramento, correctional officers handcuffed more than one hundred inmates, including the twelve shown here.

In "Folsom Prison Blues," country singer Johnny Cash told the story of a murderer who laments, "I know I can't be free," as he hears the whistle of a train passing outside his cell window.[1] Most inmates, however, will at some point "be free," following their release from incarceration. The Delancey Street Foundation, a self-supporting rehabilitation program headquartered in San Francisco, about two hours south of Folsom State Prison, helps released prisoners adjust to their newfound freedom. The foundation offers ex-convicts a place to live, job training, and employment at one of the businesses owned by the group. Roderick Davis, who has worked at the Delancey Street Restaurant for more than ten years since his release from prison, credits Delancey Street with accepting him despite "all the horrible and terrible things I've done in my life." He adds, "Nobody judged me because I did those things."[2]

In this chapter, we will look at the life of the imprisoned convict, starting with the realities of an existence behind bars and finishing with the challenges of returning to free society. Along the way, we will discuss violence in prison, correctional officers, women's prisons, the mechanics of release, and several other issues that are at the forefront of the

American corrections system today. To start, we must understand the forces that shape prison culture and how those forces affect the overall operation of the correctional facility.

PRISON CULTURE

Learning Objective 1 Explain the concept of a prison as a total institution.

Any institution, whether a school, a bank, or a police department, has an organizational culture—a set of values that help the people in the organization understand what actions are acceptable and what actions are unacceptable. According to a theory put forth by the influential sociologist Erving Goffman, prison cultures are unique because prisons are **total institutions** that encompass every aspect of an inmate's life. Unlike a student or a bank teller, a prisoner cannot leave the institution or have any meaningful interaction with outside communities. Others arrange every aspect of daily life, and all prisoners are required to follow this schedule in the same manner.[3]

Inmates develop their own argot, or language (see Figure 12.1 below). They create their own economy, which, in the absence of currency, is based on the barter of valued items such as food, contraband, and sexual favors. They establish methods of determining power, many of which, as we shall see, involve violence. Isolated and heavily regulated, prisoners create a social existence that is, out of both necessity and design, separate from the outside world.

ADAPTING TO PRISON SOCIETY

On arriving at prison, each convict attends an orientation session and receives a "Resident's Handbook." The handbook provides information such as meal and official count times, disciplinary regulations, and visitation guidelines. The norms and values of the prison society, however, cannot be communicated by the staff or learned from a handbook. As first described by Donald Clemmer in his classic 1940 work, *The Prison Community*, the process of **prisonization**—or adaptation to the prison culture—advances as the inmate gradually understands what constitutes acceptable behavior in the institution. For the most part, such behavior is defined not by prison officials but by other inmates.[4]

In studying prisonization, criminologists have focused on two areas: how prisoners change their behavior to adapt to life behind bars, and how life behind bars has changed because of inmate behavior. Sociologist John Irwin has identified several patterns of inmate behavior, each one driven by the inmate's personality and values:

Total Institution An institution, such as a prison, that provides all of the necessities for existence to those who live within its boundaries.

Prisonization The socialization process through which a new inmate learns the accepted norms and values of the prison culture.

FIGURE 12.1 Prison Slang

Ace Another word for "dollar."

Bang A fight to the death, or shoot to kill.

Base head A cocaine addict.

B.G. "Baby gangster," or someone who has never shot another person.

Booty bandit An incarcerated sexual predator who preys on weaker inmates, called "punks."

Bug A correctional staff member, such as a psychiatrist, who is deemed untrustworthy or unreliable.

Bumpin' titties Fighting.

Catch cold To get killed.

Chiva Heroin.

Dancing on the blacktop Getting stabbed.

Diddler Child molester or pedophile.

Green light Prison gang term for a contract killing.

Hacks Correctional officers.

Jug-up Mealtime.

Lugger An inmate who smuggles in and possesses illegal substances.

Punk An inmate subject to rape, usually more submissive than most inmates.

Ride with To perform favors, including sexual favors, for a convict in return for protection or prison-store goods.

Shank Knife.

Tits-up An inmate who has died.

Topped Committed suicide.

Source: www.insideprison.com/glossary.asp.

1. Professional criminals adapt to prison by "doing time." In other words, they follow the rules and generally do whatever is necessary to speed up their release and return to freedom.

2. Some convicts, mostly state-raised youths or those frequently incarcerated in juvenile detention centers, are more comfortable inside prison than outside. These inmates serve time by "jailing," or establishing themselves in the power structure of prison culture.

3. Other inmates take advantage of prison resources such as libraries or drug treatment programs by "gleaning," or working to improve themselves to prepare for a return to society.

4. Finally, "disorganized" criminals exist on the fringes of prison society. These inmates may have mental impairments or low levels of intelligence and find it impossible to adapt to prison culture on any level.[5]

The process of categorizing prisoners has a theoretical basis, but it serves a practical purpose as well, allowing administrators to reasonably predict how different inmates will act in certain situations. An inmate who is "doing time" generally does not present the same security risk as one who is "jailing."

WHO IS IN PRISON?

The culture of any prison is heavily influenced by its inmates. Their values, beliefs, and experiences will be reflected in the social order that exists behind bars. As we noted in the last chapter, the past three decades have seen incarceration rates of women and minority groups rise sharply. Furthermore, the arrest patterns of inmates have changed over that time period. A prisoner today is much more likely to have been incarcerated on a drug charge or immigration violation than was the case in the 1980s. Today's inmate is also more likely to behave violently behind bars—a situation that will be addressed shortly.

AN AGING INMATE POPULATION In recent years, the most significant demographic change in the prison population involves age. Although the majority of inmates are still under thirty-four years old, the number of state and federal prisoners over the age of fifty-five has increased dramatically since 1995, from 32,600 to 119,000.[6] Several factors have contributed to this upsurge, including "get tough on crime" measures that impose mandatory sentences (discussed in Chapter 9), high rates of recidivism, higher levels of murder and sex crimes committed by older offenders, and the aging of the U.S. population as a whole.[7]

Given that older inmates will experience more health-related problems, prisons and jails are now housing more people with medical issues than in the past. Poor health is the cause of nine of every ten deaths of inmates in state prisons, with heart disease and cancer accounting for nearly half of these fatalities.[8] About 40 percent of state and federal prisoners suffer from at least one form of illness other than a cold, the most common ailments being arthritis, hypertension, tuberculosis, and asthma.[9] Not surprisingly, corrections budgets are straining under the financial pressures caused by the health-care needs of aging inmates. According to the American Civil Liberties Union, it costs three times as much to house an elderly inmate as a younger one.[10] (The feature *A Question of Ethics—The Million-Dollar Man* on page 340 addresses the issue of whether the government is obligatted to provide criminals with expensive medical care at taxpayers' expense.)

MENTAL ILLNESS BEHIND BARS Another factor in rising correctional health-care costs is the high incidence of mental illness in American prisons and jails. During the 1950s and 1960s, nearly 600,000 mental patients lived in public hospitals, often against their will. A series of scandals spotlighting the poor medical services and horrendous living conditions in these institutions led to their closure and the elimination of much of the nation's state-run mental health infrastructure.[11] Many mentally ill people now receive no supervision whatsoever, and some inevitably commit deviant or criminal acts.

As a result, in the words of criminal justice experts Katherine Stuart van Wormer and Clemens Bartollas, jails and prison have become "the dumping grounds for people whose bizarre behavior lands them behind bars."[12] Nationwide, 60 percent of jail inmates and 56 percent of state prisoners suffer from some form of mental illness.[13] For reasons that should become clear over the course of this chapter, correctional facilities are not designed to foster mental well-being, and, indeed, inmates with mental illnesses often find that their problems are exacerbated by the prison environment.[14]

REHABILITATION AND PRISON PROGRAMS

In Chapter 9, we saw that rehabilitation is one of the basic theoretical justifications for punishment. **Prison programs,** which include any organized activities designed to foster rehabilitation, benefit inmates in several ways. On a basic level, these programs get prisoners out of their cells and alleviate the boredom that marks prison and jail life. The programs also help inmates improve their health and skills, giving them a better chance of reintegration into society after release. Consequently, nearly every federal and state prison in the United States offers some form of rehabilitation.[15]

The primary goal of rehabilitation programs, from an administrative standpoint, is to reduce recidivism. Research does demonstrate that offenders who earn a high school equivalency diploma behind bars are more likely to find employment after release, and therefore are less likely to be rearrested. Prison drug treatment programs can also be beneficial, reducing the probability of relapse in the "real world."[16] Given their budget constraints, however, prison systems are often forced to limit their vocational, educational, and treatment programs. Many inmates suffering from mental illness would benefit from medication and twenty-four-hour psychiatric care. Yet these services are quite rare behind bars, mostly due to their high costs.[17]

VIOLENCE IN PRISON CULTURE

Until the 1970s, prison culture emphasized "noninterference" and did not support inmate-on-inmate violence. Prison "elders" would themselves punish any of their peers who showed a proclivity toward assaulting fellow inmates. Today, in contrast, violence is used to establish the prisoner hierarchy by separating the powerful from the weak. Humboldt State University's Lee H. Bowker has identified several other reasons for violent behavior:

- It provides a deterrent against being victimized, as a reputation for violence may eliminate an inmate as a target of assault.
- It enhances self-image in an environment that does not respect other attributes, such as intelligence.
- In the case of rape, it gives sexual relief.
- It serves as a means of acquiring material goods through extortion or outright robbery.[18]

Why is it beneficial for prisoners such as these two Colorado state inmates, seen working on mannequin heads during a cosmetology class, to receive job training while still incarcerated?

AP Photo/*Daily Record*, Jeff Shane

Prison Programs Organized activities for inmates that are designed to improve their physical and mental health, provide them with vocational skills, or simply keep them busy while incarcerated.

Learning Objective 2 Indicate some of the reasons for violent behavior in prisons.

Deprivation Model A theory that inmate aggression is the result of the frustration inmates feel at being deprived of freedom, consumer goods, sex, and other staples of life outside the institution.

Relative Deprivation The theory that inmate aggression is caused when freedoms and services that the inmate has come to accept as normal are decreased or eliminated.

The **deprivation model** can be used to explain the high level of prison violence. According to this model, the stressful and oppressive conditions of prison life lead to aggressive behavior on the part of inmates. Prison researcher Stephen C. Light found that when conditions such as overcrowding worsen, inmate misconduct often increases.[19] In these circumstances, the violent behavior may not have any express purpose—it may just be a means of relieving tension.

LEVELS OF PRISON VIOLENCE Simply put, prisons and jails are dangerous places to live. Each year, federal correctional officers are subjected to about eighty assaults and 1,500 less-serious attacks such as pushing and shoving.[20] About five inmates in state prisons and twenty-one inmates in local jails are killed by fellow inmates each year.[21] (Note that this homicide rate is lower than the national average.) As many as 216,000 inmate-on-inmate sexual assaults take place annually, a number that is certainly artificially low because of reluctance on the part of both prisoners and correctional officials to report rapes to authorities.[22] With nothing but time on their hands, prisoners have been known to fashion deadly weapons out of everyday items. During the New Folsom riot discussed at the beginning of the chapter, inmates attacked each other with contraband razors and sharpened toothbrushes.

RIOTS As we pointed out earlier, riots—defined as situations in which a number of prisoners are beyond institutional control—are relatively rare. Researchers have addressed the seeming randomness of these incidents by turning to the concept of **relative deprivation.** This theory focuses on the gap between what is expected in any given living environment and the realities of that environment. Criminologist Peter C. Kratcoski has argued that because prisoners enjoy such meager privileges to begin with, any further deprivation can spark disorder.[23] A number of prison experts have noted that collective violence often

A QUESTION OF ETHICS: *The Million-Dollar Man*

THE SITUATION Prisoner X is serving fourteen years in a California prison for robbery. He has fallen ill, and only a heart transplant will save his life. Although many Americans who need organ transplants cannot afford such an expensive procedure, the California Department of Corrections is considering whether to spend more than $1 million for Prisoner X's operation and recovery.

THE ETHICAL DILEMMA At the time Prisoner X fell ill, more than 4,100 names were on the national waiting list for a new heart. Many California taxpayers—who would ultimately pay for Prisoner X's operation—were outraged that a convicted criminal could receive a new heart before other, law-abiding patients. In 1976, however, the United States Supreme Court ruled that prisoners have a right to "adequate" medical care, which has been interpreted to mean the same level of care they would receive if they were not behind bars. According to Michael A. Grodin, director of medical ethics at the Boston University School of Medicine

and Public Health, "[B]ecause someone is incarcerated, we have a higher obligation to provide them with health care because we have deprived them of their liberty." As the wife of a patient who was below Prisoner X on the heart transplant waiting list put it, "Since when is it unethical to save someone's life?"

WHAT IS THE SOLUTION? A number of states do not provide their prisoners with organ transplants or will do so only if the prisoner can pay for the operation. What should California do with Prisoner X?* What options do state prison officials have if they decide not to cover the costs of the transplant? Would it be ethical to release Prisoner X or any other inmate simply to avoid the burden of his or her medical bills?

*In the actual case, California did provide Prisoner X with a new heart, but his body rejected the transplanted organ, and he died within a year.

occurs in response to heightened measures of security at corrections facilities.[24] Thus, such violence may be the angry response to an additional reduction in freedom for inmates, who enjoy very little freedom to begin with.

ISSUES OF RACE AND ETHNICITY

Race plays a major role in prison life, and prison violence is often an outlet for racial tension. As prison populations have changed over the past three decades, with African Americans and Hispanics becoming the majority in many penal institutions, issues of race and ethnicity have become increasingly important to prison administrators and researchers. Leo Carroll, professor of sociology at the University of Rhode Island, has written extensively about how today's prisoners are divided into hostile groups, with race determining nearly every aspect of an inmate's life, including friends, job assignments, and cell location.[25] Carroll's research has also shown how minority groups in prison have seized on race to help form their prison identities.[26]

A correctional official displays a set of homemade knives, also known as *shivs*, made by inmates at Attica Correctional Facility in Attica, New York. What are some of the reasons why violence flourishes behind bars? AP Photo/David Duprey

PRISON GANGS In many instances, racial and ethnic identification is the primary focus of the **prison gang**—a clique of inmates who join together in an organizational structure. Gang affiliation is often the cause of inmate-on-inmate violence. Folsom State Prison, discussed in the opening of this chapter, is plagued by various gangs such as the Mexican Mafia, composed of U.S.-born inmates of Mexican descent, and their enemies, a spin-off organization called La Nuestra Familia.

In part, the prison gang is a natural result of life in the modern prison. As one expert says of these gangs:

> Their members have done in prison what many people do elsewhere when they feel personally powerless, threatened, and vulnerable. They align themselves with others, organize to fight back, and enhance their own status and control through their connection to a more powerful group.[27]

In addition to their important role in the social structure of correctional facilities, prison gangs participate in a wide range of illegal economic activities within these institutions, including prostitution, drug selling, gambling, and loan sharking. A study released in 2011 by Alan J. Drury and Matt DeLisi of Iowa State University found that gang members were more likely to be involved in prison misconduct than those offenders who had been convicted of murder.[28]

Prison Gang A group of inmates who band together within the corrections system to engage in social and criminal activities.

THE PREVALENCE OF PRISON GANGS Recent research places the rate of gang membership at 11.7 percent in federal prisons, 13.4 percent in state prisons, and 15.6 percent in jails.[29] When the National Gang Crime Research Center surveyed prison administrators, however, almost 95 percent said that gang recruitment took place at their institutions, so the overall prevalence of gangs is probably much higher.[30] Los Angeles correctional officials believe that eight out of every ten inmates in their city jails are gang affiliated. Although the stereotypical gang is composed of African Americans or Hispanics, the majority of large prisons also have white, or "Aryan," gangs. One of the largest federal capital prosecutions in U.S. history, involving thirty-two counts of murder, focused on a major prison gang known as the Aryan Brotherhood.

SELFASSESSMENT

Fill in the blanks and check your answers on page 361.

Prison culture is different from the cultures of schools or workplaces because prison is a _____ _____ that dominates every aspect of the inmate's life. In recent decades, the prison culture has been affected by the increased average _____ of inmates, which has led to higher _____-_____ costs for corrections systems. Some researchers rely on the _____ model, which focuses on the stressful and oppressive conditions of incarceration, to explain general prison violence. The concept of _____ _____, based on the gap between an inmate's expectations and reality, is used to explain the conditions that lead to prison riots.

CORRECTIONAL OFFICERS AND DISCIPLINE

In high-security prisons, correctional officers such as these two at the supermax prison in Tamms, Illinois, monitor even the most mundane of inmate activities, including working, exercising, eating, and showering. How might this constant surveillance contribute to tension between correctional officers and prisoners?

John Smierciak/MCT/Landov

Ideally, the presence of correctional officers—the standard term used to describe prison guards—has the effect of lessening violence in American correctional institutions. Practically speaking, this is indeed the case. Without correctional officers, the prison would be a place of anarchy. But in the highly regulated, oppressive environment of the prison, correctional officers must use the threat of violence, if not actual violence, to instill discipline and keep order. Thus, the relationship between prison staff and inmates is marked by mutual distrust. Consider the two following statements, the first made by a correctional officer and the second by a prisoner:

[My job is to] protect, feed, and try to educate scum who raped and brutalized women and children . . . who, if I turn my back, will go into their cell, wrap a blanket around their cellmate's legs, and threaten to beat or rape him if he doesn't give sex, carry contraband, or fork over radios, money, or other goods willingly. And they'll stick a shank in me tomorrow if they think they can get away with it.[31]

The pigs in the state and federal prisons . . . treat me so violently, I cannot possibly imagine a time I could ever have anything but the deepest, aching, searing hatred for them. I can't begin to tell you what they do to me. If I were weaker by a hair, they would destroy me.[32]

It may be difficult for an outsider to understand the emotions that fuel such sentiments. French philosopher Michel Foucault (1926–1984) pointed out that discipline, both in prison and in the general community, is a means of social organization as well as punishment.[33]

Discipline is imposed when a person behaves in a manner that is contrary to the values of the dominant social group. Correctional officers and inmates have different concepts of the ideal structure of prison society, and, as the two quotations just cited demonstrate, this conflict generates intense feelings of fear and hatred, which often lead to violence.

RANK AND DUTIES OF CORRECTIONAL OFFICERS

After local officials shut down the Montague County (Texas) Jail several years ago because it had become something of an "Animal House" behind bars, much of the blame fell on the correctional staff. Security at the facility had become lax, to put it mildly. With little interference, inmates were allowed to have sex with their girlfriends, bring in comfortable furniture from home, take drugs, and chat on cell phones.

To avoid such problems, correctional facilities generally provide their employees with clearly delineated ranks and duties. The custodial staff at most prisons, for example, is organized according to four general ranks—captain, lieutenant, sergeant, and officer. In keeping with the militaristic model, captains are primarily administrators who deal directly with the warden on custodial issues. Lieutenants are the disciplinarians of the prison, responsible for policing and transporting the inmates. Sergeants oversee platoons of officers in specific parts of the prison, such as various cell blocks or work spaces.

Lucien X. Lombardo, professor of sociology and criminal justice at Old Dominion University, has identified six general job categories among correctional officers:[34]

1. *Block officers.* These employees supervise cell blocks containing as many as several hundred inmates, as well as the correctional officers on block guard duty. In general, the block officer is responsible for the well-being of the inmates. She or he makes sure the inmates do not harm themselves or other prisoners and also acts as something of a camp counselor, dispensing advice and seeing that inmates understand and follow the rules of the facility.

2. *Work detail supervisors.* In many penal institutions, the inmates work in the cafeteria, the prison store, the laundry, and other areas. Work detail supervisors oversee small groups of inmates as they perform their tasks.

3. *Industrial shop and school officers.* These officers perform maintenance and security functions in workshop and educational programs. Their primary responsibility is to make sure that inmates are on time for these programs and do not cause any disturbances during the sessions.

4. *Yard officers.* Officers who work the prison yard usually have the least seniority, befitting the assignment's reputation as dangerous and stressful. These officers must be constantly on alert for breaches in prison discipline or regulations in the relatively unstructured environment of the prison yard.

5. *Tower guards.* These officers spend their entire shifts, which usually last eight hours, in isolated, silent posts high above the grounds of the facility. Although their only means of communication are walkie-talkies or cellular devices, the safety benefits of the position can outweigh the loneliness that comes with the job.

6. *Administrative building assignments.* Officers who hold these positions provide security at prison gates, oversee visitation procedures, act as liaisons for civilians, and handle administrative tasks such as processing the paperwork when an inmate is transferred from another institution.

Learning Objective 3 List and briefly explain the six general job categories among correctional officers.

Black Creek/TSI PRISM

Tracking Inmates

Technology has added significantly to correctional officers' ability to keep prisons safe and orderly. Walk-through metal detectors and X-ray body scanners, for example, can detect weapons or other contraband hidden on the body of an inmate. The most promising new technology in this field, however, relies on radio frequency identification (RFID). About the size of two grains of rice, an RFID tag consists of a glass capsule that contains a computer chip, a tiny copper antenna, and an electrical device known as a "capacitor" that transmits the data in the chip to an outside scanner. In the prison context, RFID works as a high-tech head count: inmates wear bracelets tagged with the microchips while correctional officers wear small RFID devices resembling pagers.

Guided by a series of radio transmitters and receivers, the system is able to pinpoint the location of inmates and guards within twenty feet. Every two seconds, radio signals "search out" the location of each inmate and guard, and relay this information to a central computer. On a grid of the prison, an inmate shows up as a yellow dot and a correctional officer as a blue dot. Many RFID systems also store all movements in a database for future reference. "[RFID] completely revolutionizes a prison because you know where everyone is—not approximately but exactly where they are," remarked an official at the National Institute of Justice.

THINKING ABOUT RFID TRACKING: Review the discussion of crime mapping and "hot spots" on pages 139–141 in Chapter 5. Drawing on your knowledge of crime-mapping technology, discuss how RFID technology can reduce violence and other misconduct such as drug sales in prisons.

DISCIPLINE

As Erving Goffman noted in his essay on the "total institution," in the general society adults are rarely placed in a position where they are "punished" as a child would be.[35] Therefore, the strict disciplinary measures imposed on prisoners come as something of a shock and can provoke strong defensive reactions. Correctional officers who must deal with these responses often find that disciplining inmates is the most difficult and stressful aspect of their job.

SANCTIONING PRISONERS As mentioned earlier, one of the first things that an inmate receives on entering a correctional facility is a manual that details the rules of the prison or jail, along with the punishment that will result from rule violations. These handbooks can be quite lengthy—running one hundred pages in some instances—and specific. Not only will a prison manual prohibit obvious misconduct such as violent or sexual activity, gambling, and possession of drugs or currency, but it also addresses matters of daily life such as personal hygiene, dress codes, and conduct during meals.

Correctional officers enforce the prison rules in much the same way that a highway patrol officer enforces traffic regulations. For a minor violation, the inmate may be "let off easy" with a verbal warning. More serious infractions will result in a "ticket," or a report forwarded to the institution's disciplinary committee.[36] The disciplinary committee generally includes several correctional officers and, in some instances, outside citizens or even inmates. Although, as we shall see, the United States Supreme Court has ruled that an inmate must be given a "fair hearing" before being disciplined,[37] in reality he or she has very little ability to challenge the committee's decision.

SOLITARY CONFINEMENT Depending on the seriousness of the violation, sanctions can range from a loss of privileges in regard to family members to the extreme unpleasantness of **solitary confinement**. Although conditions may vary, in general this term refers to the confinement of an inmate alone in a small cell with minimal environmental stimulation or social interaction. In the past, solitary confinement was primarily a disciplinary tool. Today, however, prison officials use it as a form of preventive detention for inmates, such as gang members, who are deemed a security risk to themselves or others.[38] According to estimates, approximately 4.5 percent of the American prison population—about 60,000 inmates—are in solitary confinement at any given time.[39]

Solitary Confinement The isolation of an inmate in a separate cell, either as punishment or to remove the inmate from the general prison population for security reasons.

USE OF FORCE Generally, courts have been unwilling to put too many restrictions on the use of force by correctional officers. As we saw with police officers in Chapter 5, correctional officers are also given great leeway to use their experience to determine when force is warranted. In *Whitley v. Albers* (1986),[40] the Supreme Court held that the use of force by prison officials violates an inmate's Eighth Amendment protections only if the force amounts to "the unnecessary and wanton infliction of pain." Excessive force can be considered "necessary" if the legitimate security interests of the penal institution are at stake. Consequently, an appeals court ruled that when officers at a Maryland prison formed an "extraction team" to remove the leader of a riot from his cell, beating him in the process, the use of force was justified given the situation.[41]

The judicial system has not, however, given correctional officers total freedom of discretion to apply force. In *Hudson v. McMillan* (1992),[42] the Supreme Court ruled that minor injuries suffered by a convict at the hands of a correctional officer following an argument did violate the inmate's rights, because there was no security concern at the time of the incident. In other words, the issue is not *how much* force was used, but whether the officer used the force as part of a good faith effort to restore discipline or acted "maliciously and sadistically" to cause harm. This "malicious and sadistic" standard has been difficult for aggrieved prisoners to meet: in the ten years following the *Hudson* decision, only about 20 percent of excessive force lawsuits against correctional officials were successful.[43]

Social Media and CJ CorrectionsOne.com bills itself as the "#1 Resource" for America's correctional officers. To access the site's Twitter Web page, which provides a near constant flow of corrections information, visit the *Criminal Justice CourseMate* at cengagebrain.com and select the *Web Links* for this chapter.

FEMALE CORRECTIONAL OFFICERS

Security concerns were the main reason why, for many years, prison administrators refused to hire women as correctional officers in men's prisons. The consensus was that women were not physically strong enough to subdue violent male inmates and that their mere presence in the predominantly masculine prison world would cause disciplinary breakdowns.[44] As a result, in the 1970s a number of women brought lawsuits against state corrections systems, claiming that they were being discriminated against on the basis of their gender. For the most part, these legal actions were successful in opening the doors to men's prisons for female correctional officers (and vice versa).[45] Today, more than 150,000 women work in correctional facilities, many of them in constant close contact with male inmates.[46]

As it turns out, female correctional officers have proved just as effective as their male counterparts in maintaining discipline in men's prisons.[47] Furthermore, evidence

shows that women prison staff can have a calming influence on male inmates, thus lowering levels of prison violence.[48] The primary problem caused by women working in male prisons, it seems, involves sexual misconduct. According to the federal government, nearly 60 percent of prison staff members who engage in sexual misconduct are female, suggesting a disturbing amount of consensual sex with inmates.[49]

PROTECTING PRISONERS' RIGHTS

The general attitude of the law toward inmates is summed up by the Thirteenth Amendment to the U.S. Constitution:

> Neither slavery nor involuntary servitude, except as a punishment for crime whereof the party shall have been duly convicted, shall exist within the United States.

About a quarter of the security staff at Sing Sing Correctional Facility in Ossining, New York—shown here—are women. What are some of the challenges that face female correctional officers who work in a men's maximum security prison?

Susan Farley/*New York Times*/Redux Pictures

In other words, inmates do not have the same guaranteed rights as other Americans. For most of the nation's history, courts have followed the spirit of this amendment by applying the **"hands-off" doctrine** of prisoner law. This (unwritten) doctrine assumes that the care of inmates should be left to prison officials and that it is not the place of judges to intervene in penal administrative matters.

At the same time, the United States Supreme Court has stated that "[t]here is no iron curtain between the Constitution and the prisons of this country."[50] Consequently, like so many other areas of the criminal justice system, the treatment of prisoners is based on a balancing act—here, between the rights of prisoners and the security needs of the correctional institutions. Of course, as just noted, inmates do not have the same civil rights as do other members of society. In 1984, for example, the Supreme Court ruled that arbitrary searches of prison cells are allowed under the Fourth Amendment because inmates have no reasonable expectation of privacy.[51] (See page 171 in Chapter 6 for a review of the privacy expectation.)

THE "DELIBERATE INDIFFERENCE" STANDARD As for those constitutional rights that inmates do retain, in 1976 the Supreme Court established the **"deliberate indifference"** standard. In the case in question, *Estelle v. Gamble,*[52] an inmate had claimed to be the victim of medical malpractice. In his majority opinion, Justice Thurgood Marshall wrote that prison officials violated a convict's Eighth Amendment rights if they "deliberately" failed to provide him or her with necessary medical care. At the time, the decision was hailed as a victory for prisoners' rights, and it continues to ensure that a certain level of health care is provided. Defining "deliberate" has proved difficult, however. Does it mean that prison officials "should have known" that an inmate was placed in harm's way, or does it mean that officials purposefully placed the inmate in that position?

The Supreme Court seems to have taken the latter position. In *Wilson v. Seiter* (1991),[53] for example, inmate Pearly L. Wilson filed a lawsuit alleging that certain conditions of his confinement were cruel and unusual. These conditions included overcrowding, excessive noise, inadequate temperature control and ventilation, and unsanitary bathroom and dining facilities. The Court ruled against Wilson, stating that he had failed to prove that these conditions, even if they existed, were the result of "deliberate indifference" on the part of prison officials.

"Hands-Off" Doctrine The unwritten judicial policy that favors noninterference by the courts in the administration of prisons and jails.

"Deliberate Indifference" The standard for violation of an inmate's Eighth Amendment rights, requiring that prison officials be aware of harmful conditions in a correctional institution *and* fail to take steps to remedy those conditions.

"IDENTIFIABLE HUMAN NEEDS" In its *Wilson* decision, the Supreme Court created the **"identifiable human needs"** standard for determining Eighth Amendment violations. The Court asserted that a prisoner must show that the institution has denied her or him a basic need such as food, warmth, or exercise.[54] The Court mentioned only these three needs, however, forcing the lower courts to determine for themselves what other needs, if any, fall into this category. The Court's 2011 ruling in *Brown v. Plata* regarding the California corrections system, discussed in the previous chapter, seems to have expanded the identifiable human needs standard. Essentially, the Court found that severe overcrowding in California state prisons denied inmates satisfactory levels of mental and physical health care and therefore amounted to unconstitutional cruel and unusual punishment.[55]

THE FIRST AMENDMENT IN PRISON The First Amendment reads, in part, that the federal government "shall make no law respecting an establishment of religion, or prohibiting the free exercise thereof; or abridging the freedom of speech." In the 1970s, the prisoners' rights movement forced open the "iron curtain" to allow the First Amendment behind bars. In 1974, for example, the Supreme Court held that prison officials can censor inmate mail only if doing so is necessary to maintain prison security.[56] The decade also saw court decisions protecting inmates' access to group worship, instruction by clergy, special dietary requirements, religious publications, and other aspects of both mainstream and nonmainstream religions.[57]

Judges will limit some of these protections when an obvious security interest is at stake. In 2010, for example, a Pennsylvania prison was allowed to continue banning religious headscarves because of legitimate concerns that the scarves could be used to conceal drugs or strangle someone.[58] In general, however, the judicial system's commitment to freedom of speech and religion behind bars remains strong. (This commitment may have a particularly dangerous side effect, as you can see in the feature *Anti-Terrorism in Action— Prislam* on the following page.)

Learning Objective 4 Describe the hands-off doctrine of prisoner law and indicate two standards used to determine if prisoners' rights have been violated.

"Identifiable Human Needs" The basic human necessities that correctional facilities are required by the Constitution to provide to inmates.

SELFASSESSMENT

Fill in the blanks and check your answers on page 361.

Correctional officers known as _____ _____ are responsible for the daily well-being of the inmates in their cells. Perhaps the most stressful and important aspect of a correctional officer's job is enforcing _____ among the inmates. To do so, the officers may use force when a _____ security interest is being served. Courts will not, however, accept any force that is "_____ and sadistic." To prove that prison officials violated the _____ Amendment's prohibitions against cruel and unusual punishment, the inmate must first show that the officials acted with "_____ indifference" in taking or not taking an action.

INSIDE A WOMEN'S PRISON

When the first women's prison in the United States opened in 1839 on the grounds of New York's Sing Sing institution, the focus was on rehabilitation. Prisoners were prepared for a return to society with classes on reading, knitting, and sewing. Early women's reformatories had few locks or bars, and several included nurseries for the inmates' young children. Today, the situation is dramatically different. "Women's institutions are literally men's institutions, only we pull out the urinals," remarks Meda Chesney-Lind, a criminologist at the University of Hawaii.[59] Given the different circumstances surrounding male and female incarceration, this uniformity can have serious consequences for the women imprisoned in this country.

CHARACTERISTICS OF FEMALE INMATES

Male inmates outnumber female inmates by approximately nine to one, and there are only about a hundred women's correctional facilities in the United States. Consequently, most research concerning the American corrections system focuses on male inmates and men's prisons. Enough data exist, however, to provide a useful portrait of women behind bars. Female inmates are typically low income and undereducated, and have a history of unemployment. Like male inmates, female prisoners are disproportionately African American, although the percentage of white female inmates has increased over the past two decades. Female offenders are much less likely than male offenders to have committed a violent offense. Most are incarcerated for a nonviolent drug or property crime (see Figure 12.2 on the facing page).

ANTI-TERRORISM IN ACTION

PRISLAM

Islam is the fastest-growing religion in the American prison system. According to one U.S. Justice Department study, about 30,000 to 40,000 federal prisoners convert to Islam each year. For the vast majority of inmates who choose "Prislam," as correctional officials have come to call the practice, the conversion is not political. Rather, the religion acts as a stabilizing force in their lives, helping them break the destructive patterns that caused them to be incarcerated in the first place.

From time to time, however, Prislam finds itself tainted by the specter of radical Islamic terrorism. In May 2009, for example, four Muslim men were accused of planning to bomb synagogues and shoot down military aircraft with Stinger missiles in the New York City area. Two of the plotters—Laguerre Payen and Onta Williams—are believed to have converted while in prison. Also, about a decade ago the Islamic terrorist group Jam'yyat Al-Islam Al Saheeh (JIS), which was formed in Sacramento's Folsom Prison, launched a conspiracy to "kill infidels" in Southern California. Additionally, both Richard Reid, the "shoe bomber" who attempted to blow up an international flight in 2001, and José Padilla, convicted in 2007 of aiding terrorists, were prison converts to Islam.

PEOPLE SHOULD BE WORRIED

Many American Muslims discount the connection between Islamic inmates and terrorist activity. If a radical prisoner

with terrorist tendencies is "an unreformed sociopath who happens to be a Muslim, [then] Islam is not to be blamed for his condition," says Iman Talib Abdur-Rashid, a chaplain in the New York City prison system.

Still, the Federal Bureau of Prisons is taking steps to prevent the radicalization of federal inmates, including monitoring religious meetings and screening written religious materials. The worry is that the degradations and frustrations of prison life will drive unstable prisoners toward terrorism. "People should be worried about us. People in prison feel there is no way out," says Jehmahl, a murderer who converted to Islam while behind bars and subsequently joined JIS. "This is not so much about Islam. I'm radical. Radical means that you're holding no foundation. That's what the suicide bombers do. There's nothing but God left so let's go find a bomb."

FOR CRITICAL ANALYSIS The United States Supreme Court has held that prisoners retain a constitutional right to religious freedom. At the same time, prison administrators may regulate religious activities for security reasons. What steps do you think correctional officials should take to limit the spread of Islamic extremism in the nation's prisons?

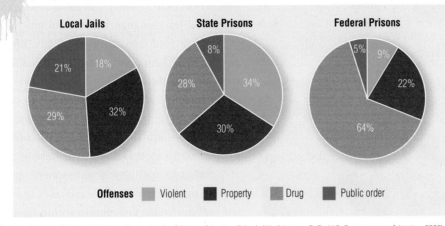

FIGURE 12.2 Offenses of Women in Jail and Prison

Local Jails
- 18%
- 32%
- 29%
- 21%

State Prisons
- 8%
- 34%
- 30%
- 28%

Federal Prisons
- 5%
- 9%
- 22%
- 64%

Offenses ■ Violent ■ Property ■ Drug ■ Public order

Sources: Bureau of Justice Statistics, *Sourcebook of Criminal Justice,* 3d ed. (Washington, D.C.: U.S. Department of Justice, 2003), Table 6.56, page 519; Bureau of Justice Statistics, *Profile of Jail Inmates, 2002* (Washington, D.C.: U.S. Department of Justice, July 2004), Table 4, page 4; and Bureau of Justice Statistics, *Prisoners in 2010* (Washington, D.C.: U.S. Department of Justice, December 2011), Appendix table 17a, page 29.

The single factor that most distinguishes female prisoners from their male counterparts is a history of physical or sexual abuse. A self-reported study conducted by the federal government indicates that 55 percent of female jail inmates have been abused at some point in their lives, compared with only 13 percent of male jail inmates.[60] Fifty-seven percent of women in state prisons and 40 percent of women in federal prisons report some form of past abuse—both figures are significantly higher than those for male prisoners.[61] Health experts believe that these levels of abuse are related to the significant amount of drug and/or alcohol addiction that plagues the female prison population, as well as to the mental illness problems that such addictions can cause or exacerbate.[62]

THE MOTHERHOOD PROBLEM

Drug and alcohol use within a women's prison can be a function of the anger and depression many inmates experience due to being separated from their children. An estimated seven out of every ten female prisoners have at least one minor child. About 150,000 American children have a mother who is under correctional supervision.[63] Given the scarcity of women's correctional facilities, inmates are often housed at great distances from their children. One study found that almost two-thirds of women in federal prison are more than five hundred miles from their homes.[64]

Further research indicates that an inmate who serves her sentence more than fifty miles from her residence is much less likely to receive phone calls or personal visits from family members. For most inmates and their families, the costs of "staying in touch" are too high.[65] This kind of separation can have serious consequences for the children of inmates. When a father goes to prison, his children are likely to live with their mother. When a mother is incarcerated, however, her children are likely to live with other relatives or, in about 11 percent of the cases, be sent to foster care.[66] Only six states—California, Indiana, Nebraska, New York, Ohio, and Washington—provide facilities where inmates and their infant children can live together, and even in these facilities nursery privileges generally end once the child is eighteen months old.

THE CULTURE OF WOMEN'S PRISONS

After spending five years visiting female inmates in the Massachusetts Correctional Institution (MCI) at Framingham, journalist Cristina Rathbone observed that the

Female inmates at the Women's Eastern Reception, Diagnostic and Correctional Center in Vandalia, Missouri, visit with their daughters and granddaughters. Why is it difficult for many mothers behind bars to see their children?

AP Photo/Whitney Curtis

medium-security facility seemed "more like a high school than a prison."[67] The prisoners were older and tougher than high school girls, but they still divided into cliques, with the "lifers" at the top of the hierarchy and "untouchables" such as child abusers at the bottom. Unlike in men's prisons, where the underground economy revolves around drugs and weapons, at MCI-Framingham the most treasured contraband items are clothing, food, and makeup.[68]

Although both men's and women's prisons are organized with the same goals of control and discipline, the cultures within the two institutions are generally very different. As we have seen, male prison society operates primarily on the basis of power. Deprived of the benefits of freedom, male prisoners tend to create a violent environment that bears little relation to life on the outside.[69] In contrast, researchers have found that women prisoners prefer to re-create their outside identities by forming social networks that resemble the traditional family structure.[70] In these pseudofamilies, inmates often play specific roles, with the more experienced convicts acting as "mothers" to younger, inexperienced "daughters." As one observer noted, the younger women rely on their "moms" for emotional support, companionship, loans, and even discipline.[71]

SELFASSESSMENT

Fill in the blanks and check your answers on page 362.

The majority of female inmates are members of _____ groups who have been arrested for nonviolent _____ or property crimes. On admission to a correctional facility, women report much higher levels of physical and sexual _____ than their male counterparts, and female inmates often suffer from depression because they are separated from their _____.

PAROLE AND RELEASE FROM PRISON

Parole The conditional release of an inmate before his or her sentence has expired.

At any given time, more than 840,000 Americans are living in the community on **parole,** or the *conditional* release of a prisoner after a portion of his or her sentence has been served. Parole allows the corrections system to continue to supervise an offender who is no longer incarcerated. As long as parolees follow the conditions of their parole, they are allowed to finish their terms outside the prison. If parolees break the terms of their early release, however, they face the risk of being returned to a penal institution.

Parole is based on three concepts:[72]

1. *Grace.* The prisoner has no right to be given an early release, but the government has granted her or him that privilege.
2. *Contract of consent.* The government and the parolee enter into an arrangement whereby the latter agrees to abide by certain conditions in return for continued freedom.
3. *Custody.* Technically, though no longer incarcerated, the parolee is still the responsibility of the state. Parole is an extension of corrections. (The phonetic and

administrative similarities between probation and parole can be confusing. See *Mastering Concepts—Probation versus Parole* below for clarification.)

Because of good-time credits and parole, most prisoners do not serve their entire sentence in prison. In fact, the average felon serves only about half of the term handed down by the court.

DISCRETIONARY RELEASE

As you may recall from Chapter 9, corrections systems are classified by sentencing procedure—indeterminate or determinate. Indeterminate sentencing occurs when the legislature sets a range of punishments for particular crimes, and the judge and the parole board exercise discretion in determining the actual length of the prison term. For that reason, states with indeterminate sentencing are said to have systems of **discretionary release**. Until the mid-1970s, all states and the federal government operated in this manner.

ELIGIBILITY FOR PAROLE Under indeterminate sentencing, parole is not a right but a privilege. This is a crucial point, as it establishes the terms of the relationship between the inmate and the corrections authorities during the parole process. In *Greenholtz v. Inmates of the Nebraska Penal and Correctional Complex* (1979),[73] the Supreme Court ruled that inmates do not have a constitutionally protected right to expect parole, thereby giving states the freedom to set their own standards for determining parole eligibility.

Not all convicts are eligible for parole. As we saw in Chapter 9, offenders who have committed the most serious crimes often receive life sentences without the possibility

Discretionary Release The release of an inmate into a community supervision program at the discretion of the parole board within limits set by state or federal law.

MASTERINGCONCEPTS

PROBATION VERSUS PAROLE

Probation and parole have many aspects in common. In fact, probation and parole are so similar that many jurisdictions combine them into a single agency. There are, however, some important distinctions between the two systems, as noted below.

	PROBATION	PAROLE
Basic Definition	An **alternative to imprisonment** in which a person who has been convicted of a crime is allowed to serve his or her sentence in the community subject to certain conditions and supervision by a probation officer.	An **early release** from a correctional facility, in which the convicted offender is given the chance to spend the remainder of her or his sentence under supervision in the community.
Timing	The offender is sentenced to a probationary term in place of a prison or jail term. If the offender breaks the conditions of probation, he or she is sent to prison or jail. Therefore, **probation generally occurs before imprisonment.**	Parole is a form of early release. Therefore, **parole occurs *after* an offender has spent time behind bars.**
Authority	**Probation is under the domain of the judiciary.** A judge decides whether to sentence a convict to probation, and a judge determines whether a probation violation warrants revocation and incarceration.	**Parole often falls under the domain of the parole board.** This administrative body determines whether the prisoner qualifies for early release and the conditions under which the parole must be served.
Characteristics of Offenders	As a number of studies have shown, probationers are normally less involved in the criminal lifestyle. Most of them are **first-time offenders who have committed nonviolent crimes.**	Many parolees have **spent months or even years in prison** and, besides abiding by conditions of parole, must make the difficult transition to "life on the outside."

of early release. In general, life without parole is reserved for those who have committed first degree murder or are defined by statute as habitual offenders. Also, officials can set conditions for parole eligibility. In 2011, for example, Mississippi governor Haley Barbour agreed to the conditional release of sisters Jamie and Gladys Scott, who were both serving life sentences for armed robbery, if Gladys would donate a kidney to Jamie.

PAROLE PROCEDURES A convict does not apply for parole. Rather, different jurisdictions have different procedures for determining discretionary release dates. In many states, the offender is eligible for discretionary release at the end of her or his minimum sentence minus good-time credits (see page 257). For instance, in 2012, Michael Claudy was sentenced to five to ten years in prison for harassing female students at Shippensburg University in Pennsylvania. This means that he will become eligible for parole after serving five years, less good time. In other states, parole eligibility is measured at either one-third or one-half of the maximum sentence, or it is a matter of discretion for the parole authorities.

In most, but not all, states, the responsibility for making the parole decision falls to the **parole board**, whose members are generally appointed by the governor. Most parole boards are small, made up of three to seven members. In many jurisdictions, board members' terms are limited to between four and six years. The requirements for board members vary. Nearly half the states have no prerequisites, while others require a bachelor's degree or some expertise in the field of criminal justice.

THE PAROLE DECISION Parole boards use a number of criteria to determine whether the convict should be given discretionary release. These criteria include the nature of the underlying offense, any prior criminal record, the inmate's behavior behind bars, and the attitude of the victim or the victim's family. In a system that uses discretionary parole, the actual release decision is made at a **parole grant hearing.** During this hearing, the entire board or a subcommittee reviews relevant information on the convict. Sometimes, but not always, the offender is interviewed. Because the board members have only limited knowledge of each offender, key players in the case are often notified in advance of the parole hearing and asked to provide comments and recommendations. These participants include the sentencing judge, the attorneys at the trial, the victims, and the victim's family, and any law enforcement officers who may be involved. After these preparations, the typical parole hearing itself is very short—usually lasting just a few minutes.

As parole has become a more important tool for decarceration, as discussed in the previous chapter, corrections authorities are making greater efforts to ensure that the process does not endanger the community. Each of Michigan's approximately 43,000 state prisoners, for example, is subjected to an annual evaluation to determine her or his "risk potential." As this numerical score improves, so do the inmate's chances for parole. State corrections officials are highly motivated to succeed in finding potential parolees: parole supervision costs about $2,130 a year, compared with about $34,000 a year for an offender in state prison.[74]

PAROLE DENIAL If parole is denied, the entire process is replayed at the next "action date," which depends on the nature of the offender's crimes and all relevant laws. In 2012, for example, Mark David Chapman was denied parole for the seventh time. Three decades earlier, Chapman had been convicted of murder for fatally shooting musician John Lennon in New York City and sentenced to twenty years to life in prison. Although Chapman had not had an infraction behind bars since 1994, the three parole board

Parole Board A body of appointed civilians that decides whether a convict should be granted conditional release before the end of his or her sentence.

Parole Grant Hearing A hearing in which the entire parole board or a subcommittee reviews information, meets the offender, and hears testimony from relevant witnesses to determine whether to grant parole.

members told him that they still had concerns "about the disregard you displayed for the norms of our society and the sanctity of human life."[75] Chapman's chances for release are also hurt by the continuing wishes of Yoko Ono, Lennon's widow, that parole be denied. (See the feature *You Be the Parole Board Member—Cause for Compassion?* below to learn more about the process of discretionary release.)

PAROLE GUIDELINES

Nearly twenty states have moved away from discretionary release systems to procedures that provide for **mandatory release.** Under mandatory release, offenders leave prison only when their prison terms have expired, minus adjustments for good time. No parole board is involved in this type of release, which is designed to eliminate discretion from the process.

Instead, in mandatory release, corrections officials rely on **parole guidelines** to determine the early release date. Similar to sentencing guidelines (see Chapter 9), parole guidelines determine a potential parolee's risk of recidivism using a mathematical equation. Under this system, inmates and corrections authorities know the *presumptive parole date* soon after the inmate enters prison. So long as the offender does not experience any disciplinary or other problems while incarcerated, he or she can be fairly sure of the time of release.[76]

Mandatory Release
Release from prison that occurs when an offender has served the full length of his or her sentence, minus any adjustments for good time.

Parole Guidelines
Standards that are used in the parole process to measure the risk that a potential parolee will recidivate.

YOU BE THE PAROLE BOARD MEMBER

Cause for Compassion?

THE SITUATION Thirty-seven years ago, Susan was convicted of first degree murder and sentenced to life in prison for taking part in a grisly killing spree in Los Angeles. Over the course of two days, Susan and her accomplices killed seven people. Susan stabbed one of the victims—a pregnant woman—sixteen times and wrote the word "PIG" on a door using another woman's blood. During her trial, Susan testified that "I was stoned, man, stoned on acid" at the time of her crimes. Now sixty-one years old, Susan is before your parole board, requesting release from prison. For most of her time behind bars, she has been a model prisoner, and she has apologized numerous times for her wrongdoing. Furthermore, her left leg has been amputated, the left side of her body is paralyzed, and she has been diagnosed with terminal brain cancer.

THE LAW You have a great deal of discretion in determining whether a prisoner should be paroled. Some of the factors you should consider are the threat the prisoner would pose to the community if released, the nature of the offense, and the level of remorse. In addition, California allows for "compassionate release" when an inmate is "terminally ill."

YOUR DECISION Susan obviously poses no threat to the community and is a viable candidate for compassionate release. Should she be set free on parole? Or are some crimes so horrific that the convict should never be given parole, no matter what the circumstances? Explain your vote.

[To see how a California parole board voted in a similar situation, go to Example 12.1 in Appendix B.]

Rasmus Rasmusson/iStockphoto/Photodisc/Photodisc/Shutterstock/James Stadl/iStockphoto

PAROLE SUPERVISION

The term *parole* has two meanings. The first, as we have seen, refers to the establishment of a release date. The second relates to the continuing supervision of convicted felons after they have been released from prison. Whether paroled through discretionary or mandatory release procedures, all parolees are subject to supervision.

CONDITIONS OF PAROLE Many of the procedures and issues of parole supervision are similar to those of probation supervision. Like probationers, parolees who are granted parole are placed under the supervision of parole officers and required to follow certain conditions. Some of these conditions are fairly uniform. All parolees, for example, must comply with the law, and they are generally responsible for reporting to their parole officer at certain intervals. The frequency of these visits, along with the other terms of parole, is spelled out in the **parole contract,** which sets out the agreement between the state and the paroled offender. Under the terms of the contract, the state agrees to conditionally release the inmate, and the future parolee agrees that her or his conditional release will last only as long as she or he abides by the contract.

Each jurisdiction has its own standard parole contract, although the parole board can add specific provisions if it sees the need (see Figure 12.3 below). Besides common restrictions, such as no illegal drug use, no association with known felons, and no change of address without notifying authorities, parolees have on occasion been ordered to lose weight and even to undergo chemical castration. Professional football player Michael Vick, who spent eighteen months in federal prison from 2007–2009 for running a pit bull–fighting operation in Virginia, was prohibited from owning a dog as a condition of his early release.

PAROLE REVOCATION If convicts follow the conditions of their parole until the *maximum expiration date,* or the date on which their sentence ends, then they are discharged from supervision. A large number—about one-quarter—return to incarceration before their maximum expiration date, most because they were convicted of a new offense or had their parole revoked.[77] **Parole revocation** is similar in many aspects to probation revocation. If the parolee commits a new crime, then a return to prison is very likely.

If, however, the individual breaks a condition of parole, known as a *technical violation,* the parole authorities have discretion as to whether revocation proceedings should be initiated. An example of a technical violation would be failure to report a change in address to parole authorities. A number of states, including Michigan, Missouri, and New York, have taken steps to avoid reincarcerating parolees for technical violations as part of continuing efforts to reduce prison populations.[78]

PAROLE AND DUE PROCESS Until the early 1970s, parole officers had the power to arbitrarily revoke parole status for technical violations. A parolee who was returned to prison had little or no recourse. In *Morrissey v. Brewer* (1972),[79] the Supreme Court changed this

Parole Contract An agreement between the state and the offender that establishes the conditions of parole.

Parole Revocation When a parolee breaks the conditions of parole, the process of withdrawing parole and returning the person to prison.

FIGURE 12.3 Standard Conditions of Parole

The parolee must do the following:
- Stay within a certain area.
- Obtain permission before changing residence or employment.
- Obtain and maintain employment.
- Maintain acceptable, nonthreatening behavior.
- Not possess firearms or weapons.
- Report any arrest within twenty-four hours.

- Not use illegal drugs or alcohol or enter drinking establishments.
- Not break any state or local laws.
- Allow contacts by parole officers at home or employment without obstruction.
- Submit to search of person, residence, or motor vehicle at any time by parole officers.

Source: West Virginia Division of Corrections.

by holding that a parolee has a "liberty interest" in remaining on parole. In other words, before parolees can be deprived of their liberty, they must be afforded a measure of due process at a parole revocation hearing.

Although this hearing does not provide the same due process protections as a criminal trial, the parolee does have the right to be notified of the charges, to present witnesses, to speak in his or her defense, and to question any hostile witnesses (so long as such questioning would not place them in danger). In the first stage of the hearing, the parole board determines whether there is probable cause that a violation occurred. Then, the board decides whether to return the parolee to prison.

OTHER TYPES OF PRISON RELEASE

The vast majority of all inmates leaving prison—about 80 percent—do so through one of the parole mechanisms discussed in the chapter. Of the remaining 20 percent, most are given an **expiration release.**[80] Also known as "maxing out," expiration release occurs when an inmate has served the maximum amount of time on the initial sentence, minus reductions for good-time credits, and is not subjected to community supervision. Another, quite rare unconditional release is a **pardon,** a form of executive clemency. The president (on the federal level) and the governor (on the state level) can grant a pardon, or forgive a convict's criminal punishment.

Most states have a board of pardons—affiliated with the parole board—that makes recommendations to the governor in cases in which it believes a pardon is warranted. Most pardons involve obvious miscarriages of justice, though sometimes a governor will pardon an individual to remove the stain of conviction from her or his criminal record.

Certain temporary releases also exist. Some inmates, who qualify by exhibiting good behavior and generally proving that they do not represent a risk to society, are allowed to leave the prison on **furlough** for a certain amount of time, usually between a day and a week. At times, a furlough is granted because of a family emergency, such as a funeral. Furloughs can be particularly helpful for an inmate who is nearing release and can use them to ease the readjustment period Finally, *probation release* occurs following a short period of incarceration at the back end of shock probation, which we discussed in Chapter 10. Generally, however, as you have seen, probationers experience community supervision in place of a prison term.

SELFASSESSMENT

Fill in the blanks and check your answers on page 362.

Parole refers to the _____ release of an inmate from prison before the end of his or her _____. In jurisdictions that have systems of discretionary release, a _____ _____ makes the parole decision. In contrast, with a _____ release, the inmate will not leave prison until her or his sentence has expired, minus good-time credits. Once an inmate has been released from prison, the terms of his or her release are spelled out in a parole _____, and a _____ violation of these terms or, especially, the commission of a new crime will almost certainly result in a return to prison.

Expiration Release The release of an inmate from prison at the end of his or her sentence without any further correctional supervision.

Pardon An act of executive clemency that overturns a conviction and erases mention of the crime from the person's criminal record.

Furlough Temporary release from a prison for purposes of vocational or educational training, to ease the shock of release, or for personal reasons.

On April 27, 2012, a parole board in Deer Lodge, Montana, rejected eighty-one-year-old Don Nichols's request for early release. Nichols is spending eighty-five years behind bars for kidnapping biathlete Kari Swenson in 1984 to be a wife for his son. Why might a judge hand down a sentence with a "max out" date that is well beyond the defendant's life expectancy?

AP Photo/Matt Gouras

REENTRY INTO SOCIETY

Learning
Objective **7** Explain
the goal
of prisoner
reentry
programs.

David Pederson had spent nearly half of his thirty-one years behind bars for various crimes when he was released, probably for the last time, in July 2011. Four months later, Pederson was again in prison, having gone on a "vicious, vile reign of terror"[81] through the Pacific Northwest that claimed at least four murder victims, including his father. Ex-inmates such as Pederson and the troubles they bring with them present a crucial challenge for the criminal justice system. Each year, more than 700,000 persons leave prison and return to the community. What steps can be taken to lessen the possibility that these ex-convicts will continue to harm society following their release?

Efforts to answer that question have focused on programs that help inmates make the transition from prison to the outside. In past years, these programs would have come under the general heading of "rehabilitation," but today corrections officials and criminologists refer to them as part of the strategy of **prisoner reentry.** The concept of reentry has come to mean many things to many people. For our purposes, keep in mind the words of Joan Petersilia of the University of California at Irvine, who defines *reentry* as encompassing "all activities and programming conducted to prepare ex-convicts to return safely to the community and to live as law abiding citizens."[82] In other words, whereas rehab is focused on the individual offender, *reentry* encompasses the released convict's relationship with society.

BARRIERS TO REENTRY

Prisoner Reentry A corrections strategy designed to prepare inmates for a successful return to the community and to reduce their criminal activity after release.

Perhaps the largest obstacle to successful prisoner reentry is the simple truth that life behind bars is very different from life on the outside. As one inmate explains, the "rules" of prison survival are hardly compatible with good citizenship:

> An unexpected smile could mean trouble. A man in uniform was not a friend. Being kind was a weakness. Viciousness and recklessness were to be respected and admired.[83]

The prison environment also insulates inmates. They are not required to make the day-to-day decisions that characterize a normal existence beyond prison bars. Depending on the length of incarceration, a released inmate must adjust to an array of economic, technological, and social changes that took place while she or he was behind bars. Common acts such as using an ATM or smartphone may be completely alien to someone who has just completed a long prison term.

CHALLENGES OF RELEASE Other obstacles hamper reentry efforts. Housing can be difficult to secure, as many private property owners refuse to rent to someone with a criminal record, and federal and state laws restrict public housing options for ex-convicts. A criminal past also limits the ability to find employment, as does the lack of job skills of someone who has spent a significant portion of his or her life in prison. Felix Mata, who works with ex-convicts in Baltimore, Maryland, estimates that the average male prisoner returning to that city has only $50 in his pocket and owes $8,000 in child support. Furthermore, these men generally have no means of transportation, no place to live, and no ability to gain employment. At best, most ex-prisoners can expect to earn no more than $10,000 annually the first few years after being released.[84]

These economic barriers can be complicated by the physical and mental condition of the freed convict. We discussed the high incidence of substance abuse among prisoners and the health-care needs of aging inmates earlier in this chapter. In addition, one study concluded that as many as one in five Americans leaving jail or prison is seriously mentally ill.[85]

THE THREAT OF RELAPSE All of these problems conspire to make successful reentry difficult to achieve. Perhaps it is not surprising that research conducted by the Pew Center on the States found that 43 percent of ex-prisoners are back in prison or jail within three years of their release dates.[86] These figures highlight the problem of recidivism among those released from incarceration.

Even given the barriers to reentry we have discussed, these rates of recidivism seem improbably high. Regardless of their ability to find a job or housing, many ex-convicts are fated to run afoul of the criminal justice system. Psychologists Edward Zamble and Vernon Quinsey explain the phenomenon as a *relapse process.*[87] Take the hypothetical example of an ex-convict who gets in a minor automobile accident while driving to work one morning. The person in the other car gets out and starts yelling at the ex-convict, who "relapses" and reacts just as he would have in prison—by punching the other person in the face. The ex-convict is then convicted of assault and battery and given a harsh prison sentence because of his criminal record.

PROMOTING DESISTANCE

One ex-inmate compared the experience of being released to entering a "dark room, knowing that there are steps in front of you and waiting to fall."[88] The goal of reentry is to act as a flashlight for convicts by promoting **desistance,** a general term used to describe the continued abstinence from offending and the reintroduction of offenders into society. Preparation for reentry starts behind bars. In addition to the rehabilitation-oriented prison programs discussed earlier in the chapter, most correctional facilities offer "life skills" classes to inmates. This counseling covers topics such as finding and keeping a job, locating a residence, understanding family responsibilities, and budgeting.

After release, however, former inmates often find it difficult to continue with educational programs and counseling as they struggle to readjust to life outside prison. More than two dozen *reentry courts* have been established in the United States to help offenders deal with this struggle. At the Santa Clara County (California) Reentry Court, for example, parolees who have committed technical violations get the opportunity to avoid reincarceration by taking court-ordered remedial action, usually drug treatment and increased contact with their parole officers.[89]

WORK RELEASE Work and lodging are crucial components of desistance. Corrections officials have several options in helping certain parolees—usually low-risk offenders—find employment and a place to live during the supervision period. Nearly a third of correctional facilities offer **work release programs,** in which prisoners nearing the end of their sentences are given permission to work in the community.[90]

HALFWAY HOUSE Inmates on work release must either return to the correctional facility in the evening or live in community residential facilities known as **halfway houses.** These facilities, also available to other parolees and those who have finished their sentences, are often remodeled hotels or private homes. They provide a less institutionalized living environment than a prison or jail for a small number of offenders (usually between ten and twenty-five). Halfway houses can be tailored to the needs of the former inmate. Many communities, for example, offer substance-free transitional housing for those whose past criminal behavior was linked to drug or alcohol abuse.

> "I don't see prison as prison. I see prison as a cage. A dog cage, or monkey cage. It's an animal cage, period. I refuse. I will not live my life like that anymore."
>
> —**Alissa,** ex-inmate

Desistance The process through which criminal activity decreases and reintegration into society increases over a period of time.

Work Release Program Temporary release of convicts from prison for purposes of employment. The offenders may spend their days on the job but must return to the correctional facility at night and during the weekend.

Halfway House A community-based form of early release that places inmates in residential centers and allows them to reintegrate with society.

CAREERS IN CJ

JULIE HOWE
HALFWAY HOUSE PROGRAM MANAGER

Early on in my career, I felt a bit intimidated by the clients simply because of my discomfort, not by their behavior. I started out very stern and learned later that it was better to start strong and to lighten up later rather than the reverse. The clients respect you more and know to take you seriously. My first client as a case manager was a real eye-opener. He was in his fifties, and I was in my early twenties. Earning his trust was quite a challenge. In the end he learned to respect me, and I learned different techniques when working with offenders.

My favorite part of my job is that I know that I have an impact on people's lives. If I can assist someone to become sober, responsible, employed, and self-sufficient, I am also having an impact on the community and those whom my clients' lives touch. I never get tired of hearing clients say thanks and knowing their lives are forever changed when they realize their potential and value. I also love that I have the opportunity to influence the behavior of others and shape their future. What an awesome responsibility!

Social Media Career Tip
Don't misrepresent facts or tell lies of omission online. Doing so in front of millions of online viewers virtually ensures you will be caught, and such untruths can fatally damage career possibilities. **f** **Linked in** ▼

FAST FACTS

HALFWAY HOUSE PROGRAM MANAGER, JOB DESCRIPTION:

- Coordinate recreational, educational, and vocational counseling and other programs for residents.
- Maintain the security of the house and residents.

WHAT KIND OF TRAINING IS REQUIRED?

- A bachelor's degree or master's degree in social work, career counseling, criminal justice, or psychology.
- Also helpful are internships, volunteer work with a halfway house, and community service work with an agency.

ANNUAL SALARY RANGE?

- $29,390–$45,552

THE SPECIAL CASE OF SEX OFFENDERS

Despite the beneficial impact of reentry efforts, one group of wrongdoers has consistently been denied access to such programs: those convicted of sex crimes. The eventual return of these offenders to society causes such high levels of community anxiety that the criminal justice system has not yet figured out what to do with them. (A Gallup poll found that 66 percent of the respondents were "very concerned" about child molesters, compared with 52 percent who expressed such concern about violent crime and 36 percent about terrorism.[91])

Part of the problem is that efforts to reform sex offenders have produced inconsistent results. In one of the few long-term studies of the issue, researchers found that sex offenders who took part in therapy programs in California were actually more likely to reoffend than those who received no treatment whatsoever.[92] Thus, corrections officials are caught between public demands for protection from "these monsters" and the insistence of medical professionals that sex offenders represent a public health problem, albeit one without any ready solution. Not surprisingly, strategies to control sex offenders on their release from prison have frustrated both the public and medical professionals.

SEX OFFENDER NOTIFICATION LAWS In the summer of 1994, seven-year-old Megan Kanka of Hamilton Township, New Jersey, was raped and murdered by a twice-convicted pedophile (an adult sexually attracted to children). The offender had moved into her neighborhood after being released from prison on parole. The next year, in response to public outrage, the state passed a series of laws known collectively as the New Jersey Sexual Offender Registration Act, or "Megan's Law."[93] Today, all fifty states and the federal government have their own version of Megan's Law, or a **sex offender notification law,** which requires local law authorities to alert the public when a sex offender has been released into the community.

Protests by relatives and friends of Donna Jou forced California state officials to delay the scheduled April 2011 release of John Steven Burgess, a convicted sex offender who drugged and accidentally killed Jou four years earlier. Why might notification laws sometimes fail to protect the community from sex offenders such as Burgess?

ZUMA Press/Newscom

ACTIVE AND PASSIVE NOTIFICATION No two sex offender notification laws have exactly the same provisions, but all are designed with the goal of allowing the public to learn the identities of convicted sex offenders living in their midst. In general, the laws demand that a paroled sex offender notify local law enforcement authorities on taking up residence in a state. In Georgia, for example, paroled sex offenders are required to present themselves to both the local sheriff and the superintendent of the public school district where they plan to live.[94] This registration process must be renewed every time the parolee changes his or her address.

The authorities, in turn, notify the community of the sex offender's presence through the use of one of two models. Under the "active" model, the authorities directly notify the community or community representatives. Traditionally, this notification has taken the form of bulletins or posters, distributed and posted within a certain distance from the offender's home. Now, a number of states use e-mail alerts to fulfill notification obligations. In the "passive" model, information on sex offenders is made open and available for public scrutiny. All fifty states operate Web sites that provide citizens with data on registered sex offenders in their jurisdiction.

Sex Offender Notification Law Legislation that requires law enforcement authorities to notify people when convicted sex offenders are released into their neighborhood or community.

CONDITIONS OF RELEASE Generally, sex offenders are supervised by parole officers and are subject to the same threat of revocation as other parolees. Paroled child molesters usually have the following conditions of release:

Learning Objective 8 Indicate typical conditions for release for a paroled child molester.

- Must have no contact with children under the age of sixteen.
- Must continue psychiatric treatment.
- Must receive permission from the parole officers to change residence.
- Must stay a certain distance from schools or parks where children are present.
- Cannot own toys that may be used to lure children.
- Cannot have a job or participate in any activity that involves children.

In addition, of course, they are required to register through the proper authorities. Today, more than 715,000 registered sex offenders live throughout the United States. Finally, more than half of the states and hundreds of municipalities have passed *residency restrictions* for convicted sex offenders. These laws ban sex offenders from living within a certain distance from places where children naturally congregate. In New Jersey, for example, "high-risk" offenders cannot take up residence within 3,000 feet of any school, park or campground, church, theater, bowling alley, library, or convenience store.[95]

SELFASSESSMENT

Fill in the blanks and check your answers on page 362.

Ex-convicts often struggle to succeed after being released from prison because their limited skills make it difficult to find _____. The resulting financial troubles hamper the offender's ability to secure _____, which makes it more likely that he or she will recidivate. Corrections officials promote _____, or the process by which a former inmate stops committing crimes, by allowing certain low-risk offenders to live in _____ houses, where they can receive specialized treatment. Sex offender _____ laws, also known as Megan's laws, mandate that law enforcement officials must alert the public when a sex offender has moved into the community.

CHAPTER SUMMARY

Learning Objective 1 **Explain the concept of prison as a total institution.** Although many people spend time in partial institutions—schools, companies where they work, and religious organizations—only in prison is every aspect of an inmate's life controlled, and that is why prisons are called total institutions. Every detail for every prisoner is fully prescribed and managed.

Learning Objective 2 **Indicate some of the reasons for violent behavior in prisons.** (a) To separate the powerful from the weak and establish a prisoner hierarchy; (b) to minimize one's own probability of being a target of assault; (c) to enhance one's self-image; (d) to obtain sexual relief; and (e) to obtain material goods through extortion or robbery.

Learning Objective 3 **List and briefly explain the six general job categories among correctional officers.** (a) Block officers, who supervise cell blocks or are on block guard duty; (b) work detail supervisors, who oversee the cafeteria, prison store, and laundry, for example; (c) industrial shop and school officers, who generally oversee workshop and educational programs; (d) yard officers, who patrol the prison yard when prisoners are allowed there; (e) tower guards, who work in isolation; and (f) those who hold administrative building assignments, such as prison gate guards and overseers of visitation procedures.

Learning Objective 4 **Describe the hands-off doctrine of prisoner law and indicate two standards used to determine if prisoners' rights have been violated.** The hands-off doctrine assumes that the care of prisoners should be left to prison officials and that it is not the place of judges to intervene. Nonetheless, the Supreme Court has created two standards to be used by the courts in determining whether a prisoner's Eighth Amendment protections against cruel and unusual punishment have been violated. Under the "deliberate indifference" standard, prisoners must show that prison officials were aware of harmful conditions at the facility but failed to remedy them. Under the "identifiable human needs" standard, prisoners must show that they were denied a basic need such as food, warmth, or exercise.

Learning Objective 5 **Contrast probation, parole, expiration release, pardon, and furlough.** Probation is an alternative to incarceration. Parole is an early release program for those incarcerated. Expiration release occurs when the inmate has served the maximum time for her or his initial sentence minus good-time credits. A pardon can be given only by the president or one of the fifty governors. Furlough is a temporary release while in jail or prison.

Learning Objective 6 **Describe typical conditions of parole.** Parolees must not use illegal drugs, not associate with known felons, not change their addresses without notifying authorities, and report to their parole officer at specified intervals. (These terms are usually set out in the parole contract.)

Learning Objective 7 **Explain the goal of prisoner reentry programs.** Based on the ideals of rehabilitation, these programs have two main objectives: (a) to prepare a prisoner for a successful return to the community, and (b) to protect the community by reducing the chances that the ex-convict will continue her or his criminal activity after release from prison.

Learning Objective 8 **Indicate typical conditions for release for a paroled child molester.** (a) Have no contact with children under the age of sixteen; (b) continue psychiatric treatment; (c) obtain permission from a parole officer to change residence; (d) keep away from schools or parks where children are present; (e) cannot own toys that may be used to lure children; and (f) cannot have a job or participate in any activity that involves children.

QUESTIONS FOR CRITICAL ANALYSIS

1. The principle of least eligibility holds that inmates should not receive any benefits that are unavailable to the least advantaged members of outside society. Do you agree with the principle of least eligibility? If so, do you believe that prison programs such as substance abuse treatment and vocational training should be discontinued? Why or why not? If you disagree with the principle, how can you justify such programs beyond their benefits for individual inmates? Explain your answers.

2. In 2011, a Florida inmate sued the state corrections system, claiming that his soy-based diet was cruel and unusual punishment. Under what circumstances, if any, do you think that unpleasant prison food can violate an inmate's constitutional rights?

3. Do you agree with prison policies that prohibit male correctional officers from patting down and strip-searching female inmates? Why or why not? Under what circumstances might such policies be unrealistic?

4. In many jurisdictions, parolees can be stopped and searched by parole or police officers at any time, even if there is no probable cause that the parolee has committed a crime. What is the justification for such a policy?

5. The town of Dyersville, Iowa, has one of the strictest residency requirements in the country: no sex offenders can live anywhere within its limits. What is your opinion of this strategy? How do you feel about residency laws in general?

KEY TERMS

"deliberate indifference" 346
deprivation model 340
desistance 357
discretionary release 351
expiration release 355
furlough 355
halfway house 357
"hands-off" doctrine 346
"identifiable human needs" 347

mandatory release 353
pardon 355
parole 350
parole board 352
parole contract 354
parole grant hearing 352
parole guidelines 353
parole revocation 354
prison gang 341

prison programs 339
prisoner reentry 356
prisonization 337
relative deprivation 340
sex offender notification law 359
solitary confinement 345
total institution 337
work release program 357

SELF ASSESSMENT ANSWER KEY

Page 342: **i.** total institution; **ii.** age; **iii.** health-care; **iv.** deprivation; **v.** relative deprivation

Page 347: **i.** block officers; **ii.** discipline; **iii.** legitimate; **iv.** malicious; **v.** Eighth; **vi.** deliberate

Page 350: **i.** minority; **ii.** drug; **iii.** abuse; **iv.** children

Page 355: **i.** conditional; **ii.** sentence; **iii.** parole board; **iv.** mandatory; **v.** contract; **vi.** technical

Page 360: **i.** employment; **ii.** housing; **iii.** desistance; **iv.** halfway; **v.** notification

COURSEMATE

For online help and access to resources that accompany *Criminal Justice in Action: The Core,* go to **www.cengage-brain.com/shop/ISBN/978-1-285-06915-9**. Click "Access Now," where you will find flashcards, an online quiz, and other helpful study aids. If you have an access code for CourseMate, log in and go to the chapter of your choice for additional online study aids.

NOTES

1. Johnny Cash, "Folsom Prison Blues" (Sun Records, 1955).

2. Roderick Davis, "The Road from Prison to Rehabilitation," *New York Times* (January 21, 2011), at **www.nytimes.com/interactive/2011/01/22/opinion/20110122_Fixes_Delancey.html?emc=eta1**.

3. Erving Goffman, "On the Characteristics of Total Institutions," in *Asylums: Essays on the Social Situation of Mental Patients and Other Inmates* (New York: Doubleday, 1961), 6.

4. Donald Clemmer, *The Prison Community* (Boston: Christopher, 1940).

5. John Irwin, *Prisons in Turmoil* (Boston: Little, Brown, 1980), 67.

6. Bureau of Justice Statistics, *Prisoners in 2003* (Washington, D.C.: U.S. Department of Justice, November 2004), Table 10, page 8; and Bureau of Justice Statistics, *Prisoners in 2010* (Washington, D.C.: U.S. Department of Justice, December 2011), Appendix table 13, page 26.

7. *Old behind Bars: The Aging Prison Population in the United States* (New York: Human Rights Watch, January 2012), 24–42.

8. Bureau of Justice Statistics, *Prison and Jail Deaths in Custody, 2000–2009—Statistical Tables* (Washington, D.C.: U.S. Department of Justice, December 2011), 3.

9. Bureau of Justice Statistics, "Medical Problems of Prisoners," April 2008, "Highlights" and Table 2, at **www.ojp.usdoj.gov/bjs/pub/pdf/mpp.pdf**.

10. Nicholas K. Geranios, "Aging Inmates Straining State Prison System," *Associated Press* (November 10, 2010).

11. Michael Vitiello, "Addressing the Special Problems of Mentally Ill Prisoners: A Small Piece of the Solution to Our Nation's Prison Crisis," *Denver University Law Review* (Fall 2010), 57–62.

12. Katherine Stuart van Wormer and Clemens Bartollas, *Women and the Criminal Justice System,* 3d ed. (Upper Saddle River, NJ: Pearson Education, 2011), 143.

13. Bureau of Justice Statistics, *Mental Health Problems of Prison and Jail Inmates* (Washington, D.C.: U.S. Department of Justice, September 2006), 1.

14. William Kanapaux, "Guilty of Mental Illness," *Psychiatric Times* (January 1, 2004), at **www.psychiatrictimes.com/forensic-psych/content/article/10168/47631**.

15. Bureau of Justice Statistics, *Census of State and Federal Correctional Facilities, 2005* (Washington, D.C.: U.S. Department of Justice, October 2008), 6.

16. Joan Petersilia, "Beyond the Prison Bubble," *Wilson Quarterly* (Winter 2011), 29.

17. Todd R. Clear, George F. Cole, and Michael D. Reisig, *American Corrections,* 9th ed. (Belmont, CA: Wadsworth Cengage Learning, 2011), 381.

18. Lee H. Bowker, *Prison Victimization* (New York: Elsevier, 1981), 31–33.

19. Stephen C. Light, "The Severity of Assaults on Prison Officers: A Contextual Analysis," *Social Science Quarterly* 71 (1990), 267–284.

20. Federal Bureau of Prisons report, cited in Kevin Johnson, "Report Points to Prison Security Failures," *USA Today* (June 8, 2009), 3A.

21. Bureau of Justice Statistics, *Prison and Jail Deaths in Custody, 2000–2009,* Table 1, page 5; and Table 13, page 16.

22. David Kaiser and Lovisa Stannow, "Prison Rape and the Government," *New York Review of Books* (March 24, 2011), at **www.nybooks.com/articles/archives/2011/mar/24/prison-rape-and-government**.

23. Randy Martin and Sherwood Zimmerman, "A Typology of the Causes of Prison Riots and an Analytical Extension to the 1986 Virginia Riot," *Justice Quarterly* 7 (1990), 711–737.

24. Bert Useem, "Disorganization and the New Mexico Prison Riot of 1980," *American Sociological Review* 50 (1985), 677–688.

25. Leo Carroll, "Race, Ethnicity, and the Social Order of the Prison," in *The Pains of Imprisonment,* ed. R. Johnson and H. Toch (Beverly Hills, CA: Sage, 1982).

26. Leo Carroll, *Hacks, Blacks, and Cons: Race Relations in a Maximum-Security Prison* (Lexington, MA: Lexington Books, 1988), 78.

27. Craig Haney, "Psychology and the Limits of Prison Pain," *Psychology, Public Policy, and Law* (December 1977), 499.

28. Alan J. Drury and Matt DeLisi, "Gangkill: An Exploratory Empirical Assessment of Gang Membership, Homicide Offending, and Prison Misconduct," *Crime & Delinquency* (January 2011), 130–146.

29. *A Study of Gangs and Security Threat Groups in America's Adult Prisons and Jails* (Indianapolis: National Major Gang Task Force, 2002).

30. George W. Knox, *The Problem of Gangs and Security Threat Groups (STGs) in American Prisons Today: Recent Research Findings from the 2004 Prison Gang Survey,* available at **www.ngcrc.com/corr2006.html**.

31. Quoted in John J. DiIulio, Jr., *No Escape: The Future of American Corrections* (New York: Basic Books, 1991), 268.

32. Jack Henry Abbott, *In the Belly of the Beast* (New York: Vintage Books, 1991), 54.

33. Michel Foucault, *Discipline and Punish: The Birth of the Prison* (New York: Pantheon Books, 1977), 128.

34. Lucien X. Lombardo, *Guards Imprisoned: Correctional Officers at Work* (Cincinnati, OH: Anderson Publishing Co., 1989), 51–71.

35. Goffman, 7.

36. Clear, Cole, and Reisig, 333.

37. *Wolff v. McDonnell,* 418 U.S. 539 (1974).

38. Colin Dayan, "Barbarous Confinement," *New York Times* (July 18, 2011), A19.

39. Camille Graham Camp and George M. Camp, eds., *The Corrections Yearbook, 2000* (New York: Criminal Justice Yearbook, 2000), 26.

40. 475 U.S. 312 (1986).

41. *Stanley v. Hejirika,* 134 F.3d 629 (4th Cir. 1998).

42. 503 U.S. 1 (1992).

43. Darrell L. Ross, "Assessing *Hudson v. McMillan* Ten Years Later," *Criminal Law Bulletin* (September/October 2004), 508.

44. Van Wormer and Bartollas, 387.

45. Cristina Rathbone, *A World Apart: Women, Prison, and a Life behind Bars* (New York: Random House, 2006), 46.

46. Carl Nink et al., *Women Professionals in Corrections: A Growing Asset* (Centerville, UT: MTC Institute, August 2008), 1.

47. Denise L. Jenne and Robert C. Kersting, "Aggression and Women Correctional Officers in Male Prisons," *Prison Journal* (1996), 442–460.

48. Nink et al., 8–9.

49. Matt Gouras, "Female Prison Guards Often Behind Sex Misconduct," *Associated Press* (March 14, 2010).

50. *Wolff v. McDonnell*, 539.

51. *Hudson v. Palmer*, 468 U.S. 517 (1984).

52. 429 U.S. 97 (1976).

53. 501 U.S. 294 (1991).

54. *Wilson v. Seiter*, 501 U.S. 294, 304 (1991).

55. 563 U.S. ___ (2011).

56. *Procunier v. Martinez*, 416 U.S. 396 (1974).

57. *Cruz v. Beto*, 405 U.S. 319 (1972); *Gittlemacker v. Prasse*, 428 F.2d 1 (3d Cir. 1970); and *Kahane v. Carlson*, 527 F.2d 492 (2d Cir. 1975).

58. Maryclaire Dale, "Court Says Pa. Prison Can Ban Muslim Scarf," *Associated Press* (August 2, 2010).

59. Quoted in Alexandra Marks, "Martha Checks in Today," *Seattle Times* (October 8, 2004), A8.

60. Bureau of Justice Statistics, *Profile of Jail Inmates, 2002* (Washington, D.C.: U.S. Department of Justice, July 2004), 10.

61. Bureau of Justice Statistics, *Prior Abuse Reported by Inmates and Probationers* (Washington, D.C.: U.S. Department of Justice, April 1999), 2.

62. *Caught in the Net: The Impact of Drug Policies on Women and Families* (Washington, D.C.: American Civil Liberties Union, 2004), 18–19.

63. Jessica Meyerson, Christa Otteson, and Krysten Lynn Ryba, *Childhood Disrupted: Understanding the Features and Effects of Maternal Incarceration* (St. Paul, MN: Wilder Research, November 2010), 1.

64. Kelly Bedard and Eric Helland, "Location of Women's Prisons and the Deterrent Effect of 'Harder' Time," *International Review of Law and Economics* (June 2004), 152.

65. *Ibid.*

66. Sarah Schirmer, Ashley Nellis, and Marc Mauer, *Incarcerated Parents and Their Children: Trends 1991–2007* (Washington, D.C.: The Sentencing Project, February 2009), 5.

67. Rathbone, 4.

68. *Ibid.*, 158.

69. Van Wormer and Bartollas, 137–138.

70. Barbara Bloom and Meda Chesney-Lind, "Women in Prison," in *It's a Crime: Women and Justice,* 4th ed. Roslyn Muraskin (Upper Saddle River, NJ: Prentice Hall, 2007), 542–563.

71. Piper Kerman, *Orange Is the New Black: My Year in a Women's Prison* (New York: Spiegal and Grau, 2011), 131.

72. Clear, Cole, and Reisig, 408.

73. 442 U.S. 1 (1979).

74. "Michigan Lets Prisoners Go—and Saves a Bundle," *Bloomberg Businessweek* (December 11, 2011), 16.

75. Quoted in "Chapman Strikes Out Again in Parole Bid," *Chicago Tribune* (September 8, 2010), 15.

76. Clear, Cole, and Reisig, 420–421.

77. Bureau of Justice Statistics, *Probation and Parole in the United States, 2010* (Washington, D.C.: U.S. Department of Justice, November 2011), Table 6, page 9.

78. Joseph Walker, "Rules May Help Parolees Avoid Jail for Small Errors," *New York Times* (January 5, 2012), at **cityroom.blogs. nytimes.com/2012/01/05/rating-a-parol- ees-risk-before-a-return-to-prison**.

79. 408 U.S. 471 (1972).

80. Bureau of Justice Statistics, "Reentry Trends in the U.S.," at **bjs.ojp.usdoj.gov/content/ reentry/releases.cfm**.

81. Jonathan Cooper, "3rd Body Linked to Northwest Supremacists' Alleged Crime Spree," *Associated Press* (October 9, 2011).

82. Joan Petersilia, *When Prisoners Come Home: Parole and Prisoner Reentry* (New York: Oxford University Press, 2003), 39.

83. Victor Hassine, *Life without Parole: Living in Prison Today,* ed. Thomas J. Bernard and Richard McCleary (Los Angeles: Roxbury Publishing Co., 1996), 12.

84. John H. Tyler and Jeffrey R. King, "Prison-Based Education and Reentry into the Mainstream Labor Market," in *Barriers to Reentry? The Labor Market for Released Prisoners in Post-Industrial America,* ed. Shawn D. Bushway, Michael A. Stoll, and David F. Weiman (New York: Russell Sage Foundation, 2007), 237.

85. *Ill Equipped: U.S. Prisons and Offenders with Mental Illness* (New York: Human Rights Watch, 2003).

86. Pew Center on the States, *State of Recidivism: The Revolving Door of America's Prisons* (Washington, D.C.: The Pew Charitable Trusts, April 2011), 2.

87. Edward Zamble and Vernon Quinsey, *The Criminal Recidivism Process* (Cambridge, England: Cambridge University Press, 1997).

88. Quoted in Kevin Johnson, "After Years of Solitary, Freedom Is Hard to Grasp," *USA Today* (June 9, 2005), 2A.

89. Dorothy Korber, *"A Courtroom Unlike Any Other": Santa Clara County's Parolee Reentry Court Is a Case Study in Reducing Recidivism* (Sacramento, CA: California Senate Office of Oversight and Outcomes, June 2011).

90. Bureau of Justice Statistics, *Census of State and Federal Correctional Facilities, 2005,* Table 6, page 5.

91. "The Greatest Fear," *The Economist* (August 26, 2006), 25.

92. Janice Marques, Mark Wiederanders, David Day, Craig Nelson, and Alice Ommeren, "Effects of a Relapse Prevention Program on Sexual Recidivism: Final Results from California's Sex Offender Treatment and Evaluation Project (SOTEP)," *Sexual Abuse: A Journal of Research and Treatment* (January 2005), 79–107.

93. New Jersey Revised Statute Section 2C:7-8(c) (1995).

94. Georgia Code Annotated Section 42-9-44.1(b) (1).

95. New Jersey Statutes Annotated Section 2C: 7-3.

CHAPTER

13

The Juvenile Justice System

Aaron Josefczyk/Reuters/Landov

LEARNING OBJECTIVES

After reading this chapter, you should be able to...

1 Describe the child-saving movement and its relationship to the doctrine of *parens patriae*.

2 List the four major differences between juvenile courts and adult courts.

3 Identify and briefly describe the single most important Supreme Court case with respect to juvenile justice.

4 Describe the one variable that always correlates highly with juvenile crime rates.

5 Indicate some of the reasons why youths join gangs.

6 Describe the four primary stages of pretrial juvenile justice procedure.

7 Explain the distinction between an adjudicatory hearing and a disposition hearing.

8 List the four categories of residential treatment programs.

Throughout the chapter you will see each learning objective repeated in the margin next to the content it relates to. The chapter summary on pages 389 and 390 includes all of the learning objectives for review.

CHAPTER OUTLINE

- The Evolution of American Juvenile Justice
- Determining Delinquency Today
- Trends in Juvenile Delinquency
- Factors in Juvenile Delinquency
- First Contact: The Police and Pretrial Procedures
- Trying and Punishing Juveniles

365

THE END OF INNOCENCE

Omer Ninham was fourteen years old when he and several friends saw young Zong Vang riding a bicycle in Green Bay, Wisconsin. "Let's mess with this kid," said thirteen-year-old Richard Crapeau, one of Ninham's companions. Crapeau pulled Vang off his bike, and Ninham punched the smaller boy in the face. Vang then fled to the top of a nearby parking garage before Crapeau and Ninham caught up with him. Ninham grabbed Vang's wrists and Crapeau held his ankles, and they swung Vang toward the edge of the building. With their friends urging them on, the two boys let go, hurling Vang to his death five stories below. Both Crapeau and Ninham were sentenced to life in prison for first degree murder, with one crucial difference: unlike Crapeau, Ninham was not given the opportunity for early release through parole.

During Ninham's sentencing, jurors were unmoved by testimony that he had suffered repeated physical and mental abuse at home and was drinking alcohol regularly by age ten. Nine years later, when Ninham was twenty-three, a prison psychologist noted that he had "grown into a thoughtful young man whose prognosis for successful reentry into the community, and absence of recidivism, is very good." About that time, attorneys from the nonprofit Equal Justice Initiative took Ninham's case to state court, arguing that a sentence of life without parole for a fourteen-year-old is "cruel and unusual" under the Eighth Amendment. "Children and adolescents are not adults in miniature," Ninham's lawyers argued. "Their youth makes them less capable to recognize the consequences of their decisions, yet more capable of extraordinary, positive growth as they develop into adults."

In May 2011, the Wisconsin Supreme Court rejected this argument and upheld Ninham's life-without-parole sentence. "Under the circumstances of this case, Ninham's punishment is severe, but not disproportionately so," wrote state justice Anne Ziegler in her majority opinion.

Omer Ninham, convicted of first degree murder at fourteen years old, is serving a sentence of life-without-parole in the Wisconsin corrections system.

Courtesy Equal Justice Initiative/www.eji.org

Omer Ninham's lawyers pointed out that only about seventy inmates are presently serving life-without-parole sentences in the United States for murders committed when they were fourteen or younger. Thus, they claimed, there is a "national consensus" against such sentences. The Wisconsin Supreme Court countered that the punishment is rarely handed down because fourteen-year-olds rarely engage in the kind of "horrific and senseless" behavior for which Ninham was convicted.[1] The Wisconsin justices did not, however, have the final word on this issue. In June 2012, the United States Supreme Court banned laws in about twenty states that required life-without-parole sentences for juveniles such as Ninham who have been found guilty of committing murder.[2]

While making its decision, the Supreme Court confronted the difficult question—asked every time a young offender commits an "adultlike" act of violence—that lies at the heart of the juvenile justice debate. That is, should criminal acts by youths be given the same weight as those committed by adults, or should they be seen as "mistakes" that can be "corrected" by care and counseling? The American juvenile justice system generally operates as an uneasy compromise between "rehabilitation and punishment, treatment and custody." In this chapter, we will discuss the successes and failures of this compromise and examine the aspects of the juvenile justice system that differentiate it from the criminal justice system.

THE EVOLUTION OF AMERICAN JUVENILE JUSTICE

In a recent poll, about 90 percent of Americans expressed the belief that rehabilitation and treatment for youthful offenders would help prevent them from committing future crimes.[3] To a certain degree, such opinions reflect the founding principles of the American juvenile justice system. At the beginning of the 1800s, juvenile offenders were treated the same as adult offenders—they were judged by the same courts and sentenced to the same severe penalties. This situation began to change soon after, as urbanization and industrialization created an immigrant underclass that was, at least in the eyes of many reformers, predisposed to deviant activity. Certain members of the Progressive movement, known as the child savers, began to take steps to "save" children from these circumstances, introducing the idea of rehabilitating delinquents in the process.

> "When our children make mistakes, are we going to lock them up and throw away the key?"
>
> —**Brian Gowdy,**
> defense attorney

THE CHILD-SAVING MOVEMENT

In general, the child savers favored the doctrine of *parens patriae,* which holds that the state has not only a right but also a duty to care for children who are neglected, delinquent, or in some other way disadvantaged. Juvenile offenders, the child savers believed, required treatment, not punishment, and adherents were horrified at the thought of placing children in prisons with hardened adult criminals. In 1967, then Supreme Court justice Abe Fortas said of the child savers:

> They believed that society's role was not to ascertain whether the child was "guilty" or "innocent," but "What is he, how has he become what he is, and what had best be done in his interest and in the interest of the state to save him from a downward career." The child—essentially good, as they saw it—was made "to feel that he is the object of [the government's] care and solicitude," not that he was under arrest or on trial.[4]

Child-saving organizations convinced local legislatures to pass laws that allowed them to take control of children who exhibited criminal tendencies or had been neglected by their parents. To separate these children from the environment in which they were raised, the organizations created a number of institutions, the best known of which was New York's House of Refuge. Opening in 1825, the House of Refuge implemented many of the same reformist measures popular in the penitentiaries of the time, meaning that its charges were subjected to the healthful influences of hard study and labor. Although the House of Refuge was criticized for its harsh discipline (which caused many boys to run away), similar institutions sprang up throughout the Northeast during the middle of the 1800s.

Learning Objective 1 Describe the child-saving movement and its relationship to the doctrine of *parens patriae.*

Parens Patriae A doctrine that holds that the state has a responsibility to look after the well-being of children and to assume the role of parent if necessary.

THE ILLINOIS JUVENILE COURT

The efforts of the child savers culminated with the passage of the Illinois Juvenile Court Act in 1899. The Illinois legislature created the first court specifically for juveniles, guided by the principles of *parens patriae* and based on the belief that children are not fully responsible for criminal conduct and are capable of being rehabilitated.[5]

The Illinois Juvenile Court and juvenile courts in other states that followed in its path were (and, in many cases, remain) drastically different from adult courts:

- *No juries.* The matter was decided by judges who wore regular clothes instead of black robes and sat at a table with the other participants rather than behind a bench. Because the primary focus of the court was on the child and not the crime, the judge had wide discretion in disposing of each case.
- *Different terminology.* To reduce the stigma of criminal proceedings, "petitions" were issued instead of "warrants." The children were not "defendants," but "respondents," and they were not "found guilty" but "adjudicated delinquent."
- *No adversarial relationship.* Instead of trying to determine guilt or innocence, the parties involved in the juvenile court worked together in the best interests of the child, with the emphasis on rehabilitation rather than punishment.
- *Confidentiality.* To avoid "saddling" the child with a criminal past, juvenile court hearings and records were kept sealed, and the proceedings were closed to the public.

By 1945, every state had a juvenile court system modeled after the first Illinois court. For the most part, these courts were able to operate without interference until the 1960s and the onset of the juvenile rights movement.

JUVENILE DELINQUENCY

After the first juvenile court was established in Illinois, the Chicago Bar Association described its purpose as, in part, to "exercise the same tender solicitude and care over its neglected wards that a wise and loving parent would exercise with reference to his [or her] own children under similar circumstances."[6] In other words, the state was given the responsibility of caring for those minors whose behavior seemed to show that they could not be controlled by their parents. As a result, many **status offenders** found themselves in the early houses of refuge and continue to be placed in state-run facilities today. A status offense is an act that, if committed by a juvenile, is considered illegal and grounds for possible state custody. The same act, if committed by an adult, does not warrant law enforcement action. (See Figure 13.1 below for a list of the most common status offenses.)

In contrast, **juvenile delinquency** refers to conduct that would also be criminal if committed by an adult. According to federal law and the laws of most states, a juvenile delinquent is someone who has not yet reached his or her eighteenth birthday—the age of adult criminal responsibility—at the time of the offense in question. In two states (New York and North Carolina), persons aged sixteen and older are considered adults, and eleven other states confer adulthood on seventeen-year-olds for purposes of criminal law. Under certain circumstances, discussed later in this chapter, children under these ages can be tried in adult courts and incarcerated in adult prisons and jails. Remember that Omer Ninham was fourteen years old when he was convicted as an adult for the murder of Zong Vang, described on page 366.

Status Offender A juvenile who has engaged in behavior deemed unacceptable for those under a certain statutorily determined age.

Juvenile Delinquency Behavior that is illegal under federal or state law that has been committed by a person who is under an age limit specified by statute.

FIGURE 13.1 Status Offenses

1. Smoking cigarettes	5. Running away from home
2. Drinking alcohol	6. Violating curfew
3. Being truant (skipping school)	7. Participating in sexual activity
4. Disobeying teachers	8. Using profane language

CONSTITUTIONAL PROTECTIONS AND THE JUVENILE COURT

Although the ideal of the juvenile court seemed to offer the "best of both worlds" for juvenile offenders, in reality the lack of procedural protections led to many children being arbitrarily punished not only for crimes, but for status offenses as well. Juvenile judges were treating all violators similarly, which led to many status offenders being incarcerated in the same institutions as violent delinquents. In response to a wave of lawsuits demanding due process rights for juveniles, the United States Supreme Court issued several rulings in the 1960s and 1970s that significantly changed the juvenile justice system.

A Port Authority (New York) police officer speaks to a girl who has run away from her home. Why is leaving home considered a status offense and not a crime?

James Estrin/*New York Times*/Redux

KENT V. UNITED STATES The first decision to extend due process rights to children in juvenile courts was *Kent v. United States* (1966).[7] The case concerned sixteen-year-old Morris Kent, who had been arrested for breaking into a woman's house, stealing her purse, and raping her. Because Kent was on juvenile probation, the state sought to transfer his trial for the crime to an adult court (a process to be discussed later in the chapter).

Without giving any reasons for his decision, the juvenile judge consented to this judicial waiver, and Kent was sentenced in the adult court to a thirty- to ninety-year prison term. The United States Supreme Court overturned the sentence, ruling that juveniles have a right to counsel and a hearing in any instance in which the juvenile judge is considering sending the case to an adult court. The Court stated that, in such cases, a child receives "the worst of both worlds," getting neither the "protections accorded to adults" nor the "solicitous care and regenerative treatment" offered in the juvenile system.[8]

IN RE GAULT The *Kent* decision provided the groundwork for *In re Gault* one year later. Considered by many the single most important case concerning juvenile justice, *In re Gault* involved a fifteen-year-old boy who was arrested for allegedly making a lewd phone call while on probation.[9] (See the feature *Landmark Cases: In re Gault* on the following page.) In its decision, the Supreme Court held that juveniles are entitled to many of the same due process rights granted to adult offenders, including notice of charges, the right to counsel, the privilege against self-incrimination, and the right to confront and cross-examine witnesses.

Learning Objective 3 Identify and briefly describe the single most important Supreme Court case with respect to juvenile justice.

OTHER IMPORTANT COURT DECISIONS Over the next ten years, the Supreme Court handed down three more important rulings on juvenile court procedure. The ruling in *In re Winship* (1970)[10] required the government to prove "beyond a reasonable doubt" that a juvenile had committed an act of delinquency, raising the burden of proof from a "preponderance of the evidence." In *Breed v. Jones* (1975),[11] the Court held that the Fifth Amendment's double jeopardy clause prevented a juvenile from being tried in an adult court for a crime that had already been adjudicated in juvenile court. In contrast, the decision in *McKeiver v. Pennsylvania* (1971)[12] represented an instance in which the Court did not move the juvenile court further toward the adult model. In that case, the Court ruled that the Constitution did not give juveniles the right to a jury trial.

SELFASSESSMENT
Fill in the blanks and check your answers on page 390.

At its inception, the American juvenile justice system was guided by the principles of _____ _____, which holds that the state has a responsibility to look after children when their parents cannot do so. In general, juveniles are involved in two types of wrongdoing: (1) acts that would not be crimes if committed by adults, or _____ _____, and (2) acts that would be crimes if committed by an adult, or juvenile _____.

LANDMARK CASES: *In Re Gault*

In 1964, fifteen-year-old Gerald Gault and a friend were arrested for making lewd telephone calls to a neighbor in Gila County, Arizona. Gault, who was on probation, was placed under custody with no notice given to his parents. The juvenile court in his district held a series of informal hearings to determine Gault's punishment. During these hearings, no records were kept, Gault was not afforded the right to counsel, and the complaining witness was never made available for questioning. At the close of the hearing, the judge sentenced Gault to remain in Arizona's State Industrial School until the age of twenty-one. Gault's lawyers challenged this punishment, arguing that the proceedings denied their client his due process rights. Eventually, the matter was taken up by the United States Supreme Court.

In re Gault
United States Supreme Court
387 U.S. 1 (1967)
supreme.justia.com/us/387/1/case.html

IN THE WORDS OF THE COURT...
JUSTICE FORTAS, MAJORITY OPINION

* * * *

From the inception of the juvenile court system, wide differences have been tolerated—indeed insisted upon—between the procedural rights accorded to adults and those of juveniles. In practically all jurisdictions, there are rights granted to adults which are withheld from juveniles.

* * * *

Accordingly, the highest motives and most enlightened impulses led to a peculiar system for juveniles, unknown to our law in any comparable context. The constitutional and theoretical basis for this peculiar system is—to say the least—debatable. And in practice, as we remarked in the *Kent* case, the results have not been entirely satisfactory. * * * The absence of substantive standards has not necessarily meant that children receive careful, compassionate, individualized treatment. The absence of procedural rules based upon

constitutional principle has not always produced fair, efficient, and effective procedures. Departures from established principles of due process have frequently resulted not in enlightened procedure, but in arbitrariness.

* * * *

Ultimately, however, we confront the reality of that portion of the Juvenile Court process with which we deal in this case. A boy is charged with misconduct. The boy is committed to an institution where he may be restrained of liberty for years. * * * His world becomes a "building with whitewashed walls, regimented routine and institutional hours. . . ." Instead of mother and father and sisters and brothers and friends and classmates, his world is peopled by guards, custodians, state employees, and "delinquents" confined with him for anything from waywardness to rape and homicide. In view of this, it would be extraordinary if our Constitution did not require the procedural regularity and the exercise of care implied in the phrase "due process." Under our Constitution, the condition of being a boy does not justify a kangaroo court.

Decision
The Court held that juveniles facing a loss of liberty were entitled to the basic procedural safeguards afforded by the U.S. Constitution, including the right to counsel, the right to confront and cross-examine witnesses, and the privilege against self-incrimination. The decision marked a turning point in juvenile justice in this country: no longer would informality and paternalism be the guiding principles of juvenile courts. Instead, due process would dictate the adjudication process, much as in an adult court.

FOR CRITICAL ANALYSIS
What might be some of the negative consequences of the *In re Gault* decision for juveniles charged with committing delinquent acts? Can you think of any reasons why juveniles should not receive the same due process protections as adult offenders?

DETERMINING DELINQUENCY TODAY

In the eyes of many observers, the net effect of the Supreme Court decisions during the 1966–1975 period was to move juvenile justice away from the ideals of the child savers. As a result of these decisions, many young offenders would find themselves in a formalized system that was often indistinguishable from its adult counterpart. Although the Court has recognized that minors charged with crimes possess certain constitutional rights, it has failed to dictate at what age these rights should be granted. Consequently, the legal status of children in the United States varies depending on where they live, with each state making its own policy decisions on the crucial questions of age and competency.

THE AGE QUESTION

On March 1, 2011, a twelve-year-old boy was playing with toy trucks and planes in the backyard of his family's Burlington, Colorado, home. Minutes later, he fatally shot his parents, Charles and Marilyn Long, with a .357 Magnum revolver. In Chapter 3 (page 83), we saw that early American criminal law recognized infancy as a defense against criminal charges. At that time, on attaining fourteen years of age, a youth was considered an adult and treated accordingly by the criminal justice system. Today, as Figure 13.2 below shows, the majority of states, including Colorado, (as well as the District of Columbia), allow for the prosecution of juveniles under the age of thirteen as adults. Thus, Colorado officials had the option of prosecuting the Longs' son for murder as an adult, despite his tender years.

Instead, despite the wishes of some Long family members, district attorney Robert E. Watson decided to keep the boy in the state's juvenile justice system. "If you're looking for an adult explanation for why this kid went from playing in dirt to commit murder you'll never get one," said Watson. "This lies in the mind of a very immature twelve-year-old."[13]

FIGURE 13.2 The Minimum Age at Which a Juvenile Can Be Tried as an Adult

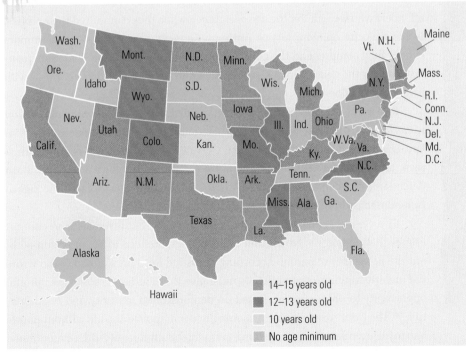

Legend:
- 14–15 years old
- 12–13 years old
- 10 years old
- No age minimum

Source: National Center for Juvenile Justice.

For the most part, when juveniles who remain in juvenile court are found guilty, they receive "limited" sentences. Under these circumstances, they cannot remain incarcerated in juvenile detention centers past their eighteenth or twenty-first birthday. Consequently, a Colorado juvenile judge eventually sentenced the boy who shot his parents to seven years in juvenile detention.

THE CULPABILITY QUESTION

Many researchers believe that by the age of fourteen, an adolescent has the same ability as an adult to make a competent decision.[14] Nevertheless, according to some observers, a juvenile's ability to theoretically understand the difference between "right" and "wrong" does not mean that she or he should be held to the same standards of competency as an adult.

JUVENILE BEHAVIOR A study released by the Research Network on Adolescent Development and Juvenile Justice found that 33 percent of juvenile defendants in criminal courts had the same low level of understanding of legal matters as mentally ill adults who had been found incompetent to stand trial.[15] Legal psychologist Richard E. Redding believes that

> adolescents' lack of life experience may limit their real-world decision-making ability. Whether we call it wisdom, judgment, or common sense, adolescents may not have nearly enough.[16]

Juveniles are generally more impulsive, more likely to engage in risky behavior, and less likely to calculate the long-term consequences of any particular action. Adolescents are also far more likely to respond to peer pressure than are adults. The desire for acceptance and approval may drive them to commit crimes: juveniles are arrested as part of a group at much higher rates than adults.[17] Furthermore, juveniles are less likely than adults to display remorse immediately following a violent act. As a result, they are often penalized by the courts for showing "less grief than the system demands."[18]

DIMINISHED GUILT The "diminished culpability" of juveniles was one of the reasons given by the United States Supreme Court in its landmark decision in *Roper v. Simmons* (2005).[19] As we saw in Chapter 9, that case forbade the execution of offenders who were under the age of eighteen when they committed their crimes. In his majority opinion, Justice Anthony Kennedy wrote that because minors cannot fully comprehend the consequences of their actions, the two main justifications for the death penalty—retribution and deterrence—do not "work" with juvenile wrongdoers.[20]

Five years later, the Supreme Court applied the same reasoning in *Graham v. Florida* (2010).[21] The case involved two defendants who had committed violent crimes as juveniles: Joe Sullivan, who raped a woman when he was thirteen, and Terrance Graham, who committed armed burglary at sixteen. Both defendants claimed that their life-without-parole sentences violated the Eighth Amendment's prohibition of "cruel and unusual punishment."

By a close 5–4 vote, the Court agreed, holding that juveniles who commit crimes that do not involve murder may not be sentenced to life in prison without the possibility of parole. According to Justice Anthony Kennedy, who wrote the majority opinion, state officials must give these inmates "some meaningful opportunity to obtain release based on demonstrated maturity and rehabilitation."[22] The Court used similar reasoning when it applied the life without parole ban to all juveniles—including murderers—in the summer of 2012, as mentioned earlier in the chapter.

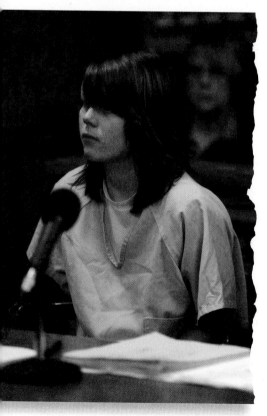

In February 2012, a Cole County (Missouri) judge sentenced Alyssa Bustamante to life in prison with the possibility of parole. Three years earlier, when she was fifteen years old, Bustamante had brutally murdered her nine-year-old neighbor so she could find out what it felt like to kill. Do you think that juvenile murderers such as Bustamante should be given a chance at parole? Why or why not?

AP Photo/Kelley McCall, Pool, File

The age at which a child can be held criminally responsible for his or her actions differs from _____ to _____. Many experts believe that minors should not be held to the same level of competency as adults, partially because they are more _____ and more likely to respond to _____ pressure. This "diminished culpability" was one of the reasons the United States Supreme Court gave for prohibiting the _____ _____ for offenders who were under the age of eighteen when they committed their crimes.

TRENDS IN JUVENILE DELINQUENCY

When asked, juveniles will admit to a wide range of illegal or dangerous behavior, including carrying weapons, getting involved in physical fights, driving after drinking alcohol, and stealing or deliberately damaging school property.[23] Has the juvenile justice system been effective in controlling and preventing this kind of misbehavior, as well as more serious acts?

To answer this question, many observers turn to the Federal Bureau of Investigation's Uniform Crime Report (UCR), initially covered in Chapter 2. Because the UCR breaks down arrest statistics by age of the arrestee, it has been considered the primary source of information on the presence of juveniles in America's justice system. This does not mean, however, that the UCR is completely reliable when it comes to measuring juvenile delinquency. The process measures only those juveniles who were caught and therefore does not accurately reflect all delinquent acts in any given year. Furthermore, it measures the number of arrests but not the number of arrestees, meaning that—due to repeat offenders—the number of juveniles actually in the system could be below the number of juvenile arrests.

DELINQUENCY BY THE NUMBERS

With these cautions in mind, UCR findings are helpful in determining the extent of juvenile offending in the United States today. In 2011, juveniles accounted for 12.7 percent of violent crime arrests and 11.8 percent of criminal activity arrests in general.[24] According to the 2011 UCR, juveniles were responsible for

- 8 percent of all murder arrests.
- 19 percent of all aggravated assault arrests.
- 14 percent of all forcible rapes.
- 18 percent of all weapons arrests.
- 22 percent of all robbery arrests.
- 20 percent of all Part I property crimes.
- 19 percent of all drug offenses.

THE RISE AND FALL OF JUVENILE CRIME

As Figure 13.3 on the following page shows, juvenile arrest rates for violent crimes have fluctuated dramatically over the past three decades. In the 2000s, with a few exceptions, juvenile crime in the United States has decreased at a rate similar to that of adult crime, as discussed earlier in this textbook. Furthermore, after peaking in 1997, juvenile court delinquency caseloads declined 12 percent over the next decade.[25] Not surprisingly, the drop in juvenile arrests and court appearances has led to fewer juveniles behind bars. The

FIGURE 13.3 Arrest Rates of Juveniles

After rising dramatically from 1985 to 1994, arrest rates for juveniles have fallen steadily since, with a few exceptions.

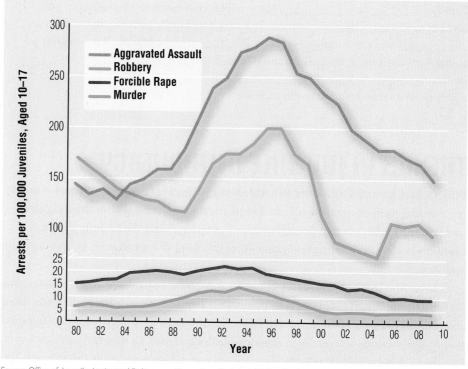

Source: Office of Juvenile Justice and Delinquency Prevention, *Statistical Briefing Book*, at **www.ojjdp.ncjrs.org** /ojstatbb/crime/JAR.asp.

national population of juvenile inmates decreased 12 percent between 2006 and 2008, allowing officials in some states, including California, Ohio, and Texas, to close juvenile detention facilities.[26]

A number of theories have been put forth to explain this downturn in juvenile offending. Some observers point to the increase in police action against "quality-of-life" crimes such as loitering, which they believe stops juveniles before they have a chance to commit more serious crimes. Similarly, about 80 percent of American municipalities enforce juvenile curfews, which restrict the movement of minors during certain hours, usually after dark.[27] In 2011, law enforcement made nearly 60,000 arrests for curfew and loitering law violations.[28]

Furthermore, thousands of local programs designed to educate children about the dangers of drugs and crime operate across the country. The results of such community-based efforts are difficult, if not impossible, to measure—it cannot be assumed that children would have become delinquent if they had not participated. Still, these programs are generally considered a crucial element of keeping youth crime under control.[29]

GIRLS IN THE JUVENILE JUSTICE SYSTEM

Although overall rates of juvenile offending have been dropping, arrest rates for girls are declining more slowly than those for boys. Between 1995 and 2005, violent crime arrests for juvenile males dropped 28 percent, while violent crime arrests for juvenile females dropped only 10 percent.[30] Self-reported studies show, however, that there has been little change in girls' violent behavior over the past few decades.[31] Why, then, is the presence of girls in the juvenile and criminal justice system increasing relative to their male counterparts?

A GROWING PRESENCE Although girls have for the most part been treated more harshly than boys for status offenses,[32] a "chivalry effect" (see page 264) has traditionally existed in other areas of the juvenile justice system. In the past, police were likely to arrest offending boys while allowing girls to go home to the care of their families for similar behavior. This is no longer the case. According to the National Center for Juvenile Justice, juvenile courts handled more than twice as many cases involving girls in 2008 as they did in 1985.[33] A particular problem area for girls appears to be the crime of assault. In 2011, females accounted for 24 percent of all juvenile arrests for aggravated assault and 36 percent of those arrests for simple assault—higher percentages than for other crimes involving violence or the threat of violence.[34]

FAMILY-BASED DELINQUENCY Criminologists disagree on whether rising arrest rates for female juveniles reflect a change in behavior or a change in law enforcement practices. A significant amount of data supports the latter proposal, especially research showing that police are much more likely to make arrests in situations involving domestic violence than they were even a decade ago. Experts have found that girls are four times more apt to fight with parents or siblings than are boys, who usually engage in violent encounters with strangers. Consequently, a large percentage of female juvenile arrests for assault arise out of family disputes—arrests that until relatively recently would not have been made.[35]

Evidence also shows that law enforcement agents continue to treat girls more harshly for status offenses. More girls than boys are arrested for the status offense of running away from home, for example, even though studies show that male and female juveniles run away from home with equal frequency.[36] Criminologists who focus on issues of gender hypothesize that such behavior is considered normal for boys, but is seen as deviant for girls and therefore more deserving of punishment.[37]

SCHOOL VIOLENCE AND BULLYING

One Monday morning in February 2012, seventeen-year-old T.J. Lane walked into the cafeteria of Chardon High School in Chardon, Ohio, and opened fire on a table of students, killing three of them and wounding two others. The incident is every student's (and parent's and teacher's) worst nightmare. Like other episodes of school violence, it received heavy media coverage, fanning fears that our schools are unsafe.

SAFE SCHOOLS Research does show that juvenile victimization and delinquency rates increase during the school day. In addition, the most common juvenile crimes, such as simple assaults, are more likely to take place on school grounds than elsewhere.[38] This is not the case, however, with violent crimes such as the one committed by T.J. Lane. In fact, school-age youths are more than fifty times more likely to be murdered away from school than on a campus.[39] Furthermore, between 1995 and 2010, victimization rates of students for nonfatal crimes at school declined significantly, meaning that in general, schools are safer today than they were in the recent past.[40]

For the most part, these statistics mirror the downward trend of all criminal activity in the United States since the mid-1990s. In addition, since the fatal shootings of fourteen students and a teacher at Columbine High School near Littleton, Colorado, in 1999, many schools have improved security measures. From 1999 to 2011, the percentage of American schools using security cameras to monitor their campuses increased from 19 to 61 percent. Today, 92 percent of public schools control access to school buildings by locking or monitoring their doors.[41]

Bullying Overt acts taken by students with the goal of intimidating, harassing, or humiliating other students.

"BULLIED TO DEATH" **Bullying** can be broadly defined as repeated, aggressive behavior with physical (hitting, punching, and spitting) and verbal (teasing, name calling, and spreading false rumors) aspects. Such behavior has traditionally been seen more as an inevitable rite of passage than as potentially criminal. In recent years, however, society has become more aware of the negative consequences of bullying, underscored by a number of high-profile "bullycides." In March 2010, for example, thirteen-year-old Jon Carmichael of Cleburne, Texas, hanged himself after multiple acts of torment by fellow students, including being thrown into a trash can and having his head flushed in a toilet. That September, four teenage boys in different parts of the country committed suicide after being bullied about their sexuality.

According to data gathered by the federal government, 28 percent of students aged twelve to eighteen have been victims of bullying.[42] In particular, gay students are targeted—nine out of ten report being bullied each year.[43] As a response to this problem, forty-five states have passed antibullying legislation. These laws focus mostly on "soft" measures, such as training school personnel how to recognize and respond to bullying.[44]

As yet, state legislatures have been reluctant to take "harder" measures such as specifically defining bullying as a crime. Such harder measures may ultimately come in response to dozens of civil lawsuits filed by parents of bullied children across the country. On the anniversary of their son's death in 2011, for example, Jon Carmichael's parents sued the Joshua Independent School District for $20 million, claiming that staff and students were aware of the bullying on school grounds and did nothing to prevent it.[45]

CJ&TECHNOLOGY

Cheryl E. Davis/Shutterstock

Cyberbullying

Although it is not clear whether bullying in general is more prevalent now than in the past, one form of bullying is definitely on the rise. As the Internet, texting, and social networking sites such as Facebook and Twitter have become integral parts of youth culture, so, it seems, has cyberbullying. Studies have shown that between one-fifth and one-third of American teenagers are targets of cyberbullying, which occurs when a person uses computers, smartphones, or other electronic devices to inflict willful and repeated emotional harm. One of the incidents involving Jon Carmichael (discussed above)—in which he was stripped nude, tied up, and placed in a trash can—was posted on YouTube.

To many, cyberbullying can be even more devastating than "old school" bullying. Not only does the anonymity of cyberspace seem to embolden perpetrators, causing them to be more vicious than they might be in person, but, as one expert points out, when bullying occurs online, "you can't get away from it."

THINKING ABOUT CYBERBULLING: How should the criminal justice system respond to cyberbullying, if at all?

The crime rate for juveniles has generally been _____ for more than a decade. Despite this trend, more _____ are getting involved with the juvenile justice system today than at any time in recent history. _____ violence is another area in which crime rates have dropped since the 1990s, thanks, in part, to greater security measures such as surveillance cameras and locked building doors. _____, in both its traditional and electronic forms, remains a problem, however, and is increasingly being addressed by school administrators and state legislators.

FACTORS IN JUVENILE DELINQUENCY

As we discussed in Chapter 2, an influential study conducted by Professor Marvin Wolfgang and several colleagues in the early 1970s introduced the concept of the "chronic 6 percent" to criminology. The researchers found that out of one hundred boys, six will become chronic offenders, meaning that they are arrested five or more times before their eighteenth birthdays.

Furthermore, Wolfgang and his colleagues determined that these chronic offenders are responsible for half of all crimes and two-thirds of all violent crimes within any given cohort (a group of persons who have similar characteristics).[46] Does this "6 percent rule" mean that no matter what steps society takes, six out of every hundred juveniles are "bad seeds" and will act delinquently? Or does it point to a situation in which a small percentage of children may be more likely to commit crimes under certain circumstances?

Most criminologists favor the second interpretation. In this section, we will examine the four factors that have traditionally been used to explain juvenile criminal behavior and violent crime rates: age, substance abuse, family problems, and gangs. Keep in mind, however, that the factors influencing delinquency are not limited to these topics (see Figure 13.4 on the following page). Researchers are constantly interpreting and reinterpreting statistical evidence to provide fresh perspectives on this very important issue. For example, criminologists continue to debate the consequences of dropping out of high school. Although adolescents who do so are statistically at a higher risk for coming into contact with the juvenile justice system, does leaving school *cause* delinquency and criminal behavior? Or do adolescents drop out of high school for the same reasons that they become involved in crime, such as low self-control and substance abuse?[47]

Aging Out A term used to explain the fact that criminal activity declines with age.

THE AGE-CRIME RELATIONSHIP

Crime statistics are fairly conclusive on one point: the older a person is, the less likely she or he will exhibit criminal behavior. Self-reported studies confirm that most people are involved in some form of criminal behavior—however "harmless"—during their early years. In fact, Terrie Moffitt of Duke University has said that "it is statistically aberrant to refrain from crime during adolescence."[48] So, why do the vast majority of us not become chronic offenders? According to many criminologists, particularly Travis Hirschi and Michael Gottfredson, any group of at-risk persons—regardless of gender, race, intelligence, or class—will commit fewer crimes as they grow older.[49]

This process is known as **aging out** (or, sometimes, *desistance,* a term we first encountered in the previous chapter). Professor Robert J. Sampson and his colleague John H. Laub believe that this phenomenon is explained by certain events, such as marriage, employment, and military service, that force delinquents to "grow up" and forgo criminal acts.[50]

Learning Objective 4 Describe the one variable that always correlates highly with juvenile crime rates.

FIGURE 13.4 Risk Factors for Juvenile Delinquency

The characteristics listed here are generally accepted as "risk factors" for juvenile delinquency. In other words, if one or more of these factors are present in a juvenile's life, he or she has a greater chance of exhibiting delinquent behavior—though such behavior is by no means a certainty.

Family	• Single parent/lack of parental role model • Parental or sibling drug/alcohol abuse • Extreme economic deprivation • Family members in a gang
School	• Academic frustration/failure • Learning disability • Negative labeling by teachers • Disciplinary problems
Community	• Social disorganization (see Chapter 2) • Presence of gangs and obvious drug use in the community • Availability of firearms • High crime/constant feeling of danger • Lack of social and economic opportunities
Peers	• Delinquent friends • Friends who use drugs or who are members of gangs • Lack of "positive" peer pressure
Individual	• Tendency toward aggressive behavior • Inability to concentrate or focus/easily bored/hyperactive • Alcohol or drug use • Fatalistic/pessimistic viewpoint

Age of Onset The age at which a juvenile first exhibits delinquent behavior.

Another view sees the **age of onset,** or the age at which the youth begins delinquent behavior, as a consistent predictor of future criminal behavior. One study compared recidivism rates between juveniles first judged to be delinquent before the age of fifteen and those first adjudicated delinquent after the age of fifteen. Of the seventy-one subjects who made up the first group, 32 percent became chronic offenders. Of the sixty-five who made up the second group, none became chronic offenders.[51] Furthermore, according to the Office of Juvenile Justice and Delinquency Prevention, the earlier a youth enters the juvenile justice system, the more likely he or she will become a violent offender.[52] This research suggests that juvenile justice resources should be concentrated on the youngest offenders, with the goal of preventing crime and reducing the long-term risks for society.

SUBSTANCE ABUSE

As we have seen throughout this textbook, substance abuse plays a strong role in criminal behavior for adults. The same can certainly be said for juveniles. According to the University of Michigan's Institute for Social Research, 27 percent of American tenth-graders and 40 percent of American twelfth-graders are regular alcohol drinkers, increasing their risks for violent behavior, delinquency, academic problems, and unsafe sexual behavior.[53] Regular marijuana use among high school seniors reached a thirty-year high in 2011, and more juveniles are abusing synthetic drugs (described on pages 57–58) than ever before.[54]

A STRONG CORRELATION As with adults, substance abuse among juveniles seems to play a major role in offending. Drug use is associated with a wide range of antisocial and illegal behaviors by juveniles, from fist fights to large-scale theft.[55] Nearly all young offenders (94 percent) entering juvenile detention self-report drug use at some point in their lives, and 85 percent have used drugs in the previous six months.[56] According to the Arrestee Drug Abuse Monitoring Program, nearly 60 percent of male juvenile detainees and 46 percent of female juvenile detainees test positive for drug use at the time of their offense.[57] Drug use is a particularly strong risk factor for girls: 75 percent of young women incarcerated in juvenile facilities report regular drug and alcohol use—starting at the age of fourteen—and one study found that 87 percent of female teenage offenders need substance abuse treatment.[58]

A STRONG CAUSATION? The correlation between substance abuse and offending for juveniles seems obvious. Does this mean that substance abuse *causes* juvenile offending? Researchers make the point that most youths who become involved in antisocial behavior do so before their first experience with alcohol or drugs. Therefore, it would appear that substance abuse is a form of delinquent behavior rather than its cause.[59] Still, a recent study of adolescent offenders did find that substance abuse treatment reduces criminal behavior in the short term, suggesting that, at the least, the use of illegal drugs is an integral component of the juvenile delinquent lifestyle.[60]

CHILD ABUSE AND NEGLECT

Abuse by parents also plays a substantial role in juvenile delinquency. **Child abuse** can be broadly defined as the infliction of physical or emotional damage on a child. Similar though not the same, **child neglect** refers to deprivations—of love, shelter, food, and proper care—children undergo by their parents. According to the National Survey of Children's Exposure to Violence, one in ten children in the United States suffers from mistreatment at the hands of a close family member.[61] Children in homes characterized by violence or neglect suffer from a variety of physical, emotional, and mental health problems at a much greater rate than their peers.[62] This, in turn, increases their chances of engaging in delinquent behavior.

One survey of violent juveniles showed that 75 percent had suffered severe abuse by a family member and 80 percent had witnessed violence in their homes.[63] Nearly half of all juveniles—and 80 percent of girls—sentenced to life in prison suffered high rates of abuse.[64] Cathy Spatz Widom, currently a professor of psychology at John Jay College of Criminal Justice, compared the arrest records of two groups of subjects—one made up of 908 cases of substantiated parental abuse and neglect and the other made up of 667 children who had not been abused or neglected. Widom found that those who had been abused or neglected were 53 percent more likely to be arrested as juveniles than those who had not.[65] Simply put, according to researchers Janet Currie of Columbia University and Erdal Tekin of Georgia State University, "child maltreatment roughly doubles the probability that an individual engages in many types of crime."[66]

Child Abuse Mistreatment of children by causing physical, emotional, or sexual damage without any plausible explanation, such as an accident.

Child Neglect A form of child abuse in which the child is denied certain necessities such as shelter, food, care, and love.

Youth Gang A self-formed group of youths with several identifiable characteristics, including a gang name and other recognizable symbols, a geographic territory, and participation in illegal activities.

GANGS

When youths cannot find the stability and support they require in the family structure, they will often turn to their peers. This is just one explanation for why juveniles join **youth gangs.** Although jurisdictions may have varying definitions, for general purposes a youth gang is viewed as a group of three or more persons who (1) self-identify as an entity separate from the community by special clothing, vocabulary, hand signals, and names and (2) engage in criminal activity within a geographic territory. According to an exhaustive survey of law enforcement agencies, there are probably around 33,000 gangs with more than one million members in the United States.[67]

Juveniles who have experienced the risk factors discussed in this section are more likely to join a gang, and once they have done so they are more likely to engage in delinquent and violent behavior than non–gang members.[68] Statistics show high levels of gang involvement in weapons trafficking, burglary, assault, and motor vehicle theft, and more than 50 percent of all youth gangs are believed to be involved in drug sales.[69] One-third of all murders in Chicago and one-third of all murders in Los Angeles are gang related.[70] (See Figure 13.5 below.)

WHO JOINS GANGS? The average gang member is seventeen to eighteen years old, though members tend to be older in cities with long traditions of gang activity, such as Chicago and Los Angeles. Although it is difficult to determine with any certainty the makeup of gangs as a whole, one recent survey found that 49 percent of all gang members in the United States are Hispanic, 35 percent are African American, and 9 percent are white, with the remaining 7 percent belonging to other racial or ethnic backgrounds.[71]

Although gangs tend to have racial or ethnic characteristics—that is, one group predominates in each gang—many researchers do not believe that race or ethnicity is the dominant factor in gang membership. Instead, gang members seem to come from lower-class or working-class communities, mostly in urban areas but with an increasing number from the suburbs and rural counties. In addition, researchers are finding that adolescents who will eventually join a gang display significantly higher levels of delinquent behavior than those who will never become involved in gang activity.[72]

Learning Objective 5 Indicate some of the reasons why youths join gangs.

WHY DO YOUTHS JOIN GANGS? Gang membership often appears to be linked with status in the community. Many teenagers, feeling alienated from their families and communities, join gangs for the social relationships and the sense of identity a gang can provide.[73]

A number of youths, especially those who live in high-crime neighborhoods, see gang membership as a necessity—joining a gang is a form of protection against violence from other gangs. For example, Mara Salvatrucha (MS-13) was formed by the children of immigrants who fled the civil war of El Salvador for Los Angeles in the 1980s. Finding themselves easy prey for the established local gangs, these young Salvadorans started MS-13 as a protective measure.

FIGURE 13.5 Comparison of Gang and Nongang Delinquent Behavior

Taking self-reported surveys of subjects aged thirteen to eighteen in the Seattle area, researchers for the Office of Juvenile Justice and Delinquency Prevention found that gang members were much more likely to exhibit delinquent behavior.

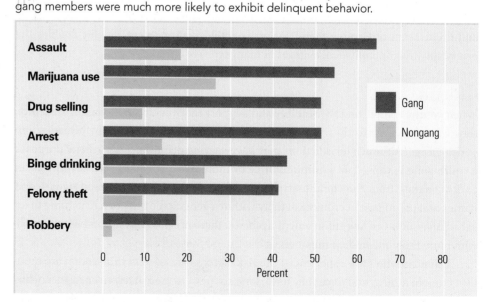

Source: Karl G. Hill, Christina Lui, and J. David Hawkins, *Early Precursors of Gang Membership: A Study of Seattle Youth* (Washington, D.C.: Office of Juvenile Justice and Delinquency Prevention, December 2001), Figure 1, page 2.

Excitement is another attraction of the gang life, as is the economic incentive of enjoying the profits from illegal gang activities such as dealing drugs or robbery. Finally, some teenagers are forced to join gangs by the threat of violence from gang members.

SELFASSESSMENT

Fill in the blanks and check your answers on page 390.

Criminologists have identified a number of _____ factors that increase the probability of juvenile misbehavior. One is youth. Studies of a process called _____ _____ show that children commit fewer offenses as they grow older. According to two researchers, _____ _____ at the hands of parents or guardians doubles the chances of delinquency. Youth who become involved in _____ _____ also more likely to engage in criminal activity than those who do not.

In Los Angeles, a gang member signifies his allegiance to the "Street Villains" through a series of elaborate tattoos. What role does identity play in a juvenile's decision to join a gang?
Kevork Djansezian/Getty Images

FIRST CONTACT: THE POLICE AND PRETRIAL PROCEDURES

Until recently, most police departments allocated few resources to dealing with juvenile crime. The number of violent crimes committed by youths under the age of eighteen has, however, provided a strong incentive for departments to set up special services for children. The standard bearer for these operations is the *juvenile officer,* who operates either alone or as part of a juvenile unit within a department.

The initial contact between a juvenile and the criminal justice system, however, is usually handled by a regular police officer on patrol, who either apprehends the juvenile while he or she is committing a crime or answers a call for service. (See Figure 13.6 on the following page for an overview of the juvenile justice process.) The youth is then passed on to the juvenile officer, who must decide how to handle the case.

POLICE DISCRETION AND JUVENILE CRIME

Police arrest about 1.1 million youths under the age of eighteen each year. In most states, police officers must have probable cause to believe that the minor has committed an offense, just as they would if the suspect were an adult. Police power with regard to juveniles is greater than with adults, however, because police can take youths into custody for status offenses, such as possession of alcohol or truancy. In these cases, the officer is acting *in loco parentis,* or in the place of the parent. The officer's role is not necessarily to punish the youths, but to protect them from harmful behavior.

Police officers also have a great deal of discretion in deciding what to do with juveniles who have committed crimes or status offenses. Juvenile justice expert Joseph Goldstein labels this discretionary power **low-visibility decision making** because it relies on factors that the public is not generally in a position to understand or criticize. When a grave offense has taken place, a police officer may decide to formally arrest the juvenile, send him or her to juvenile court, or place the youth under the care of a social-service organization.

Low-Visibility Decision Making A term used to describe the discretionary power police have in determining what to do with misbehaving juveniles.

FIGURE 13.6 The Juvenile Justice Process

This diagram shows the possible tracks that a young person may take after her or his first contact with the juvenile justice system (usually a police officer).

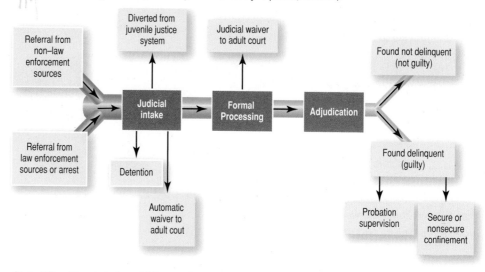

Source: Office of Juvenile Justice and Delinquency Prevention.

Referral The notification process through which a law enforcement officer or other concerned citizen makes the juvenile court aware of a juvenile's unlawful or unruly conduct.

Intake The process by which an official of the court must decide whether to file a petition, release the juvenile, or place the juvenile under some other form of supervision.

In less serious situations, the officer may simply issue a warning or take the offender to the police station and release the child into the custody of her or his parents.

In making these discretionary decisions, police generally consider the following factors:

- The nature of the child's offense.
- The offender's past history of involvement with the juvenile justice system.
- The setting in which the offense took place.
- The ability and willingness of the child's parents to take disciplinary action.
- The attitude of the offender.
- The offender's race and gender.

Law enforcement officers notify the juvenile court system that a particular young person requires its attention through a process known as a **referral.** Anyone with a valid reason, including parents, relatives, welfare agencies, and school officials, can refer a juvenile to the juvenile court. The vast majority of cases in juvenile courts, however, are referred by the police.[74]

Learning Objective 6 Describe the four primary stages of pretrial juvenile justice procedure.

INTAKE

Following arrest, if a police officer feels the offender warrants the attention of the juvenile justice process and thus refers the youth to juvenile court, a complaint is filed with a special division of the juvenile court. Then, the **intake** process begins. Intake may be followed by diversion to a community-based program, transfer to an adult court, or detention to await trial in juvenile court. Thus, intake, diversion, transfer, and detention are the four primary stages of pretrial juvenile justice procedure.

During intake, an official of the juvenile court—usually a probation officer, but sometimes a judge—must decide, in effect, what to do with the offender. The intake officer has several options during intake:

1. Simply dismiss the case, releasing the offender without taking any further action.
2. Divert the offender to a social-services program, such as drug rehabilitation or anger management.

3. File a **petition** for a formal court hearing. The petition is the formal document outlining the charges against the juvenile.

4. Transfer the case to an adult court, where the offender will be tried as an adult.

With regard to status offenses, judges have sole discretion to decide whether to process the case or *divert* the youth to another juvenile service agency.

PRETRIAL DIVERSION

In the early 1970s, Congress passed the first Juvenile Justice and Delinquency Prevention (JJDP) Act, which ordered the development of methods "to divert juveniles from the traditional juvenile justice system."[75] Within a few years, hundreds of diversion programs had been put into effect. Today, diversion refers to the process of removing low-risk offenders from the formal juvenile justice system by placing them in community-based rehabilitation programs.

A juvenile court judge makes a ruling in her courtroom at the Juvenile Court of Memphis and Shelby County (Tennessee). What are some of the reasons that juvenile judges might choose to divert status offenders into social-service programs?

ZUMA Press/Newscom

Diversion programs vary widely, but fall into three general categories:

1. *Probation.* In this program, the juvenile is returned to the community, but placed under the supervision of a juvenile probation officer. If the youth breaks the conditions of probation, he or she can be returned to the formal juvenile system.

2. *Treatment and aid.* Many juveniles have behavioral or medical conditions that contribute to their delinquent behavior, and many diversion programs offer remedial education, drug and alcohol treatment, and other forms of counseling to alleviate these problems.

3. *Restitution.* In these programs, the offender "repays" her or his victim, either directly or symbolically through community service.[76]

Increasingly, juvenile justice practitioners are relying on principles of restorative justice (see Chapter 9) to divert adolescents from formal institutions. For example, in Barron County, Wisconsin, delinquents have access to victim-offender conferences, underage drinking and anger management workshops, and group intervention courses for chronic offenders.[77] Juvenile drug courts, modeled on the adult drug courts we discussed in Chapter 10, have also had some success in this area.[78] Proponents of diversion programs include many labeling theorists (see Chapter 2), who believe that contact with the formal juvenile justice system "labels" the youth a delinquent, which leads to further delinquent behavior.

Petition The document filed with a juvenile court alleging that the juvenile is a delinquent or a status offender and requesting that the court either hear the case or transfer it to an adult court.

Judicial Waiver The process in which the juvenile judge, based on the facts of the case at hand, decides that the alleged offender should be transferred to adult court.

TRANSFER TO ADULT COURT

One side effect of diversionary programs is that the youths who remain in the juvenile courts are more likely to be seen as "hardened" and thus less amenable to rehabilitation. This, in turn, increases the likelihood that the offender will be transferred to an adult court, a process in which the juvenile court waives jurisdiction over the youth.

There are three types of transfer laws, and most states use more than one of them depending on the jurisdiction and the seriousness of the offense.[79] Juveniles are most commonly transferred to adult courts through **judicial waiver,** in which the juvenile judge is given the power to determine whether a young offender's case will be waived to adult court. The judge makes this decision based on the offender's age, the nature of the offense, and any criminal history. All but five states employ judicial waiver. About nine thousand delinquency cases are waived to adult court by judges annually—1 percent of all cases that reach juvenile court.[80] As you might guess, those juveniles who commit the most violent felonies are the most likely to be transferred.

Twenty-nine states have taken the waiver responsibility out of judicial hands through **automatic transfer,** also known as *legislative waiver.* In these states, the legislatures have designated certain conditions—usually involving serious crimes such as murder and rape—under which a juvenile case is automatically "kicked up" to adult court. In Rhode Island, for example, a juvenile aged sixteen or older with two prior felony adjudications will automatically be transferred on being accused of a third felony.[81] Fifteen states also allow for **prosecutorial waiver,** in which prosecutors are allowed to choose whether to initiate proceedings in juvenile or criminal court when certain age and offense conditions are met.

DETENTION

Once the decision has been made that the offender will face adjudication in a juvenile court, the intake official must decide what to do with him or her until the start of the trial. Generally, the juvenile is released into the custody of parents or a guardian—most jurisdictions favor this practice in lieu of setting money bail for youths. The intake officer may also place the offender in **detention,** or temporary custody in a secure facility, until the disposition process begins. Once a juvenile has been detained, most jurisdictions require that a **detention hearing** be held within twenty-four hours. During this hearing, the offender has several due process safeguards, including the right to counsel, the right against self-incrimination, and the right to cross-examine and confront witnesses.

In justifying its decision to detain, the court will usually address one of three issues:

1. Whether the child poses a danger to the community.
2. Whether the child will return for the adjudication process.
3. Whether detention will provide protection for the child.

The Supreme Court upheld the practice of preventive detention (see Chapter 8) for juveniles in *Schall v. Martin* (1984)[82] by ruling that youths can be detained if they are deemed a "risk" to the safety of the community or to their own welfare. Partly as a result, the number of detained juveniles increased by 41 percent between 1985 and 2008.[83]

SELFASSESSMENT

Fill in the blanks and check your answers on page 391.

If the circumstances are serious enough, a police officer can formally _____ an offending juvenile. Otherwise, the officer can _____ the juvenile to the juvenile court system or place her or him in the care of a _____-service organization. During the _____ process, a judge or juvenile probation officer decides the immediate fate of the juvenile delinquent. One of the options is _____, in which low-risk offenders are placed in community rehabilitation programs. If the judge believes that the seriousness of the offense so warrants, she or he can transfer the juvenile into the adult court system through a process called judicial _____.

TRYING AND PUNISHING JUVENILES

Over the past forty years, the one constant in the juvenile justice system has been change. Supreme Court rulings in the wake of *In re Gault* (1967) have increased the procedural formality and the overriding punitive philosophy of the juvenile court.

Automatic Transfer The process by which a juvenile is transferred to adult court as a matter of state law.

Prosecutorial Waiver A procedure used in situations where the prosecutor has discretion to decide whether a case will be heard by a juvenile court or an adult court.

Detention The temporary custody of a juvenile in a secure facility after a petition has been filed and before the adjudicatory process begins.

Detention Hearing A hearing to determine whether a juvenile should be detained, or remain detained, while waiting for the adjudicatory process to begin.

Diversion policies have worked to remove many status offenders from the juvenile court's jurisdiction, and waiver policies ensure that the most violent juveniles are tried as adults. Some observers feel these adjustments have "criminalized" the juvenile court, effectively rendering it indistinguishable both theoretically and practically from adult courts.[84] Just over half of the states, for example, permit juveniles to request a jury trial under certain circumstances. As the *Mastering Concepts* feature below explains, however, juvenile justice proceedings may still be distinguished from the adult system of criminal justice, and these differences are evident in the adjudication and disposition of the juvenile trial.

Adjudicatory Hearing The process through which a juvenile court determines whether there is sufficient evidence to support the initial petition.

ADJUDICATION

During the adjudication stage of the juvenile justice process, a hearing is held to determine whether the offender is delinquent or in need of some form of court supervision. Most state juvenile codes dictate a specific set of procedures that must be followed during the **adjudicatory hearing,** with the goal of providing the respondent with "the essentials of due process and fair treatment." Consequently, the respondent in an adjudicatory hearing has the right to notice of charges, counsel, and confrontation and cross-examination, as well as the privilege against self-incrimination. Furthermore, "proof beyond a reasonable doubt" must be established to find the child delinquent. When the

Learning Objective 7 Explain the distinction between an adjudicatory hearing and a disposition hearing.

MASTERINGCONCEPTS
THE JUVENILE JUSTICE SYSTEM VERSUS THE CRIMINAL JUSTICE SYSTEM

When the juvenile justice system was first established in the United States, its participants saw it as being separate from the adult criminal justice system. Indeed, the two systems remain separate in many ways. There are, however, a number of similarities between juvenile and adult justice. Here, we summarize both the similarities and the differences.

SIMILARITIES	DIFFERENCES		
		Juvenile System	**Adult System**
• The right to receive the *Miranda* warning.	Purpose	Rehabilitation of the offender.	Punishment.
• Procedural protections when making an admission of guilt.	Arrest	Juveniles can be arrested for acts (status offenses) that are not criminal for adults.	Adults can be arrested only for acts made illegal by the relevant criminal code.
• Prosecutors and defense attorneys play equally important roles.	Wrongdoing	Considered a "delinquent act."	A crime.
• The right to be represented by counsel at the crucial stages of the trial process.	Proceedings	Informal; closed to public.	Formal and regimented; open to public.
• Access to plea bargains.	Information	Courts may *not* release information to the public.	Courts *must* release information to the public.
• The right to a hearing and an appeal.	Parents	Play significant role.	Play no role.
	Release	Into parent/guardian custody.	May post bail when appropriate.
• The standard of evidence is proof beyond a reasonable doubt.	Jury trial	In some states, juveniles do *not* have this right.	All adults have this right.
• Offenders can be placed on probation by the judge.	Searches	Juveniles can be searched in school without probable cause.	No adult can be searched without probable cause.
• Offenders can be held before adjudication if the judge believes them to be a threat to the community.	Records	Juvenile's record is sealed at age of adult criminal responsibility.	Adult's criminal record is permanent.
	Sentencing	Juveniles are placed in separate facilities from adults.	Adults are placed in county jails or state or federal prisons.
• Following trial, offenders can be sentenced to community supervision.	Death penalty	No death penalty.	Death penalty for certain serious crimes under certain circumstances.

child admits guilt—that is, admits to the charges of the initial petition—the judge must ensure that the admission was voluntary.

At the close of the adjudicatory hearing, the judge is generally required to rule on the legal issues and evidence that have been presented. Based on this ruling, the judge determines whether the respondent is delinquent or in need of court supervision. Alternatively, the judge can dismiss the case based on a lack of evidence. It is important to remember that finding a child delinquent is *not* the same as convicting an adult of a crime. A delinquent does not face the same restrictions imposed on adult convicts in some states, such as limits on the right to vote (discussed in Chapter 11).

DISPOSITION

Once a juvenile has been adjudicated delinquent, the judge must decide what steps will be taken toward treatment and/or punishment. Most states provide for a *bifurcated* process in which a separate **disposition hearing** follows the adjudicatory hearing. Depending on state law, the juvenile may be entitled to counsel at the disposition hearing.

SENTENCING JUVENILES

In an adult trial, the sentencing phase is primarily concerned with the needs of the community to be protected from the convict. In contrast, a juvenile judge uses the disposition hearing to determine a sentence that will serve the needs of the child. For assistance in this crucial process, the judge will order the probation department to gather information on the juvenile and present it in the form of a **predisposition report.** The report usually contains information concerning the respondent's family background, the facts surrounding the delinquent act, and interviews with social workers, teachers, and other important figures in the child's life.

JUDICIAL DISCRETION

In keeping with the rehabilitative tradition of the juvenile justice system, juvenile judges generally have a great deal of discretion in choosing one of several disposition possibilities. A judge can tend toward leniency, delivering only a stern reprimand or warning before releasing the juvenile into the custody of parents or other legal guardians. Otherwise, the choice is among incarceration in a juvenile correctional facility, probation, or community treatment. In most cases, the seriousness of the offense is the primary factor used in determining whether to incarcerate a juvenile, though history of delinquency, family situation, and the offender's attitude are all relevant.

JUVENILE CORRECTIONS

In general, juvenile corrections are based on the concept of **graduated sanctions**—that is, the severity of the punishment should fit the crime. Consequently, status and first-time offenders are diverted or placed on probation, repeat offenders find themselves in intensive community supervision or treatment programs, and serious and violent offenders are placed in correctional facilities.

As society's expectations of the juvenile justice system have changed, so have the characteristics of its corrections programs. In some cities, for example, juvenile probation officers join police officers on the beat. Because the former are not bound by the same search and seizure restrictions as other law enforcement officials, this interdepartmental teamwork provides more opportunities to fight youth crime aggressively. Juvenile correctional facilities are also changing their operations to reflect public mandates that they should both reform and punish.

Disposition Hearing
Similar to the sentencing hearing for adults, a hearing in which the juvenile judge or officer decides the appropriate punishment for a youth found to be delinquent or a status offender.

Predisposition Report A report prepared during the disposition process that provides the judge with relevant background material to aid in the disposition decision.

Graduated Sanctions The practical theory in juvenile corrections that a delinquent or status offender should receive a punishment that matches in seriousness the severity of the wrongdoing.

Social Media and CJ
The **Campaign for Youth Justice** is a special interest organization dedicated to removing juvenile offenders from the adult criminal justice system. To access its Twitter Web page, visit the *Criminal Justice CourseMate* at cengagebrain.com and select the *Web Links* for this chapter.

JUVENILE PROBATION The most common form of juvenile corrections is probation. The majority of all adjudicated delinquents (nearly 60 percent) will never receive a disposition more severe than being placed on probation.[85] These statistics reflect a general understanding among juvenile court judges and other officials that a child should normally be removed from her or his home only as a last resort.

The organization of juvenile probation is very similar to adult probation (see Chapter 10), and juvenile probationers are increasingly subjected to electronic monitoring and other supervisory tactics. The main difference between the two programs lies in the attitude toward the offender. Adult probation officers have an overriding responsibility to protect the community from the probationer, while juvenile probation officers are expected to take the role of a mentor or a concerned relative in looking after the needs of the child.

CONFINING JUVENILES About 81,000 American youths (up from 30,000 at the end of the 1970s) are incarcerated in public and private juvenile correctional facilities in the United States.[86] Most of these juveniles have committed crimes against people or property, but a significant number (about 15 percent) have been incarcerated for technical violations of their probation or parole agreements.[87] After deciding that a juvenile needs to be confined, the judge has two sentencing options: nonsecure juvenile institutions and secure juvenile institutions.

Nonsecure Confinement Some juvenile delinquents do not require high levels of control and can be placed in **residential treatment programs.** These programs, run by probation departments or social-services departments, allow their subjects freedom of movement in the community. Generally, this freedom is predicated on the juveniles following certain rules, such as avoiding illegal drugs and alcohol and returning to the facility for curfew. Residential treatment programs can be divided into four categories:[88]

1. *Foster care programs,* in which the juveniles live with a couple who act as surrogate parents.
2. *Group homes,* which generally house between twelve and fifteen youths and provide treatment, counseling, and education services by a professional staff.
3. *Family group homes,* which combine aspects of foster care and group homes, meaning that a single family, rather than a group of professionals, looks after the needs of the young offenders.
4. *Rural programs,* which include wilderness camps, farms, and ranches where between thirty and fifty children are placed in an environment that provides recreational activities and treatment programs.

Secure Confinement Secure facilities are comparable to the adult prisons and jails we discussed in Chapters 11 and 12. These institutions go by a confusing array of names depending on the state in which they are located, but the two best known are boot camps and training schools. A **boot camp** is the juvenile variation of shock probation. As we noted in Chapter 10, boot camps are modeled after military training for new recruits. Boot camp programs are based on the theory that by giving wayward youths a taste of the "hard life" of military-like

Residential Treatment Program A government-run facility for juveniles whose offenses are not deemed serious enough to warrant incarceration in a training school.

Boot Camp A variation on traditional shock incarceration in which juveniles (and some adults) are sent to secure confinement facilities modeled on military basic training camps instead of prison or jail.

Learning Objective 8 List the four categories of residential treatment programs.

Juvenile inmates prepare to enter a dormitory at Texas's Marlin Orientation and Assessment Unit. What might be some of the reasons that juvenile correctional facilities often operate similarly to adult prisons and jails?

Michael Ainsworth/*Dallas Morning News*/Corbis

CAREERS IN CJ

CARL McCULLOUGH, SR.
RESIDENT YOUTH WORKER

I had a shot in the NFL, playing for the Buffalo Bills and the Minnesota Vikings, but that lasted only a short time. Today, I work at the Hennepin County (Minnesota) Juvenile Detention Center, where I'm responsible for a group of twelve young men, aged thirteen to eighteen, who are awaiting trial, waiting for placements, or just being held in a secure place due to the high-profile nature of their cases. I'm with the kids every day and every other weekend from 6:30 A.M. to 2:30 P.M. I do everything from helping with homework to supervising their leisure time, running group programs, and just being a positive, caring adult with whom to talk.

Having the NFL experience is a huge icebreaker with the residents. "Why are you here?" they always ask me, and I tell them I am here because I care about them, because I want to see a change, and because I'd like to help them believe that something better is possible. To do this job well, you have to be good at building relationships. It helps to know how to work with different cultures as well. Then you have to have patience; without it you won't last long. You know they are going to test you, to see what they can and can't get away with. You also have to be willing to learn a few things from them. You have to be a good listener.

Social Media Career Tip

Potential employers want information about you, but they do not want your life story. Take advantage of the two things that social media excel at when making career contacts: (1) personalize your message, and (2) be concise. **f** **Linked in**.

FAST FACTS

RESIDENT YOUTH WORKER, JOB DESCRIPTION:

- Provide safety, security, custodial care, discipline, and guidance. Play a critical role in the rehabilitation of youth and, as a result, have a potentially great impact on a youth's success during and after his or her incarceration.

WHAT KIND OF TRAINING IS REQUIRED?

- A bachelor's degree in human services, behavioral science, or a related field.
- Professional and respectful verbal communication skills.

ANNUAL SALARY RANGE?

- $16,840 – $44,940

Training School A correctional institution for juveniles found to be delinquent or status offenders.

training for short periods of time, usually no longer than 180 days, they will be "shocked" out of a life of crime. New York's Camp Monterey Shock Incarceration Facility is typical of the boot camp experience. Inmates are grouped in platoons and live in dormitories. They spend eight hours a day training, drilling, and doing hard labor, and also participate in programs such as basic adult education and job skills training.[89]

No juvenile correctional facility is called a "prison." This does not mean they lack a strong resemblance to prisons. The facilities that most closely mimic the atmosphere at an adult correctional facility are **training schools,** alternatively known as youth camps, youth development centers, industrial schools, and several other similar titles. Whatever the name, these institutions claim to differ from their adult countparts by offering a variety of programs to treat and rehabilitate the young offenders. In reality, training schools are plagued by many of the same problems as adult prisons and jails, including high levels of inmate-on-inmate violence, substance abuse, gang wars, and overcrowding.

AFTERCARE Juveniles leave correctional facilities through an early release program or because they have served the length of their sentences. Juvenile corrections officials recognize that many of these children, like adults, need assistance in readjusting to the outside world. Consequently, released juveniles are often placed in **aftercare** programs. Based on the same philosophy that drives the prisoner reentry movement (discussed in the previous chapter), aftercare programs are designed to offer services for the juveniles, while at the same time supervising them to reduce the chances of recidivism. The ideal aftercare program includes community support groups, aid in finding and keeping employment, and continued monitoring to ensure that the juvenile is able to deal with the demands of freedom.

Aftercare The variety of therapeutic, educational, and counseling programs made available to juvenile delinquents (and some adults) after they have been released from a correctional facility.

SELFASSESSMENT

Fill in the blanks and check your answers on page 391.

A juvenile offender's delinquency is determined during the _____ hearing, which is similar in many ways to an adult trial. If the juvenile is found to be delinquent, her or his sentence is determined during the _____ hearing. The most common form of juvenile corrections is _____. If the judge decides that the juvenile needs more stringent supervision, he or she can sentence the offender to a _____ facility such as a residential treatment program. If the juvenile's offense has been particularly serious, she or he will most likely be sent to a secure confinement facility such as a _____ camp or a _____ school.

CHAPTER SUMMARY

Learning Objective 1 **Describe the child-saving movement and its relationship to the doctrine of *parens patriae*.** Under the doctrine of *parens patriae*, the state has a right and a duty to care for neglected, delinquent, or disadvantaged children. The child-saving movement, based on the doctrine of *parens patriae*, started in the 1800s. Its followers believed that juvenile offenders require treatment rather than punishment.

Learning Objective 2 **List the four major differences between juvenile courts and adult courts.** (a) No juries, (b) different terminology, (c) no adversarial relationship, and (d) confidentiality.

Learning Objective 3 **Identify and briefly describe the single most important Supreme Court case with respect to juvenile justice.** The case was *In re Gault*, decided by the Supreme Court in 1967. In this case a minor was arrested for allegedly making an obscene phone call. His parents were not notified and were not present during the juvenile court judge's decision-making process. In this case, the Supreme Court held that juveniles are entitled to many of the same due process rights granted to adult offenders, including notice of charges, the right to counsel, the privilege against self-incrimination, and the right to confront and cross-examine witnesses.

Learning Objective 4 **Describe the one variable that always correlates highly with juvenile crime rates.** The older a person is, the less likely he or she will exhibit criminal behavior. This process is known as aging out. Thus, persons in any at-risk group will commit fewer crimes as they get older.

Learning Objective 5 **Indicate some of the reasons why youths join gangs.** Some alienated teenagers join gangs for the social relationships and the sense of identity that gangs can provide. Youths living in high-crime neighborhoods join gangs as a form of protection. The excitement of belonging to a gang is another reason to join.

Learning Objective 6 **Describe the four primary stages of pretrial juvenile justice procedure.** (a) Intake, in which an official of the juvenile court engages in a screening process to determine what to do with the youthful offender; (b) pretrial diversion, which may consist of probation, treatment and aid, and/or restitution; (c) jurisdictional waiver to an adult court, in which case the youth leaves the juvenile justice system; and (d) some type of detention, in which the youth is held until the disposition process begins.

Learning Objective 7 **Explain the distinction between an adjudicatory hearing and a disposition hearing.** An adjudicatory hearing is essentially a "trial." Defense attorneys may be present during the adjudicatory hearing in juvenile courts. In many states, once adjudication has occurred, there is a separate disposition hearing that is similar to the sentencing phase in an adult court. At this point, the court, often aided by a predisposition report, determines the sentence that serves the "needs" of the child.

Learning Objective 8 **List the four categories of residential treatment programs.** Foster care, group homes, family group homes, and rural programs such as wilderness camps, farms, and ranches.

QUESTIONS FOR CRITICAL ANALYSIS

1. What is the difference between a status offense and a crime? What punishments do you think should be imposed on juveniles who commit status offenses?

2. Several years ago, eight Florida teenagers ranging in age from fourteen to eighteen beat a classmate so badly that she suffered a concussion. According to law enforcement officials, the teenagers recorded the assault so that they could post it on the Internet. If you were a prosecutor and could either waive these teenagers to adult court or refer them to the juvenile justice system, which option would you choose? What other information would you need to make your decision?

3. Forty-four states have enacted parental responsibility statutes, which make parents responsible for the offenses of their children. Seventeen of these states hold parents criminally liable for their children's actions, punishing the parents with fines, community service, and even incarceration. What is your opinion of these laws—particularly those with criminal sanctions for parents?

4. Do you think that bullying should be punishable as a felony along the same lines as assault? (For the definition of assault, see page 33.) Why or why not?

5. Research shows that judges in adult criminal courts impose a "juvenile penalty" during the sentencing process. That is, they tend to punish juveniles who have been transferred to adult court more harshly than young adults (nineteen- and twenty-year-olds) who have been convicted of similar crimes. Why do you think judges behave in this manner?

KEY TERMS

adjudicatory hearing **385**
aftercare **389**
age of onset **378**
aging out **377**
automatic transfer **384**
boot camp **387**
bullying **376**
child abuse **379**
child neglect **379**

detention **384**
detention hearing **384**
disposition hearing **386**
graduated sanctions **386**
intake **382**
judicial waiver **383**
juvenile delinquency **368**
low-visibility decision making **381**
parens patriae **367**

petition **383**
predisposition report **386**
prosecutorial waiver **384**
referral **382**
residential treatment
    program **387**
status offender **368**
training school **388**
youth gang **379**

SELF ASSESSMENT ANSWER KEY

Page 370: i. *parens patriae;* **ii.** status offenses; **iii.** delinquency

Page 373: i. state; **ii.** state; **iii.** impulsive; **iv.** peer;
    v. death penalty

Page 377: i. declining; **ii.** girls; **iii.** School; **iv.** Bullying

Page 381: i. risk; **ii.** aging out; **iii.** child abuse/child neglect;
    iv. youth gangs

Page 384: **i.** arrest; **ii.** refer; **iii.** social; **iv.** intake; **v.** diversion; **vi.** waiver

Page 389: **i.** adjudicatory; **ii.** disposition; **iii.** probation; **iv.** nonsecure; **v.** boot; **vi.** training

COURSEMATE

For online help and access to resources that accompany *Criminal Justice in Action: The Core*, go to **www.cengage-brain.com/shop/ISBN/978-1-285-06915-9**. Click "Access Now," where you will find flashcards, an online quiz, and other helpful study aids. If you have an access code for CourseMate, log in and go to the chapter of your choice for additional online study aids.

NOTES

1. Bruce Vielmetti, "Sentence of Life without Parole for Teen Upheld," *Milwaukee Journal Sentinel* (May 22, 2011), B1.

2. *Miller v. Alabama*, 567 U.S. ____ (2012).

3. *Polling on Public Attitudes about the Treatment of Young Offenders* (Washington, D.C.: National Juvenile Justice Network, 2010).

4. *In re Gault*, 387 U.S. 1, at 15 (1967).

5. Samuel Davis, *The Rights of Juveniles: The Juvenile Justice System,* 2d ed. (New York: C. Boardman Co., 1995), Section 1.2.

6. Quoted in Anthony Platt, *The Child Savers* (Chicago: University of Chicago Press, 1969), 119.

7. 383 U.S. 541 (1966).

8. *Ibid.,* 556.

9. 387 U.S. 1 (1967).

10. 397 U.S. 358 (1970).

11. 421 U.S. 519 (1975).

12. 403 U.S. 528 (1971).

13. Quoted in "Colo. Boy Pleads Guilty to Killing Parents," *Associated Press* (September 29, 2011).

14. Gary B. Melton, "Toward 'Personhood' for Adolescents: Autonomy and Privacy as Values in Public Policy," *American Psychology* 38 (1983), 99–100.

15. Research Network on Adolescent Development and Juvenile Justice, *Youth on Trial: A Developmental Perspective on Juvenile Justice* (Chicago: John D. & Catherine T. MacArthur Foundation, 2003), 1.

16. Richard E. Redding, "Juveniles Transferred to Criminal Court: Legal Reform Proposals Based on Social Science Research," *Utah Law Review* (1997), 709.

17. Howard N. Snyder and Melissa Sickmund, *Juvenile Offenders and Victims: A National Report* (Washington, D.C.: U.S. Department of Justice, 1995), 47.

18. Martha Grace Duncan, "'So Young and So Untender': Remorseless Children and the Expectations of the Law," *Columbia Law Review* (October 2002), 1469.

19. 543 U.S. 551 (2005).

20. *Ibid.,* 567.

21. 560 U.S. ____ (2010).

22. *Ibid.*

23. *Surveillance Summaries: Youth Risk Behavior Surveillance—United States, 2001* (Washington, D.C.: Centers for Disease Control and Prevention, June 28, 2002).

24. Federal Bureau of Investigation, *Crime in the United States, 2011* (Washington, D.C.: U.S. Department of Justice, 2012), at **www.fbi.gov/about-us/cjis/ucr/crime-in-the-u.s/2011/crime-in-the-u.s.-2011/tables/table-38.**

25. Charles Puzzanchera, Benjamin Adams, and Melissa Sickmund, *Juvenile Court Statistics 2008* (Pittsburgh, PA: National Center for Juvenile Justice, July 2011), 6.

26. Office of Juvenile Justice and Delinquency Prevention, *Juvenile Residential Facility Census, 2008: Selected Findings* (Washington, D.C.: U.S. Department of Justice, July 2011), 1; and Todd Richmond, "Fewer Young Criminals Push States to Close Prisons," *Associated Press* (June 7, 2010).

27. David McDowell, "Juvenile Curfew Laws and Their Influence on Crime," *Federal Probation* (December 2006), 58.

28. *Crime in the United States, 2011,* at **www.fbi.gov/about-us/cjis/ucr/crime-in-the-u.s/2011/crime-in-the-u.s.-2011/tables/table-38.**

29. Office of Juvenile Justice and Delinquency Prevention, "Community Prevention Grants Program," at **www.ojjdp.gov/cpg.**

30. Margaret A. Zahn et al., *Girls Study Group: Understanding and Responding to Girls' Delinquency* (Washington, D.C.: Office of Juvenile Justice and Delinquency Prevention, October 2008), 3.

31. Sara Goodkind et al., "Are Girls Really Becoming More Delinquent? Testing the Gender Convergence Hypothesis by Race and Ethnicity, 1976-2005," *Children and Youth Services Review* (August 2009), 885–889.

32. Kimberly Kempf-Leonard and Lisa Sample, "Disparity Based on Sex: Is Gender-Specific Treatment Warranted?" *Justice Quarterly* 17 (2000), 89–128.

33. Puzzanchera, Adams, and Sickmund, *Juvenile Court Statistics 2008,* 12.

34. *Crime in the United States, 2011,* at **www.fbi.gov/about-us/cjis/ucr/crime-in the-u.s/2011/crime-in-the-u.s.-2011/tables/table-33.**

35. Zahn et al., 3.

36. Melissa Sickmund and Howard N. Snyder, *Juvenile Offenders and Victims: 1999 National Report* (Washington, D.C.: Office of Juvenile Justice and Delinquency Prevention, 1999), 58.

37. Meda Chesney-Lind, *The Female Offender: Girls, Women, and Crime* (Thousand Oaks, CA: Sage Publications, 1997).

38. Denise C. Gottfredson and David A. Soulé, "The Timing of Property Crime, Violent Crime, and Substance Abuse among Juveniles," *Journal of Research in Crime and Delinquency* (February 2005), 110–120.

39. National Center for Education Statistics and Bureau of Justice Statistics, *Indicators of School Crime and Safety: 2011* (Washington, D.C.: U.S. Department of Justice, February 2012), 6.

40. *Ibid.,* 10–15.

41. *Ibid.,* 82–83.

42. *Ibid.,* 44.

43. Jessica Bennett, "From Lockers to Lockup," *Newsweek* (October 11, 2010), 39.

44. Adam J. Speraw, "No Bullying Allowed: A Call for a National Anti-Bullying Statute to Promote a Safer Learning Environment in American Public Schools," *Valparaiso University Law Review* (Summer 2010), 1151–1198.

45. Natalie DiBlasio, "More Cases of Bullying Are Ending Up in Court," *USA Today* (September 12, 2011), 3A.

46. Marvin E. Wolfgang, *From Boy to Man, from Delinquency to Crime* (Chicago: University of Chicago Press, 1987).

47. Gary Sweeten, Shawn D. Bushway, and Raymond Paternoster, "Does Dropping Out of School Mean Dropping into Delinquency?" *Criminology* (February 2009), 47–88.

48. Quoted in John H. Laub and Robert J. Sampson, "Understanding Desistance from Crime," in *Crime and Justice: A Review of Research* (Chicago: University of Chicago Press, 2001), 6.

49. Travis Hirschi and Michael Gottfredson, "Age and the Explanation of Crime," *American Journal of Sociology* 89 (1982), 552–584.

50. Robert J. Sampson and John H. Laub, "A Life-Course View on the Development of Crime," *Annals of the American Academy of Political and Social Science* (November 2005), 12.

51. David P. Farrington, "Offending from 10 to 25 Years of Age," in *Prospective Studies of Crime and Delinquency,* ed. Katherine Teilmann Van Dusen and Sarnoff A. Mednick (Boston: Kluwer-Nijhoff Publishers, 1983), 17.

52. Office of Juvenile Justice and Delinquency Prevention, *Juveniles in Court* (Washington, D.C.: U.S. Department of Justice, June 2003), 29.

53. Lloyd D. Johnston et al., *Monitoring the Future: National Results on Adolescent Drug Use—Overview of Key Findings, 2011* (Ann Arbor, MI: Institute for Social Research, February 2012), 36.

54. Anahad O'Connor, "Regular Marijuana Use by High School Students Hits New Peak, Report Finds," *New York Times* (December 15, 2011), A16.

55. Carl McCurley and Howard Snyder, *Co-occurrence of Substance Abuse Behaviors in Youth* (Washington, D.C.: Office of Juvenile Justice and Delinquency Prevention, 2008).

56. Gary McClelland, Linda Teplin, and Karen Abram, "Detection and Prevalence of Substance Abuse among Juvenile Detainees," *Juvenile Justice Bulletin* (Washington, D.C.: Office of Juvenile Justice and Delinquency Prevention, June 2004), 10.

57. Arrestee Drug Abuse Monitoring Program, *Preliminary Data on Drug Use and Related Matters among Adult Arrestees and Juvenile Detainees* (Washington, D.C.: National Institute of Justice, 2003).

58. National Mental Health Association, "Mental Health and Adolescent Girls in the Justice System," at **www.nmha.org/children/justjuv/girlsjj.cfm**.

59. Larry J. Siegel and Brandon C. Welsh, *Juvenile Delinquency: The Core,* 4th ed. (Belmont, CA: Wadsworth Cengage Learning, 2011), 268.

60. Edward P. Mulvey, *Highlights from Pathways to Desistance: A Longitudinal Study of Serious Adolescent Offenders* (Washington, D.C.: Office of Juvenile Justice and Delinquency Prevention, March 2011), 1–3.

61. Sherry Hamby, David Finkelhor, Heather Turner, and Richard Ormrod, *Juvenile Justice Bulletin: Children's Exposure to Intimate Partner Violence and Other Family Violence* (Washington, D.C.: Office of Juvenile Justice and Delinquency Prevention, October 2011), 1.

62. Anne Dannerbeck and Jiahui Yan, "Missouri's Crossover Youth: Examining the Relationship between Their Maltreatment History and Their Risk of Violence," *Journal of Juvenile Justice* (Fall 2011), 85.

63. Grover Trask, "Defusing the Teenage Time Bombs," *Prosecutor* (March/April 1997), 29.

64. Ashley Nellis, *The Lives of Juvenile Lifers: Findings from a National Survey* (Washington, D.C.: The Sentencing Project, March 2012), 2.

65. Cathy Spatz Widom, *The Cycle of Violence* (Washington, D.C.: National Institute of Justice, October 1992).

66. Janet Currie and Erdal Tekin, *Does Child Abuse Cause Crime?* (Atlanta, GA: Andrew Young School of Policy Studies, April 2006), 27–28.

67. Arlen Egley, Jr., and James C. Howell, *Highlights of the 2009 National Youth Gang Survey* (Washington, D.C.: Office of Juvenile Justice and Delinquency Prevention, June 2011), 1.

68. Chris Melde and Finn-Aage Esbensen, "Gang Membership as a Turning Point in the Life Course," *Criminology* (August 2011), 513–546.

69. *National Gang Threat Assessment 2009* (Washington, D.C.: National Gang Intelligence Center, January 2009), iii.

70. James C. Howell et al., *National Gang Center Bulletin: U.S. Gang Problem Trends and Seriousness, 1996–2009* (Washington, D.C.: Office of Juvenile Justice and Delinquency Prevention, May 2011), Chart 1, page 10.

71. "Race/Ethnicity of Gang Members," *National Youth Gang Survey Analysis* (Institute for Intergovernmental Research/National Youth Gang Center, 2009), at **www.iir.com/nygc/nygsa**.

72. Rachel A. Gordon, Benjamin B. Lahey, Eriko Kawai, Rolf Loeber, and Magda Stouthamer-Loeber, "Antisocial Behavior and Youth Gang Membership: Selection and Socialization," *Criminology* (February 2004), 55–89.

73. Anthony Pinizzotto, Edward Davis, and Charles Miller, "Street-Gang Mentality: A Mosaic of Remorseless Violence and Relentless Loyalty," *FBI Law Enforcement Bulletin* (September 2007), 1–6.

74. "Charles Puzzanchera, Benjamin Adams, and Melissa Sickmund, *Juvenile Court Statistics 2006–2007* (Washington, D.C.: National Center for Juvenile Justice, March 2010), 31.

75. 42 U.S.C. Sections 5601–5778 (1974).

76. S'Lee Arthur Hinshaw II, "Juvenile Diversion: An Alternative to Juvenile Court," *Journal of Dispute Resolution* (1993), 305.

77. Ted Gordon Lewis, "Barron County Restorative Justice Programs: A Partnership Model for Balancing Community and Government Resources for Juvenile Justice Services," *Journal of Juvenile Justice* (Fall 2011), 17–32.

78. Audrey Hickert et al., "Impact of Juvenile Drug Courts on Drug Use and Criminal Behavior," *Journal of Juvenile Justice* (Fall 2011), 60–77.

79. Patrick Griffin et al., *Trying Juveniles as Adults: An Analysis of State Transfer Laws and Reporting* (Washington, D.C.: Office of Juvenile Justice and Delinquency Prevention, September 2011), 1–3.

80. Puzzanchera, Adams, and Sickmund, *Juvenile Court Statistics 2008*, 58.

81. Rhode Island General Laws Section 14-1-7.1 (1994 and Supp. 1996).

82. 467 U.S. 253 (1984).

83. Puzzanchera, Adams, and Sickmund, *Juvenile Court Statistics 2006–2007*, 32.

84. Barry C. Feld, "Criminalizing the American Juvenile Court," *Crime and Justice* 17 (1993), 227–254.

85. Puzzanchera, Adams, and Sickmund, *Juvenile Court Statistics 2008*, 55.

86. Office of Juvenile Justice and Delinquency Prevention, *Juvenile Residential Facility Census, 2008: Selected Findings* (Washington, D.C.: U.S. Department of Justice, July 2011), 2.

87. Howard N. Snyder and Melissa Sickmund, *Juvenile Offenders and Victims: 2006 National Report* (Washington, D.C.: National Center for Juvenile Justice, March 2006), 98.

88. Sickmund and Snyder, 182.

89. Dean John Champion, *The Juvenile Justice System: Delinquency, Processing, and the Law,* 5th ed. (Upper Saddle River, NJ: Pearson Prentice Hall, 2007), 581–582.

CHAPTER

14

Today's Challenges in Criminal Justice

AP Photo/Delcia Lopez, File

LEARNING OBJECTIVES

After reading this chapter, you should be able to...

1 Identify three important trends in international terrorism.

2 Explain how American law enforcement agencies have used "preventive policing" to combat terrorism.

3 Explain how the Patriot Act has made it easier for federal agents to conduct searches during terrorism investigations.

4 Describe the three following forms of malware: (a) botnets, (b) worms, and (c) viruses.

5 Explain how the Internet has contributed to piracy of intellectual property.

6 Explain the difference between a temporary visa and a green card.

7 Indicate some of the ways in which white-collar crime is different from violent or property crime.

8 Explain the concept of corporate violence.

Throughout the chapter you will see each learning objective repeated in the margin next to the content it relates to. The chapter summary on page 423 includes all of the learning objectives for review.

CHAPTER OUTLINE

- Homeland Security
- Cyber Crime
- The Criminalization of Immigration Law
- White-Collar Crime

THE HACKTIVIST

The front page of the *Chicago Sun-Times* shows Jeremy Hammond dressed eccentrically, sitting on a rooftop, working on a computer. Above him, a headline asks the rhetorical question, "Evil Genius?" Indeed, Hammond does seem to be something of a genius when it comes to computers. Growing up in Glendale Heights, Illinois, he began programming video games at age nine and worked for an Apple specialist as a teenager. Hammond's attorney compared his talent to that of a "comic book character's superpower, like Superman's X-ray vision."

Hammond's attorney also said that his client had "some extreme opinions and thoughts" but that he "used his social and political views for good." It is true that Hammond volunteered for the Salvation Army, built bicycles for charity, and helped prepare free meals for the poor. At the same time, he was an active "hacktivist," illegally using his computer skills to further his political viewpoints. In 2005, he was convicted of stealing credit-card data from Protest Warrior, a conservative Web site, and spent nearly two years in prison. Then, several years ago, Hammond joined up with Anonymous, a leaderless group of Internet activists who use computers to break into corporate and government databases around the world.

According to federal authorities, in early 2012, Hammond and several Anonymous colleagues breached the security of Strategic Forecasting (Stratfor), a Texas-based company that provides critical information on global business affairs. The hackers then released the account information of nearly 860,000 Stratfor subscribers, including former vice president Dan Quayle (1989–1993) and hundreds of government, law enforcement, and military officials. In a statement, Anonymous called on the "armies of darkness" to use the information "to wreak unholy havoc upon the systems and personal accounts of these rich and powerful oppressors." On March 7, 2012, Federal Bureau of Investigation (FBI) agents arrested Hammond at his Chicago, apartment. If found guilty of participating in the Stratfor operation, Hammond would face ten years in federal prison.

In March 2012, federal agents arrested Jeremy Hammond for using his computer skills to breach the security of corporate Web sites.

AFP/Getty Images/Newscom

The offshoot of Anonymous that was responsible for breaking into Stratfor's database called itself LulzSec, playing on the Internet slang for "laughs" and "security." The group is more than a collection of mere Internet pranksters, however. Jeremy Hammond allegedly made more than $700,000 in authorized charges using the credit-card numbers stolen from Stratfor accounts. Furthermore, in February 2012, an Irish Anonymous member intercepted a telephone conference between the FBI and British law enforcement officials and published the transcript online.[1]

Over the past thirteen chapters, we have touched on cyber crime and homeland security, two subjects highlighted by the exploits of Hammond and his Anonymous associates. In this final chapter of the textbook, we will look more closely at these matters, which provide two of the greatest challenges to the American criminal justice system in the 2000s. We will also explore two other hot topics in the field: (1) the increasingly blurred—and controversial—distinction between criminal law and immigration law, and (2) white-collar crime, a form of criminal activity that has received part of the blame for the worst economic downturn in the United States since the Great Depression of the 1930s.

HOMELAND SECURITY

One day after the arrests of Jeremy Hammond and four of his colleagues, Robert S. Mueller III, the director of the FBI, warned that terrorist groups would surely employ such computer tactics against the United States in the near future. "These adaptations of the terrorist threat make the FBI's counterterrorism mission that much more difficult and challenging," Mueller said.[2] Such unpredictability is one of the most striking, and unnerving, aspects of life in the United States post–September 11. Terrorism and its uncertainties have been a theme throughout this textbook, and we have seen a number of instances in which law enforcement, the courts, and corrections have had to evolve to meet the challenge. Now, we will focus more closely on the criminal justice system's role in *homeland security,* defined by the federal government as

> a concerted national effort to prevent terrorist attacks within the United States, reduce America's vulnerability to terrorism, and minimize the damage and recover from attacks that do occur.[3]

We start with an introduction to the phenomenon of terrorism—the driving force behind the homeland security movement in the United States.

THE GLOBAL CONTEXT OF TERRORISM

Generally, terrorist acts are not the acts of nations or legally appointed governments. Rather, terror is the realm of **nonstate actors,** free of control by or allegiance to any nation, that use violence to further their own goals. Today, the dominant strain of terrorism mixes political ambitions with very strong religious affiliations.

Nonstate Actor An entity that plays a role in international affairs but does not represent any established state or nation.

Modern terrorism is also characterized by extreme levels of violence. The January 24, 2011, suicide bombing at Russia's busiest airport, in Moscow, killed at least 37 people and injured almost 180 more. The three-day November 2008 raid on the financial district of Mumbai, India, left 173 dead and more than 300 wounded. And, of course, the September 11, 2001, attacks on New York and Washington, D.C., claimed nearly 3,000 lives. Indeed, the power of terrorism is a direct result of the fear caused by this violence—not only the fear that such atrocities will be repeated but also that next time, they will be much worse.

DEFINING TERRORISM Terrorism has always had a subjective quality, summed up by the useful cliché "one person's terrorist is another person's freedom fighter." Because it means different things to different people in different situations, politicians, academics, and legal experts alike have long struggled to determine which acts of violence qualify as terrorism and which do not. The FBI defines terrorism as

> the unlawful use of force or violence against persons or property to intimidate or coerce a government, the civilian population, or any segment thereof, in furtherance of political or social objectives.[4]

This definition is useful for our purposes because it is relatively straightforward and easy to understand. It is inadequate, however, in that it fails to capture the wide scope of international terrorism in the twenty-first century. Today, many observers are asking whether the state should consider terrorist violence merely "unlawful," as in the FBI definition, or an act of war. Generally, wars are considered military actions undertaken by one state or nation against another. This would seem to remove terrorism from the realm of warfare, given that its instigators are nonstate actors, as mentioned earlier.

Professor David A. Westbrook of the University of Buffalo (New York) points out, however, that the large scale and financial resources of some modern terrorist organizations

Rescue workers tend to a victim of the suicide bomber who struck Moscow's Domodevo International Airport on January 24, 2011. Russian officials blamed the attack, which killed at least 37 and wounded nearly 180 more, on militant Islamists. How are such acts of terrorism distinguished from acts of war?

AP Photo/Ivan Sekretarev

make them as powerful as many nations, if not more so. In addition, the high body counts associated with the worst terrorist acts seem better described in terms of war than of crime, which in most cases involves two people—the criminal and the victim.[5] Thus, perhaps the most satisfying definition of terrorism describes it as a "supercrime" that incorporates many of the characteristics of warfare.

AL QAEDA VERSUS THE UNITED STATES On May 1, 2011, a team of U.S. Navy Seals in helicopters descended on a three-story house in Abbottabad, a town located about thirty miles northeast of Islamabad, the capital of Pakistan. Forty minutes later, they left with the body of Osama bin Laden, whom they had killed after a shootout with his bodyguards. "Justice has been done," said President Barack Obama, echoing the sentiments of many Americans for whom the event marked a symbolic triumph in the struggle against international terrorism.[6] Experts, however, doubted that bin Laden's death would have much practical impact. Al Qaeda, the movement he had helped to start, was already moving on without him.

Osama bin Laden and al Qaeda Osama bin Laden's al Qaeda organization grew out of a network of volunteers who migrated to Afghanistan in the 1980s to rid that country of its Communist occupiers. (Ironically, in light of later events, bin Laden and his comrades received significant American financial aid at that time.) For bin Laden, these efforts took the form of *jihad,* a controversial term that has been the subject of much confusion.

Contrary to what many think, *jihad* does not mean "holy war." Rather, it refers to three kinds of struggle, or exertion, required of the Muslim faithful: (1) the struggle against the evil in oneself, (2) the struggle against the evil outside oneself, and (3) the struggle against nonbelievers.[7] Many Muslims believe that this struggle can be achieved without violence and denounce the form of *jihad* practiced by al Qaeda. Clearly, however, bin Laden and his followers rejected the notion that *jihad* can be accomplished through peaceable efforts.

In the 1990s, bin Laden began to turn his attention to the United States, and al Qaeda set its sights on American interests abroad. In 1998, for example, the organization bombed two U.S. embassies in Africa, killing 231 people. Two years later, al Qaeda agents launched a suicide attack on the U.S.S. *Cole,* a Navy destroyer docked in Aden, a port in the small Middle Eastern country of Yemen, during which seventeen U.S. sailors died. About a year after the September 11, 2001, attacks, bin Laden wrote a letter to the American people outlining the reasons behind al Qaeda's opposition to our government. These included American support for Israel, which is widely seen as an enemy to Muslims, and U.S. exploitation of Islamic countries for their oil. Furthermore, bin Laden criticized the presence of U.S. military forces in the Middle East, "spreading your ideology and thereby polluting the hearts of our people."[8]

A Continuing Threat Two years before his death, Osama bin Laden boasted that his disciples would "continue *jihad* for another seven years, seven years after that, and even seven years more after."[9] Two days after his death, al Qaeda posted a statement on the Internet that echoed this prediction: "Sheik Osama didn't build an organization to die when he dies," it said. "The soldiers of Islam will continue in groups and united, plotting and planning . . . with determination, without giving up until striking a blow."[10] More and more often, these "soldiers of Islam" resemble José Pimental, a U.S. citizen arrested in November 2011 for planning to use pipe bombs to attack banks and government buildings in New York City. Such "homegrown" extremists present a grave new challenge for law enforcement. Because they have grown up in the United States, they know how to operate on American soil. Because they possess U.S. passports, they can move freely in and out of the country.

Actions like those planned by Pimental have traditionally been described as **domestic terrorism** because they involved a local terrorist acting against his or her own people with no direct foreign involvement. More frequently, however, homegrown American terrorists are relying on foreign support. In some instances, this support comes from pro-*jihadist* Web sites, which offer training manuals, audio and video propaganda, and communication with like-minded individuals through chat rooms. In other instances, the encouragement is "hands-on." For example, Faisal Shahzad, who tried to detonate a car bomb in New York City's Times Square in 2010, received five days of explosives training and $15,000 from an extremist group operating out of northwest Pakistan.

TERRORISM TRENDS FOR THE FUTURE Smaller operations involving American-born terrorists influenced by international sources reflect several trends in this area identified by homeland security expert Brian M. Jenkins. As the list below shows, each of Jenkins' trends de-emphasizes the importance of any single, dominant organization such as al Qaeda.[11]

1. *Terrorists have developed more efficient methods of financing their operations* through avenues such as Internet fund-raising, drug trafficking, and money laundering schemes.
2. *Terrorists have developed more efficient organizations* based on the small-business model, in which individuals are responsible for different tasks including recruiting, planning, propaganda, and social services such as supporting the families of suicide bombers. These "employees" do not answer to a single leader but rather function as a network that is quick to adjust and difficult to infiltrate.
3. *Terrorists have exploited new communications technology to mount global campaigns,* relying on the Internet for immediate, direct communication among operatives and as a crucial recruiting tool. Furthermore, large numbers of "jihobbyists" are operating online, disseminating extremist writings and videos and using social media to spread the terrorist message in cyberspace.

As you may have noted, each of these trends favors the global terrorism movement. Indeed, Jenkins finds that today's *jihadists* are dangerous, resilient survivors who have achieved some strategic results and are determined to continue attacking their enemies. "Destroying their terrorist enterprise," he concludes, "will take years."[12]

THE ANTITERRORISM AND EFFECTIVE DEATH PENALTY ACT

America's first important step toward destroying terrorist enterprises actually predated the September 11, 2001, attacks. Signed into law by President Bill Clinton on April 24, 1996, the **Antiterrorism and Effective Death Penalty Act (AEDPA)** was passed

Domestic Terrorism Acts of terrorism that take place within the territorial jurisdiction of the United States without direct foreign involvement.

Antiterrorism and Effective Death Penalty Act of 1996 (AEDPA) Legislation giving law enforcement officers the power to arrest and prosecute any individual who provides "material support or resources" to a "foreign terrorist organization."

Learning Objective 1 Identify three important trends in international terrorism.

"Terrorism cannot be 'defeated,' because it is a tactic and not an enemy."

—**Nora Bensahel,** political scientist

in response to the 1995 truck bombing of the Alfred P. Murrah Federal Building in Oklahoma City, Oklahoma. The primary goal of the AEDPA is to hamper terrorist organizations by cutting off their funding from outside sources. The law prohibits persons from "knowingly providing material support or resources" to any group that the United States has designated a "foreign terrorist organization," or FTO.[13] Each year, the U.S. secretary of state is required to provide Congress with a list of these FTOs, loosely defined to cover organizations that (1) are foreign, (2) engage in terrorist activity, and (3) threaten the security of U.S. citizens or the United States itself.[14] The latest edition of this list included forty-four such organizations, most of them based in the Middle East.[15]

"Material support" is defined very broadly in the legislation, covering funding, financial services, lodging, training, expert advice or assistance, communications equipment, transportation, and other physical assets.[16] The "knowingly" requirement applies to all material support except for direct monetary donations to FTOs—this act is a strict liability crime (see pages 79–80). Consequently, even if a person is unaware that the recipient of charitable giving is involved in terrorist activity, she or he can be prosecuted under the AEDPA.[17]

THE PATRIOT ACT

Patriot Act Legislation passed in the wake of the September 11, 2001, terrorist attacks that greatly expanded the ability of government agents to monitor and apprehend suspected terrorists.

The original AEDPA did not include the provision making a donation to an FTO a strict liability crime. This amendment was part of the far-reaching scope of the **Patriot Act,** signed into law by President George W. Bush on October 26, 2001, just six weeks after the September 11 terrorist attacks.[18] As we have seen throughout this textbook, the emphasis on the rights of the accused in the American criminal justice system often makes it difficult to arrest and convict suspected criminals. The Patriot Act is the result of a strong impulse in Washington, D.C., and elsewhere to "level the playing field" when it comes to terrorists.

The legislation makes it easier for law enforcement agents to collect information about those suspected of committing terrorist acts or having knowledge of terrorist activity and then detain them based on that information. It enhances the power of the federal government to keep noncitizens under suspicion of having terrorist sympathies from entering the United States, and, as we have seen, it targets the fund-raising of terrorist enterprises. (See Figure 14.1 below for an overview of the Patriot Act.)

FIGURE 14.1 Selected Provisions of the Patriot Act

A massive piece of legislation, the Patriot Act is difficult to summarize. Selected aspects of it are listed here to provide a general idea of the statute's goals, as well as its methods of achieving them.

- The act relaxes restrictions on information sharing between various U.S. law enforcement agencies and other governmental departments concerning suspected terrorists.
- It creates the crime of knowingly harboring a terrorist.
- It allows law enforcement agents greater freedom in seizing the e-mail records of suspected terrorists.
- It authorizes funds to triple the number of border patrol agents, customs inspectors, and immigration enforcement officers along the United States' northern border with Canada.
- It allows the federal government to detain non-U.S. citizens suspected of terrorist activity for up to seven days without informing them of the charges on which they are being held.
- It eliminates the statute of limitations (see page 228) for prosecution of the most serious terrorism-related crimes.

Source: Jane A. Bullock, George Haddow, and Damon P. Coppola, *Introduction to Homeland Security*, 4th ed. (Waltham, MA: Butterworth-Heinemann, 2012), 45–46.

THE DEPARTMENT OF HOMELAND SECURITY

While the Patriot Act transformed the legal landscape of America's counterterrorism efforts, the Homeland Security Act of 2002 had a similar effect on the inner workings of the U.S. government. Prior to this legislation, disaster management at the federal level was primarily the responsibility of the Federal Emergency Management Agency (FEMA). The Patriot Act placed FEMA, as well as twenty-one other federal agencies, under the control of the Department of Homeland Security (DHS). The antiterrorism responsibilities of the DHS are, for the most part, concentrated in seven agencies. Three of these agencies—U.S. Customs and Border Protection (CBP), U.S. Immigration and Customs Enforcement (ICE), and the U.S. Secret Service—were discussed in Chapter 4 (see pages 117–118). The other four agencies also play a crucial role in preventing and responding to terrorist-related activity:

In March 2012, U.S. Coast Guard agents offload 3,500 pounds of confiscated cocaine at Base Miami Beach, Florida. Besides traditional duties such as illegal drug interdiction, in what ways might the Coast Guard contribute to the country's homeland security efforts?

U.S. Coast Guard photo by Petty Officer 2nd Class Nick Ameen

- The *U.S. Coast Guard* defends the nation's coasts, ports, and inland waterways. It also combats illegal drug shipping and enforces immigration law at sea.
- The *Transportation Security Administration (TSA)* is responsible for the safe operation of our airline, rail, bus, and ferry services.
- *U.S. Citizenship and Immigration Services (USCIS)* handles the "paperwork" side of U.S. immigration law. The agency processes the more than 20 million applications made each year by individuals who want to visit the United States or to reside or work in this country.
- *FEMA* retains its position as the lead federal agency in preparing for and responding to disasters such as hurricanes, floods, terrorist attacks, and *infrastructure* concerns. **Infrastructure** includes all of the facilities and systems that provide the daily necessities of modern life, such as electric power, food, water, transportation, and telecommunications.

FEDERAL AGENCIES OUTSIDE THE DHS

The DHS does not directly control all federal efforts to combat terrorism. Since September 11, 2001, the FBI, a branch of the Department of Justice, has been the "lead federal agency" for all terrorism-related matters. Its Strategic Information Operations Center serves as an information clearinghouse for federal, state, and local law enforcement agents who want to share information on terrorism-related matters. Indeed, the agency now lists "protecting the United States from terrorist attack" as its highest organizational priority.[19]

The *intelligence* agencies of the U.S. government also play an important role in antiterrorism efforts. In contrast to a law enforcement agency, which works to solve crimes that have already occurred, an **intelligence agency** works to prevent crimes or other undesirable acts by gathering information, or intelligence, on potential wrongdoers and stopping the illegal conduct in the planning stage. Intelligence operations rely on the following strategies to collect information:

1. *Electronic surveillance* of phone, social media, and e-mail communications, as well as advanced recording devices placed on satellites, aircraft, and land-based technology centers.

Infrastructure The services and facilities that support the day-to-day needs of modern life, such as electricity, food, transportation, and water.

Intelligence Agency An agency that is primarily concerned with gathering information about potential criminal or terrorist events to prevent those acts from taking place.

2. *Human-source collection*, which refers to the recruitment of foreign agents and interviews with people who have particular knowledge about areas of interest.
3. *Open-source collection*, or close attention to "open" data sources such as books, newspapers, radio and television transmissions, and Internet sites.
4. *Intelligence sharing* with friendly foreign intelligence services.
5. *Counterintelligence*, which involves placing undercover agents in a position to gain information from hostile foreign intelligence services.[20]

In particular, two intelligence agencies are integral to American antiterrorism efforts. The first is the **Central Intelligence Agency (CIA),** which is responsible for gathering and analyzing information on foreign governments, corporations, and individuals, and then passing that information on to the upper echelons of our federal government. The second, the **National Security Agency (NSA),** is also in the business of gathering and analyzing information, but it focuses primarily on communications. NSA agents eavesdrop on foreign conversations, whatever form they might take, while at the same time working to ensure that sensitive messages sent by the U.S. government are not subjected to similar scrutiny.

COUNTERTERRORISM CHALLENGES AND STRATEGIES

A government commission that investigated the circumstances leading to the September 11, 2001, terrorist attacks found that the federal government "did not have an effective intelligence collection effort" with regard to terror cases.[21] Over the past decade, the government has expended significant resources to remedy this situation. In 2001, the CIA's Counterterrorism Center had three hundred employees. Today, it has more than two thousand.[22] The FBI is now more likely to investigate security threats than ordinary crimes. Between 2009 and 2011, FBI agents completed nearly 43,000 "assessments" of people or groups to determine any possible ties to terrorism.[23]

A similar shift can be seen in local police departments, for whom "intelligence used to be a dirty word," according to David Carter, a professor of criminal justice at Michigan State University.[24] Today, financial support from the federal government has helped create more than one hundred state and local police intelligence units, with at least one unit in every state.[25] As we saw in Chapter 4, the federal government has established more than seventy *fusion centers* to allow for better cooperation with local police forces in this area. Indeed, intelligence gathering has become crucial in apprehending the "lone wolf" terrorist, as described below.

PREVENTIVE POLICING On February 17, 2012, a Moroccan immigrant named Amine El Khalifi was arrested near the U.S. Capitol Building in Washington, D.C. El Khalifi, who had bragged that he "would be happy killing thirty people," was carrying an automatic weapon and wearing a suicide vest packed with what he thought were explosives.[26] In Chapter 3, we saw that criminal law generally requires intent and action. A person must have both intended to commit a crime and taken some steps toward doing so. In most cases, criminal law also requires that a harm has been done and that the criminal act caused the harm.

According to federal officials, however, no evidence showed that El Khalifi had made any successful contacts with established terrorist groups. The gun El Khalifi was carrying was inoperable, and the explosives were inert. Both had been provided to him by an FBI undercover agent acting as an al Qaeda operative. Indeed, El Khalifi had been under FBI surveillance for more than a year.

No Immediate Threat The case of Amine El Khalifi represents a growing trend in the criminal justice system brought about by the new challenges of fighting terrorism. The

---

Central Intelligence Agency (CIA) The U.S. government agency that is responsible for collecting and coordinating foreign intelligence operations.

National Security Agency (NSA) The intelligence agency that is responsible for protecting U.S. government communications and producing intelligence by monitoring foreign communications.

Learning Objective 2 Explain how American law enforcement agencies have used "preventive policing" to combat terrorism.

goal for many law enforcement agencies is no longer to solve crimes after they have occurred but rather to prevent them from happening in the first place. Even though El Khalifi posed no immediate threat to the public, federal authorities were not willing to take the risk that he might eventually develop into a dangerous terrorist. Although some observers claim that law enforcement officials are exaggerating the threat posed by many of these accused plotters, the government points to a record of successes to justify this new approach. From the beginning of 2009 to February 2012, law enforcement agencies arrested nearly forty lone wolf terrorist suspects similar to El Khalifi.[27]

Informants and Entrapment Because makeshift terrorist cells often need help to procure the weaponry necessary for their schemes, they are natural targets for well-placed informants and undercover agents (both discussed in Chapter 5). With their amateur approach to terrorist activities, these suspects are natural targets for well-placed "insiders." The resulting intelligence reports have been crucial in helping authorities identify potential terrorists. According to the Center on Law and Security at New York University, 62 percent of the federal government's most significant terrorism prosecutions have relied on evidence provided by informants.[28]

These tactics have drawn criticism from some quarters. Amine El Khalifi, critics point out, could never have hatched his plot without the aid of the fake al Qaeda operatives "Hussein," a confidential informer, and "Yusuf," an FBI undercover agent. One observer sarcastically called El Khalifi's efforts another case of "law-enforcement-assisted terrorism."[29] As you learned in Chapter 3, entrapment is a possible defense for criminal behavior when a government agent plants the idea of committing a crime in a defendant who would not have considered it on his or her own. Although the entrapment defense has often been raised in terrorism cases involving informants or undercover agents, it has yet to succeed. In every instance, judges and juries have found that the defendant was predisposed to terrorist behavior without any help from the government.[30]

EMERGENCY PREPAREDNESS AND RESPONSE *Preparedness* is also an integral part of homeland security. The White House defines **preparedness** as the "existence of plans, procedures, policies, training, and equipment necessary at the federal, state, and local level to maximize the ability to prevent, respond to, and recover from major events."[31] The term has come to describe a wide variety of actions taken at different governmental levels to protect a community not only against terrorist attacks but also against natural disasters such as hurricanes, tornadoes, and floods. The Oakland County (Michigan) Emergency Operations Center, for example, combines the contributions of thirty-four different local agencies, each one organized and prepared for a different type of emergency.

A necessary complement to preparedness is *response,* or the actions taken after an incident has occurred. Because the federal government is usually unable to respond rapidly to any single incident, the burden of response initially falls on local emergency personnel such as police officers, firefighters, and emergency medical technicians. These aptly named **first responders** have several important duties, including the following:

Preparedness An umbrella term for the actions taken by governments to prepare for large-scale catastrophic events such as terrorist attacks or environmental disasters.

First Responders Those individuals, such as firefighters, police officers, and emergency medical technicians, who are responsible for the protection and preservation of life and property during the early stages following a disaster.

Members of a hazardous materials team wear protective suits as they respond to an anthrax scare in Centennial, Colorado. Why are these emergency personnel called *first responders*? What role do first responders play in homeland security?

John Moore/Getty Images

- Securing the scene of the incident by maintaining order.
- Rescuing and treating any injured civilians.
- Containing and suppressing fires or other hazardous conditions that have resulted from the incident.
- Retrieving those who have been killed.[32]

First responders show great bravery in carrying out their duties under extremely dangerous circumstances. On September 11, 2001, 343 firefighters and 75 police officers were killed in the line of duty.

BORDER SECURITY People and goods legally enter the United States through checkpoints at airports, seaports, and guarded land stations. At these regulated points of entry, government agents check documents such as passports and *visas* and inspect luggage and cargo to ensure compliance with immigration and trade laws. (A **visa** is a document issued by the U.S. State Department that indicates the conditions under which a holder can enter and travel within the United States.) The task is immense. Close to 90 million foreign visitors arrive at America's more than one hundred international airports each year, with millions more passing through patrol stations along our borders with Mexico and Canada.

Increased Scrutiny One of the hard lessons of the September 11 attacks was that regulation of points of entry does not ensure security. Every one of the nineteen hijackers involved in those attacks entered the United States legally—that is, with a valid visa. They were also able to easily board the airplanes that they used as flying bombs. Consequently, one of the hallmarks of homeland security has been increased scrutiny at points of entry—particularly airports.

The DHS Transportation Security Administration (TSA) has overseen significant changes in the way airports screen passengers, luggage, and cargo. Border personnel, both at home and abroad, have been trained to scrutinize all foreigners entering the United States for "terrorist risk factors." The FBI's Terrorist Screening Center has also compiled a "no fly" list of individuals who are deemed to pose a risk of terrorist activity and therefore are not allowed to board flights leaving or entering the United States.

Unregulated Border Entry Every year hundreds of thousands of non-U.S. citizens, unable to legally obtain visas, enter the country illegally by crossing the large, unregulated stretches of our borders with Mexico and Canada. Securing these border areas has proved problematic, if not impossible, for the various homeland security agencies. As a result, the border areas provide a conduit for illegal drugs, firearms and other contraband, illegal immigrants, and, possibly, terrorists to be smuggled into the country.

The main problem for the U.S. Border Patrol and local law enforcement agents in trying to stem this flow is logistics. The U.S.-Canadian border extends for 3,957 miles (not counting Alaska), and the border with Mexico stretches for 1,954 miles. Much of the borderland consists of uninhabited plains and woodland to the north and desert and scrubland to the south. To compensate, the homeland security presence on the Mexican border has never been greater.

Today, approximately 21,500 Border Patrol agents are monitoring the area, up from 9,000 in 2001. This increase in personnel seems to have acted as a deterrent for those who would otherwise try to enter the United States illegally. In 2011, about 325,000 illegal crossers were apprehended on the Mexican and Canadian borders. A decade earlier, that number was close to 1.6 million.[33] (The recent economic downturn in the United States, which has removed some of the economic incentives for illegal crossing, has probably also affected these figures.)

Visa Official authorization allowing a person to travel to and within the issuing country.

SECURITY VERSUS CIVIL LIBERTIES

Many of the informants who have provided crucial intelligence regarding homegrown terrorists have come from the Muslim American community. Ties between that community and law enforcement became strained in late 2011, however, when national media outlets began reporting on the New York Police Department's Demographics Unit. With the help of the CIA, this secret team of sixteen officers had infiltrated Muslim communities in New York, New Jersey, and Connecticut, gathering information on thousands of American citizens without any proof of wrongdoing.[34]

This strategy caused widespread outrage and a reluctance among those in the affected communities to cooperate with the police.[35] It has also raised the issue of racial profiling, which we first discussed in Chapter 6. Still, polls have found that a relatively high percentage of Americans favor using Muslim identity as a trigger for government surveillance, particularly at the nation's airports.[36] (To learn about a country where such profiling is national policy, see the feature *Comparative Criminal Justice—The Not-So-Friendly Skies* below.)

As we have seen throughout this textbook, the need to balance the rights of society and the rights of the individual is a constant in the criminal justice system. As we will see in this section, nowhere is this challenge more fraught with difficulty than in the struggle against terrorism.

SEARCHES, SURVEILLANCE, AND SECURITY The Fourth Amendment protects against unreasonable searches and seizures. According to the United States Supreme Court, the purpose of this amendment is to "prevent arbitrary and oppressive interference by

> ### "As terrible as 9/11 was, it didn't repeal the Constitution."
> —**Rosemary S. Pooler,**
> U.S. circuit judge

COMPARATIVE CRIMINAL JUSTICE

THE NOT-SO-FRIENDLY SKIES

El Al, the national airline of Israel, has an impressive security record. Despite Israel's near-constant state of conflict with one or more of its neighbors in the Middle East, and the country's status as a favored target for terrorist attacks, no El Al airplane has been hijacked in three decades. The Israeli government credits this success to its profiling strategy, which is based on the principle that it is "essential to focus on a very small percentage of passengers with terrorist intent."

Whereas American security procedures are designed to find weapons, the Israelis focus on finding terrorists. At Ben Gurion International Airport, outside Tel Aviv, travelers are stopped several times before they reach their gate. During these encounters, airport security personnel ask a series of questions and evaluate the security risk of each passenger. In doing so, screening agents take into account a traveler's country of origin and skin color. Most Jewish Israeli citizens are waived through this process rather quickly. Arab Israelis and other non-Jewish passengers, however, are generally taken aside for lengthy questioning, as well as a thorough luggage check and physical examination.

Saleh Yaaqubi, an Arab Israeli student, called the security check at Ben Gurion "the most offensive and humiliating experience I have ever had." Americans, too, are often taken aback by the experience. Writer Matthew Yglesias noted that the one African American traveling with his group was singled out for intense scrutiny, and he criticized the Ben Gurion staff for "the most unpleasant encounter I've had with airport security in a decade." Israeli terrorism experts dismiss such complaints as shortsighted. "How many blonde, blue-eyed ladies have brought down planes in the last twenty years?" asked one security consultant. "They were all fanatic Muslims. So, if you are a Muslim, we have to find out if you are a fanatic or not."

FOR CRITICAL ANALYSIS Would you be in favor of instituting Israeli screening methods in American airports? Why or why not?

enforcement officials with the privacy and personal security of individuals."[37] In practice, this has meant that a "neutral and detached" judge must, in most circumstances, decide whether a search or surveillance of a suspect's person or property is warranted. Law enforcement has often chafed against these restrictions, and this tension has only been exacerbated by the demands of counterterrorism search and surveillance strategies.

Learning Objective **3** Explain how the Patriot Act has made it easier for federal agents to conduct searches during terrorism investigations.

The Patriot Act and Searches In a 2011 poll, 34 percent of those questioned about the Patriot Act felt that the law "goes too far and poses a threat to civil liberties," while 42 percent considered it a "necessary tool that helps the government fight terrorism."[38] The legislation has certainly made it easier for law enforcement agents to conduct searches. For example, previously, to search a suspect's apartment and examine the contents of his or her computer, agents needed a court order based on probable cause that a crime had taken place or was about to take place. The Patriot Act amends the law to allow the FBI or other federal agencies to obtain warrants for "terrorism" investigations, "chemical weapons" investigations, or "computer fraud and abuse" investigations as long as agents can prove that such actions have a "significant purpose."[39] In other words, no proof of criminal activity need be provided.

The Patriot Act and Surveillance The Patriot Act gives intelligence agents more leeway when conducting surveillance. The Foreign Intelligence Surveillance Act of 1978 (FISA) allowed for surveillance of a suspect without a warrant as long as the "primary purpose" of the surveillance was to investigate foreign spying and not to engage in criminal law enforcement.[40] The Patriot Act amends FISA to allow for searches and surveillance if a "significant purpose" of the investigation is intelligence gathering or any other type of antiterrorist activity.[41] The statute also provides federal agents with "roving surveillance authority," allowing them to continue monitoring a terrorist suspect on the strength of the original warrant even if the suspect moves to another jurisdiction.[42]

Furthermore, the Patriot Act makes it much easier for law enforcement agents to avoid the notification requirements of search warrants. This means that a person whose home has been the target of a search and whose voice mails or computer records have been seized may not be informed of these activities until weeks after they have taken place.[43]

Congress and Wiretapping Following a series of controversies concerning the ability of the National Security Agency (NSA) to monitor telephone and e-mail communications of terrorism suspects, several years ago Congress passed an amended version of FISA.[44] The new law allows the NSA to wiretap for seven days, without a court order, any person "reasonably believed" to be outside the United States, if necessary to protect national security. It also permits the wiretapping of Americans for seven days without a court order, if the attorney general has probable cause to believe that the target is linked to terrorism. Supporters of the amendments claim that the average American has nothing to fear from the law "unless you have al Qaeda on your speed dial." Critics, however, see it as a further erosion of Fourth Amendment protections in the name of homeland security.[45]

DUE PROCESS AND INDEFINITE DETENTION The Fifth Amendment provides that no *person* shall be deprived of life, liberty, or property without due process of law. (See pages 89–91 for a review of due process.) More than a century ago, the United States Supreme Court ruled that, because the amendment uses the word *person* and not *citizen,* due process protections extend to non-U.S. citizens under the jurisdiction of the U.S. government.[46] Immediately after the September 11, 2001, attacks, however, the Office of the U.S. Attorney

**Social Media and CJ
The Department of
Homeland Security**
operates a Facebook page that provides up-to-date information on its many organizations and operations. To access this Web site, visit the *Criminal Justice CourseMate* at **cengagebrain.com** and select the *Web Links* for this chapter.

General set forth regulations that allowed homeland security officials to detain non-U.S. citizens of "special interest" without first charging them with any crime. The new rules also allowed for the indefinite detention of such suspects in the event of "emergency or other extraordinary circumstance."[47]

Detention at GTMO More than eight hundred of these "enemy combatants" were eventually sent to a U.S. military detention center at the U.S. Naval Base in Guantánamo Bay, Cuba (GTMO). At the time, American officials insisted that because these al Qaeda and Taliban operatives had been captured during military operations, they could be held indefinitely without being charged with any wrongdoing.[48] The detainees were denied access to legal representation or family members and were subjected to harsh interrogation tactics such as waterboarding, sleep and food deprivation, physical stress positions, and isolation.[49] Because of the conditions at GTMO, the U.S. government came under a great deal of international criticism. In particular, Arab and Muslim governments have condemned GTMO, as have officials from those non-Muslim nations, such as Australia and Great Britain, whose citizens were being held at the detention center.

Detainees in orange jumpsuits sit in a holding area at the U.S. Naval Base in Guantánamo Bay, Cuba. Do you think non-U.S. citizens who are in the custody of the U.S. military should be protected by our Constitution? Why or why not?
Reuters NewMedia, Inc./Corbis

As of January 2012, 171 detainees remained incarcerated at GMTO, many of the others having been returned to their home countries. At least fifty of the remaining prisoners are considered too dangerous for release. Federal officials will review their status periodically, but in theory they could be held indefinitely.[50] At present, no alternative site for these men has been identified. Consequently, despite continuing criticism of GTMO, the facility appears likely to remain open and operational for the foreseeable future.

Military Justice A large number of GTMO detainees—about 120—will be given the chance to prove their innocence in regard to terrorist charges. Initially, the Obama administration favored adjudicating these cases in civilian courts on U.S. soil, where the detainees would have enjoyed all of the rights available to any criminal defendant. However, following negative reaction to the criminal trial of Ahmed Khalfan Ghailani (described on page 230), federal authorities decided that **military tribunals** would be the primary means for trying GTMO detainees. In May 2012, for instance, a military tribunal at GTMO commenced proceedings against Khalid Sheikh Mohammed, the "mastermind" behind the September 11, 2001, attacks, and four of his colleagues.

Military Tribunal A court that is operated by the military rather than the criminal justice system and is presided over by military officers rather than judges.

Such tribunals, operating out of a $12 million, high-tech courtroom located at the Guantánamo Bay facilities, offer a more limited set of protections than do civilian criminal courts. In a tribunal, the accused does not have the right to a trial by jury, as guaranteed by the Sixth Amendment. Instead, a panel of at least five military commissioners acts in place of the judge and jury and decides questions of both fact and law. Only two-thirds of the panel members need to agree for a conviction, in contrast to the unanimous jury required by criminal trials. Furthermore, evidence that would be inadmissible in criminal court, such as some forms of hearsay testimony (pages 238–239) and "fruit of the poisoned tree" from unreasonable searches and seizures (page 163), is allowed before these tribunals.[51]

CYBER CRIME

The Craigslist advertisement—offering $300 a week and a free trailer to "watch over a 688-acre patch of hilly farmland and feed a few cows"—acted like a beacon to the unemployed and the desperate. The ad drew more than one hundred responses, and four men traveled to the property in rural southern Ohio for a final "interview." Only one of them survived, a man who alerted local law enforcement after a close escape on November 6, 2011. The bodies of the three other men were found in shallow graves, leaving authorities perplexed as to the motives of the two suspects in the crime, Richard J. Beasley and high school student Brogan Rafferty.[52]

Using false names, Beasley and Rafferty were allegedly able to attract applicants from across the United States (one of the victims was from Virginia, another from South Carolina) for a job that did not exist on land they did not own. Access and anonymity are two of the hallmarks of Internet technology, which has transformed daily life in the twenty-first century. Nearly three-fourths of all American households now own a computer, and the proliferation of handheld Internet devices has made it possible to be online at almost any time or in any "place." Furthermore, nearly every business in today's economy relies on computers to conduct its daily affairs and to provide consumers with easy access to its products and services. In short, the Internet has become a place where large numbers of people interact socially and commercially. As in any such environment, wrongdoing has an opportunity to flourish.

Computer Crime Any wrongful act that is directed against computers and computer parts or that involves wrongful use or abuse of computers or software.

COMPUTER CRIME AND THE INTERNET

The U.S. Department of Justice broadly defines **computer crime** as "any violation of criminal law that involves a knowledge of computer technology for [its] perpetration, investigation, or prosecution."[53] More specifically, computer crimes can be divided into three categories, according to the computer's role in the particular criminal act:[54]

1. The computer is the *object* of a crime, such as when the computer itself or its software is stolen.
2. The computer is the *subject* of a crime, just as a house is the subject of a burglary. This type of computer crime occurs, for example, when someone "breaks into" a computer to steal personal information such as a credit-card number.

"You know, you can do this just as easily online."

P.C. Vey/Conde Nast Publications/www.cartoonbank.com

3. The computer is the *instrument* of a crime, as was the case with the alleged plot of Richard J. Beasley and Brogan Rafferty in Ohio.

In this chapter, we will be using a broader term, **cyber crime,** to describe any criminal activity occurring via a computer in the virtual community of the Internet. It is very difficult, if not impossible, to determine how much cyber crime actually takes place. Often, people never know that they have been the victims of this type of criminal activity. Furthermore, businesses sometimes fail to report such crimes for fear of losing customer confidence. Nonetheless, in 2011, the Internet Crime Complaint Center (IC3), operated as a partnership between the FBI and the National White Collar Crime Center, received about 315,000 complaints.[55] According to the Norton Cybercrime Report, nearly 70 percent of all adults who use the Internet have been victimized by cyber crime, with annual global losses exceeding $380 billion.[56]

CYBER CRIMES AGAINST PERSONS AND PROPERTY

Most cyber crimes are not "new" crimes. Rather, they are existing crimes in which the Internet is the instrument of wrongdoing. In the Ohio Craigslist case described above, for example, the suspects were charged with a variety of crimes ranging from murder to kidnapping to wire fraud, the same charges that would have been filed if they had placed their bogus advertisements in a newspaper.

The challenge for law enforcement is to apply traditional laws, which were designed to protect persons from physical harm or to safeguard their physical property, to crimes committed in cyberspace. This challenge is made all the greater by two aspects of the Internet that may aid the perpetrators of cyber crimes—the anonymity it provides and the ease with which large amounts of information may be transferred quickly. In the pages that follow, we look at several types of activity that constitute "updated" crimes against persons and property: online consumer fraud, cyber theft, and cyberstalking.

CYBER CONSUMER FRAUD The expanding world of e-commerce has created many benefits for consumers. It has also led to some challenging problems, including fraud conducted via the Internet. In general, fraud is any misrepresentation knowingly made with the intention of deceiving another person. Furthermore, the victim must reasonably rely on the fraudulent information to her or his detriment. **Cyber fraud,** then, is fraud committed over the Internet. Scams that were once conducted solely by mail or phone can now be found online, and new technology has led to increasingly more creative ways to commit fraud. Online dating scams, for example, have increased dramatically in recent years, with fraudsters creating fake profiles to deceive unwitting romantic partners. In one case, a fictitious American solider in Iraq convinced his online "sweetheart" that he had been kidnapped and needed $250,000 from her to buy his freedom.

As you can see in Figure 14.2 alongside, two widely reported forms of cyber crime are *advance fee fraud* and *online auction fraud.* In the simplest form of advance fee fraud, consumers order and pay for items that are never delivered. Online auction fraud is also fairly straightforward. A person puts up an item for auction, on either a legitimate or a fake auction site, and then refuses to send the product after receiving payment. In 2012, for example, the FBI uncovered a scheme in which an Oregon couple took photos of items on store shelves, offered them for auction on the Internet, and collected more than $300,000

Cyber Crime A crime that occurs online, in the virtual community of the Internet, as opposed to taking place in the physical world.

Cyber Fraud Any misrepresentation knowingly made over the Internet with the intention of deceiving another and on which a reasonable person would and does rely to his or her detriment.

FIGURE 14.2 Criminal Activities Online

The list below shows the five most common types of cyber crime reported to the Internet Crime Complaint Center in 2011.

1. FBI-related scams, where the offender poses as an FBI agent to defraud victims.
2. Identify theft, described on page 410.
3. Advance fee fraud, described on this page.
4. Online auction fraud, described on this page.
5. Overpayment fraud, in which the victim is notified of non-existent overpayments and asked to return the funds.

Source: Internet Crime Complaint Center, *IC3 2011 Internet Crime Report* (Glen Allen, VA: National White Collar Crime Center, 2012), 10.

from unsuspecting bidders. As a variation, the wrongdoer may send the purchaser a forgery or an item that is worth less than the one offered in the auction.

CYBER THEFT In cyberspace, thieves are not subject to the physical limitations of the "real" world. A thief can steal data stored in a networked computer with network access from anywhere on the globe. Only the speed of the connection and the thief's computer equipment limit the quantity of data that can be stolen.

Identity Theft This freedom from physical limitations has led to a marked increase in **identity theft,** which occurs when the wrongdoer steals a form of identification—such as a name, date of birth, or Social Security number—and uses the information to access the victim's financial resources. According to the federal government, about 7 percent of American households have at least one member who has been the victim of identity theft.[57]

This crime existed to a certain extent before the widespread use of the Internet. Thieves would "steal" calling-card numbers by watching people using public telephones, or they would rifle through garbage to find bank account or credit-card numbers. The identity thief would then use the calling-card or credit-card number or withdraw funds from the victim's account until the theft was discovered.

The Internet has provided even easier access to personal data. Frequent Web surfers surrender a wealth of information about themselves without knowing it. Many Web sites use "cookies" to collect data on those who visit their sites. The data can include the areas of the site the user visits and the links the user clicks on. Furthermore, Web browsers often store information such as the consumer's name and e-mail address. Finally, every time a purchase is made online, the item is linked to the purchaser's name, allowing Web retailers to amass a database of who is buying what.

Phishing A distinct form of identity theft known as **phishing** has added a different wrinkle to the identity theft. In a phishing attack, the perpetrators "fish" for financial data and passwords from consumers by posing as a legitimate business such as a bank or credit-card company. The "phisher" sends an e-mail asking the recipient to "update" or "confirm" vital information, often with the threat that an account or some other service will be discontinued if the information is not provided. Once the unsuspecting target enters the information, the phisher can use it to masquerade as the person or to drain his or her bank or credit account. Over the past several years, dozens of companies, including Amazon.com, AT&T, and Zappos.com, have been forced to warn consumers that fraudulent e-mails asking for personal and financial information had been sent in the companies' names.

Phishing scams have also spread to other areas, such as text messaging and social-networking sites. Nearly 13 percent of all phishing, for example, takes place using Facebook alerts.[58] A new form of this fraud, called spear phishing, is much more difficult to detect because the messages seem to have come from co-workers, friends, or family workers. "It's a really nasty tactic because it's so personalized," explains security expert Bruce Schneier. "It's an e-mail from your mother saying she needs your Social Security number for the will she's doing."[59]

CYBER AGGRESSION AND THE NEW MEDIA The growing use of mobile devices such as smartphones and tablets has added another outlet for online criminal activity. About 10 percent of cyber crime now targets such devices.[60] In particular, widespread smartphone use seems to have exacerbated cyberbullying, which we discussed in the context of school crime in the previous chapter (see page 376). According to a recent survey, American teen-

Identity Theft The theft of personal information, such as a person's name, driver's license number, or Social Security number.

Phishing Sending an unsolicited e-mail that falsely claims to be from a legitimate organization in an attempt to acquire sensitive information such as passwords or credit-card details from the recipient.

agers who consider themselves "heavy users" of their cell phones are much more likely to experience cyberbullying than those who consider themselves "normal users" of the devices.[61]

Cyberstalking In 2009, the U.S. Department of Justice released a landmark study that shed light on the high incidence of stalking in the United States. Defined as a "credible threat" that puts a person in reasonable fear for her or his safety or the safety of the person's immediate family, stalking, according to the study, affects approximately 3.4 million Americans each year.[62] About one in four of these victims experiences a form of **cyberstalking,** in which the perpetrator uses e-mail, social media, text messages, or some other form of electronic communication to carry out his or her harassment.[63]

Session Hijacking Another growing threat to the privacy of Internet users is *session hijacking,* in which an outside party gains unauthorized access to Web activity. In most instances, the goal of session hacking is to steal code names and passwords for sensitive Web sites in order to gain access to bank accounts or Facebook pages, for example.

In some instances, though, this kind of privacy invasion can be a very effective form of cyber aggression. Following a dispute with his neighbors, for example, Barry Ardolf of Blaine, Minnesota, gained illegal access to their Wi-Fi (wireless) Internet server and drastically misrepresented them on the Internet. Over the course of two years, among other things, Ardolf created a Myspace page covered with child pornography and threatened the vice president of the United States using his neighbors' identities. In 2011, Ardolf was arrested and sentenced to eighteen years in prison for his actions. (For the most part, this form of identity theft can be avoided by password protecting private Wi-Fi networks and avoiding public ones.)

CYBER CRIMES IN THE BUSINESS WORLD

Just as cyberspace can be a dangerous place for consumers, it presents a number of hazards for businesses that wish to offer their services on the Internet. The same circumstances that enable companies to reach a wide number of consumers also leave them vulnerable to cyber crime. For example, in 2011, Rogelio Hackett, Jr., of Lithonia, Georgia, pleaded guilty to fraud and identity theft for stealing more than 675,000 credit-card accounts from online businesses. Hackett would sell these accounts for as little as $20 to third parties, who used them to make fraudulent charges of more than $36 million.

HACKERS Rogelio Hackett, Jr., is a particular type of cyber criminal known as a *hacker.* (So is Jeremy Hammond, whose misdeeds were described in the opening of this chapter.) **Hackers** are people who use one computer to illegally access another. The danger posed by hackers has increased significantly because of **botnets,** or networks of computers that have been appropriated by hackers without the knowledge of their owners. A hacker will secretly install a program on thousands, if not millions, of personal computer "robots," or "bots," that allows her or him to forward transmissions to an even larger number of systems. The program attaches itself to the host computer when someone operating the computer opens a fraudulent e-mail.

The Zeus Trojan, or Zbot, for example, employs a technique called *keystroke logging* to embed itself in a victim's computer and then record user names and passwords. Using

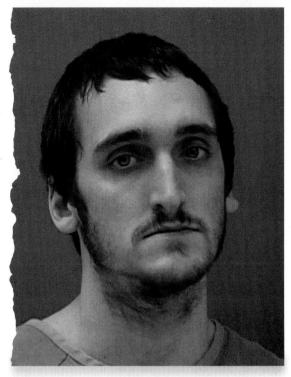

In January 2012, Patrick Macchione was sentenced to four years in prison for cyberstalking fellow University of Central Florida student Kristen Pratt. Macchione sent death threats to Pratt using Twitter, posted lewd messages to her Facebook account, and directed nearly thirty threatening videos at her on YouTube. Do you agree that cyberstalking can cause just as much "reasonable fear" in a victim as physical stalking? Why or why not?

Photo Courtesy of Seminole County Sheriff's Office

Cyberstalking The crime of stalking, committed in cyberspace through the use of e-mail, text messages, or another form of electronic communication.

Hacker A person who uses one computer to break into another.

Botnet A network of computers that have been appropriated without the knowledge of their owners and used to spread harmful programs via the Internet; short for *robot network.*

Learning
Objective **4** Describe the
three following
forms of
malware:
(a) botnets,
(b) worms, and
(c) viruses.

this "banking Trojan," cyberthieves stole $4 million from American bank accounts in 2010.[64] Computer security experts also worry that fake apps containing botnets will find their way onto the increasingly popular smartphones and tablet computers, allowing hackers to harvest personal information from those devices.

MALWARE Programs that create botnets are one of the latest forms of *malware*, a term that refers to any program that is harmful to a computer or, by extension, a computer user. A **worm,** for example, is a software program that is capable of reproducing itself as it spreads from one computer to the next. A **virus,** another form of malware, is also able to reproduce itself, but it must be attached to an "infested" host file to travel from one computer network to another. Worms and viruses can be programmed to perform a number of functions, such as prompting host computers to continually "crash" and reboot, or otherwise infect the system.

Over the past few years, malware has increasingly been used to target specific companies or organizations. In 2011, for example, hackers used malware to carry out a targeted attack on Sony's PlayStation network, thus gaining access to personal information and, possibly, the credit-card numbers of 77 million online gamers worldwide. Sony, a Japanese company, was forced to shut down the network for twenty-four days, costing the company $170 million. The Ponemon Institute, a private research organization, estimates that individual American businesses each lose an average of $5.9 million a year because of malware and other cyber crime.[65]

THE SPREAD OF SPAM Businesses and individuals alike are targets of **spam,** or unsolicited "junk e-mails" that flood virtual mailboxes with advertisements, solicitations, and other messages. Considered relatively harmless in the early days of the Internet, by 2011 nearly 150 billion spam messages were being sent each day, accounting for about 75 percent of all e-mails. Far from being harmless, the unwanted files can wreak havoc with computer systems. Bot networks, described earlier, are responsible for about 90 percent of spam e-mail.[66]

Spam is also the preferred method of phishing, the identity theft scam described earlier. By sending millions or even billions of these fraudulent e-mails, phishers need only entice a few users to "take the bait" to ensure a successful and lucrative operation. "Social" spam is becoming more common on social-networking sites such as Facebook. This form of hacking relies on fake messages, such as "hey, check out this free iPad," that appear to be from a friend rather than an unknown company. The message includes a link to download a coupon for the free product. In reality, however, by clicking on the link, the unsuspecting user may have allowed malware to infect his or her computer.[67]

Worm A computer program that can automatically replicate itself over a network such as the Internet and interfere with the normal use of a computer. A worm does not need to be attached to an existing file to move from one network to another.

Virus A computer program that can replicate itself over a network such as the Internet and interfere with the normal use of a computer. A virus cannot exist as a separate entity and must attach itself to another program to move through a network.

Spam Bulk e-mails, particularly of commercial advertising, sent in large quantities without the consent of the recipient.

CJ&TECHNOLOGY

Hacking Cars

There are more than a quarter billion automobiles on the roads of the United States, and many of them could accurately be described as computers on wheels. The "electronic brains" in cars control everything from air bags to stereos to brake systems. Like any other computer, these computers can be hacked. Several years ago, for example, a team of researchers from Rutgers University and the University of South Carolina were able to commandeer a car's wireless tire pressure-monitoring system while that car was traveling at sixty miles per hour.

Another academic experiment, conducted in 2011, showed that high-tech car thieves could cause an automobile to wirelessly divulge its GPS coordinates and vehicle identification number. Then, using those data, the crooks could issue a series of wireless orders "telling" the vehicle to unlock its doors and start its engines. As automobiles and other vehicles become more reliant on computers to function, say experts, the likelihood of "car hacking" becomes more of a real-world threat.

THINKING ABOUT HACKING CARS: Using your imagination, describe how the possibility of hacking car computers could be a threat to homeland security.

PIRATING INTELLECTUAL PROPERTY ONLINE Most people think of wealth in terms of houses, land, cars, stocks, and bonds. Wealth, however, also includes **intellectual property,** which consists of the products that result from intellectual, creative processes. The government provides various forms of protection for intellectual property, such as copyrights and patents. These protections ensure that a person who writes a book or a song or who creates a software program is financially rewarded if that product is sold in the marketplace.

Intellectual property such as books, films, music, and software is vulnerable to "piracy"—the unauthorized copying and use of the property. In the past, copying intellectual products was time consuming, and the quality of the pirated copies was clearly inferior. In today's online world, however, things have changed. Simply clicking a mouse can now reproduce millions of unauthorized copies, and pirated duplicates of copyrighted works obtained via the Internet are often exactly the same as the original, or close to it. The Business Software Alliance estimates that 29 percent of all business software is pirated, costing software makers more than $59 billion in 2010.[68]

Intellectual Property Property resulting from intellectual, creative processes.

CYBER CRIMES AGAINST THE COMMUNITY

One of the greatest challenges cyberspace presents for law enforcement is how to enforce laws governing activities that are prohibited under certain circumstances but are not always illegal. Such laws generally reflect the will of the community, which recognizes behavior as acceptable under some circumstances and unacceptable under others. Thus, while it is legal in many areas to sell a pornographic video to a fifty-year-old, it is never legal to sell the same item to a fifteen-year-old. Similarly, placing a bet on a football game with a bookmaker in Las Vegas, Nevada, is legal, but doing the same thing with a bookmaker in Cleveland, Ohio, is not. Of course, in cyberspace it is often impossible to know whether the customer buying porn is age fifty or fifteen, or if the person placing the bet is in Las Vegas or Cleveland.

Consequently, the Internet has been a boon to both the pornography and the gambling industries. Twelve percent of all Web sites have pornographic content, and these sites generate $4.2 billion in revenue a year.[69] Although no general figures are available, the Internet has undoubtedly also greatly aided those who illegally produce and sell material depicting sexually explicit conduct involving a child—child pornography. Furthermore, even though all states have statutes that regulate gambling—defined as any scheme that

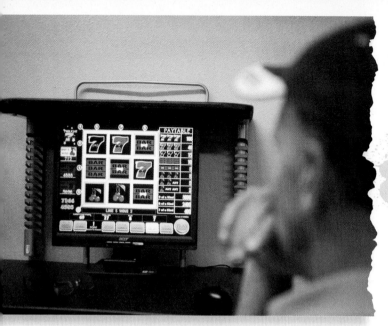

In 2012 several states, including California and Texas, considered legalizing many forms of Internet gambling in order to collect taxes on the activity. What would be the benefits and drawbacks if all states legalized online poker, slots (as shown here), and other Internet games of chance?

Cassi Alexandra/New York Times/Redux Pictures

involves the distribution of property by chance—the United States is the largest online betting market in the world, with some $6 billion wagered illegally each year.[70]

SELFASSESSMENT

Fill in the blanks and check your answers on page 424.

One common cyber crime is online _____ fraud, which occurs when a consumer pays for a product that is not delivered. Web thieves have opportunities to practice _____ theft because of the large amount of personal financial information that is stored on the Internet. A _____ is someone who gains illegal access to one computer using another computer. These wrongdoers sometimes use _____, or networks of hijacked computers, to carry out various improper online activities, including the illegal spread of junk e-mails known as _____.

THE CRIMINALIZATION OF IMMIGRATION LAW

Given that Hispanics make up the majority of both legal and illegal immigrants in the United States, this demographic has received a great deal of attention when it comes to immigration law topics. As we noted in Chapter 11, Hispanics are the fastest growing group among inmates in federal prisons, mostly as a result of immigration offenses. On the state level, as we saw in Chapter 6, efforts to police illegal immigrants have led to debate, outrage, and charges of racial profiling.

At the outset, it is important to understand two crucial aspects of immigration law:

1. It is a *civil* regulatory system. Violations of immigration law are civil infractions, not criminal infractions. America's criminal justice and immigration systems are separate entities.
2. The U.S. Constitution gives the power to admit, exclude, or expel non-U.S. citizens to the *federal* government, not the state governments.

Historically, then, immigration law has generally been considered a civil and federal matter. In recent decades, however, a process labeled "crimmigration" by some observers has drastically changed the immigration law landscape. According to its critics, this process has resulted in a hybrid system in which non-U.S. citizen civil law violators are treated as criminals while state and local law enforcement officers increasingly take on immigration law enforcement responsibilities.[71] For supporters of crimmigration measures, such developments are not only welcome but also long overdue.

IMMIGRATION LAW BASICS

Fundamentally, immigration law acts as a screening process. It determines which non-U.S. citizens may come into this country, how long they can stay, and when they must leave. People violate immigration law in two ways: by entering the United States without proper authorization from the federal government or by staying in the country after that authorization becomes invalid.

VISA BASICS An **alien** is someone who is not a citizen of the country in which she or he is located. As we saw on page 404, proper authorization for an alien to enter the United States usually comes in the form of a *visa.* The most common types of visas allow aliens to visit this country for purposes of employment, tourism, education, or medical treatment. Such visas are *temporary* and allow only a limited stay in the United States. When a visa expires, the non-U.S. citizen must either renew it or leave the country immediately.

Nontemporary visas are also available to certain foreign citizens who want to live in the United States on a permanent basis. Most of those who succeed in obtaining a nontemporary visa—known as a **green card** even though the document itself is no longer green—do so with the help of a U.S. citizen family member or an American employer. Green card holders, or **permanent residents,** enjoy many of the same rights as U.S. citizens to live and work in this country. Permanent residents are still aliens, however, and must carry their green cards with them at all times.[72] Furthermore, they are subject to *removal* from the United States if they violate the terms of their visas.

REMOVAL BASICS As we noted earlier in the chapter, hundreds of thousands of non-U.S. citizens try to enter the United States each year without first obtaining a visa, mostly by crossing the U.S. border with Mexico. By definition, those who succeed are inadmissible (unauthorized) and can be removed by American immigration authorities at any time. **Removal** is a legal proceeding in which the U.S. government formally declares that a legal alien or an unauthorized alien has violated immigration law and therefore does not enjoy the right to stay in the United States. Generally, removal results in the alien's being returned to his or her home country.

The mere presence of an unauthorized alien on U.S. soil, if detected by immigration authorities, will almost always lead to his or her removal. In contrast, a permanent resident must have violated immigration law in a specific way to become eligible for deportation, another form of removal. Examples of such violations include lying to a federal immigration agent or encouraging another alien to enter the United States illegally. Criminal convictions also put permanent residents in danger of being removed.[73] Indeed, of the nearly 400,000 aliens removed by ICE in 2011, about 55 percent had criminal convictions.[74] (See Figure 14.3 below for a breakdown of those criminal convictions.) Keep in mind that removal proceedings are separate from the criminal court proceedings you have been studying in this textbook. When an alien faces removal, she or he is involved in a civil process with its own courtrooms, judges, and opportunities for appeal.

Learning Objective 6 Explain the difference between a temporary visa and a green card.

Alien A person who is not a citizen of the country in which he or she is found and therefore does not enjoy the same rights as a citizen of that country.

Green Card A document—no longer green—that indicates the holder's status as a lawful permanent resident of the United States.

Permanent Resident An alien who has been granted permission by the U.S. government to live and work in the United States on a permanent basis.

Removal The process used by the federal government to expel an alien from the United States.

FIGURE 14.3 Removal of Criminal Immigrants

As this figure shows, immigrants removed from the United States because of prior criminal convictions in 2011 were most likely to have been involved with drug- or alcohol-related wrongdoing.

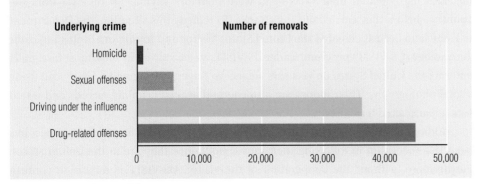

Source: Immigration and Customs Enforcement.

CAREERS IN CJ

PAUL MORRIS
CUSTOMS AND BORDER PROTECTION AGENT

The most memorable day of my career was, without a doubt, September 11, 2001. That morning, as I watched the fall of the Twin Towers, I knew that things were going to be different. Personally, the attacks left me with a resolve to ensure, to the maximum extent possible, that nothing similar ever happens again. Professionally, that day marked a sea charge with respect to how the federal border agencies viewed border security. Ever since, our antiterrorism mission has been elevated above our other responsibilities, such as controlling illegal immigration, protecting our agricultural interests, and stopping the flow of illegal narcotics into this country.

www.dhs.gov

To be sure, as each of these tasks is crucially important, the extra burdens of antiterrorism pose a significant challenge. With the volume of vehicles, cargo, and persons crossing our borders, there can be no guarantees that a potential terrorist or weapon of mass destruction cannot slip across the border. Nevertheless, with advanced identification technology, increased personnel, and a more efficient infrastructure, I am confident that the possibility of such a breach is low.

Social Media Career Tip

Consider setting up personal and career-oriented Facebook pages or Twitter accounts and keeping your posts on each separated. Remember, though, that just because material is on your "personal" page or account, it still may be seen by others outside your network. **f** **Linked** **in**

FAST FACTS

CUSTOMS AND BORDER PROTECTION AGENT, JOB DESCRIPTION:

- Make sure that laws are observed when goods or people enter the U.S. Work at ports of entry and all along the border to prevent smuggling and the entrance of unauthorized immigrants.

WHAT KIND OF TRAINING IS REQUIRED?

- Be under age 40, be a U.S. citizen and resident of the United States, and possess a valid state driver's license.
- Be fluent in Spanish or be able to learn the Spanish language.

ANNUAL SALARY RANGE?

- $36,600 – $46,500

ILLEGAL PRESENCE As noted earlier, the September 11 plot exposed, among other homeland security failures, several weaknesses in America's immigration system. One such shortcoming was an inability to track foreigners who failed to conform to the terms of their visas and were therefore illegally present in the United States. Five of the 9/11 hijackers had violated their visas—and were therefore eligible for removal from the country—before they carried out the attacks. To remedy this situation, the Department of Homeland Security created the United States Visitor and Immigrant Status Indicator Technology (US-VISIT) program. Under US-VISIT, which started in 2004, most foreigners entering the United States on visas are subject to fingerprinting and a facial scan using digital photography. Their names are also checked against criminal records and watch lists for suspected terrorists.

Although the program has been effective in recording the entry of foreigners, it has been less successful in following their movements once they are in the United States. Furthermore, without the cooperation of the visitor, US-VISIT is unable to confirm when, or if, she or he has left the country. As a result, about 200,000 non-U.S. citizens intentionally overstay their visas each year.[75] Amine El Khalifi, whose foiled plot to attack the U.S. Capitol Building in Washington, D.C., was discussed earlier in the chapter, had overstayed his visa by twelve years at the time of his arrest.

ENFORCING IMMIGRATION LAW

About 11.2 million unauthorized aliens are living in the United States, according to research conducted by the nonpartisan Pew Hispanic Center.[76] The vast majority of these aliens are law-abiding individuals who have come to this country for no other reason than to make a better life for themselves and their families. Nevertheless, some aliens—both legal and unauthorized—do commit crimes, and American law enforcement has developed strategies to combat this criminal behavior. Increasingly, these strategies have focused on a particular vulnerability of criminal unauthorized aliens: their immigrant status.

OPERATION COMMUNITY SHIELD In matters of criminal justice, the U.S. Constitution does not differentiate on the basis of citizenship. Before, during, and after a criminal trial, both U.S. citizens and non-U.S. citizens are protected by the Fourth, Fifth, and Sixth Amendments.[77] This "equality principle" does not apply to the enforcement of immigration law, however. For example, an ICE agent can arrest a person for violating immigration law even if no probable cause exists. The agent needs to have only an "articulable," or explainable, suspicion of a violation for the arrest to be valid.[78] Immigration law violators also have no right to receive the *Miranda* warning before custodial interrogations and have no right to an attorney when appearing before an immigration judge.[79]

Detainer A document that gives U.S. Immigration and Customs Enforcement custody of an immigration law violator following the disposition of that person's case by the criminal justice system.

As we have discussed, the probable cause requirement places significant restrictions on law enforcement's ability to arrest suspects (see pages 161–163). Facing no such restraints when it comes to immigration law, federal agents can prove useful partners for their counterparts in local law enforcement. The benefits of such a partnership are evident in Operation Community Shield, launched in 2005 by ICE to "target violent transnational street gangs" by arresting and removing alien gang members.[80] The mechanics of Operation Community Shield are fairly simple. First, local police officers identify street gang members who are also in the country illegally. Then, ICE agents use immigration law to remove these gang members, a process that, as we have noted, is much quicker and easier than criminal prosecution.

Overall, in its first five years, Operation Community Shield resulted in the arrest of more than 17,500 gang members.[81] Although about 70 percent of these aliens were ultimately removed because of immigration law violations,[82] a significant number of them had violent criminal histories, as well.

In March 2011, ICE agents and local law enforcement officers teamed up as part of Project Southern Tempest. The operation resulted in the arrests of more than 400 non-U.S. citizen gang members throughout the nation. What advantages do ICE agents have when apprehending gang members who are in the country illegally?

Belmarie Campos/Senior Forensic Photographer/Medical Examiner Dept./Miami-Dade County/ICE

SECURE COMMUNITIES The most ambitious cooperative effort between the federal government and state and local law enforcement is the Secure Communities initiative. Under this program, started in 2008, information on every suspect arrested by state and local police officers is transmitted electronically to the Department of Homeland Security during the booking process. If this instant background check shows that the suspect has a history of criminal or immigration law violations that makes him or her eligible for removal, ICE will issue a **detainer.** This document allows ICE to take custody of

the suspect at the conclusion of his or her contact with the criminal justice system, usually after the suspect has been released by police or has completed a jail or prison sentence. As of April 2012, nearly 2,600 state and local law enforcement agencies had access to Secure Communities software, and the program had resulted in the removal of about 130,00 non-U.S. citizens.[83]

SELFASSESSMENT

Fill in the blanks and check your answers on page 424.

Immigration violations are a matter of _____, rather than criminal, law, and such violations have traditionally come under the jurisdiction of the _____ government, not the states. When the holder of a green card, also known as a _____ resident, violates immigration law, then he or she is subject to _____.

WHITE-COLLAR CRIME

> "My morals were for sale."
>
> —**Justin Paperny,**
> who served eighteen months in prison for misleading investment clients (2010)

A woman in Huntsville, Alabama, squanders $60,000 in student loans on house bills and "entertainment." The owners of the Glory Pharmacy in Hernando County, Florida, knowingly accept 1,400 fake prescriptions for the painkiller oxycodone. A New Jersey defense contractor sells the U.S. Army faulty helicopter parts. A former Massachusetts state treasurer is indicted for using lottery funds to finance an unsuccessful campaign to become governor.

These court cases represent a variety of criminal behavior with different motives, different methods, and different victims. Yet they all fall into the category of *white-collar crime*, an umbrella term for wrongdoing marked by deceit and scandal rather than violence. As we mentioned in Chapter 1, white-collar crime has a broad impact on the global economy, causing American businesses alone approximately $300 billion in losses each year.[84] Despite its global and national importance, however, white-collar crime has consistently challenged a criminal justice system that struggles to define the problem, much less effectively combat it.

WHAT IS WHITE-COLLAR CRIME?

White-collar crime is not an official category of criminal behavior measured by the federal government in the Uniform Crime Report. Rather, it covers a broad range of illegal acts involving "lying, cheating, and stealing," according to the FBI's Web site on the subject.[85] To give a more technical definition, white-collar crimes are financial activities characterized by deceit and concealment that do not involve physical force or violence. Figure 14.4 on the facing page lists and describes some common types of white-collar crime.

Learning Objective 7 Indicate some of the ways in which white-collar crime is different from violent or property crime.

DIFFERENT TECHNIQUES To differentiate white-collar crime from "regular" crime, criminologists Michael L. Benson of the University of Cincinnati and Sally S. Simpson of the University of Maryland focus on technique. For example, in an ordinary burglary, a criminal uses physical means, such as picking a lock, to get somewhere he or she should not be—someone else's home—to do something that is clearly illegal. Furthermore, the victim is a specific identifiable individual—the homeowner. In contrast, white-collar criminals usually (1) have legal access to the place where the crime occurs, (2) are spatially separated from the victim, who is often unknown, and (3) behave in a manner that is, at least superficially, legitimate.[86]

FIGURE 14.4 White-Collar Crimes

Embezzlement

Embezzlement is a form of employee fraud in which an individual uses her or his position within an organization to *embezzle,* or steal, the employer's funds, property, or other assets. Pilferage is a less serious form of employee fraud in which the individual steals items from the workplace.

Tax Evasion

Tax evasion occurs when taxpayers underreport (or do not report) their taxable income or otherwise purposely attempt to evade a tax liability.

Credit-Card and Check Fraud

Credit-card fraud involves obtaining credit-card numbers through a variety of schemes (such as stealing them from the Internet) and using the numbers for personal gain. Check fraud includes writing checks that are not covered by bank funds, forging checks, and stealing traveler's checks.

Mail and Wire Fraud

This umbrella term covers all schemes that involve the use of mail, radio, television, the Internet, or a telephone to intentionally deceive in a business environment.

Securities Fraud

Securities fraud covers illegal activity in the stock market. Stockbrokers who steal funds from their clients are guilty of securities fraud, as are those who engage in *insider trading,* which involves buying or selling securities on the basis of information that has not been made available to the public.

Bribery

Also known as *influence peddling,* bribery occurs in the business world when somebody within a company sells influence, power, or information to a person outside the company who can benefit. A county official, for example, could give a construction company a lucrative county contract to build a new jail. In return, the construction company would give some of the proceeds, known as a *kickback,* to the official.

Consumer Fraud

This term covers a wide variety of activities designed to defraud consumers, from selling counterfeit art to offering "free" items, such as electronic devices or vacations, that include a number of hidden charges.

Insurance Fraud

Insurance fraud involves making false claims in order to collect insurance payments. Faking an injury in order to receive payments from a workers' compensation program, for example, is a form of insurance fraud.

Benson and Simpson also identify three main techniques used by white-collar criminals to carry out their crimes:[87]

1. *Deception.* White-collar crime almost always involves a party who deceives and a party who is deceived. For example, in 2009, Congress passed legislation giving first-time home buyers an $8,000 tax credit. By 2010, federal agents had uncovered more than 100,000 instances of deception involving this benefit—applicants were lying about being first-time home buyers or were misusing the funds.[88]

2. *Abuse of trust.* A white-collar criminal often operates in a position of trust and misuses that trust for personal benefit. Dishonest stockbrokers, for example, may steal funds from clients rather than investing those funds in the stock market as promised.

3. *Concealment and conspiracy.* To continue their illegal activities, white-collar criminals need to conceal those activities. In *odometer fraud,* for example, an automobile dealership "rolls back" the odometers of used cars so that a higher price can be charged for the vehicles. When the fraud is discovered, the scheme normally can no longer succeed.

VICTIMS OF WHITE-COLLAR CRIME   As the above examples show, sometimes the victim of a white-collar crime is obvious. A fraudulent stockbroker is stealing directly from her or his clients, and odometer fraud denies consumers the actual value of their purchased automobiles. But who was victimized when the tax credit for first-time home buyers was fraudulently claimed? In that instance, the "victims" were the U.S. taxpayers, who collectively had to cover the cost of the unwarranted benefits. Often, white-collar crime does not target individuals but rather large groups or even abstract concepts such as "society" or "the environment."

Corporate Violence Physical harm to individuals or the environment that occurs as the result of corporate policies or decision making.

Regulation Governmental control of society through rules and laws enforced by administrative agencies.

Compliance The state of operating in accordance with governmental standards.

What role did the Environmental Protection Agency (EPA) play in monitoring efforts to clean up the oil slick from the Deepwater Horizon oil spill in the spring of 2010? Why is the EPA considered a regulatory agency and not a law enforcement agency?

Ted Jackson/*Times-Picayune*/Landov

REGULATING AND POLICING WHITE-COLLAR CRIME

Several years ago, Guidant Corporation was found guilty of deliberately selling flawed heart defibrillators, which employ electric energy to correct irregular heart rhythms. Because six people who used the faulty devices died, Guidant was fined nearly $300 million and placed on three years' probation, during which time its operations would be subject to regular government inspections.[89]

The deaths of six people because of Guidant Corporation's heart defibrillators are an example of *corporate violence.* In contrast to assaults committed by individual people, **corporate violence** is a result of policies or actions undertaken by a corporation. In the United States, parallel regulatory and criminal systems have evolved to prevent corporate violence and other forms of white-collar crime.

THE REGULATORY JUSTICE SYSTEM Although most white-collar crimes cause harm, these harms are not necessarily covered by criminal statutes. Indeed, more often they are covered by *administrative* laws, which we first encountered in Chapter 3 (see page 69). Such laws make up the backbone of the U.S. regulatory system, through which the government attempts to control the actions of individuals, corporations, and other institutions. The goal of **regulation** is not prevention or punishment as much as **compliance,** or the following of regulatory guidelines.[90] For example, following the Deepwater Horizon oil spill off the coast of Louisiana in April 2010, BP (the corporation that operated the faulty oil-drilling rig) used special types of chemicals called dispersants to aid in the cleanup. Agents from the Environmental Protection Agency (EPA) monitored the levels of these chemicals to ensure that further damage was not done to the Gulf of Mexico (see the photo below).

The EPA—which regulates practices relating to air quality, water quality, and toxic waste—is one of the federal administrative agencies whose compliance oversight brings them into contact with white-collar crime. Another, the Occupational Safety and Health Administration (OSHA), enforces workplace health and safety standards. In 2011, OSHA cited Texas' Taft Grain and Elevator for noncompliance and fined the company $188,000 after one of its employees was killed in a grain bin accident.[91] In addition, the Federal Trade Commission regulates business interactions, and the Securities and Exchange Commission (SEC) ensures that financial markets such as the New York Stock Exchange operate in a fair manner.

LAW ENFORCEMENT AND WHITE-COLLAR CRIME Two years after the Deepwater Horizon accident referred to above, in which eleven workers were killed, federal prosecutors charged a former BP engineer with intentionally deleting two hundred text messages relating to the accident. In general, when officials at a regulatory agency find that criminal prosecution is needed to punish a particular violation, they will refer the matter to the U.S. Department of Justice. Either through such referrals or at their own discretion, federal officials prosecute white-collar crime using the investigatory powers of several different federal law enforcement agencies. The FBI has become the lead agency when it comes to white-collar crime, particularly in response to high-profile financial scandals. The U.S. Postal Inspection Service is also quite active in such investigations, as fraudulent activities often involve the U.S. mail and Internet wire fraud. In addition, the Internal Revenue Service's Criminal Investigative Division has jurisdiction over a wide variety of white-collar crimes, including tax fraud, and operates perhaps the most effective white-collar crime lab in the country.

Local and state agencies also investigate white-collar crimes, but because of the complexity and costs of such investigations, most are handled by the federal government. Federal prosecutors are also in a unique position to enforce the federal Racketeer Influenced and Corrupt Organizations Act (RICO), which we discussed briefly in Chapter 10. Originally designed to combat organized crime, RICO makes it illegal to receive income through a pattern of *racketeering*.[92] The definition of **racketeering** is so inclusive—basically covering any attempt to earn illegal income involving more than one person—that it can be used against a broad range of white-collar wrongdoing. In 2011, for example, federal prosecutors used RICO to convict eleven tobacco companies for misleading the American public about the addictive qualities of cigarettes.

Racketeering The criminal action of being involved in an organized effort to engage in illegal business transactions.

WHITE-COLLAR CRIME IN THE 2000s

The decade that ended in 2010 was marked by two periods of financial scandal. First, in 2001 and 2002, fraudulent accounting practices led to the demise of giant corporations such as Enron and Worldcom, costing investors tens of billions of dollars. Then, near the end of the decade, the collapse of the subprime mortgage market caused millions of Americans to lose their homes to foreclosure and led to the collapse of major financial institutions such as Lehman Brothers and Washington Mutual. In the latter period, headlines focused on widespread *mortgage fraud,* or dishonest practices relating to home loans, along with the misdeeds of Bernard Madoff. Before his 2008 arrest, Madoff managed to defraud thousands of investors out of approximately $65 billion.

As has often occurred in U.S. history, these scandals and the concurrent economic downturns led to greater regulation and criminalization of white-collar crime. In 1934, for example, in the wake of the Great Depression, Congress established the SEC to watch over the American economy.[93] Similarly, in 2002, Congress passed legislation which, among other things, enhanced the penalties for those convicted of white-collar crimes.[94] (See the feature *Myth versus Reality—Soft Time for White-Collar Crime* on the following page.) In response to the "Great Recession" of 2008 and 2009, the FBI created the National Mortgage Fraud Team and began to crack down on a variety of white-collar crimes. Indeed, FBI agents are increasingly using aggressive tactics such as going undercover, planting wiretaps, and raiding offices—tactics previously reserved for drug dealers, mobsters, and terrorists—against white-collar criminals.[95]

SELFASSESSMENT

Fill in the blanks and check your answers on page 424.

According to the FBI, white-collar crimes are economic activities characterized by _____ and concealment that do not involve _____ . Administrative agencies such as the _____ Protection Agency make up the backbone of the U.S. regulatory system, which combats white-collar crime by requiring _____ with certain guidelines. A powerful tool for law enforcement in combating white-collar crimes, _____ can be used against groups or organizations that attempt to earn income illegally.

MYTH vs. REALITY

Soft Time for White-Collar Crime

During the 1980s, the nation was rocked by a series of financial scandals, including the "savings and loan crisis." As a result of this debacle, dozens of financial institutions failed, eventually costing American taxpayers more than $160 billion. To the outrage of many, the high-profile white-collar criminals from the era received relatively light prison sentences for their fraudulent behavior. Corrupt Louisiana financier Herman K. Beebe spent less than a year in prison. Michael Milken, "the junk bond king" who pleaded guilty to violating securities laws, was released after twenty-two months. Bank president Charles Keating, Jr., whose actions wiped out the savings of more than 20,000 customers, served four and a half years.

THE MYTH White-collar criminals, with their high-priced lawyers and friends in high places, receive light penalties. Even though their wrongdoing causes a great deal of suffering, they are not treated as harshly by the criminal justice system as petty thieves or low-level drug dealers.

THE REALITY The political response to the financial scandals of the early 2000s focused on increasing penalties for white-collar criminals. In November 2001, the U.S. Sentencing Commission increased its recommended punishments for businesspersons who commit fraud, particularly when the misdeeds involve losses in excess of $100 million. Then, in 2002, Congress passed the White Collar Crime Penalty Enhancement Act, which doubled the maximum sentences for some kinds of corporate fraud.

The results have been striking. In 2009, Edward Hugh Okun was sentenced to 120 years for stealing $126 million from clients, and Richard Harkless received 100 years for defrauding investors out of nearly $40 million. In December 2011, a U.S. district judge sentenced Judith Negron to thirty-five years in prison for cheating federal government programs that provide health care to the elderly and disabled out of $205 million. Bernie Madoff, mentioned in

the text, received a 150-year prison term. Although judges still have great leeway to depart from the guidelines when sentencing white-collar criminals, public outrage at white-collar crime has apparently created an environment in which harsh punishments are the rule rather than the exception.

FOR CRITICAL ANALYSIS What are some of the justifications for punishing white-collar criminals such as Judith Negron and Bernie Madoff so harshly? Are there any reasons to be lenient with those whose crimes do not physically harm their victims?

Bernie Madoff, left center, was sentenced to 150 years in prison for stealing tens of billions of dollars from investment clients.

Timothy A. Clary/AFP/Getty Images

CHAPTER SUMMARY

Learning Objective 1 **Identify three important trends in international terrorism.** (a) Terrorists have developed more efficient methods of financing their operations. (b) Terrorists have developed more efficient organizations based on the small-business model. (c) Terrorists have exploited new communications technology to mount global campaigns.

Learning Objective 2 **Explain how American law enforcement agencies have used "preventive policing" to combat terrorism.** American law enforcement agencies are no longer willing to take the chance that nascent terrorist plots will lose momentum rather than develop into significant security threats. Therefore, they are taking steps to stop these plots in the planning stages, even if the dangers posed by the conspirators are minimal.

Learning Objective 3 **Explain how the Patriot Act has made it easier for federal agents to conduct searches during terrorism investigations.** In requesting a search warrant for investigations of terrorism, federal agents no longer need to provide probable cause of wrongdoing. They must only prove that their actions have a "significant purpose," which means that no proof of criminal activity need be provided.

Learning Objective 4 **Describe the three following forms of malware: (a) botnets, (b) worms, and (c) viruses.** (a) A botnet is a network of computers that have been hijacked without the knowledge of their owners and used to spread harmful programs across the Internet. (b) A worm is a damaging software program that reproduces itself as it moves from computer to computer. (c) A virus is a damaging software program that must be attached to an "infested" host file to transfer from one computer to the next.

Learning Objective 5 **Explain how the Internet has contributed to piracy of intellectual property.** In the past, copying intellectual property such as films and music was time consuming, and the quality of the pirated copies was vastly inferior to that of the originals. On the Internet, however, millions of unauthorized copies of intellectual property can be reproduced at the click of a mouse, and the quality of these items is often the same as that of the original, or close to it.

Learning Objective 6 **Explain the difference between a temporary visa and a green card.** A temporary visa is a document that gives a non-U.S. citizen permission to visit the United States for a limited amount of time and for a limited purpose. A green card, or nontemporary visa, confers on the holder the status of permanent resident, and he or she enjoys many of the same rights as U.S. citizens to live and work in this country.

Learning Objective 7 **Indicate some of the ways in which white-collar crime is different from violent or property crime.** A wrongdoer committing a standard crime usually uses physical means to get somewhere she or he legally should not be in order to do something clearly illegal. Also, the victims of violent and property crimes are usually easily identifiable. In contrast, a white-collar criminal usually has legal access to the crime scene where he or she is doing something seemingly legitimate. Furthermore, victims of white-collar crimes are often unknown or unidentifiable.

Learning Objective 8 **Explain the concept of corporate violence.** Corporate violence occurs when a corporation implements policies that ultimately cause physical harm to individuals or the environment.

QUESTIONS FOR CRITICAL ANALYSIS

1. Using your own words, what is the definition of *terrorism?*

2. According to Donna Marsh, whose pregnant daughter was killed on September 11, 2001, in New York City, it is "unconscionable" to hold terrorism suspects for nearly a decade without trial, and it "demeans the United States' justice system" to say these suspects cannot be tried in civilian courts. What is your opinion of these statements?

3. Consider the following proposed state law: *It is unlawful for any person, with intent to terrify, intimidate, threaten, harass, annoy, or offend, to use ANY ELECTRONIC OR DIGITAL DEVICE and use any obscene, lewd, or profane language.* What is your opinion of this statute? What might be some of its unforeseen consequences?

4. Guy, who was born in Haiti, has lived in Miami, Florida, for fifteen years and is a permanent resident, meaning

that he has a green card. One night Guy gets in a fight with a neighbor and is eventually convicted of simple assault. Even if a judge sentences him to probation rather than jail time, how might this conviction affect Guy's ability to continue living in the United States legally?

5. Law enforcement agencies have extensively employed antiracketeering laws such as RICO in combating drug dealers and criminal gangs. (To review RICO, go to page 421.) Why would such legislation be useful in prosecuting these non-white-collar criminals?

KEY TERMS

alien **415**

Antiterrorism and Effective Death
    Penalty Act of 1996 (AEDPA) **399**

botnet **411**

Central Intelligence Agency
    (CIA) **402**

compliance **420**

computer crime **408**

corporate violence **420**

cyber crime **409**

cyber fraud **409**

cyberstalking **411**

detainer **417**

domestic terrorism **399**

first responders **403**

green card **415**

hacker **411**

identity theft **410**

infrastructure **401**

intellectual property **413**

intelligence agency **401**

military tribunal **407**

National Security Agency (NSA) **402**

nonstate actor **397**

Patriot Act **400**

permanent resident **415**

phishing **410**

preparedness **403**

racketeering **421**

regulation **420**

removal **415**

spam **412**

virus **412**

visa **404**

worm **412**

SELF ASSESSMENT ANSWER KEY

Page 408: i. nonstate; **ii.** prevent; **iii.** intelligence; **iv.** probable; **v.** significant

Page 414: i. retail; **ii.** identity; **iii.** hacker; **iv.** botnets; **v.** spam

Page 418: i. civil; **ii.** federal; **iii.** permanent; **iv.** removal

Page 421: i. deceit; **ii.** violence/physical force; **iii.** Environmental; **iv.** compliance; **v.** RICO/antiracketeering laws

COURSEMATE

For online help and access to resources that accompany *Criminal Justice in Action: The Core*, go to **www.cengage-brain.com/shop/ISBN/978-1-285-06915-9**. Click "Access Now," where you will find flashcards, an online quiz, and other helpful study aids. If you have an access code for CourseMate, log in and go to the chapter of your choice for additional online study aids.

NOTES

1. "Anonymous Hacks Cyber Cops," *Associated Press* (February 6, 2012).

2. Quoted in Michael S. Schmidt, "FBI Director Warns against Terrorist Hacking," *New York Times* (March 8, 2012), A16.

3. *National Strategy for Homeland Security* (Washington, D.C.: Office of Homeland Security, 2002), 2.

4. "Domestic Terrorism Program," at **baltimore. fbi.gov/domter.htm.**

5. David A. Westbrook, "Bin Laden's War," *Buffalo Law Review* (December 2006), 981–1012.

6. Quoted in Kimberly Dozier and David Espo, "U.S. Kills Osama bin Laden Decade after 9/11 Attacks," *Associated Press* (May 2, 2011).

7. Ahmed S. Hashim, "Al-Qaida: Origins, Goals, and Grand Strategy," in *The McGraw-Hill Homeland Security Handbook*, ed. David G. Kamien (New York: McGraw-Hill, 2006), 24.

8. Quoted in *ibid.*, 9.

9. Quoted in "The Growing, and Mysterious, Irrelevance of al Qaeda," *The Economist* (January 24, 2009), 64.

10. Quoted in Maggie Michael, "Al-Qaida Confirms Osama bin Laden's Death," *Associated Press* (May 6, 2011).

11. Brian Michael Jenkins, "The New Age of Terrorism," in *The McGraw-Hill Homeland Security Handbook*, ed. David G. Kamien (New York: McGraw-Hill, 2006), 117–129.

12. *Ibid.,* 128.

13. 18 U.S.C. Section 2339B(a)(1) (1996).

14. 8 U.S.C. Section 1182(a)(3)(B) (Supp. I 2001); and 8 U.S.C. Section 1189(a)(1)(C) (Supp. I 2001).

15. U.S. Department of State, "Country Reports on Terrorism," at **www.state.gov/s/ct/rls/crt/2008/122449.htm**.

16. 18 U.S.C. Section 2339A(b) (Supp. I 2001).

17. 8 U.S.C. Section 1182(a)(3)(B)(iv)(VI) (Supp. I 2001), amended by the Patriot Act of 2001, Pub. L. No. 107-56, Section 411(a), 115 Stat. 272.

18. Uniting and Strengthening America by Providing Appropriate Tools Required to Intercept and Obstruct Terrorism Act of 2001, Pub. L. No. 107-56, 115 Stat. 272 (2001).

19. Federal Bureau of Investigation, "Facts and Figures: FBI Priorities," at **www.fbi.gov/priorities/priorities.htm**.

20. Jane A. Bullock et al., *Introduction to Homeland Security,* 4th ed. (Waltham, MA: Butterworth-Heinemann, 2012), 182–183.

21. National Commission on Terrorist Attacks upon the United States, *The 9/11 Commission Report: Executive Summary* (Washington, D.C.: National Commission on Terrorist Attacks upon the United States, 2004), 77.

22. Greg Miller and Julie Tate, "CIA Focus Shifts to Killing Targets," *Washington Post* (September 1, 2010), A1.

23. Charlie Savage, "FBI Focusing on Security over Ordinary Crime," *New York Times* (August 24, 2011), A15.

24. Quoted in "Spies Among Us," *U.S. News & World Report* (May 8, 2006), 43.

25. *Ibid.,* 41–43.

26. Richard A. Serrano, "D.C. Bomb Plot Foiled," *Baltimore Sun* (February 18, 2012), 10A.

27. Debbie Siegelbaum, "Authorities Foil Planned Suicide Bombing Attack on Capitol Building," *The Hill* (February 17, 2012), at **thehill.com/homenews/news/211447-authorities-foil-planned-suicide-bombing-attack-on-capitol-building**.

28. Center on Law and Security, *Terrorist Trial Report Card: September 11, 2001–September 11, 2009* (New York: New York University School of Law, January 2010), 42–44.

29. Carl Strock, "How Far Was Terrorist an FBI Creation?" *Daily Gazette (Schenectady, NY)* (February 21, 2012), B1.

30. Eric Schmitt and Charlie Savage, "In U.S. Sting Operations, Questions of Entrapment," *New York Times* (November 30, 2010), A22.

31. "Homeland Security Presidential Directive/HSPD-8," at **www.fas.org/irp/offdocs/nspd/hspd-8.html**.

32. Bullock et al., 334.

33. Marc Lacey, "At the Border, on the Night Watch," *New York Times* (October 13, 2011), A17.

34. Adam Goldman and Matt Puzo, "Inside the Spy Unit That NYPD Says Doesn't Exist," *Associated Press* (August 31, 2011).

35. Chris Hawley and Eileen Sullivan, "Angry over Spying, Muslims Say 'Don't Call NYPD,'" *Associated Press* (November 14, 2011).

36. "Anti-Muslim Sentiments Fairly Commonplace," Gallup Poll (August 10, 2006), at **www.gallup.com/poll/24073/antimuslim-sentiments-fairly-commonplace.aspx**.

37. *INS v. Delgado,* 466 U.S. 215 (1983).

38. Pew Research Center for the People and the Press, "Public Remains Divided over the Patriot Act" (February 15, 2011), at **pewresearch.org/pubs/1893/poll-patriot-act-renewal**.

39. Pub. L. No. 107-56, Section 201-2-2, 115 Stat. 272, 278 (2001).

40. 50 U.S.C. Section 1803 (2000).

41. Patriot Act, Section 203(d)(1), 115 Stat. 272, 280 (2001).

42. Patriot Act, Section 206, amending Section 105(c)(2)(B) of the Foreign Intelligence Surveillance Act.

43. Patriot Act, Section 213.

44. FISA Amendments Act of 2008, Pub. L. No. 110-261, 122 Stat. 2436 (2008).

45. Eric Lichtblau, "Senate Approves Bill to Broaden Wiretap Powers," *New York Times* (July 10, 2008), A1.

46. *Wong Wing v. United States,* 163 U.S. 228 (1896).

47. 66 *Federal Register* 48334 (September 20, 2001).

48. Richard M. Pious, *The War on Terrorism and the Rule of Law* (Los Angeles: Roxbury Publishing Co., 2006), 165–166.

49. Michael Greenberger, "You Ain't Seen Nothin' Yet: The Inevitable Post-Hamdan Conflict between the Supreme Court and the Political Branches," *Maryland Law Review* 66 (2007), 805, 807.

50. Charlie Savage, "U.S. Prepares to Lift Ban on Guantanamo Cases," *New York Times* (January 20, 2011), A1.

51. Military Commission Act of 2009, Pub. L. No. 111-84, Sections 1801–1807, 123 Stat. 2190 (2009).

52. Erica Goode, "Craigslist Used in Deadly Plot to Lure Victims to Ohio," *New York Times* (December 2, 2011), A16.

53. National Institute of Justice, *Computer Crime: Criminal Justice Resource Manual* (Washington, D.C.: U.S. Department of Justice, 1989), 2.

54. *Ibid.*

55. Internet Crime Complaint Center, *IC3 2011 Internet Crime Report* (Glen Allen, VA: National White Collar Crime Center, 2012), 9.

56. Symantec, press release, "Norton Study Calculates Cost of Global Cybercrime" (September 7, 2011), at **ww.symantec.com/about/news/release/article.jsp?prid=20110907_02**.

57. Bureau of Justice Statistics, *Identity Theft Reported by Households, 2005–2010* (Washington, D.C.: U.S. Department of Justice, November 2011), 1.

58. Benny Evangelista and Alejandro Martinez-Cabrera, "Big Jump in Number of People on Twitter," *San Francisco Chronicle* (September 4, 2010), D2.

59. Quoted in Matt Richtel and Verne G. Kopytoff, "E-Mail Fraud Hides behind Friendly Face," *New York Times* (June 3, 2011), A1.

60. Ben Rooney, "Cybercrime Exacts a Daily Toll," *Wall Street Journal* (September 12, 2011), 29.

61. Openet, press release, "Openet-Sponsored Study Reveals 41 Percent of Teenagers Experience Cyber-bullying" (January 18, 2012), at **www.openet.com/company/news-events/press-releases?id=482**.

62. Bureau of Justice Statistics, *Stalking Victimization in the United States* (Washington, D.C.: U.S. Department of Justice, January 2009), 1.

63. *Ibid.*

64. Geraldine Baum and Stuart Pfeifer, "Dozens Charged in Bank Thefts," *Los Angeles Times* (October 1, 2010), B1.

65. *Second Annual Cost of Cyber Crime Study: Benchmark Study of U.S. Companies* (Traverse City, MI: Ponemon Institute, August 2011), 1.

66. *Symantec Global Internet Security Threat Report: Trends for 2009* (Mountain View, CA: Symantec, April 2010), 16.

67. Geoffrey A. Fowler, Shaundi Raice, and Amir Efrati, "Spam Finds a New Target," *Wall Street Journal* (January 4, 2012), B1.

68. *Eighth Annual BSA and IDC Global Software Piracy Study* (Washington, D.C.: Business Software Alliance, May 2011), 2.

69. "The Internet Porn 'Epidemic': By the Numbers," *The WEEK* (June 17, 2010), at **theweek.com/article/index/204156/the-internet-porn-epidemic-by-the-numbers**.

70. Steve Chapman, "More Freedom Is a Sound Bet," *Chicago Tribune* (August 1, 2010), 21.

71. Teresa A. Miller, "Lessons Learned, Lessons Lost: Immigration Enforcement's Failed Experiment with Penal Severity," *Fordham Urban Law Journal* (November 2010), 217.

72. 8 U.S.C.A. Section 1304(e).

73. 8 U.S.C.A. Section 1227(a).

74. Immigration and Customs Enforcement, "Removal Statistics," at **www.ice.gov/removal-statistics**.

75. James C. McKinley, Jr., and Julia Preston, "U.S. Can't Trace Foreign Visitors on Expired Visas," *New York Times* (October 12, 2009), A1.

76. John S. Passel and D'Vera Cohn, "Unauthorized Immigrant Population: National and State Trends, 2010," *Pew Hispanic Center* (February 1, 2011), at **pewhispanic.org/reports/report.php?ReportID=133**.

77. *Wong Wing v. United States,* 163 U.S. 228 (1895).

78. 8 C.F.R. Section 287.3(a)-(b).

79. *Ibid.;* and *Samayoa-Martinez v. Holder,* 558 F.3d 897, 901–902 (9th Cir. 2009).

80. U.S. Immigration and Customs Enforcement, "Operation Community Shield/Transnational Gangs," at **www.ice.gov/community-shield**.

81. James Walsh, "Feds Arrest Eighteen Gang Members," *Star Tribune (Minneapolis–St. Paul)* (July 9, 2010), 4B.

82. Jon Freere and Jessica Vaughan, "Taking Back the Streets: ICE and Local Law Enforcement Target Immigrant Gangs," Center for Immigration Studies, September 2008, at **www.cis.org/immigrantgangs**.

83. Immigration and Customs Enforcement, "Activated Jurisdictions," at **www.ice.gov/doclib/secure-communities/pdf/sc-activated.pdf**.

84. The Federal Bureau of Investigation, Seattle Division, "What We Investigate," at **www.fbi.gov/seattle/about-us/what-we-investigate/priorities**.

85. The Federal Bureau of Investigation, "White-Collar Crime" at **www.fbi.gov/about-us/investigate/white_collar/whitecollar crime**.

86. Michael L. Benson and Sally S. Simpson, *White-Collar Crime: An Opportunity Perspective* (New York: Routledge, 2009), 79–80.

87. *Ibid.*, 81–87.

88. Anton R. Valukas, "White-Collar Crime and Economic Recession," *University of Chicago Legal Forum* (2010), 5.

89. U.S. Department of Justice, "Medical Device Manufacturer Guidant Sentenced for Failure to Report Defibrillator Safety Problems to FDA" (January 12, 2011), at **www.justice.gov/opa/pr/2011/January/11-civ-035.html**.

90. Benson and Simpson, 189.

91. Occupational Safety & Health Administration, "US Labor Department's OSHA Cites Grain Elevator Operator with Safety Violations Following Worker Death in Taft, Texas" (May 9, 2011), at **www.osha.gov/pls/oshaweb/owadisp.show_document?p_table=NEWS_RELEASES&p_id=19764**.

92. Lawrence Salinger, *Encyclopedia of White-Collar and Corporate Crime,* 2d ed. (Thousand Oaks, CA: Sage, 2004), 361.

93. 15 U.S.C. Sections 78a *et seq.*

94. White-Collar Crime Penalty Enhancement Act of 2002, 18 U.S.C. Sections 1341, 1343, 1349–1350.

95. Peter Lattman and William K. Rashbaum, "A Trader, an F.B.I. Witness, and Then a Suicide," *Reuters* (June 2, 2011)

APPENDIX A: The Constitution of the United States

PREAMBLE

We the People of the United States, in Order to form a more perfect Union, establish Justice, insure domestic Tranquility, provide for the common defence, promote the general Welfare, and secure the Blessings of Liberty to ourselves and our Posterity, do ordain and establish this Constitution for the United States of America.

ARTICLE I

Section 1. All legislative Powers herein granted shall be vested in a Congress of the United States, which shall consist of a Senate and House of Representatives.

Section 2. The House of Representatives shall be composed of Members chosen every second Year by the People of the several States, and the Electors in each State shall have the Qualifications requisite for Electors of the most numerous Branch of the State Legislature.

No Person shall be a Representative who shall not have attained to the Age of twenty five Years, and been seven Years a Citizen of the United States, and who shall not, when elected, be an Inhabitant of that State in which he shall be chosen.

Representatives and direct Taxes shall be apportioned among the several States which may be included within this Union, according to their respective Numbers, which shall be determined by adding to the whole Number of free Persons, including those bound to Service for a Term of Years, and excluding Indians not taxed, three fifths of all other Persons. The actual Enumeration shall be made within three Years after the first Meeting of the Congress of the United States, and within every subsequent Term of ten Years, in such Manner as they shall by Law direct. The Number of Representatives shall not exceed one for every thirty Thousand, but each State shall have at Least one Representative; and until such enumeration shall be made, the State of New Hampshire shall be entitled to chuse three, Massachusetts eight, Rhode Island and Providence Plantations one, Connecticut five, New York six, New Jersey four, Pennsylvania eight, Delaware one, Maryland six, Virginia ten, North Carolina five, South Carolina five, and Georgia three.

When vacancies happen in the Representation from any State, the Executive Authority thereof shall issue Writs of Election to fill such Vacancies.

The House of Representatives shall chuse their Speaker and other Officers; and shall have the sole Power of Impeachment.

Section 3. The Senate of the United States shall be composed of two Senators from each State, chosen by the Legislature thereof, for six Years; and each Senator shall have one Vote.

Immediately after they shall be assembled in Consequence of the first Election, they shall be divided as equally as may be into three Classes. The Seats of the Senators of the first Class shall be vacated at the Expiration of the second Year, of the second Class at the Expiration of the fourth Year, and of the third Class at the Expiration of the sixth Year, so that one third may be chosen every second Year; and if Vacancies happen by Resignation, or otherwise, during the Recess of the Legislature of any State, the Executive thereof may make temporary Appointments until the next Meeting of the Legislature, which shall then fill such Vacancies.

No Person shall be a Senator who shall not have attained to the Age of thirty Years, and been nine Years a Citizen of the United States, and who shall not, when elected, be an Inhabitant of that State for which he shall be chosen.

The Vice President of the United States shall be President of the Senate, but shall have no Vote, unless they be equally divided.

The Senate shall chuse their other Officers, and also a President pro tempore, in the Absence of the Vice President, or when he shall exercise the Office of President of the United States.

The Senate shall have the sole Power to try all Impeachments. When sitting for that Purpose, they shall be on Oath or Affirmation. When the President of the United States is tried, the Chief Justice shall preside: And no Person shall be convicted without the Concurrence of two thirds of the Members present.

Judgment in Cases of Impeachment shall not extend further than to removal from Office, and disqualification to hold and enjoy any Office of honor, Trust, or Profit under the United States: but the Party convicted shall nevertheless be liable and subject to Indictment, Trial, Judgment, and Punishment, according to Law.

Section 4. The Times, Places and Manner of holding Elections for Senators and Representatives, shall be prescribed in each State by the Legislature thereof; but the Congress may at any time by Law make or alter such Regulations, except as to the Places of chusing Senators.

The Congress shall assemble at least once in every Year, and such Meeting shall be on the first Monday in December, unless they shall by Law appoint a different Day.

Section 5. Each House shall be the Judge of the Elections, Returns, and Qualifications of its own Members, and a Majority of each shall constitute a Quorum to do Business; but a smaller Number may adjourn from day to day, and may be authorized to compel the Attendance of absent Members, in such Manner, and under such Penalties as each House may provide.

Each House may determine the Rules of its Proceedings, punish its Members for disorderly Behavior, and, with the Concurrence of two thirds, expel a Member.

Each House shall keep a Journal of its Proceedings, and from time to time publish the same, excepting such Parts as may in their Judgment require Secrecy; and the Yeas and Nays of the Members of either House on any question shall, at the Desire of one fifth of those Present, be entered on the Journal.

Neither House, during the Session of Congress, shall, without the Consent of the other, adjourn for more than three days, nor to any other Place than that in which the two Houses shall be sitting.

Section 6. The Senators and Representatives shall receive a Compensation for their Services, to be ascertained by Law, and paid out of the Treasury of the United States. They shall in all Cases, except Treason, Felony and Breach of the Peace, be privileged from Arrest during their Attendance at the Session of their respective Houses, and in going to and returning from the same; and for any Speech or Debate in either House, they shall not be questioned in any other Place.

No Senator or Representative shall, during the Time for which he was elected, be appointed to any civil Office under the Authority of the United States, which shall have been created, or the Emoluments whereof shall have been increased during such time; and no Person holding any Office under the United States, shall be a Member of either House during his Continuance in Office.

Section 7. All Bills for raising Revenue shall originate in the House of Representatives; but the Senate may propose or concur with Amendments as on other Bills.

Every Bill which shall have passed the House of Representatives and the Senate, shall, before it become a Law, be presented to the President of the United States; If he approve he shall sign it, but if not he shall return it, with his Objections to the House in which it shall have originated, who shall enter the Objections at large on their Journal, and proceed to reconsider it. If after such Reconsideration two thirds of that House shall agree to pass the Bill, it shall be sent together with the Objections, to the other House, by which it shall likewise be reconsidered, and if approved by two thirds of that House, it shall become a Law. But in all such Cases the Votes of both Houses shall be determined by Yeas and Nays, and the Names of the Persons voting for and against the Bill shall be entered on the Journal of each House respectively. If any Bill shall not be returned by the President within ten Days (Sundays excepted) after it shall have been presented to him, the Same shall be a Law, in like Manner as if he had signed it, unless the Congress by their Adjournment prevent its Return in which Case it shall not be a Law.

Every Order, Resolution, or Vote, to which the Concurrence of the Senate and House of Representatives may be necessary (except on a question of Adjournment) shall be presented to the President of the United States; and before the Same shall take Effect, shall be approved by him, or being disapproved by him, shall be repassed by two thirds of the Senate and House of Representatives, according to the Rules and Limitations prescribed in the Case of a Bill.

Section 8. The Congress shall have Power To lay and collect Taxes, Duties, Imposts and Excises, to pay the Debts and provide for the common Defence and general Welfare of the United States; but all Duties, Imposts and Excises shall be uniform throughout the United States;

To borrow Money on the credit of the United States;

To regulate Commerce with foreign Nations, and among the several States, and with the Indian Tribes;

To establish an uniform Rule of Naturalization, and uniform Laws on the subject of Bankruptcies throughout the United States;

To coin Money, regulate the Value thereof, and of foreign Coin, and fix the Standard of Weights and Measures;

To provide for the Punishment of counterfeiting the Securities and current Coin of the United States;

To establish Post Offices and post Roads;

To promote the Progress of Science and useful Arts, by securing for limited Times to Authors and Inventors the exclusive Right to their respective Writings and Discoveries;

To constitute Tribunals inferior to the supreme Court; To define and punish Piracies and Felonies committed on the high Seas, and Offenses against the Law of Nations;

To declare War, grant Letters of Marque and Reprisal, and make Rules concerning Captures on Land and Water;

To raise and support Armies, but no Appropriation of Money to that Use shall be for a longer Term than two Years;

To provide and maintain a Navy;

To make Rules for the Government and Regulation of the land and naval Forces;

To provide for calling forth the Militia to execute the Laws of the Union, suppress Insurrections and repel Invasions;

To provide for organizing, arming, and disciplining, the Militia, and for governing such Part of them as may be employed in the Service of the United States, reserving to the States respectively, the Appointment of the Officers, and the Authority of training the Militia according to the discipline prescribed by Congress;

To exercise exclusive Legislation in all Cases whatsoever, over such District (not exceeding ten Miles square) as may, by Cession of particular States, and the Acceptance of Congress, become the Seat of the Government of the United States, and to exercise like Authority over all Places purchased by the Consent of the Legislature of the State in which the Same shall be, for the Erection of Forts, Magazines, Arsenals, dock-Yards, and other needful Buildings;—And

To make all Laws which shall be necessary and proper for carrying into Execution the foregoing Powers, and all other Powers vested by this Constitution in the Government of the United States, or in any Department or Officer thereof.

Section 9. The Migration or Importation of such Persons as any of the States now existing shall think proper to admit, shall not be prohibited by the Congress prior to the Year one thousand eight hundred and eight, but a Tax or duty may be imposed on such Importation, not exceeding ten dollars for each Person.

The privilege of the Writ of Habeas Corpus shall not be suspended, unless when in Cases of Rebellion or Invasion the public Safety may require it.

No Bill of Attainder or ex post facto Law shall be passed.

No Capitation, or other direct, Tax shall be laid, unless in Proportion to the Census or Enumeration herein before directed to be taken.

No Tax or Duty shall be laid on Articles exported from any State.

No Preference shall be given by any Regulation of Commerce or Revenue to the Ports of one State over those of another: nor shall Vessels bound to, or from, one State be obliged to enter, clear, or pay Duties in another.

No Money shall be drawn from the Treasury, but in Consequence of Appropriations made by Law; and a regular Statement and Account of the Receipts and Expenditures of all public Money shall be published from time to time.

No Title of Nobility shall be granted by the United States: And no Person holding any Office of Profit or Trust under them, shall, without the Consent of the Congress, accept of any present, Emolument, Office, or Title, of any kind whatever, from any King, Prince, or foreign State.

Section 10. No State shall enter into any Treaty, Alliance, or Confederation; grant Letters of Marque and Reprisal; coin Money; emit Bills of Credit; make any Thing but gold and silver Coin a Tender in Payment of Debts; pass any Bill of Attainder, ex post facto Law, or Law impairing the Obligation of Contracts, or grant any Title of Nobility.

No State shall, without the Consent of the Congress, lay any Imposts or Duties on Imports or Exports, except what may be absolutely necessary for executing its inspection Laws: and the net Produce of all Duties and Imposts, laid by any State on Imports or Exports, shall be for the Use of the Treasury of the United States; and all such Laws shall be subject to the Revision and Controul of the Congress.

No State shall, without the Consent of Congress, lay any Duty of Tonnage, keep Troops, or Ships of War in time of Peace, enter into any Agreement or Compact with another State, or with a foreign Power, or engage in War, unless actually invaded, or in such imminent Danger as will not admit of delay.

ARTICLE II

Section 1. The executive Power shall be vested in a President of the United States of America. He shall hold his Office during the Term of four Years, and, together with the Vice President, chosen for the same Term, be elected, as follows:

Each State shall appoint, in such Manner as the Legislature thereof may direct, a Number of Electors, equal to the whole Number of Senators and Representatives to which the State may be entitled in the Congress; but no Senator or Representative, or Person holding an Office of Trust or Profit under the United States, shall be appointed an Elector.

The Electors shall meet in their respective States, and vote by Ballot for two Persons, of whom one at least shall not be an Inhabitant of the same State with themselves. And they shall make a List of all the Persons voted for, and of the Number of Votes for each; which List they shall sign and certify, and transmit sealed to the Seat of the Government of the United States, directed to the President of the Senate. The President of the Senate shall, in the Presence of the Senate and House of Representatives, open all the Certificates, and the Votes shall then be counted. The Person having the greatest Number of Votes shall be the President, if such Number be a Majority of the whole Number of Electors appointed; and if there be more than one who have such Majority, and have an equal Number of Votes, then the House of Representatives shall immediately chuse by Ballot one of them for President; and if no Person have a Majority, then from the five highest on the List the said House shall in like Manner chuse the President. But in chusing the President, the Votes shall be taken by States, the Representation from each State having one Vote; A quorum for this Purpose shall consist of a Member or Members from two thirds of the States, and a Majority of all the States shall be necessary to a Choice. In every Case, after the Choice of the President, the Person having the greater Number of Votes of the Electors shall be the Vice President. But if there should remain two or more who have equal Votes, the Senate shall chuse from them by Ballot the Vice President.

The Congress may determine the Time of chusing the Electors, and the Day on which they shall give their Votes; which Day shall be the same throughout the United States.

No person except a natural born Citizen, or a Citizen of the United States, at the time of the Adoption of this Constitution, shall be eligible to the Office of President; neither shall any Person be eligible to that Office who shall not have attained to the Age of thirty five Years, and been fourteen Years a Resident within the United States.

In Case of the Removal of the President from Office, or of his Death, Resignation or Inability to discharge the Powers and Duties of the said Office, the same shall devolve on the Vice President, and the Congress may by Law provide for the Case of Removal, Death, Resignation or Inability, both of the President and Vice President, declaring what Officer shall then act as President, and such Officer shall act accordingly, until the Disability be removed, or a President shall be elected.

The President shall, at stated Times, receive for his Services, a Compensation, which shall neither be increased nor diminished during the Period for which he shall have been elected, and he shall not receive within that Period any other Emolument from the United States, or any of them.

Before he enter on the Execution of his Office, he shall take the following Oath or Affirmation: "I do solemnly swear (or affirm) that I will faithfully execute the Office of President of the United States, and will to the best of my Ability, preserve, protect and defend the Constitution of the United States."

Section 2. The President shall be Commander in Chief of the Army and Navy of the United States, and of the Militia of the several States, when called into the actual Service of the United States; he may require the Opinion, in writing, of the principal Officer in each of the executive Departments, upon any Subject relating to the Duties of their respective Offices, and he shall have Power to grant Reprieves and Pardons for Offenses against the United States, except in Cases of Impeachment.

He shall have Power, by and with the Advice and Consent of the Senate to make Treaties, provided two thirds of the Senators present concur; and he shall nominate, and by and with the Advice and Consent of the Senate, shall appoint Ambassadors, other public Ministers and Consuls, Judges of the supreme Court, and all other Officers of the United States, whose Appointments are not herein otherwise provided for, and which shall be established by Law; but the Congress may by Law vest the Appointment of such inferior Officers, as they think proper, in the President alone, in the Courts of Law, or in the Heads of Departments.

The President shall have Power to fill up all Vacancies that may happen during the Recess of the Senate, by granting Commissions which shall expire at the End of their next Session.

Section 3. He shall from time to time give to the Congress Information of the State of the Union, and recommend to their Consideration such Measures as he shall judge necessary and expedient; he may, on extraordinary Occasions, convene both Houses, or either of them, and in Case of Disagreement between them, with Respect to the Time of Adjournment, he may adjourn them to such Time as he shall think proper; he shall receive Ambassadors and other public Ministers; he shall take Care that the Laws be faithfully executed, and shall Commission all the Officers of the United States.

Section 4. The President, Vice President and all civil Officers of the United States, shall be removed from Office on Impeachment for, and Conviction of, Treason, Bribery, or other high Crimes and Misdemeanors.

ARTICLE III

Section 1. The judicial Power of the United States, shall be vested in one supreme Court, and in such inferior Courts as the Congress may from time to time ordain and establish. The Judges, both of the supreme and inferior Courts, shall hold their Offices during good Behaviour, and shall, at stated Times, receive for their Services a Compensation, which shall not be diminished during their Continuance in Office.

Section 2. The judicial Power shall extend to all Cases, in Law and Equity, arising under this Constitution, the Laws of the United States, and Treaties made, or which shall be made, under their Authority;—to all Cases affecting Ambassadors, other public Ministers and Consuls;—to all Cases of admiralty and maritime Jurisdiction;—to Controversies to which the United States shall be a Party;—to Controversies between two or more States;—between a State and Citizens of another State;—between Citizens of different States;—between Citizens of the same State claiming Lands under Grants of different States, and between a State, or the Citizens thereof, and foreign States, Citizens or Subjects.

In all Cases affecting Ambassadors, other public Ministers and Consuls, and those in which a State shall be a Party, the supreme Court shall have original Jurisdiction. In all the other Cases before mentioned, the supreme Court shall have appellate Jurisdiction, both as to Law and Fact, with such Exceptions, and under such Regulations as the Congress shall make.

The Trial of all Crimes, except in Cases of Impeachment, shall be by Jury; and such Trial shall be held in the State where the said Crimes shall have been committed; but when not committed within any State, the Trial shall be at such Place or Places as the Congress may by Law have directed.

Section 3. Treason against the United States, shall consist only in levying War against them, or, in adhering to their Enemies, giving them Aid and Comfort. No Person shall be convicted of Treason unless on the Testimony of two Witnesses to the same overt Act, or on Confession in open Court.

The Congress shall have Power to declare the Punishment of Treason, but no Attainder of Treason shall work Corruption of Blood, or Forfeiture except during the Life of the Person attainted.

ARTICLE IV

Section 1. Full Faith and Credit shall be given in each State to the public Acts, Records, and judicial Proceedings of every other State. And the Congress may by general Laws prescribe the Manner in which such Acts, Records and Proceedings shall be proved, and the Effect thereof.

Section 2. The Citizens of each State shall be entitled to all Privileges and Immunities of Citizens in the several States.

A Person charged in any State with Treason, Felony, or other Crime, who shall flee from Justice, and be found in another State, shall on Demand of the executive Authority of the State from which he fled, be delivered up, to be removed to the State having Jurisdiction of the Crime.

No Person held to Service or Labour in one State, under the Laws thereof, escaping into another, shall, in Consequence of any Law or Regulation therein, be discharged from such Service or Labour, but shall be delivered up on Claim of the Party to whom such Service or Labour may be due.

Section 3. New States may be admitted by the Congress into this Union; but no new State shall be formed or erected within the Jurisdiction of any other State; nor any State be formed by the Junction of two or more States, or Parts of States, without the Consent of the Legislatures of the States concerned as well as of the Congress.

The Congress shall have Power to dispose of and make all needful Rules and Regulations respecting the Territory or other Property belonging to the United States; and nothing in this Constitution shall be so construed as to Prejudice any Claims of the United States, or of any particular State.

Section 4. The United States shall guarantee to every State in this Union a Republican Form of Government, and shall protect each of them against Invasion; and on Application of the Legislature, or of the Executive (when the Legislature cannot be convened) against domestic Violence.

ARTICLE V

The Congress, whenever two thirds of both Houses shall deem it necessary, shall propose Amendments to this Constitution, or, on the Application of the Legislatures of two thirds of the several States, shall call a Convention for proposing Amendments, which, in either Case, shall be valid to all Intents and Purposes, as part of this Constitution, when ratified by the Legislatures of three fourths of the several States, or by Conventions in three fourths thereof, as the one or the other Mode of Ratification may be proposed by the Congress; Provided that no Amendment which may be made prior to the Year One thousand eight hundred and eight shall in any Manner affect the first and fourth Clauses in the Ninth Section of the first Article; and that no State, without its Consent, shall be deprived of its equal Suffrage in the Senate.

ARTICLE VI

All Debts contracted and Engagements entered into, before the Adoption of this Constitution shall be as valid against the United States under this Constitution, as under the Confederation.

This Constitution, and the Laws of the United States which shall be made in Pursuance thereof; and all Treaties made, or which shall be made, under the Authority of the United States, shall be the supreme Law of the Land; and the Judges in every State shall be bound thereby, any Thing in the Constitution or Laws of any State to the Contrary notwithstanding.

The Senators and Representatives before mentioned, and the Members of the several State Legislatures, and all executive and judicial Officers, both of the United States and of the several States, shall be bound by Oath or Affirmation, to support this Constitution; but no religious Test shall ever be required as a Qualification to any Office or public Trust under the United States.

ARTICLE VII

The Ratification of the Conventions of nine States shall be sufficient for the Establishment of this Constitution between the States so ratifying the Same.

AMENDMENT I [1791]

Congress shall make no law respecting an establishment of religion, or prohibiting the free exercise thereof; or abridging the freedom of speech, or of the press; or the right of the people peaceably to assembly, and to petition the Government for a redress of grievances.

AMENDMENT II [1791]

A well regulated Militia, being necessary to the security of a free State, the right of the people to keep and bear Arms, shall not be infringed.

AMENDMENT III [1791]

No Soldier shall, in time of peace be quartered in any house, without the consent of the Owner, nor in time of war, but in a manner to be prescribed by law.

AMENDMENT IV [1791]

The right of the people to be secure in their persons, houses, papers, and effects, against unreasonable searches and seizures, shall not be violated, and no Warrants shall issue, but upon probable cause, supported by Oath or affirmation, and particularly describing the place to be searched, and the persons or things to be seized.

AMENDMENT V [1791]

No person shall be held to answer for a capital, or otherwise infamous crime, unless on a presentment or indictment of a Grand Jury, except in cases arising in the land or naval forces, or in the Militia, when in actual service in time of War or public danger; nor shall any person be subject for the same offence to be twice put in jeopardy of life or limb; nor shall be compelled in any criminal case to be a witness against himself, nor be deprived of life, liberty, or property, without due process of law; nor shall private property be taken for public use, without just compensation.

AMENDMENT VI [1791]

In all criminal prosecutions, the accused shall enjoy the right to a speedy and public trial, by an impartial jury of the State and district wherein the crime shall have been committed, which district shall have been previously ascertained by law, and to be informed of the nature and cause of the accusation; to be confronted with the witnesses against him; to have compulsory process for obtaining witnesses in his favor, and to have the Assistance of Counsel for his defence.

AMENDMENT VII [1791]

In Suits at common law, where the value in controversy shall exceed twenty dollars, the right of trial by jury shall be preserved, and no fact tried by jury, shall be otherwise reexamined in any Court of the United States, than according to the rules of the common law.

AMENDMENT VIII [1791]

Excessive bail shall not be required, nor excessive fines imposed, nor cruel and unusual punishments inflicted.

AMENDMENT IX [1791]

The enumeration in the Constitution, of certain rights, shall not be construed to deny or disparage others retained by the people.

AMENDMENT X [1791]

The powers not delegated to the United States by the Constitution, nor prohibited by it to the States, are reserved to the States respectively, or to the people.

AMENDMENT XI [1798]

The Judicial power of the United States shall not be construed to extend to any suit in law or equity, commenced or prosecuted against one of the United States by Citizens of another State, or by Citizens or Subjects of any Foreign State.

AMENDMENT XII [1804]

The Electors shall meet in their respective states, and vote by ballot for President and Vice-President, one of whom, at least, shall not be an inhabitant of the same state with themselves; they shall name in their ballots the person voted for as President, and in distinct ballots the person voted for as Vice-President, and they shall make distinct lists of all persons voted for as President, and of all persons voted for as Vice-President, and of the number of votes for each, which lists they shall sign and certify, and transmit sealed to the seat of the government of the United States, directed to the President of the Senate;—The President of the Senate shall, in the presence of the Senate and House of Representatives, open all the certificates and the votes shall then be counted;—The person having the greatest number of votes for President, shall be the President, if such number be a majority of the whole number of Electors appointed; and if no person have such majority, then from the persons having the highest numbers not exceeding three on the list of those voted for as President, the House of Representatives shall choose immediately, by ballot, the President. But in choosing the President, the votes shall be taken by states, the representation from each state having one vote; a quorum for this purpose shall consist of a member or members from two-thirds of the states, and a majority of all states shall be necessary to a choice. And if the House of Representatives shall not choose a President whenever the right of choice shall devolve upon them, before the fourth day of March next following, then the Vice-President shall act as President, as in the case of the death or other constitutional disability of the President.—The person having the greatest number of votes as Vice-President, shall be the Vice-President, if such number be a majority of the whole number of Electors appointed, and if no person have a majority, then from the two highest numbers on the list, the Senate shall choose the Vice-President; a quorum for the purpose shall consist of two-thirds of the whole number of Senators, and a majority of the whole number shall be necessary to a choice. But no person constitutionally ineligible to the office of President shall be eligible to that of Vice-President of the United States.

AMENDMENT XIII [1865]

Section 1. Neither slavery nor involuntary servitude, except as a punishment for crime whereof the party shall have been duly convicted, shall exist within the United States, or any place subject to their jurisdiction.

Section 2. Congress shall have power to enforce this article by appropriate legislation.

AMENDMENT XIV [1868]

Section 1. All persons born or naturalized in the United States, and subject to the jurisdiction thereof, are citizens of the United States and of the State wherein they reside. No State shall make or enforce any law which shall abridge the privileges or immunities of citizens of the United States; nor shall any State deprive any person of life, liberty, or property, without due process of law; nor deny to any person within its jurisdiction the equal protection of the laws.

Section 2. Representatives shall be apportioned among the several States according to their respective numbers, counting the whole number of persons in each State, excluding Indians not taxed. But when the right to vote at any election for the choice of electors for President and Vice President of the United States, Representatives in Congress, the Executive and Judicial officers of a State, or the members of the Legislature thereof, is denied to any of the male inhabitants of such State, being twenty-one years of age, and citizens of the United States, or in any way abridged, except for participation in rebellion, or other crime, the basis of representation therein shall be reduced in the proportion which the number of such male citizens shall bear to the whole number of male citizens twenty-one years of age in such State.

Section 3. No person shall be a Senator or Representative in Congress, or elector of President and Vice President, or hold any office, civil or military, under the United States, or under any State, who having previously taken an oath, as a member of Congress, or as an officer of the United States, or as a member of any State legislature, or as an executive or judicial officer of any State, to support the Constitution of the United States, shall have engaged in insurrection or rebellion against the same, or given aid or comfort to the enemies thereof. But Congress may by a vote of two-thirds of each House, remove such disability.

Section 4. The validity of the public debt of the United States, authorized by law, including debts incurred for payment of pensions and bounties for services in suppressing insurrection or rebellion, shall not be questioned. But neither the United States nor any State shall assume or pay any debt or obligation incurred in aid of insurrection or rebellion against the United States, or any claim for the loss or emancipation of any slave; but all such debts, obligations and claims shall be held illegal and void.

Section 5. The Congress shall have power to enforce, by appropriate legislation, the provisions of this article.

AMENDMENT XV [1870]

Section 1. The right of citizens of the United States to vote shall not be denied or abridged by the United States or by any State on account of race, color, or previous condition of servitude.

Section 2. The Congress shall have power to enforce this article by appropriate legislation.

AMENDMENT XVI [1913]

The Congress shall have power to lay and collect taxes on incomes, from whatever source derived, without apportionment among the several States, and without regard to any census or enumeration.

AMENDMENT XVII [1913]

Section 1. The Senate of the United States shall be composed of two Senators from each State, elected by the people thereof, for six years; and each Senator shall have one vote. The electors in each State shall have the qualifications requisite for electors of the most numerous branch of the State legislatures.

Section 2. When vacancies happen in the representation of any State in the Senate, the executive authority of such State shall issue writs of election to fill such vacancies: *Provided,* That the legislature of any State may empower the executive thereof to make temporary appointments until the people fill the vacancies by election as the legislature may direct.

Section 3. This amendment shall not be so construed as to affect the election or term of any Senator chosen before it becomes valid as part of the Constitution.

AMENDMENT XVIII [1919]

Section 1. After one year from the ratification of this article the manufacture, sale, or transportation of intoxicating liquors within, the importation thereof into, or the exportation thereof from the United States and all territory subject to the jurisdiction thereof for beverage purposes is hereby prohibited.

Section 2. The Congress and the several States shall have concurrent power to enforce this article by appropriate legislation.

Section 3. This article shall be inoperative unless it shall have been ratified as an amendment to the Constitution by the legislatures of the several States, as provided in the Constitution, within seven years from the date of the submission hereof to the States by the Congress.

AMENDMENT XIX [1920]

Section 1. The right of citizens of the United States to vote shall not be denied or abridged by the United States or by any State on account of sex.

Section 2. Congress shall have power to enforce this article by appropriate legislation.

AMENDMENT XX [1933]

Section 1. The terms of the President and Vice President shall end at noon on the 20th day of January, and the terms of Senators and Representatives at noon on the 3d day of January, of the years in which such terms would have ended if this article had not been ratified; and the terms of their successors shall then begin.

Section 2. The Congress shall assemble at least once in every year, and such meeting shall begin at noon on the 3d day of January, unless they shall by law appoint a different day.

Section 3. If, at the time fixed for the beginning of the term of the President, the President elect shall have died, the Vice President elect shall become President. If the President shall not have been chosen before the time fixed for the beginning of his term, or if the President elect shall have failed to qualify, then the Vice President elect shall act as President until a President shall have qualified; and the Congress may by law provide for the case wherein neither a President elect nor a Vice President elect shall have qualified, declaring who shall then act as President, or the manner in which one who is to act shall be selected, and such person shall act accordingly until a President or Vice President shall have qualified.

Section 4. The Congress may by law provide for the case of the death of any of the persons from whom the House of Representatives may choose a President whenever the right of choice shall have devolved upon them, and for the case of the death of any of the persons from whom the Senate may choose a Vice President whenever the right of choice shall have devolved upon them.

Section 5. Sections 1 and 2 shall take effect on the 15th day of October following the ratification of this article.

Section 6. This article shall be inoperative unless it shall have been ratified as an amendment to the Constitution by the legislatures of three-fourths of the several States within seven years from the date of its submission.

AMENDMENT XXI [1933]

Section 1. The eighteenth article of amendment to the Constitution of the United States is hereby repealed.

Section 2. The transportation or importation into any State, Territory, or possession of the United States for delivery or use therein of intoxicating liquors, in violation of the laws thereof, is hereby prohibited.

Section 3. This article shall be inoperative unless it shall have been ratified as an amendment to the Constitution by conventions in the several States, as provided in the Constitution, within seven years from the date of the submission hereof to the States by the Congress.

AMENDMENT XXII [1951]

Section 1. No person shall be elected to the office of the President more than twice, and no person who has held the office of President, or acted as President, for more than two years of a term to which some other person was elected President shall be elected to the office of President more than once. But this Article shall not apply to any person holding the office of President when this Article was proposed by the Congress, and shall not prevent any person who may be holding the office of President, or acting as President, during the term within which this Article becomes operative from holding the office of President or acting as President during the remainder of such term.

Section 2. This article shall be inoperative unless it shall have been ratified as an amendment to the Constitution by the legislatures of three-fourths of the several States within seven years from the date of its submission to the States by the Congress.

AMENDMENT XXIII [1961]

Section 1. The District constituting the seat of Government of the United States shall appoint in such manner as the Congress may direct:

A number of electors of President and Vice President equal to the whole number of Senators and Representatives in Congress to which the District would be entitled if it were a State, but in no event more than the least populous state; they shall be in addition to those appointed by the states, but they shall be considered, for the purposes of the election of President and Vice President, to be electors appointed by a state; and they shall meet in the District and perform such duties as provided by the twelfth article of amendment.

Section 2. The Congress shall have power to enforce this article by appropriate legislation.

AMENDMENT XXIV [1964]

Section 1. The right of citizens of the United States to vote in any primary or other election for President or Vice President, for electors for President or Vice President, or for Senator or Representative in Congress, shall not be denied or abridged by the United States, or any State by reason of failure to pay any poll tax or other tax.

Section 2. The Congress shall have power to enforce this article by appropriate legislation.

AMENDMENT XXV [1967]

Section 1. In case of the removal of the President from office or of his death or resignation, the Vice President shall become President.

Section 2. Whenever there is a vacancy in the office of the Vice President, the President shall nominate a Vice President who shall take office upon confirmation by a majority vote of both Houses of Congress.

Section 3. Whenever the President transmits to the President pro tempore of the Senate and the Speaker of the House of Representatives his written declaration that he is unable to discharge the powers and duties of his office, and until he transmits to them a written declaration to the contrary, such powers and duties shall be discharged by the Vice President as Acting President.

Section 4. Whenever the Vice President and a majority of either the principal officers of the executive departments or of such other body as Congress may by law provide, transmit to the President pro tempore of the Senate and the Speaker of the House of Representatives their written declaration that the President is unable to discharge the powers and duties of his office, the Vice President shall immediately assume the powers and duties of the office as Acting President.

Thereafter, when the President transmits to the President pro tempore of the Senate and the Speaker of the House of Representatives his written declaration that no inability exists, he shall resume the powers and duties of his office unless the Vice President and a majority of either the principal officers of the executive department or of such other body as Congress may by law provide, transmit within four days to the President pro tempore of the Senate and the Speaker of the House of Representatives their written declaration that the President is unable to discharge the powers and duties of his office. Thereupon Congress shall decide the issue, assembling within forty-eight hours for that purpose if not in session. If the Congress, within twenty-one days after receipt of the latter written declaration, or, if Congress is not in session, within twenty-one days after Congress is required to assemble, determines by two-thirds vote of both Houses that the President is unable to discharge the powers and duties of his office, the Vice President shall continue to discharge the same as Acting President; otherwise, the President shall resume the powers and duties of his office.

AMENDMENT XXVI [1971]

Section 1. The right of citizens of the United States, who are eighteen years of age or older, to vote shall not be denied or abridged by the United States or by any State on account of age.

Section 2. The Congress shall have power to enforce this article by appropriate legislation.

AMENDMENT XXVII [1992]

No law, varying the compensation for the services of the Senators and Representatives, shall take effect, until an election of Representatives shall have intervened.

APPENDIX B: You Be The _____: Actual Outcomes and Court Decisions

1.1 SENATOR In 2009, New York Senator Charles Schumer introduced the Avoiding Life-Endangering and Reckless Texting by Drivers Act (ALERT), which would deny federal highway funds to states that fail to ban texting while driving. As of November 2012, Congress has failed to pass ALERT, and states continue to have the freedom to decide this issue without federal intrusion.

3.1 JUDGE The appellate court refused to throw out the charges. Although Emil was unconscious at the time his car struck the schoolgirls, he had made the initial decision to get behind the wheel despite the knowledge that he suffered from epileptic seizures. In other words, the *actus reus* in this crime was not Emil's driving into the girls, but his decision to drive in the first place. That decision was certainly voluntary and therefore satisfies the requirements of *actus reus*. Note that if Emil had never had an epileptic seizure before, and had no idea that he suffered from that malady, the court's decision would probably have been different.

4.1 POLICE COMMISSIONER Boston Police Commissioner Edward F. Davis gave the order to clear the Greenway. Police officers forced protestors onto their stomachs, cable-tied their hands, and dragged them into police vans. "We have been very accommodating to everyone's right to demonstrate peaceably," Boston police spokeswoman Elaine Driscoll said of Davis's decision. "But when unpredictability starts to enter the scenario, we are obligated to maintain public order and protect public safety." Some protestors claimed that the Boston police were unnecessarily rough in making these arrests, but both sides seemed to have learned from the encounter. A month later, Occupy Boston made a peaceful march on the Charlestown Bridge that avoided any confrontation with city law enforcement.

5.1 SHERIFF'S DEPUTY As these events actually played out, fifteen Cincinnati law enforcement officers had surrounded a suspect named Lorenzo Collins when he brandished the brick, and the two officers closest to Collins fatally shot him. The two officers were cleared of any wrongdoing, given that a reasonable officer in their position could have seen the brick as an instrument that could cause death or serious bodily harm. The court of public opinion, however, was against the police officers, who were accused by members of the community of needlessly killing a mentally unstable man who was carrying a brick, not a knife or a gun.

6.1 JUDGE Federal district judge Aleta Trauger ruled that the drug task force agent did not have probable cause to stop the car—actually driven by two cousins named Luis and Gerardo Ruiz. Therefore, the half-kilo of heroin was "fruit of the poisoned tree" and was not allowed as evidence. Trauger clearly did not believe that the cousins had broken any traffic laws, and suggested that the arresting officer had changed his story only after realizing that the "video showed that the Ruiz vehicle was not speeding." Note that Trauger did not address the question of racial profiling in this case, though the defendants' Hispanic origins most likely gave him further reason to suspect the law enforcement officer's motives and behavior.

8.1 DEFENSE ATTORNEY In defending Daniel Aguilar against charges regarding Christopher Ash's murder, defense attorney Antonio Bestard's primary argument was that his client did not know that Ash was going to be killed in the garage. After all, they were best friends. Along the same lines, Bestard argued that Aguilar was forced to lure his friend to the garage by older gang members, who would have killed Aguilar had he refused. Bestard also attacked the credibility of the main witness, José Covarrubias, who not only was under the influence of drugs on the night of the murder and sleeping with the victim's sister, but also had received a lighter sentence of twenty-two years in return for testifying against fellow gang members. Bestard suggested that Covarrubias had an incentive to lie to law enforcement officials to get a lighter sentence. In the end, however, the jury found Aguilar guilty of first degree murder, and he was sentenced to life in prison without parole.

10.1 PROBATION OFFICER Alain LeConte's probation officer did not take any steps to revoke his probation. The issue became moot, however, when LeConte was arrested for killing a gas station attendant during an armed robbery in Norwalk, Connecticut. The crime took place between his first and second failed drug tests. LeConte's probation officer came under a great deal of criticism for failing to revoke his probation, but she received support from her supervisor. "We can only do so much," he said. "[LeConte's] probation officer went out of her way to assist this young man, but unfortunately it wasn't successful." The supervisor also pointed out that LeConte had no known history of violent behavior and had been a generally cooperative probationer when it came to getting treatment. This case underscores the difficult aspects of a probation officer's job. A misjudgment, even if it was based on a reasonable evaluation of the situation, can end in tragedy.

12.1 PAROLE BOARD MEMBER

Susan Atkins was a disciple of cult leader Charles Manson and, in the summer of 1969, participated in one of the most sensationalized mass murders in American history. The woman Atkins stabbed sixteen times was Sharon Tate, an actress and the wife of film director Roman Polanski. On September 2, 2009, the California Board of Parole unanimously denied compassionate release for Atkins, marking the eighteenth time she had been refused parole. Three months later, Atkins died of brain cancer. Her case highlights the extent to which parole boards are often swayed by the nature of the crime above all other considerations.

APPENDIX C: Table of Cases

A

Adamson v. California (1947), 229
Allen v. United States (1896), 243
Argersinger v. Hamlin (1972), 208
Arizona v. Fulminante (1991), 182
Arizona v. Gant (2009), 175
Atkins v. Virginia (2002), 273, 277

B

Barker v. Wingo (1972), 227
Batson v. Kentucky (1986), 232
Baze v. Rees (2008), 274, 275
Bell v. Wolfish (1979), 326
Bennis v. Michigan (1996), 298
Benton v. Maryland (1969), 91
Berger v. United States (1935), 205
Boykin v. Alabama (1969), 226
Breed v. Jones (1975), 369
Brewer v. Williams (1977), 164
Brown v. Entertainment Merchants Association (EMA), 51, 52
Brown v. Plata (2011), 347
Burger v. New York (1967), 176

C

California v. Greenwood (1988), 171
Carroll v. United States (1925), 174
Chimel v. California (1969), 173
Coolidge v. New Hampshire (1971), 175
County of Riverside v. McLaughlin (1991), 163

D

Duncan v. Louisiana (1968), 91, 228

E

Escobedo v. Illinois (1964), 91
Estelle v. Gamble (1976), 346

F

Florida v. Powell (2010), 182
Furman v. Georgia (1972), 197, 271, 276

G

Gagnon v. Scarpelli (1973), 293
Gault, In re (1967), 91, 208, 369, 370, 384
Georgia v. McCollum (1992), 234
Gideon v. Wainwright (1963), 91, 196, 208
Graham v. Connor (1989), 148
Graham v. Florida (2010), 372
Greenholtz v. Inmates of the Nebraska Penal and Correctional Complex (1979), 351
Gregg v. Georgia (1976), 197

H

Herring v. United States (2009), 164
Howes v. Fields (2012), 182
Hudson v. McMillan (1992), 345
Hudson v. Michigan (2006), 169–170

I

In re _____. See name of party

J

J. E. B. v. Alabama ex rel. T. B. (1994), 234

K

Katz v. United States (1967), 171, 176
Kentucky v. King (2011), 160–161, 163
Kent v. United States (1966), 369

K

Klopfer v. North Carolina (1967), 91
Knights, United States v. (2001), 291

L

Leon v. United States (1984), 164
Lockyer v. Andrade (2003), 267

M

Malloy v. Hogan (1964), 91
Mapp v. Ohio (1961), 91
Maryland v. Shatzer (2010), 197
McClesky v. Kemp (1987), 277
McKeiver v. Pennsylvania (1971), 369
Mempa v. Rhay (1967), 293
Minnesota v. Murphy (1984), 294
Miranda v. Arizona (1966), 29, 91, 179, 180, 196, 244
Montana v. Egelhoff (1996), 86
Moran v. Burbine (1986), 182
Morrissey v. Brewer (1972), 293, 354–355

N

New York v. Benton (1981), 174–175
New York v. Quarles (1984), 182
Nix v. Williams (1984), 164

O

Oliver, In re (1948), 91

P

Parker v. Gladden (1966), 91
Payton v. New York (1980), 170
Pointer v. Texas (1965), 91
Powers v. Ohio (1991), 234

Q

Quirk, In re (1997), 291

R

Ring v. Arizona (2002), 272
Robinson, v. United States (1973), 173
Rochin v. California (1952), 91
Roper v. Simmons (2005), 273, 277, 372
Rovario v. United States (1957), 134
Rummel v. Estelle (1980), 267

S

Santobello v. New York (1971), 225
Schall v. Martin (1984), 384
Schneckcloth v. Bustamonte (1973), 174
Steagald v. United States (1981), 170
Swain v. Alabama (1965), 232

T

Tennessee v. Garner (1985), 147–148
Terry v. Ohio (1968), 165–166, 167, 168, 171
Texas v. Cobb (2001), 182

U

United States v. _____. See name of opposing party

W

Weems v. United States (1910), 271, 273
Whitley v. Albers (1986), 345
Wilson v. Arkansas (1995), 169
Wilson v. Seiter (1991), 346
Winship, In re (1970), 230, 369

Z

Zolin, v. United States (1989), 210

GLOSSARY

A

acquittal A declaration following a trial that the individual accused of the crime is innocent in the eyes of the law and thus is absolved of the charges.

actus reus (pronounced *ak*-tus *ray*-uhs). A guilty (prohibited) act.

adjudicatory hearing The process through which a juvenile court determines whether there is sufficient evidence to support the initial petition.

administrative law The body of law created by regulatory (administrative) agencies (in the form of rules, regulations, orders, and decisions) in order to carry out their duties and responsibilities.

affidavit A written statement of facts, confirmed by the oath or affirmation of the party making it and made before a person having the authority to administer the oath or affirmation.

affirmative action A hiring or promotion policy favoring those groups, such as women, African Americans, or Hispanics, who have suffered from discrimination in the past or continue to suffer from discrimination.

aftercare The variety of therapeutic, educational, and counseling programs made available to juvenile delinquents (and some adults) after they have been released from a correctional facility.

age of onset The age at which a juvenile first exhibits delinquent behavior.

aggravating circumstances Any circumstances accompanying the commission of a crime that may justify a harsher sentence.

aging out A term used to explain the fact that criminal activity declines with age.

alien A person who is not a citizen of the country in which he or she is found and therefore does not enjoy the same rights as a citizen of that country.

Allen **Charge** An instruction by a judge to a deadlocked jury with only a few dissenters that asks the jurors in the minority to reconsider the majority opinion.

anomie A condition in which the individual suffers from the breakdown or absence of social norms.

Antiterrorism and Effective Death Penalty Act of 1996 (AEDPA) Legislation giving law enforcement officers the power to arrest and prosecute any individual who provides "material support or resources" to a "foreign terrorist organization."

appeal The process of seeking a higher court's review of a lower court's decision for the purpose of correcting or changing this decision.

appellate courts Courts that review decisions made by lower courts, such as trial courts.

arraignment A court proceeding in which the suspect is formally charged with the criminal offense stated in the indictment.

arrest To take into custody a person suspected of criminal activity.

arrest warrant A written order, based on probable cause and issued by a judge or magistrate, commanding that the person named on the warrant be arrested by the police.

assault A threat or an attempt to do violence to another person that causes that person to fear immediate physical harm.

attempt The act of taking substantial steps toward committing a crime while having the ability and the intent to commit the crime, even if the crime never takes place.

attendant circumstances The facts surrounding an event that must be proved to convict the defendant of the underlying crime.

attorney-client privilege A rule of evidence requiring that communications between a client and his or her attorney be kept confidential, unless the client consents to disclosure.

attorney general The chief law officer of a state; also, the chief law officer of the nation.

authority The power designated to an agent of the law over a person who has broken the law.

automatic transfer The process by which a juvenile is transferred to adult court as a matter of state law.

B

bail The dollar amount or conditions set by the court to ensure that an individual accused of a crime will appear for further criminal proceedings.

bail bond agent A businessperson who agrees, for a fee, to pay the bail amount if the accused fails to appear in court as ordered.

ballistics The study of firearms, including the firing of the weapon and the flight of the bullet.

ballot initiative A procedure in which citizens, by collecting enough signatures, can force a public vote on a proposed change to state or local law.

battery The act of physically contacting another person with the intent to do harm, even if the resulting injury is insubstantial.

bench trial A trial conducted without a jury, in which a judge determines the defendant's guilt or innocence.

beyond a reasonable doubt The degree of proof required to find the defendant in a criminal trial guilty of committing the crime. The defendant's guilt must be the only reasonable explanation for the criminal act before the court.

Bill of Rights The first ten amendments to the U.S. Constitution.

biology The science of living organisms, including their structure, function, growth, and origin.

biometrics Methods to identify a person based on his or her unique physical characteristics, such as fingerprints or facial configuration.

blue curtain A metaphorical term that refers to the secrecy and the general mistrust of the outside world shared by many police officers.

boot camp A variation on traditional shock incarceration in which juveniles (and some adults) are sent to secure confinement facilities modeled on military basic training camps instead of prison or jail.

botnet A networks of computers that have been appropriated without the knowledge of their owners and used to spread harmful programs via the Internet; short for robot network.

***Boykin* form** A form that must be completed by a defendant who pleads guilty. The defendant states that she or he has done so voluntarily and with full comprehension of the consequences.

broken windows theory Wilson and Kelling's theory that a neighborhood in disrepair signals that criminal activity is tolerated in the area. By cracking down on quality-of-life crimes, police can reclaim the neighborhood and encourage law-abiding citizens to live there.

bullying Overt acts taken by students with the goal of intimidating, harassing, or humiliating other students.

bureaucracy A hierarchically structured administrative organization that carries out specific functions.

burglary The act of breaking into or entering a structure (such as a home or office) without permission for the purpose of committing a crime.

burnout A mental state that occurs when a person suffers from exhaustion and has difficulty functioning normally as a result of overwork and stress.

C

capital crime A criminal act that makes the offender eligible to receive the death penalty.

capital punishment The use of the death penalty to punish wrongdoers for certain crimes.

case attrition The process through which prosecutors, by deciding whether to prosecute each person arrested, effect an overall reduction in the number of persons prosecuted.

case law The rules of law announced in court decisions.

caseload The number of individual probationers or parolees under the supervision of a probation or parole officer.

causation The relationship in which a change in one measurement or behavior creates a recognizable change in another measurement or behavior.

Central Intelligence Agency (CIA) The U.S. government agency that is responsible for collecting and coordinating foreign intelligence operations.

challenge for cause A *voir dire* challenge for which an attorney states the reason why a prospective juror should not be included on the jury.

charge The judge's instructions to the jury following the attorneys' closing arguments.

child abuse Mistreatment of children by causing physical, emotional, or sexual damage without any plausible explanation, such as an accident.

child neglect A form of child abuse in which the child is denied certain necessities such as shelter, food, care, and love.

chronic offender A delinquent or criminal who commits multiple offenses and is considered part of a small group of wrongdoers who are responsible for a majority of the antisocial activity in any given community.

circumstantial evidence Indirect evidence that is offered to establish, by inference, the likelihood of a fact that is in question.

citizen oversight The process by which citizens review complaints brought against individual police officers or police departments.

civil law The branch of law dealing with the definition and enforcement of all private or public rights, as opposed to criminal matters.

civil liberties The basic rights and freedoms for American citizens guaranteed by the U.S. Constitution, particularly in the Bill of Rights.

classification The process through which prison officials determine which correctional facility is best suited to the individual offender.

clearance rate A comparison of the number of crimes cleared by arrest and prosecution with the number of crimes reported during any given time period.

closing arguments Arguments made by each side's attorney after the cases for the prosecution and the defense have been presented.

coercion The use of physical force or mental intimidation to compel a person to do something—such as confess to committing a crime—against her or his will.

cold case A criminal investigation that has not been solved after a certain amount of time

cold hit The establishment of a connection between a suspect and a crime, often through the use of DNA evidence, in the absence of an ongoing criminal investigation.

community corrections The correctional supervision of offenders in the community as an alternative to sending them to prison or jail.

community policing A policing philosophy that emphasizes community support for and cooperation with the police in preventing crime.

competency hearing A court proceeding to determine whether the defendant is mentally well enough to understand the charges filed against her or him and cooperate with a lawyer in presenting a defense.

compliance The state of operating in accordance with governmental standards.

computer crime Any wrongful act that is directed against computers and computer parts or that involves wrongful use or abuse of computers or software.

concurrent jurisdiction The situation that occurs when two or more courts have the authority to preside over the same criminal case.

concurring opinions Separate opinions prepared by judges who support the decision of the majority of the court but who want to make or clarify a particular point or to voice disapproval of the grounds on which the decision was made.

confidential informant (CI) A human source for police who provides information concerning illegal activity in which he or she is involved.

conflict model A criminal justice model in which the content of criminal law is determined by the groups that hold economic, political, and social power in a community.

confrontation clause The part of the Sixth Amendment that guarantees all defendants the right to confront witnesses testifying against them during the criminal trial.

congregate system A nineteenth-century penitentiary system in which inmates were kept in separate cells during the night but worked together in the daytime under a code of enforced silence.

consensus model A criminal justice model in which the majority of citizens in a society share the same values and beliefs. Criminal acts are acts that conflict with these values and beliefs and that are deemed harmful to society.

consent searches Searches by police that are made after the subject of the search has agreed to the action. In these situations, consent, if given of free will, validates a warrantless search.

conspiracy A secret plot by two or more people to carry out an illegal or harmful act.

constitutional law Law based on the U.S. Constitution and the constitutions of the various states.

control theory A series of theories that assume that all individuals have the potential for criminal behavior, but are restrained by the damage that such actions would do to their relationships with family, friends, and members of the community.

coroner The medical examiner of a county, usually elected by popular vote.

corporate violence Physical harm to individuals or the environment that occurs as the result of corporate policies or decision making.

corpus delicti The body of circumstances that must exist for a criminal act to have occurred.

correlation The relationship between two measurements or behaviors that tend to move in the same direction.

courtroom work group The social organization consisting of the judge, prosecutor, defense attorney, and other court workers.

crime An act that violates criminal law and is punishable by criminal sanctions.

crime control model A criminal justice model that places primary emphasis on the right of society to be protected from crime and violent criminals.

crime mapping Technology that allows crime analysts to identify trends and patterns of criminal behavior within a given area.

criminal justice system The interlocking network of law enforcement agencies, courts, and corrections institutions designed to enforce criminal laws and protect society from criminal behavior.

criminologist A specialist in the field of crime and the causes of criminal behavior.

criminology The scientific study of crime and the causes of criminal behavior.

cross-examination The questioning of an opposing witness during trial.

custodial interrogation The questioning of a suspect after that person has been taken into custody. In this situation, the suspect must be read his or her *Miranda* rights before interrogation can begin.

custody The forceful detention of a person, or the perception that a person is not free to leave the immediate vicinity.

cyber crime A crime that occurs online, in the virtual community of the Internet, as opposed to in the physical world.

cyber fraud Any misrepresentation knowingly made over the Internet with the intention of deceiving another and on which a reasonable person would and does rely to his or her detriment.

cyberstalking The crime of stalking, committed in cyberspace through the use of e-mail, text messages, or another form of electronic communication.

D

dark figure of crime A term used to describe the actual amount of crime that takes place. The "figure" is "dark," or impossible to detect, because a great number of crimes are never reported to the police.

day reporting center (DRC) A community-based corrections center to which offenders report on a daily basis for treatment, education, and rehabilitation.

deadly force Force applied by a police officer that is likely or intended to cause death.

defendant In a civil court, the person or institution against whom an action is brought. In a criminal court, the person or entity who has been formally accused of violating a criminal law.

defense attorney The lawyer representing the defendant.

delegation of authority The principles of command on which most police departments are based, in which personnel take orders from and are responsible to those in positions of power directly above them.

"deliberate indifference" The standard for violation of an inmate's Eighth Amendment rights, requiring that prison officials be aware of harmful conditions in a correctional institution and fail to take steps to remedy those conditions.

departure A stipulation in many federal and state sentencing guidelines that allows a judge to adjust his or her sentencing decision based on the special circumstances of a particular case.

deprivation model A theory that inmate aggression is the result of the frustration inmates feel at being deprived of freedom, consumer goods, sex, and other staples of life outside the institution.

desistance The process through which criminal activity decreases and reintegration into society increases over a period of time.

detainer A document that gives U.S. Immigration and Customs Enforcement custody of an immigration law violator following the disposition of that person's case by the criminal justice system.

detective The primary police investigator of crimes.

detention The temporary custody of a juvenile in a secure facility after a petition has been filed and before the adjudicatory process begins.

detention hearing A hearing to determine whether a juvenile should be detained, or remain detained, while waiting for the adjudicatory process to begin.

determinate sentencing A period of incarceration that is fixed by a sentencing authority and cannot be reduced by judges or other corrections officials

deterrence The strategy of preventing crime through the threat of punishment.

deviance Behavior that is considered to go against the norms established by society.

differential response A strategy for answering calls for service in which response time is adapted to the seriousness of the call.

directed patrol A patrol strategy that is designed to focus on a specific type of criminal activity at a specific time.

direct evidence Evidence that establishes the existence of a fact that is in question without relying on inference.

direct examination The examination of a witness by the attorney who calls the witness to the stand to testify.

direct supervision approach A process of prison and jail administration in which correctional officers are in continuous physical contact with inmates during the day.

discovery Formal investigation by each side prior to trial.

discretion The ability of individuals in the criminal justice system to make operational decisions based on personal judgment instead of formal rules or official information.

discretionary release The release of an inmate into a community supervision program at the discretion of the parole board within limits set by state or federal law.

discrimination The illegal use of characteristics such as gender or race by employers when making hiring or promotion decisions.

disposition hearing Similar to the sentencing hearing for adults, a hearing in which the juvenile judge or officer decides the appropriate punishment for a youth found to be delinquent or a status offender.

dissenting opinions Separate opinions in which judges disagree with the conclusion reached by the majority of the court and expand on their own views about the case.

diversion In the context of corrections, a strategy to divert those offenders who qualify away from prison and jail and toward community-based sanctions.

DNA fingerprinting The identification of a person based on a sample of her or his DNA, the genetic material found in the cells of all living things.

docket The list of cases entered on a court's calendar and thus scheduled to be heard by the court.

domestic terrorism Acts of terrorism that take place within the territorial jurisdiction of the United States without direct foreign involvement.

double jeopardy To twice place at risk (jeopardize) a person's life or liberty. The Fifth Amendment to the U.S. Constitution prohibits a second prosecution for the same court for the same criminal offense.

double marginality The double suspicion that minority law enforcement officers face from their white colleagues and from members of the minority community to which they belong.

drug Any substance that modifies biological, psychological, or social behavior; in particular, an illegal substance with those properties.

drug abuse The use of drugs that results in physical or psychological problems for the user, as well as disruption of personal relationships and employment.

Drug Enforcement Administration (DEA) The federal agency responsible for enforcing the nation's laws and regulations regarding narcotics and other controlled substances.

dual court system The separate but interrelated court system of the United States, made up of the courts on the national level and the courts on the state level.

due process clause The provisions of the Fifth and Fourteenth Amendments to the Constitution that guarantee that no person shall be deprived of life, liberty, or property without due process of law.

due process model A criminal justice model that places primacy on the right of the individual to be protected from the power of the government.

duress Unlawful pressure brought to bear on a person, causing the person to perform an act that he or she would not otherwise perform.

duty The moral sense of a police officer that she or he should behave in a certain manner.

duty to retreat The requirement that a person claiming self-defense prove that she or he first took reasonable steps to avoid the conflict that resulted in the use of deadly force.

E

electronic monitoring A technique of probation supervision in which the offender's whereabouts are kept under surveillance by an electronic device.

electronic surveillance The use of electronic equipment by law enforcement agents to record private conversations or observe conduct that is meant to be private.

entrapment A defense in which the defendant claims that he or she was induced by a public official—usually an undercover agent or police officer—to commit a crime that he or she would not otherwise have committed.

ethics The moral principles that govern a person's perception of right and wrong.

evidence Anything that is used to prove the existence or nonexistence of a fact.

exclusionary rule A rule under which any evidence that is obtained in violation of the accused's rights, as well as any evidence derived from illegally obtained evidence, will not be admissible in criminal court.

exigent circumstances Situations that require extralegal or exceptional actions by the police.

expert witness A witness with professional training or substantial experience qualifying her or him to testify on a certain subject.

expiration release The release of an inmate from prison at the end of his or her sentence without any further correctional supervision.

extradition The process by which one jurisdiction surrenders a person accused or convicted of violating another jurisdiction's criminal law to the second jurisdiction.

F

Federal Bureau of Investigation (FBI) The branch of the Department of Justice responsible for investigating violations of federal law.

federalism A form of government in which a written constitution provides for a division of powers between a central government and several regional governments.

felony A serious crime, usually punishable by death or imprisonment for a year or longer.

felony-murder An unlawful homicide that occurs during the attempted commission of a felony.

field training The segment of a police recruit's training in which he or she is removed from the classroom and placed on the beat, under the supervision of a senior officer.

first responders Those individuals, such as firefighters, police officers, and emergency medical technicians, who are responsible for the protection and preservation of life and property during the early stages following a disaster.

forensics The application of science to establish facts and evidence during the investigation of crimes.

forfeiture The process by which the government seizes private property attached to criminal activity.

formal criminal justice process The model of the criminal justice process in which participants follow formal rules to create a smoothly functioning disposition of cases from arrest to punishment.

frisk A pat-down or minimal search by police to discover weapons.

fruit of the poisoned tree Evidence that is acquired through the use of illegally obtained evidence and is therefore inadmissible in court.

furlough Temporary release from a prison for purposes of vocational or educational training, to ease the shock of release, or for personal reasons.

G

general patrol A patrol strategy that relies on police officers monitoring a certain area with the goal of detecting crimes in progress or preventing crime by their presence.

"good faith" exception The legal principle that evidence obtained with the use of a technically invalid search warrant is admissible during trial if the police acted in good faith when they sought the warrant from the judge.

"good time" A reduction in time served by prisoners based on good conduct, conformity to rules, and other positive behavior.

graduated sanctions The practical theory in juvenile corrections that a delinquent or status offender should receive a punishment that matches in seriousness the severity of the wrongdoing.

grand jury The group of citizens called to decide whether probable cause exists to believe that a suspect committed the crime with which she or he has been charged.

green card A document—no longer green—that indicates the holder's status as a lawful permanent resident of the United States.

gun control Efforts by a government to regulate or control the sale of guns.

H

habeas corpus An order that requires correctional officials to bring an inmate before a court or a judge and explain why he or she is being held in prison.

habitual offender laws Statutes that require lengthy prison sentences for those who are convicted of multiple felonies.

hacker A person who uses one computer to break into another.

halfway house A community-based form of early release that places inmates in residential centers and allows them to reintegrate with society.

"hands-off" doctrine The unwritten judicial policy that favors noninterference by the courts in the administration of prisons and jails.

hate crime law A statute that provides for greater sanctions against those who commit crimes motivated by bias against an individual or a group based on race, ethnicity, religion, gender, sexual orientation, disability, or age.

hearsay An oral or written statement made by an out-of-court speaker that is later offered in court by a witness (not the speaker) concerning a matter before the court. Hearsay usually is not admissible as evidence.

home confinement A community-based sanction in which offenders serve their terms of incarceration in their homes.

homeland security A concerted national effort to prevent terrorist attacks within the United States and reduce the country's vulnerability to terrorism.

hormone A chemical substance, produced in tissue and conveyed in the bloodstream, that controls certain cellular and bodily functions such as growth and reproduction.

hot spots Concentrated areas of high criminal activity that draw a directed police response.

hung jury A jury whose members are so irreconcilably divided in their opinions that they cannot reach a verdict.

hypothesis A possible explanation for an observed occurrence that can be tested by further investigation.

I

"identifiable human needs" The basic human necessities that correctional facilities are required by the Constitution to provide to inmates.

identity theft The theft of personal information, such as a person's name, driver's license number, or Social Security number.

incapacitation A strategy for preventing crime by detaining wrongdoers in prison, thereby separating them from the community and reducing criminal opportunities.

inchoate offenses Conduct deemed criminal without actual harm being done, provided that the harm that would have occurred is one the law tries to prevent.

incident-driven policing A reactive approach to policing that emphasizes a speedy response to calls for service.

indeterminate sentencing An indeterminate term of incarceration in which a judge decides the minimum and maximum terms of imprisonment.

indictment A charge or written accusation, issued by a grand jury, that probable cause exists to believe that a named person has committed a crime.

"inevitable discovery" exception The legal principle that illegally obtained evidence can be admitted in court if police using lawful means would have "inevitably" discovered it.

infancy A condition that, under early American law, excused young wrongdoers of criminal behavior because presumably they could not understand the consequences of their actions.

informal criminal justice process A model of the criminal justice system that recognizes the informal authority exercised by individuals at each step of the criminal justice process.

information The formal charge against the accused issued by the prosecutor after a preliminary hearing has found probable cause.

infraction In most jurisdictions, a noncriminal offense for which the penalty is a fine rather than incarceration.

infrastructure The services and facilities that support the day-to-day needs of modern life such as electricity, food, transportation, and water.

initial appearance An accused's first appearance before a judge or magistrate following arrest.

insanity A defense for criminal liability that asserts a lack of criminal responsibility due to mental instability.

intake The process by which an official of the juvenile court decides whether to file a petition, release the juvenile, or place the juvenile under some other form of supervision.

intellectual property Property resulting from intellectual, creative processes.

intelligence agency An agency that is primarily concerned with gathering information about potential criminal or terrorist events to prevent those acts from taking place.

intelligence-led policing An approach that measures the risk of criminal behavior associated with certain individuals or locations so as to predict when and where such criminal behavior is most likely to occur in the future.

intensive supervision probation (ISP) A punishment-oriented form of probation in which the offender is placed under stricter and more frequent surveillance and control than in conventional probation by probation officers with limited caseloads.

intermediate sanctions Sanctions that are more restrictive than probation and less restrictive than imprisonment.

internal affairs unit (IAU) A division within a police department that receives and investigates complaints of wrongdoing by police officers.

interrogation The direct questioning of a suspect to gather evidence of criminal activity and try to gain a confession.

intoxication A defense for criminal liability in which the defendant claims that the taking of intoxicants rendered him or her unable to form the requisite intent to commit a criminal act.

involuntary manslaughter A negligent homicide, in which the offender had no intent to kill his or her victim.

irresistible-impulse test A test for the insanity defense under which a defendant who knew his or her action was wrong may still be found insane if he or she was unable, as a result of a mental deficiency, to control the urge to complete the act.

J

jail A facility, usually operated by the county government, used to hold persons awaiting trial or those who have been found guilty of misdemeanors.

judicial review The power of a court—particularly the United States Supreme Court—to review the actions of the executive and legislative branches and, if necessary, declare those actions unconstitutional.

judicial waiver The process in which the juvenile judge, based on the facts of the case at hand, decides that the alleged offender should be transferred to adult court.

jurisdiction The authority of a court to hear and decide cases within an area of the law or a geographic territory.

jury trial A trial before a judge and a jury.

just deserts A sanctioning philosophy based on the assertion that criminals deserve to be punished for breaking society's rules.

justice The quality of fairness that must exist in the processes designed to determine whether individuals are guilty of criminal wrongdoing.

juvenile delinquency Behavior that is illegal under federal or state law that has been committed by a person who is under an age limit specified by statute.

L

larceny The act of taking property from another person without the use of force with the intent of keeping that property.

lay witness A witness who can truthfully and accurately testify on a fact in question without having specialized training or knowledge.

learning theory The hypothesis that delinquents and criminals must be taught both the practical and emotional skills necessary to participate in illegal activity.

liability In a civil court, legal responsibility for one's own or another's actions.

life course criminology The study of crime based on the belief that behavioral patterns developed in childhood can predict delinquent and criminal behavior later in life.

lockdown A disciplinary action taken by prison officials in which all inmates are ordered to their quarters and nonessential prison activities are suspended.

low-visibility decision making A term used to describe the discretionary power police have in determining what to do with misbehaving juveniles.

M

***M'Naghten* rule** A common law test of criminal responsibility, derived from *M'Naghten's* Case in 1843, that relies on the defendant's inability to distinguish right from wrong.

magistrate A public civil officer or official with limited judicial authority within a particular geographic area, such as the authority to issue an arrest warrant.

mala in se A descriptive term for acts that are inherently wrong, regardless of whether they are prohibited by law.

mala prohibita A descriptive term for acts that are made illegal by criminal statute and are not necessarily wrong in and of themselves.

malice aforethought A depraved state of mind in which the offender's behavior reflected a wanton disregard for the well-being of his or her victim.

mandatory release Release from prison that occurs when an offender has served the full length of his or her sentence, minus any adjustments for good time.

mandatory sentencing guidelines Statutorily determined punishments that must be applied to those who are convicted of specific crimes.

master jury list The list of citizens in a court's district from which a jury can be selected; compiled from voter registration lists, driver's license lists, and other sources.

maximum-security prison A correctional institution designed and organized to control and discipline dangerous felons, as well as prevent escape.

medical model A model of corrections in which the psychological and biological roots of an inmate's criminal behavior are identified and treated.

medium-security prison A correctional institution that houses less dangerous inmates and therefore uses less restrictive measures to prevent violence and escapes.

mens rea (pronounced *mehns ray*-uh). Mental state, or intent. A wrongful mental state is usually as necessary as a wrongful act to establish criminal liability.

methamphetamine (meth) An easily produced, relatively inexpensive stimulant that creates a strong feeling of euphoria in the user and is highly addictive.

military tribunal A court that is operated by the military rather than the criminal justice system and is presided over by military officers rather than judges.

minimum-security prison A correctional institution designed to allow inmates, most of whom pose low security risks, a great deal of freedom of movement and contact with the outside world.

Miranda **rights** The constitutional rights of accused persons taken into custody by law enforcement officials, such as the right to remain silent and the right to counsel.

misdemeanor A criminal offense that is not a felony; usually punishable by a fine and/or a jail term of less than one year.

Missouri Plan A method of selecting judges that combines appointment and election.

mitigating circumstances Any circumstances accompanying the commission of a crime that may justify a lighter sentence.

morals Principles of right and wrong behavior, as practiced by individuals or by society.

murder The unlawful killing of one human being by another.

N

National Security Agency (NSA) The intelligence agency that is responsible for protecting U.S. government communications and producing intelligence by monitoring foreign communications.

necessity A defense against criminal liability in which the defendant asserts that circumstances required her or him to commit an illegal act.

negligence A failure to exercise the standard of care that a reasonable person would exercise in similar circumstances.

neurotransmitter A chemical that transmits nerve impulses between nerve cells and from nerve cells to the brain.

new-generation jail A jail that is distinguished architecturally by a design that encourages interaction between inmates and jailers and that offers greater opportunities for treatment.

night watch system An early form of American law enforcement in which volunteers patrolled their community from dusk to dawn to keep the peace.

noble cause corruption Knowing misconduct by a police officer with the goal of attaining what the officer believes is a "just" result.

nolo contendere Latin for "I will not contest it." A criminal defendant's plea, in which she or he chooses not to challenge, or contest, the charges brought by the government.

nonpartisan elections Elections in which candidates are presented on the ballot without any party affiliation.

nonstate actor An entity that plays a role in international affairs but does not represent any established state or nation.

O

opening statements The attorneys' statements to the jury at the beginning of the trial.

opinions Written statements by the judges expressing the reasons for the court's decision in a case.

oral arguments The verbal arguments presented in person by attorneys to an appellate court.

organized crime Illegal acts carried out by illegal organizations engaged in the market for illegal goods or services, such as illicit drugs or firearms.

P

pardon An act of executive clemency that overturns conviction and erases mention of the crime from the person's criminal record.

parens patriae A doctrine that holds that the state has a responsibility to look after the well-being of children and to assume the role of parent if necessary.

parole The conditional release of an inmate before his or her sentence has expired.

parole board A body of appointed civilians that decides whether a convict should be granted conditional release before the end of his or her sentence.

parole contract An agreement between the state and the offender that establishes the conditions of parole.

parole grant hearing A hearing in which the entire parole board or a subcommittee reviews information, meets the offender, and hears testimony from relevant witnesses to determine whether to grant parole.

parole guidelines Standards that are used in the parole process to measure the risk that a potential parolee will recidivate.

parole revocation When a parolee breaks the conditions of parole, the process of withdrawing parole and returning the person to prison.

Part I offenses Crimes reported annually by the FBI in its Uniform Crime Report. Part I offenses include murder, rape, robbery, aggravated assault, burglary, larceny, motor vehicle theft, and arson.

Part II offenses All crimes recorded by the FBI that do not fall into the category of Part I offenses. These crimes include both misdemeanors and felonies.

partisan elections Elections in which candidates are affiliated with and receive support from political parties.

Patriot Act Legislation passed in the wake of the September 11, 2001, terrorist attacks that greatly expanded the ability of government agents to monitor and apprehend suspected terrorists.

patronage system A form of corruption in which the political party in power hires and promotes police officers, receiving job-related "favors" in return.

penitentiary An early form of correctional facility that emphasized separating inmates from society and from each other.

peremptory challenges *Voir dire* challenges to exclude potential jurors from serving on the jury without any supporting reason or cause.

permanent resident An alien who has been granted permission by the U.S. government to live and work in the United States on a permanent basis.

petition The document filed with a juvenile court alleging that the juvenile is a delinquent or a status offender and requesting that the court either hear the case or transfer it to an adult court.

phishing Sending an unsolicited e-mail that falsely claims to be from a legitimate organization in an attempt to acquire sensitive information such as passwords or credit-card details from the recipient.

plaintiff The person or institution that initiates a lawsuit in civil court proceedings by filing a complaint.

plain view doctrine The legal principle that objects in plain view of a law enforcement agent who has the right to be in a position to have that view may be seized without a warrant.

plea bargaining The process by which the accused and the prosecutor work out a mutually satisfactory conclusion to the case, subject to court approval.

police corruption The abuse of authority by a law enforcement officer for personal gain.

police subculture The values and perceptions that are shared by members of a police department and, to a certain extent, by all law enforcement agents.

precedent A court decision that furnishes an example or authority for deciding subsequent cases involving similar facts.

predisposition report A report prepared during the disposition process that provides the judge with relevant background material to aid in the disposition decision.

preliminary hearing An initial hearing in which a magistrate decides if there is probable cause to believe that the defendant committed the crime with which he or she is charged.

preparedness An umbrella term for the actions taken by governments to prepare for large-scale catastrophic events such as terrorist attacks or environmental disasters.

preponderance of the evidence The degree of proof required to decide in favor of one side or the other in a civil case. In general, this requirement is met when a plaintiff proves that a fact more likely than not is true.

prescription drugs Medical drugs that require a physician's permission for purchase.

presentence investigative report An investigative report on an offender's background that assists a judge in determining the proper sentence.

pretrial detainees Individuals who cannot post bail after arrest and are therefore forced to spend the time prior to their trial incarcerated in jail.

pretrial diversion program An alternative to trial offered by a judge or prosecutor, in which the offender agrees to participate in a specified counseling or treatment program in return for withdrawal of the charges.

preventive detention The retention of an accused person in custody due to fears that she or he will commit a crime if released before trial.

prisoner reentry A corrections strategy designed to prepare inmates for a successful return to the community and to reduce their criminal activity after release.

prison gang A group of inmates who band together within the corrections system to engage in social and criminal activities.

prisonization The socialization process through which a new inmate learns the accepted norms and values of the prison population.

prison programs Organized activities for inmates that are designed to improve their physical and mental health, provide them with vocational skills, or simply keep them busy while incarcerated.

private prisons Correctional facilities operated by private corporations instead of the government and, therefore, reliant on profits for survival.

private security The practice of private corporations or individuals offering services traditionally performed by police officers.

proactive arrests Arrests that occur because of concerted efforts by law enforcement agencies to respond to a particular type of criminal or criminal behavior.

probable cause Reasonable grounds to believe the existence of facts warranting certain actions, such as the search or arrest of a person.

probation A criminal sanction in which a convict is allowed to remain in the community rather than be imprisoned.

probationary period A period of time at the beginning of a police officer's career during which she or he may be fired without cause.

problem-oriented policing A policing philosophy that requires police to identify potential criminal activity and develop strategies to prevent or respond to that activity.

procedural criminal law Rules that define the manner in which the rights and duties of individuals may be enforced.

procedural due process The constitutional requirement that the law must be carried out in a fair and orderly manner.

professional model A style of policing advocated by August Vollmer and O. W. Wilson that emphasizes centralized police organizations, increased use of technology, and a limitation of police discretion through regulations and guidelines.

property bond An alternative to posting bail in cash, in which the defendant gains pretrial release by providing the court with property valued at the bail amount as assurance that she or he will return for trial.

prosecutorial waiver A procedure used in situations where the prosecutor has discretion to decide whether a case will be heard by a juvenile court or an adult court.

psychoactive drugs Chemicals that affect the brain, causing changes in emotions, perceptions, and behavior.

psychology The scientific study of mental processes and behavior.

public defenders Court-appointed attorneys who are paid by the state to represent defendants who are unable to hire private counsel.

public order crime Behavior that has been labeled criminal because it is contrary to shared social values, customs, and norms.

public prosecutor An individual, acting as a trial lawyer, who initiates and conducts cases in the government's name and on behalf of the people.

R

racial profiling The practice of targeting people for police action based solely on their race, ethnicity, or national origin.

racketeering The criminal action of being involved in an organized effort to engage in illegal business transactions.

rational choice theory A school of criminology that holds that wrongdoers act as if they weigh the possible benefits of criminal or delinquent activity against the expected costs of being apprehended.

reactive arrests Arrests that come about as part of the ordinary routine of police patrols and responses to calls for service.

real evidence Evidence that is brought into court and seen by the jury, as opposed to evidence that is described for a jury.

"real offense" The actual offense committed, as opposed to the charge levied by a prosecutor as the result of a plea bargain.

reasonable force The degree of force that is appropriate to protect the police officer or other citizens and is not excessive.

rebuttal Evidence given to counteract or disprove evidence presented by the opposing party.

recidivism The act of committing a new crime after a person has already been punished for a previous crime by being convicted and sent to jail or prison.

recklessness The state of being aware that a risk does or will exist and nevertheless acting in a way that consciously disregards this risk.

recruitment The process by which law enforcement agencies develop a pool of qualified applicants from which to select new members.

referral The notification process through which a law enforcement officer or other concerned citizen makes the juvenile court aware of a juvenile's unlawful or unruly conduct.

regulation Governmental control of society through rules and laws enforced by administrative agencies.

rehabilitation The philosophy that society is best served when wrongdoers are provided the resources needed to eliminate criminality from their behavioral pattern.

reintegration A goal of corrections that focuses on preparing the offender for a return to the community unmarred by further criminal behavior.

relative deprivation The theory that inmate aggression is caused when freedoms and services that the inmate has come to accept as normal are decreased or eliminated.

release on recognizance (ROR) A judge's order that releases an accused from jail with the understanding that he or she will return for further proceedings of his or her own will.

relevant evidence Evidence tending to make a fact in question more or less probable than it would be without the evidence. Only relevant evidence is admissible in court.

removal The process used by the federal government to expel an alien from the United States.

residential treatment program A government-run facility for juveniles whose offenses are not deemed serious enough to warrant incarceration in a training school.

response time The rapidity with which calls for service are answered.

restitution Monetary compensation for damages done to the victim by the offender's criminal act.

restorative justice An approach to punishment designed to repair the harm done to the victim and the community by the offender's criminal act.

retribution The philosophy that those who commit criminal acts should be punished based on the severity of the crime and that no other factors need be considered.

robbery The act of taking property from another person through force, threat of force, or intimidation.

rule of four A rule of the United States Supreme Court that the Court will not issue a writ of *certiorari* unless at least four justices approve of the decision to hear the case.

S

search The process by which police examine a person or property to find evidence that will be used to prove guilt in a criminal trial.

searches and seizures The legal term, as found in the Fourth Amendment of the U.S. Constitution, that generally refers to the searching for and the confiscating of evidence by law enforcement agents.

searches incidental to arrests Searches for weapons and evidence that are conducted on persons who have just been arrested.

search warrant A written order, based on probable cause and issued by a judge or magistrate, commanding that police officers or criminal investigators search a specific person, place, or property to obtain evidence.

seizure The forcible taking of a person or property in response to a violation of the law.

self-defense The legally recognized privilege to protect one's self or property from injury by another.

self-reported survey A method of gathering crime data that relies on participants to reveal and detail their own criminal or delinquent behavior.

sentencing discrimination A situation in which the length of a sentence appears to be influenced by a defendant's race, gender, economic status, or other factor not directly related to the crime he or she committed.

sentencing disparity A situation in which those convicted of similar crimes do not receive similar sentences.

sentencing guidelines Legislatively determined guidelines that judges are required to follow when sentencing those convicted of specific crimes.

separate confinement A nineteenth-century penitentiary system in which inmates were kept separate from one another at all times, with daily activities taking place in individual cells.

sex offender notification law Legislation that requires law enforcement authorities to notify people when convicted sex offenders are released into their neighborhood or community.

sexual assault Forced or coerced sexual intercourse (or other sexual acts).

sheriff The primary law enforcement officer in a county, usually elected to the post by a popular vote.

shock incarceration A short period of incarceration that is designed to deter further criminal activity by "shocking" the offender with the hardships of imprisonment.

social conflict theories A school of criminology that views criminal behavior as the result of class conflict.

social disorganization theory The theory that deviant behavior is more likely in communities where social institutions such as the family, schools, and the criminal justice system fail to exert control over the population.

socialization The process through which a police officer is taught the values and expected behavior of the police subculture.

social process theories A school of criminology that considers criminal behavior to be the predictable result of a person's interaction with his or her environment.

sociology The study of the development and functioning of groups of people who live together within a society.

solitary confinement The isolation of an inmate in a separate cell, either as punishment or to remove the inmate from the general prison population for security reasons.

spam Bulk e-mails, particularly of commercial advertising, sent in large quantities without the consent of the recipient.

specialty courts Lower courts that have jurisdiction over one specific area of criminal activity, such as illegal drugs or domestic violence.

split sentence probation A sentence that consists of incarceration in a prison or jail, followed by a probationary period in the community.

status offender A juvenile who has engaged in behavior deemed unacceptable for those under a certain statutorily determined age.

statute of limitations A law limiting the amount of time prosecutors have to bring criminal charges against a suspect after the crime has occurred.

statutory law The body of law enacted by legislative bodies.

statutory rape A strict liability crime in which an adult engages in a sexual act with a minor.

stop A brief detention of a person by law enforcement agents for questioning.

strain theory The assumption that crime is the result of frustration felt by individuals who cannot reach their financial and personal goals through legitimate means.

street gang A group of people, usually three or more, who share a common identity and engage in illegal activities.

stressors The aspects of police work and life that lead to feelings of stress.

strict liability crimes Certain crimes, such as traffic violations, in which the defendant is guilty regardless of her or his state of mind at the time of the act.

substantial-capacity test (ALI/MPC test) A test for the insanity defense that states that a person is not responsible for criminal behavior when he or she "lacks substantial capacity" to understand that the behavior is wrong or know how to behave properly.

substantive criminal law Law that defines the rights and duties of individuals with respect to one another.

substantive due process The constitutional requirement that laws used to accuse and convict persons of crimes must be fair.

supermax prison A correctional facility reserved for those inmates who have extensive records of misconduct in maximumsecurity prisons.

supremacy clause A clause in the U.S. Constitution establishing that federal law is the "supreme law of the land" and shall prevail when in conflict with state constitutions or statutes.

suspended sentence A judicially imposed condition in which an offender is sentenced after being convicted of a crime, but is not required to begin serving the sentence immediately.

sworn officer A law enforcement agent who has been authorized to make arrests and use force, including deadly force, against civilians

system A set of interacting parts that, when functioning properly, achieve a desired result.

T

technical violation An action taken by a probationer that, although not criminal, breaks the terms of probation as designated by the court.

terrorism The use or threat of violence to achieve political objectives.

testimony Verbal evidence given by witnesses under oath.

testosterone The hormone primarily responsible for the production of sperm and the development of male secondary sex characteristics such as the growth of facial and pubic hair and the change of voice pitch.

theory An explanation of a happening or circumstance that is based on observation, experimentation, and reasoning.

time served The period of time a person denied bail (or unable to pay it) has spent in jail prior to her or his trial.

total institution An institution, such as a prison, that provides all of the necessities for existence to those who live within its boundaries.

trace evidence Evidence such as a fingerprint, blood, or hair found in small amounts at a crime scene.

training school A correctional institution for juveniles found to be delinquent or status offenders.

trial courts Courts in which most cases usually begin and in which questions of fact are examined.

truth-in-sentencing laws Legislative attempts to ensure that convicts will serve approximately the terms to which they were initially sentenced.

U

Uniform Crime Report (UCR) An annual report compiled by the FBI to give an indication of criminal activity in the United States.

U.S. Customs and Border Protection (CBP) The federal agency responsible for protecting U.S. borders and facilitating legal trade and travel across those borders.

U.S. Immigration and Customs Enforcement (ICE) The federal agency that enforces the nation's immigration and customs laws.

U.S. Secret Service A federal law enforcement organization with the primary responsibility of protecting the president, the president's family, the vice president, and other important political figures.

V

venire The group of citizens from which the jury is selected.

verdict A formal decision made by the jury.

victim impact statement (VIS) A statement to the sentencing body (judge, jury, or parole board) in which the victim is given the opportunity to describe how the crime has affected her or him.

victimology A school of criminology that studies why certain people are the victims of crimes and the optimal role for victims in the criminal justice system.

victim surveys A method of gathering crime data that directly surveys participants to determine their experiences as victims of crime.

virus A computer program that can replicate itself over a network such as the Internet and interfere with the normal use of a computer. A virus cannot exist as a separate entity and must attach itself to another program to move through a network.

visa Official authorization allowing a person to travel to and within the issuing country.

voir dire The preliminary questions that the trial attorneys ask prospective jurors to determine whether they are biased or have any connection with the defendant or a witness.

voluntary manslaughter A homicide in which the intent to kill was present in the mind of the offender, but malice was lacking.

W

warden The prison official who is ultimately responsible for the organization and performance of a correctional facility.

warrantless arrest An arrest made without first seeking a warrant for the action.

white-collar crime Nonviolent crimes committed by business entities or individuals to gain a personal or business advantage.

widen the net The criticism that intermediate sanctions designed to divert offenders from prison actually increase the number of citizens who are under the control and surveillance of the American corrections system.

work release program Temporary release of convicts from prison for purposes of employment. The offenders may spend their days on the job but must return to the correctional facility at night and during the weekend.

worm A computer program that can automatically replicate itself over a network such as the Internet and interfere with the normal use of a computer. A worm does not need to be attached to an existing file to move from one network to another.

writ of *certiorari* A request from a higher court asking a lower court for the record of a case. In essence, the request signals the higher court's willingness to review the case.

wrongful conviction The conviction, either by verdict or by guilty plea, of a person who is factually innocent of the charges.

Y

youth gang A self-formed group of youths with several identifiable characteristics, including a gang name and other recognizable symbols, a geographic territory, and participation in illegal activities.

NAME INDEX

A

Abbott, Jack Henry, 342
Abdur-Rashid, Talib, 348
Abram, Karen, 378
Adam, Jean, 192
Adam, Scott, 192
Adams, Benjamin, 42, 373, 375, 382, 384, 387
Agnew, Robert, 35, 50
Alarcon, Arthur L., 90
al-Awlaki, Anwar, 90, 191
Albonetti, Celesta, 206
Alderden, Megan, 142
Alison, Laurence, 48
Alito, Samuel, 160
Alpert, Geoffrey P., 103
Alschuler, Albert W., 225, 226
Alvarez, Danielle A., 259
Alvarez, W., 146
Amabile, John, 210
Anastasia, George, 188
Andenaes, Johannes, 76
Anderson, Dale, 175
Anderson, Eddie Leroy, 86
Andrade, Leandro, 267–268
Anglin, Deirdre, 146
Anglin, M. Douglas, 295
Anthony, Casey, 24, 237
Anthony, Caylee, 24
Ardolf, Barry, 411
Arkin, William M., 107
Arpaio, Joe, 328
Ashenfeiter, David, 298

B

Bader, Ruth Ginsburg, 161, 203
Bainbridge, J. S., Jr., 265
Baissus, Jean-Marc, 202
Baker, John S., Jr., 68
Baker, Thomas J., 18
Baldwin, William A., 82
Banks, Elizabeth, 17
Barbour, Haley, 352
Barch, Krys, 6
Barr, Bob, 262
Barry, Rob, 5
Barthe, Emmanuel P., 103
Bartollas, Clemens, 111, 339, 345
Baskin, Deborah, 134
Basu, G., 47
Baum, Geraldine, 412
Bayley, David H., 131
Baze, Ralph, 275
Beasley, Richard J., 408
Beattie, James M., 311
Beck, Allen J., 315
Becker, Howard S., 56
Becker, Ronald F., 134, 151, 152
Beebe, Herman K., 422
Beebe, Paul, 81
Beh, Hazel Glenn, 150
Beiner, Theresa B., 203
Bell, Arnold E., 119

Bello, Marisol, 24
Bennett, Jessica, 376
Benoit, Carl A., 173
Benson, Bruce L., 120
Benson, Michael L., 418, 420
Berk, Richard, 274
Berkowitz, Scott, 32
Berns, Walter, 269
Bhati, Avinash Singh, 254–255
Bianchi, Herman, 6, 48
Biggs, David C., 77
bin Laden, Osama, 398
Bittner, Egon, 99
Black, Antwain, 264
Black, Julia L., 266
Black, Kevin, 73
Blackstone, William, 32
Blair, J. Pete, 128
Blake, Martha, 136
Blakely, Curtis R., 324
Blitstein, Ryan, 221
Bloom, Barbara, 350
Bloomberg, Michael, 4
Blumberg, Mark, 39
Blumstein, Alfred, 18, 19
Bogard, David, 329
Boland, Barbara, 222
Boruchowitz, Robert C., 209
Borukhova, Mazoltuv, 236
Bourke, Michael L., 252
Bousquet, Steve, 325
Bouza, Anthony, 132
Bowker, Lee H., 339
Bowling, Ralph, 275
Boyer, Barbara, 137
Boyle, Douglas J., 299
Braccialarghe, Randolph, 210
Braga, Anthony, 287
Braiden, Chris, 103
Brantingham, Jeff, 105
Bratton, William, 101
Breivik, Anders Behring, 255
Bright, Stephen, 269
Brockway, Zebulon, 313
Broeder, David W., 242
Brown, Charles, 139
Brown, Robbie, 324
Bruck, David, 269
Brucker, Joseph, 239
Bullock, Jane A., 402, 404
Bumphus, Vic W., 324
Burchfield, Keri B., 55
Burgess, John Steven, 359
Burk, Lauren, 273
Burkhart, Harry, 218
Burnett, Ernest, 228
Burns, Jeffrey M., 47
Bush, George W., 315, 400
Bush, Jeb, 4
Bushway, Shawn D., 377
Bustamante, Alyssa, 372
Butterfield, Fox, 326, 330

C

Caldero, Michael A., 151–152
Camp, Camille Graham, 345
Camp, George M., 345
Campbell, Howard, 58
Canter, David, 48
Capone, Al, 120
Carlson, Kenneth, 324
Carlsten, Annika, 234
Carmichael, Jon, 376
Carr, Craig L., 87
Carroll, Leo, 341
Carter, David, 142, 402
Cary, Mary Kate, 278
Casady, Tom, 142
Cash, Johnny, 336
Cassell, Paul, 267
Chahal, Shirin, 178
Champion, Dean John, 388
Chapman, Mark David, 352
Chapman, Steve, 414
Chapman, Warner, 216
Chase, Monique, 202
Chen, Edward M., 203
Chenoweth, James H., 107
Chermak, Steven, 98
Chesney-Lind, Meda, 45, 347–348, 350, 375
Churchill, Vicki, 261
Claudy, Michael, 352
Clear, Todd R., 55, 219, 255, 266, 287, 300, 319, 339, 344, 350, 353
Clementi, James, 188
Clementi, Tyler, 188, 207, 238
Clemmer, Donald, 334, 337
Clifford, Mary, 302
Clinton, Bill, 315, 399
Cloninger, Dale O., 139
Cloud, John, 24
Cnaan, Ram, 22
Cochran, John K., 40
Coffee, John C., 265
Cohen, Larry, 53–54
Cohen, Neil P., 291
Cohen, Richard, 20
Cohn, D'Vera, 417
Cohn, Scott, 324
Cole, Dave, 175
Cole, David, 315
Cole, George F., 219, 266, 300, 319, 339, 344, 350, 353
Cole, Simon A., 135
Collier, Acurie, 293
Collier, Linda J., 169
Cooksey, Kazi, 74
Cooper, Alexia, 42
Cooper, Jonathan, 278, 356
Cordner, Gary W., 132
Coscarelli, Kate, 299
Cottrell, Leonard S., 49
Cox, Steven M., 111, 112
Crank, John P., 151–152

Crapeau, Richard, 366
Crew, Keith, 264
Cronin, Ingrid, 252
Cronin, James M., 134
Crumbley, Nikolaus, 135
Cullen, Francis T., 53, 314
Cunningham, William C., 121
Curran, Christopher, 138
Currie, Janet, 379
Cury, Colleen, 239
Cushing, M. A., 145

D

Dale, Maryclaire, 347
Dannerbeck, Anne, 379
Daranciang, Nelson, 324
David, Kenneth Culp, 149
Davis, Edward, 379
Davis, Kenneth Culp, 221
Davis, Roderick, 336
Davis, Samuel, 367
Davis, Shawn, 204
Day, David, 358
Day, Nathan, 310
Dayan, Colin, 345
Dean, Mensah M., 286
Decker, Scott, 25
DeCorrell, Dee, 66
Deise, Jerome, 268
Deitz, A. Steven, 142
Delaney, Ruth, 315
del Carmen, Rolando V., 163, 164, 168, 172, 181
DeLisi, Matt, 341
DeMichele, Matthew T., 293
Dempsey, John S., 100, 113, 130, 145
Deutsch, Linda, 200
Dewey, Robert, 23
Dezhbakhsh, Hashem, 274
Diamond, John L., 70
DiBlasio, Natalie, 376
Dieckman, Duane, 139
Dieter, Richard C., 278
DiIulio, John, 325
DiIulio, John J., Jr., 342
Donger, Rand D., 43
Donohue, John J., 274
Doob, Anthony N., 315, 316
Downing, Michael, 107
Downing, Rondal G., 202
Dozier, Kimberly, 398
Dressler, Joshua, 84
Drury, Alan J., 341
Dubois, Amber, 225
Duff, H. Wayne, 153
Duncan, Martha Grace, 372
Dunham, Roger G., 103
Durkheim, Emile, 49–50
Dwyer, Pete, 98

E

Earley, Eddie, 275
Earley, Tina, 275

Egley, Arlen, Jr., 19, 379
Ehrlich, Isaac, 254
Elabed, Hanni, 324
Elgion, John, 223
El Khalifi, Amine, 402, 403, 417
Emshwiller, John R., 86
Enker, Arnold N., 87
Enzbrenner, David, 144
Erazo-Rodriguez, Jenny, 83
Erez, Edna, 268, 301
Eron, Leonard D., 51
Esbensen, Finn-Aage, 379
Espo, David, 398
Evangelista, Benny, 410

F

Fahim, Kareem, 264
Falkenberg, Lisa, 288
Farbiarz, Russell E., 256
Farnell, Dee Anna, 258
Farrington, David P., 378
Feinberg, Joel, 70
Feinman, Clarice, 264
Feld, Barry C., 385
Felson, Marcus, 37, 53–54
Felson, Richard, 55, 223
Ferdinand, Anton, 6
Fernandez, Manny, 128, 144
Fields, Gary, 86
Figlio, Robert, 55
Fine, Bernie, 228
Finkelhor, David, 379
Fisher, Jeffrey L., 181
Fletcher, Connie, 131, 133
Fletcher, George P., 15
Foglia, Michael, 239
Forst, Brian, 254, 262
Forst, Linda S., 100, 113, 130, 145
Fortas, Abe, 367, 370
Foucault, Michel, 342
Fowler, Geoffrey A., 412
Fox, James A., 42
Frana, John F., 53
Franklin, Christopher, 137
Franklin, Lonnie, Jr., 137
Franklin, Sharon B., 178
Freere, Jon, 417
Freud, Sigmund, 48
Friedman, Lawrence M., 71, 146, 216
Friend, Zach, 140
Funes, Muaricio, 164
Fyfe, James, 128

G

Gable, Robert S., 300
Gallo, Andrew, 254
Gallo, Leonard, 150
Garcia, Greyston, 5
Gardner, John Albert, 225
Gartner, Rosemary, 315, 316
Garza, Tony, 58
Gault, Gerald, 370
Gay, William, 131–132
Geller, William A., 144
Geranios, Nicholas K., 338
Gershman, Bennett L., 205
Ghailani, Ahmed Khalfan, 228, 407
Gibson, Tammy, 82

Gill, F. W., 72
Gilmore, Gary, 272
Giordano, Peggy C., 53
Gittings, R. Kaj, 274
Glaze, Lauren E., 22
Gobert, James J., 291
Goffman, Erving, 337
Goldman, Adam, 405
Goldstein, Herman, 142–143
Goldstein, Joseph, 15, 16, 381
Goldstein, Steven, 188
Gonzalez, Jaime, 128, 143
Gonzalez, Jaime, Sr., 128
Gonzalez, Noralva, 128
Goode, Erica, 98, 140, 252, 316, 408
Goodkind, Sara, 374
Goodnough, Abby, 57, 58
Gordon, Rachel A., 379
Gottfredson, Denise C., 375
Gottfredson, Michael, 53, 377
Gouras, Matt, 345
Grace, Anthony A., 57
Graham, Terrance, 372
Greenberger, Michael, 407
Greene, Edith, 268
Greene, Jack, 99
Greenman, Emma, 202
Greenwald, Glenn, 90
Greenwood, Peter W., 133
Gribble, Christopher, 48
Griffin, Patrick, 383
Griffiths, Elizabeth, 19
Grodin, Michael A., 340
Groff, Elizabeth R., 140
Grove, Walter R., 40
Guirguis, Michael, 146
Gupta, Sarika, 288

H

Hackett, Rogelio, Jr., 411
Hahn, Paul H., 287–288, 293
Haigh, Susan, 150
Halbert, Terry, 77
Haller, Mark H., 103
Hamby, Sherry, 379
Hammond, Jeremy, 396
Haney, Craig, 341
Harkless, Richard, 422
Harlan, John, Jr., 171
Harlow, Caroline Wolf, 43
Harris-Moore, Colton, 261
Hart, Henry, 70
Harvey, Brian, 177
Hashim, Ahmed S., 398
Hassine, Victor, 356
Hastie, Reid, 235
Haughney, Christine, 15, 16
Hawken, Angela, 295
Hawkins, Angela, 295
Hawkins, Gordon, 330
Hawkins, Karen, 137
Hawley, Chris, 405
Hehre, Robert, 202
Heinz, John, 13
Henrichson, Christian, 315
Hermann, Peter, 54
Hernandez, Andres E., 252
Hernstein, Richard J., 46

Hess, Karen M., 130–131, 138, 165
Heumann, Milton, 225–226
Hibberd, James, 145
Hickert, Audrey, 383
Hightower, Kyle, 88, 237
Hinkle, D. P., 109
Hinshaw, S'Lee Arthur, II, 383
Hipp, John R., 42
Hirschi, Travis, 51–52, 53, 377
Hirsh, Milton, 222
Holcomb, Jayme W., 174
Holland, Jesse J., 181
Hollander, Lee, 252
Holleran, David, 263, 264
Holmes, James, 8
Horowitz, M. J., 146
Householder, Jason, 259
Howe, Julie, 358
Howe, William, 162
Howell, James C., 19, 379
Huesmann, L. Rowell, 51
Huguely, George, 216
Hutchinson, Virginia A., 329
Hutson, H. Range, 146
Hymon, Elton, 147

I

Ibarra, Peter R., 301
Ifill, Sherrilyn A., 203
Ingraham, Barton L., 229
Ingulli, Elaine, 77
Iontcheva, Jena, 260
Irwin, John, 327, 337, 338
Israel, Jerold H., 170
Izzo, Tony, 320

J

Jackson, Michael, 75, 200
Jacobs, James B., 316
Jayaraman, Mythri, 286
Jenkins, Brian M., 399
Jenkins, Philip, 252
Jenne, Denise L., 345
Jesilow, Paul, 254
Johnson, Alex, 137
Johnson, Brian, 264
Johnson, Donald, 134
Johnson, Kevin, 54, 357
Johnston, Lloyd D., 378
Jones, Antoine, 178
Jones, Christopher, 81
Jones, Mark, 303
Jonson, Cheryl L., 314
Jou, Donna, 359
Joy, Peter A., 208
Justin-Jinich, Johanna, 83

K

Kaczynski, Ted, 321
Kagan, Elena, 203
Kaiser, David, 340
Kaltreider, N. B., 146
Kalven, Harry, 235
Kanapaux, William, 339
Kane, Robert J., 150
Kanka, Megan, 359
Kaplan, Harold I., 47
Kaplan, John, 210
Kappeler, Victor E., 39

Karmen, Andrew, 53
Katehis, John, 244
Katz, Jack, 46
Kauder, Neal B., 266
Kawai, Eriko, 379
Kazerounian, Salmun, 166
Keating, Charles, Jr., 422
Keel, Timothy G., 134
Kelling, George L., 52, 55, 101–102,
    103, 105, 130, 139, 140–141,
    142
Kelly, Raymond, 106–107
Kemmler, William, 269
Kempf-Leonard, Kimberly, 375
Ken, Rogers L., 128
Kenneally, Christine, 138
Kennedy, Anthony, 167, 372
Kennedy, David, 54
Kennedy, Robert, 117
Kent, Morris, 369
Kerman, Piper, 350
Kerr, Orin, 160
Kersting, Robert C., 345
Keve, Paul W., 258, 289
Kidwell, Keith, 241
Kimball, Peter, 318
King, Hollis, 160
King, Jeffrey R., 356
King, Nancy J., 260
King, Rodney, 146
Kirkham, Chris, 325
Kitzhaber, John, 278
Kleiman, Mark, 295
Kleinig, John, 16–17
Klockars, Carl, 99, 101, 292
Knox, George W., 341
Kochly, Robert, 222
Koenigs, Michael, 207
Koppel, Nathan, 288
Kopytoff, Verne G., 410
Korber, Dorothy, 357
Korey, Jason, 239
Koski, Douglas D., 235
Kramer, John, 264
Kraska, Peter B., 56
Kratcoski, Peter C., 340
Kreuz, L. E., 47
Kubrin, Charis E., 18
Kuehnel, Julie, 47, 48, 255
Kurlychek, Megan, 8
Kurtz, Josh, 301
Kyriacou, Demetrious N., 146

L

Lacey, Marc, 404
LaFond, John Q., 80
Lahey, Benjamin B., 379
Lake, Eli, 191
Lane, T. J., 375
Lanier, Mark M., 260
Lappin, Harley G., 324
Larson, Berry, 323
Larson, Robin, 151
Lasser, Mitchell, 202
Latessa, Edward J., 314
Lattman, Peter, 421
Laub, John H., 53, 377
Lee, Henry K., 222

Lee, Jason Vaughn, 142
LeFave, Wayne R., 170
LeVin, Ryan, 303
Levitt, Steven, 254, 314
Lewis, Ted Gordon, 383
Lewter, Judith E., 135
Lichtblau, Eric, 406
Light, Stephen C., 340
Lincoln, Abraham, 269
Lindgren, James, 19
Lininger, Tom, 223
Liptak, Adam, 161, 175, 276
Lockhart, Courtney, 273
Loeber, Rolf, 379
Logan, Charles, 317
Lohan, Lindsay, 40
Lombardo, Lucien X., 343
Long, Charles, 371
Long, Marilyn, 371
Longmore, Monica A., 53
Longshore, Douglas, 295
Loughner, Jared, 48, 85
Love, Jack, 301
Love, Yeardley, 216
Lozier, James E., 202
Lum, Cynthia, 140
Lurie, Norman A., 301
Lynch, Mary, 302

M

Macchione, Patrick, 411
Mac Donald, Heather, 43
Madden, Shanterrica, 231
Madoff, Bernard, 421, 422
Mahanna, Paul, 222
Manikas, Peter, 13
Manning, Peter K., 103
Markus, David Oscar, 222
Marques, Janice, 358
Marseca, Steve, 252
Marshall, Thurgood, 203, 346
Marsico, Edward M., 178
Martin, Randy, 340
Martin, Susan, 112
Martin, Trayvon, 4, 88
Martinez-Cabrera, Alejandro, 410
Martinson, Robert, 313
Mata, Felix, 356
Mauer, Marc, 258, 315, 330, 349
McCamey, William P., 111, 112
McCarthy, Peggy, 296
McClelland, Gary, 378
McClure, David, 17
McClure, Julie, 188
McConnell, Mitch, 230
McCord, David, 277
McCoy, David, 106
McCue, Colleen, 106
McCullough, Carl, Sr., 388
McCullough, Jack Daniel, 228
McCurley, Carl, 378
McDonald, Douglas C., 324
McDonald, Ricky, 74
McDowell, David, 374
McEwen, Tom, 134
McGlone, Tim, 266
McIntyre, Douglas, 49
McKay, Henry, 49

McKinley, James C., Jr., 417
McKinley, Jesse, 137
McMunigal, Kevin C., 208
McNulty, Paul J., 106
McTaggart, Kelli C., 170
Meadows, Robert J., 47, 48, 255
Meier, Robert, 43, 50
Meisner, Jason, 293
Melde, Chris, 379
Melton, Gary B., 372
Menard, James, 80
Meranze, Michael, 311
Merton, Robert K., 50
Meyerson, Jessica, 349
Michael, Maggie, 399
Milazzo, Carl, 198
Milken, Michael, 422
Miller, Charles, 379
Miller, Claud H., III, 260
Miller, Greg, 402
Miller, Laurence, 146
Miller, R. L., 329
Miller, Teresa A., 414
Miranda, Ernesto, 180
Mitchell, Brian David, 233
Mitchell, Paula M., 90
Mocan, Naci, 274
Moeller, Marguerite, 44
Moffitt, Terrie, 377
Mohammed, Khalid Sheikh, 230, 407
Mohler, Henry Calvin, 312
Moise-Titus, Jessica, 51
Molloy, Donald, 68
Montague, Don, 128
Moore, Mark H., 102, 103, 105, 130, 141
Moore, Richard, 73
Morenoff, Jeffrey, 42, 44
Morgan, Stephen, 83
Morris, Paul, 416
Morton, Michael, 245
Moskos, Peter C., 112
Mroz, Jacqueline, 111
Mueller, Robert S., III, 397
Muller, Eric L., 233
Mullins, Harry J., 144
Mulvey, Edward P., 379
Murphy, Christopher K., 177
Murphy, Gerard R., 134
Murray, Conrad, 74–75, 200
Murray, Henry L., 301
Myers, Bryan, 268
Myers, David G., 56

N

Nagy, Pamela S., 271
Nalla, M. K., 102
Napolitano, Janet, 117
Nees, H., 129
Negron, Judith, 422
Nellis, Ashley, 330, 349, 379
Nelson, Craig, 358
Neubauer, David W., 244
Newman, G. R., 102
Nichols, Don, 355
Nichols, Terry, 321
Ninham, Omer, 366

Nink, Carl, 345, 346
Noble, Rosevelt L., 260

O

Obama, Barack, 90, 230, 398, 407
Oceant, Emose, 264
O'Connor, Anahad, 378
O'Connor, Sandra Day, 203, 268
Okun, Edward Hugh, 422
Olson, Wendy, 86
Omar, Mohamud Said, 191
Ommeren, Alice, 358
O'Neil, J. L., 145
Oppel, Richard, Jr., 18
O'Reilly, Gregory W., 258
Orlin, David, 170
Ormrod, Richard, 379
Ormsby, Thayne, 229
Osmakac, Sami, 22
Ostrom, Brian J., 266
O'Sullivan, Julie R., 261
Otteson, Christa, 349
Owens, John B., 120

P

Packer, Herbert, 13–14, 17, 189, 253
Padilla, José, 348
Page, Douglas, 320
Palazzolo, Joe, 5
Palmer, Ted, 300, 313
Palumbo, Dennis, 302
Pare, Paul-Philippe, 223
Parent, Dale, 300
Parker, Andre, 106
Parker, Ian, 188
Passel, John S., 417
Pastor, Michael, 200
Pate, Tony, 139
Paternoster, Ray, 268, 377
Payen, Laguerre, 348
Payne, William, 135
Paynter, Ben, 58
Peak, Ken, 103
Pearl, James, 170
Pederson, David, 356
Peel, Sir Robert "Bobbie," 102
Pellegrino, Evan, 137
Penn, William, 311
Pennington, Nancy, 235
Pepinsky, Harold, 254
Percival, Robert V., 216
Persky, H., 47
Persons, Vicci, 329
Pescatore, Joanne, 286
Petersilia, Joan, 133, 290, 299, 315, 339, 356
Peterson, Joseph, 134
Pettigrew, Charles A., 321
Pfeifer, Stuart, 412
Pimental, José, 399
Pinizzotto, Anthony, 379
Pious, Richard M., 407
Platt, Anthony, 368
Podolski, Cheryl-Lynn, 51
Pollak, Louis H., 200
Pollock, Joycelyn, 128, 151, 152
Potter, Gary W., 39
Pound, Roscoe, 189

Powers, Pamela, 164
Pratt, C. E., 149
Preston, Julia, 417
Pridemore, William A., 43
Priest, Dana, 107
Puzo, Matt, 405
Puzzanchera, Charles, 42, 373, 375, 382, 384, 387

Q

Quagliana, Rhonda, 216
Quinsey, Vernon, 357

R

Rafferty, Brogan, 408
Raftery, Isolde, 261
Rankin, Bill, 269
Rashbaum, William K., 223, 421
Ratcliffe, Jerry H., 140
Rathbone, Cristina, 345, 348–350
Raudenbush, Stephen W., 42, 44
Ravi, Dharun, 188, 207, 227, 238
Ray, James Arthur, 66, 78
Redding, Richard E., 372
Reed, Thomas J., 238
Rehnquist, William, 166, 181
Reichel, Philip L., 328
Reid, Richard, 348
Reiman, Jeffery, 36
Reisig, Michael D., 219, 300, 319, 339, 344, 350, 353
Reyes, Jessica Wolpaw, 45
Ri, Luis, 66
Rice, Phillip, 146
Richardson, Robert C., 273
Richtel, Matt, 410
Ritchie, Lauren, 4
Ritter, Nancy, 137
Robbins, Ira P., 325
Robert, David J., 107
Roberts, John G., Jr., 98, 275
Robinson, Marcus, 277
Robinson, Paul H., 83
Rochester, Stephanie, 47
Rodriguez, Francisco, 133
Rodriguez, Orlando, 128
Rookey, Bryan D., 45
Rooney, Ben, 410
Rose, R. M., 47
Rosenbloom, Deborah D., 169
Rosenfeld, Richard, 42
Ross, Darrell L., 345
Rossman, Shelli B., 297
Roth, Mitchell P., 102
Rowe, David C., 47
Rozas, Angela, 54
Rubin, Joel, 105
Rubin, Paul H., 274
Ryba, Krysten Lynn, 349

S

Sadock, Benjamin J., 47
Sadock, Virginia A., 47
Salinger, Lawrence, 421
Sample, Lisa, 375
Sampson, Robert J., 42, 44, 53, 377
Sanders, Kerry, 188
Sandusky, Jerry, 33
Sauter, Michael, 49

Savage, Charlie, 33, 36, 316, 402, 403, 407
Scalia, Antonin, 16, 52, 170
Scaramella, Gene L., 111, 112
Schack, Stephen, 131–132
Schaible, Catherine, 286, 288
Schaible, Herbert, 286, 288
Schaible, Kent, 286
Schaller, Barry R., 200
Schell, Theodore, 131–132
Schirmer, Sarah, 330, 349
Schmidt, Michael S., 397
Schmitt, Eric, 403
Schmitt, John, 288
Schneider, Mike, 88
Schneier, Bruce, 410
Schroeder, Ryan D., 53
Schulhofer, Stephen J., 226
Schultz, Ray, 98
Schumann, Cynthia, 98
Schwartz, Adam, 76
Schwartz, Jennifer, 45
Schwartz, John, 80
Scones, Ronald, 222
Scott, Eric J., 131
Scott, Gladys, 352
Scott, Jamie, 352
Scott, Michael S., 144
Seffrin, Patrick M., 53
Seligman, Dan, 329
Sellin, Thorsten, 55
Serrano, Richard A., 402
Seymour, Anne, 270
Shahzad, Faisal, 321, 399
Shaw, Clifford R., 49
Shearer, John D., 312
Shelton, Donald E., 237
Shepherd, Joanna M., 274
Sherman, Lawrence, 55, 140, 150, 256
Shern, Ian, 207
Shilton, Mary, 288
Sias, Ben, 151
Sickmund, Melissa, 42, 372, 373, 375, 382, 384, 387
Siegel, Larry J., 190, 208, 379
Siegelbaum, Debbie, 403
Sigala, Joey, 98
Simon, Darran, 137
Simons, Kenneth W., 86
Simons, Ronald L., 43
Simpson, Sally S., 418, 420
Sims, Barbara, 303
Singer, Richard G., 80
Siprut, Joseph, 177
Sklansky, David Alan, 112
Skogan, Wesley, 140, 142
Skolnick, Jerome, 101
Smith, Erica L., 42
Smith, Juan, 206

Smith, K., 47
Snyder, Howard N., 20, 44, 372, 375, 378, 387
Snyder-Joy, Zoann K., 302
Sommers, Ira, 134
Sotomayor, Sonia, 203, 206, 207
Soulé, David A., 375
Souter, David H., 268
Spahr, Lisa L., 134
Speraw, Adam J., 376
Spohn, Cassia, 263, 264
Stannow, Lovisa, 340
Steffensmeier, Darrell, 44, 264
Steinbeck, Margaret, 264
Sterling, Eric, 262
Stevens, John Paul, 113
Stevens, Robert, 197
Stewart, Eric A., 43
Stewart, Potter, 271
Stith, Kate, 259, 260
Stockdale, Charles, 49
Stockum, John, 259
Stouthamer-Loeber, Magda, 379
Stracner, Jenny, 170–171
Strang, Heather, 256
Strauchs, John J., 121
Strauss-Kahn, Dominique, 223
Streifel, Cathy, 264
Strock, Carl, 403
Strote, Jared, 146
Subban, P. K., 6
Sullivan, Eileen, 48, 405
Sullivan, Joe, 372
Sutherland, Edwin H., 51
Sutherland, George, 205–206
Swatt, Marc L., 42
Sweeten, Gary, 377
Swerdlow, Russell H., 47

T
Tabor, Diana, 12
Tanigughi, Travis, 140
Tate, Julie, 402
Taylor, Gregory, 267
Teeters, Negley K., 311, 312
Tekin, Erdal, 379
Temin, Carolyn Engel, 286, 289
Teplin, Linda, 53, 378
Terry, John, 6
Thiessen, Jacob, 170
Thomas, Aaron, 135
Thomas, Andre, 85
Thomas, Cal, 310
Thomas, Clarence, 203
Thurman, Quint C., 142
Tiffany, Lawrence P., 85
Tiffany, Mary, 85
Tita, George E., 19
Tittle, Charles, 43
Toliver, Jessica L., 134

Tonry, Michael, 287, 302
Toporek, Lisa, 170
Torres-Spelliscy, Ciara, 202
Torrey, E. Fuller, 48
Trask, Grover, 379
Trojanowicz, Robert C., 142
Tunison, John, 324
Turley, Jonathan, 288
Turner, Heather, 379
Turner, Susan, 290, 299
Tyler, John H., 356

U
Urada, Darren, 295
Useem, Bert, 318, 340
Uviller, H. Richard, 179

V
Valukas, Anton R., 419
van den Haag, Ernest, 274
Van Dorn, Tom, 170
Vang, Zong, 366
Van Meter, Clifford W., 121
van Wormer, Katherine Stuart, 339, 345
Vara, Vauhini, 327
Vaughan, Jessica, 417
Velman, Gerald F., 190
Vick, Michael, 193, 354
Vielmetti, Bruce, 366
Vilca, Daniel, 252
Violanti, John, 145
Vitiello, Michael, 339
Vogt, Mike, 145
Vollmer, August, 103, 109

W
Wakefield, Sara, 330
Walker, Jacob, 273
Walker, Jeffrey T., 168
Walker, Joseph, 354
Walker, Samuel, 103, 129, 131, 150, 311
Wallace, George, 117
Wallenstein, Arthur, 326
Walshk, James, 417
Warner, Kris, 288
Warren, Earl, 180
Warren, Patricia Y., 42
Watson, Richard A., 202
Watson, Robert E., 371
Weber, George, 244
Weger, Richard E., 134
Wei, Molly, 188
Weinstein, Jack, 266
Weisburd, David, 17, 140
Weiss, Alexander, 98
Welch, Jennifer, 237
Wellford, Charles, 262
Wells, Christina, 80–81
Wells, Mike, 80–81

Welsh, Brandon C., 379
Wertsch, Teresa Lynn, 111
Westbrook, David A., 397, 398
Westly, William, 144
Wheeler, Russell, 189, 202
Whitcomb, Howard, 189
White, Bobby, 327
White, Byron, 208
White, Michael D., 150
White, Sarah, 166
Wides-Munoz, Laura, 117
Widom, Cathy Spatz, 379
Wiederanders, Mark, 358
Wildeman, Christopher, 330
Williams, Onta, 348
Williams, Robert, 164
Wilner, N., 146
Wilson, David B., 18
Wilson, James A., 40
Wilson, James Q., 13, 18, 41, 46, 52, 55, 101–102, 140–141, 254
Wilson, Jeffrey M., 101
Wilson, O. W., 103
Wilson, Pearly L., 346
Winick, Bruce J., 85
Witkin, Gordon, 128
Wolf, Robert V., 297
Wolfers, Justin, 274
Wolfgang, Marvin, 55, 377
Wood, Jennifer D., 140
Wood, Peter B., 40
Woodson, Michael, 165
Wortmon, Maggie Jean, 79
Wortmon, Michael, 79
Wrobleski, Henry M., 130–131

Y
Yan, Jiahui, 379
Yellen, David, 253
Yeoman, Barry, 45

Z
Zacharias, Fred C., 225
Zahn, Margaret A., 374
Zamble, Edward, 357
Zeisel, Hans, 235
Zezima, Katie, 58
Zhao, Jihong, 142
Ziegler, Anne, 366
Zimbardo, Philip, 48, 51
Zimmerman, George, 4, 5, 88
Zimmerman, Paul R., 274
Zimmerman, Sherwood, 340
Zimring, Franklin, 41, 315, 316, 326, 330
Zraick, Karen, 264
Zuidema, Brandon V., 153

SUBJECT INDEX

A

Aberdeen Police Department, 151
Abuse, child, 379
Accomplice liability, 80
Acquittal, 229
Actus reus
   attempt, 77
   defined, 77
   legal duty, 77
Adams County Correctional Center, 324
Adjudicatory hearing, 385–386
Administrative building assignment, 343
Administrative duties, of patrol officer, 132
Administrative law, 69, 420
Administrative Office of the United States
   Courts, 201
Adultery, 6
Advance fee fraud, 409
Affidavit, 172
Affirmative action, 110–111
Affirmative defense, 240
African Americans
   consequences of high incarceration rate, 330
   crime statistics and, 42
   death penalty and, 276–277
   drug offenses, 42, 43
   female inmates, 348
   incarceration rate, 23–24
   jury selection, 232–234
   as law enforcement officers, 110–113
   low representation on Supreme Court,
     202–203
   murder rate and, 42
   poor relations with police, 104
   prison violence and, 341
   sentencing discrimination, 264
Aftercare programs, 389
Age
   crime and, 377–378
   juveniles tried as adults and, 371–372
   of prison population, 338
Age of onset, 378
Aggravated assault
   average length of sentence, 290
   by juveniles, 373–374
   as Part I offense, 37
   sentence outcome for guilty plea, 226
   sentencing disparity, 263
Aggravating circumstances, 261
Aging out, 377
Alcohol, juvenile delinquency and, 378
Alcohol, Tobacco, Firearms and Explosives
   (ATF), Bureau of, 11
   responsibilities of, 116, 118–119
Alibi defense, 240
Alien, 415
ALI/MPC test, 84
Allen Charge, 243
al Qaeda, 398–399
   history of, 398–399
Alternative sanctions, as form of punishment, 259
American Bar Association (ABA), on defending
   the guilty, 208

American Law Institute, 84
Ankle bracelet, 301
Anomie, 49–50
Anonymous, 396
Anti-terrorism. *See also* Homeland security
   challenges of, 106–107
   cost of, 107
   Prislam, 348
   prosecution of terrorists, 230
   suspicious activity defined, 106
Antiterrorism and Effective Death Penalty Act
   (AEDPA), 399–400
Apology, 256, 259
Appeals
   double jeopardy, 244
   habeas corpus, 244–245
   percentage of cases, 244
   reasons for, 244
   steps in, 245
   wrongful conviction, 245
Appellate courts
   jurisdiction, 192
   state court system, 195–196
   U. S., 196
Appellate jurisdiction, 192
Arizona, S.B. 1070, 166–167
Arm's reach doctrine, 173
Arraignment, 218, 223
Arrestee Drug Abuse Monitoring Program, 378
Arrests
   authority to, 169
   compared to stop, 168
   crime rate and, 140–141
   elements of, 168–169
   entering a dwelling, 169
   exigent circumstances, 169
   intent, 168
   knock and announce rule, 169–170
   proactive, 140
   reactive, 140
   seizure or detention, 169
   understanding of, 169
   waiting period, 169–170
   with a warrant, 169–170
   without a warrant, 170
Arrest warrant, 169–170
Arson, 33
   as Part I offense, 37
Aryan Brotherhood, 341
Asian Americans, as law enforcement officers,
   110–113
Assaults
   defined, 33
   gangs and, 380
   as Part II offense, 38
Assistant prosecutors, 206
Association, probable cause based on, 163
Attempt, 77
Attendant circumstance, 81–82
Attica Correctional Facility, 319
Attorney-client privilege
   defense attorneys, 209–210
   defined, 210

exceptions to, 210
Attorney general, 206
Attorneys. *See* Defense attorneys; Prosecutors
Auburn Prison, 312
Auburn system, 312
Authority
   as element of arrest, 169
   of law enforcement officers, 146
   of probation officer, 292–293
   use of force and, 146–148
Automatic License Plate Recognition, 104, 177
Automatic transfer, 384
Automobiles, searches of, 174–175

B

Bail
   average amounts, 219
   posting, 219
   purpose of, 217–219
   reasonable, 217
Bail bond agent, 219
Bailiff, 204–205
Bail tariffs, 217
Ballistics, 135
Ballot initiatives, 68–69
Baltimore Police Department, 102
Bath salts, 58
Battery, 33, 82
Beat, 130
Bench trial, 228
Berkeley Police Department, 103
Beyond a reasonable doubt, 73
Bias intimidation, 188
Bifurcated death penalty process, 271–272
Bigamy, 70, 75
Bill of Rights, 21. *See also* Constitution, United
   States; individual amendments
   procedural safeguards and, 89
bin Laden, Osama, al Qaeda and, 398
Biology, trait theory and, 47–48
Biometrics, 18
Block officers, 343
Blue curtain, 144
Booking, 218
Boot camps, 259, 300, 387–388
Border Patrol, 117
   totality of circumstances test, 166
Border security
   increased scrutiny, 404
   regulated ports of entry, 404
   unregulated ports of entry, 404
Boston Police Department, 102
Botnets, 411
Boykin form, 226
Brain, crime and, 47–48
Bribery, 149, 419
   during political era of policing, 103
Bridewell Place, 311
Broken windows theory, 52, 55, 140–141
Broward County Sheriff Department, 151
Brownsville Texas Police Department, 128,
   143–144

Brown v. Entertainment Merchants Association (EMA), 52
Bullycides, 376
Bullying, 376
  cyber, 410–411
Burden of proof
  civil cases, 73
  criminal cases, 73
Bureaucracy, 129
  function of courts and, 190
Bureau of Prisons (BOP), 322, 329
Burglary
  average length of sentence, 290
  defined, 33
  degree of crime and, 74
  as Part I offense, 37
  sentence outcome for guilty plea, 226
  sentencing disparity, 263
Burnout, 145
Bush, George W.
  creation of Homeland Security, 116
  federalize gun possession crimes, 315
  Patriot Act, 400
Business Software Alliance, 413

C

Calls for service, 132
Camden Police Department, number of officers and crime, 137
Capital crime, 23
Capital offense, 74
Capital punishment. *See also* Death penalty
  defined, 269
  as form of punishment, 258
Case citations, reading, 29
Case law, 69
Caseload, 293
Cases
  case attrition, 221–222
  priorities, 222–223
Causation, 45, 80–81
Cell blocks, 320, 321
Cell phones, banning texting while driving, 10
Central Intelligence Agency (CIA), counterterrorism efforts, 402
Chain of command
  police departments and, 129–130
  prisons, 318
Challenges for cause, 232
Charge to jury, 242
Charging conference, 242
Chemical spray, 146–147
Chicago Police Department, 102
Child abuse, 379
Child neglect, 379
Children. *See also* Juveniles
  abuse of, 379
  infancy defense, 83
  neglect of, 379
  parens patriae, 367
  pornography, 252, 413–414
Child savers, 367
Chivalry effect, 264
Christopher Commission, 146
Chronic offender, 55
Chronic 6 percent, 55, 377

Cincinnati Police Department, 102, 130, 151
Circumstantial evidence, 237
City attorney, 205
Civil law
  burden of proof, 73
  vs. criminal law, 72
  defined, 72
  responsibility and, 73
Civil liberties, 21
Civil rights, counterterrorism actions and, 405–407
Civil Rights Act, 110
Civil suits, double jeopardy, 244
Classification process, prisons, 319
Clean Water Act, 69
Clearance rates, 134
Clerk of the court, 205
Closed-circuit television (CCTV) cameras, 177–178
Closing arguments, 241
Coast Guard, 116
  under Homeland Security Department, 401
Cockfighting, 70–71
CODIS, 136
Coercion
  confession and, 179
  inherent, 179
Cold cases, 134
Cold hit, 135–136
Cole, U.S.S., 398
Commercialized vice, 38
Community corrections, 286–303
  cost of, 288
  defined, 15, 286
  diversion, 287–288
  intermediate sanctions, 295–302
  justification for, 287–288
  low-cost alternative, 288
  number of people in, 286, 288, 289
  paradox of, 303
  probation, 288–295
  reintegration, 287
Community dispute resolution centers, 297
Community era of policing, 104–105
Community policing, 101
  defined, 141
  historical perspective on, 103, 105
Community service, as form of punishment, 259
Community services, provided by police, 100–101, 131
Competency hearing, 85
Compliance, 420
CompStat, 140
Computer crime, 408. *See also* Cyber crimes
Concurrence, 80
Concurrent jurisdiction, 193
Concurring opinions, 199
Confessions
  attorney-client privilege and, 210
  coercion and, 179
  recording, 182
  as self-incrimination, 179
Confidential informant, 134
Conflict model, 6–7
Confrontation clause, 239
Congregate system, 312
Connecticut State Police, 115

Consensus model, 5–6
Consent
  electronic surveillance, 176–177
  searches with, 173–174
Consent decree, 111
Consent searches, 173–174
Constitution, United States. *See also* specific amendments
  Bill of Rights, 89
  choice of defense attorney, 209
  cruel and unusual punishment, 89
  double jeopardy, 89
  due process, 89–91
  excessive bail and fines, 89
  federalism, 9
  Fourth Amendment, 161–165
  juveniles and, 369–370
  Miranda warning, 180–182
  prisoners' rights, 346–347
  private prisons, 325
  public trial, 89
  right to bear arms, 19
  right to lawyer, 89
  as source for criminal law, 67
  speedy trial, 89
  Supreme Court as interpreter of, 197–198
  as supreme law of land, 67
  unreasonable searches and seizure, 89
  warrants for searches, 89
  witness incrimination, 89
Constitutional law, 67. *See also* Constitution, United States
Consumer fraud, 419
  cyber, 409–410
Continuity theory of crime, 53
Controlled Substances Act, 118
Control theory, 51–52
Coroner, 115
Corporate violence, 420
Corpus delicti, 77, 81, 238
Correctional officers
  discipline by, 344–345
  duties of, 343
  female, 345–346
  protecting prisoners' rights, 346–347
  rank of, 343
  sanctioning prisoners, 344–345
  use of force, 345
Corrections
  community-based, 15
  jail, 13
  juvenile, 386–389
  probation, 13
Corrections Corporation of America (CCA), 322
Correlation, 45
Corruption
  bribery, 149
  defined, 148
  mooching, 149
  payoffs, 149
  in police subculture, 150
  during political era of policing, 103
  shakedowns, 149
  stages of, 150
Cortisol, 145
Counterfeiting, 38
Counterintelligence, 402

County attorney, 205
Court reporters, 205
Courtroom work group, 203–210
  defense attorney, 207–210
  docket, 201
  judge in, 205
  members of, 204–205
  prosecutor, 205–207
Courts
  appellate, 192
  criminal, 12
  drug courts, 297
  dual system of, 11–12
  federal court system, 196–199
  functions of
    bureaucratic, 190
    crime control, 189–190
    due process, 189
    rehabilitation, 190
  problem-solving, 297
  state court system, 194–196
  trial, 192
  United States Supreme Court, 196–199
  work group in, 203–210
Credit-card and check fraud, 419
Crime control, function of courts and, 189–190
Crime control model, 17
Crime in the United States, 36
Crime-mapping technology, 140, 141
Crime prevention, by police officers, 101
Crime rate
  arrest rate and, 140–141
  defined, 36
  drop in, 17–18, 41–42
  economy and, 41
  imprisonment and, 41
  increased incarceration and, 315, 317
  law enforcement impact on, 17–18
  percentage change, 36
  women and, 44–45
  youth populations and, 41
Crime(s). *See also* Crime theories; specific types
    of crimes
  actus reus, 77
  attendant circumstances, 81–82
  broken windows theory, 52, 55
  capital, 23
  causation, 80–81
  class and, 42–44
  classification of, 71–76
  concurrence, 80
  conflict model of, 6–7
  consensus model of, 5–6
  cyber, 408–414
  dark figure of, 37–38
  defined, 5–7
  degree of, 33, 74–75
  deliberate, 74
  vs. deviance, 7
  dropping crime rate, 17–18, 41–42
  drug-crime relationship, 55–58
  elements of, 77–82
  ethnicity and, 44
  felonies, 74–75
  fortresses of crime, 49, 50
  guns and, 19
  harm, 82

hate, 81–82
high-tech, 34
illegal drugs and, 20
increased incarceration and rate of, 315
mala in se, 75–76
mala prohibita, 75–76
measuring, 35–45
mens rea, 77–80
misdemeanor, 75
organized, 34
premeditated crime, 74
property, 33
public order, 33–34
race and, 42
rate, 17–18
seduction of, 46–47
seriousness of, and sentencing, 260–261
street gangs and, 19
trends today, 40–45
types of, 33–34
victimless, 34
violent, 33
white-collar, 34, 418–422
women and, 44–45
Crime scene photographer, 12
Crime statistics
  dropping crime rate, 41–42
  gangs and, 380
  on juveniles, 373–374
  race and poverty, 42–44
  self-reported surveys, 39–40
  Uniform Crime Report (UCR), 36–38
  victim surveys, 37–39
  women and, 44–45
Crime theories, 45–53
  continuity theory of crime, 53
  control theory, 51–52
  correlation and causation, 45
  learning theory, 51
  life course theories, 52–53
  rational choice theory, 46–47
  role of theory, 46
  routine activities theory, 53–54
  self-control theory, 53
  social conflict theory, 50
  social disorganization theory, 49, 50
  social process theories, 51–52
  strain theory, 49–50
  trait theory, 47–49
Criminal act, 77–80
Criminal court system, dual court system, 193
Criminal harm, 70
Criminal justice process
  as assembly line, 13–15
  discretion in, 15–16
  formal, 14
  informal, 15
Criminal justice system
  compared to juvenile justice system, 384–385
  courtroom work group, 203–210
  crime control model, 17
  defined, 7
  discretion in, 15–16
  due process model, 17
  federal court system, 196–199
  federalism and, 9
  goals of, 8

judges in court system, 199–203
jurisdiction, 191–192
local, state and federal employees of, 10–11
process of, 13–15
purpose of, 7–9
social media's impact on, 24–25
state court system, 194–196
structure of, 9–15
trail and appellate courts, 192
Criminal law, 67–91
  burden of proof, 73
  vs. civil law, 72
  defenses under, 82–88
  due process, 89–91
  elements of crime, 77–80
  guilt and, 73
  legal function of, 70
  procedural, 88–91
  purposes of, 70–71
  safeguards, 88–91
  social function of, 70–71
  substantive, 88
  written sources of, 67–69
Criminals
  career criminal, 55
  victim-offender connection, 54
Criminal trials. *See also* Trials
  impartial jury, 228
  presumption of innocence, 229
  privilege against self-incrimination, 229
  special features of, 227–231
  speedy trial, 227–228
  strict standard of proof, 230
Criminologists, 35, 45
Criminology, 45
Crimmigration, 414
Cross-examination, 239
Cruel and unusual punishment
  defined, 271
  deliberate indifference standard, 346
  juveniles and, 372
  method of execution and, 270–271
  Supreme Court on, 271, 274
  three-strikes laws, 267–268
Crush videos, 197
CSI effect, 237
Curfew, home confinement and, 300
Curfew violations, 38
Custodial interrogation, 179
Custody, defined, 179
Customs and Border Protection (CBP)
  agent, 416
  Border Patrol, 117
  under Homeland Security, 117, 401
  responsibilities of, 116, 117
Cyberbullying, 376, 410–411
Cyber crimes, 408–414
  in business world
    hackers, 396–397, 411–412
    pirating intellectual property, 413
    spam, 412
    worms and viruses, 412
  against the community, 413–414
    gambling and pornography, 413–414
  defined, 409
  homeland security and, 396–397
  incidence of, 409

against persons and property
consumer fraud, 409–410
cyberbullying, 410–411
cyberstalking, 411
identity theft, 410
phishing, 410
session hijacking, 411
Cyber fraud, 34, 409–410
Cyberstalking, 411
Cyber theft, 410

D

Dallas Police Department, 177
Operation Heat Wave, 143
Dark figure of crime, 37–38
Day-fines, 298
Day reporting centers, 299
Deadly force
defined, 147
justifiable use of, 87–88
Death penalty, 269–278
Antiterrorism and Effective Death Penalty Act
(AEDPA), 399–400
arbitrariness of, 276
bifurcated process, 271–272
choice theory and, 47
in colonies, 311
continued support for, 278
cost of, 277–278
cruel and unusual punishment, 270–271,
273–274
decline in executions, 277–278
decrease in death sentences, 23
defined, 269
deterrence argument, 274
discriminatory effect, 276–277
DNA evidence and, 23
Eighth Amendment, 270, 271, 272, 273
executions by state, 276
fallibility and, 274–275
as form of punishment, 258
future of, 277–278
historical perspective on, 269–270
incapacitation argument, 254
insanity, 273
jury and, 260, 268
juveniles and, 273, 372
mentally handicapped and, 273
methods of execution, 269–270
mitigating circumstances, 273
number of executions 1976 to 2011, 271
number of prisoners on death row, 269
persons sentenced and later found to be
innocent, 275
Sixth Amendment and, 273
Supreme Court rulings and, 197, 270–274
victim impact evidence and sentencing, 268
Death Penalty Information Center, 275
Death row, number of prisoners on, 269
Decarceration, 316
parole and, 352
Deception, 419
Deepwater Horizon, 420
Defendants
appeals, 244–245
arraignment, 223

attorney-client privilege and, 209–210
in civil case, 73
defined, 73
Fifth amendment, 229
plea bargaining and, 225, 226
presumption of innocence, 229
self-incrimination, 229
Defense(s)
affirmative defense, 240
alibi, 240
creating reasonable doubt, 239
duress, 86–87, 240
entrapment, 88, 240
infancy, 83
insanity, 83–85, 240
intoxication, 85–86
justifiable use of force, 87–88
mistake, 86
necessity, 88
self-defense, 87–88, 240
Defense attorneys, 207–210
attorney-client privilege, 209–210
charging conference, 242
closing arguments, 241
constitutional right to, 89
creating reasonable doubt, 239
cross-examination, 239
defending the guilty, 208
defense strategies, 240
evidence and, 236
hearsay, 238–239
jury selection, 232
opening statements, 235
plea bargaining and, 225–226
preliminary hearing, 220
private attorneys, 208
public defenders, 208
recross-examination, 239
responsibilities of, 207–208
in sentencing process, 260
social media and, 24
surrebuttal, 241
Delancey Street Foundation, 336
Delegation of authority, 129–130
Deliberate crime, 74
Deliberate indifference standard, 346
Delinquency in a Birth Cohort (Wolfgang, Figlio
and Sellin), 55
Department of Homeland Security (DHS).
See Homeland Security, Department
of (DHS)
Departure, 266
Deprivation model, 340
Desistance, 357, 377
Detainer, 417–418
Detective, 133, 162
Detention
as element of arrest, 169
of juveniles, 384
pretrial, 217–219
preventive, 218–219, 384
Detention hearing, 384
Determinate sentencing, 257, 258
Deterrence
death penalty as, 274
general, 254
patrol officers, 131

as purpose of sentencing, 254
specific, 254
Deviance, 7
DHS. *See* Homeland Security, Department
of (DHS)
Differential association, theory of, 51
Differential response, 138
Directed patrol, 139
Direct evidence, 236–237
Direct examination, 238
Direct supervision approach, 329
Discipline
by correctional officers, 344–345
role in society, 342–343
Discovery, 220
Discretion
in criminal justice system, 15–16
defined, 15
ethics and, 16–17, 152
in Japanese courts and, 224
judicial, 258, 259, 262, 265, 291, 386
juveniles and, 381–382
prosecutorial, 206, 221–223
Discrimination
death penalty, 276–277
hiring of women and minorities as police
officers, 110–111
selection of judges for Supreme Court and,
202–203
sentencing and, 263–264
Disorderly conduct, 38, 75
Disposition hearing, 386
Dispositions, 258
Dissenting opinions, 199
District, 130
District attorney, 205
District Courts, U.S., 196
Diversion
community corrections as, 287–288
pretrial diversion programs, 297
pretrial programs, 383
probation as, 383
treatment and aid, 383
DNA data
CODIS and cold hits, 136
death penalty and, 23
DNA fingerprinting, 135
familial searches, 137
touch DNA, 136–137
DNA profiling, 18
Docket, 201
Domestic court, 195
Domestic terrorism, 399
Domestic violence, uncooperative victim, 223
Dopamine, 47–48
drug addiction and, 57
Double jeopardy, 89, 244
civil suits, 244
hung jury, 244
juveniles, 369
limits of, 244
possibility and risk of retrial, 244
Driving under the influence, 38
Drug abuse
defined, 56
dopamine and addiction, 57
juvenile delinquency and, 378–379

synthetic drugs, 57–58
Drug courts, 195, 297
Drug Enforcement Administration (DEA), 11, 114
    employees and budget, 118
    responsibilities of, 116, 118
Drug offenses
    average length of sentence, 290
    increases in prison population and, 314–315
    by juveniles, 373
    race and, 42, 43
    sentence outcome for guilty plea, 226
    sentencing disparity, 263
Drugs
    crime and, 20, 55–58
    habits/categories of illegal drug users, 21
    mandatory sentencing guidelines, 267
    Mexican drug cartels, 58
    psychoactive, 20
Drug trafficking
    average length of sentence, 290
    sentence outcome for guilty plea, 226
    sentencing disparity, 263
Drug use
    addiction and dependency, 56–57
    drug-crime relationship, 57–58
    learning theory, 56
    methamphetamine, 57
    prescription drugs, 57
    social disorganization theory and, 56
Drug Use Forecasting Program, 39
Drunkenness offenses, 38
Dual court system, 11–12, 193
Due process
    constitutional guarantee of, 89–91
    defined, 89
    function of courts and, 189
    indefinite detention and war on terrorism, 406–407
    juveniles and, 369, 370
    parole and, 354–355
    procedural, 90
    revocation process, 293–294
    substantive, 90–91
    Supreme Court's role in, 91
Due process model, 17
Duress
    as defense, 86–87, 240
    defined, 86
Duty, ethical dilemmas of, 152
Duty to aid statutes, 77
Duty to retreat, 88

E

East Coast Rapist, 135
Eastern Penitentiary, 312
East Haven Police Department, 149–150
Eavesdropping Act, 76
Economy, crime rate variations and, 41
Eighth Amendment, 89
    death penalty and, 270, 271, 272, 273
    deliberate indifference standard, 346
    identifiable human needs, 347
    juveniles and, 372
    reasonable bail, 217
    three-strikes laws, 267

use of force by prison officials, 345
Electric chair, 270
Electronic monitoring
    ankle bracelet, 301
    defined, 300
    technological advances in, 301
    types of, 301
Electronic surveillance, 259
    closed-circuit television (CCTV) cameras, 177–178
    consent and probable cause, 176–177
    defined, 176
    as force multiplier, 177
    traffic cameras, 177
Elmira Reformatory, 312–313, 319
El Paso County Sheriff's Department, 114
El Salvador, gangs and firm hand laws, 164
Embezzlement, 38, 419
Emergency preparedness and response, 403–404
England, early police experience and, 102
Entrapment, 88
    homeland security and, 403
Entrapment defense, 240
Environmental Protection Agency (EPA), 69, 420
Equal Employment Act, 110
Ethics
    defined, 16
    discretion and, 16–17, 152
    duty, 152
    elements of, 152
    encouraging ethical policing, 153
    ethical dilemmas, 151–152
    honesty, 152
    justice and, 16–17
    kidney compensation, 68
    loyalty, 152
    police corruption, 149–150
Ethnicity, crime and, 44
Evidence
    circumstantial, 237
    CSI effect, 237
    defined, 235
    direct, 236–237
    exclusionary rule, 163–165
    fingerprint matches, 200
    fruit of the poisoned tree, 163
    good faith exception, 164–165
    hearsay, 238–239
    inevitable discovery exception, 162
    prejudicial, 237–238
    probable cause based on, 163
    real evidence, 235–236
    relevance, 237
    role in trial, 235–237
    testimonial, 235
    victim impact evidence, 268
Exclusionary rule, 222
    defined, 163
    exceptions to, 163–165
    good faith exception, 164–165
    inevitable discovery exception, 162
    purpose of, 163
Excuse defenses
    duress, 86–87
    infancy, 83
    insanity, 83–85
    intoxication, 85–86

mistake, 86
overview, 83
Exigent circumstances, arrests and, 169
Expert witness, 236
Expiration release, 355
Extradition, 191

F

Facebook, 24, 25, 376
    searches and, 178
Faith-based neglect, 288
Familial searches, 137
Family
    child abuse and juvenile delinquency, 379
    crime and, 51
Family group homes, 387
Federal Bureau of Investigation (FBI), 11
    careers in, 119
    counterterrorism efforts, 401–402
    creation of, 118
    definition of terrorism, 397
    employees and budget, 118
    fingerprint matches, 200
    responsibilities of, 116, 118
    Safe Streets initiative, 19
    Strategic Information Operations Center, 401–402
    Terrorist Screening Center and "no fly" list, 404
    Uniform Crime Report (UCR), 36–38
Federal Bureau of Prisons (BOP), 316
Federal Circuit, 196, 197
Federal court system
    in dual court system, 193
    judges, 196
    selection of judges, 201
    Supreme Court, 196–199
    U.S. Courts of Appeal, 196
    U.S. District Court, 196
Federal Emergency Management Agency (FEMA), under Homeland Security Department, 401
Federal Food, Drug and Cosmetic Act, 69
Federal government, law enforcement and, 11
Federalism, 9
Federal law enforcement agencies, 116–120
    Bureau of Alcohol, Tobacco, Firearms and Explosives (ATF), 118–119
    Customs and Border Protection (CBP), 117
    Drug Enforcement Administration (DEA), 118
    Federal Bureau of Investigation (FBI), 118
    Homeland Security, 116–118
    Immigration and Customs Enforcement (ICE), 117
    Justice Department, 118–120
    number of officers in, 116
    Secret Service, 117–118
    Treasury Department, 120
    U.S. Marshals Service, 119–120
Federal Reporter, 29
Federal Rules of Evidence, 238
Federal statutes, 67
Federal Supplement, 29
Federal Trade Commission (FTC), 420
Felony
    case attrition, 221, 222

defined, 74
degrees of, 74
felony-murder, 80
initial appearance, 217
jury trials, 229
Felony-murder, 80
Female police officers. *See* Women police officers
Field services
　defined, 130
　investigations, 133–137
　patrol, 131–133
Field training, 110
Field training officer (FTO), 110
Fifth Amendment, 89
　arraignment, 223
　double jeopardy, 244
　due process and indefinite detention, 406–407
　juveniles and, 369
　Miranda warning, 179, 180, 181, 182
　pretrial detention, 217
　privilege against self-incrimination, 229
　probation officer meeting with probationer, 295
　witnesses and, 229
Fines
　day-fines in Sweden, 298
　as form of punishment, 259, 296–297
Fingerprinting, 135
　new techniques for, 200–201
Fingerprint matches, 200–201
Fire marshals, 10–11
First Amendment, 5
　abusive speech, 6
　crush videos, 197
　freedom of speech, 21
　prisoners' rights, 347
First responders, 403–404
Flag burning, 68
Flash-rob, 25
Folsom State Prison, 319, 336, 341
Food and Drug Administration (FDA), 69
Force
　deadly, 87, 147
　duty to retreat, 88
　justifiable use of, 87–88
　misuse of, 146–147
　nondeadly, 147
　by prison officials, 345
　reasonable, 147
　reasonable belief and, 87
　Supreme Court decisions on, 147–148
　types of, 147
　use of force matrix, 146–147
Force multipliers, 177
Foreign Intelligence Surveillance Act (FISA), 406
Foreign terrorist organization (FTO), 400
Forensics, 134–137
　ballistics, 135
　databases and cold hits, 135–136
　DNA fingerprinting, 135
　trace evidence, 134–135
Forensic scientist, 136
Forfeiture, 297–298
Forgery, 38
Formal criminal justice process, 14
Fortresses of crime, 49

Fort Smith Police Department, 151
Foster care programs, 387
Four Loko, 7
Fourteenth Amendment, 89
Fourth Amendment, 21, 89, 161–165
　arbitrary searches of prison cells, 346
　automobile searches, 174
　closed-circuit television cameras and, 178
　electronic surveillance, 176
　exclusionary rule, 163–165
　garbage searches and, 170–171
　good faith exception, 164–165
　inevitable discovery exception, 162
　prisoners' rights, 346
　probable cause, 161–163
　reasonableness, 161
　search warrants, 172
　war on terrorism and, 405–406
Fraud
　consumer, 419
　credit-card and check, 419
　cyber, 34, 409–410
　insurance, 419
　mail and wire, 419
　mortgage, 421
　as Part II offense, 38
　securities, 419
Freedom of speech, 21
Fresno Police Department, budget cuts and, 137
Frisk, 167
Fruit of the poisoned tree, 163, 182
Furlough, 355
Fusion centers, 402

G
Gambling, 38
　online, 413–414
Gang investigator, 72
Gangs
　characteristics of members of, 380
　crime and, 19
　defined, 379
　firm hand laws in El Salvador, 164
　in prison, 341
　reasons for joining, 380–381
　as risk factor for juvenile delinquency, 379–380
Gender
　jury selection, 234–235
　juvenile delinquency and, 473–475
　sentencing discrimination, 264
General deterrence, 254
General jurisdiction, 195
General patrol, 139
General Theory of Crime, A (Gottfredson and Hirschi), 53
GEO Group, Inc., 322
Good faith exception, 164–165
Good time, 257, 319
Google+, 24
GPS, 301–302
Graduated sanctions, 386
Grand jury, 218, 220–221
Great Britain, abusive speech, 6
Great Law, 311

Great Recession, 421
Green card, 415
Grim Sleeper, 137
Gross misdemeanor, 75
Group homes, 387
Guantánamo Bay, Cuba (GTMO), 407
Guidant Corporation, 420
Guilty
　beyond a reasonable doubt, 230
　guilty but mentally ill, 84
　plea bargaining, 224–227
　pleading, 223–224
Guilty act, 77
Guilty plea, 218, 223–224
　juveniles and, 386
　misdemeanor cases at initial appearance, 217
Gun control, 19
Gun Control Act, 118
Gun court, 195
Guns
　ATF responsibilities and, 118–119
　concealed weapon statutes, 70
　control vs. right debate, 19
　crime and, 19
　federalization of gun possession crimes and prison populations, 315

H
Habeas corpus, 244–245
Habitual Criminal Sterilization Act, 91
Habitual offender laws, 267
Hacking, 396–397, 411–412
　cars, 412–413
Hacktivist, 396
Halfway house, 357
Halfway house program manager, 358
Hallcrest Report II, 121
Hands-off doctrine, 346
Harm, 81–82
Hate crimes
　incidence of, 82
　laws against, 81–82
Hawaii's Opportunity Probation with Enforcement (HOPE) program, 295
Hearsay, 238–239
High-tech crime, 34
Highway patrol, 10–11
　number of agencies, 115
　purpose and duties of, 115
Hillsborough (New Jersey) Police Department, 24
Hispanics
　crime rate and, 44
　immigration law and increase in prison population, 315, 414
　incarceration rate and, 24
　as law enforcement officers, 110–113
　low representation on Supreme Court, 202–203
　prison violence and, 341
　sentencing discrimination, 264
Home confinement, 300–301
　defined, 300
　levels of, 300
Home detention, 300
Home incarceration, 300

Homeland security, 397–407. *See also* Anti-
terrorism; Terrorism
Antiterrorism and Effective Death Penalty Act
(AEDPA), 399–400
counterterrorism challenges and strategies,
402–404
cyber crime and, 396–397
defined, 20, 397
Department of Homeland Security, 401
federal agencies outside DHS, 401–402
global context of terrorism, 397–399
homegrown extremists, 399
informants and entrapment, 403
lone wolf terrorist, 402–403
Patriot Act, 400
security vs. civil liberties, 405–407
state and local counterterrorism efforts, 402
Homeland Security, Department of (DHS), 401
agencies under, 401
creation of, 11, 116, 401
Customs and Border Protection (CBP), 117
federal agencies outside, 401–402
Immigration and Customs Enforcement (ICE),
117
organization of, 401
Secret Service, 117–118
United States Visitor and Immigrant Status
Indicator Technology (US-VISIT)
program, 416
Homeland Security Act, 401
Homeless, attacks against, 46–47
Homicide. *See also* Murder
justifiable, 5
Honor killings, 76
Hormones, 47
Hot-spot policing, 18
Hot spots, 140
House arrest, 259
House of Refuge, 367
Human-source collection, 402
Hung jury, 239, 243
double jeopardy, 244
Hypothesis, 46

I

Idaho Correctional Center (ICC), 324
Identifiable human needs, 347
Identity theft, 410
Illinois Juvenile Court Act, 367–368
I-Max maximum security prison, 320
Immigration and Customs Enforcement (ICE)
under Homeland Security Department, 117,
401
responsibilities of, 116, 117
Immigration and Naturalization Service (INS),
117
Immigration law
as civil regulatory system, 414
crimmigration, 414
enforcing, 417–418
as federal matter, 414
growth in prison population and, 315, 414
number of unauthorized aliens, 417
Operation Community Shield, 417
removal, 415

Secure Communities initiative, 417–418
United States Visitor and Immigrant Status
Indicator Technology (US-VISIT)
program, 416
visa basics of, 415
Impartial jury, 228
Imprisonment
crime rate variations and, 41
as form of punishment, 258
Incapacitation, as purpose of sentencing, 254–255
Incarceration
high rate of, in U.S., 314–315, 317
increased probability of, 314–315
of juveniles, 387–389
shock, 259, 289
Incarceration rate, race and, 23–24
Inchoate offenses, 82
Incident-driven policing, 138
Indeterminate sentencing
defined, 256
historical perspective of, 258
individualized justice, 258
rehabilitation and, 256–257, 258
Indictment, 218, 221
Individualized justice, 258
Industrial schools, 388
Industrial shop and school officers, 343
Inevitable discovery exception, 162
Infancy defense, 83, 371
Informal criminal justice process, 15
Informants
homeland security and, 403
probable cause based on, 163
Information
defined, 220
issued by prosecutor, 220
probable cause based on, 162
Infraction, 75
Infrastructure, 401
Inherent coercion, 179
Initial appearance, 217
In loco parentis, 381
Inmates. *See* Prisoners
Innocence, presumption of, 229
Innocence Project, 245
Insanity
ALI/MPC test, 84
death penalty and, 273
as defense under criminal law, 83–85
determining competency, 84–85
guilty but mentally ill, 84
irresistible-impulse test, 84
measuring, 83–84
M'Naghten rule, 83–84
substantial-capacity test, 84
use of, as defense, 8, 85
Insanity defense, 240
Insurance fraud, 419
Intake, 382
Intellectual property, 413
Intelligence agency, 401
Intelligence-led policing, 105–107
Intelligence operations, types of, 401–402
Intensive supervision probation, 299
Intent, 77, 79, 80, 81
as element of arrest, 168

Intermediate sanctions, 295–302
boot camps, 300
day-fines, 297, 298
day reporting centers, 299
defined, 295
drug courts, 297
electronic monitoring, 300–301
forfeiture, 297–298
home confinement, 300–301
intensive supervision probation, 299
judicially administered, 296–298
pretrial diversion programs, 297
shock incarceration, 299–300
in Sweden, 298
widen the net, 302
Intermittent incarceration, 289
Internal affairs unit (IAU), 150
Internal Revenue Service (IRS), 114, 120, 421
responsibilities of, 116
Internet. *See also* Cyber crimes
pornography, 252
Internet Crime Complaint Center (IC$_3$), 409
Interrogation process
custodial interrogation, 179
inherent coercion, 179
Miranda rights and, 178–182
recording, 182
Intoxication
as defense under criminal law, 85–86
involuntary, 85
voluntary, 85
Investigations, 133–137
ballistics, 135
clearance rates, 134
confidential informant, 134
databases and cold hits, 135–136
DNA fingerprinting, 135
forensics, 134–137
presentence, 259–260, 292
trace evidence, 134–135
undercover operations, 133–134
Involuntary intoxication, 85
Involuntary manslaughter, 74–75, 79
Irresistible-impulse test, 84
Islam, conversion to in prison, 348

J

Jails, 325–330
administration, 328
characteristics of population, 325–326
compared to prisons, 325–326, 327
defined, 13, 326
direct supervision approach, 329
function of, 326
new-generation jails, 328–329
pretrial detainees, 326
sentenced jail inmates, 327
sociology of, 327–328
Japan, discretion in courts and, 224
Jihad, meaning of term, 398
Judges
charge to jury, 242
discretion and, 16, 258, 259, 262, 265, 291
federal, 196
in France, 202

intermediate sanctions, 296–298
Missouri Plan, 201–202
roles
in courtroom work group, 205
of trial judges, 199–201
selection of, 201–202
sentencing, 259–260
departures, 266
factors in, 260–262
individualized justice, 258
sentencing disparity, 262–263
victim impact evidence, 268
Supreme Court, 196–199
Judicial discretion, 386
Judicial review, 197
Judicial system
courtroom work group, 203–210
dual court system, 193
federal court system, 196–199
judges in court system, 199–203
state court system, 194–196
trail and appellate courts, 192
Judicial waiver, 383
Jurisdiction
appellate, 192
concurrent, 193
defined, 191
general, 192, 195
geographic, 191
international, 191–192
limited, 192, 194–195
original, 192
subject-matter, 192
of Supreme Court, 198
universal, 192
Jury
Allen Charge, 243
charge to, 242
death penalty and, 260, 268
deliberations, 242
hung, 239, 243
impartial, 228
instructions, 242
requirements for, 231
right to trial by, 21
role of, 228–229
selection
challenges for cause, 232
goal of, 231
master jury list, 231
peremptory challenges, 232
race and, 232–234
venire, 231
voir dire, 231–232
women, 234–235
sentencing process and, 260
sequestered, 242
Jury instructions, 242
Jury pool, 231
Jury selection, 231–235
Jury trials, 228. *See also* Trials
juveniles, 369
Just deserts, 253
Justice
defined, 8
ethics and, 16–17
maintaining, 8

Justice Department, 118–120
law enforcement agencies of, 118–120
Justifiable homicide, 5
Justifiable use of force, 87–88
Justification defenses, 86–88
duress, 86–87
entrapment, 88
necessity, 88
overview, 86
self-defense, 87–88
Juveniles. *See also* Children; Juvenile
delinquency; Juvenile justice system
age tried as adults, 371–372
bullying, 376
constitutional protections, 369–370
crimes committed by, 373–374
culpability and, 372
death penalty and, 273, 372
detention, 384
incarceration
aftercare programs, 389
boot camps, 387–388
nonsecure confinement, 387
residential treatment programs, 387
secure confinement, 387–389
training schools, 388
infancy defense, 83, 371
life-without-parole sentences, 366
parens patriae, 367
police and, 381–382
probation for, 387
school violence, 375
status offender, 368
on trial, 384–386
Juvenile corrections, 386–389
Juvenile courts, 195
age tried as an adult, 371–372
constitutional protections, 369–370
double jeopardy, 369
due process, 369, 370
establishment of, 367–368
Fifth Amendment, 369
Illinois Juvenile Court Act, 367–368
jury trial, 369
reasonable double standard, 369
tried as an adult, 367, 369, 371–372, 383–384,
385
Juvenile delinquency
chronic 6 percent, 377
defined, 368
family-based delinquency, 375
girls, 374–375
rise and fall of crime rate for, 373–374
risk factors, 377–381
age, 377–378
child abuse and neglect, 379
gang involvement, 379–381
low self-control, 377
overview, 378
substance abuse, 378–379
vs. status offenders, 368
trends in, 373–376
UCR data on, 373
Juvenile Justice and Delinquency Prevention
Act, 383
Juvenile justice system
compared to criminal justice system, 384–385

evolution of
child-saving movement, 367
constitutional protections, 369
Illinois Juvenile Court, 367–368
status offenses vs. juvenile delinquency, 368
girls in, 374–375
pretrial procedures, 381–384
detention, 384
intake, 382–383
overview of, 382
petition, 383
police discretion and, 381–382
pretrial diversion, 383
referral, 382
transfer to adult court, 383–384
on trial, 384–386
adjudication, 385–386
disposition hearing, 386
sentencing, 386
Juvenile officer, 381

K
Kansas City Preventive Patrol Experiment, 139
Keystroke logging, 411–412
Kidney transplant, 68
Knapp Commission, 149
Knock and announce rule, 169–170
Knock and talk strategy, 174

L
La Familia Michoacana drug cartel, 114
Lake Erie Correctional Institute, 325
La Nuestra Familia, 341
Larceny, 33
as Part I offense, 37
Law enforcement
federal, 11
impact on crime rate, 17–18
local, 10
state, 10–11
Law enforcement agencies, 114–121
benefit of cultural diversity, 113
counterterrorism efforts, 402–403
federal agencies, 116–120
municipal agencies, 114
number of, 114
sheriffs and county, 114–115
state police and highway patrol, 115
Law Enforcement Code of Ethics, 100
Law enforcement officers
academy training, 109
accountability, 150
broken windows theory, 140–141
community policing, 141–142
community services provided,
100–101, 131
corruption by, 149–150
crime prevention, 101
cultural diversity and, 113
educational requirements for, 109
enforcing laws, 99–100
ethics, 151–152
field training, 110
general and directed patrol strategies, 139
incident-driven policing, 138

investigations, 133–137
juveniles and, 381–382
killed in the line of duty, 144–145
minorities as, 110–113
patrol, 131–133
peacekeeping role, 101–102
physical dangers of police work, 144–145
probationary period, 109
problem-oriented policing, 142–143
reactive and proactive arrest strategies,
140–141
recruitment for, 107–110
requirements for, 108–109
response time to 911 calls, 138
responsibilities of, 99–102
salary, 108
stress and mental dangers, 145–146
subculture of, 144
undercover officers, 133–134
women as, 111
Laws. *See also* Criminal law
administrative, 69
ballot initiatives and, 68–69
case, 69
constitutional, 67
legal function of, 70
police enforcing, 99–100
social function of, 70–71
statutory, 67–69
Lay witness, 236
Leading questions, 238
Learning theory, 51
drug use and, 56
Legal duty, 77
Legislative sentencing authority, 256–258
Legislative waiver, 384
Lehman Brothers, 421
Less-lethal weapons, 146–147
Lethal injection, 270, 273–274
Lexington-Fayette Police Department, 160
Liability, 73
Liable, 73
Life course criminology, 52–53
Life-without-parole sentence, 352
juveniles and, 366, 372
Limited jurisdiction, 192, 194–195
Line services, 130
Liquor laws, 38
Local government, law enforcement, 10
Local police departments. *See* Municipal law
enforcement agencies
Lockdown, 321
Loitering laws, 38
London Metropolitan Police, 102
Lone wolf terrorist, 402–403
Los Angeles County Men's Central Jail, 328
Los Angeles County Sheriff's Department,
number of employees, 114
Low-visibility decision making, 381
Loyalty, ethical dilemmas of, 152
LulzSec, 396
Lynchburg Police Department, 153

M

Magistrate, 195
Mail and wire fraud, 419

Mala in se crimes, 75–76
Mala prohibita crimes, 75–76
Malice aforethought, 74
Malware, 412
Mandatory release, 353
Mandatory sentencing guidelines, 267–268
Manhattan Bail Project, 219
Manslaughter
involuntary, 74–75, 79
voluntary, 74
Mara Salvatrucha, 164
Marijuana, 58
for medical use, 68–69
Marriage, bigamy, 70
Marshals Service, responsibilities of, 116
Massachusetts Correctional Institution at
Framingham, 349–350
Master jury list, 231
Maximum-security prison, 319–321
Medical examiner, 115
Medical marijuana, 68
Medical model, 313
Medium-security prison, 321
Megan's Law, 359
Mens rea, 66
accomplice liability, 80
categories of, 78
criminal liability, 79
defined, 77
duress, 86
intoxication and, 85–86
murder and, 79
negligence, 78–79
recklessness, 79
strict liability, 79–80
Mental illness, prison population and, 338–339
Mentally handicapped, death penalty and, 273
Methadone, 57
Methadrone crystals, 58
Methamphetamine, 57
Mexican drug cartels, 58
Mexican Mafia, 341
Mexico, border patrol and, 404
Military tribunals, 407
Minimum-security prison, 321–322
Minorities
consequences of high incarceration rate, 330
jury selection, 232–234
low representation on Supreme Court, 202–203
sentencing discrimination, 263–264
Minority law enforcement officers
antidiscrimination law and affirmative action,
110–111
benefits of diverse police force, 113
double marginality, 112–113
numbers of, 110, 111–112
Miranda warning
erosion of, 181–182
fourteen day invocation, 197–198
future of, 181–182
legal basis for, 179
recording confessions, 182
voluntary statements, 181–182
waiving rights, 181
when not required, 180–181
when required, 179
wording of, 179

Misdemeanors
degrees of, 75
gross, 75
initial appearance, 217
petty, 75
punishment for, 75
Missouri Plan, 201–202
Mistake
as defense under criminal law, 86
of fact, 86
of law, 86
Mistrial, 243
Misuse of force, 146–147
Mitigating circumstances
death penalty, 273
defined, 261
as factor in sentencing, 273
M'Naghten rule, 83–84
Mobile Offender Recognition and Identification
System (MORIS), 18–19
Model Penal Code, 74, 84
Mooching, 149
Morality, public, 70
Morals, 6
Mortgage fraud, 421
Moscow airport bombing, 397
Motor vehicle theft, 33
as Part I offense, 37
sentencing disparity, 263
MS-13, 164, 380
Mumbai financial district raid, 397
Municipal court judges, 195
Municipal law enforcement agencies
authority of, 114
population served, 114
vs. sheriff department, 115
Murder
African Americans and, 42
average length of sentence for, 290
clearance rate for, 134
defined, 33
degree of, 74, 79
felony-murder, 80
first degree, 74, 79
gangs and, 380
intent and, 79
involuntary manslaughter, 79
by juveniles, 373–374
vs. manslaughter, 74–75
mens rea, 79
as Part I offense, 37
second degree, 74, 79
sentence outcome for guilty plea, 226
sentencing disparity, 263
Muslims
conversion to Islam, in prison, 348
terrorist profiling, 405
MySpace, 107

N

National Advisory Commission on Civil
Disorders, 104
National Center for Victims of Crime, 270
National Combined DNA Index System (CODIS),
136
National Crime Information Center (NCIC), 118

National Crime Victimization Survey (NCVS), 38–39
National Gang Crime Research Center, 341
National Mortgage Fraud Team, 421
National Reporter System, 29
National Security Agency (NSA), 402
  counterterrorism efforts, 406
National White Collar Crime Center, 409
Necessity defense, 88
Negligence
  defined, 78
  mens rea, 78–79
Neurons, 47
Neurotransmitters, 47–48
New Folsom, 336
Newgate Prison, 312
New-generation jails, 328–329
New Orleans Police Department, 102
New York Police Department (NYPD)
  corruption in, 149
  crime-mapping system, 140
  establishment of, 102
  internal affairs investigation department, 150
  number of employees, 114
  stops and race, 166
New York system, 312
Night watch system, 102
911 calls, response time to, 138
Nolle prosequi, 221
Nolo contendere plea, 224
Nondeadly force, 147
Nonpartisan elections, 201
Nonstate actors, 397
Norepinephrine, 47–48
Norway, sentencing and rehabilitation focus, 255
Notification laws, sex offenders, 359

O

Obama, Barack
  bin Laden's death, 398
  military tribunals, 407
  prosecuting terrorists, 230
Occupational Safety and Health Administration (OSHA), 69
Occupy Boston, 100
Officers. *See* Law enforcement officers
Oklahoma City bombing, 400
Oleoresin capsicum, 146–147
Online auction fraud, 409
Online child pornography, 413–414
Online gambling, 413–414
Opening statement, 235
Open-source collection, 402
Operation Community Shield, 417
Operation Heat Wave, 143
Operations, 130
Opinions, 192
Oral arguments, 198
Organized crime, 34
Original jurisdiction, 192
Orlando Police Department, 147
OxyContin, 57

P

Pardon, 355
Parens patriae, 367

Parole
  authority, 351
  characteristics of offenders, 351
  compared to probation, 289, 351
  conditions of, 354
  defined, 13, 350, 351
  due process and, 354–355
  eligibility for, 257, 351–352
  guidelines for, 353
  life-without-parole sentences, 352
  mandatory release, 353
  parole contract, 354
  parole grant hearing, 352–353
  parole officer and, 354–355
  presumptive parole date, 353
  promoting desistance, 357
  revocation of, 354–355
  supervision, 354–355
  technical violation, 354
  timing, 351
  work release programs and halfway houses, 357
Parole board, 257
  defined, 352
  good time and, 257
  indeterminate sentencing and, 257
  parole hearing, 352
Parole contract, 354
Parole grant hearing, 352–353
Parole guidelines, 353
Parole officers, 354–355
  presentence investigation report, 259–260, 292
Parole revocation, 354–355
Part I offenses, 36–37
Part II offenses, 37–38
Partisan elections, 201
Patriot Act, 400
  criticism of, 21
  key provisions of, 20
  overview of, 400
  searches and, 406
  surveillance and, 406
Patrol, 131–133
  activities on, 131–133
  administrative duties, 132
  calls for service, 132
  community services, 131
  directed, 139
  general, 139
  officer-initiated activities, 132
  preventive patrol, 132
  purpose of, 131
  strategies for, 139
Patronage system, 103
Payoffs, 149
Peacekeeping role of police, 101–102
Penal harm movement, 314
Penitentiary, 311. *See also* Prisons
Penitentiary Administrative Maximum (ADX), 321
Pennsylvania System, 312
Peremptory challenges, 232
Permanent residents, 415
Persistent offender, 267
Petition, 383
Petty misdemeanor, 75
Petty offense, 75

Philadelphia Police Department, 102
Phishing, 410
Physical agility exam, 108–109
Physician-assisted suicide, 7, 9
Piracy, 413
Pittsburgh Police Department, 139
Plaintiff, 72
Plain view doctrine, 175–176
Platoons, 130
Plea bargaining
  defendants and, 225, 226
  defense attorneys and, 225–226
  defined, 224
  at initial appearance, 218
  motivations for, 225–227
  prosecutors and, 225
  role in justice system, 224–225
  sentence outcome for, 225, 226
Police. *See also* Law enforcement officers
  accountability, 150
  citizen oversight, 150
  corruption, 149–150
  discretion and, 15–16
  ethics and, 151–152
  historical perspective
    anti-terrorism, 106–107
    community era, 104–105
    early American experience, 102
    first police department, 102
    intelligence-led, 105–107
    political era and corruption, 103, 105
    professionalism, 103
    reform era, 103, 105
    technology and, 105–106
  municipal government and, 10
Police academy, 109
Police Code of Conduct, 151
Police corruption, 149–150
  bribery, 149
  defined, 149
  mooching, 149
  payoffs, 149
  shakedowns, 149
  stages of, 150
Police departments
  bureaucratic model for, 129
  chain of command, 129–130
  compared to prisons, 318
  delegation of authority, 129–130
  effective strategies for, 137–143
  organization of, 129
  patrol, 131–133
  structure of, 129–131
Police Executive Research Forum, 142
Police Services Study, 131
Police strategies
  broken windows theory and, 140–141
  community policing, 141–142
  general and directed patrol strategies, 139
  hot-spot policing, 18
  incident-driven policing, 138
  predictive policing and crime mapping, 139–140
  proactive policing, 18
  problem-oriented, 142–143
  reactive and proactive arrest strategies, 140–141

response time to 911 calls, 138
Police subculture
    authority and use of force, 146–148
    blue curtain, 144
    corruption and, 150
    defined, 144
    physical danger of police work and, 144–145
    socialization, 144
    stress and mental dangers, 145–146
Political era of policing, 103
Pornography
    child, 252
    online, 252, 413–414
Postal Inspectors, 116, 421
Postpartum psychosis, 47
Post-traumatic stress disorder (PTSD),
        145–146
Poverty, crime and, 42–44, 49, 50
Precedent, 69
Precincts, 130
Predictive policing, 139–140
Predisposition report, 386
Prejudicial evidence, 237–238
Preliminary hearing, 218
    to establish probable cause, 220
    pretrial diversion programs, 297
    revocation of probation, 293–294
    waiving, 220
Premeditated crime, 74
Preparedness, 403
Preponderance of the evidence, 73
Prescription drugs, 57
Presentence investigation report, 259–260, 292
President's Commission on Law Enforcement
        and Administration of Justice, 13, 37–38
Pretrial detainees, 326
Pretrial detention, 217–219
    bail bond agent, 219
    initial appearance, 217
    posting bail, 219
    preventive detention, 218–219
    purpose of bail, 217–219
    release on recognizance, 219
Pretrial diversion programs, 297
Pretrial procedures
    arraignment, 223–224
    plea bargaining, 224–227
    prosecutorial screening process, 221–223
Preventive detention, 218–219
Preventive patrol, 132
Preventive policing, counterterrorism strategy,
        402–403
Prima facie case, 233
Prislam, 348
Prison Community, The (Clemmer), 337
Prisoner reentry, 356–360
Prisoners, 336–360. *See also* Prisons
    adapting to prison society, 337–338
    age of, 338
    classification process, 319
    culture of, 337–341
    discipline, 344–345
    gangs, 341
    health and health care for, 338–339
    in prison vs. jail, 326, 327
    recidivism rate, 23, 357
    rehabilitation and prison programs, 339

release of, 350–355
    challenges of, 356
    conditional, 350
    discretionary, 351–353
    expiration release, 355
    furlough, 355
    pardon, 355
    parole, 350–355
    probation release, 355
    promoting desistance, 357
    sex offenders, 358–360
    temporary release, 355
    threat of relapse, 357
    work release programs and halfway houses,
        357
rights of, 346–347
    deliberate indifference standard, 346
    First Amendment, 347
    hands-off doctrine, 346
    identifiable human needs, 347
slang, 337
solitary confinement, 345
violence and
    deprivation model, 340
    incidence of, 340
    prison conditions and, 336
    in prison culture, 339–341
    race and ethnicity, 341
    relative deprivation model, 340–341
    riots, 340–341
women, 347–350
Prison gang, 341
Prisonization, 337
Prisons, 310–325. *See also* Prisoners
    average length of sentence, 290
    average sentence length vs. time served, 257
    classification process, 319
    community corrections as low-cost alternative
        to, 288
    compared to jails, 325–326, 327
    conditions in, and violence, 336
    congregate system, 312
    consequences of high incarceration rate, 330
    correctional officers, 342–347
    cost of, 22–23, 288, 315–316
    decarceration, 316
    defined, 13
    designs of, 320
    as form of punishment, 258
    gangs, 341
    good time, 257
    growth of inmate population of, 314–315
    high rate of incarceration in U.S., 314–315,
        317
    history of
        in colonies, 311
        first penitentiary, 311
        high rate of incarceration, 314–315
        Pennsylvania vs. New York systems,
            311–312
        reassertion of punishment, 313
        reformers and progressives, 312–313
    medical model, 313
    organization and management, 316–318
        chain of command, 318
        compared to police department, 318
        governing, 318

        management structure, 318
        organizational chart for, 319
        types of offenses of federal and state
            inmates, 316–317, 318
        warden and, 318, 319
    penal harm movement, 314
    population of
        aging, 338
        ailing, 338–339
        decarceration, 316
        decrease in, 310
        growth in, 314–315
        high rate of incarceration and, 314–315,
            317
        immigration law and, 315, 414
        leveling off of, 22, 23
        mental illness and, 338–339, 356
    private prisons, 322–325
        arguments against, 324–325
        cost efficiency, 322–324
        future of, 325
        outsourcing inmates, 324
        overcrowding, 324
        philosophical concerns, 325
        profitability of, 325
        reasons for, 322–324
        safety concerns, 324
    rehabilitation and prison programs, 339
    riots, 340–341
    separate confinement, 312
    technology and tracking inmates, 344
    as total institutions, 337
    truth-in-sentencing laws, 257–258
    types of
        maximum-security, 319–321
        medium-security, 321
        minimum-security, 321–322
        security measures in, 320–321
        supermax, 321
    violence in, 339–341
    women in, 315, 347–350
Privacy
    closed-circuit television (CCTV) cameras,
        177–178
    garbage searches and, 171
    prisoners' rights, 346
    reasonable expectation of, 171
    role in searches, 171
Private prisons, 322–325
Private security, 120–121
    defined, 120
    demand for, 120
    growth in, 121
Proactive arrests, 140
Proactive policing, 18
Probable cause, 161–163
    electronic surveillance, 176–177
    establishing, 220–221
    framework, 163
    grand jury, 220–221
    preliminary hearing, 220
    search warrant and, 171
    sources of, 161–163
Probation, 286–303
    authority, 351
    average length of, 290
    caseload and, 293

characteristics of offenders, 351
compared to parole, 289, 351
conditions for, 290–292
defined, 13, 289, 351
diversion, 288
in diversion programs, 383
effectiveness of, 295
eligibility for, 290
as form of punishment, 258–259
intensive supervision probation, 299
juveniles, 387
as low-cost alternative to prison, 288
new models of, 295
number of people under, 286, 288, 289
principles of, 291
vs. prison, 13
probation officer's supervisory role in, 292–293
revocation of, 291, 293–295
shock probation, 289
split sentence, 289
successful completion of, 293
suspended sentence, 289
timing of, 351
Probationary period, 109
Probation officers
authority of, 292–293
as career, 296
caseloads and, 293
presentence investigative report, 259–260
supervisory role, 292–293
Problem-oriented policing, 142–143
Problem-solving courts, 297
Procedural criminal law, 88–91
Procedural due process, 90
Professional model of policing, 103
Progressive movement, 312–313
Project Delirium, 114
Project 54, 104
Property bonds, 219
Property crime
defined, 33
by juveniles, 373
Prosecuting attorney, 205
Prosecutorial waiver, 384
Prosecutors, 205–207
assistant prosecutors, 206
attorney general, 206
burden of proving guilt, 229–230
case attrition, 221–222
case priorities, 222–223
charging conference, 242
closing arguments, 241
direct examination of witnesses, 238
discretion and, 206, 221–223, 266
double jeopardy, 244
as elected official, 206–207
establishing probable cause pretrial, 220–221
evidence and, 236
grand jury, 220–221
hearsay, 238–239
information issued by, 220
jury selection, 232
office of, 206
opening statements, 235

organization of, 206
plea bargaining and, 225
power of, 205–206
preliminary hearing, 220
pretrial diversion programs, 297
rebuttal, 241
redirect examination, 239
screening process, 221–223
in sentencing process, 260
social media and, 24
strict standard of proof, 230–231
Prostitution, 38, 76
Psychoactive drugs, 20
Psychology, 47
crime and, 48
Public defenders
defined, 208
eligibility issues, 208–209
job description, 234
role of, 208
Public morality, 70
Public order crime, 33–34
Public policy
rational choice theory and, 47
trait theory, 48–49
Public prosecutors, 205–206
Punishment
choice theory and, 47
cruel and unusual punishment, 270–271, 273–274
forms of, 258–259
intermediate sanctions, 295–302
probation as, 289

R

Race
consequences of high incarceration rate, 330
crime and, 42
drug offenses and, 42, 43
incarceration rate and, 23–24
prison violence and, 341
stops and, 166–167
Racial profiling
defined, 166
stops and, 166
terrorist profiling, 405
Racketeer Influenced and Corrupt Organizations Act (RICO), 297–298, 421
Racketeering, 421
Radio frequency identification (RFID), 344
Rape
definition of, 32, 33
incidence of, 32
by juveniles, 373–374
as Part I offense, 36
Prison rape, 340
statutory, 80
Rational choice theory, 46–47
Reactive arrests, 140
Real evidence, 235–236
Real offense, 261
Reasonable bail, 217
Reasonable belief, 87
Reasonable doubt standard, 230
juveniles and, 369, 385

Reasonable force, 147
Reasonable suspicion
frisk, 167
Terry case, 165–166
totality of the circumstances test, 166
Rebuttal, 241
Recidivism, 23
Recklessness, 79
Recruitment, of police officers, 107–110
Redirect examination, 239
Reentry courts, 357
Referral, 382
Reform era of policing, 103, 129–130
Regulation, 420
Regulatory agency, 69
Rehabilitation
criticism of, by Martinson, 313
day reporting centers, 299
function of courts and, 190
indeterminate sentencing and, 256–257, 258
Pennsylvania and first penitentiary, 311
of prisoners and prison programs, 339
Progressives and, 312–313
as purpose of sentencing, 254
reintegration through community corrections, 287
Reintegration, community corrections, 287
Relapse process, 357
Relative deprivation, 340–341
Release on recognizance, 219
Relevant evidence, 237
Religion, prisoners' rights and, 347
Removal, immigration law and, 415
Research Network on Adolescent Development and Juvenile Justice, 372
Residential treatment programs, 387
Resident youth worker, 388
Response time
to 911 calls, 138
defined, 138
Restitution, 256
as form of punishment, 259
in pretrial diversion program, 383
Restorative justice, 383
defined, 256
as form of punishment, 259
purpose of sentencing and, 256
Retribution
as purpose of sentencing, 253–254
state sentencing guidelines, 265
Reviewing court, 195
Revocation, of probation, 293–294
Revocation hearing, 294
Revocation sentencing, 294
Riots, prison, 340–341
Robbery
average length of sentence, 290
defined, 33
gangs and, 380
by juveniles, 373–374
as Part I offense, 37
sentence outcome for guilty plea, 226
sentencing disparity, 263
Routine activities theory, 53–54
Rule of four, 198
Rural programs, 387

S

San Jose Police Department, 151
San Quentin State Prison, 319
Santa Clara County Reentry Court, 357
Santa Cruz Police Department, 140
Santa Fe Police Department, 114
S.B. 1070, 166–167
    Supreme Court ruling, and, 167
Schizophrenia, 48
Schools
    bullying, 376
    violence in, 375
Scientific method, 46
Screening process, 222–223
Search(es). *See also* Search and seizure
    arm's reach doctrine, 173
    automobiles, 174–175
    with consent, 173–174
    defined, 171
    incidental to arrest, 173
    knock and talk strategy, 174
    social media searches, 178
Search and seizure
    arm's reach doctrine, 173
    automobiles, 174–175
    with consent, 173–174
    electronic surveillance, 176–178
    exclusionary rule, 163–165
    good faith exception, 164–165
    incidental to arrest, 173
    inevitable discovery exception, 162
    knock and talk strategy, 174
    Patriot Act, 406
    plain view doctrine, 175–176
    probable cause, 161–163
    reasonableness, 161, 172
    role of privacy in, 171
    search warrants, 171–172
    thermal imagers, 175–176
    war on terrorism and, 405–406
    without warrant, 172–174
Search warrants
    defined, 171
    exceptions to requirements for, 174
    particularity requirements, 172
    probable cause and, 171
    purpose of, 172
    search and seizure without, 172–174
Secret Service, 11
    under Homeland Security, 117–118, 401
    responsibilities of, 116, 117–118
Secure Communities initiative, 417–418
Secure Continuous Remote Alcohol Monitor
    (SCRAM), 40
Securities and Exchange Commission (SEC), 420
Securities fraud, 419
Security. *See* Private security
Security Housing Unit (SHU), 321
Seduction of crime, 46–47
Seizure. *See also* Search and seizure
    categories of items for, 172
    defined, 172
    as element of arrest, 169
    plain view doctrine, 175–176
Self-control theory, 53
Self-defense, 76
    as defense, 87, 240

Self-incrimination
    confession as, 179
    privilege against, 229
    witnesses, 229
Self-reported surveys, 39–40
Sentences
    average length of, 290
    split, 289
    suspended, 289
Sentencing, 253–268
    average sentence length vs. time served, 257
    chivalry effect, 264
    community service, 296
    determinate, 257, 258
    discrimination in, 263–264, 276–277
    disparity in, 262–263
    factors in
        judicial philosophy, 262
        mitigating and aggravating circumstances,
            261
        real offense, 261
        seriousness of crime, 260–261
    fines, 296–297
    forfeiture, 297–298
    forms of punishment, 258–259
    good time, 257
    growth in prison population and, 315
    guidelines, 265–267
    indeterminate, 256–257
    individualized justice and judge, 258
    juveniles, 386
    presentence investigative report, 259–260
    probation, 289–290
    process of, 259–260
    purpose of
        deterrence, 254
        incapacitation, 254–255
        rehabilitation, 255
        restitution, 256
        restorative justice, 256
        retribution, 253–254
    reform, 265–268
    restitution, 296
    revocation sentencing, 294
    structure of
        judicial authority, 258–259
        legislative authority, 256–258
    truth-in-sentencing laws, 257–258, 315
    victim impact evidence and, 268
Sentencing discrimination, 263–264
Sentencing disparity, 262–263
Sentencing guidelines
    federal, 265–266
    habitual offender laws, 267
    judicial departures from, 266–267
    mandatory, 267–268
    state, 265
    three-strike laws, 267–268
Sentencing Guidelines Commission, 265
Sentencing reform, 265–268
    departure, 266
    sentencing guidelines, 265–267
    victim impact evidence, 268
Sentencing Reform Act (SRA), 264, 265–266, 315
Separate confinement, 312
September 11, 2001 attacks, 397
    anti-terrorism and policing, 106–107

    first responders killed in, 404
    Homeland Security, 20
    Patriot Act, 20–21, 400
Sequestration, 242
Serotonin, 47–48
Session hijacking, 411
Sex offender notification law, 359
Sex offenders
    conditions of release, 359–360
    Megan's Law, 359
    release of, 358–360
    residency restrictions, 360
    sex offender notification law, 359
Sex offenses, 38
Sexual assault
    average length of sentence, 290
    defined, 33
    sentence outcome for guilty plea, 226
    sentencing disparity, 263
Shakedowns, 149
Sheriffs
    county law enforcement, 10
    defined, 114
    vs. local police departments, 115
    number of departments, 114
    political aspect of, 114
    size and responsibility of departments,
        114–115
Shifts, 130
Shock incarceration, 259, 289
    boot camps, 300
    defined, 299
    value of, 300
Shock probation, 289
Sing Sing Correctional Facility, 319, 347
Sixth Amendment, 21, 89
    cross-examination, 239
    death penalty, 273
    defense attorneys and, 207, 208
    impartial jury, 228
    military tribunals, 407
    pretrial detention, 217
    speedy trial, 227, 228
Social conflict theory, 50
Social disorganization theory, 49, 50
Socialization, 144
Social media, impact on criminal justice system,
    24–25
Social networking, collecting intelligence on,
    107
Social process theories, 51–52
Social psychology, 48
Societal boundaries, 71
Sociology, 49
Solitary confinement, 345
Spam, 412
Special prosecution, 206
Specialty courts, 195
Specific deterrence, 254
Speedy trial, 227–228
Speedy Trial Act, 228
Split sentence probation, 289
Spoils system, 103
Stalking, cyber, 411
Standard of proof
    civil cases, 73
    criminal cases, 73

Stand Your Ground statute, 4, 5
State court systems
    courts of appeal, 195–196
    courts of limited jurisdiction, 194–195
    in dual court system, 193
    organization of, 194
    selection of judges, 201–202
    specialty courts, 195
    trial courts of general jurisdiction, 195
State police, 10–11
    number of departments, 115
    purpose and duties of, 115
State prosecutor, 205
States, law enforcement and, 10–11
State statutes, 67
Station, 130
Status offenders, 368
    treatment of girls, 375
Statute of limitations, 228
Statutes
    ballot initiatives, 68–69
    as source of law, 67
Statutory law, 67–69
Statutory rape, 80
Stolen property, 38
Stop-and-identify laws, 167
Stops
    compared to arrests, 168
    defined, 167
    race and, 166–167
    racial profiling, 166
    Terry case, 165–166
    totality of the circumstances test, 166
Strain theory, 49–50
Strategic Forecasting, 396
Strategic Information Operations Center, 401–402
Street gangs, 19. See also Gangs
Stress, of police work, 145–146
Stress hormone, 145
Stressors, 145
Strict liability crimes, 79–80
Subculture. See Police subculture
Substance abuse, juvenile delinquency and, 378–379
Substance Abuse and Crime Prevention Act, 295
Substantial-capacity test, 84
Substantive criminal law, 67, 88
Substantive due process, 90–91
Suicide
    bullycides, 376
    physician-assisted suicide, 7, 9
Supermax prison, 321
Supremacy clause, 68
Supreme Court, state, jurisdiction on, 195
Supreme Court, United States, 67
    Allen Charge, 243
    appeals process, 244
    arrests, 168
    automobile searches, 174–175
    cases heard by, 198
    choice of defense attorney, 209
    concurring opinions, 199
    counsel at criminal trials, 196
    cruel and unusual punishment, 271, 274
    crush videos, 197
    death penalty, 197, 270–274
    death penalty for juveniles, 372

deliberate indifference standard, 346
dissenting opinions, 199
diversity on bench, 202–203
due process and, 91
electronic surveillance, 176–177
federal mandatory sentencing guidelines, 267–268
flag burning, 68
forfeiture, 298
good faith exception, 164–165
hands-off approach, 346
identifiable human needs, 347
impact of, 196–197
indefinite detention, 406–407
initial appearance, 217
interpreter of law, 197–198
judicial review, 197
jurisdiction, 191, 198
jury selection, 232–234
juveniles and, 369–370
knock and announce rule, 169–170
Miranda warning, 180–182, 197–198
number of cases heard by, 198
oral arguments before, 198
parole, 351
parole revocation and due process, 354–355
plain view doctrine, 175–176
plea bargaining, 225
pretrial detainees, 326
preventive detention, 384
prisoners medical care, 340
prisoners' rights, 346–347
privacy, 171
probable cause, 163
process of reaching a decision, 198–199
reasonable doubt standard, 230
reasonable search, 161
rule of four, 198
searches incidental to arrest, 173
self-incrimination, 229
speedy trial, 227
stops, 165–166, 167
totality of the circumstances test, 166
use of force by law enforcement officials, 147–148
use of force by prison officials, 345
victim impact evidence, 268
warrantless arrest, 170
writ of certiorari, 198
Supreme Court justices
    appointment and terms of, 196
    diversity on bench, 202–203
    impact of past discrimination, 203
Supreme Court Reporter, 29
Surrebuttal, 241
Surveillance, war on terrorism and, 405–406
Suspended sentence, 289
Suspicious Activity Report (SAR), 106
Sweden, day-fines, 298
Sworn officers, 131
Synthetic drugs, 57–58
System, 13

T

Taft Correctional Institution, 324
Taft Grain and Elevator, 420

Taser, 146, 147
Tax evasion, 419
Technical violation, 293
    parole, 354
Technology
    Automatic License Plate Recognition, 104, 177
    closed-circuit television (CCTV) cameras, 177–178
    crime-mapping, 140, 141
    electronic eavesdropping, 76
    fingerprinting techniques, 200–201
    GPS, 301–302
    hacking cars, 412–413
    patrol cars and, 104
    Project 54, 104
    radio frequency identification (RFID), 344
    self-surveillance, 151
    social media and criminal justice system, 24–25
    thermal imagers, 175–176
    tracking inmates and, 344
    transdermal alcohol testing, 40
    wireless devices in courtroom, 243
Television, aggression and televised violence, 51, 52
Tenth Amendment, 67
Terrorism, 396–423. See also Homeland security
    characteristics of, 397
    civil liberties and
        due process and indefinite detention, 406–407
        military tribunals, 407
        searches, surveillance and security, 405–406
        terrorist profiling, 405
    counterterrorism strategies
        border security, 404
        emergency preparedness and response, 403–404
        preventive policing, 402–403
    defined, 20
    domestic, 399
    foreign terrorist organization list, 400
    global context of, 397–399
    homegrown extremists, 399
    homeland security
        Antiterrorism and Effective Death Penalty Act (AEDPA), 399–400
        counterterrorism challenges and strategies, 402–404
        Department of Homeland Security, 401
        federal agencies outside DHS, 401–402
        informants and entrapment, 403
        lone wolf terrorist, 402–403
        Patriot Act, 400
        security vs. civil liberties, 405–407
    homeland security response
        FBI, CIA, NSA efforts, 401–402
        state and local antiterrorism efforts, 402
    jihad, 398
    Osama bin Laden and al Qaeda, 398
    Patriot Act and, 20–21
    police department and anti-terrorism, 106–107
    prosecution of terrorists, 230
    supercrime of, 398

trends in, 399
violence of, 397
as warfare, 397–398
Testimony
defined, 235
as evidence, 235
Testosterone, 47
Texas Department of Public Safety, 114
Texting, banning while driving, 10
Theft
cyber, 410
gangs and, 380
identity, 410
motor vehicle, 33
as Part I offense, 37
property crime, 33
Theories, 46. *See also* Crime theories
Thermal imagers, 175–176
Thirteenth Amendment, prisoners' rights, 346
Three-strike laws, 55, 267–268, 315
Three-strikes laws, 69
Thrill offenders, 46–47
Time served, 327
Tokenism, 111
Total institution, 337
Totality of the circumstances test, 166
Touch DNA, 136–137
Tours, 130
Tower guards, 343
Trace evidence, 134–135
Traffic cameras, 177
Traffic laws, 71
Training schools, 388
Trait theory, 47–49
biochemical conditions and, 47–48
psychology and crime, 48
public policy and, 48–49
Transactional Records Access Clearinghouse,
267
Transdermal alcohol testing, 40
Transportation Security Administration (TSA)
airport screening, 404
under Homeland Security Department, 401
Treasury Department, 120
Treasury Police Force, 118
Trespassing, 75
Trial courts, jurisdiction, 192
Trial judges
administrative role of, 201
roles and responsibilities of, 199–201
before trial, 199–200
during trial, 200
Trials
bench, 228
change of venue, 229
elements of
appeals, 244–245
closing arguments, 241–242
cross-examination, 239
defendant's case, 239–240
jury deliberation, 242
opening statements, 235
prosecution's case, 238–239
rebuttal and surrebuttal, 241
role of evidence, 235–238
verdict, 243
jury selection, 231–235

pleading guilty, 223–224
pretrial procedures, prosecutorial screening
process, 221–223
special features of criminal trials, 227–231
impartial jury, 228–229
presumption of innocence, 229
privilege against self-incrimination,
229
role of jury, 228–229
speedy trial, 227–228
strict standard of proof, 230–231
speedy, 227–228
statute of limitations, 227
steps leading to, 218
wireless devices in courtroom, 243
Truth-in-sentencing laws, 257–258, 315
Twitter, 24, 25, 98, 107, 376
searches and, 178
Two Rivers Correctional Institution, 320

U

UCR. *See* Uniform Crime Report (UCR)
Undercover officers, 133–134
Uniform Code of Military Justice, 192
Uniform Crime Report (UCR), 36–38, 99
defined, 36
dropping crime rate, 41–42
juvenile delinquency and, 373
Part I offenses, 36–37
Part II offenses, 37–38
United States Citizenship and Immigration
Services (USCIS), under Homeland
Security Department, 401
United States Reports, 29
United States Visitor and Immigrant Status
Indicator Technology (US-VISIT) program,
416
Universal jurisdiction, 192
Unreasonable searches and seizures, 21
Use of force. *See* Force
Use of force matrix, 146, 147
U.S. Marshals Service
creation of, 119
responsibilities of, 120

V

Vagrancy, 38
Vandalism, 38
Vehicles, searches of, 174–175
Venire, 231
Verdict, 243
Vicodin, 57
Victim impact statements (VISs), 268
Victimless crimes, 34
Victim-offender mediation, 256
Victimology, 53
Victims
civil lawsuits brought by, 244
demographics of, 54
drug use and, 55
reasonable doubt about credibility, 223
risks of, 53–54
routine activities theory, 53–54
uncooperative, 223
unreliable, 223

victim impact evidence and sentencing,
268
victim-offender connection, 54
victim-offender mediation, 256
of white-collar crime, 419
Victim surveys, 37–39
Video games, violent, 51, 52
Violence
corporate, 420
in prisons, 339–341
in schools, 375
Violent crimes
categories of, 33
defined, 33
demographics of victims, 54
drop in crime rate, 17–18, 41–42
juveniles, 373–374
Part I offenses, 36–37
Virus, 412
Visa, 404, 415
Voir dire, 231–232
Voluntary intoxication, 85
Voluntary manslaughter, 74

W

Waiver
automatic, 384
judicial, 383
legislative, 384
prosecutorial, 384
Wake County Sheriff Department, 149
Walnut Street Jail, 311, 329
War, terrorism as act of, 397–398
Warden, 318, 319, 323
War on drugs, 43
Warrantless arrest, 170
Warrants
arrests with, 169–170
arrests without, 170
probable cause and, 161
Washington, George, 119
Washington Mutual, 421
Wealth, crime and, 42–44
Weapons, violations, 38
Wedding cake model, 216–217
Western Penitentiary, 312
White-collar crime
in 2000s, 421
defined, 34, 418
law enforcement and, 420–421
penalties for, 422
regulating, 420
types of, 418–419
victims of, 419
White Collar Crime Penalty Enhancement Act,
422
Widen the net, 302
Willful, 79
Wilmington Police Department, 99
Wiretapping, 406
Witnesses
cross-examination of, 239
direct examination of, 238
expert, 236
Fifth amendment, 229
granted immunity, 229

hearsay, 238–239
lay, 236
redirect examination, 239
self-incrimination, 229
Women
chivalry effect, 264
as correctional officers, 345–346
crime and, 44–45
girls in juvenile justice system, 374–375
honor killings, 76
increasing number of incarcerated, 315
jury selection, 234–235
low representation on Supreme Court, 202–203
sentencing discrimination, 264
Women police officers
added scrutiny of, 111
antidiscrimination law and affirmative action,
110–111
benefits of diverse police force, 113
effectiveness of, 112
in leadership positions, 111
numbers of, 110, 111–112
tokenism, 111
Women's prisons
characteristics of inmates, 348–349
culture of, 349–350
history of abuse, 349
motherhood problems, 349
number of inmates, 44
pseudo-family, 350
Work detail supervisors, 343
Work release programs, 357

Worm, 412
Writ of *certiorari*, 198
Wrongful convictions, 245

Y

Yard officers, 343
Youth camps, 388
Youth development centers, 388
Youth gangs, 379–381
Youth populations, crime rate variations and, 41

Z

Zero-tolerance theory, 101–102